GENETICS

Charlotte J. Avers
Rutgers University

Revised Edition

D. Van Nostrand Company
New York/Cincinnati/Toronto/London/Melbourne

To David

D. Van Nostrand Company Regional Offices:
New York   Cincinnati

D. Van Nostrand Company International Offices:
London   Toronto   Melbourne

Published by D. Van Nostrand Company
135 West 50th Street, New York, N.Y. 10020

10 9 8 7 6 5 4 3 2 1

Preface

Genetics is an introductory text for students who have completed college-level courses in biology and chemistry. My goal has been to provide a balanced, comprehensive view of genetics in a book of reasonable length. The historical perspective used throughout the book emphasizes the debt owed by later workers to those geneticists and biochemists who earlier paved the way through ingenious experimental design and their talented use of new methods to probe gene structure, function, and regulation. Insofar as possible, I have included current studies and discussed their significance.

Each chapter concludes with a set of problems and questions (answers in the back of the book) and a list of pertinent references. Students benefit from the problem-solving experience and can better appreciate the logic and discipline of thinking in genetic terms about biological topics. References for each chapter include those cited directly in the chapter and others from which students can benefit by reading original research literature.

I could not have written this book without the prodigious efforts and patient prodding of Dave Axelrod, who helped me to sharpen my focus time and again as the project took shape. I greatly appreciated comments and helpful suggestions by reviewers of the manuscript: Sally Allen, University of Michigan at Ann Arbor; William Birky, Ohio State University; Philip Hedrick, University of Kansas; William Moore, Wayne State University; Simon Silver, Washington University; Herbert Wiesmeyer, Vanderbilt University. I am grateful to other friends and colleagues who contributed to this book and to the literary executor of the late Sir Ronald A. Fisher, F. R. S., to Dr. Frank Yates, F. R. S., and to Longman Group, Ltd., London, for permission to reprint Table II from *Statistical Tables for Biological, Agricultural and Medical Research*, by Fisher and Yates.

For the preparation of this Revised Edition, the author acknowledges the helpful comments and suggestions of users of the original edition.

Charlotte J. Avers

Contents

Gregor Johann Mendel, 1822–1884

1

Mendelian Inheritance

The foundations of genetic analysis were established by Gregor Mendel in his published report of 1866, describing experimental observations and interpretations based on eight years of breeding garden peas differing in seven traits. Mendel established the particulate nature of inheritance. He proposed that inheritance was based on units (genes), that each unit of inheritance existed in two alternative forms (alleles), and that one member of a pair of alleles behaved as a dominant to its recessive alternative allele. The two Laws of Mendelian inheritance which we still rely upon today are: (1) members of a pair of alleles segregate from one another during reproduction; and (2) members of different pairs of alleles undergo independent assortment during reproduction.

The particular ratios of phenotypes and genotypes in F_2 progeny reflect inherited differences due to one gene or more than one gene. The F_2 phenotypic ratio of 3 dominant:1 recessive indicates single-gene inheritance; the F_2 phenotypic ratio of 9:3:3:1 indicates inheritance based on two independent genes governing the appearance of progeny individuals. The testcross experimental design is a powerful tool to show the occurrence of monohybrid or dihybrid or trihybrid inheritance, since the ratios are 1:1, 1:1:1:1, and 1:1:1:1:1:1:1:1, respectively, and each phenotypic class is represented by a unique genotype. Variations on these phenotypic ratios were reported soon after Mendel's work was rediscovered in 1900, and each of these variations was shown to conform to Mendelian Laws of inheritance: alleles segregated and underwent independent assortment in reproduction. Mendelian rules of inheritance continue to serve as the basic foundations of genetic analysis.

Inheritance patterns are influenced by environmental as well as genetic factors, but the transmission of genes from parents to progeny provides the experimental basis for analyzing these patterns and for understanding their variations. The continuous study of genetics since 1900 can be traced back directly to the intellectual contributions made by Mendel in 1865-1866.

MENDELIAN RULES OF INHERITANCE

The breeding experiments reported by Gregor Mendel in 1865 defined a method of genetic analysis which is historically significant and which is still in use. Before Mendel's time there was a general appreciation and recognition of inheritance, which was the basis for selective breeding of crops and domestic animals. People in general recognized inheritance; for example, the rule for circumcision of a Jewish boy could be waived if there was a history of bleeding problems in other boys in the family. In these cases there was often a practical approach to some particular problem, but there was little generalization to allow for an understanding of inherited traits or of predicting their occurrence. Mendel developed an experimental approach which would allow other biologists to analyze many inheritance problems, regardless of the particular characteristic in question.

Mendel's conclusions have been shown to apply to all organisms, including humans. He was unappreciated in his own time, however, because his interpretations of the inheritance of familiar traits, such as height or color, were put into abstract terms of hypothetical units of inheritance. There was no biological framework into which his hypothetical units could be placed, since the nucleus was not yet recognized as a significant component of heredity in 1865. We can appreciate Mendel's methods and interpretations today, because we expect carefully designed experiments, carefully chosen experimental organisms, and a systematic approach to exploring the unknown. We should appreciate them even more when we realize how much of a pioneer Mendel was over 100 years ago.

1.1   The Systematic Approach

Mendel collected strains of garden peas (*Pisum sativum*) that differed in seven particular characteristics, with pairs of strains showing contrasting expressions for these characteristics. One strain produced tall plants and a contrasting strain produced short plants; strains bearing round seeds were contrasted with strains producing wrinkled seeds, and so forth for five other traits (Table 1.1). During the first two years of the eight years spent on his experiments, Mendel tested a larger number of varieties and characteristics and chose plants that bred true for one particular type. The final collection of pea varieties was therefore a carefully selected group with easily distinguished characteristics occurring in unambiguously contrasting pairs; for

Table 1.1
Seven traits studied in garden peas by Mendel, and results of crosses between strains with contrasting features for each of these traits.

Trait	Crosses between plants of alternative characteristics	Characteristics of F$_1$ progeny plants
Height	tall × short	tall
Seed shape	round × wrinkled	round
Cotyledon color	yellow × green	yellow
Seed coat color	gray × white	gray
Pod shape	inflated × constricted	inflated
Pod color	green × yellow	green
Position of flowers	axial × terminal	axial

example, the tall plants were 6-7 feet in height while the short plants were less than 2 feet tall in every generation. In addition to his thoroughness in selecting experimental plants, Mendel also kept accurate records of breeding results. He followed a program of experimental design which checked and double-checked his observations and the hypotheses based on these observations.

When Mendel performed the crosses between contrasting strains he made each combination **reciprocally**, that is, tall female parents were crossed with short males and short females with tall males. The pea flower is so constructed that it is normally self-fertilizing, a feature to which Mendel paid careful attention in deciding on the plant species to use. Although the work of emasculating flowers and hand-pollinating is tedious, Mendel used relatively large numbers of individual flowers for each of the seven sets of reciprocal crosses. His results in progenies of the first filial (F_1) generation were consistent in all cases: each F_1 progeny resembled only one of the two parents; for example, if one parent was tall and the other short, all the progeny were tall.

Mendel then proceeded to allow flowers of the F_1 plants to self-fertilize as they normally do, and he grew plants of the second filial (F_2) generation from the seeds produced on F_1 plants after self-fertilization. He continued this program of selfings up to the F_6 generation, testing each kind of plant in the successive progenies to determine the consistency of results and the pattern of inheritance he had deduced from these results. Using the same procedures and experimental designs, Mendel analyzed the progenies from parents differing in one, two, or three of the seven characteristics involved.

1.2 Monohybrid Crosses

The F_2 progenies from F_1 self-fertilizations in each of the seven sets of single-character crosses were consistent: (1) there were plants representing both parental types, whereas only one of these had appeared in the F_1; and (2) the parental type which had been expressed in the F_1 now appeared in three times the number of the contrasting parental type, or in a ratio of 3:1 (Table 1.2). Mendel called the character expressed in the F_1 and in 3/4 of the F_2 **dominant**, and the alternative expression was called **recessive**. The recessive character was not apparent in the F_1 generation, but it had not been lost because it reappeared in some of the F_2 progeny.

Table 1.2
Data from some of Mendel's monohybrid crosses showing numbers and ratios of F_2 progeny types after self-fertilizations of F_1 plants.

Appearance of F_1 plants	Numbers of F_2 plants observed	F_2 ratios calculated
round seeds	5474 round:1850 wrinkled	2.96:1
yellow cotyledons	6022 yellow:2001 green	3.01:1
gray seed coats	705 gray:224 white	3.15:1
inflated pods	882 inflated:299 constricted	2.95:1
green pods	428 green:152 yellow	2.85:1
axial flowers	651 axial:207 terminal	3.14:1
tall plants	787 tall:277 short	2.84:1

By carrying the experiments on to the F_3, F_4, F_5, and F_6 generations, Mendel was able to show that in each generation there were two types of progeny, whose appearance resembled the two parent types. When self-fertilized, all recessive appearing plants gave rise only to recessive progeny, but only 1/3 of the plants with the dominant appearance gave rise exclusively to dominant progeny, while the other 2/3 of the dominants produced both dominants and recessives. Mendel's deductions on the mechanisms of inheritance, based on these results, were: (1) inheritance was based on discrete, particulate factors which were sorted out in sexual reproduction and were grouped in all possible combinations at random in the offspring; and (2) there was no change in these factors as they were passed from one generation to another.

By applying simple arithmetic, Mendel arrived at generalizations which held firm in each case, regardless of the characteristic studied or the absolute numbers of individuals of each type in a progeny. He put forward the important concept that *inheritance was based on units*, which were inherited and passed on unchanged from generation to generation. Today we call this unit of inheritance a **gene**. Mendel's conceptual achievement provides the cornerstone for all of genetics. It also led others later on to focus on the gene as the unit of inheritance and as the basis for the transmission of similarities and differences from parents to progeny in successive generations.

The F_2 ratio of 3 dominants to 1 recessive was shown to be a ratio of 1 true-breeding dominant parental type:2 segregating hybrid types:1 true-breeding recessive parental type in successive generations. The F_2 ratio is easily derived by considering each pair of unit factors to be independent alternatives which segregate and then reassort at random in all possible combinations. As Mendel pointed out and verified by particular tests which we will discuss shortly, there must be eggs and pollen of each inherited type produced in equal proportions in the parents; and an equal chance for each of the possible combinations of factors to appear in their offspring. If we consider the characteristic of plant height, we can call the dominant factor T and its recessive alternative t, and we can calculate events as follows:

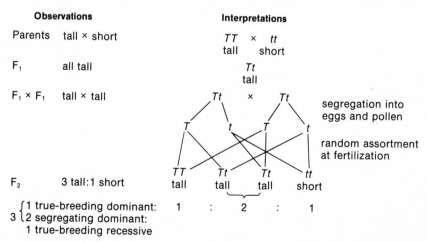

Observations		Interpretations	
Parents	tall × short	TT × tt tall short	
F_1	all tall	Tt tall	
F_1 × F_1	tall × tall	Tt × Tt	segregation into eggs and pollen
		T t T t	random assortment at fertilization
F_2	3 tall:1 short	TT Tt Tt tt tall tall tall short	
	3 { 1 true-breeding dominant: 2 segregating dominant: 1 true-breeding recessive	1 : 2 : 1	

Since F₁ plants produce T and t germ cells (whether eggs or pollen) in equal numbers, and since the F₂ progeny ratio is 1:2:1, it must mean that each of the three possible combinations arises by chance alone. Fertilizations take place at random, regardless of the factor carried, and in enough trials there will be a large enough number of individuals produced to reveal the simple ratio which reflects the pattern of inheritance. Mendel was keenly aware of the need for adequate numbers of trials and individuals for analysis.

We would predict for each case of single-gene, or **monohybrid**, inheritance that the classes of F₂ progeny would be produced in a ratio that is an outcome of the simple probability that particular events occur at random. If we have F₁ parents, each having one dominant and one recessive factor for height, Tt, then the chance for T going into a gamete is 1/2, and the chance for the alternative t is also 1/2 for *each* parent. If the chance for two gametes having the T factor is 1/2 for each, then the probability of two such gametes coming together will be 1/2 × 1/2, or 1/4. Since each gamete is an independent event, the probability of two independent events coming together at the same time is the *product of the separate probabilities*.

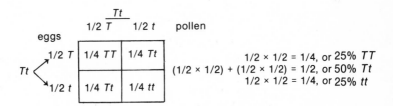

If we look at the three combinations (TT, Tt, tt) in a slightly different way and ask how often we may expect at least one of the two gametes to have the factor T, then we see that the chances are 1/4 + 1/2 = 3/4 or 75% probability. Stated in terms of the ratio of F₂ phenotypes, we expect a series of crosses between Tt and Tt to give a ratio of 3T-:1 tt (where T- stands for either TT or Tt), or 3 tall:1 short. The repeatability of these results is due to the same laws of probability that tell us we have a 50% chance to toss a coin heads up, and a 25% chance to toss two coins together and have them both land heads up (0.5 × 0.5 = 0.25). If we toss one coin often enough we expect an average of 1/2 heads:1/2 tails, and if we have enough trials with two coins we expect 1/4 heads:1/2 heads + tails:1/4 tails. These are average results expected on the basis of chance alone, whether the independent events deal with alternative inheritance factors or heads and tails on coins.

Before continuing it will be easier if we introduce modern terminology as we follow Mendel's other experiments on the particulate nature of inheritance. The unit of inheritance is the **gene**, which exists in alternative forms called **alleles.** Using simple symbols to identify genes and their allelic forms, we can say that the gene for plant height occurs in the form of a dominant allele governing tallness (T) and an alternative recessive allele (t) governing shortness. The capital letter usually indicates the dominant, and the lower-case stands for the alternative recessive allele. We distinguish between the actual gene constitution, or **genotype**, and the visible expression of a characteristic, or **phenotype**. When different alleles of a gene coexist in the same individual, as in *Tt*, the combination or individual is **heterozygous**. If both alleles of a gene are identical in an individual, as in *TT* or *tt*, the genotype or individual is **homozygous dominant** or **homozygous recessive**, respectively. We often refer to the individuals as **heterozygotes** or **homozygotes**.

Individuals may have the same phenotype but different genotypes, for example, tall plants may be either *TT* or *Tt*. The allele expressed in the heterozygotes is the dominant allele, and it masks the expression of the recessive allele which is also present. Dominance and recessiveness can therefore be determined by crossing parents with contrasting alleles for the same gene or characteristic and observing the phenotype of their heterozygous progeny. True-breeding individuals or strains must be homozygous since they produce only their own kind in successive generations. Hybrid or heterozygous individuls or strains produce more than one kind of offspring because different alleles segregate and reassort in reproduction.

These results led Mendel to conclude what we now call **Mendel's First Law of Inheritance:** there is a *segregation of alleles* during sexual reproduction.

1.3   Dihybrid Crosses

Mendel studied the inheritance of the seven characteristics of peas in combinations of twos and threes, as well as singly. In every case he found that the dominant and recessive alternatives behaved the same whether studied singly or in combination with other genes. His analysis of **dihybrid** (two-gene) F_2 and F_3 data revealed that each of the observed ratios could be explained using the same simple rules of probability as in monohybrid crosses. By continuing to the F_3 generation Mendel could again identify the true-breeding and segregating classes having the same phenotype in F_2 progeny (Table 1.3).

When studied in single-gene inheritance, tall was dominant to short and round seeds was dominant to wrinkled seeds. In combination, tall and

Table 1.3
Predicted phenotypes of F_3 progeny resulting from self-fertilizations of F_2 progeny individuals segregating for seed color and seed shape

F_2 phenotypes	Proportion of F_2 phenotypes	Postulated F_2 genotypes		Predicted phenotypes of F_3 progeny from self-fertilized F_2 individuals
yellow, round	9/16	1/16 *YYRR*	→	all yellow, round
		2/16 *YYRr*	→	3 yellow, round:1 yellow, wrinkled
		2/16 *YyRR*	→	3 yellow, round:1 green, round
		4/16 *YyRr*	→	9:3:3:1 ratio, as in F_2 generation
yellow, wrinkled	3/16	1/16 *YYrr*	→	all yellow, wrinkled
		2/16 *Yyrr*	→	3 yellow wrinkled:1 green, wrinkled
green, round	3/16	1/16 *yyRR*	→	all green, round
		2/16 *yyRr*	→	3 green, round:1 green, wrinkled
green, wrinkled	1/16	1/16 *yyrr*	→	all green, wrinkled

round were still dominant to their recessive alternatives. Whether the parental cross was *tall, round × short, wrinkled* or *tall, wrinkled × short, round*, the F_2 ratio of phenotypes was:

9/16 tall, round
3/16 tall, wrinkled
3/16 short, round
1/16 short, wrinkled

The observed 9:3:3:1 ratio of phenotypes is explained most simply if each characteristic is inherited independently of the other. We expect 3/4 tall:1/4 short and 3/4 round:1/4 wrinkled in monohybrid F_2 progenies. If each character is inherited independently of the other (height and seed shape), we would expect to find the following in the F_2:

3/4 tall × 3/4 round   = 9/16 tall, round
3/4 tall × 1/4 wrinkled   = 3/16 tall, wrinkled
1/4 short × 3/4 round   = 3/16 short, round
1/4 short × 1/4 wrinkled = 1/16 short, wrinkled

When F_3 plants were raised from F_2 individuals which had self-fertilized, Mendel saw that there were nine different genotypes among the four F_2 phenotypic classes (Fig. 1.1).

Figure 1.1 Mendelian ratios in F_2 for a dihybrid cross between homozygous parents differing in plant height and seed shape. Upon self fertilization the various F_2 types would produce F_3 offspring in the ratios shown. These F_3 ratios provide the main basis for interpreting specific genotypes of F_2 individuals, even when genotypically different individuals have the same phenotype.

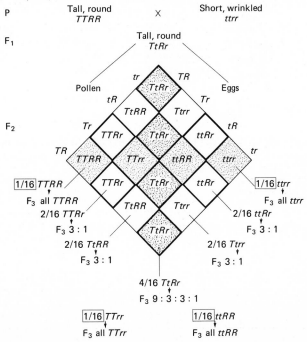

Table   1.4
Relationship between the number of pairs of alleles and the number of kinds of gametes, gamete combinations at fertilization, genotypic classes, and phenotypic classes that can be produced by heterozygotes.

Number of allele pairs (genes)	Number of kinds of gametes formed by each sex	Number of gamete combinations produced by random fertilization	Number of genotypic classes in the progeny	Number of phenotypic classes in the progeny
1	2	4	3	2
2	4	16	9	4
3	8	64	27	8
4	16	256	81	16
5	32	1,024	243	32
6	64	4,096	729	64
7	128	16,384	2,187	128
8	256	65,536	6,561	256
9	512	262,144	19,683	512
10	1,024	1,048,576	59,043	1,024
n	2^n	4^n	3^n	2^n

In crosses involving peas differing in three characteristics (**trihybrid crosses**), the general principle was confirmed that *inheritance was based on discrete units existing in alternative forms.* In a monohybrid cross there were 3 genotypes, in dihybrid crosses there were 9 genotypes, and in trihybrid crosses there were 27 different genotypes, as determined from analyses of the F_3 generations. The simple relationship is 3^n **genotypic classes**, where n is the number of different pairs of alleles involved in a cross between heterozygous parents: $3^1 = 3$ genotypes for 1 pair of alleles of 1 gene, $3^2 = 9$ genotypes for 2 pairs of alleles, and $3^3 = 27$ genotypes for 3 different pairs of alleles. This simple, consistent relationship was interpreted to mean that inheritance was particulate and not the result of blending or mixing of responsible elements.

The observed ratios of F_2 phenotypic classes in monohybrid, dihybrid, and trihybrid crosses were 3:1, 9:3:3:1, and 27:9:9:9:3:3:3:1, respectively. The relationship can be expressed as 2^n **phenotypic classes**, where n is the number of different genes involved: $2^1 = 2$, $2^2 = 4$, and $2^3 = 8$ F_2 phenotypic classes in this series (Table 1.4).

These results led to what is called **Mendel's Second Law of Inheritance**: members of different pairs of alleles undergo *independent assortment* during sexual reproduction.

1.4   Confirming a Prediction by Testcrosses

One important assumption in these interpretations leading to the two laws of inheritance was that egg cells and pollen cells of different genetic types must be produced in approximately equal percentages. When we calculate the F_2 ratio of phenotypes and genotypes we *assume* equal proportions of all kinds of reproductive cells by each parent. We don't mark these numerical values in the usual diagrammatic presentations because we expect them to be equal. We could just as easily show these values when describing crosses involving any genes. For the hypothetical two pairs of alleles *A* and *a*, and *B* and *b*, we would write:

Monohybrid $F_1 \times F_1$ *Aa* × *Aa*   *Bb* × *Bb*

	1/2 *A*	1/2 *a*
1/2 *A*	1/4 *AA*	1/4 *Aa*
1/2 *a*	1/4 *Aa*	1/4 *aa*

	1/2 *B*	1/2 *b*
1/2 *B*	1/4 *BB*	1/4 *Bb*
1/2 *b*	1/4 *Bb*	1/4 *bb*

F_2

Dihybrid $F_1 \times F_1$ *AaBb* × *AaBb*

	1/4 *AB*	1/4 *Ab*	1/4 aB	1/4 *ab*
1/4 *AB*	1/16 *AABB*	1/16 *AABb*	1/16 *AaBB*	1/16 *AaBb*
1/4 *Ab*	1/16 *AABb*	1/16 *AAbb*	1/16 *AaBb*	1/16 *Aabb*
1/4 *aB*	1/16 *AaBB*	1/16 *AaBb*	1/16 *aaBB*	1/16 *aaBb*
1/4 *ab*	1/16 *AaBb*	1/16 *Aabb*	1/16 *aaBb*	1/16 *aabb*

F_2

Mendel tested this assumption of equal proportions of germ cells of different genetic types by making reciprocal crosses between doubly heterozygous F_1 plants, such as *AaBb*, with their homozygous *AABB* and *aabb* parental types. These are called **backcrosses** (of progeny to parent or parent type). The particular kind of backcross which is most informative is the **testcross**, which specifically refers to interbreeding progeny and the recessive parent or parent type, as in the dihybrid testcross between a doubly-heterozygous progeny and a doubly-recessive parent: *AaBb × aabb*. The testcross is a basic design in genetic analysis to the present day, and we will refer to it often in coming chapters.

Mendel predicted each of the expected results in a series of backcrosses involving various characteristics. We can look at the example of dihybrid backcrosses involving the pair of alleles for height, *T* and *t*, and the pair of alleles for seed shape, *R* (round) and *r* (wrinkled). The particularly significant crosses were made *reciprocally* between doubly-heterozygous tall, round (*TtRr*) and doubly-recessive short, wrinkled (*ttrr*) plants. If the hereditary units existed in pairs and were separated cleanly into the reproductive cells in equal proportions, then four different phenotypic classes would have to be produced in the testcross progeny *in equal proportions*, on the average:

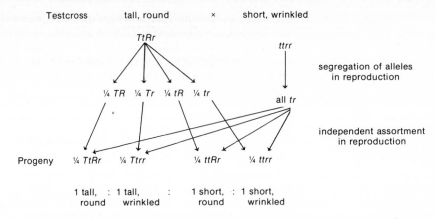

Testcross   tall, round   ×   short, wrinkled

TtRr   *ttrr*

segregation of alleles
in reproduction

¼ *TR*   ¼ *Tr*   ¼ *tR*   ¼ *tr*   all *tr*

independent assortment
in reproduction

Progeny   ¼ *TtRr*   ¼ *Ttrr*   ¼ *ttRr*   ¼ *ttrr*

1 tall, round	:	1 tall, wrinkled	:	1 short, round	:	1 short, wrinkled

Similarly, in a trihybrid testcross involving the alleles for height, for seed shape, and for seed color (*Y*, dominant allele for yellow; *y*, recessive allele for green), we can predict eight phenotypic classes occurring in equal proportions. Using the checkerboard notation, we would have:

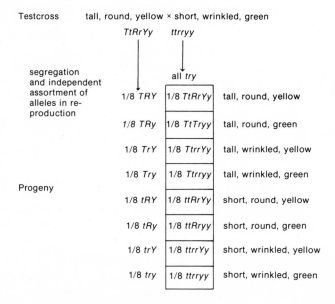

Testcross   tall, round, yellow × short, wrinkled, green

TtRrYy   *ttrryy*

segregation
and independent
assortment of
alleles in re-
production

all *try*

1/8 *TRY*	1/8 *TtRrYy*	tall, round, yellow
1/8 *TRy*	1/8 *TtTryy*	tall, round, green
1/8 *TrY*	1/8 *TtrrYy*	tall, wrinkled, yellow
1/8 *Try*	1/8 *Ttrryy*	tall, wrinkled, green
1/8 *tRY*	1/8 *ttRrYy*	short, round, yellow
1/8 *tRy*	1/8 *ttRryy*	short, round, green
1/8 *trY*	1/8 *ttrrYy*	short, wrinkled, yellow
1/8 *try*	1/8 *ttrryy*	short, wrinkled, green

Progeny

Testcross ratio = 1:1:1:1:1:1:1:1

In order to verify the factors that were present in these testcross progenies, Mendel allowed individuals to self-fertilize. The nature of each class was shown to be exactly as he had predicted. The enormous value of the testcross can be seen in the two examples above: *each phenotypic class is represented by only one genotype.* Simple inspection of testcross progeny can therefore show the genotypes present, without the trouble of proceeding to another generation as Mendel had to do when he was establishing the principles. Whenever a phenotype can be correctly interpreted on a genotypic basis, time and effort are saved. The convenience of the testcross and its accurate interpretation have made it a basic method in the breeding analysis of many organisms. Testcross phenotypic ratios of 1:1, 1:1:1:1, and 1:1:1:1:1:1:1:1, for 1, 2, and 3 pairs of alleles, respectively, are evidence for segregation of alleles and their independent assortment during sexual reproduction.

1.5   Mendel Was Ignored and Later "Rediscovered"

When Mendel's 1865 report to the Brünn Natural History Society appeared in print in 1866, there were few scientists who could appreciate his abstract symbolism interpreting inheritance to be based on particulate factors. Although they could follow the simple algebraic logic which was used, they did not have a biological context into which these symbols and phenomena would fit. The phenotype could be observed directly; the genes had to be postulated. Mendel's incisive analysis, painstaking attention to detail, and widely applicable experimental procedures finally were recognized and valued as much as his conceptual achievement, as the science of genetics progressed after 1900.

Mendel's work essentially lay dormant and unappreciated until 1900, when Carl Correns in Germany, Hugo DeVries in Holland, and Ernst von Tschermak in Austria cited Mendel's 1866 report, independently of one another. Each of these men pointed out how Mendel's units of inheritance, which occur in pairs and which segregate and reassort at random, could also explain the patterns of phenotypes they had observed in their own studies of inheritance. We mark 1900 as the beginning of genetic studies because work in this science has continued uninterruptedly since that year. By 1900 a lot had been learned about cells and their internal construction, and the nucleus had been strongly implicated as the central focus for inheritance and the site of the postulated gene. Not only could other biologists immediately plunge into their own breeding experiments using Mendel's procedures, but his abstractions could be translated into concrete biological premises which also could be analyzed and related to observed patterns of inheritance in various organisms. Events moved very swiftly in the early years of the 20th century, so that before 1920 geneticists had already located genes on chromosomes in the nucleus and mapped them there.

VARIATIONS IN MENDELIAN PHENOTYPIC RATIOS

Very soon after 1900 there were reports of inheritance patterns which gave different phenotypic ratios than those established by Mendel. In every case, the apparent "exceptions" proved to strengthen and broaden the basis of Mendelian inheritance. There were variations observed in (1) dominance and recessiveness relationships between a pair of alleles, (2) the number of alleles of a gene, and (3) in the specific ratio of phenotypic classes found in various progenies and generations. A few examples will serve to illustrate these variations in inheritance patterns, and how each of these differences in phenotypic ratios was explained by Mendelian principles.

1.6   Variations Involving a Single Gene

Mendel had shown that one allele was dominant to its recessive alternative, since all the F_1 resembled only one of the parents and since there were only two phenotypic classes in the ratio of 3 dominant:1 recessive in F_2 progeny. In studies of some flowering plants, such as the four-o'clock, it was found that red flowers × white flowers produced pink-flowered F_1 progeny that did not resemble either parent, and it appeared as though the alleles had not segregated in reproduction. But when pink F_1 plants were interbred to give the F_2 progeny, there were three phenotype classes: 1/4 red:1/2 pink:1/4 white, in reciprocal crosses (Fig. 1.2). The observed pattern implied a segregation of phenotypes, which suggested that the alleles for red and white were passed on, unchanged, to the different generations. If inheritance had not been based on particulate units which segregated and assorted at random, then flower color should have become paler and paler as pinks were interbred, or when pinks were testcrossed to the white-flowered parent. Instead, each set of crosses clearly followed the Mendelian rule for segregation and assortment of red and white alleles for the flower-color gene.

The variations in F_1 and F_2 phenotypic ratios can easily be explained if we realize that heterozygotes show **incomplete dominance** of the red allele over the white allele. In this case and in similar cases described to the present day, genes behave like particulate units but their expression may be reduced when one allele is present, as in pink Rr heterozygotes compared with RR homozygous types which produced red flowers.

Figure 1.2   Incomplete dominance in four o'clocks is evident from the pink-flowered F_1 progeny and from the 1:2:1 ratio of genotypes and phenotypes in the F_2.

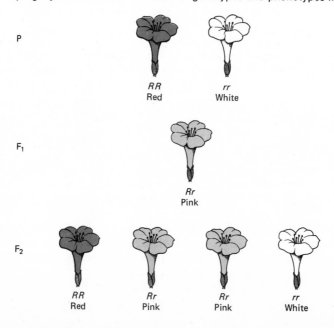

We can illustrate two variations in Mendelian inheritance in the patterns displayed for the major human blood groups: **co-dominance** of two alleles of the same gene and the existence of **multiple alleles** for one gene (Fig. 1.3). There are four phenotypic classes of human blood types: A, B, AB, and O. These classes are the result of the behavior of three alleles of the blood group gene. The alleles for blood types A and B are co-dominant, so an individual with only the A allele or only the B allele is phenotypically different from a person with an A and a B allele, since such a person is type AB. The type O phenotypic class consists of homozygous recessive individuals who carry two copies of the third allele, which is recessive to both the A and B alleles of the gene. There are many examples of multiple alleles, and we know that each gene theoretically may exist in many allelic forms. The human blood group gene is typical, not exceptional.

In many cases of multiple alleles, only one of the alleles is dominant and the others are recessive. The usual inheritance pattern which identifies such a group of multiple alleles can be illustrated by the eye-color gene in *Drosophila melanogaster*, the common fruit fly. There are more than three alleles for this particular gene, but the principle can be shown just as easily with the minimum number of three. When red-eyed flies are crossed with white-eyed flies, the F_1 has red eyes. When red-eyed flies are crossed with apricot-eyed flies, the F_1 has red eyes. There is a phenotypic ratio in the F_2 of each cross showing 3 red:1 white, or 3 red:1 apricot (Fig. 1.4). This shows single-gene inheritance in both sets of crosses, and it seems that the allele for red is the dominant in each case. We might expect two different eye-color genes to be involved, and to test this possibility we would cross apricot- and white-eyed flies. In the F_1 progeny of apricot × white, all the flies have pale apricot eye color. When we interbreed these F_1 progeny, we find a pheno-

Figure 1.3 Inheritance of the ABO blood groups in humans is based on multiple alleles of one gene, with alleles I^A and I^B codominant and the i^O allele recessive to both I^A and I^B. Blood group genotypes and phenotypes will vary in proportion, depending on the particular genotypes of the parents in each case.

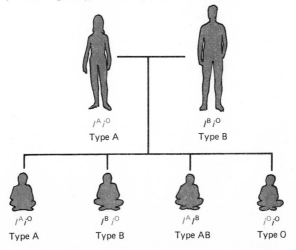

	Phenotypes	Genotypes
P	red X apricot	w^+w^+ X $\underline{w}^a\underline{w}^a$
F_1	red	$w^+\underline{w}^a$
F_2	3 red: 1 apricot	w^+w^+ w^+w^a w^+w^a w^aw^a
P	red X white	w^+w^+ X ww
F_1	red	w^+w
F_2	3 red: 1 white	w^+w^+ w^+w w^+w ww
P	apricot X white	w^aw^a X ww
F_1	apricot	w^aw
F_2	3 apricot: 1 white	w^aw^a w^aw w^aw ww

Figure 1.4   Monohybrid inheritance pattern for multiple alleles of a gene governing eye color in *Drosophila melanogaster*. From the 3:1 ratio of phenotypes in the F_2 it is clear that red eyes is dominant over its alternatives and that all these variants are allelic to each other. Dihybrid or more complex ratios would occur if two or more nonallelic genes were involved in phenotypic development of color.

typic ratio in the F_2 of 3 apricot:1 white. The 3:1 F_2 phenotypic ratio in this cross, as in the other two crosses, indicates single-gene inheritance. The simplest explanation of how all three phenotypes can show monohybrid inheritance in all possible crosses, is that the phenotypes must be the result of expressions of three different alleles of the same single gene. If there had been two different genes for eye color, the F_2 phenotypic ratio would have reflected the 9:3:3:1 ratio in the F_2 progeny in which two pairs of alleles segregated and underwent independent assortment in reproduction, as seen in Fig. 1.5.

Figure 1.5   Inheritance of eye color due to different genes. Two of the significant clues to this dihybrid inheritance pattern are: (1) mutant × mutant yields red-eyed (dominant phenotype) F_1 progeny, and (2) 9/16 of the F_2 progeny are red-eyed, in the typical 9:3:3:1 phenotypic ratio for dihybrid crosses.

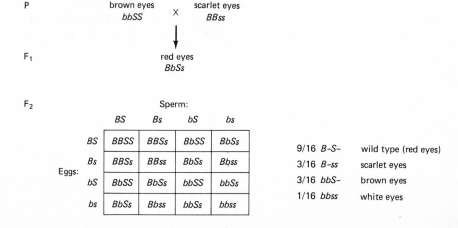

P   brown eyes   scarlet eyes
              bbSS   X   *BBss*

F_1 red eyes
                        BbSs

F_2 Sperm:

		BS	Bs	bS	bs
	BS	*BBSS*	*BBSs*	*BbSS*	*BbSs*
	Bs	*BBSs*	*BBss*	*BbSs*	*Bbss*
Eggs:	bS	*BbSS*	*BbSs*	*bbSS*	*bbSs*
	bs	*BbSs*	*Bbss*	*bbSs*	*bbss*

9/16 *B–S–*   wild type (red eyes)
3/16 *B–ss*   scarlet eyes
3/16 *bbS–*   brown eyes
1/16 *bbss*   white eyes

1.7 Nonallelic Gene Interactions

There are a number of examples of different genes which contribute to the same phenotype. In the illustration which follows, the particular interaction between different (nonallelic) genes in the development of a particular phenotype is referred to as **epistasis**. In some epistatic interactions, at least one dominant allele for each of two different genes must be present if an individual is to develop the dominant phenotype. If there is only one gene whose dominant allele is present, or if neither gene is represented by a dominant allele (homozygous recessive), then the recessive phenotype will be expressed. Such an epistatic interaction has been found in white clover plants.

Some clover strains have high cyanide (HCN, hydrocyanic acid) content while others have lower levels of cyanide in their leaves. Cattle do not seem to be affected by the cyanide they consume when eating these plants. The usual result of crossing high-cyanide and low-cyanide strains of clover is a uniform F_1 with high cyanide and an F_2 which segregates 3 high:1 low cyanide. Such results point to a single pair of alleles of one gene, with low-cyanide recessive to its alternative. We would therefore expect crosses between homozygous recessive low-cyanide strains to produce progeny consisting only of low-cyanide phenotypes. In some crosses, however, both the F_1 and F_2 progeny are different from the expected:

Parents	low strain-1 × low strain-2
F_1	high-cyanide
F_2	9 high-cyanide:7 low-cyanide

Looking at this carefully you can see that the F_2 ratio must be modified from the usual 9:3:3:1 such that 9/16 are high-cyanide and 7/16 (3/16 + 3/16 + 1/16) are low-cyanide. The fact that the F_1 are all high-cyanide further indicates that this expression must be dominant to low-cyanide. If we look for a common feature among the 7/16 which are low-cyanide, one which does not occur in the 9/16 high-cyanide or in the F_1, we can put the story together more easily. The common feature among 7/16 of an F_2 progeny is the presence of one pair of recessive alleles as a minimum; 9/16 of a dihybrid F_2 progeny have at least one dominant allele for each of the two genes involved:

9/16 are *A-B-* (- stands for either allele)
3/16 are *A-bb*
3/16 are *aaB-*
1/16 are *aabb*

If we construct the breeding scheme to allow two different genes to govern the same characteristic of cyanide content, so that both genes must be present in the dominant form for high cyanide content to develop, we have the following:

$$A\text{-} = \text{high} \qquad B\text{-} = \text{high}$$
$$aa = \text{low} \qquad bb = \text{low}$$

P
$$AAbb \times aaBB$$
$$\text{low} \qquad \text{low}$$

F_1
$$AaBb$$
$$\text{high}$$

F_2 9 $A\text{-}B\text{-}$: 3 $A\text{-}bb$: 3 $aaB\text{-}$: 1 $aabb$

9 high: 7 low

In this particular case, two different chemical compounds must be produced in order to get high cyanide levels. Each compound is made only when each gene is represented by at least one dominant allele ($A\text{-}B\text{-}$). The A-bb low-cyanide strain can make only one of these compounds, and the aaB- can make only the other compound; $aabb$ can't make either compound. In all three genotypes producing the low-cyanide phenotype, therefore, the chemical reactions leading to high cyanide content do not take place.

There are other variations on nonallelic interactions involving two different genes which produce modified 9:3:3:1 F_2 phenotypic ratios. Some of these epistatic systems will be presented in the Problems at the end of this chapter. In all these cases, the rules of Mendelian inheritance can be demonstrated. There are pairs of alleles which undergo segregation and independent assortment as expected. The variation is reflected only in the F_2 phenotypic ratio due to gene interactions in development and not to a change in behavior of the pairs of alleles during reproduction.

1.8   Discontinuous and Continuous Phenotypic Variation

The characteristics studied by Mendel and many other geneticists early in this century could easily be assigned to discrete phenotypic classes, such that plants were either tall or short and flowers were either red, pink, or white. This kind of variation is **discontinuous**, that is, the phenotypic classes are distinct, different, and not overlapping. Many other traits show a gradual or **continuous variation** from one extreme to another, however, and when this is the case it is difficult or impossible to separate individuals into specific phenotype classes. For example, traits such as stature usually vary from one extreme of shortness to the other extreme of tallness (Fig. 1.6). Mendel's tall and short peas were somewhat exceptional. In most cases we cannot easily separate increments of height differences into anything other than arbitrary categories.

Many important features, such as crop yield, milk production, height, weight, intelligence, and other traits, exhibit continuous variation. It was therefore important to know whether Mendelian inheritance was responsible for continuous variation as it had been shown to be for discontinuous inherited variation. Plant geneticists such as H. Nilsson-Ehle in Sweden and R. A. Emerson and E. East in the United States provided the first genetic analyses and explanations in Mendelian terms for the inheritance of continuously variable traits. Their studies still stand as the major experimental basis for understanding **quantitative inheritance**, which is

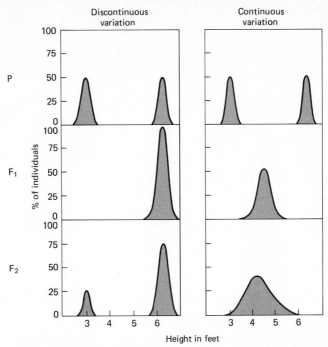

Figure 1.6 Discrete phenotypic classes are characteristic of discontinuous variation, while most continuously variable traits, such as height, are distributed across a continuous gradation between one phenotypic extreme and the other.

the term generally used to identify transmission of traits showing continuous variation in phenotypic expression.

Nilsson-Ehle, Emerson, East, and others proposed that quantitative traits were expressions due to the *additive* influence of three or more genes which governed the same phenotypic characteristic. Each gene was postulated to contribute a portion of the total inheritance, that is, **multiple genes** or **polygenes** as they are called today, were responsible for inheritance of quantitative traits. In Nilsson-Ehle's experiments, kernel color in wheat was analyzed genetically. We can use his information to see how the principles of quantitative inheritance were derived.

When different strains of wheat (*Triticum vulgare*) were crossed, the F_2 progenies could yield 3:1, 15:1, or 63:1 ratios of red:white kernels. These ratios reflect monohybrid, dihybrid, and trihybrid phenotypic ratios, respectively, in which white kernels are produced only by plants containing one, two, or three pairs of recessive alleles. If the dihybrid F_2 progeny plants were examined more carefully, five phenotypic classes could be identified instead of just the two classes of red and white. In addition to kernels that were as dark a red or as white as the two parental types, there were three intermediate classes showing gradually lighter red-colored kernels, in a phenotypic ratio of 1:4:6:4:1 (Fig. 1.7). Similarly, the trihybrid ratio of 63 red:1 white could be characterized instead by 1:6:15:20:15:6:1, according to the different shades of red which were observed.

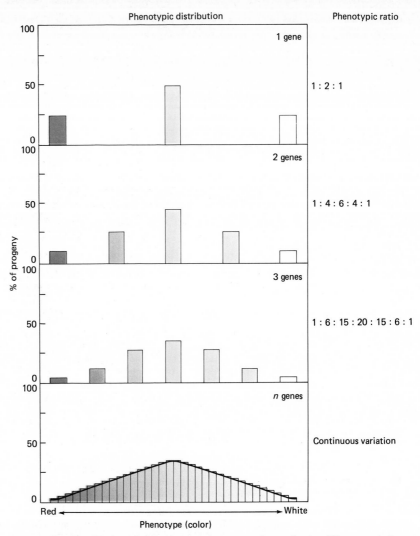

Figure 1.7 Distribution of phenotypes across a spectrum of color differences between the extreme of darkest red to the other extreme of white, according to the number of genes involved in the phenotypic expression. As the number of governing genes increases so does the number of phenotypes. With multiple genes (polygenes) the numerous phenotypic classes merge into a spectrum showing continuous (graduated) variation in color, between red and white.

With three genes interacting additively to produce a phenotype it is still possible to see slight discontinuities between classes. These can be interpreted in typical Mendelian terms according to segregation and independent assortment of pairs of alleles during reproduction (Fig. 1.8). If more than three genes contribute to the expression of a phenotypic trait, the discontinuities become smaller and smaller, until we cannot resolve the separate phenotypic classes. Variation in the trait will appear to range continuously across a gradation of expressions going from one extreme to the

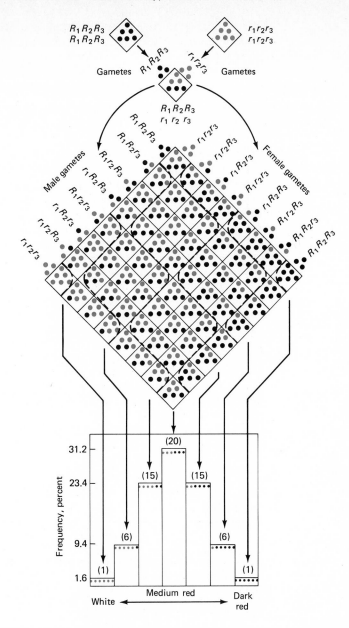

Figure 1.8 Segregation and independent assortment of three pairs of alleles (R_1/r_1, R_2/r_2, and R_3/r_3) governing kernel color in wheat. Homozygous parental lines are crossed and the F_1 undergoes self-fertilization to give the F_2 distribution of color shown in the histogram (bar diagram). The alleles interact additively such that progressively more red color is produced according to the number of R alleles, from 0–6. Seven phenotypic classes arise, in the ratio shown. (From *Genetics*, 2nd ed., by M. Strickberger, Macmillian Publishing Co., New York. Copyright © 1976 by M. W. Strickberger.)

other within the entire progeny or population. By extension of the multiple gene hypothesis derived from studies of 1, 2, or 3 genes, we can theoretically accommodate situations in which more than three genes influence a single quantitative trait. When we obtain a measure of some quantitative trait for each individual in a population sample, and then group these according to the frequency of individuals of different measurements, the distribution approximates a bell-shaped curve of continuous variation. Such a bell-shaped curve is typical of a **normal distribution** of continuous variation (Fig. 1.9).

It is sometimes possible to estimate the number of genes involved in determining a quantitative trait. We saw that the proportions of the two extreme classes were progressively reduced as the number of genes increased from one to three for red kernel color in wheat. With one pair of alleles there were 1/4 red and 1/4 white in the F_2, with two pairs of alleles there were 1/16 red and 1/16 white, and with three pairs of alleles there were 1/64 red and 1/64 white. In other words, when F_1 parents are heterozygous at n gene loci for a single phenotypic trait, $(1/4)^n$ of the F_2 progeny will resemble one of the original homozygous parents. As n increases, the value of $(1/4)^n$ becomes vanishingly smaller and the number of extreme phenotypes may only be determined from large populations or from adequate samples of such populations. Since the number of phenotypic classes covering the range of variation also increases, it becomes virtually impossible to distinguish separate classes. Variation is therefore observed to be essentially continuous, since clear-cut discontinuities cannot be resolved except on an arbitrary basis.

In human beings, a number of different genes are assumed to be responsible for skin color variations between blacks and whites. This estimate is based on family histories, or pedigree analysis, among the earliest of which was reported by C. B. Davenport in 1913. Davenport

Figure 1.9 Bell-shaped curve typical of a normal distribution of frequencies of a continuously variable phenotypic trait. Such a curve is typical of polygenically inherited quantitative traits.

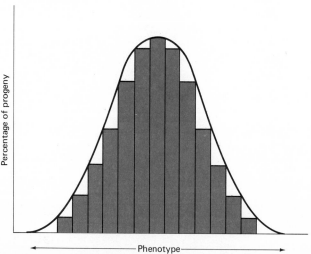

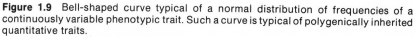

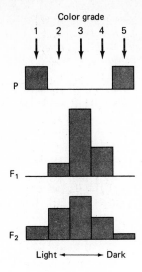

Figure 1.10 C. B. Davenport postulated the occurrence of five phenotypic classes of skin color, with the distribution shown. Such a distribution of F_1 and F_2 phenotypic classes led to the interpretation that skin pigmentation in humans was due to the equal and additive effects of two different pairs of alleles. (See Fig. 1.7 for general reference.)

recognized five grades of pigmentation in different individuals, and he then investigated a number of marriages between blacks and whites. He found that the F_1 offspring were exactly intermediate in skin color to both parents. He interpreted these observations as showing that pigmentation differences arose from additive effects of different genes governing this phenotypic trait (Fig. 1.10). From distributions of skin color measurements among 32 offspring of $F_1 \times F_1$ matings, the frequencies of all five color grades were interpreted to be due to two genes governing skin color, since there was approximately a 1:4:6:4:1 phenotype ratio in the F_2.

Davenport's classification of five color grades was rather arbitrary, however, and more recent information on skin color reflectance measured photometrically has shown that there is a continuous gradation of skin color from light to dark rather than a stepwise distribution (Fig. 1.11). From wider samplings of American populations, it appears that more than two genes are involved in pigmentation. The best estimate at present is that four or five different genes all contribute to skin color differences between blacks and whites.

Pigmentation is clearly a quantitative trait based on polygenic inheritance. There is at least some additive effect of these genes in producing the final phenotype. Two individuals each having some alleles for dark skin can produce children as dark or somewhat lighter or darker than themselves. It is genetically unlikely that two light-skinned parents will produce a very dark child, however, since there is no reliable evidence showing that alleles for dark skin are fully recessive to alleles for white skin color.

Figure 1.11 Mean reflectance from the skin of Europeans, Africans, and various hybrid groups as measured with a reflectance spectrophotometer using filters of selected wavelengths (in nm) of visible light. The percentage reflectance at each selected wavelength, according to the filter used, is shown for each phenotypic class. (From Harrison, G., and J. Owen. 1964. *Ann. Human Genet.* **28**:27.)

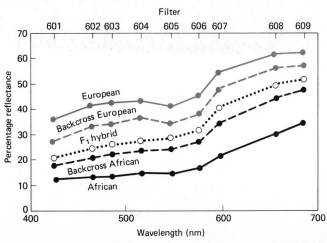

1.9 Environmental Influences on Phenotypic Development

Phenotypic expression usually depends on both the genotype and the environment in which the organism develops. For example, tall plants will develop if the genotype is *TT* or *Tt* and if there are suitable conditions for growth. A genotypically tall plant may develop into a short, stunted plant, despite its alleles, if it grows in unfavorable conditions of lighting, watering, and soil quality.

One of the axioms of scientific analysis is the need to establish and maintain experimental conditions which are *standard*, or consistent, and *optimum* for the system being studied. By reducing the variability of the system and its surroundings we can place more confidence in the differences we may observe under controlled manipulation of the experiment. Mendel followed these simple rules by pre-testing pea varieties and selecting those which showed consistent development of characteristics to be studied, and by growing the plants under the best possible conditions for their development. Any variations he observed in the experiments could then be related to inherited variation and not to random effects caused by unknown features of the plants or changes in their surroundings.

This general approach can also help to show whether an inherited feature behaves differently in different environmental conditions, once it has been established that the feature is inherited and its pattern of inheritance is known. In the high- and low-cyanide strains of white clover we saw that the expression of one gene could be influenced by another gene in the individual. This is an example of variation in phenotypic expression in relation to the genotype, or the genetic environment. There are numerous examples of variations in phenotypic expression in relation to the physical environment in which the individual develops, such as a stunted plant with genes for *potential* development of tallness. Phenotypic development is the outcome of a cooperative interaction between genes and nongenic environmental factors. To put this into a familiar axiom or slogan, development is the result of *nature plus nurture*, not nature *or* nurture.

Phenylketonuria (PKU) in humans is a condition which is inherited as a simple recessive trait, and it can lead to extreme mental retardation. The primary effect in recessives is failure to metabolize the amino acid phenylalanine properly into tyrosine during protein processing and degradation:

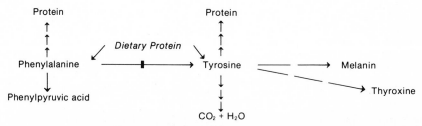

If such a child is given a suitable low-protein diet during the first six years or so of its life, so that there is relatively little phenylalanine to metabolize, the devastating effects of mental retardation can be avoided.

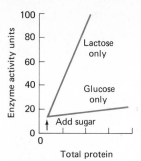

Figure 1.12 *E. coli* synthesizes little detectable β-galactosidase when glucose is in the growth medium, but makes substantial amounts of the enzyme if lactose is present instead. Different phenotypes (amount of enzyme made) may therefore arise among genotypically identical cells in different environments.

Afterward, there seems to be relatively little danger of mental retardation in youngsters with the recessive genotype. Babies are tested routinely in a large part of the United States to determine whether or not they are PKU-positive and, if they are, they are placed on a low-protein diet immediately. PKU-positives excrete large amounts of phenylalanine and phenylpyruvic acid in the urine, whereas individuals who are homozygous or heterozygous for the dominant allele can process phenylalanine to tyrosine and have normal levels of these amino acids in their urine. By modifying the environment, through diet, the phenotypic expression of mental retardation can be avoided. Regardless of their diet, however, PKU-positives retain the recessive genotype and can transmit recessive alleles to their own children. Modification of the environment does not alter the gene or the genotype, but it can alter the phenotype in PKU-positives.

In experimental studies we find similar situations in which one genotype can give rise to two phenotypes in two different environments. In the common colon bacillus, *Escherichia coli*, the milk sugar lactose and related compounds can be processed to simpler metabolites. Normal *E. coli* has the inherited ability to synthesize the enzyme β-galactosidase for lactose metabolism. When *E. coli* cells are incubated in nutrient media containing the sugar glucose, very little enzyme activity can be detected (Fig. 1.12). When such cells are incubated in lactose-containing media, in the absence of glucose, β-galactosidase activity increases sharply and rapidly as enzyme protein is synthesized in the cells. Synthesis of this enzyme must be under gene control because there exist mutant strains in which the enzyme is not synthesized under any conditions. But normal *E. coli* may or may not synthesize the enzyme depending on its environmental surroundings (Table 1.5). Such gene-environment interactions are a common feature of cell metabolism in all species studied. These observed interactions form the basis for the important concept that ultimate phenotypic expression is the outcome of many prior steps involving interactions between genes, and between genes and environment, during development and differentiation of the organism.

Table 1.5

Phenotypes, observed as presence or absence of the enzyme β-galactosidase, in genetically different strains of *E. coli* grown in the presence of the sugars glucose or lactose in their environment.

Sugar	Genotype	
	+	−
Glucose	no enzyme	no enzyme
Lactose	enzyme	no enzyme

PREDICTING OUTCOME OF CROSSES

We have seen that genotypes resulting from a cross can be diagrammed in a checkerboard or some equivalent system. The methods are tedious and subject to inadvertent error, and a shortcut would be desirable. The use of probabilities provides such a convenient shortcut method for predicting the frequency of any genotypic or phenotypic class arising from a cross, regardless of the number of genes involved.

1.10   Probability Formulations

Individuals of genotype Aa can produce two kinds of gametes in equal numbers, such that the frequency of these are $1/2A$ and $1/2a$. Based on this frequency, the probability that a type A egg or sperm will participate in a fertilization event is $1/2$, and the probability that a type a gamete will be involved is also $1/2$. Since fertilizations are random events based on chance encounters between eggs and sperm, the chance that any given egg will be fertilized by any given sperm is the product of their separate probabilities. In this way, the chances for all possible fertilizations involving two heterozygous parents in a cross $Aa \times Aa$ are

egg A will be fertilized by sperm A is $1/2 \times 1/2$ or $1/4$, giving $1/4AA$ progeny
egg A will be fertilized by sperm a is $1/2 \times 1/2$ or $1/4$, giving $1/4Aa$ progeny
egg a will be fertilized by sperm A is $1/2 \times 1/2$ or $1/4$, giving $1/4Aa$ progeny
egg a will be fertilized by sperm a is $1/2 \times 1/2$ or $1/4$, giving $1/4aa$ progeny

These calculations of probabilities lead us to derive the familiar genotypic ratio of $1/4AA:1/2Aa:1/4aa$ among progeny of a monohybrid cross between two heterozygous parents. If we look at this ratio in another way, we can predict that the probability or chance of obtaining a heterozygote from any fertilization involving these parental types is $1/2$, and the probability that any individual offspring will be either homozygous AA or aa is $1/4$. We can also make predictions about the phenotype of an individual produced in this cross. For alleles showing complete dominance we can conclude that the probability of a fertilization producing an individual with the dominant trait is $3/4$, while the probability of obtaining the homozygous recessive phenotype is $1/4$.

These relatively simple considerations of probability can be used to make predictions in cases involving two or more genes which assort independently. In the cross $AaBb \times AaBb$, where alleles A and B are dominants, either pair of alleles will be observed in the progeny in 1:2:1 genotypic and 3:1 phenotypic ratios because the pairs of alleles assort independently of one another. By applying the mathematical rule that the chance of two independent events occurring simultaneously is the product of their separate probabilities, we can use simple arithmetic instead of a checkerboard diagram to predict the genotypic and phenotypic frequencies resulting from this cross. We know the expected frequency of genotypes and phenotypes for each pair of alleles considered separately. These separate probabilities are multiplied together to obtain the overall probability that the separate events will occur simultaneously, by chance. We can then predict the outcome of the cross $AaBb \times AaBb$. The proportion of their progeny that will show

both dominant traits is 3/4 × 3/4 or 9/16
dominant trait A and recessive trait b is 3/4 × 1/4 or 3/16
recessive trait a and dominant trait B is 1/4 × 3/4 or 3/16
both recessive traits is 1/4 × 1/4 or 1/16

The proportion of the progeny expected to be of a particular genotype can also be determined in this way. For example, the proportion that will be of genotype $Aabb$ is $1/2 \times 1/4$ or 1/8; the proportion of genotype $AaBb$ will be $1/2 \times 1/2$ or 1/4; the proportion of genotype $aabb$ will be $1/4 \times 1/4$ or 1/16, and so forth.

Probabilities can be used to predict the outcome of any type of cross, as long as these conform to two simple premises: (1) the genetic events under consideration are independent of one another, and (2) the simultaneous occurrence of two or more such events is due to chance alone. Let us consider the cross $AabbCcDd \times AaBBccDd$ as an example, dealing with each gene separately. For the alleles A and a, the cross is between heterozygotes and we can expect a genotypic ratio of $1/4AA{:}1/2Aa{:}1/4aa$ and a 3:1 phenotypic ratio. For the alleles B and b, the cross is between a homozygous recessive and a homozygous dominant, and all the progeny will be heterozygous for this pair of alleles and identical genotypically and phenotypically. For alleles C and c, the cross is a testcross which will produce a 1:1 genotypic and phenotypic ratio. For alleles D and d, the cross involves two heterozygotes and we expect a 1:2:1 genotypic ratio and a 3:1 phenotypic ratio in the progeny. To predict the proportion of progeny which will show the dominant phenotype for all four traits, our calculation would be $3/4 \times 1 \times 1/2 \times 3/4$ or 9/32. The proportion that will show the dominant phenotype for A and B and the recessive phenotype for c and d will be $3/4 \times 1 \times 1/2 \times 1/4$ or 3/32. We can also calculate the proportion of the progeny that will show some particular genotype. We would expect the genotype $aaBbccDd$ to be produced with the frequency of $1/4 \times 1 \times 1/2 \times 1/2$ or 1/16, and the genotype $AaBbCcDd$ to be produced with the frequency of $1/2 \times 1 \times 1/2 \times 1/2$ or 1/8. Each of the possible genotypes can be predicted to occur in this cross with a particular frequency using the same calculations.

Using these simple probability formulations we can predict the outcome of genetic crosses involving genes which assort independently of one another during reproduction. These formulations, therefore, provide a shortcut which is valuable in making predictions for cases which conform to the two basic premises mentioned above. When different pairs of alleles assort independently of one another and their simultaneous occurrence is due to chance alone, the probability that different events will occur randomly at the same time is the product of their separate probabilities.

The same probability formulations apply to any sets of separate events occurring simultaneously, not just to genetic crosses. We have already mentioned that since the chance of tossing a coin heads up is 1/2 and the chance of tossing it tails up is 1/2, the probability that two coins will land heads up is $1/2 \times 1/2$ or 1/4. The mathematical principles which underlie predictions of outcome of independent events occurring at the same time apply equally well to nonbiological and biological systems.

1.11   The Chi-Square Test

The **chi-square test** (χ^2) is a simple statistical test which is used to determine whether or not a given set of data fits a particular ratio. In genetic analysis, we expect some particular ratio of genotypes and phenotypes to be produced among the progeny, according to a particular hypothesis concerning the distribution of alleles from parents to progeny. For example, if our hypothesis is that height in peas is governed by a single gene and that the allele for tall is dominant to the allele for short, we would expect a phenotypic ratio in the F_2 generation of 3 tall:1 short. These ratios are based on actual counts of the different kinds of offspring produced in any cross, and the ratios enable us to deduce the genotypes of the progeny. In Mendel's crosses there were 787 tall:277 short plants in the F_2 generation, yielding a phenotypic ratio of 2.84:1. Is this calculated ratio close enough to the expected ratio of 3:1 based on the hypothesis of monohybrid inheritance where tallness is completely dominant to shortness? The answer to this question can be determined objectively rather than intuitively by use of the chi-square statistical test of the hypothesis for this cross.

The formula for chi-square is:

$$\chi^2 = \Sigma(d^2/e)$$

where Σ stands for "the sum of", d stands for deviation, and e is the expected value. To use the chi-square test we must first establish the hypothesis to be tested. Our hypothesis is that tall and short appear in the ratio of 3:1, respectively. If the total progeny conformed exactly to the expected 3:1 ratio, we would expect the F_2 of 1064 individual plants to consist of 798 tall and 266 short plants. The expected values differ somewhat from the observed values of 787 tall and 277 short plants. This difference between what was observed and what was expected for each phenotypic class is the deviation (d) for each class. Sometimes the deviation (d) is expressed more specifically as observed (o) minus expected (e), or ($o - e$). These values are used in the chi-square test as follows:

χ^2 **Test for a Progeny of 1064**

Hypothesis	3 tall	1 short
Observed (o)	787	277
Expected (e)	798	266
Deviation (d) or ($o - e$)	−11	11
d^2 or ($o - e$)^2	121	121
d^2/e	121/798 = 0.152	121/266 = 0.455
$\chi^2 = 0.152 + 0.455 = 0.607$		

After the χ^2 value has been calculated we must determine one other value, the **degrees of freedom** (df), before we can use the table of chi-squares to interpret our data, in relation to the hypothesis of a 3:1 phenotypic ratio in the F_2. From these data, the number of degrees of freedom is always one less than the number of classes in the ratio. This is because we calculate the expected number (*e*) for all but one class, which must therefore contain all remaining progeny. For the case of only two classes, as in our example, we may assign the data to either class. But once that class is designated, the other class is automatically determined. For example, once we assign an expected value of 798 for the tall phenotypic class, the other class must include the remaining 266 individuals in the progeny of 1064 plants. In our present example, therefore, one degree of freedom is available.

Once we have calculated the values for χ^2 and degrees of freedom, we can turn to the table of chi-squares and determine the **probability** (*P*) that our data fit the ratio and that the deviations observed can be attributed to chance (Table 1.6). We compare the calculated χ^2 value with those given horizontally in the table for one degree of freedom. After finding a reasonable match between the calculated χ^2 value and a tabulated value, the heading at the top of the table is consulted for the corresponding probability value. In the present case, our chi-square value of 0.607 corresponds to a probability of between 0.5 and 0.3. This means that the probability of finding a deviation as great as that observed would be expected to occur by chance in 30-50% of the same kind of crossing experiments, or, in 30 to 50 out of 100 such crosses.

The arbitrary criterion for interpreting the meaning of the *P* value is that when *P* is greater than 0.05, the deviation is not statistically significant and such a deviation can be expected on the basis of chance alone. If *P* is 0.05 or less, the deviation between the expected and observed ratios is statistically significant and must be due to some particular factor other than chance. In other words, if the probability of obtaining the observed ratio is equal to or less than five in 100 ($P \leq 0.05$), some factor other than chance may be involved. A significant deviation may indicate that the hypothesis is incorrect, or that individuals in one of the phenotypic classes are less likely to survive, or that the environment favors one class more than another, or that some other non-chance factor is operating. In general, the occurrence of a deviation by chance alone in 5% of the trials or experiments

Table 1.6
Table of χ^2 (chi-square)*

df	P = 0.95	0.90	0.70	0.50	0.30	0.20	0.10	0.05	0.01
1	0.004	0.016	0.148	0.455	1.074	1.642	2.706	3.841	6.635
2	0.103	0.211	0.713	1.386	2.408	3.219	4.605	5.991	9.210
3	0.352	0.584	1.424	2.366	3.665	4.642	6.251	7.816	11.345
4	0.711	1.064	2.195	3.357	4.878	5.989	7.779	9.488	13.277
5	1.145	1.610	3.000	4.351	6.064	7.289	9.236	11.070	15.086
6	1.635	2.204	3.828	5.348	7.231	8.558	10.645	12.592	16.812
7	2.167	2.833	4.671	6.346	8.383	9.803	12.017	14.067	18.475
8	2.733	3.490	5.527	7.344	9.524	11.030	13.362	15.507	20.090
9	3.325	4.168	6.393	8.343	10.656	12.242	14.684	16.919	21.666
10	3.940	4.865	7.267	9.342	11.781	13.442	15.987	18.307	23.209

*Abridged from Table II of Fisher and Yates, *Statistical Tables for Biological, Agricultural and Medical Research* (1953), published by Longman; with permission of the authors and publishers.

is to be heeded, but many statisticians consider $P = 0.05$ to be borderline. In this case, some investigators prefer to establish a one percent probability ($P = 0.01$) as the cutoff point between statistically significant and nonsignificant deviation from the expected. If there is only one chance in 100 that a deviation could be due to chance, then everyone will agree that such a deviation is significant. Not everyone will agree that $P = 0.05$ is the cutoff point for significance, but they will look very carefully at the data and at the hypothesis nevertheless.

The chi-square test can be used for ratios containing more than two terms. For example, in a dihybrid cross in which the hypothesis predicts a phenotypic ratio of 9:3:3:1 in the F_2 generation, we can calculate how closely the data fit the predictions when three degrees of freedom are available. We can use data from one of Mendel's experiments to illustrate the situation.

χ^2 **Test for a Progeny of 556 F_2 Plants**

Hypothesis	9 round, yellow	3 round, green	3 wrinkled, yellow	1 wrinkled, green
Observed	315	101	108	32
Expected (e)	313	104	104	35
Deviation (d)	2	–3	4	–3
d^2	4	9	16	9
d^2/e	0.013	0.086	0.154	0.257

$\chi^2 = 0.013 + 0.086 + 0.154 + 0.257 = 0.510$
$df = 3$
$P = {>}0.9$

There is better than a 90% probability that the observed deviation is due to chance, and we can conclude that Mendel's data fit the hypothesis very closely.

Chi-square therefore provides a valuable objective basis by which data may be tested for **goodness of fit** to a proposed hypothesis. The progeny or population samples that are so tested must be sufficiently large and representative if the statistical test is to be meaningful. In general, the chi-square test can only be used in cases where the smallest class contains five or more individuals. It is most useful, therefore, in genetic analysis when controlled matings are possible and when progeny size can be planned in advance to include an adequate number of individuals representative of all the expected phenotypic classes.

1.12   Predicting Risk in Human Inheritance

The knowledge of Mendelian ratios and Mendelian patterns of inheritance can be applied to human beings as well as to other species. One particular instance in which this knowledge is of great practical importance is in predicting risk of occurrence of some inherited affliction in a family. In essence, we can predict the outcome of matings in terms of the risk or probability that two parents will produce a child who is normal or who has inherited some affliction which is known to run in the family according to its past history. Such predictions are of importance to the families of afflicted individuals, as well as to these individuals themselves.

Suppose two normal parents have produced a child with the inherited disease cystic fibrosis. The condition is inherited as a simple recessive, and the phenotype is concerned with defects in mucus secretion and subsequent respiratory problems and susceptibility to various diseases. There is a greatly shortened life expectancy for people who have cystic fibrosis, but with improved medical care many individuals survive into their early twenties. The parents would want to know whether or not they may expect another child with the same disease.

Mendelian ratios can be used to predict the risk of children exhibiting genetic defects inherited from their parents. In our example, both parents are normal, and therefore must each have a dominant allele of the gene. But since their child has the disease, each parent must have contributed one recessive allele to produce a child with the recessive phenotype. Each parent must therefore be heterozygous for the alleles of this gene.

The risk of the couple having another child with cystic fibrosis can be calculated on the basis of $Cc \times Cc$, which represents the parental genotypic situation. On the average, three-fourths of the progeny of many such pairs of heterozygous parents would be C- and one-fourth cc. The same 3:1 phenotypic ratio can be used to predict risk, or the chance or probability, of the birth of a normal versus a diseased child. The crucial point is that *each* birth is an independent event, and there is a probability in *each* birth of 75% (3/4) for C- and 25% (1/4) for cc:

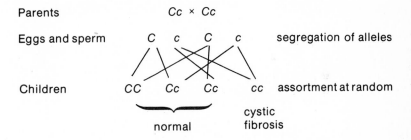

It makes no difference whether the couple has previously had a normal child or one with the disease. In each conception there is a statistical probability for an egg carrying the C or c allele to be fertilized by a sperm carrying C or c. On the basis of four possible allele combinations, produced randomly, there is a 25% probability (risk, in this case) for conception to lead to the cc genotype and to cystic fibrosis in such a child.

We will discuss this topic further in Chapter 3, but this example does show how a knowledge of basic Mendelian principles can be put to practical use in human societies. The methods for establishing a genetic basis for some characteristic, and for determining the pattern of inheritance, rely on the principles first established by Mendel. It is rare to be able to set such a firm date and identify one individual responsible for a field of study; genetics is one such field which we trace specifically to Gregor Mendel in 1865. It is all the more remarkable that the same principles he established are applied to new genetic situations, to the present day. Mendel's scientific contribution stands as an intellectual milestone in human history.

NONGENETIC PATTERNS THAT MIMIC INHERITANCE

There are many examples of family traits which are not determined by genes. In some cases there may seem to be an inherited basis to the appearance of a trait or condition, but further study will show a nongenetic factor to be involved. This is particularly true with certain diseases, where a dietary or pathogenic agent rather than genes can be shown to be the cause. For example, years ago there was a general notion that tuberculosis was an inherited disease because it appeared in some families for generations. Once the tuberculosis bacterium was identified and shown to be the infectious agent, the cause of the disease was identified. There was a pattern of occurrence in some families and not in others because members of families usually lived in similar conditions. The risk of infection may have been similarly high or low for successive generations of particular family groups.

Various **birth defects**, also called **congenital defects**, are due to genes or to chromosome abnormalities, while others are entirely nongenetic. The phenotypes may be the same in inherited and noninherited situations. For example, there is an inherited form of deafness in human beings, but there is also deafness due to accident or disease at any time in life, including before or at birth. Isolated instances of disease or affliction are often difficult to analyze, but the persistent occurrence of some condition in every generation of a family is often taken as preliminary evidence of dominant inheritance (Fig. 1.13). In dominant inheritance, the phenotype may be expressed when the individual is heterozygous or homozygous for the dominant allele. These phenotypes would usually appear in some family members in each generation.

There are a number of inherited neurological disorders which affect an individual during childhood or adulthood. Recently, at least two such disorders were shown to be nongenetic even though in each case the patterns seemed to be those of dominant phenotype expression due to a single gene. The disease called Kuru, an invariably fatal neurological degenerative disease found in some parts of New Guinea, appeared in several generations of some families, but most often in adult females and children of both sexes. D. Gajdusek discovered that the disease could be transmitted to monkeys, our primate relatives, by inoculating their brains with brain tissue from Kuru patients. Clearly, the disease was caused by an infectious agent and not by a gene. From his results with monkeys, Gajdusek was led to look for a nongenetic basis to explain the observed pattern of the disease. He found that Kuru developed in successive generations of families in New Guinea as the result of the ritual consumption of the brains of the dead, especially by

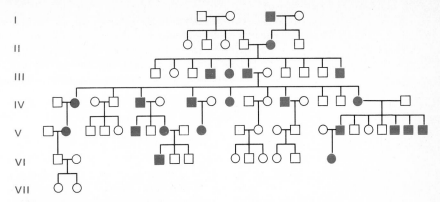

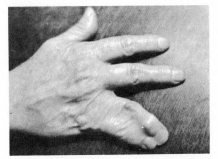

Figure 1.13 Pedigree of syndactyly in one family. Circles (♀♀) and squares (♂♂) are solid for affected individuals and open for normal members of the family. The trait seems to be due to dominant inheritance, since syndactylous children may be produced when only one parent is affected but usually not when both parents are normal. Usually two fingers are joined by a fold of skin, but occasionally three fingers may be syndactylous (held together by skin folds).

women and children. The infectious agent was consumed in this way and ultimately caused the disease.

This convincing analysis has led to a reexamination of the basis for other fatal brain diseases which appeared to have a genetic basis according to family histories. One of these is Creutzfeldt-Jakob disease, which is clinically similar to Kuru and which was discovered in four generations of a family. The condition is rare, except for populations of Libyan Jews living in Israel, who consider sheep's brains to be a dietary delicacy. Clinical studies have now clearly shown that the condition can be transmitted by eating infected food, as well as by other nongenetic means during surgery.

Because these two diseases have been shown to be nongenetic in origin, it isn't necessarily the case that all apparently inherited nervous disorders are caused by infectious agents or other noninherited factors. Each disease must be analyzed individually in order to make a specific determination of cause. It does point out, however, that some patterns of a nongenetic nature can mimic truly genetic situations. Just because there is a pattern of occurrence in every generation does not automatically mean that the pattern is one of genetic transmission from parents to offspring. Through genetic analysis, as we will see in the next few chapters, it is usually possible to determine whether or not an inheritance pattern exists. If it does, we can determine whether it is due to one or more genes, to dominant, recessive, or co-dominant alleles, to epistatic interactions between different genes, and to other aspects of gene behavior.

QUESTIONS AND PROBLEMS

1.1. Tomatoes can be either yellow or red. Plants of these two phenotypes were crossed as follows:

Parents	Progeny
red × red	61 red
red × red	47 red, 16 yellow
red × yellow	58 red
yellow × yellow	64 yellow
red × yellow	33 red, 36 yellow

a. What phenotype is dominant?

b. What are the genotypes of the parents and progeny in each
cross?

1.2. In *Drosophila,* scarlet eye color is produced in homozygous recessive
flies, while normal flies have red eyes.

a. If homozygous red-eyed females are crossed with scarlet males,
what will be the eye color of the offspring?

b. If males and females of the F_1 progeny are interbred, what
phenotypes can we expect in the F_2 and in what proportions?

c. If an F_1 female is crossed to a scarlet male, what kinds of progeny will be produced and in what proportions?

1.3. A black guinea pig was crossed to a white guinea pig, and the litter
consisted entirely of black offspring. The F_1 offspring were used in
the following crosses:

Parents	Progeny
F_1 black × P_1 black	10 black
F_1 black × F_1 black	8 black, 3 white
F_1 black × P_1 white	5 black, 4 white

a. Which is the dominant and which is the recessive phenotype?

b. If *B* represents the dominant allele and *b* the recessive allele,
what are the genotypes of the original parents?

c. What are the genotypes of the F_1 black guinea pigs?

d. What are the genotypes of the black progeny in the third cross?

e. If F_1 black was crossed to F_2 white, what kinds of offspring
would be produced and in what proportions?

1.4. You have a single black guinea pig of unknown parentage. How
would you determine whether the animal is homozygous or heterozygous for coat color?

1.5. In corn, yellow seedlings (*g*) is recessive to green seedlings (*G*), and
waxy endosperm (*wx*) is recessive to starchy endosperm (*Wx*). The
two genes assort independently. A cross between a homozygous
green, waxy plant and a homozygous yellow, starchy plant produced F_1 progeny that were phenotypically green, starchy.

a. If F_1 individuals are interbred, what phenotypes would be found
in the F_2 generation and in what proportions?

b. If some F_1 plants are crossed to plants from the green, waxy variety, what genotypes and phenotypes would be found in their progeny and in what ratios?

c. If particular F_2 plants are self-fertilized in an experiment, such F_2 plants could produce F_3 progeny as listed below.

F_2 phenotype	F_3 progeny
green, starchy	33 green, starchy; 10 green, waxy
green, starchy	51 green, starchy
green, starchy	101 green, starchy; 34 green, waxy; 35 yellow, starchy; and 12 yellow, waxy
green, starchy	44 green, starchy; 15 yellow, starchy

What is the genotype of each of the four self-fertilizing F_2 plants listed?

1.6. A cross between two snapdragon plants produced 83 plants with pink flowers, 35 with red flowers, and 36 with white flowers.
   a. What is the genotype and phenotype of each parent?
   b. What phenotypes would you expect and in what proportions among the progeny of the following crosses?

   (1) pink × pink   (2) red × red   (3) red × white
   (4) pink × white

1.7. In chickens there are two genes involved in comb shape, such that genotype *R-P-* gives walnut comb, *R-pp* rose comb, *rrP-* pea comb, and *rrpp* single comb.
   a. How many different genotypes will produce a rose phenotype? What are these genotypes?
   b. If you obtain a progeny of 31 walnut, 28 rose, 10 pea, and 9 single from crosses between walnut and rose parents, what are the genotypes of these parents?

1.8. Five samples of *Drosophila* heterozygous for the recessive genes black body (*b*) and rough eyes (*ro*), were inbred and the following data were obtained:

Sample	Normal eye Normal color	Normal color Rough eye	Black color Normal eye	Black color Rough eye
1	190	58	34	6
2	276	94	64	26
3	226	66	74	18
4	304	120	110	42
5	124	60	42	30

   a. Calculate for each sample the χ^2. Which of the ratios fits a 9:3:3:1 distribution?
   b. Is there a significant deviation in any of these cases?

1.9. In mice the Brachyury allele (*T*) causing short tail is dominant over the wild type allele (+) causing long tail. Homozygous *TT* is a lethal condition and such mice do not survive. An allele at this locus, called *t*, is recessive to the wild type but is also lethal when homozygous. The heterozygote *Tt* is viable.
   a. In a cross between *Tt* heterozygotes, what would be the genotype(s) and phenotype(s) of the viable progeny?

     b. If the normal litter size was 24, how many living mice would be born?

1.10. Ectrodactyly or lobster claw is an inherited physical defect in humans, occurring in homozygous recessive individuals.

     a. If two normal parents had a daughter affected with this condition, and a normal son, what is the probability that the son will be a carrier of the recessive allele?

     b. If this son married a normal woman whose brother was afflicted with lobster claw, what is the probability that a second child would be afflicted if the first child born to these two people had this physical defect?

1.11. Four babies, two of which were fraternal twins (produced from two different fertilized eggs), were born in a hospital during the same night. Their blood types were found to be A, B, AB, and O. The three parents were:

AB and O

A and B

B and O

Assign the four babies to their parents and list the genotypes for each parent and baby.

1.12. From repeated matings between two mice each having a tail length of 12.5 cm, the following progeny were found to have tail lengths as indicated:

Length of tail, cm	2.5	7.5	12.5	17.5	22.5
No. of progeny	9	37	57	34	12

     a. How many pairs of alleles would regulate this characteristic?

     b. Give the expected ratio of each class of tail length, and the proportion of alleles in each genotype that would produce the above results.

     c. What offspring phenotypes would be expected from a mating between progeny having tail lengths of 2.5 cm and 17.5 cm?

1.13. Two white-kernel strains of corn were crossed. All the F_1 progeny were red, while F_2 progeny consisted of 91 red and 69 white. What is the inheritance pattern in this case? Calculate the χ^2 to test your hypothesis.

1.14. In crosses between large and small true-breeding gerbils, all F_1 progeny are intermediate in size. Among 452 F_2 progeny, 106 are large and 108 are small. Assuming the simplest case of polygenic inheritance, how many alleles contribute to gerbil size?

REFERENCES

Correns, C. 1900. G. Mendels Regel über das Verhalten der Nachkommenschaft der Rassenbastarde. *Ber. deutsch. bot. Ges.* **18**: 158-168. (English translation in *Genetics* **35**, Suppl. to No. 5, Part 2, pp. 33-41, 1950.)

Dunn, L. C. 1965. *A Short History of Genetics.* New York: McGraw-Hill.

East, E. M. 1910. A Mendelian interpretation of variation that is apparently continuous. *Amer. Nat.* **44**:65.

McKusick, V. A., and R. Claiborne, Eds. 1973. *Medical Genetics.* New York: HP Publications.

Mendel, G. 1866. Versuche über Pflanzen Hybriden. *Verh. naturf. Ver. in Brünn, Abhandlungen, iv.* (English translation in J. A. Peters, ed. 1959. *Classic Papers in Genetics.* Englewood Cliffs, N. J.: Prentice-Hall.)

Nilsson-Ehle, H. 1909. Kreuzungsuntersuchungen an Hafer und Weizen. *Lunds Univ. Aarskr, N. F. Afd.*, Ser. 2, Vol. 5, No. 2, pp. 1-122.

Ravin, A. W. 1965. *The Evolution of Genetics.* New York: Academic Press.

Stent, G. Dec. 1972. Prematurity and uniqueness in scientific discovery. *Sci. Amer.* **227**:84.

Cellular Reproduction and Inheritance

Experiments by breeding analysis can be accomplished without knowing the details of gene location or gene distribution mechanisms in organisms, as we saw in Mendel's work. The foundations of genetic analysis, however, are woven together with the knowledge of cellular and organismal reproductive systems. A major factor in the quick understanding of Mendel's abstract inheritance factors by 1900 was the ease with which these units could be incorporated into the biological framework discovered by microscopists shortly before and after Mendel's death in 1884. During meiosis, alleles on chromosomes are segregated and assorted independently into the gametes. The parallel behaviors of genes and chromosomes still underlie our understanding of various genetic systems today.

Each new cell or individual must receive a complete set of genetic instructions for development. Identical copies of genes are distributed to a new asexual generation by mitosis. Different combinations of alleles leading to a variety of genotypes in a new generation arise in sexual cycles punctuated by meiosis and fertilization. The nuclear division processes of mitosis and meiosis are characteristic of eukaryotes, organisms with a membrane-bounded nucleus, but are absent from prokaryotes, organisms lacking a membrane-bounded nucleus. Viruses are not cellular, and their reproduction is very different from asexual or sexual reproduction in cellular life forms.

Particular attention must be paid to the events of meiotic divisions of the nucleus. The behavior of chromosomes during meiosis provides the essential foundation for understanding patterns of inheritance, independent assortment and recombinations of members of pairs of alleles, and gene mapping methods.

In order to exploit organisms with particular advantages for genetic analysis, we must also know their life cycles as well as processes taking place in individual cells. Suitable examples are described in the second half of this chapter.

CELLULAR DISTRIBUTION OF GENES

All cellular organisms can be classified as **prokaryote** or **eukaryote**, according to their cellular plan of organization. Prokaryotes include all the bacteria and blue-green algae; all other cellular organisms are eukaryotes (Table 2.1). In prokaryotes, genes are localized in a region of the cell called the **nucleoid**, which is surrounded by cytoplasm encased in a plasma membrane and bounded by a cell wall (Fig. 2.1). There is no permanent membrane other than the plasma membrane, and the nucleoid is not separated from the cytoplasm by a nuclear membrane. A membrane-bounded nucleus characterizes eukaryotic cells. This is the basic distinction between the two groups of cellular organisms: *presence or absence of a membrane-bounded nucleus.*

Mitosis, meiosis, and fertilization are eukaryotic processes exclusively. Mitosis is one phase in a cycle of cellular events which leads to a new generation of identical cells or organisms, which arise by **asexual reproduction**. In sexual species there are, in addition to mitotic activities, meiosis and fertilization. During **sexual reproduction** gametes are produced, and when gametes fuse at fertilization the new sexual generation is initiated. *Genetic constancy* characterizes asexual reproduction, while *genetic variety* may arise from sexual reproduction.

2.1 Mitosis and the Cell Cycle

Each new generation of cells or individuals is the result of reproduction. Since progeny resemble their parents, there must be mechanisms that

Table 2.1
Kingdom classification systems*

"Traditional"	Dodson, 1971	Whittaker, 1969
Plantae	**Monera**	**Monera**
Bacteria	Bacteria	Bacteria
Blue-green algae	Blue-green algae	Blue-green algae
Chrysophytes	**Plantae**	**Protista**
Green algae	Chrysophytes	Chrysophytes
Red algae	Green algae	Protozoa
Brown algae	Red algae	**Fungi**
Slime molds	Brown algae	Slime molds
True fungi	Slime molds	True fungi
Bryophytes	True fungi	**Plantae**
Tracheophytes	Bryophytes	Green algae
Animalia	Tracheophytes	Red algae
Protozoa	**Animalia**	Brown algae
Metazoa	Protozoa	Bryophytes
	Metazoa	Tracheophytes
		Animalia
		Metazoa

*References: Dodson, E. O. 1971. The kingdoms of organisms. *Systematic Zoology* 20:265-281; and Whittaker, R.H. 1969. New concepts of the kingdoms of organisms. *Science* 163:150-160.

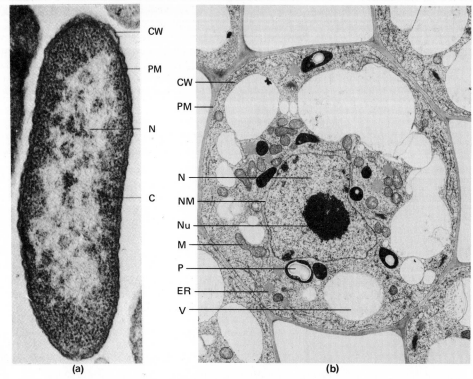

Figure 2.1 Electron micrographs of thin-sections of a prokaryotic and a eukaryotic cell type: (a) Rod-shaped bacterium (*Pseudomonas aeruginosa*) showing typical prokaryotic cellular plan of a nucleoid (N) region surrounded by cytoplasm (C), all enclosed within the plasma membrane (PM); the living protoplast is surrounded by a cell wall (CW). × 60,000 (Photograph by H.-P. Hoffmann). (b) Mature root cell from the eukaryotic species *Potamogeton natans*, a flowering plant, showing the nucleus (N) containing a nucleolus (Nu) and enclosed by a nuclear membrane (NM) system. The cytoplasm surrounding the nucleus is filled with various differentiated components, including mitochondria (M), plastids containing starch (P), endoplasmic reticulum (ER), and prominent vacuoles (V). The plasma membrane (PM) is surrounded by a cell wall (CW). × 7,500 (Courtesy of M. C. Ledbetter)

ensure faithful *increase* and *transmission* of genetic information. Increase is essential because more copies of the **genome** (one set of genes) must be made if progeny are to get all the information they need to grow up and produce their own offspring in turn. Once multiplied, the genes must be delivered from parents to progeny with great accuracy. Unless the processes of gene increase and gene transfer were accomplished with considerable fidelity, progeny would not resemble their parents, as they in fact do.

Our understanding of the mechanics of gene and chromosome replication came from a healthy infusion of biochemistry into biological study, but we can easily see the chromosomes themselves by microscopy. From combined studies using biochemistry, genetics, and cytology (the study of cells by microscopy), we know that chromosome replication is accomplished

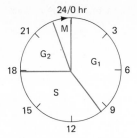

Figure 2.2 In a cell cycle, which may be 24 hr long, the interval of mitosis (M) is relatively brief. During interphase between successive mitotic divisions, G_1 is variable in duration but it is the time when preparations get under way for chromosome replication; S is the phase of chromosome replication; and G_2 is the post-replication phase when preparations are made to deliver sets of chromosomes to daughter nuclei by mitosis.

at a different time in the **cell cycle** from the delivery of replicated chromosomes during mitosis (Fig. 2.2).

The whole interval between one mitosis and the next is subdivided into three separate phases called G_1, S, and G_2. During G_1 preparations get under way for replication of the chromosomes. During S the new chromosomes are made through processes of replication, and during G_2 preparations get

Figure 2.3 Mitosis. Chromosomes replicate during interphase, and begin to condense in prophase. The nuclear membrane usually disappears, as do nucleoli, by the end of prophase. The spindle forms, and during prometaphase the chromosomes move toward the equatorial plane of the spindle and become aligned there in metaphase. Sister chromatids of each replicated chromosome separate toward opposite poles in anaphase, and nuclei are reorganized in telophase. Afterward, each nucleus enters the interphase state, and may or may not undergo other mitotic divisions.

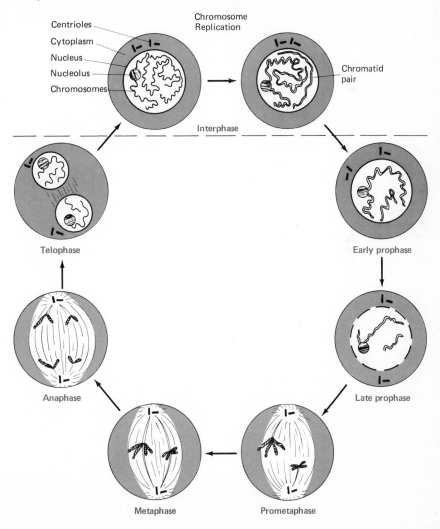

under way for delivery of the parental and progeny chromosomes to two daughter cells. The actual process of delivery is mitosis.

Genes are found on chromosomes and they are passed on to new cells; chromosomes are duplicated and then distributed to new cells. In each cell cycle, we see chromosomal events, but we relate these events directly to gene increase and gene transfer to the progeny. Mitosis is an asexual process by which daughter cells are virtually assured of receiving equal and identical copies of all the genes from the parent cell. Mitosis is the only mechanism available in asexually reproducing eukaryotes for the transfer of genetic information to successive generations. In sexual species of multicellular eukaryotes, mitosis is responsible for accurate delivery of the genes in each somatic (body cell) nuclear division event. The trillions of cells in one human being arise by countless mitotic divisions of the original fertilized egg during development. Replacement of old cells by new cells during a lifetime also takes place by mitotic divisions. The unique combinations of alleles in each person are accurately copied and accurately delivered in every cell cycle in each part of the individual.

2.2   The Stages of Mitosis

The continuous sequence of events in mitosis is conventionally divided into arbitrary stages (Fig. 2.3): **prophase** (*pro*, before), **metaphase** (*meta*, between), **anaphase** (*ana*, back), and **telophase** (*telo*, end). The entire interval between mitotic divisions is called **interphase**, and it includes the G_1, S, and G_2 phases of a somatic cell cycle.

Figure 2.4 Sister chromatids of a replicated chromosome are more likely to separate toward opposite poles since their individual centromeres are oriented toward opposite poles of the cell during metaphase. The sister centromeres are held together in a common centromere region until anaphase separation begins.

As prophase begins, the stringy tangle of chromosomes in the interphase nucleus begins to shorten and thicken. By about mid-prophase individual chromosomes can be seen and recognized as double (duplicated) structures. As mitosis proceeds, the chromosomes continue to condense until they line up at the equatorial plane of the **spindle**, and metaphase begins. Each metaphase chromosome can clearly be seen as a replicated structure made up of two **chromatids** (half-chromosomes) held together at the common **centromere region** (Fig. 2.4). Each sister chromatid of a chromosome has its own **centromere**, and the two centromeres are so situated as to face opposite poles of the cell. When anaphase begins, sister chromatids separate toward opposite poles because of their initial metaphase orientation on the spindle, aided by spindle fibers extending from the centromere to one pole of the cell. When chromatids separate from each other, each becomes a full-fledged and independent chromosome, no longer acting together with its sister. During the final stage of telophase, the condensed chromosomes in each daughter nucleus unfold and gradually assume their interphase appearance. Nuclear reorganization takes place, and the sequence ends with two new interphase nuclei produced from the original parent nucleus (Fig. 2.5).

Each daughter nucleus contains an identical set of chromosomes and genes, which is also identical to that of the parent nucleus, replication

Interphase

Prophase

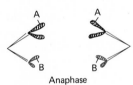

Metaphase

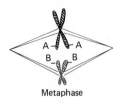

Anaphase

Daughter nuclei

Figure 2.5 Each daughter nucleus has an identical set of chromosomes and genes, unchanged from the original parental nucleus which underwent chromosome replication and subsequent mitosis.

having taken place during the preceding interphase, producing two identical sets of chromosomes, which were distributed accurately during mitosis itself. The *same distribution mechanism* operates for eukaryotic cells regardless of their chromosome number, the number of chromosome sets, or aberrancies in number (Table 2.2). The fidelity of distribution is responsible for ensuring identical chromosome complements and, therefore, for *genetic constancy* in mitotic generations. Variations can arise by mutation or by other random modifications of chromosomes, but these variations in turn will be replicated and transmitted faithfully to all descendants of the modified cell or individual. Asexually reproducing species are therefore genetically rather uniform.

Each body (somatic) cell in a multicellular organism is essentially identical in genetic content. Differences in cell appearance, function, and activity arise during development and differentiation through regulation of gene action, a topic to be covered in depth in Chapters 9 and 13, and elsewhere in this book. For now, the main point is to realize that mitosis delivers the genes on chromosomes during reproduction, while other processes then direct the expression of genetic potential into the variety of cells, tissues, and organs of the individual. The genetic consequence of mitosis is that the two new cells contain identical copies of the same kinds of genes, and that these genes are the same as the ones which were present in the cell from which they came.

Table 2.2
Chromosome numbers found in various organisms

Organism	Diploid no.
Human *(Homo sapiens)*	46
Chimpanzee *(Pan troglodytes)*	48
Rhesus monkey *(Macaca mulatta)*	42
Dog *(Canis familiaris)*	78
Cat *(Felis domestica)*	76
Horse *(Equus caballus)*	64
Toad *(Xenopus laevis)*	36
Housefly *(Musca domestica)*	12
Mosquito *(Culex pipiens)*	6
Nematode *(Caenorhabditis elegans)*	11♂,12♀
Tobacco *(Nicotiana tabacum)*	48
Cotton *(Gossypium hirsutum)*	52
Kidney bean *(Phaseolus vulgaris)*	22
Broad bean *(Vicia faba)*	12
Onion *(Allium cepa)*	16
Potato *(Solanum tuberosum)*	48
Tomato *(Lycopersicon esculentum)*	24
Bread wheat *(Triticum aestivum)*	42
Rice *(Oryza sativa)*	24
Baker's yeast *(Saccharomyces cerevisiae)*	34

2.3   An Overview of Meiosis

Only sexually reproducing species have cells which can switch from mitotic divisions to meiotic divisions of the nucleus, at specified times in a life cycle. Unicellular eukaryotes also switch to meiosis during a sexual phase, from a previous phase of asexual or vegetative multiplication by mitosis. The prokaryotic bacteria and blue-green algae have different gene delivery systems, and the acellular viruses reproduce by methods which are unique to them. Examples of these kinds of organisms will be discussed later in the chapter in order to underscore the direct relationship between systems for gene transmission and reproduction in a life cycle.

There are two consecutive divisions which make up the total process of nuclear division by meiosis. Cells which are **haploid** (having one set of chromosomes) normally do not undergo meiosis, whereas cells with two sets (**diploid**) or more than two sets (**polyploid**) of chromosomes have meiotic

Figure 2.6   Meiosis. Chromosomes proceed through an extended prophase in division I (1–5), followed by movement to the spindle equator (6), alignment at the equator (7), and separation (8) and possible reorganization of the two nuclei (9) when Meiosis I ends. During Meiosis II, conventional prophase (10), metaphase (11), and anaphase (12) activities eventually lead to a quartet of nuclear products of the original meiotic nucleus. Significant events include chromosome pairing at zygonema (2), reduction of chromosome number by one-half at anaphase I (8), and reduction of gene numbers or DNA content in anaphase II (12) to one-half the level that was present in the premeiotic nucleus. In this example the chromosome number has been reduced from $2n = 4$ to $n = 2$.

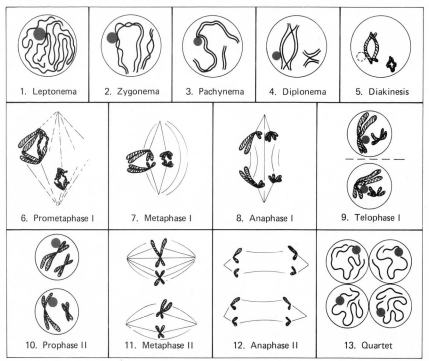

potential. In a typical diploid species, such as garden peas or human beings, the diploid number of chromosomes is *reduced by one-half*, to the haploid number, by meiosis (Fig. 2.6).

If reduction in chromosome number is the only criterion, we may wonder why there is a second division, because chromosome number is reduced by one-half at the end of the first of the two meiotic divisions. The answer lies in a consideration of the number of copies of the genome when meiosis begins and when it is concluded.

During interphase before meiosis begins, chromosomes replicate and the number of genome copies is doubled in the mother cell nucleus. Since the mother cell is usually diploid, there are 2 copies of the genome before replication and 4 copies afterward. The chromosome number remains diploid, however, since sister chromatids remain associated in the replicated chromosomes. When meiosis begins, therefore, there are 2 replicated chromosomes of every kind so that 4 genomes of every kind are distributed among the pairs of chromatids in the diploid nucleus (Fig. 2.7). When anaphase of the first meiotic division takes place, partner chromosomes separate to opposite poles and the chromosome number is reduced by one-half. Each chromosome consists of two chromatids, however, so that each anaphase nucleus has two copies of each set of genes. This is the same as in the original mother cell before replication, so *gene number* has not yet been reduced by one-half (the haploid level). The second meiotic division leads to separation of sister chromatids and the alleles they carry into different nuclei. Each product of the second phase of meiosis thus ends up with one set of chromosomes carrying one copy of the genome. Reduction from the genetic diploid to the genetic haploid state therefore requires two consecutive divisions for one complete meiotic cycle.

The four products of a meiotic cell, or **meiocyte**, can be genetically different from one another (see Fig. 2.7). This provides the biological basis for Mendel's deductions from breeding analysis that all possible kinds of germ cells are produced in equal numbers, on the average, by each parent in a cross. If we follow one pair of alleles alone, for example A/a, there would be equal proportions of the two alleles of the gene in the meiotic products. If we follow two pairs of alleles, we find AB, Ab, aB, and ab in equal proportions. With three pairs of alleles in triply heterozygous meiotic cells, there will be eight different genotypes among the meiotic products of a random sampling of meiocytes (Fig. 2.8). Each pair of chromatids can be oriented in two different ways, on the basis of purely random alignment on the metaphase plate in the first meiotic division.

The genetic consequence of meiosis is segregation and the random assortment of members of pairs of alleles into the germ cells, leading to various combinations of alleles in the gametes. When gamete fusions take place at random in the fertilization phase of a sexual cycle, a variety of genotypes can arise among the progeny.

2.4   The First Meiotic Division

The meiotic nucleus proceeds through a sequence of prophase, metaphase, anaphase, and telophase stages in a continuing series of events. These

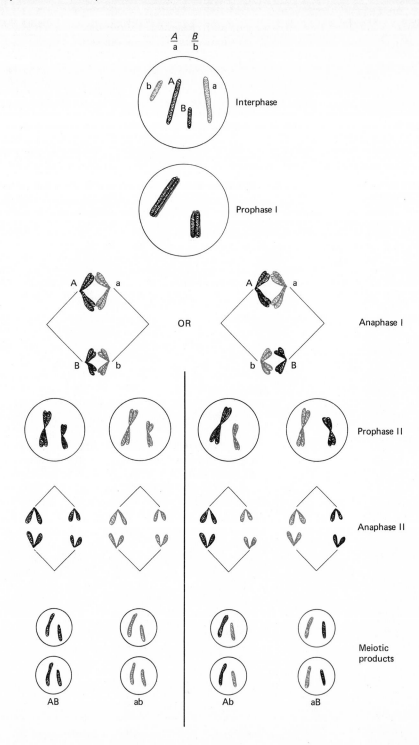

Figure 2.7 During meiosis the chromosome number in the nuclear products is reduced to one-half the number present in the parent meiocyte nucleus. Reduction of chromosome number and of gene number require two consecutive divisions. At the end of meiosis, genetically different progeny nuclei may arise from a meiocyte with heterozygous loci.

$$\frac{A}{a} \quad \frac{B}{b} \quad \frac{C}{c}$$

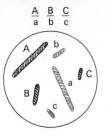

Figure 2.8 Equal proportions of eight possible genotypic combinations may be found in a random sampling of meiotic products arising from triply heterozygous meiocytes. Segregation of members of a pair of alleles and independent assortment of different pairs of alleles, which are the Mendelian laws of inheritance, are the genetic consequences of meiosis. Distributions of chromosomes carrying A/a, B/b, and C/c are independent of one another and they assort at random into all possible combinations of genotypes which, therefore, are produced in approximately equal proportions among the meiotic products.

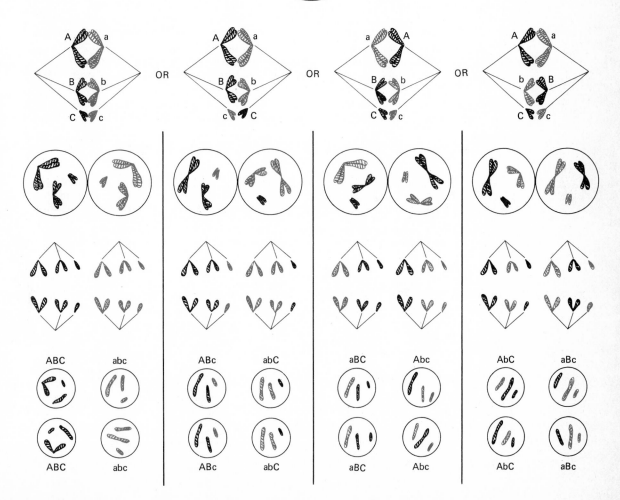

designations are made for convenience in analysis and discussion, and not because there are interruptions in the division process. Because the prophase of **Meiosis I** (the first division) is the most complex, protracted, and genetically significant interval, it has been further subdivided for convenience into the substages of **leptonema** ("slender thread"), **zygonema** ("yoked thread"), **pachynema** ("thick thread"), **diplonema** ("double thread"), and **diakinesis** ("divided across"). When using an adjective to describe some feature of the first four substages, we will use the terms **leptotene**, **zygotene**, **pachytene**, and **diplotene**. For example, leptotene chromosomes pair during zygonema to produce pachytene bivalents of four chromatids each.

Meiosis begins in the replicated nucleus with leptonema, the first of the substages of **prophase I**. The tangled jumble of beaded, slender threads soon begin to pair at various places along their length in the process of **synapsis**, as zygonema begins. Synapsis is a specific process which only involves pairing between **homologous** chromosomes or parts of chromosomes (Fig. 2.9). A complex structure called the **synaptonemal complex** begins to form between paired chromosome regions. It runs completely down the length of each chromosome pair when zygonema ends and all parts of homologous chromosomes have synapsed. The synaptonemal complex is responsible for keeping paired homologous chromosomes together and in register throughout pachynema, the next stage of prophase I (Fig. 2.10). Such a pair of synapsed chromosomes is called a **bivalent**.

Each pachytene bivalent looks unreplicated but is actually made up of four chromatids, two per chromosome in the pair. Pachynema is one of the significant parts of prophase I because exchanges take place between chromatid segments in the bivalents. The process of exchange of homolo-

Figure 2.9 Synapsis involves only two homologous chromosome segments at any particular pairing site, even when more than two homologous regions are present in the nucleus. In this example of a trivalent (three homologous, synapsed chromosomes) in castor bean (*Ricinus communis*) meiosis, the photograph of trivalent chromosome 9 (a) is interpreted in the drawing (b) as having only two-by-two pairings, with one of the chromosomes (2) paired with parts of the other two homologues (1, 3). (Courtesy of G. Jelenkovic)

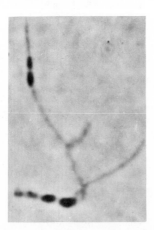
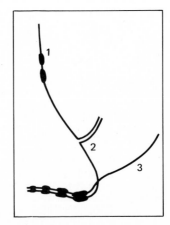

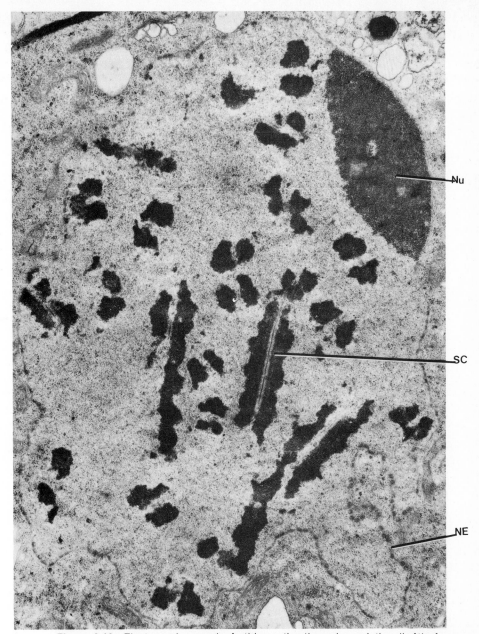

Figure 2.10 Electron micrograph of a thin-section through a meiotic cell of the fungus *Neottiella*, a member of the Ascomycetes. One of the pachytene bivalents has been sectioned favorably and it displays the synaptonemal complex (SC) in the space between the paired homologous chromosomes. The nuclear envelope (NE) is visible, as well as a prominent nucleolus (Nu). × 16,000. (Courtesy of D. von Wettstein, from Westergaard, M., and D. von Wettstein. 1970. *Compt. rend. Lab. Carlsberg* **37**:239, Fig. 1).

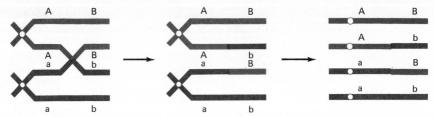

Figure 2.11 Crossing over in a pachytene bivalent heterozygous at two gene loci. The homologous chromosomes are held in register and are closely paired as a result, which increases the probability that one or more exchanges may take place between homologous chromosomes. New genotypic combinations may arise in this way (*Ab*, *aB*), as well as parental types (*AB*, *ab*).

gous chromosome segments is called **crossing over**, during which new combinations of alleles on the *same* chromosome pair may arise. The process of crossing over leading to recombinations between pairs of alleles in the same chromosome is a critical feature in recombination analysis and in gene mapping, as we will see in Chapters 4 and 5. The presence of the synaptonemal complex is essential for crossing over to take place, since homologous chromosomes may separate before crossing over occurs unless they remain in register and closely paired during pachynema (Fig. 2.11).

When diplonema begins it is signaled by **opening-out** of the bivalents at various places along their length. The homologues remain associated only at places called **chiasmata** (sing., **chiasma**), which are believed to be the first visible evidence of previous crossing-over events within the bivalents. From genetic analysis, to be described later, it is quite clear that *each* crossover event involves only two of the four chromatids in a bivalent. In favorable cytological materials such as insect spermatocytes, it can clearly be seen that two chromatids participate in each exchange, but that all four chromatids can be involved in multiple exchange events in a bivalent (Fig. 2.12).

During diplonema, the synaptonemal complex is shed everywhere along the bivalent except at chiasmata. Even these fragments of the complex are usually shed before diplonema is over. Diplonema may last for weeks, months, or years in some species, particularly during oocyte development leading to egg production. In the human female embryo all the oocytes are produced for a lifetime, but they remain suspended in diplonema until the girl reaches the age of puberty. Between puberty and menopause, when a woman is biologically capable of reproduction, per menstrual cycle an oocyte resumes meiosis and completes the first division. It is in this stage that the oocyte (usually but inaccurately called the egg or ovum at this stage) is released from the ovary during ovulation, midway through a menstrual cycle. The second meiotic division will not take place unless the oocyte is penetrated by a sperm. Once this occurs, the oocyte nucleus completes the second meiotic division. The resulting single egg nucleus fuses with the sperm nucleus to form the first nucleus of the new individual, which begins as a **fertilized egg cell**. The situation is different in human males, since sperm production in the testes does not begin until the boy

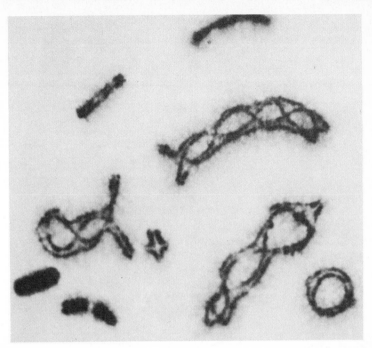

Figure 2.12 Diplotene bivalents in grasshopper spermatocyte. Each chiasma (site of a previous crossover event) involves two of the four chromatids in a bivalent, but all four chromatids may be involved in multiple exchange events in a bivalent. (Courtesy of B. John)

reaches puberty. Sperm are then produced in the hundreds of millions every day, until relative old age (Fig. 2.13). If there is no fertilization or sperm release, eggs and sperm disintegrate within a relatively short time and are resorbed into the tissues, just like any other kind of wornout cell. In general, gametes do not undergo further development in any sexual species unless they unite at fertilization. They are highly specialized reproductive cells with no other known function.

Chromosomes continue to condense until they reach their most contracted state during diakinesis. Bivalents are short and thick, chiasmata are plainly evident, and the individual bivalents are relatively well spaced within the nucleus. Chromosome counts are easily made at this stage in many species, and aberrant chromosomes or chromosome rearrangements are seen most readily here.

When the meiotic bivalents come into alignment on the spindle equator at metaphase I, the ends of the chromosome arms are positioned at the equator while centromeres of homologous chromosomes are as far apart as physically possible. This is just the opposite of the situation during mitotic metaphase, when centromeres are aligned at the equator and chromosome arms wave about in all directions on either side of this zone (compare Figs. 2.3 and 2.6). This orientation at metaphase I makes it highly likely that homologous centromeres will move to opposite poles of the cell.

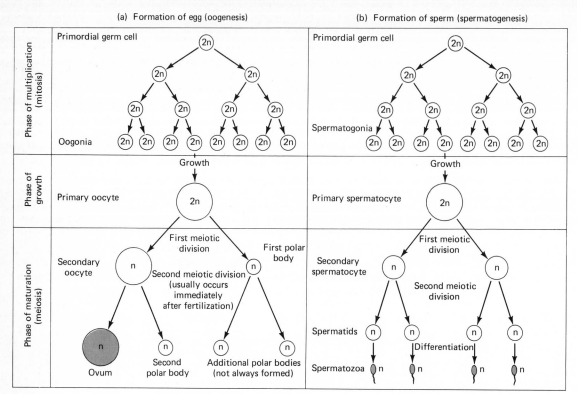

Figure 2.13 In humans and other animals (a) oogenesis leads to one functional egg per oocyte, whereas (b) spermatogenesis results in four functional sperm per spermatocyte at the conclusion of meiosis.

Each pair of sister chromatids making up one chromosome of a bivalent is called a **dyad**. We can therefore say that separation of one dyad from its sister dyad is almost guaranteed by the simple mechanism of centromere positioning at the equatorial plane of the metaphase spindle. Mistakes do occur on occasion; for example, both dyads of the bivalent may move to the same pole. We will discuss such errors later on.

Anaphase begins when homologous chromosomes (dyads, or pairs of chromatids, or replicated chromosomes) separate and move to opposite poles of the cell. Each chromosome is a double structure, containing two copies of the genome. On the basis of chromosome number, however, reduction to one-half has been achieved.

Telophase is a stage of nuclear reorganization, just as in mitosis. There is considerable variability among species in the events between anaphase I and metaphase of the second meiotic division. In some cases nuclei in anaphase I enter almost directly into metaphase II. At the other extreme there are species which proceed through anaphase I, telophase I, interphase between divisions, and prophase II, before entering metaphase II. Every variation between these two extremes has been observed in one or more species.

2.5   The Second Meiotic Division

There is nothing particularly striking or unusual about **Meiosis II**. Nuclei proceed through conventional stages not unlike mitosis, but it is not mitosis at all; it is the concluding phase of meiosis.

The main result of Meiosis II is separation of the chromatids of each dyad into different nuclei, at which time each chromatid becomes a full-fledged chromosome acting independently from other chromosomes. Since there is now one genome in every nucleus, reduction to one-half the content of the chromosomes, DNA, and genes has been accomplished. Reduction division is complete only at this point.

In most cases, separation of the four nuclear products of meiosis into four separate cells takes place at the end of Meiosis II. In other cases there may be a cell division after Meiosis I to produce two cells, each of which will divide again at the end of Meiosis II. In both situations there are four products of meiosis, and the fate of these four cells varies among different groups of eukaryotes. In the more complex plants and animals, there is only one functional product among the four produced by a meiocyte in the female, since the other three are aborted, but in males all four products of a meiocyte are functional (see Fig. 2.13).

2.6   Genetic Consequences of Meiosis

Meiosis leads to segregation of members of pairs of alleles into the gametes which sooner or later develop from the meiotic products. Subsequent fertilization allows new and different combinations of alleles in every sexual generation. Almost every individual in a sexual species has a unique genotype even though all the members of a species have the same genes; the differences are due to the variety of combinations of alleles for these genes.

Mendel's First Law is explained by meiosis: the two members of each pair of alleles are segregated into different gametes when homologous chromosomes are segregated into separate haploid nuclei. Mendel's Second Law is also explained by meiosis: different pairs of alleles are assorted independently from other allele pairs since non-homologous chromosomes align independently and are segregated independently into haploid gametes.

If 3^n is the theoretically possible number of different genotypes when n = the number of chromosome pairs, each carrying one pair of heterozygous alleles, then peas may produce 3^7 different genotypes when differing in only 7 pairs of alleles on their 7 pairs of chromosomes in diploids. In human beings with 23 pairs of chromosomes, 3^{23} different genotypes are possible when only one pair of heterozygous alleles is present on each pair of chromosomes. Since there are thousands of genes in the human genome, and since many of these exist in the heterozygous state, it is statistically almost impossible for identical genotypes to arise by chance. Except for identical twins and other identical siblings, no two people have, ever have had, or are ever likely to have the same genotype by chance alone. From such considerations we can see that sexual reproduction is a system that essentially guarantees *genetic variety* in every generation.

Asexually reproducing species are relatively uniform within a population, since meiosis and fertilization are absent. Mitosis in eukaryotes is dedicated to accurate delivery of genome copies, and progeny resemble their parent in such species. Variation arises primarily by **mutation**, leading to some differences between populations of asexual species. Mutation is a random event and the chances are that different mutations arise in different populations at different times. Mutations also occur in sexual species, enhancing the degree of variability and providing the new genetic information which is tested during evolution. According to many biologists, the greater the genetic variability, the better the chances that some inherited features will prove advantageous and provide the foundation for change leading toward adaptation during evolutionary time. According to this idea, the explosive increase in life forms over the past billion years was due in large measure to the appearance of sexual reproduction in certain ancestral populations. For the first 3 billion years or so, life was present in limited variety according to the fossil record.

LIFE CYCLES OF SOME SEXUALLY REPRODUCING SPECIES

In animals and a number of other kinds of organisms the haploid cells resulting from meiosis function directly as sex cells, called **gametes**. The first cell formed by gamete fusion is the diploid **zygote**, and this is the cell which develops into the new individual in diploid species through development and differentiation of mitotic cell lineages. In the diploid land plants, there is an intermediate stage in the life cycle when haploid **spores** are produced by meiosis in the **sporophyte** phase of the cycle. These spores subsequently develop into structures or systems called **gametophytes**, which later produce gametes by mitotic divisions of haploid cells (Fig. 2.14). Gamete fusion restores the diploid state and the zygote develops into the diploid plant through many mitotic divisions. In all of these cases, gametes arise only from cells which are meiocytes, or which can be traced back directly to meiocyte divisions by meiosis.

In haploid eukaryotic organisms, the diploid phase of the life cycle may be only the zygote nucleus or cell, which immediately undergoes meiosis and restores the haploid state. The products of such meiotic divisions are not gametes; they are ordinary vegetative cells or spores with the haploid chromosome number. But two such haploid nuclei or their mitotic descendants can unite, under suitable conditions, to produce another zygote and another generation of the species by sexual processes.

In multicellular sexually reproducing organisms, therefore, the sexual cycle of gamete fusion—fertilization—gamete fusion occupies only a part of the life cycle. The mitotic divisions giving rise to new cells, and development and differentiation of the organism, very often take up the major part of a life cycle, that is, the time between the start of one generation and initiation of the next generation.

The selected sampling of organisms to be described represent: (1) a few of the species which have an important place in genetic research, and (2) those which are fairly typical of their group.

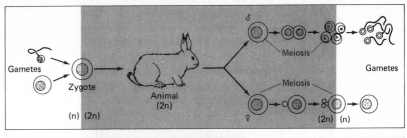

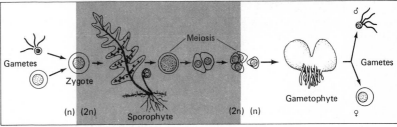

Figure 2.14 Comparison of animal and plant life cycles, showing differences in structures and in the time of meiosis in sexual reproduction. The events shown for animals are typical of almost all animal species, but some differences in detail characterize various plant groups.

2.7   Drosophila

Both the vertebrate and invertebrate animals share the common feature of spending almost all of their life cycle in the diploid state (Fig. 2.15). The only haploid cells are the gametes themselves, which restore the diploid state when they unite at fertilization and initiate the new generation. Many invertebrates, including insects like Drosophila, and most of the amphibians, undergo relatively little embryonic development before the egg hatches into an immature, or juvenile stage. The juvenile tadpole or larval form undergoes additional mitotic divisions and a series of developmental changes during **metamorphosis**, and finally emerges in the adult form of the species.

One of the great advantages in genetic studies of Drosophila is that each of these developmental stages can easily be collected for detailed analysis of chromosomal activities and for the time when the effect of mutant alleles occurs. The giant, banded chromosomes in nuclei of the larval salivary glands and some other organs can be studied at a level of detail which is almost impossible with other species (Fig. 2.16). These huge chromosomes are important in gene mapping studies, in studies of the molecular organization of chromosome structure, and in relating the activity of a particular gene with its phenotypic expression at a particular time in larval development.

Drosophila melanogaster was the experimental organism in the laboratory of Thomas Hunt Morgan, the first geneticist to receive the Nobel prize for his pioneering studies during the early decades of this century.

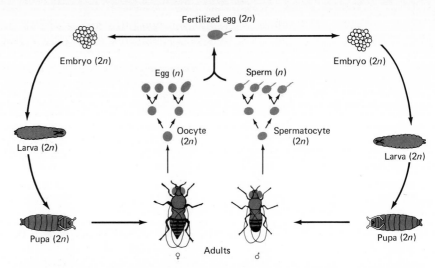

Figure 2.15   Life cycle of *Drosophila melanogaster*, showing the succession of developmental stages leading from fertilized egg to embryo, larva, and pupa, before emergence of the adult fly, or imago. Females have five dark stripes across the dorsal surface of the abdomen, while males have only three dark stripes. Except for the gametes, all other cells are diploid (2*n*).

Figure 2.16   Light micrograph of the salivary gland chromosomes of *Drosophila melanogaster*, stained to show the band patterns in high contrast. The individual chromosomes or chromosome arms have been identified (chromosomes X, 2-4; Right and Left arms, where appropriate). × 1,000.

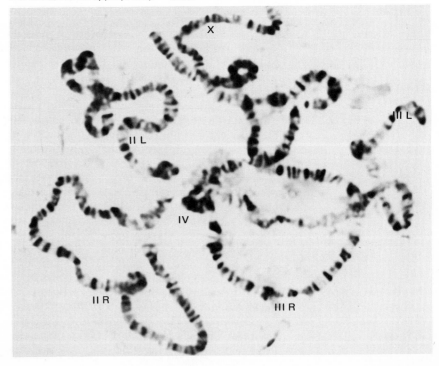

Morgan and his colleagues had been studying the embryology of Drosophila and continued to analyze the well-known system from a genetic standpoint. The generation time of about two weeks is relatively short; large numbers of flies could be raised in relatively little space, and numerous mutants could be analyzed by breeding tests and chromosome study. Females are easily recognized by their markings of five bands on the upper surface of the abdomen, in contrast to three bands in males. Knowing that after fertilization females store sperm in an organ called a **spermotheca**, it is essential to use virgin females which are recently hatched from pupae and kept isolated until they are put together with appropriate males for breeding analysis.

2.8   Corn (Maize)

The agricultural importance of *Zea mays* made this species an organism of choice for geneticists associated with agricultural schools and experiment stations. We probably know more about the genetics of corn than any other seed plant, and the general features of its life cycle are fairly typical of other flowering plants, or angiosperms, like peas, tobacco, tomato, and other genetically exploited species (Fig. 2.17).

Among the advantages of studying corn, despite its relatively long life cycle and the need for acres of space and a warm climate, are: (1) large num-

Figure 2.17 Life cycle of corn, or maize (*Zea mays*). Male flowers in the tassel and female flowers in the ear produce a succession of reproductive cells and structures which lead to fruit (kernel) formation. Each kernel contains a single seed, which includes the 2n embryo from which the new corn plant will develop, and the 3n endosperm tissue which nourishes the growing embryo and young seedling during germination. The sporophyte is conspicuous whereas male and female gametophytes are microscopic in size. See details in text.

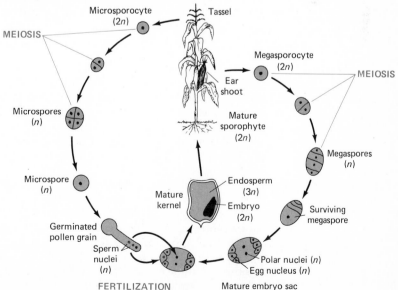

bers of mutant characteristics are known and mapped on chromosomes; (2) the relative ease of controlled matings; (3) large numbers of progeny can be obtained from the seeds on a single ear of corn; and (4) its suitability for cytogenetic analysis because of the large size and distinctive morphology of the ten chromosomes making up the genome.

The prominent corn plant is a sporophyte in which female flowers are borne in the *ears* along the stem and male flowers in the *tassel* at the top of the plant. Corn is **monoecious**, which means that there are separate male and female flowers, which, however, are produced on the same plant. Peas and most other flowering plants, on the other hand, have **perfect** flowers in which both the male (pollen-bearing anthers of the stamens) and female (egg-bearing ovules of the pistils) structures occur in the same flower. When mating genetically different parents in corn, it is simply a matter of putting a bag over the ears to prevent alien pollen from reaching the female flowers, and adding the desired pollen taken from tassels of designated male parent plants. Corn is normally cross-fertilizing so that precautions must be taken in every experimental generation, unlike peas in which self-fertilizations produce F_2, F_3, and other progenies from gametes known to come from the same flower.

The corn sporophyte produces **megaspores** in female structures and **microspores** in male flower parts, by meiosis. Megaspores undergo three successive mitotic divisions to produce eight nuclei, one of which is enclosed in the egg cell of the **embryo sac**, which is the name given to the gametophyte produced by megaspore development during mitoses. Microspores give rise to **pollen** grains, which are the male gametophytes, containing a tube nucleus and two sperm nuclei. Both the female and male gametophytes of flowering plants are therefore inconspicuous, and both grow within and at the expense of the green sporophyte plant.

When mature pollen is carried by wind, gravity, or the experimenter to the ear-shoot, pollen germinates to produce a long pollen tube which grows down through the silks (female receptive flower parts) to the embryo sac within the ovule in the ovary, into which the two sperm nuclei penetrate. One sperm nucleus fuses with the egg nucleus to produce the zygote, the first cell of the new sporophyte, and the second sperm unites with two polar nuclei to form an **endosperm nucleus** in the embryo sac. The zygote is diploid, and develops by many mitotic divisions into an embryo; the endosperm nucleus is triploid (three genomes) and gives rise by successive mitoses to endosperm tissue which nourishes the embryo in the seed and young seedling. Upon germination, the embryo develops into the new corn plant. The endosperm is used up shortly after seedling growth begins. Each kernel on an ear of corn has developed from a separate female flower and therefore represents a different individual. Hundreds of kernels on a single ear can develop into comparable hundreds of individuals of the next generation. In corn there is one embryo sac produced per female flower, and one seed which can therefore arise. In many plants, including peas, more than one embryo sac is produced in the same flower meaning that more than one seed can develop within a common fruit such as the pea pod. Each seed, however, contains a unique embryo produced from an independent fertilization between sperm from a pollen grain and the egg in an embryo sac.

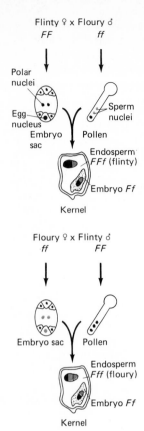

Flinty ♀ x Floury ♂
FF   *ff*

Polar
nuclei

Egg
nucleus

Sperm
nuclei

Embryo
sac

Pollen

Endosperm
FFf (flinty)

Embryo *Ff*

Kernel

Floury ♀ x Flinty ♂
ff   *FF*

Embryo sac

Pollen

Endosperm
Fff (floury)

Embryo *Ff*

Kernel

Figure 2.18 The triploid endosperm tissue can be examined directly on the ear of corn and be phenotypically identified. In reciprocal crosses between diploid *FF* and *ff* parents, flinty or floury endosperm develops according to the numbers of *F* and *f* alleles present. Two dominant alleles in this case are required to mask the expression of one recessive allele (*FFf* produces flinty, *Fff* produces floury endosperm).

In most plants and animals it is impossible to verify by direct tests that pairs of alleles segregate 1:1 at meiosis; we presume this to be true on the basis of genotypic and phenotypic ratios of many progeny as Mendel did. In corn, however, a direct test of 1:1 segregation of alleles can be made in pollen grains and in female gametophytes as well. For instance, the kernel phenotypes *waxy* and *nonwaxy* have different kinds of starch present, and can be distinguished by simple treatment with an iodine solution; *waxy* pollen stains red and *nonwaxy* pollen stains blue in iodine. The characters are controlled by a single pair of alleles; *Wx* is the normal allele for nonwaxy and *wx* is its mutant alternative for waxy pollen. If pollen from a hetero-zygous *Wx wx* plant is stained with iodine, about half stain red and half blue; 3,437 blue and 3,482 red-stained pollen were recorded in one particular test. Similar direct proof of 1:1 segregation of a pair of alleles has been obtained from female gametophytes of *Wx wx* heterozygotes, which not only demonstrates the predicted ratio, but which also shows that the sur-viving megaspore of a meiotic division may be of either allelic type, occur-ring equally often by chance in a large enough sampling.

While most of the characters in corn are sporophytic, good use has been made of inherited features expressed in the endosperm of the corn kernel. Since endosperm is triploid, there is an opportunity to analyze the inter-

Figure 2.19 Starchy and sugary endosperm segregants can be identified directly by examination of the kernels produced in ears on the female parent plant. Approximately 3/4 of the kernels shown here are starchy and about 1/4 are sugary. Only *su su su* endosperm develops the sugary phenotype, since one, two, or three *Su* alleles produce starchy phenotypes.

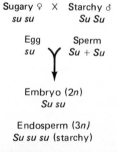

Sugary ♀   X   Starchy ♂
su su   *Su Su*

Egg   Sperm
su   *Su + Su*

Embryo (2*n*)
Su su

Endosperm (3*n*)
Su su su (starchy)

actions among three allelic copies of a gene in the same nucleus. Heterozygous endosperm has two identical alleles from the polar nuclei of the
embryo sac and the alternative third allele is derived from the sperm
nucleus with which the two polar nuclei fused initially. By crossing *flinty*
(*F*) females and *floury* (*f*) males, *FFf* endosperm is produced; while the
reciprocal cross gives rise to seeds with *Fff* endosperm (Fig. 2.18). The endosperm character can be observed directly in the seeds on the ear, so seeds
need not be planted before the breeding results are recorded. The *FFf*
genotype determined flinty endosperm, and *Fff* was floury. In this case, it
takes two dominant alleles to mask the expression of the *f* allele. This is not
always the case, since starchy (*Su*) endosperm is produced with either *Su
Su su* or *Su su su* genotypes, and only the triple recessive has sugary endosperm (Fig. 2.19).

2.9   Neurospora

Important breakthroughs were made in biochemical genetics during the
1940s and afterward when the filamentous fungus *Neurospora crassa* took
its place in the lineup of genetically studied species. There are four species of
Neurospora, but virtually all studies have used *N. crassa*, and this is the
species meant when no other is specified. Neurospora belongs to the Ascomycetes, a group of fungi characterized by reproducing sexually to produce
ascospores in a sac called an **ascus**, and reproducing asexually to produce
salmon-pink spores called **conidia** (Fig. 2.20). The conidia are produced in
fantastic numbers on the haploid filamentous body of the fungus, which is a
mass of tubular **hyphae** making up a **mycelium**. The common name of
"red bread mold" comes from its color due to masses of conidia on the
mycelium, and because it once was a nasty contaminant in bakeries.

Neurospora has two mating types, *A* and *a*, which are determined by a
pair of alleles of the mating type gene. Sexual reproduction can only take
place when haploid nuclei in cells of opposite mating type unite, producing
the diploid fusion nucleus or zygote. The zygote is the only diploid stage in
Neurospora, since meiosis begins shortly after nuclear fusion and leads to
haploid meiotic products within the ascus. These four nuclei divide again by
mitosis, and thick spore walls soon form around each nucleus until every
ascus has a set of eight ascospores ripe for release. The ascus is a slender sac
with no space for nuclei to slip past one another. The four nuclei formed
after meiosis or the eight nuclei formed when each of these has completed
mitosis remain in a linear row within an ascus. While the initial four products of meiosis may be genetically distinct, depending on their alleles, the
two members of a pair of ascospores are allelically identical because they
arose by mitosis. When ascospores are released spontaneously or after manipulation from the ascus, each ascospore may germinate to produce a new
haploid mycelium whose genotype was determined during segregation and
reassortment of alleles.

The linear ordering of ascospores provided an unusual opportunity to
recover and analyze all four products of meiosis (called a tetrad) from an
individual fusion nucleus. By **tetrad analysis** it was possible to get geno-

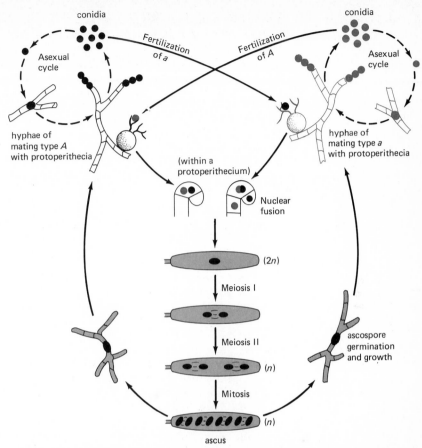

Figure 2.20 Life cycle of *Neurospora crassa*, showing asexual and sexual systems. In the sexual phase, fertilization occurs when haploid nuclei of opposite mating type (*A*, *a*) unite to produce the 2*n* zygote nucleus. Haploidy is reinstituted by meiosis, producing four nuclei per ascus. Each haploid nucleus undergoes mitosis, producing a final linear array of eight (four pairs) ascospores ordered precisely in the sequence in which the nuclei arose during meiosis and mitosis. Each ascospore can germinate asexually to produce a new haploid mycelium.

typic and phenotypic ratios directly for *single* meiotic events, rather than relying on statistical samplings exclusively. Using a microscope and a fine needle, individual ascospores could be dissected *in the order of their alignment within an ascus* and transferred in known sequence to tubes of culture media for germination and growth (Fig. 2.21). By lining up the set of eight tubes it is possible to refer the phenotypes directly to segregation of alleles at meiosis. Each culture is haploid, so there is no masking or masked allele of a pair as there is in a heterozygous diploid in other species; each phenotype is developed from one genome and can therefore be related directly to the haploid genotype present in the culture.

Cultures which produce pink spores are genetically different from cultures producing colorless spores; each breeds true in both sexual and

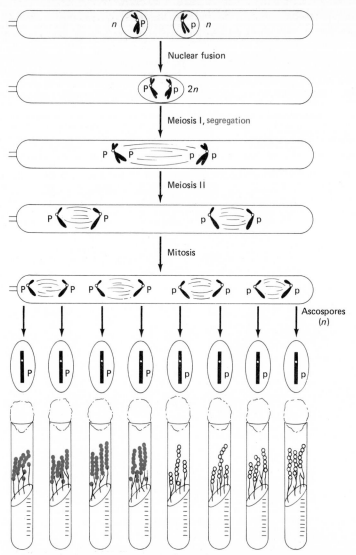

Figure 2.21 First-division segregation within an ascus of *Neurospora crassa*. The behavior of the pair of homologous chromosomes carrying alleles *P* and *p* (conidiospore color) provide the basis for understanding arrangements of ascospore types within an ascus. Ascospores are dissected in the order of their arrangement within the ascus, and are placed individually on growth media in separate test tubes. When the mold develops, conidiospore color can be related back to the particular order of alleles on chromosomes within the ascus. Knowing about chromosome behavior at meiosis, one can see that *P* and *p* segregated at Meiosis I in the heterozygous *Pp* diploid nucleus. Centromeres are shown as clear circles on chromosomes.

asexual reproduction. When *pink* × *colorless* crosses are analyzed, each ascus can be shown to have 4 pink and 4 colorless products of ascospore development. The ratio of 1 pink:1 colorless is read out directly as segrega-

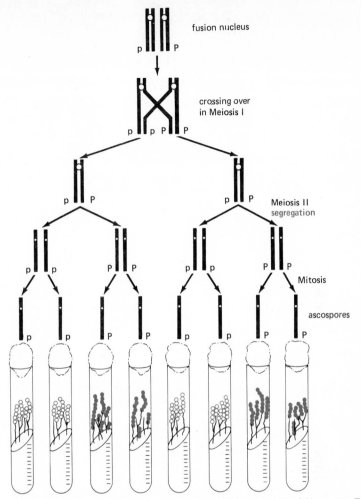

fusion nucleus

crossing over
in Meiosis I

Meiosis II
segregation

Mitosis

ascospores

Figure 2.22 Second-division segregation within an ascus of *N. crassa*. Each nucleus produced during Meiosis I is still heterozygous (*Pp*); *P* and *p* alleles do not segregate (assort into separate nuclei) until Meiosis II in this case. Ascospore order can be determined from culture growth in the eight ordered test tubes, and be related back to the distribution of alleles during meiosis. Second-division segregations result when an exchange occurs between gene locus and centromere of two chromatids in the bivalent during meiosis.

tion of *P* and *p* alleles at meiosis. The alignment of these alleles from one end of an ascus to the other included:

arrangement no.	order of ascospores	
1	*P P P P p p p p*	
2	*p p p p P P P P*	
3	*P P p p p P P p p*	(all are 4 *P*:4 *p*
4	*p p P P p p P P*	or, 1:1 ratio of
5	*P P p p p p P P*	the two alleles)
6	*p p P P P P p p*	

From Fig. 2.21 you can see how arrangements 1 and 2 can arise when homologous chromosomes segregate at the first meiotic division; then, during Meiosis II, each Meiosis I nucleus produces an identical partner nucleus and each of these, in turn, undergoes mitosis. The explanation for the ascospore ordering in examples 3 and 4 can be found in Fig. 2.22. An exchange of non-sister chromatid segments (crossover) between the gene and the centromere took place giving rise to what are called **second-division segregations**. Arrangements 1 and 2 result from **first-division segregations**. Information from the proportion of these two kinds of segregation patterns can be used to estimate the distance between the gene and the centromere of a chromosome, and to map the likely position of the centromere itself. Since it is very difficult to study the small Neurospora chromosomes by microscopy, genetic analysis of the ascospores is the principal means for discovering cytological information in this organism. We have not explained the chromosomal events leading to arrangements 5 and 6. Can you diagram the probable basis for these two arrangements?

In addition to tetrad analysis and its many uses, another general test method used with Neurospora and some other organisms is the **complementation test**. The hyphae are filaments of multinucleate cells, which can undergo localized fusions that allow nuclear exchanges. When mycelia of genetically marked cultures are put together in the same medium, nuclear exchanges usually lead to **heterokaryons**, whose cells have more than one genetic type of haploid nucleus. This situation is comparable to heterozygous organisms whose homologous genomes may contain different alleles of the same genes. There is one important difference, however. The genomes are within the same nucleus and all the nuclei are identical in a multicellular heterozygote; heterokaryons have different alleles in different haploid nuclei in the same cells or hyphae (Fig. 2.23).

Wild type Neurospora is cultured in a **minimal medium** containing all its growth requirements. Many mutants have been found with one or more additional growth requirements, due to modified biochemistry and metabolism governed by mutant alleles of the wild type genes. When a mutant requiring the amino acid arginine is grown in culture, arginine must be added to the minimal medium or there is no growth; the same situation is true for a histidine-requiring mutant. When the two mutant strains are cultured together, the hyphae fuse to form a heterokaryon with different haploid nuclei in the same cells. The resulting heterokaryon is able to grow in minimal medium unsupplemented with arginine or histidine. The two mutants complement each other's deficiencies. This must mean that the arginine mutant has the wild type allele for histidine and the histidine mutant must have the wild type allele for arginine (Fig. 2.24). Each kind of nucleus in the heterokaryotic hyphae governs synthesis for one of these amino acids in the cytoplasm, so that both amino acids are available in the common cytoplasm for normal development of the heterokaryon in minimal medium.

It is not particularly surprising that different phenotypes have different genotypes. But in cases of heterokaryons formed from different strains with the same phenotype, we may find one of two possible alternatives as the simplest explanations: (1) neither can grow either separately or together in

Figure 2.23 Different alleles of genes would be present in the same nuclei in a diploid heterozygote (*AaBb*), while different alleles would be present in separate nuclei in a haploid heterokaryon (*Ab + aB*).

Cytoplasm   Nucleus

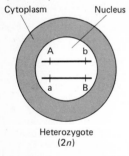

Heterozygote
(2*n*)

Cytoplasm   Nucleus

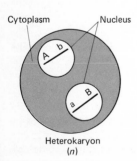

Heterokaryon
(*n*)

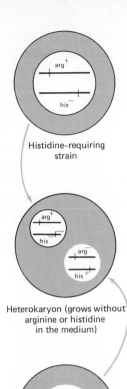

Histidine–requiring
strain

Heterokaryon (grows without
arginine or histidine
in the medium)

Arginine–requiring
strain

Figure 2.24 Mutant strains of *Neurospora* require supplements in the nutrient medium in order to grow. Heterokaryons formed from strains with different growth requirements may grow in media without supplements. Each mutant nucleus **complements** the other in the heterokaryon, which indicates that the *his⁻* nucleus must carry *arg⁺*, and the *arg⁻* nucleus must carry *his⁺*. With *arg⁺* and *his⁺* alleles in heterokaryons, growth is possible on minimal media.

minimal medium, or (2) both can grow together in minimal medium but only in supplemented media when cultured singly. Depending on whether or not the phenotypically similar strains can complement each other and grow on minimal medium, we can make the preliminary determination of whether the phenotypes are governed by the same gene or by different genes.

When two independently isolated arginine-requiring strains, called arginine-1 and arginine-2, form heterokaryons which do complement each other, it must mean that there are at least two different genes governing arginine metabolism, and that each strain has the wild type allele for one of the genes and the mutant allele for the other, or $arg\text{-}1^+arg\text{-}2^- + arg\text{-}1^-arg\text{-}2^+$. If the two arginine-requiring strains do not complement each other, we have preliminary evidence that each strain has the same mutant allele for a single gene and the deficiency cannot be remedied. The evidence in the second case is negative, that is, nothing happened. There could be other reasons for such negative results; for example, hyphal fusions do not occur between certain strains of Neurospora. But further investigation is warranted in order to establish the basis for noncomplementation.

Complementation in heterozygous diploids of various species can also be tested when appropriate crosses are made. The discovery of **multiple alleles**, that is, more than two alleles for the same gene, was based on finding that *mutant × mutant → mutant* phenotype, versus *mutant × mutant → wild type* phenotype, as follows:

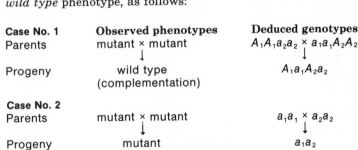

Case No. 1	Observed phenotypes	Deduced genotypes
Parents	mutant × mutant	$A_1A_1a_2a_2 \times a_1a_1A_2A_2$
	↓	↓
Progeny	wild type (complementation)	$A_1a_1A_2a_2$

Case No. 2		
Parents	mutant × mutant	$a_1a_1 \times a_2a_2$
	↓	↓
Progeny	mutant (no complementation)	a_1a_2

In Case No. 1 there must be two pairs of alleles governing the same phenotype, neither one of which alone can produce the wild phenotype: these alleles would be A_1 and a_1 of one gene and A_2 and a_2 for the second gene. You will recall that this situation resembles the inheritance of cyanide content in white clover (see Section 1.7).

In Case No. 2 there must be only one gene for the characteristic, and expression of the wild phenotype requires at least one dominant allele (A). When there is a mutant allele on each of the two chromosomes in the nucleus, the mutant phenotype is expressed. In this case, therefore, there are multiple alleles of one gene: two recessive mutant (a_1 and a_2), and one dominant allele for expression of the wild phenotype. This situation resembles the one described for Drosophila eye-color inheritance in Section 1.6.

REPRODUCTION IN BACTERIA AND VIRUSES

Bacteria are haploid, unicellular microorganisms which reproduce by **fission** (a form of asexual reproduction in which cells divide in two). They can be grown in culture on defined nutrient media and can be studied by all the methods of biochemistry and microscopy at our disposal. When grown in liquid media the cells remain in suspension and the medium becomes cloudier as more cells are formed. On solid nutrient media where cell movement is inhibited, individual cells continue to reproduce in place until a visible pile of cells called a **colony** appears on the surface of the medium. The group of identical cells in a colony is a **clone**, since each colony arises by fission from a single parent cell. Each colony can be analyzed as if it was the single cell from which the entire clone arose, but many studies can be done which would be impossible using only one cell.

Viruses can reproduce only inside a living host cell. There is never a sign of cellular organization or of a cell division process such as fission. Instead, the entering virus genes subvert the host metabolic machinery to make new virus genes and proteins and to stop making their own requirements. The newly synthesized virus molecules *assemble* into new viruses within the infected host cell, and mature infective virus progeny are released when the host cell bursts, or **lyses**. Each new virus can then initiate a new infection cycle in another host cell.

2.10   *Escherichia coli*

The common colon bacillus, *E. coli*, is a normal inhabitant of the human gut. It is a typical rod-shaped species with a generation time of 20 to 30 minutes, and an individual cell is about 1 millionth of an inch long. Its rapid reproduction and small size make *E. coli* as useful an experimental organism as Neurospora, but more limited in its morphological variations that are visible to the naked eye. Most of its phenotypic features are biochemical and physiological traits which can be observed in relation to colony growth on minimal versus supplemented media. Methods for counting cells in liquid culture are simple and straightforward, and based on serial dilutions or on optical readings of the cloudiness of the culture medium. Colonies on solid media are visible to the naked eye after one day's growth, and an apparently clear liquid culture will turn cloudy overnight as billions of cells arise by fission.

One of the great surprises in the history of genetics was the discovery of new combinations of traits among descendants of genetically marked bacterial parent strains grown together in liquid culture and then plated out on solid media to detect new genotypes. A brief report in 1946 by Joshua Lederberg and Edward Tatum, bcth of whom received the Nobel prize in 1960 for this and other work, opened the way to a whole new discipline of bacterial genetics. Since bacteria have no conventional means for sexual reproduction or even for mitosis as we know these processes in eukaryotic species, the way in which recombinant genotypes arose was not immediately clear and was not described until some years later. We will have ample opportunity to discuss *E. coli* genetics in various parts of this book, but for now it will be instructive to see how Lederberg and Tatum designed their experiment and how they used a general selection method which has since become a standard in microbial genetics.

Mutant cells having single nutritional deficiencies were obtained by exposing *E. coli* to mutagenic doses of x-ray or ultraviolet light. Multiple deficiencies were incorporated into individual strains by successive mutagenic treatments. Two triple mutants were studied: strain Y-10 required threonine, leucine, and thiamin supplements in minimal medium in order to grow, and strain Y-24 required biotin, phenylalanine, and cysteine. Thiamin and biotin are vitamins and the other four substances are amino acids. After a period of growth in the same liquid culture medium, samples containing many millions of cells were plated on minimal media and allowed to develop into colonies. The colonies were isolated and grown in pure culture to establish their altered genetic nature and their purity of type. Only about 1 cell per million from the original mixed culture actually formed colonies on the solid minimal medium. Because of their small size and huge populations produced within hours, the rare recombinants were detectable by this **prototroph selection** method. Prototrophs are wild type cells and their mutant alternatives are called **auxotrophs**. The prototrophic recombinants must have contained wild type alleles for all six of the observed nutritional characteristics, otherwise they could not have grown in minimal medium and maintained their new genotypes in subsequent generations in culture:

auxotrophic parents: $thr^-leu^-thi^-bio^+phe^+cys^+ \times thr^+leu^+thi^+bio^-phe^-cys^-$

prototrophic recombinants: $thr^+leu^+thi^+bio^+phe^+cys^+$

Using prototroph selection it is possible to analyze many millions of cells in a short time and a small amount of space, and to detect rare new phenotypes and genotypes. Strains carrying numerous mutant alleles can be studied by breeding tests which are unmanageable with higher organisms, since it is not desirable or convenient to examine millions upon millions of flies, corn plants, or similar species in F_1, F_2, or testcross generations. When we discuss gene mapping in Chapter 5, it will be easy to see the relative advantages of using *E. coli* as compared with most eukaryotic species.

2.11 Bacteriophage T2

Viruses which infect bacteria are called bacteriophages, or **phages** for short, and they have been studied genetically for more than 40 years. Phage T2 is one of the specific viruses infecting *E. coli*, and others are known and

Table 2.3
Some characteristics of representative viruses

Nucleic acid	Virus	Main host	Comments
DNA			
single stranded	fd	*Escherichia coli*	
double stranded	T2, T4, T6	*Escherichia coli*	
	P22	*Salmonella typhimurium*	
	herpes simplex	human	type 1 causes "fever blisters"
			type 2 causes genital herpes (a venereal disease)
	variola	human	causes smallpox
	Epstein-Barr	human	causes infectious mono-nucleosis; associated with Burkitt's lymphoma
	cauliflower mosaic	cauliflower	transmitted by aphids
RNA			
single stranded	Qβ	*Escherichia coli*	
	tobacco mosaic	tobacco	
	polio	human	
	measles	human	
	mumps	human	
	influenza A, B, C	human	
double stranded	reovirus	human	causes mild illness of respiratory and GI tracts
	wound tumor	plants	transmitted by leafhoppers

have been studied. All viruses require living host cells in which they can reproduce. The particular host species and host cell type provide two of the various bases for identifying and naming viruses (Table 2.3).

When T2 infects its host, the phage attaches by its tail to the host cell and injects its DNA into the host while leaving its empty protein coat outside (Fig. 2.25). The bacterial metabolic machinery is subverted to making new virus molecules instead of tending to its own needs. After a brief interval of synthesis, new phage particles assemble and end this **vegetative phase** of the cycle when they become mature, infective particles. Phages emerge when the bacterium **lyses**, or breaks up, to release a burst of progeny viruses. Each infective virus can initiate a new cycle using another host cell for its reproduction.

Because of their small size most viruses can be seen only by electron microscopy. They are usually studied phenotypically after growth on a lawn of bacterial cells covering the entire surface of solid nutrient medium. Under appropriate conditions, one phage infects one cell, and its progeny are released when that cell bursts. The liberated phages proceed to infect other cells around the original site, and in one day a visible clear area appears on the plate. This area is called a **plaque**. Plaque type is an inherited characteristic since different phages and strains produce clear

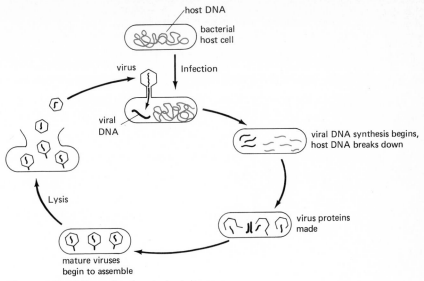

Figure 2.25   Life cycle of a virulent phage.

zones and cloudy ones, some with a sharp margin and others more jagged, some larger and others smaller, and so forth. In addition to plaque phenotypes, there are a number of other characteristics such as phage morphology, biochemical variability, and the range of host types which can be infected. Each plaque is equivalent to one virus when determining phage counts, just as each colony represents one bacterial cell in quantitative studies. The entire plaque arose from lysed bacteria that can be traced back to a single phage infecting a single bacterium on the plate.

The kind of life history shown in Fig. 2.25 is typical for a **virulent** phage, that is, one which destroys its host after infection. There also are **temperate** phages, which can infect their hosts without destroying them (Fig. 2.26). Temperate phages are transmitted from one host generation to the next, since they are integrated into the bacterial genome. On occasion, a temperate phage stops being benign and becomes infective, causing host lysis. The occasional virulent phage in a temperate population allows us to recognize the presence of integrated phages, which are called **prophages**, in the **lysogenic** host (has the ability to be lysed but carries the benign prophage). Phage production can be *induced* in certain lysogenic strains by appropriate treatments, such as ultraviolet light. From such studies it has been shown that temperate and virulent phages are essentially similar in their reproduction, but that the **latent period** is suspended before virus multiplication in lysogenic bacteria and is very brief in bacteria which are infected with virulent phages.

Phage T2 provided convincing information supporting the hypothesis that DNA was the genetic material, rather than proteins as many had believed earlier. In 1952 Alfred Hershey and Martha Chase took advantage of the knowledge of the phage reproductive cycle and of newly available

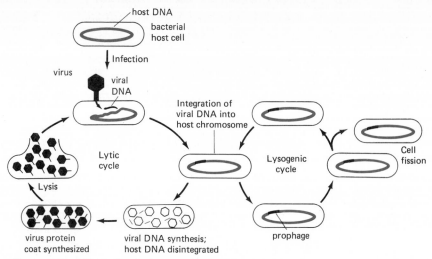

Figure 2.26 Life cycle of a temperate phage.

radioactive isotopes to determine whether DNA or protein was the genetic material in T2 (and by extension, in other species as well).

T2, like other T-even phages (T4 and T6), consists of about equal amounts of DNA and protein, exclusively. Each kind of molecule has a unique atom which is lacking in the other; DNA contains phosphorus (^{31}P) but no sulfur (^{32}S), while proteins usually have sulfur but no phosphorus. DNA in one set of T2 was labeled with radioactive P atoms [^{32}P] by growing the viruses in *E. coli* on [^{32}P]-labeled nutrient medium, and the proteins in another set of T2 were labeled with radioactive sulfur atoms [^{35}S] in a similar manner. The rationale for the experiment was rather straightforward: the new viruses which are made in infected *E. coli* are genetically identical to the original infecting phages added to these cells; therefore, whichever kind of molecule entered *E. coli* must contain genetic instructions for making progeny phages. The materials remaining outside the host cells must not have a genetic role in reproduction.

E. coli was grown in unlabeled medium (containing ^{31}P and ^{32}S) and was then infected in separate experiments by [^{32}P] DNA-labeled phages, [^{35}S] protein-labeled phages, and by **multiple infection** using both [^{32}P] and [^{35}S] viruses. After a few minutes to allow infection to take place, but before host cell lysis, the infected *E. coli* were suspended in liquid and put into an ordinary food blender. The shearing forces were enough to knock off any adhering virus materials from the cell surface but not to damage the *E. coli* cells themselves.

The suspended materials were removed from the blender and centrifuged to separate the bacterial sediment and the remaining supernatant liquid which contained any virus material that had not entered the cells during infection (Fig. 2.27). When the sedimented cells were examined they were found to contain [^{32}P] DNA and varying but much lower amounts of [^{35}S] protein. The [^{32}P]-containing DNA of the virus had apparently entered the bacterial cells. Most of the [^{35}S] protein was found in the fluid remaining after the bacterial sediment was removed, and little or no [^{32}P] DNA was present in this fluid. The [^{35}S]-containing protein did not enter the bacterial cells. From their preliminary studies of T2, Hershey and Chase had found that the phage DNA is surrounded by the protein coat of the particle. When T2 infected *E. coli*, the phage DNA entered the cells but the phage protein coats remained outside and appeared as empty ghosts attached to the bacterial wall. Using these and other lines of information, Hershey and Chase concluded that DNA must be the genetic material, since DNA entered the host cell and guided the production of virus progeny, while protein remained outside the cell for the most part.

When *E. coli* was allowed to go to the end of the cycle and burst to release mature phage progeny, some of these phages were found to contain [^{32}P] DNA but no [^{35}S]protein. On the basis of expected gene behavior in directing

Figure 2.27 Illustration of the main features in the Hershey-Chase experiments. T2 phages carrying labeled protein *or* labeled DNA were allowed to infect *E. coli*. After infection was initiated, the viruses and their host cells were separated mechanically (blender). Labeled DNA was found inside the host while labeled protein occurred primarily outside the *E. coli* cells. DNA must therefore be the genetic material, directing virus reproduction during the infection cycle in host cells.

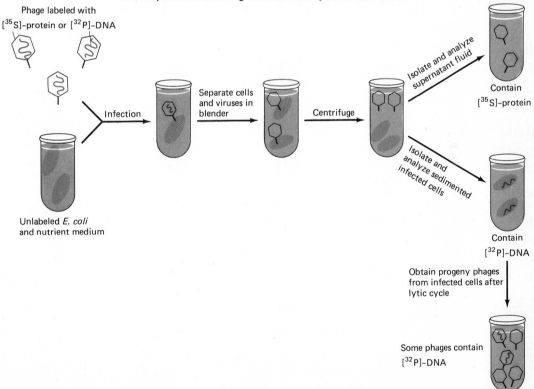

Phage labeled with [^{35}S]-protein or [^{32}P]-DNA

Unlabeled *E. coli* and nutrient medium

Infection

Separate cells and viruses in blender

Centrifuge

Isolate and analyze supernatant fluid

Contain [^{35}S]-protein

Isolate and analyze sedimented infected cells

Contain [^{32}P]-DNA

Obtain progeny phages from infected cells after lytic cycle

Some phages contain [^{32}P]-DNA

progeny formation and in maintaining genetic continuity, the only reasonable conclusion was that DNA and not protein was the genetic material. The phage DNA had directed synthesis of new phage-specific DNA, which was passed on to new generations of virus progeny.

OTHER GENETICALLY USEFUL ORGANISMS

We study the human species because we have a vital interest in our own biology, from an intellectual standpoint as well as from the practical necessity of knowing how to manipulate a situation to make it suitable or advantageous for our lives. Other organisms have been studied genetically, for many reasons. One of the most important decisions to be made by a geneticist is which experimental organism to use for a particular kind of problem. The basis for such a decision generally depends on being able to use some particular or unusual feature of a system so that it can be exploited to the maximum for the purpose of experimental study. Each of the organisms we have mentioned so far comes under these categories of usefulness. In the long run, we expect to establish general principles which apply to all life forms, although the specific information may have been obtained using a virus or Drosophila. General principles and a basic understanding of life processes are the ultimate goals of scientific inquiry.

As we proceed through this book there will be a variety of species described in relation to particular genetic topics. Vertebrate animal species of particular value or interest in genetic analysis, in addition to humans and other mammalian types, include the chicken (an avian, or bird, representative), toads (amphibian types), and a number of domesticated animals of agricultural importance, such as cattle. Among the invertebrate animals there is special emphasis on the insects, such as Drosophila and other members of the insect order called Diptera (two-winged).

Flowering plants, more than other kinds of plants, have provided a great deal of basic genetic information. In addition to corn, there is much that has been learned by studying the tomato, tobacco, wheat, and other agricultural crops, as well as wild species such as members of the sunflower family. Relatively fewer plant species have been studied than one might expect, often because of the long generation time and large space requirements in the field or the greenhouse.

For the most part, microorganisms have become favorite genetic systems for study. We have mentioned their obvious advantages in describing Neurospora, E. coli, and phages. Many species of fungi, algae, protozoa, and similar eukaryotic microorganisms are widely used in genetic analysis. Perhaps the most intensively studied organisms today, however, are a few species of bacteria and an increasing number of viruses. The particular advantages of bacteria and viruses, in addition to rapid generation times of less than an hour and the degree of control over their growth in the laboratory, is their great value in molecular analysis. DNA, RNA, and proteins can be isolated and purified from pure cultures, and large quantities of purified molecules can be subjected to the most versatile and precise analytical methods.

The development of cell culture methods has opened new avenues for study of large multicellular organisms, in conditions that are similar to those used in studying microorganisms. Cells in culture can be grown as pure clones, examined for colony or growth characteristics on solid media, and be prepared for the same kinds of genetic and molecular analyses usually expected only for microorganisms.

Advances in our understanding of genetic systems have, therefore, come from many kinds of experimental methods using various organisms. The sum of these separate studies is the clarification of biological principles which can be applied to all life, including our own species.

QUESTIONS AND PROBLEMS

2.1. Suppose you were given an electron micrograph of a section through a eukaryotic cell, but the section happened to be made of a part of the cell excluding the nucleus. How could you verify that the cell was indeed from a eukaryote?

2.2. Which phases of the cell cycle take place between telophase of one mitosis and prophase of the succeeding mitosis? What is the general nature of events taking place in these particular phases of the cell cycle?

2.3. Distinguish between two chromatids and two homologous chromosomes. During which phase of the cell cycle are sister chromatids first produced? When do they become visible by microscopy?

2.4. What are the genetic consequences of mitosis? of meiosis?

2.5. There are 23 pairs of chromosomes in humans. What proportion of human gametes will have centromeres of the following types:
   a. paternal or maternal origin only?
   b. a mixture of maternal and paternal?

2.6. How many chromosomes will be found in the following kinds of cells in humans?
   a. secondary spermatocyte
   b. spermatogonial cell
   c. primary oocyte at leptonema
   d. a polar body

2.7. The amount of DNA in a haploid nucleus of the mouse (*Mus musculus*) is about 2.5 picograms (2.5×10^{-12} g). What would be the DNA content of a nucleus in each of the following:
   a. body (somatic) cell in G_1 of a cell cycle
   b. spermatozoan
   c. primary spermatocyte at diplonema
   d. secondary spermatocyte at prophase II
   e. secondary spermatocyte at telophase II
   f. zygote at metaphase of the first mitotic division

2.8. A synaptonemal complex forms between homologous chromosomes early in prophase I of meiosis and holds the bivalent in register throughout pachynema. Why is it unlikely that the synaptonemal complex initiates synapsis of homologues at zygonema?

2.9. How does chromosome behavior during meiosis help to explain Mendel's First and Second Laws of inheritance?

2.10. *Aspergillus nidulans*, like *Neurospora*, is an ascomycetous fungus. During an experiment a yellow, adenine-requiring strain and a white, proline-requiring strain were inoculated together onto minimal medium lacking adenine and proline. Shortly afterward, growing green mycelium appeared from the inoculum. Give your interpretation of the occurrence of growth. How would you test this interpretation genetically?

2.11. In a cross between homozygous flinty (*FF*) females and floury (*ff*) males in corn, what are the genotypes of the following:
a. endosperm of the kernels produced on the female plants
b. embryo of the kernels produced on the female plants
c. sperm nuclei of germinated pollen grains
d. any nucleus of the embryo sac (female gametophyte)
e. endosperm of kernels produced on female plants of the reciprocal cross

2.12. In crosses between *Neurospora* strains which produce black spores (*B*) and others which produce tan spores (*b*), the following kinds of asci were recovered:

Ascus type	Order of ascospores
1	*b b b b B B B B*
2	*B B B B b b b b*
3	*B B b b b b B B*
4	*b b B B B B b b*
5	*b b B B b b B B*
6	*B B b b B B b b*

a. Which arrangements arise from first-division segregations and which arise from second-division segregations?
b. Diagram the events during meiosis which lead to production of ascus types 5 and 6.

2.13. Mutation rates for genes in bacteria are usually rather low, occurring on the average of about 1×10^{-7}. In the prototroph selection experiments conducted by Lederberg and Tatum using *E. coli*, what would be the probability that spontaneous prototrophic mutants of the genotype $thr^+leu^+thi^+bio^+phe^+cys^+$ would arise in either the $thr^+leu^+thi^+bio^-phe^-cys^-$ or the $thr^-leu^-thi^-bio^+phe^+cys^+$ auxotrophic parent cultures?

2.14. We usually are not particularly concerned about dominance or recessiveness of allelic genes in species like *Neurospora crassa* or *E. coli*, but we do care about these designations in organisms such as corn, mice, and *Drosophila*. Why is this true?

2.15. What evidence was provided by Hershey and Chase in experiments using phage T2 to support the hypothesis that DNA is the genetic material, and protein is not?

REFERENCES

Avers, C. J. 1976. *Cell Biology.* New York: D. Van Nostrand.

Beam, C. A., M. Himes, J. Himelfarb, C. Link, and K. Shaw. 1977. Genetic evidence of unusual meiosis in the dinoflagellate *Cryp-thecodinium cohnii. Genetics* **87**:19.

Campbell, A. Dec. 1976. How viruses insert their DNA into the DNA of the host cell. *Sci. Amer.* **235**:102.

DuPraw, E. J. 1970. *DNA and Chromosomes.* New York: Holt, Rinehart, Winston.

Hershey, A. D., and M. Chase. 1952. Independent functions of viral protein and nucleic acid in growth of bacteriophage. *J. Gen. Physiol.* **36**:39.

Mazia, D. Jan. 1974. The cell cycle. *Sci. Amer.* **230**:54.

Moens, P. B. 1978. The onset of meiosis. In *Cell Biology, A Comprehensive Treatise*, Vol. 1. L. Goldstein and D. M. Prescott, eds. New York: Academic Press, p. 93.

White, M. J. D. 1973. *The Chromosomes*, 6th ed. London: Chapman & Hall.

3

Chromosomes: Vehicles of Inheritance

In the last chapter we saw how Mendel's observations of inheritance patterns could be understood in terms of genes on chromosomes, segregating and assorting independently at meiosis. In this chapter we will consider some of the evidence for specific genes being located on specific chromosomes.

Patterns of inheritance from breeding analysis in various organisms or from family studies of human inheritance provided the major evidence that X-linked genes were located on the X chromosome, and other genes were located on nonsex chromosomes, or autosomes. Very few genes have been found on the Y chromosome in mammals or in Drosophila, and these Y-linked genes are unusual in that their sole function appears to be related to differentiation of sexual structures in the male. X-linked genes, like autosomal genes, govern many nonsexual characteristics of the individual. In human inheritance as with other species, the basic rules of Mendelian segregation and reassortment of pairs of alleles apply and form the theoretical basis for patterns which have been found. These Mendelian rules also provide probabilities, which are a basis for predicting risk of having a defective child when the prospective parents have a history of some inherited condition in one or both families.

Chromosomes are nucleoprotein bodies, whose basic unit of structure is a single, continuous chromatin fiber. The continuity of the chromatin fiber resides in the single DNA molecule which runs from one end to the other of a chromosome. Chromosomes are differentiated into functionally distinct regions, whose activities cannot be taken over by other parts of the genome. Two such differentiated regions are the centromere, needed for chromosome movement at anaphase, and the nucleolar-organizing regions where ribosomal RNA genes contribute to formation of ribosomes needed for protein synthesis.

Various studies of gene action and gene function have shown that chromosomal behavior parallels gene activity and that genes in chromosomes direct the synthesis of proteins which lead to the ultimate development of a phenotype in cells or organisms.

SEX CHROMOSOMES

There are two broad classes of chromosomes in many eukaryotic species: **sex chromosomes** and **autosomes** (nonsex chromosomes). The patterns of Mendelian inheritance of genes on the sex chromosomes are usually distinctive and recognizably different from patterns of autosomal gene inheritance. In certain inheritance patterns, there is a relationship between the sex of the individual and the development of a particular genotype into a particular phenotype. These genes usually are on autosomes and not on the sex chromosomes themselves, according to the observed inheritance pattern.

The determination of sex in animals and in some plants and eukaryotic microorganisms may be based on a chromosomal, genic, or nongenetic mechanism. In chromosomal and genic systems sex usually is determined at the moment of fertilization. In nongenetic sex determination systems, the particular sex which finally develops may be influenced by various environmental factors in the embryo or larval stages before differentiation into the adult takes place.

The historical significance of sex chromosomes is based on the fact that the first genetic studies which showed that genes were in chromosomes, and that a particular gene was specifically located in a certain chromosome, were conducted with **X-linked genes** on the X chromosome. These studies provided the first substantial genetic evidence for the Chromosome Theory of Heredity.

3.1 Discovery of the Sex Chromosomes

The first specific information on sex chromosomes came from cytological studies by C.E. McClung, E.B. Wilson, and Nettie Stevens, between 1901 and 1905. They all studied insect chromosomes, particularly in spermatocytes of grasshoppers and other members of the order Orthoptera, these being favorite materials of the early microscopists. Meiotic chromosomes are particularly well displayed in these cells. McClung noted that all the chromosomes were paired except for one "accessory" chromosome in grasshopper spermatocytes (Fig. 3.1). He suggested that this chromosome was concerned with sex determination at fertilization, since females had only paired chromosomes in oocyte meiosis and lacked the "accessory" chromosome. Wilson and Stevens straightened out the details of the story in 1905, and called McClung's "accessory" chromosome the **X chromosome**.

Female grasshoppers and most other female orthopteran insects have a pair of X chromosomes, while males have only one X. When eggs are formed at meiosis, each egg receives one X chromosome of the pair so that every egg has an X. Stevens suggested that when meiosis takes place in spermatocytes, half the sperm receive an X chromosome and half do not. When fertilization occurs, there is an even chance that an egg will be fertilized by an X-carrying sperm or by a sperm without an X chromosome; fertilized eggs may be either XX or XO (pronounced "oh", signifying no second sex chromosome is present). Because of random fertilizations, about half the zygotes will develop into females (XX) and about half into males (XO). The sex of the

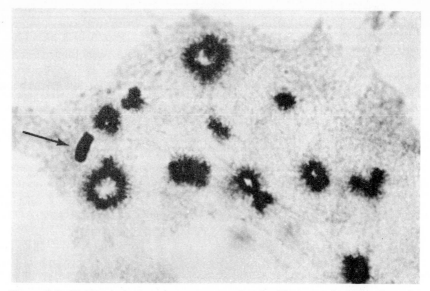

Figure 3.1 Diakinesis in grasshopper spermatocyte. There are 11 bivalents and a highly condensed, unpaired X chromosome (arrow), making a diploid chromosome count of 23 in this XX ♀/XO ♂ orthopteran species.

individual is thus determined at fertilization, by the nature of the sperm that fuses with the egg (Fig. 3.2).

Stevens, Wilson, and others described sex chromosomes in other species, including the fruit fly, *Drosophila melanogaster*. In most of these species there is a mate for the X chromosome in males, and this partner of the X was called the **Y chromosome.** In some species the Y chromosome was much

Figure 3.2 Chromosomal mechanisms of sex determination: (a) In the XX/XO system and in (b) the XX/XY system, sex is determined at fertilization in accordance with the kind of sperm fertilizing the X-carrying egg. The sex ratio, at least at birth, should be 1 ♀:1 ♂, since each of the two kinds of sperm has a 50% chance of fertilizing the egg.

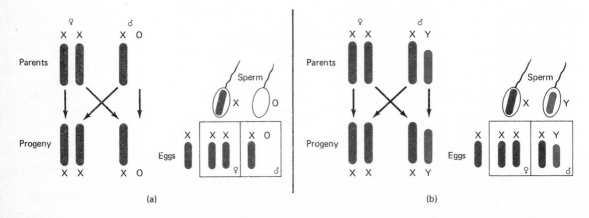

smaller than the X, as it is in human beings. In other cases the Y was different in shape but not necessarily smaller, as in Drosophila. A sex ratio of 1 female:1 male is obtained similarly in XX/XO and XX/XY species; sex is determined at fertilization according to the kind of sperm which fertilizes the egg, on a random basis. Each gamete also contributes one set of nonsex chromosomes, or autosomes, to the zygote, and these pairs of autosomes carry many pairs of alleles in the diploid nucleus.

3.2   X-Linked Inheritance in Drosophila

In 1903 Walter Sutton proposed the **Chromosome Theory of Heredity** in an essentially modern form. The parallel behavior of genes in inheritance and chromosomes in the nucleus made a powerful but circumstantial case for genes being located on chromosomes. There was no experimental evidence to support this theory until 1910, when Thomas Hunt Morgan published a brief report on the inheritance of white eyes and wild-type red eyes in Drosophila.

A white-eyed male appeared suddenly in true-breeding cultures of red-eyed flies. Morgan mated this male to its red-eyed sisters and found that all the F_1 offspring had red eyes. In the F_2 generation there were:

2,459 red-eyed females
1,011 red-eyed males
782 white-eyed males

Since the F_1 had red eyes and since the F_2 showed a reasonable Mendelian ratio of 3 red:1 white, red eyes was dominant to white eyes. Morgan noted the unusual feature that all the F_2 white-eyed flies were males.

In order to determine if females could be produced with the mutant white-eye phenotype, Morgan performed a testcross of F_1 red-eyed females with the original white-eyed male parent. In their progeny Morgan found:

129 red-eyed females
132 red-eyed males
88 white-eyed females
86 white-eyed males

Once again there is a deficiency in the recessive class which distorts the ratio, but there is a reasonable approximation of 1 red:1 white, for both males and females. The 1:1 testcross ratio verified single-gene inheritance, and also showed that white eyes could develop in females as well as in males.

Knowing that females are XX and males are XY, Morgan's results can be explained if we assume the gene is present on the X and absent from the Y chromosome (Fig. 3.3). All sons receive their only X chromosome through the eggs from their mothers. The Y chromosome, of course, comes only from their fathers. Daughters, on the other hand, get one X from their mothers and one X from their fathers. By putting the alleles on the X chromosome and following through the F_1 and F_2 generations, we can see that the pat-

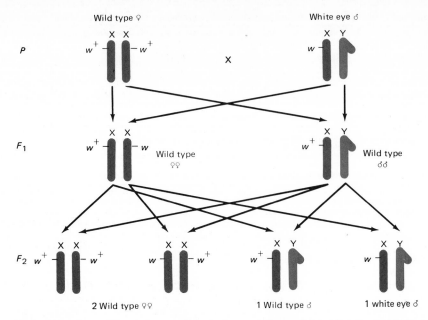

Figure 3.3 Illustration of the parallels between pattern of inheritance of X-linked alleles and pattern of transmission of the sex chromosomes in *Drosophila*.

tern of **sex-linked inheritance** parallels the pattern of transmission of the X chromosome. Males are **hemizygous** for their sex-linked alleles, having only one sex-linked allele of every kind on their one X chromosome. If the mother is heterozygous, half her eggs receive the X chromosome carrying the w^+ allele and half the eggs receive the w-carrying X, when these chromosomes segregate at meiosis. Half the sons of a w^+w mother will be red-eyed and half will be white-eyed, reflecting that half the eggs are of each genetic type.

In the testcross of the white-eyed male to his heterozygous F_1 daughters, we would predict sons with white eyes and sons with red eyes, on the same basis as just described. We would further predict the production of white-eyed females in this testcross progeny since all daughters receive an X with the w allele from their father, while half get an X from their mothers carrying the w allele and half receive the w^+ allele (Fig. 3.4). We not only would predict these kinds of females, but we would be able to say that half the females would be red-eyed and half would be white-eyed. This is just what Morgan found.

Morgan also made the reciprocal cross between white-eyed females and red-eyed males (Fig. 3.5). These results conform to the predictions made for parallel transmission of X chromosomes and sex-linked alleles on these chromosomes. They also point out two important features which distinguish sex-linked inheritance: (1) reciprocal crosses produce different progenies, and (2) sons resemble their mothers more than their fathers, revealing a "criss-cross" inheritance pattern.

The allele symbols we have just used were first proposed by Drosophila

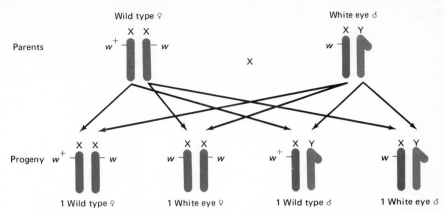

Figure 3.4 Testcross of white-eyed ♂ to his heterozygous F₁ daughters leads to the prediction that equal numbers of red-eyed and white-eyed ♂♂ and ♀♀ will be produced in this progeny, if the eye color gene is X-linked as hypothesized.

geneticists and have since been adopted for many, but not all, organisms. The gene symbol describes the mutant characteristic, w for white eyes, and its wild-type allele is indicated by a superscript +, w^+. Any other alleles at this same gene locus would be distinguished by the superscript, for example, w^e for the eosin-eye mutant allele of w^+. These symbols tell us that the wild type allele is dominant to the mutant allele(s). If we were dealing with

Figure 3.5 Reciprocal cross to one shown in Fig. 3.3, in which results conform to predictions made on the basis of parallel transmission of X chromosomes and X-linked alleles on these chromosomes.

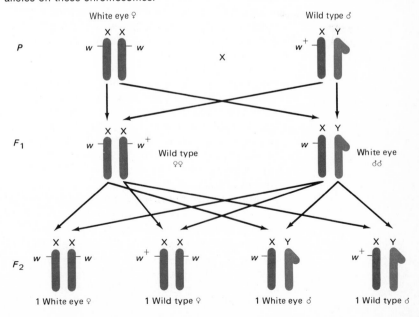

a dominant mutant allele and its wild-type recessive allele, as for bar-eyed and nonbar-eyed Drosophila, the symbols are *B* for the dominant bar-eye allele and *B*⁺ for the recessive wild type allele. By using a gene symbol describing the *mutant* characteristic we can tell at a glance if it is dominant (capital letter) or recessive (lower-case letter) to its wild type alternative (carries the + superscript).

This convention is different from the one we used for most of the discussion so far, where the wild-type allele for the dominant character appeared as the capital letter and its recessive mutant allele as a lower-case letter; for example, *T* symbolized the dominant wild type tall character and *t* its recessive short allele. Where it seems appropriate or is used for a particular species, as with corn, we will stick with the *T/t* kind of allele symbols; otherwise we will use the Drosophila convention.

In **autosomal inheritance**, such as Mendel's studies with peas, reciprocal crosses produce identical F_1 and F_2 progenies. Sons and daughters resemble either their fathers or their mothers, depending on which parent carries the dominant and which the recessive alleles. Autosomal patterns tell us that each pair of autosomes carries an equivalent set of alleles. Sex linkage, on the other hand, indicates the genetic difference between the X and Y chromosomes. What would you predict for the pattern of inheritance of genes on the Y chromosome when the X has no matching alleles? How could you distinguish X-linked and Y-linked inheritance from a pattern produced when the X and Y chromosomes carry alleles of the same gene in a species with XX females and XY males? All of these patterns have been found, which is a very good reason for using the more specific term X-linked inheritance for genes on the X chromosome. The more general term sex-linked should really be reserved for situations which have not yet been resolved to known sex chromosomes or where any sex chromosome-linked inheritance pattern is discussed, in general.

Morgan's pioneer study of the inheritance of white eyes in Drosophila opened the way to investigations of genes on chromosomes. Between 1911 and 1913 Morgan and his student Alfred Sturtevant had located six different mutant alleles on the X chromosome in Drosophila. As we will see in the next chapter, these studies of X-linked inheritance led Sturtevant to propose and develop a method for mapping genes on chromosomes, a method we use to the present day.

3.3   Other Inheritance Patterns Associated With Sex

It is fairly obvious that species having some other system of sex chromosomes can be discovered by genetic analysis, even when cytological studies are difficult or uninformative. Chickens were among the first animals to show a different pattern from the one found in Drosophila (Fig. 3.6). The inheritance of the sex-linked dominant for barred feather pattern versus nonbarred in poultry is clear from the two major features of the breeding analysis: (1) reciprocal crosses give rise to different F_1 and F_2 progenies, in direct relation to the sex having two sex chromosomes of one kind versus one of that kind; and (2) most of the progeny resemble one parent more than

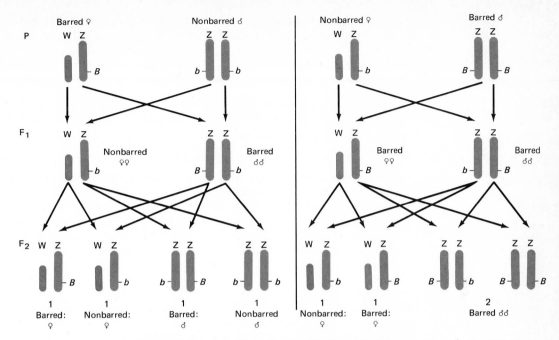

Figure 3.6 Sex-linked inheritance of feather color pattern in chickens. Barred feathers is inherited as a sex-linked dominant trait, according to the F_1 and F_2 progeny genotypic and phenotypic ratios. The particular phenotypic distribution found here is characteristic of organisms in which the female has a single X chromosome and is, therefore, the heterogametic sex. The X chromosome equivalent is often referred to as the Z chromosome, and the Y chromosome equivalent as W.

the other. In this case, however, the transmission of alleles parallels the transmission of two like sex chromosomes from the male parent rather than from the female parent.

We can tell that barred is dominant because it appears in all the F_1 of one of the reciprocal crosses and in the Mendelian 3:1 ratio in the F_2 from that cross. The 1:1 F_1 and F_2 ratios of the reciprocal cross are not informative in this respect, but they do indicate that sex-linkage determines the genotypic and phenotypic distributions when both reciprocal sets of crosses are compared.

In addition to birds, a **heterogametic** (two kinds of gametes) female and **homogametic** (one kind of gamete) male are typical of reptiles, some kinds of amphibia and fish, and the moths and butterflies (Lepidoptera). The usual convention has been to distinguish this pattern from female XX/male XY by using different letters (WZ females and ZZ males). It is just as simple to retain the letters X and Y, as long as the sex of the XX and XY individuals is specified.

Two other patterns of inheritance are associated with the sex of the individual, but the controlling genes are located on autosomes and not on sex chromosomes. The inheritance patterns are very clear for **sex-limited** phenotypic expression, since one sex expresses the two phenotypic alterna-

Genotype	♀ Phenotype ♂	
H H	hen–feathered	hen–feathered
H h	hen–feathered	hen–feathered
h h	hen–feathered	cock–feathered

Figure 3.7 Sex-limited inheritance of tail-feathering in chickens. The phenotypic ratio of 3 hen-feathered:1 cock-feathered ♂♂ in reciprocal F_2 progenies of heterozygous F_1 parents provides the basis for interpreting this characteristic to be due to autosomal, single-gene inheritance.

tives and the other sex only develops one of the two expressions regardless of its genotype (Fig. 3.7). Clearly, the characteristics usually are ones by which the males and females differ in their sexual development. In human beings, an inherited recessive condition called *testicular feminization syndrome* is only expressed in XY individuals. The mutant phenotype involves development of female genitalia and other anatomical features

Figure 3.8 Sex-influenced inheritance of pattern baldness in humans. Theoretically, different phenotypes for F_1 ♀♀ and ♂♂, and 3:1 versus 1:3 F_2 ratios for the two sexes, establishes this inheritance pattern for a single autosomal gene. The allele which is dominant in one sex is recessive in the other. Family studies have provided the evidence for sex-influenced inheritance in the case of this human trait.

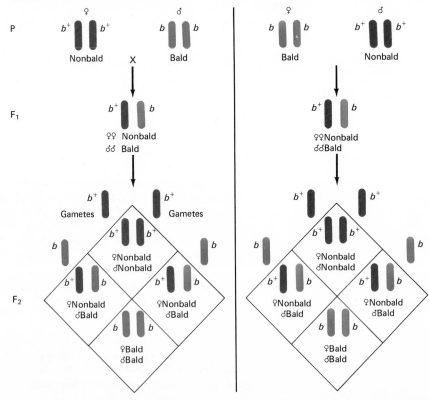

under sex-hormonal control. It can only be detected in males because these structures would develop anyway in XX females of all three genotypes. Such males are XY, and they have testes. Their insensitivity to male sex hormone produced in the embryonic testes leads to their physical development as females under the direction of female sex hormones which are produced in the adrenal glands of all males.

In **sex-influenced inheritance** of one pair of alleles, we find the Mendelian 3:1 ratio among the F_2 (Fig. 3.8). Since reciprocal crosses produce identical F_1 and F_2 progeny, inheritance must be autosomal. The difference arises in the distribution of dominant and recessive phenotypes between the sexes. There is a reversal of dominance and recessiveness of the two alleles in relation to the sex hormonal constitution of the individual. The allele which is dominant in one sex behaves as a recessive in the other sex. In human beings, pattern baldness is far more common among men than women. The phenotype is expressed in men whether they are homozygous or heterozygous for the b allele, which indicates dominance of this allele in males. Women express pattern baldness only when they have the b b genotype, which is expected in recessive inheritance. In a large sampling of heterozygote matings, we would find that 3/4 of the daughters were nonbald:1/4 balding, and among the sons there would be 1/4 nonbald:3/4 balding.

Another sex-influenced inheritance pattern in human beings involves comparative lengths of the index finger and the fourth finger on your hand. When the index finger is equal to or longer than the fourth finger, we find that the characteristic is female-dominant and male-recessive (Fig. 3.9). Can you reach this conclusion by recording the phenotype among members of your family? If the family is large enough and involves several generations, you should receive at least a hint of this inheritance pattern. A more reliable interpretation can be made if you pool your data with those from your

Figure 3.9 An autosomal sex-influenced human trait. The dominant trait in females is an index finger which is equal to, or longer than, the fourth finger; but it is the recessive condition in males. Both of the individuals photographed were heterozygous for the trait (♀, right; ♂, left).

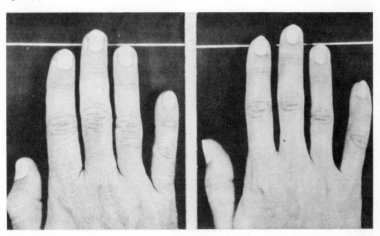

Table 3.1
Summary of the major chromosomal sex determination patterns

Females	Males	Species in which these sex chromosomes occur
XX	XY	mammals, *Drosophila,* some flowering plants
XX	XO	most grasshoppers (Orthoptera)
XY	XX	some fishes, reptiles, birds, Lepidoptera (butterflies and moths)
X	Y	liverworts (Bryophyta)

friends and classmates; a large enough sampling should reveal the genetic pattern.

In many cases of sex-influenced inheritance we can trace the differences in expression to hormonal differences during development. The behavior of an allele as a dominant or recessive is a function of the biological environment in which gene action takes place. Dominance and recessiveness are *relative behaviors*, and are not based on some chemical or physical characteristic of the alleles themselves. While we can see this more clearly in some inheritance patterns, the principle applies to all genes and their alleles.

3.4   Sex Determination Systems

The volume of genetic and chromosomal studies using Drosophila and other insects proved to be very useful in describing the sex chromosome makeup in different species, and in revealing the mechanism responsible for sex determination in these insects (Table 3.1).

Since male Drosophila and orthopterans developed whether or not a Y chromosome was present, the Y chromosome was irrelevant to sex determination in these species. Through comparisons of Drosophila strains differing in numbers of X chromosomes and sets of autosomes (A), the **Sex Balance** theory of sex determination was conceived (Table 3.2). When the ratio of X:A was 1.0 or greater, females developed; when the ratio of X:A was 0.5 or less, males developed. Females that were XXY and had two sets of

Table 3.2
Sex determination is based upon a balance between number of X chromosomes and number of autosome sets in *Drosophila melanogaster*

Sex chromosomes present	Number of sets of autosomes	Ratio of X:A	Sex of the individual
XX	2	1.00	female
XY	2	0.50	male
XXX	2	1.50	metafemale (sterile)
XXXX	3	1.33	metafemale (sterile)
XXY	2	1.00	female
XXX	4	0.75	intersex
XX	3	0.67	intersex
XY	3	0.33	metamale (sterile)
X	2	0.50	male (sterile)

autosomes were sexually equivalent to females that were XX:AA; males developed whether they were X:AA or XY:AA. Various intersex or other aberrant types appeared when the ratio deviated from X:A = 1.0 or 0.5. The determination of sex therefore depended on the ratio or balance between number of X chromosomes and number of autosome sets which came together at fertilization.

The same chromosomal mechanism for sex determination was presumed to characterize other XX female/XY male (or XY female/XX male) systems, including human beings and other mammals. Beginning in 1959, evidence was collected from cytological and genetic studies in mice which showed that XO animals were female and that XXY make-up led to males (Fig. 3.10). Female mice showing a recessive phenotype that should have been obscured if they had also inherited the dominant allele on an X chromosome from their mothers, were assumed to be XO; this was verified cytologically. Other mice were shown to be XXY males, from cytological examination and from their presumed genotype showing that one sex-linked allele must have come from each parent and that, therefore, one of their two X chromosomes had come from each parent.

From combined cytogenetic studies and from many chromosomal studies, the system of **chromosomal sex determination** in mammals was shown to be strongly Y-chromosome-determining (Table 3.3). The crucial observations were that XO = male in Drosophila but female in mammals, and XXY = female in Drosophila but male in mammals. These observations were amply supported by consistently finding that males always had at least one Y chromosome and one or more X chromosomes, while females had at least one X but no Y chromosome. All of these sex chromosome constitutions were found in individuals having two sets of autosomes. Mammalian species do not tolerate gross disturbances in their

Table 3.3
Sex chromosome anomalies and sex determination in humans

Individual designation	Chromosome constitution*	Sex
Normal male	46,XY	Male
Normal female	46,XX	Female
Turner female	45,X	Female
Triplo-X female	47,XXX	Female
Tetra-X female	48,XXXX	Female
Penta-X female	49,XXXXX	Female
Klinefelter males	47,XXY	Male
	48,XXXY	Male
	49,XXXXY	Male
	48,XXYY	Male
	49,XXXYY	Male
XYY male	47,XYY	Male

*The two-digit number indicates the total number of chromosomes in diploid cells, followed by the exact number and kinds of sex chromosomes in this complement. Two sets of autosomes are present, accounting for 44 of the total number of chromosomes in these cells.

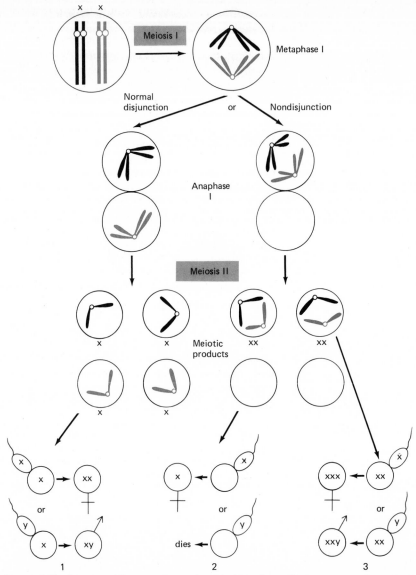

Figure 3.10 In mammalian species males develop when a Y chromosome is present, along with one or more X chromosomes. There is no Y chromosome in mammalian females. The occurrence of XO ♀♀, XXY ♂♂, and other anomalous conditions, is due to missing or extra sex chromosomes in one or both of the gametes. The phenomenon responsible for aberrant chromosome numbers is nondisjunction, a faulty distribution event in which homologous chromosomes do not separate at anaphase and are, therefore, included or excluded together in a meiotic nuclear product.

autosomal numbers, either of whole sets or of individual chromosomes, so all possible comparisons with the Drosophila pattern cannot be made. There really is little need for such extensive comparison, however, since the role of the Y chromosome in mammalian sex determination is quite clear from the data which are available.

Women who are XO show the symptoms of **Turner syndrome**, characterized in part by short stature, underdeveloped breasts and internal reproductive organs, and certain other physical traits. Men who are XXY or some variation on this constitution very often display the symptoms of **Klinefelter syndrome**, characterized by relatively long limbs in proportion to torso length, larger breast development than in XY males, and smaller testes. In general, XO women are less feminized and XXY men are more feminized in their external appearance than their XX and XY counterparts. Hormonal modifications under the influence of the sex chromosomes are clearly indicated. We will discuss these and other sex chromosomal anomalies more fully in Chapter 11.

Many species, particularly among eukaryotic microorganisms, have a **genic sex-determination** system (Fig. 3.11). We described Neurospora as having two mating types based on two alleles of the one mating type gene. This is a fairly typical pattern among many of the algae, fungi, and protists. Many variations on this theme have been found, principally showing more than 1 gene for mating types. Simpler organisms may have more than two mating types, determined by these genes. Genic sex-determination has also been found in certain fish, often operating in conjunction with sex chromosomes. In some genetic studies it has been shown that the genic and chromosomal systems can be separated so that only one or the other functions.

Various organisms have a pattern of **noninherited sex determination**, even when individuals are clearly males and females, reproductively

Figure 3.11 Whether sex determination is due to two kinds of sex chromosomes or two kinds of alleles of a gene, a sex ratio of 1 ♀:1 ♂ is expected if both kinds of gametes from the heterogametic sex (shown here as the ♂) occur in equal numbers, and if fertilization of the single kind of egg takes place at random with respect to male gamete type. Diploids are shown here, but the systems work similarly in haploid organisms.

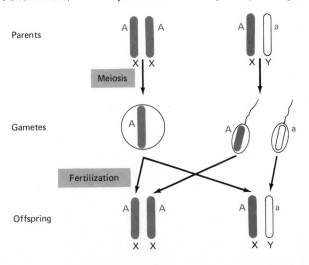

and morphologically. The marine worm *Bonnelia* provides the usually cited example of such a system. Larvae which hatch from fertilized eggs are sexually neutral. When a free-swimming larva settles on a rock or other surface, it develops into a female. Larvae which settle on a mature female, however, develop into tiny male individuals. When larvae are placed in water containing extracts of female worms, these larvae develop as males. Larvae in control media, lacking female extract, will develop into females after settling on the surface of the experimental container.

Many **hermaphroditic** species (having both ovaries and testes in the same individual) lack a sex determination system, as we would expect. Earthworms, snails, most of the flowering plants, and other bisexual organisms lack any sex-determining system of genes or chromosomes. In those few flowering plants that are **dioecious** (separate male and female flowers on separate plants), sex chromosomes may be present (Fig. 3.12). The flowering plant *Melandrium* was known for many years to have XX female and XY male differentiation, with the Y chromosome being strongly male-determining.

Still other patterns are known, in relatively great variety. We will gain little, however, by their detailed comparison at this stage in our discussion. If it is appropriate to some genetic question elsewhere in this book, one or more of these alternative patterns may be described at that time.

FAMILY STUDIES OF HUMAN INHERITANCE

It is quite obvious that analysis of human inheritance requires methods other than controlled breeding analysis. The method of choice for single-gene inheritance is to construct **family histories**, or **pedigrees**, and seek the clues which match expected patterns of allele transmission and

Figure 3.12 Metaphase I in a diploid male plant of *Melandrium* (*Lychnis*). There are 11 pairs of autosomes and one pair of sex chromosomes, seen at the left. The Y chromosome appears to be a little larger than the X chromosome.

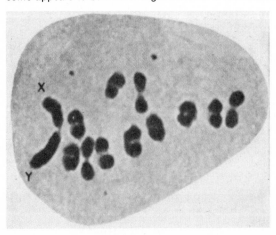

phenotypic ratios known from genetic analysis of organisms such as Drosophila, mice, and garden peas.

3.5   Autosomal Inheritance

From what we know in other species, we would expect autosomal alleles to be expressed equally in both sexes, and to show a 3:1 phenotypic ratio in heterozygote × heterozygote and a 1:1 ratio in recessive × heterozygote matings. These are equivalents of F_2 and backcross ratios, respectively. For recessive allele a:

		$a^+a \times a^+a$	
		a^+	a
a^+		a^+a^+	a^+a
a		a^+a	aa

		$a^+a \times a^+a^+$	
		a^+	
a^+		a^+a^+	
a		a^+a	

		$a^+a \times aa$	
		a	
a^+		a^+a	
a		aa	

For dominant allele A, we expect:

		$A^+A \times A^+A$	
		A^+	A
A^+		A^+A^+	A^+A
A		A^+A	AA

		$A^+A \times A^+A^+$	
		A^+	
A^+		A^+A^+	
A		A^+A	

		$A^+A \times AA$	
		A	
A^+		A^+A	
A		AA	

Let's see how these patterns can be interpreted from pedigrees for brown versus blue eyes, an autosomal recessive if we consider blue eyes and an autosomal dominant for brown eyes inheritance. We will take a family consisting of four generations (Fig. 3.13).

Several family groups in this pedigree provide the necessary clues to show that brown eyes and blue eyes are alternative phenotypes for one gene, that the allele for brown eyes is dominant to the allele for blue eyes, and that the eye color gene is autosomal.

1. *Single-gene inheritance.* We would expect a testcross ratio of 1 brown: 1 blue, or a ratio of 3 brown: 1 blue if both parents are heterozygous. We find here that brown × blue gives a 1:1 phenotypic ratio for the children of I-3 × I-4 and II-9 × II-10. Although the family is small, there is a ratio of 3 brown:1 blue among the children of I-1 × I-2.

2. *Dominance of the allele for brown.* If brown is the dominant phenotype, then we expect all the children of a homozygous dominant brown and a recessive blue to have brown eyes, as in F_1 progeny.

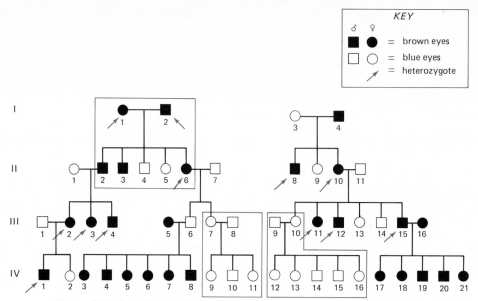

Figure 3.13 Inheritance of brown versus blue eye color in four generations of a family. Analysis of family members indicates monohybrid, autosomal inheritance, with brown dominant over blue. Some family members discussed in the text are shown boxed in red.

This is the case for the children of II-1 × II-2, and III-5 × III-6. In addition, we expect a segregation of brown and blue in the children of heterozygous parents with the dominant phenotype (I-1 × I-2), but no segregation if both parents have the recessive phenotype (III-7 × III-8 and III-9 × III-10 are blue-eyed parents whose children are all blue-eyed).

3.   *The eye color gene is autosomal.* Both males and females have brown or blue eyes equally often, which we expect for autosomal inheritance. We also expect reciprocal matings to produce identical phenotype ratios in the progeny, as seen in the families of II-1 × II-2 and III-5 × III-6.

In cases of relatively *rare* dominant or recessive mutant alleles, there are additional clues to be derived from family studies (Fig. 3.14). Since these alleles are rare in the population as a whole, and since people tend to select partners who are not relatives, we expect the following patterns to appear in **autosomal dominant inheritance:**

1.   Most matings are between heterozygotes and recessives, leading to predominantly 1:1 phenotypic ratios for all the children, regardless of sex.

2.   The dominant phenotype appears in every generation, if families are large enough to provide reasonable ratio approximations.

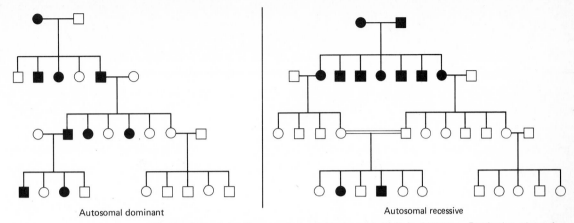

Figure 3.14 Inheritance of a relatively rare trait in humans. Particular clues for autosomal dominant inheritance and for recessive inheritance are included in these pedigrees, and are discussed in the text.

3. The phenotype may be transmitted by either parent having the dominant trait, but it is never transmitted when neither parent expresses the trait (and must therefore be recessives).

In **autosomal recessive inheritance** for some rare traits, the family patterns usually reveal the following features:

1. The trait does not appear in every generation; it "skips" generations or appears in some family member even when it was absent in a number of previous generations within the family.
2. The mutant phenotype usually is produced in children of parents with the normal phenotype (who must therefore be heterozygotes).
3. All the children will express the mutant trait when both parents have the recessive phenotype.
4. Sons and daughters are equally likely to inherit a particular autosomal allele.

3.6 X-Linked Inheritance

From our analysis of red eyes and white eyes in Drosophila, we can more easily interpret Queen Victoria's family history of hemophilia, the "bleeder's disease," as one showing X-linked inheritance of a recessive trait (Fig. 3.15). Hemophilia occurred only in the males in her family, which might seem at first glance to indicate either sex-limited or Y-chromosome inheritance. By putting the appropriate alleles on the X chromosome, we can show that only certain male relatives were hemophilic only because there were no matings between hemophilic men and either hemophilic or carrier women. In particular, we find the "criss-cross" pattern of sons receiving this

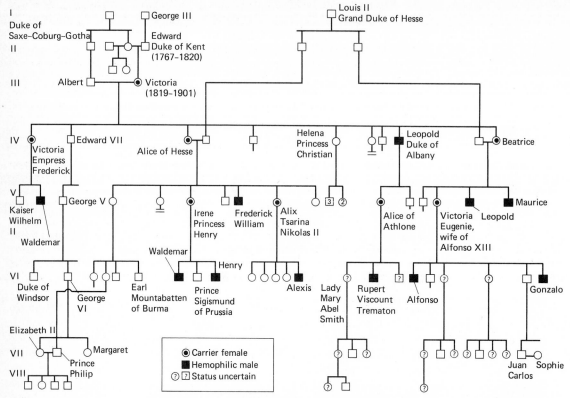

Figure 3.15 Hemophilia A (classical hemophilia) in various royal families related to Queen Victoria of Great Britain. Indications of X-linked recessive inheritance include occurrence of afflicted males and carrier females, and afflicted males have carrier mothers and afflicted male relatives, among other items.

characteristic because they have an X chromosome only from their mothers and no X from their fathers. If the characteristic were sex-limited, sons could receive the mutant allele from either father or mother. It is certainly not Y-chromosome inheritance because if it were *every* son should express the same trait as his father, and we find hemophilic sons from normal fathers and a normal son produced by Leopold, a hemophilic child of Victoria and Albert.

In **X-linked recessive inheritance**, therefore, we expect to find: (1) predominantly or only males affected, depending on the kinds of matings; (2) affected sons have carrier mothers, and male relatives (uncles, cousins, and others) with the affliction; (3) if the family is large enough we would find afflicted and normal sons about equally often among the children of carrier mothers and normal fathers; and (4) afflicted fathers produce all carrier daughters but normal sons.

In **X-linked dominant inheritance**, we have a different situation because females have twice as much chance of receiving an X chromosome carrying the dominant allele than males do (from either a carrier mother or an afflicted father; Fig. 3.16). Whether she is homozygous or heterozygous for the dominant allele, the characteristic will be expressed in the female. Sons may receive either X chromosome through the egg from a heterozygous mother, so there is a 50-50 chance for the affliction appearing in sons of such a mother. Sons cannot inherit the trait from their father because his contribution to the fertilized egg is a Y and not an X chromosome. Once again, for rare X-linked dominant alleles we would find few matings between unrelated people who both happen to carry the same rare mutant allele. Most matings would be between one parent with the trait and one with the normal phenotype.

Through studies of this kind and others to be described in Chapter 5, more than 100 genes have been shown to be X-linked. Most of these genes on the human X chromosome have nothing whatever to do with sex; hemophilia is one such example of a gene related to a nonsexual phenotypic trait. Over 1100 genes have been shown by inheritance pattern analysis and by other means to be autosomal. At least one gene has been specifically assigned to every one of the 22 autosomes in the human complement. Most of the 1100 different autosomal genes identified from inheritance studies, however, have not yet been assigned to particular autosomes. In contrast with autosomes and the X chromosome, the human Y chromosome has at least one known gene, but two more may also be present. The Y-linked human genes are entirely concerned with development of sexual reproductive structures in the male embryo after approximately 6 weeks of its growth. Biochemical studies provided the information on these early-acting genes on the Y chromosome.

PROBABILITY AND THE BINOMIAL THEOREM

We have already discussed the laws of probability in relation to predicting the outcome of Mendelian inheritance in monohybrid and dihybrid crosses. In situations involving the inheritance of afflictions, anxious parents want to know the risk or chance of their having a child with some inherited trait

Figure 3.16 X-linked dominant inheritance of vitamin D-resistant rickets in one human family. Notice that both sexes may be affected. Marriage partners are not shown, but all were normal. In patterns such as these, affected males transmit the trait only to their daughters while affected mothers transmit the trait to their sons and daughters. (From *The Metabolic Basis of Inherited Disease.* J. B. Stanbury, J. B. Wyngaarden, and D. S. Frederickson, eds. Fig. 65-12; 1978. New York: McGraw-Hill.)

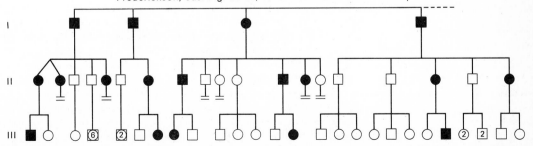

known to run in the family. We can use the same principles of probability in determining risk of the birth of one or more afflicted children in a particular family. The specific risks involved will depend on the genotypes of the parents, the nature of the inheritance pattern, dominance or recessiveness of the allele causing the affliction, and whether the allele is located on the X chromosome or an autosome.

3.7   Prediction of Risk

We briefly mentioned the Mendelian basis for predicting risk in the case of cystic fibrosis, an autosomal recessive trait, in Section 1.9. If both parents are heterozygous ($Cc \times Cc$), there is a 25% chance in *each* pregnancy for the birth of a child with this disease. If one parent is heterozygous and the other is homozygous dominant ($Cc \times CC$), the risk is zero because each child will inherit one dominant allele for normal development from the homozygous parent. There is a 50% chance for such a child to be heterozygous, and a 50% chance for it to be homozygous dominant since $Cc \times CC$ gives offspring which can only be Cc or CC, with equal probability for each genotype.

Each genetic situation provides the prediction of risk in accordance with the expected ratios of phenotypes and genotypes in single-gene inheritance (Fig. 3.17). For example, if a hemophilic son has been born in a family where the father is normal, we know the mother must be a carrier (heterozygous, Hh) and the father must be H (hemizygous for the dominant allele). The chance or risk of another hemophilic son would again be 50%, since each birth is an independent event. There is a 50% chance that the sperm carrying the H allele will fertilize an egg carrying the H allele on one of the mother's X chromosomes, or the h allele on her other X chromosome.

Suppose two people who plan to have a family want to know a range of risks they may expect knowing that hemophilia has occurred in the woman's family, among some of her male relatives. If the husband is normal, he must have the H genotype; she may be either HH or Hh. She can be tested, and if she is shown to be a carrier, the parents would be Hh and H. What is the risk of one hemophilic son? We have said it is 50%, or 1/2. What is the risk that they will have two hemophilic sons: $1/2 \times 1/2 = 1/4$, or 25%, since each birth is an independent event. What is the chance that only one of two sons might be born with hemophilia, and the other son would be normal? In this case, the chance that the first son will be hemophilic is 1/2, the chance that the second son will be hemophilic is 1/2, and the chance that only one of two sons will be a hemophiliac is also 1/2. The reason for this is that there are two sequences by which one son would be normal and the other would be a bleeder: first, a normal son followed by an abnormal son or $1/2 \times 1/2 = 1/4$; and second, an abnormal son followed by a normal son or $1/2 \times 1/2 = 1/4$. Since both of these sequences are possible, their separate probabilities must be added together to find out the total chance for obtaining a child of each type in two separate fertilizations, or $(1/2 \times 1/2) + (1/2 \times 1/2) = 1/2$.

If we substitute a for the chance of normal and b for abnormal, the chances for two normal children would be $a \times a = a^2$. The chances for two abnormal children would be $b \times b = b^2$, and the chances for one normal and

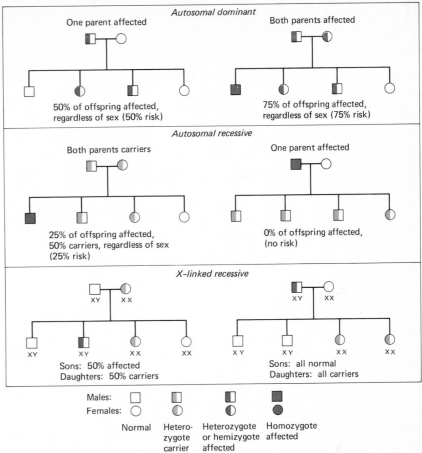

Figure 3.17 Prediction of risk of inheriting various single-gene defects depends on several items of information. Among the most important are chromosomal location of the gene; dominant, recessive, or codominant allele behavior; and the genotypes of the parents involved.

one abnormal child would be $a \times b$, or ab, and $b \times a$, or ba, which is summed up to be $2ab$. The equation for all possibilities is thus $a^2 + 2ab + b^2 = 1$. This equation is the expansion of the binomial $(a + b)^2$. In our example, the chance for a normal son is $1/2$, which is the value for a; the value for b is $1/2$, since the birth of an abnormal son is $1/2$. The chance for two normal sons $(a^2) = 1/2 \times 1/2$ or $1/4$; for one normal and one abnormal son $(2ab)$ it is $2(1/2 \times 1/2)$ or $1/2$; and for two abnormal sons (b^2) there is a $1/4$ risk.

Suppose we were dealing with two parents heterozygous for a recessive trait, such as cystic fibrosis. What is the chance for both children to be normal? The value for a is $3/4$ and the value for b is $1/4$, so the chance for two normal children is a^2 or $3/4 \times 3/4$, or $9/16$. The chances for one normal and one abnormal child are given by the binomial term $2ab$, so $2(3/4 \times 1/4)$, or $6/16$, is the chance in this case. The chances for two children with cystic fibrosis would be b^2 or $1/16$.

3.8   The Binomial Theorem

The binomial theorem provides a convenient shortcut method for determining the frequencies of genotypes and phenotypes in breeding analysis and in pedigree analysis. The theorem is useful in situations where either one of two events can occur by chance, such as normal or abnormal in the above examples. Once we know the probabilities of the two kinds of independent events, we can substitute the numerical probabilities for the values of a and b in the equation.

If we deal with two independent events, then the probability for all possible combinations is $(a + b)^2$; for three events it is $(a + b)^3$; for four events it is $(a + b)^4$. The number of individuals or individual events, therefore, determines the power to which the binomial is raised (Fig. 3.18). Depending on the number of individual events and the specific combination one desires to know, the appropriate term in the binomial expansion can be selected to gain the particular probability for the stated situation.

For relatively few events the binomial expansion serves quite well. But it becomes awkward to find the proper term when a larger number of events is involved. Whether a smaller or a larger number of individual events is in question, we can apply the following formula to determine probabilities instead of expanding the binomial to find the proper term:

$$\frac{n!}{x! \, (n\text{-}x)!} \times (a)^x (b)^{n\text{-}x}$$

The formula includes the number of events or individuals (n), the number of one type of individual or event (x), and the number of the alternative type (n-x). The symbol ! means factorial, that is, the product of all the integers to a specified term. For example, if $n = 5$, then $n! = 1 \times 2 \times 3 \times 4 \times 5$; if $x = 3$, then $x! = 1 \times 2 \times 3$. We should note that $0! = 1$. The symbols a and b stand for the probabilities of the two alternative events, just as they did in the binomial

Figure 3.18   The binomial theorem. Expansion of the binomial $(a + b)^n$, where n = the power of the binomial, $n + 1$ = the number of terms in the corresponding expansion, and $a = b = 1/2$. The coefficient of the first and last term is always 1, and the coefficient of the second and next to last term is the same as the power of the binomial in any given case. The coefficient of other terms is the sum of the coefficients above and to either side of the term in question. The values of the coefficients form a symmetrical distribution, and the number of possible combinations doubles with each successive increase in the power of the binomial.

Binomial	Power of binomial (n)	No. terms in expansion ($n + 1$)	Number of combinations	Expanded binomial
$(a + b)$	1	2	2	$a + b$
$(a + b)^2$	2	3	4	$a^2 + 2\,ab + b^2$
$(a + b)^3$	3	4	8	$a^3 + 3\,a^2b + 3\,ab^2 + b^2$
$(a + b)^4$	4	5	16	$a^4 + 4\,a^3b + 6\,a^2b^2 + 4\,ab^3 + b^4$
$(a + b)^5$	5	6	32	$a^5 + 5\,a^4b + 10\,a^3b^2 + 10\,a^2b^3 + 5\,ab^4 + b^5$
$(a + b)^6$	6	7	64	$a^6 + 6\,a^5b + 15\,a^4b^2 + 20\,a^3b^3 + 15\,a^2b^4 + 6\,ab^5 + b^6$

expansion. The first part of the factorial formula gives the number of possible orders of events, and the second part gives the probability of an order.

Suppose a family wanted to know their chances for having three boys and two girls. The probability for the birth of a girl is 1/2, and the probability for the birth of a boy is 1/2. We can substitute in the formula as follows:

$$\frac{5!}{(3!)\,(2!)} \times (\tfrac{1}{2})^3(\tfrac{1}{2})^2 = \frac{120}{12} \times (\tfrac{1}{2})^3(\tfrac{1}{2})^2 = 10(\tfrac{1}{2})^3(\tfrac{1}{2})^2 = \frac{10}{32} = 0.31, \text{ or } 31\%$$

If we had selected the term $10a^3b^2$ from the expansion of $(a + b)^5$, we would have arrived at the identical answer. You can see that because the term $10a^3b^2$ appears as $10(1/2)^3(1/2)^2$ in the solution which is calculated above using the factorial formula.

The binomial theorem is very useful in human pedigree analysis and predictions of risk, as well as in other situations. We will have occasion to refer to it again in discussions of the frequency of alleles in natural populations in Chapter 15, when we consider population genetics.

AN OVERVIEW OF CHROMOSOME ORGANIZATION AND ACTIVITY

An overall picture of chromosome morphology, types, numbers, and behavior permits us to move the gene from the realm of abstraction into the tangible world of test tubes, microscopes, and a variety of probes into its most intimate properties as part of the chromosome. At this stage in our discussions it should be helpful to paint in the broad outlines of the chemistry and organizational features of the chromosome, and touch briefly on the molecular contributions to phenotype development. We will return to this topic in greater detail beginning with Chapter 6.

3.9   Chemistry of the Chromosome

Chromosomes in most eukaryotes are rod-shaped structures which stain vividly and specifically with certain reagents. The stainable material was called **chromatin** by the early microscopists, and this continues to be a useful term today. The unreplicated chromosome consists of a single **chromatin fiber**, which is actually one continuous, linear molecule of **DNA** in association with basic **histone proteins**, acidic or neutral **non-histone proteins**, minor amounts of **RNA**, and a number of kinds of enzymes active in DNA and RNA synthesis. The chromatin fiber, therefore, is a high molecular weight, complex **nucleoprotein** fiber (Fig. 3.19). About 13-20 percent of the chromosome is DNA, and most of the remainder is protein. When the chromosome replicates, a new and identical chromatin fiber is synthesized so that each chromatid consists of one fiber carrying the same alleles as the original DNA before replication.

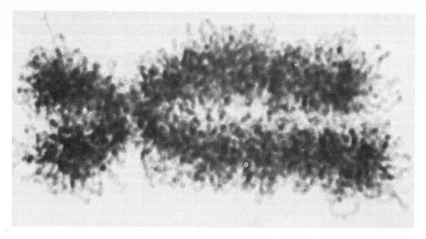

Figure 3.19 Electron micrograph of a whole mount of human chromosome 12. Each chromatid in this replicated metaphase chromosome is a single nucleoprotein, or chromatin, fiber. × 44,000. (Courtesy of E. J. DuPraw, from DuPraw, E. J. 1970. *DNA and Chromosomes*. New York: Holt, Rinehart, and Winston.)

The linear integrity of the chromosome resides in its continuous linear DNA molecule. If digestive enzyme tests are conducted, we find that the only enzyme that causes the chromosome to break up into pieces is deoxyribonuclease (**DNase**). Enzymes that digest proteins lead to an eroded appearance of the chromosome, but the structure retains its original length. These general observations have been extended recently and have provided a basis for a detailed molecular analysis of chromosome structural organization. In current studies of chromosome structure, DNase is used to fragment the chromosome into small, repeating units called **nucleosomes**. Each nucleosome unit of a chromatin fiber consists of a particular length of DNA complexed with histones. We will describe these studies and their implications starting in Chapter 7.

3.10   Functionally Different Parts of Chromosomes

Chromosomes are not just strings of genes lined up end to end; they are structures which are *differentiated* into regions with specific functions and morphology (Fig. 3.20). The **centromere** region, or **primary constriction**, is one such differentiation. Chromosomes cannot move directionally at anaphase of nuclear divisions unless a centromere is present. The centromere is a specific site for attachment of spindle fibers, and if there is no centromere spindle fibers cannot be inserted and there is no means by which the **acentric** chromosome can move directionally toward the poles (Fig. 3.21). If some rearrangement of chromosomes leads to a **dicentric** (two-centromere) chromosome, and if each centromere is oriented toward a different pole, then a "bridge" chromosome is observed at anaphase.

The centromere may be located anywhere along the length of a chromosome, even at the very tip. But each chromosome has its centromere

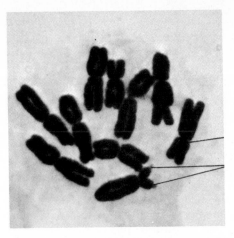

Primary
constriction

Secondary
constriction

Figure 3.20   Ten of the 16 chromosomes from onion root-tip cell. There is an obvious primary constriction (centromere region) in each replicated metaphase chromosome. One chromosome in the haploid genome has a secondary constriction at its nucleolar organizing region, and the typical satellite knob extending beyond this region on each chromatid.

in a fixed location which is constant for that chromosome. Chromosomes in a particular set can be recognized according to various criteria, including their centromere location, their relative lengths, and by the presence of **nucleolar-organizing regions** in satellited chromosomes of the complement. Each haploid complement of chromosomes must have at least one nucleolar-organizing region (**NOR**) at a fixed location on a nucleolar-organizing (**NO**)-chromosome.

The NO-chromosome has hundreds or thousands of repeated copies of the ribosomal RNA gene, arranged in tandem in the nucleolar-organizing region. There may be one NO-chromosome, as in corn (chromosome 6), or more than one in a species genome. The NO-chromosomes of the human complement are numbers 13, 14, 15, 21, and 22 (Fig. 3.22). Loss of the NOR by chromosome damage or by mutation, leading to total absence of ribosomal RNA genes, is a lethal condition. Without ribosomal RNA no ribosomes can be made, and without ribosomes no proteins can be synthesized.

3.11   Heterochromatin and X Inactivation

For over fifty years we have been aware of two kinds of chromatin, which are distinguished by their behavior during interphase between nuclear divisions. The chromatin which is greatly extended in conformation is called **euchromatin**, while **heterochromatin** remains condensed during interphase (Fig. 3.23). Knowledge of these cytological features was supplemented by genetic studies and by biochemical analysis of DNA replication during a cell cycle. The genetic studies revealed that heterochromatin is a remarkably stable form of DNA. This discovery is based on mutation

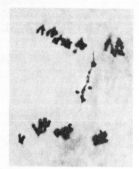

Figure 3.21 When the centromeres of a dicentric chromosome move to opposite poles, a bridge chromosome is produced at anaphase. There are two acentric fragments alongside the anaphase bridge, and neither can move directionally since neither has a centromere. (Courtesy of M. M. Rhoades)

studies in which very few mutant alleles have been mapped in heterochromatic regions as compared with the great bulk of genes mapped in euchromatic parts of chromosomes. Biochemical analysis of DNA replication showed that heterochromatin replicated late in the synthesis period, whereas euchromatin replicated earlier in this period. Heterochromatin is therefore: (1) condensed during interphase, (2) genetically stable, and (3) late-replicating.

There are two types of heterochromatin, facultative and constitutive. **Facultative heterochromatin** contains active genes, but may become condensed and genetically inactive in response to physiological and developmental conditions, and it may revert to a euchromatic state at certain times. **Constitutive heterochromatin** is permanently condensed, genetically stable, late-replicating material all of the time. The most common site for constitutive heterochromatin is around the centromere region of all chromosomes in most of the species studied so far. This kind of stable

Figure 3.22 Standardized representation of the human complement of 22 autosomes and the X and Y sex chromosomes. Chromosomes are arranged in order of decreasing size and by position of the centromere (median, submedian, or subterminal) into groups A-G. Each chromosome, however, can now be identified unambiguously according to its banding pattern after G-staining. The nucleolar-organizing chromosomes 13, 14, 15, 21, and 22, all are shown with typical satellite knobs adjacent to the nucleolar organizing region (secondary constriction). (From *Paris Conference (1971): Standardization in Human Cytogenetics*. Birth Defects: Original Article Series 8, No. 7, 1972. New York: The National Foundation.)

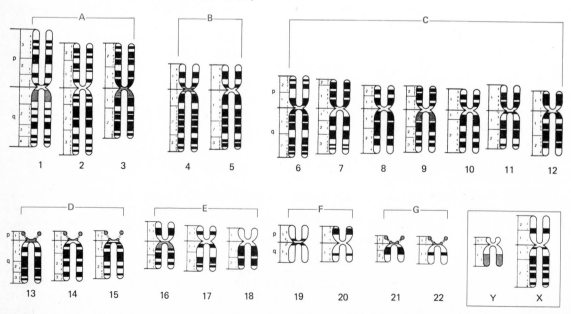

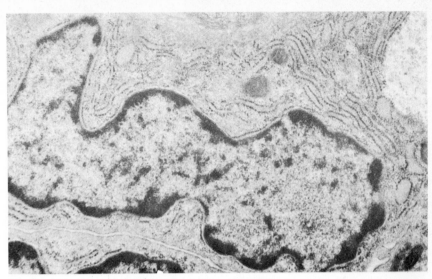

Figure 3.23 Electron micrograph of thin section of rat osteoblast. The condensed heterochromatin is located mainly at the periphery, next to the nuclear envelope. Euchromatin is dispersed in the remainder of this interphase nucleus. × 24,000. (Courtesy of M. Federman)

Figure 3.24 Barr body, or sex chromatin, in the human female. One of the two X chromosomes remains condensed during interphase, and is seen here at the periphery of one nucleus (arrow). (Courtesy of T. G. Tegenkamp)

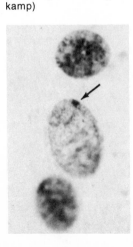

chromatin is highly desirable in a region of the chromosome which is essential for movement in the countless nuclear divisions during an individual's lifetime.

A well-known instance of facultative heterochromatin involves the mammalian X chromosome. The single X chromosome in males is almost entirely euchromatic. In females, one X chromosome remains largely euchromatic during the life of each cell, while the second X chromosome becomes condensed heterochromatin during embryonic development. The heterochromatic X chromosome is visible as a dense blob in the interphase nucleus, whereas other chromosomes are not distinguishable (Fig. 3.24). This blob is called **sex chromatin**, or a **Barr body**, and it permits a simple test for the identification of biological sex in human beings and other mammals. Females have one Barr body per nucleus, this being the condensed second X chromosome. Males have no Barr body, since their only X chromosome remains euchromatic throughout life.

In some patients with clinical symptoms that involve a sex-related characteristic, counts of Barr bodies have provided the starting point for a more detailed examination of the chromosome complement. Men with two X chromosomes (XXY) will have one Barr body in the nucleus, confirming the symptoms of Klinefelter syndrome. As the number of X chromosomes and, therefore, Barr bodies increases in a male patient, the more severe are the symptoms of Klinefelter syndrome and the greater the degree of mental retardation. Women with Turner syndrome (XO) have no Barr body, since their only X remains euchromatic. The simple relationship is: one X chromosome + n Barr bodies = the total number of X chromosomes in the nucleus. Only the euchromatic X is active and genetically functional.

The Y chromosome in mammals seems to be concerned primarily with sex determination. The few genes that have been postulated on the human Y chromosome seem to function only during early embryonic development and contribute to differentiation of the unspecified gonads into testes. In Drosophila, Y-linked genes function in sperm differentiation into swimming, active gametes. Male XO flies are sterile because they produce non-motile sperm. The X chromosome, on the other hand, carries a large number of genes needed for normal development and activities in both sexes. Total absence of X chromosomes is presumed to be lethal at very early stages in development, since neither mammalian nor Drosophila embryos or individuals have ever been found with no X chromosomes at all. Most X-linked genes have no sex-related functions.

Since only one of the two X chromosomes remains functionally euchromatic in females, there is an equivalence of *active* copies of X-linked genes in both sexes. But which of the two X chromosomes remains genetically active in females? Is it the same X or either X chromosome? If it is either X (from the mother or the father) that is inactivated while the partner X remains functional, is **X inactivation** a random (either maternal or paternal) or nonrandom (only maternal or only paternal) event?

The pattern of X-inactivation was suggested and investigated first by Mary Lyon, using genetically marked mice. That is why X-inactivation is often referred to as **Lyonization**. Through her analysis of mouse coat color patterns produced in heterozygous females carrying these X-linked alleles, she found that *either* X could be inactivated at random. These mice developed variegated (patchy) color patterns, indicating that some cell lineages expressed the normal allele and other lineages expressed the mutant allele. The mechanism of X-inactivation, however, remains to be discovered.

Figure 3.25   The X chromosome of horse and donkey are morphologically distinct, and each species produces distinctive glucose 6-phosphate dehydrogenase (GPD) protein, an X-linked trait. Female hybrids (mules) give rise to clones of body cells, about half of which show a late-replicating X^{horse} and donkey-GPD, and half of which show a late-replicating X^{donkey} and horse-GPD. These observations conform to predictions for the randomness of X inactivation, and that only the euchromatic X chromosome is genetically active in the XX cell.

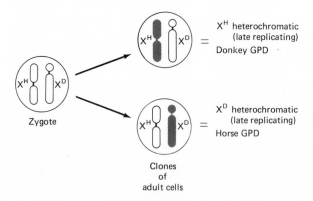

The same situation characterizes other mammalian species, as we can see from examples of two other species. In cats there is an X-linked gene governing black or orange fur color. Males are either black or orange, but heterozygous females develop the familiar calico (tortoiseshell) pattern of black and orange variegation. The black patches develop from cells in which the X carrying the orange allele was inactivated, and orange patches arise when the other X chromosome is inactivated. On rare occasions, there may be a male calico cat, and he invariably turns out to be XXY in sex chromosome constitution.

The consequences of random inactivation of X chromosomes can also be observed in human beings. One can assay skin biopsies from females who are heterozygous for some X-linked gene which governs synthesis of identifiably different proteins. Women who are heterozygous for the X-linked gene governing synthesis of the enzyme *glucose 6-phosphate dehydrogenase* have two kinds of skin cells, which contain either the normal or the altered enzyme but never both kinds in the same cell. These cells are cloned in culture and each clone breeds true for one or the other of the two protein types. It makes no difference whether the inactivated X came from the mother or the father.

In human beings, X inactivation is believed to occur at about the sixteenth day of embryonic development, according to Barr body observations. Differentiation of ovaries and other reproductive structures begins at about the twelfth week in a female fetus. According to various studies, fetal development is similar in XO and XX females, since ovarian structures are present in both the Turner and the normal female fetus. Apparently, there is degeneration of internal reproductive structures during development in a Turner female. This leads to almost total absence of internal reproductive structures in adult Turner women who have been studied. The causes of these changes during development are uncertain.

X inactivation occurs very early in mouse embryos also, perhaps in the 10-60 cell stage of the early blastocyst. It is very likely that early X inactivation is characteristic of mammalian female embryos in general.

Whole cell lineages, seen as patches of genetically identical tissue, retain their allelic distinction throughout the life of the female. The inactivated X is therefore inherited through mitosis, and each mitotic descendant of a particular cell has the same inactivated X chromosome. Different cell lineages, however, will have a different inactivated X chromosome on a purely random basis at the time the X becomes condensed (Fig. 3.25).

The mammalian X chromosome is facultatively heterochromatic, since the condensed chromosome is restored to the euchromatic state in the egg or in cells giving rise to the egg. This must be the case because both X chromosomes, the one from the egg and the one from the sperm, are euchromatic during the first sixteen days of human embryo development. In addition, the fact that X inactivation is random in the embryo also shows that the two X chromosomes are initially euchromatic and that either one of these becomes heterochromatic later on.

Although there is much to be learned about the processes of X inactivation and reactivation, we can be reasonably sure that these processes have little or nothing to do with the sex of the individual. This must be the case,

Table 3.4
Constituent units of nucleic acids

Base	Nucleoside*	Nucleotide**	Nucleic acid***
Purines:			
Adenine	Adenosine	Adenylic acid	RNA
	Deoxyadenosine	Deoxyadenylic acid	DNA
Guanine	Guanosine	Guanylic acid	RNA
	Deoxyguanosine	Deoxyguanylic acid	DNA
Pyrimidines:			
Cytosine	Cytidine	Cytidylic acid	RNA
	Deoxycytidine	Deoxycytidylic acid	DNA
Thymine	Thymidine	Thymidylic acid	DNA
Uracil	Uridine	Uridylic acid	RNA

* Consists of base + sugar (ribose or deoxyribose)
** Consists of base + sugar + phosphate, that is, unit is a nucleoside phosphate
***Polymer made up of nucleotide monomers: A, G, C, T in DNA and A, G, C, U in RNA

since X inactivation occurs in both males and females who have two or more X chromosomes, and it does not take place in males or females with one X chromosome.

3.12 Polytene Chromosome Activity and Phenotype Development

We know that the genetic material consists of **DNA**, which contains the specific information for synthesis of **proteins**. Since DNA remains bound in the chromatin fibers in the nucleus, while proteins are synthesized in the cytoplasm outside the nucleus, there must be intermediary molecules which carry copies of the information in DNA from the nucleus out into the cytoplasm. This intermediary is **RNA**. Both DNA and RNA are linear,

Figure 3.26 Genetic information in the sequence of nucleotides in DNA is copied into a complementary copy of messenger RNA in the process of transcription. The information copied into messenger RNA is then translated into a linear sequence of amino acids making up the protein molecule. Each amino acid in the protein translation is specified in type and in position in the polymer according to 3-nucleotide codewords, or codons, in DNA and its messenger RNA copy.

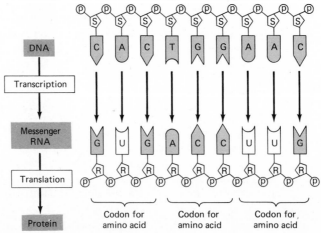

unbranched polymer chains built up from monomer units called **nucleotides**, or **nucleoside phosphates** (Table 3.4). Complementary copies of DNA sequences are built into RNA chains in the process of **transcription.** The transcribed RNA copies move out into the cytoplasm from the nucleus, and guide the synthesis of proteins from amino acids as specified in coded sequences of the original DNA (Fig. 3.26). This synthesis of protein is the process called **translation**. Both transcription and translation constitute the central dogma of the one-way flow of information as established by molecular genetics: **DNA $\longrightarrow$ RNA $\longrightarrow$ protein**. Each gene is a blueprint which specifies the kinds and sequence of amino acids in the protein polymer chain.

These events were studied by Wolfgang Beermann in giant **polytene chromosomes** of the midge *Chironomus*, a dipteran insect. The huge chromosomes develop in interphase nuclei as a consequence of repeated replications of the chromatin fiber, without subsequent mitotic segregations. The replicated strands of each chromosome remain associated and form polytene (many-stranded) structures. In addition to their large diameter, these chromosomes are greatly extended in length in the usual interphase conformations. Furthermore, interphase is metabolically the most active stage of the cell cycle, since virtually no macromolecular

Figure 3.27 Photograph taken with the phase contrast light microscope of the chromosome complement of the midge *Chironomus tentans*. The unstained chromosomes are identified by roman numerals. Each chromosome is recognizable by its morphology and band pattern. The 8 polytene chromosomes are very closely paired in this diploid cell, giving the impression of only 4 chromosomes. × 375. (Courtesy of B. Daneholt)

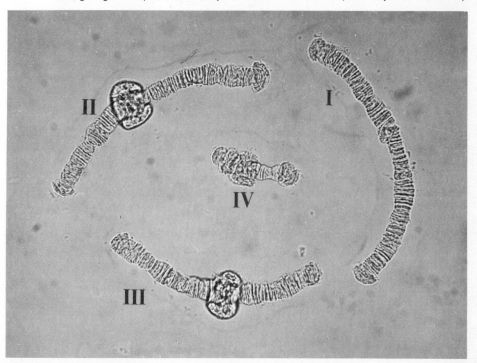

syntheses occur during chromosome delivery at mitosis. Specific chromosomes and regions of these chromosomes can easily be identified by the constant pattern of bands and interbands (Fig. 3.27). Bands can be distinguished even in unstained preparations because they are DNA-rich regions in which the continuous chromatin fiber is much more folded and compacted than in the interbands in between.

The chromosome band in all dipteran polytene chromosomes may exist in either of two alternative states: (1) compact, and as wide as the adjacent interbands; or (2) looser-stranded, swollen, and forming a puff. A **puff** is basically a localized decondensation of a chromosome band (Fig. 3.28). Using specific staining reagents to identify DNA, RNA, and both histone and nonhistone proteins, Beermann established that the principal difference between puffed and unpuffed bands was the greater amount of RNA present during puffing.

Figure 3.28 Diagrammatic representation of puff development in a polytene chromosome of *Chironomus tentans* larval salivary gland. The puff appears as a local chromosome region (probably one band) undergoes a gradual decondensation (a-f). (From Beermann, W. 1952. *Chromosoma* **5**:139.)

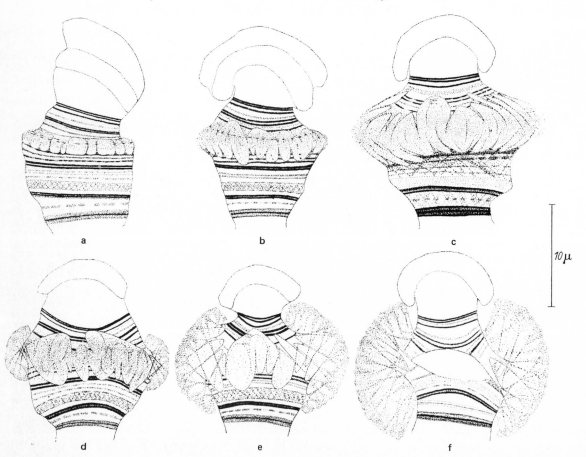

More specific information came from studies of macromolecular synthe-ses during puffing, traced by the incorporation of radioactively labeled precursors into polymers of DNA, RNA, and proteins. To see if DNA was synthesized, labeled **thymidine** was provided to the *Chironomus* larvae; labeled **uridine** was the specific precursor for RNA; and labeled **amino acids** indicated whether proteins had been synthesized in puffed bands. These labeled polymers were identified by **autoradiographs** of chromo-some preparations on microscope slides (Fig. 3.29). Silver grains which appear after the photographic emulsion is developed represent sites of radio-active events in the chromosomes beneath and, therefore, identify molecules which have incorporated the radioactively labeled precursors (Box 3.1).

These studies showed that RNA was synthesized in puffs, while little or no DNA or proteins were made in either puffed or nonpuffed bands. This indicates that transcription of DNA into RNA takes place actively during puffing, and it suggests that gene action is turned "on" during puffing but turned "off" otherwise.

A direct relationship between puffing and gene action leading to protein synthesis was reported by Beermann in 1961. He showed conclusively that a particular puff on chromosome 4 was responsible for synthesis of salivary secretion protein in *Chironomus*. The proteins were made only when this puff developed during larval growth, and only in those four cells of the salivary gland in which the puff was present (Fig. 3.30).

The transcription of genetic information and its translation into specific

Figure 3.29   Autoradiograph of polytene chromosomes of the fly *Sciara coprophila*, showing silver grains (dark spots) as evidence for incorporation of tritiated thymidine into chromosomal DNA during replication. (From Cannon, G. 1965. *J. Cell. Comp. Physiol.* **65**:163.)

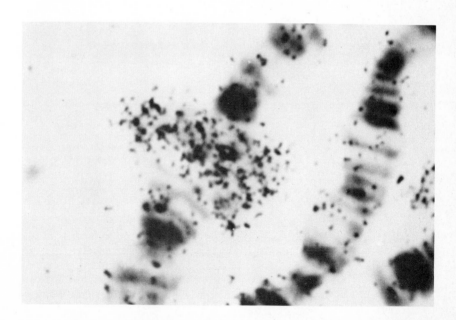

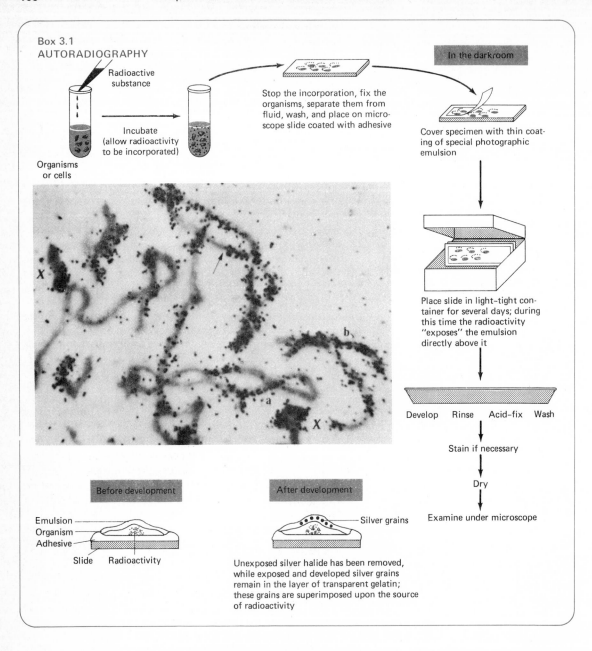

Box 3.1
AUTORADIOGRAPHY

Radioactive substance

Organisms or cells

Incubate
(allow radioactivity
to be incorporated)

Stop the incorporation, fix the
organisms, separate them from
fluid, wash, and place on microscope slide coated with adhesive

In the darkroom

Cover specimen with thin coat-
ing of special photographic
emulsion

Place slide in light-tight container for several days; during
this time the radioactivity
"exposes" the emulsion
directly above it

Develop   Rinse   Acid-fix   Wash

Stain if necessary

Dry

Examine under microscope

Before development

Emulsion
Organism
Adhesive
Slide   Radioactivity

After development

Silver grains

Unexposed silver halide has been removed,
while exposed and developed silver grains
remain in the layer of transparent gelatin;
these grains are superimposed upon the source
of radioactivity

proteins underwrite phenotypic expression. The different salivary secretions in genetically different individuals lead to differences in the kind of
"glue" used by larvae to secure themselves to a solid surface in preparation
for pupa development. This phenotype is expressed only in certain cells
when seen at the chromosomal or molecular levels, but it is a phenotypic
expression at the level of the organism when we examine the secretion

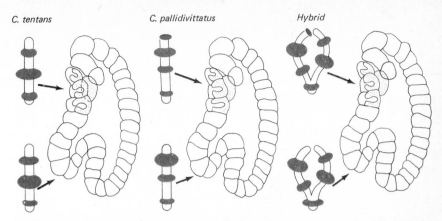

C. tentans   *C. pallidivittatus*   *Hybrid*

Figure 3.30 Diagrammatic summary of Beermann's experiments with *Chironomus*. There are four cells in the salivary gland of *Ch. pallidivittatus* that produce a granular secretion. A puff is formed at one end of chromosome-4 only in these four cells and not in the other cells of the gland (chromosomes shown to left of gland). The corresponding four cells in *Ch. tentans* produce a clear secretion lacking the granules, and no puff forms at the end of chromosome-4 in any of its gland cells. In hybrids between these two species, half as much protein granules occur in the secretion as in the *Ch. pallidivittatus* parent. Since there are structural differences in chromosome-4 in the two parent species, the hybrid chromosome pair is not closely held together and each of the two chromosomes in the pair can be identified as to its source. Only the chromosome in the hybrid that was derived from the *Ch. pallidivittatus* parent forms a puff in the four crucial gland cells. These experiments show that puffing is associated with gene action in directing synthesis of a protein that characterizes a phenotypic trait in the organism. (From Beermann, W. 1963. *Amer. Zool.* **3**:23.)

exuded by the larva just before it pupates. This same transition from synthesis of a protein to its influence on the phenotype of the organism is believed to be true for every instance of genotype ⟶ phenotype expression. We can only assume that similar chromosomal unfolding takes place at active gene sites in all eukaryotes, however, because it is difficult or impossible to see the same cytological detail in the tangle of chromatin of the typical interphase nucleus.

3.13   Chromosome-Mediated Phenotypic Expression

Genes can be mapped to specific chromosomes. We have already seen how X-linked genes can be mapped to the X chromosome from patterns of X-linked inheritance. Genes can also be mapped to specific autosomes. One method of doing this is **somatic cell hybridization**, which has provided a great deal of specific information to locate genes on all 22 autosomes and the X chromosome in human beings. We will cover human mapping studies in Chapter 5, but for now it will be useful to see how two experimental approaches have produced convincing evidence for chromosomal (and, therefore, genic) direction of phenotypic expression.

Under suitable conditions in a test tube, properly prepared somatic (body) cells of mammalian species can fuse together to form a **somatic cell-hybrid**. When the two nuclei fuse in the hybrid cell, the chromosomes of both parent cells are housed within a common nuclear envelope. In order to identify the hybrids from among the large numbers of parent cells on the solid medium to which the cells have been transferred from the test tube, each parent clone has a mutant allele for a different one of two genes needed to grow in a selective medium. These techniques are similar to those described for studying microorganisms such as *Neurospora* and *E. coli*.

The two marker genes govern synthesis of the enzymes hypoxanthine-guanosine phosphoribosyl transferase (**HPRT**) and thymidine kinase (**TK**), both of which are essential for growth in the particular selective medium which is used. If one parent has the phenotype $HPRT^- TK^+$ and the other has the phenotype $HPRT^+ TK^-$, neither can grow in the selective medium. Those cell-hybrids which are phenotypically $HPRT^+ TK^+$ can be identified because they grow and produce colonies of cells on the selective medium.

If human and mouse cells are plated together, the human-mouse cell hybrids can be tested for the HPRT and TK enzymes which are present and for the chromosomes in the nucleus. Both species make these two enzymes, but the proteins which are isolated can be distinguished as mouse or human HPRT and TK according to their migration properties in an electrical field. Mouse and human chromosomes are recognizably different when seen by microscopy, and they can be distinguished readily in cell-hybrid nuclei (Fig. 3.31).

One very useful feature of the human-mouse cell hybrid combination is that the human chromosomes tend to be lost, at random, during clonal growth while all 40 mouse chromosomes usually are retained in the nucleus. By comparing the remaining human chromosomes with the presence or absence of human HPRT or TK proteins, a direct correlation can be made between the genes on the particular chromosomes present and the synthesis of the enzymes in these cells. In this way, genes can be located in particular chromosomes of the human complement, and the chromosomal direction of protein synthesis can be established. The phenotypic consequence of such chromosomally-directed synthesis is growth of the cells in selective media. This system of locating genes on chromosomes depends on chromosome loss, which functions as a substitute for the system of chromosome segregation in sexual reproduction.

In every case studied, human HPRT is made only in cell-hybrids which retain the human X chromosome, and human TK is made only when human chromosome 17 is present. Chromosomal activities leading to phenotypic expression clearly continue even when only one or a few chromosomes of the human complement are present along with a full set of mouse chromosomes.

Deficient or defective HPRT enzyme is the primary cause of Lesch-Nyhan disease, a rare X-linked recessive condition. Afflicted children do not survive beyond their teens, so the allele is only transmitted from a carrier mother to half her sons, on the average. The abnormality in purine metabolism because of the missing or inactive enzyme leads to abnormal and self-destructive behavior in boys with this disease. The relationship between the metabolic defect and the abnormal behavior has not yet been established.

In more recent studies, chromosomes have been isolated from meta-

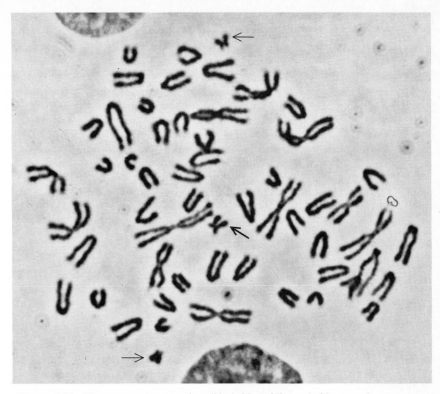

Figure 3.31 Human-mouse somatic cell hybrid retaining only 3 human chromosomes. The light arrows (top and bottom) indicate group G human chromosomes (No. 21 and 22), and the heavier arrow (center) points to a human chromosome of group E (No. 17 or 18). (From "Hybrid Somatic Cells" by B. Ephrussi and M. C. Weiss. Copyright © 1969 by Scientific American, Inc. All rights reserved.)

phase cells and purified free of contaminating cellular debris. Since there is no nuclear envelope around the highly condensed chromosomes at metaphase, the job of isolation is simplified. These purified metaphase chromosomes are then incubated with mammalian cells, usually from mouse or Chinese hamster, in selective medium in which only $HPRT^+ TK^+$ cells can grow. Apparently, the isolated chromosomes attach to the cells in culture and the cell membrane of the recipient invaginates at the site of attachment and engulfs the chromosome.

Most of the engulfed chromosomal material is fragmented or digested by the usual intracellular processes which handle foreign material routinely, and no part of the donor chromosomes can be seen in the recipient cells after a short time. The evidence supporting the presence of donor chromosome fragments comes from the demonstration that *donor-specific* HPRT or TK is produced in recipients which were phenotypiclly HPRT⁻ or TK⁻ at the start of the experiment. For example, if human chromosomes carrying the dominant *Hprt* or the dominant *Tk* allele are incubated with mouse recipient cells that are genetically recessive and have only *hprt* or *tk* alleles, phenotypically HPRT$^+$ TK$^+$ cells can develop into colonies on selective medium. When these mouse-cell colonies are analyzed, they are found to contain human HPRT or human TK, and not the mouse enzyme equivalents.

These systems for chromosome-mediated gene transfer, and the other systems we have discussed so far in this book, all build to a powerful case for genes in chromosomes and for gene-directed development of the phenotype in cells and organisms. Chromosomes are the vehicles of inheritance, since they contain the genetic material which directs the synthesis of proteins. Development of a particular phenotype in turn depends on the nature of the proteins which are made according to the genetic blueprints.

QUESTIONS AND PROBLEMS

3.1. In *Drosophila* vermilion eye color (*v*) and curved wings (*c*) are recessive to their wild type alternatives. A vermilion ♀ was crossed with a curved-wing ♂, producing the following progeny: ♀♀—½ wild type, ½ curved wing; ♂♂—½ vermilion, ½ vermilion, curved.
   a. What was the genotype of the female parent?
   b. What was the genotype of the male parent?
   c. What are the genotypes of the male and female progeny?

3.2. Red-green colorblindness in humans is recessive and sex-linked. A normal woman whose mother was colorblind marries a colorblind man. They produce a son and a daughter.
   a. What is the probability that the son is colorblind?
   b. What is the probability that the daughter is colorblind?
   c. What is the probability that both children are colorblind?

3.3. Sex determination in the cockroach is based on a balance between the number of X chromosomes to autosome sets, and the X:A ratio of 1.0 leads to female development. The somatic cells of a cockroach are examined and found to contain 23 chromosomes.
   a. What is the sex of this individual?
   b. What is the diploid number of the opposite sex?
   c. What is the usual chromosome constitution of male and female cockroaches?

3.4. In the dioecious plant *Melandrium albus* a recessive sex-linked gene is known (*l*) to be lethal when homozygous in females. When present in the hemizygous condition in males, it produces patches of yellow-green color. When females are homozygous or heterozygous for the wild type allele (*L*) or males are hemizygous for this allele, the plant develops the normal dark green color. Determine the expected genotypes and phenotypes in the progeny from the following crosses:
   a. heterozygous females × yellow-green males
   b. heterozygous females × dark green males.
   (In this species females are XX and males are XY.)

3.5. In chickens a dominant sex-linked gene (*B*) produces barred plumage and the recessive allele (*b*) leads to nonbarred plumage. Removal of the ovary leads to the development of testes in the animal, and such a "male" can produce sperm. If such a "male" with nonbarred plumage is mated to a barred female:
   a. What sex ratio will occur in their progeny?
   b. What are the genotypes and phenotypes of the progeny? (Females are XY and males are XX in birds.)

3.6. Suppose that you have two homozygous strains of *Drosophila*, one found in San Francisco (strain A) and the other in Los Angeles (strain B). Both strains have bright scarlet eyes, whereas wild-type flies have red eyes.
   a. When strain A ♂♂ are crossed with strain B ♀♀ you obtain 100 wild type ♂♂ and 100 wild type ♀♀ in the F₁ generation. From this result what can you say about the inheritance of the eye color in the two strains?
   b. When strain B ♂♂ are crossed with strain A ♀♀ you obtain 98 scarlet eyed ♂♂ and 100 wild type ♀♀ in the F₁ generation. What can you say about the inheritance of eye color from this result?
   c. When you cross members of the F₁ progeny of part (a) you obtain in the F₂

76 wild type ♀♀	63 scarlet ♂♂
24 scarlet ♀♀	37 wild type ♂♂

   Diagram the genotypes of the parents and of the F₁ offspring. Indicate the expected ratio of F₂ genotypes and phenotypes.

3.7. The following three pedigrees represent a particular family segregating for three different traits: colorblindness, glucose 6-phosphate dehydrogenase (GPD) deficiency, and XG blood group system. Use the following gene symbols.

   C for normal vision, *c* for colorblindness
   Gpd for normal GPD enzyme levels, *gpd* for GPD deficiency
   Xg for presence of XG blood group, *xg* for absence of XG blood group

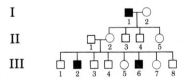 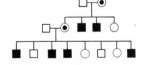 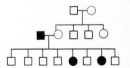

Colorblindness:	GPD deficiency:	XG blood group:
affected: black	greatly affected: black	XG present: black
normal: white	partially affected: dot	XG absent: white
	normal: white	

   a. Determine the mode of inheritance of each trait.
   b. Give the most probable genotypes of individuals I1, I2, II1, II2, III1, and III5, for all three genes.

3.8. The pedigree shown below is concerned with night blindness.

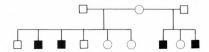

    a. What mode of inheritance best accounts for the transmission of this trait?

    b. Determine the genotypes of the members of this family according to your hypothesis.

3.9. Suppose you have the following human pedigree segregating for brachydactyly (shortened fingers) and a dental abnormality called *amelogenesis imperfecta*. Individuals with brachydactyly are indicated by a dot, and those with the dental abnormality are shown by filled squares; normal individuals are indicated by open and un-dotted squares and circles.

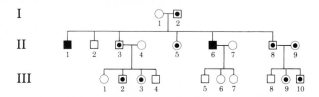

    a. What can you tell about the inheritance of brachydactyly?

    b. What can you tell about the inheritance of the dental disease?

    c. What is the probability that a child of III1 will have shortened fingers? the dental disease?

    d. What are the genotypes of individuals I1 and I2?

3.10. Harelip (incomplete fusion of upper lip) in humans appears to be dominant in men, recessive in women.

    a. What proportion of the sons of two heterozygous parents is expected to have harelip?

    b. What proportion of all their children is expected to have this trait?

3.11. A young couple have had a hemophilic son and want to know the risk of having a second hemophilic child should they plan to enlarge their family. The genetic counselor tells them there is no risk of having a hemophilic daughter but there is a predictable risk for their producing a second hemophilic son.

    a. What are the genotypes of the two parents?

    b. What is the probability that their second child will be a hemophiliac?

    c. What are their chances of having two afflicted sons in a family of only two children?

3.12. Two people plan to have five children, despite their understanding of the concept of zero population growth.

    a. What is the probability that they would produce five sons?

    b. What is the probability that they would produce five children of the same sex?

    c. What term of the binomial expansion would you select to determine the probability that they will have one son and four daughters?

    d. What is the probability that their first child will be a son and their next four children all will be female?

3.13. Two cats mate and produce a litter of 8 kittens, including 3 calico ♀♀, 2 orange ♀♀, 2 orange ♂♂, and 1 black ♂.

    a. What are the genotypes and phenotypes of the parents?

    b. Suppose one of the male kittens proved to be XXY. Would it be orange or black if nondisjunction occurred at Meiosis I? Diagram the possible sex chromosomes present in gametes that could produce such an XXY ♂ at fertilization if nondisjunction occurred at Meiosis I.

3.14. A colorblind woman and a man with normal vision have a colorblind son who is 47,XXY and shows characteristics of Klinefelter syndrome.

    a. What sex chromosomes were present in the egg and sperm that fused to produce their son?

    b. If Barr body counts are made for both parents and their son, would the son's cells resemble those from his mother or those from his father?

    c. If these two people have another son of the normal 46,XY chromosome constitution, what is the probability that he would be colorblind?

REFERENCES

Beermann, W., and U. Clever. Apr. 1964. Chromosome puffs. *Sci. Amer.* **210**:50.

Bergsma, D. (ed.). 1972. Paris conference (1971): Standardization in human cytogenetics. *Birth Defects, Original Article Series* **8** (7):1.

Brown, S. W. 1966. Heterochromatin. *Science* **151**:417.

Daneholt, B. 1975. Transcription in polytene chromosomes. *Cell* **4**:1.

Ephrussi, B., and M. C. Weiss. Apr. 1969. Hybrid somatic cells. *Sci. Amer.* **220**:26.

Epstein, C. J., S. Smith, B. Travis, and G. Tucker. 1978. Both X chromosomes function before visible X-chromosome inactivation in female mouse embryos. *Nature* **274**:500.

German, J., J. L. Simpson, R. Chaganti, R. Summitt, L. Reid, and I. Markatz. 1978. Genetically determined sex-reversal in 46,XY humans. *Science* **202**:53.

McKusick, V. A. Aug. 1965. The royal hemophilia. *Sci. Amer.* **213**: 88.

McKusick, V. A. 1969. *Human Genetics*, 2nd ed. Englewood Cliffs, N.J.: Prentice-Hall.

Moses, M. J., S. J. Counce, and D. F. Paulson. 1975. Synaptonemal complex complement of man in spreads of spermatocytes, with details of the sex chromosome pair. *Science* **187**:363.

Ohno, S. 1978. *Major Sex-Determining Genes.* New York: Springer-Verlag.

Rattner, J. B., and B. A. Hamkalo. 1979. Nucleosome packing in interphase chromatin. *J. Cell Biol.* **81**:453.

Selden, J. R., S. S. Wachtel, G. C. Koo, M. E. Haskins, and D. F. Patterson. 1978. Genetic basis of XX male syndrome and XX true hermaphroditism: Evidence in the dog. *Science* **201**:644.

Shine, I. and S. Wrobel. 1976. *Thomas Hunt Morgan: Pioneer of Genetics.* Lexington: University Press of Kentucky.

Silvers, W. K., and S. S. Wachtel. 1977. H-Y antigen: Behavior and function. *Science* **195**:956.

Sturtevant, A. H. 1913. The linear arrangement of six sex-linked factors in *Drosophila*, as shown by their mode of association. *J. Exp. Zool.* **14**:43.

Sutton, W. S. 1903. The chromosomes in heredity. *Biol. Bull.* **4**:231.

Wachtel, S. S. 1977. H-Y antigen and the genetics of sex determination, *Science* **198**:797.

Tijo, J. H., and A. Levan. 1956. The chromosome number of man. *Hereditas* **42**:1.

Winters, S. J. *et al.* 1979. H-Y antigen mosaicism in the gonad of a true 46,XX hermaphrodite. *New Engl. J. Med.* **300**:745.

4

Linkage, Recombination, and Mapping

In this chapter we will see how the methods of genetic analysis showed that there were genes on the same chromosome, or linked genes. Linked genes can be distinguished by progeny analysis from genes which undergo independent assortment in reproduction. In testcrosses, linked genes show an excess of parental and a deficit of nonparental, or recombinant, genotypes instead of equal proportions of all genotypic classes. The process which leads to new combinations of linked genes in progeny is crossing over, and recombinants are those progeny with crossover chromosomes. The frequency of recombinations is proportional to the frequency of crossing over between linked genes, and therefore to the distance between them. These data provide information which permits us to construct a map of genes in fixed positions and at specified distances from one another on the chromosome. The gene map is also called a chromosome map or a map of the linkage group (genes linked on a particular chromosome).

The chromosome map is a summary of the types of progeny obtained from particular crosses, and it has two kinds of information: order of the genes and distances between genes in the linear chromosome. The map provides the basis for accurate predictions of progenies in breeding tests. The usual method for constructing a linkage map of the genes on a chromosome is the three-point testcross. By this method we can derive a more accurate estimate of the distance between genes because we can detect recombinations which arise by double crossing over between genes in the same two chromatids of a meiotic bivalent.

Special advantage can be taken of haploid microorganisms whose four products of meiosis remain associated in a tetrad. By tetrad analysis we can use genetic methods to determine particular chromosomal events during meiosis, which are not detectable otherwise. Linkage relations can be established by tetrad analysis using the same basic rules as those derived from studies of random samples of diploid progeny in testcrosses.

Crossing over involves a physical exchange between parts of homologous chromosomes during prophase of the first meiotic division, after chromosome replication has occurred. The cytogenetic evidence which supports this statement will be described.

LINKAGE ANALYSIS

By breeding studies we can distinguish between genes which assort independently and genes which have a tendency to stay together in parental combinations of alleles more often than to separate into new combinations. Genes which stay together more often than they separate are linked on the same chromosome. When they do separate to produce new combinations, recombinants arise in proportion to the frequency of crossing over between such **linked genes**. The relationship of gene behavior in transmission from parents to progeny and the parallel behavior of chromosomes in reproduction provided strong evidence for the location of genes in chromosomes.

4.1   Linkage Versus Independent Assortment

William Bateson and R. C. Punnett were among the early geneticists to report apparent exceptions to the Mendelian Law of independent assortment in plants and animals. In monohybrid crosses between *purple* and *red* flowered sweet pea plants, and between sweet peas with *long* versus *round* pollen grains, they had found the expected 3:1 F_2 phenotypic ratios in both cases. Instead of the expected F_2 ratio of 9:3:3:1 in dihybrid crosses, however, they obtained results such as:

Parents   *PPLL*   ×   *ppll*
             purple, long   red, round

F_1 all *P-L-* (purple, long)

F_2 Progeny class	Phenotype	No. of plants Observed	No. of plants Expected (9:3:3:1 ratio)
parental	purple, long	296	240 (9/16 of 427)
recombinant	purple, round	19	80 (3/16 of 427)
recombinant	red, long	27	80 (3/16 of 427)
parental	red, round	85	27 (1/16 of 427)
		427	427

It does not require a statistical analysis, such as the chi-square test, to see that there are distortions in the numbers of plants actually observed relative to the numbers expected on an F_2 ratio distribution of all four phenotypic classes. The important observation here is that there is a substantial deviation from expected results, and there is a pattern to this deviation. There is an excess of both **parental** phenotypic classes (*purple, long* and *red, round*) and a deficiency in the **recombinant** phenotypic classes (*purple, round* and *red, long*), relative to the expected numbers for a 9:3:3:1 F_2 ratio.

The dominance-recessiveness relationships between the members of the two pairs of alleles remained unchanged, purple and long were dominant to red and round, as can be seen from the phenotype of the F_1 plants. The F_2

progeny data further show that each pair of alleles segregated in a 3:1 phenotypic ratio:

$$\text{purple: } 296 + 19 = 315 \atop \text{red: } \quad 27 + 85 = 112 = 3{:}1 \qquad \text{long: } 296 + 27 = 323 \atop \text{round: } 19 + 85 = 104 = 3{:}1$$

The genes have not changed, nor have the members of each pair of alleles. The single difference is that alleles tended to stay together in the parental combinations and did not assort independently, or there would have been a 9:3:3:1 F_2 ratio of the four phenotypic classes. The tendency of different genes to stay together in parental combinations is called **linkage**. The phenomenon of linkage is evidenced from an *excess* of parental phenotypes and a *deficiency* of recombinant phenotypes in the progeny, when compared with independently assorting pairs of alleles.

4.2   Linkage Studies Using Drosophila

Bateson and Punnett tried to explain their results according to modified ratios, but without success. The essentially modern explanation of linkage began with the studies by T. H. Morgan and his colleagues and students at Columbia University. By 1911, Morgan had isolated a number of mutants, in addition to the white-eye mutant, and he used these Drosophila strains in crosses involving two or more X-linked genes. He and his collaborators, especially Alfred Sturtevant, provided an extensive and carefully argued analysis of inheritance patterns for these X-linked genes in Drosophila. They concluded that genes on the same chromosome had a tendency to stay together in the formation of gametes, whereas genes on different chromosomes underwent independent assortment in sexual reproduction.

To follow the analysis we will use some of the original data reported between 1911 and 1913 by Morgan and Sturtevant. In particular, we will follow the inheritance of two of the six X-linked characters which they described: *gray* wild-type body color, y^+, versus mutant *yellow, y*; and *red* wild-type eye color, v^+, versus mutant *vermilion, v*.

We will use the symbols ♀ for female (♀♀ is plural) and ♂ for male (♂♂, plural) in all cases. When yellow ♀♀ were crossed to gray ♂♂, and when vermilion ♀♀ were crossed to red ♂♂, in monohybrid tests, each pair of alleles showed typical X-linked inheritance (Fig. 4.1). The behavior of these two pairs of alleles was then analyzed in dihybrid crosses.

If the members of these two pairs of X-linked alleles are inherited together, they should produce a dihybrid F_2 ratio of 1:1 in two parental phenotypic classes. In a cross between yellow, vermilion ♀♀ and gray, red ♂♂, Sturtevant found the expected F_1 phenotypes of gray, red ♀♀ and yellow, vermilion ♂♂. The F_2 progeny obtained by interbreeding these F_1 males and females included four phenotypic classes, however, in a ratio that was not 1:1:1:1 (Table 4.1).

We see in this F_2 progeny the same pattern of numerical deviation that Bateson and Punnett had found in sweet peas; there was neither a 1:1 ratio of parental phenotypes nor a 1:1:1:1 ratio of parental and recombinant

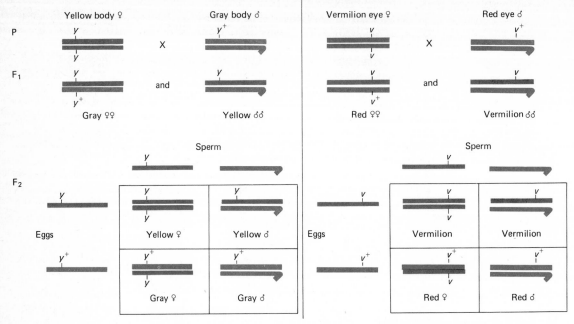

Figure 4.1 Monohybrid X-linked inheritance characterizes the y^+/y allele pair for body color and the v^+/v pair of alleles for eye color in *Drosophila melanogaster*.

phenotypic classes. Before we continue with this analysis, notice that we are on the brink of a generalization:

1. The same inheritance pattern showing linkage occurred in a representative plant and a representative animal species.

2. The same deviation from expected dihybrid F_2 proportions was found for autosomal genes in sweet peas and for X-linked genes in Drosophila.

3. There was no alteration in the linkage pattern even though Drosophila males have only one X chromosome and are hemizygous for the X-linked alleles studied in these crosses.

Table 4.1
F_2 progeny from a dihybrid cross between parental yellow, vermilion ♀♀ ($\frac{y\ v}{y\ v}$) and gray, red ♂♂ ($\frac{y^+\ v^+}{}$) of *Drosophila melanogaster*

Phenotypes	Number of females		Number of males		Total progeny	
	Observed	Expected*	Observed	Expected*	Observed	Expected*
gray, red	427	323.5	385	271	812	594.5
gray, vermilion	240	323.5	186	271	426	594.5
yellow, red	213	323.5	189	271	402	594.5
yellow, vermilion	414	323.5	324	271	738	594.5
Totals	1294	1294	1084	1084	2378	2378

*Expected for 1:1:1:1 ratio

The appearance of a consistent pattern in the inheritance of linked genes leads us to predict that there is a common basis or feature which is responsible for this consistency.

In 1911, Morgan suggested that linkage was the result of genes being on the same chromosome; this would explain the high percentage of parental types, since alleles on the same chromosome would have a tendency to be inherited together and not to assort independently. Morgan further suggested that recombinants arose as the result of **crossing over** (a term he coined in 1912), involving exchanges between paired chromosomes during meiosis. The difference in the *strength* of linkage, expressed in the varying percentages of recombination between different genes in different crosses, was postulated to be related to their distance apart along the chromosome. We will discuss this last point shortly.

Morgan based his hypothesis on a synthesis of data, observations, and ideas of his own and those of other biologists. He was fully aware of Sutton's Chromosome Theory of Heredity, and of the simple point that there must be more than one gene per chromosome because there are far more genes than chromosomes in a species. F. Janssens had suggested that chiasmata (a term he coined) might be the sites of exchange between chromosomes while they were closely paired as bivalents in meiosis. Morgan cited this idea and supported it as the physical basis for recombinations between linked genes (Fig. 4.2).

In essence, Morgan developed the concept of linkage to explain the patterns of inheritance which he had observed in breeding analysis of two or more genes which did not undergo independent assortment. The

Figure 4.2 Diakinesis in grasshopper spermatocyte, showing chiasmata. The arrow points to a bivalent with a particularly clear display of a chiasma in which only two of the four chromatids are obviously involved. × 3,000.

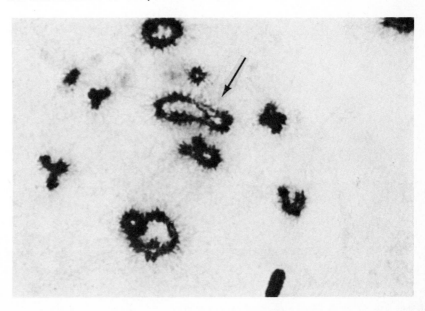

chromosomal events of crossing over which Morgan had postulated were entirely theoretical. But they provided a working hypothesis which related the behavior of chromosomes in meiosis to the pattern of gene transmission derived from his genetic analyses. The cytogenetic evidence which showed the parallel behavior of meiotic chromosomes and linked genes was still twenty years away. The power of genetic analysis was strong enough, however, to make Morgan's ideas seem attractive and viable enough for biologists to seek evidence in their support. Just as Mendel had postulated the existence of genes on the basis of particulate patterns of transmission in inheritance, Morgan postulated chromosomal events on the basis of gene transmission patterns.

The cross between yellow, vermilion and gray, red parents whose F_2 progeny are shown in Table 4.1 can now be summarized more specifically if we put the alleles on the X chromosome and follow their progress through both progeny generations (Fig. 4.3). The recombinant classes of F_2 progeny

Figure 4.3 Inheritance of two X-linked characteristics in *D. melanogaster* (see Table 4.1). For linked genes, recombinant F_2 classes arise as the result of fertilization of eggs carrying a crossover X chromosome. Parental F_2 classes contain only noncrossover X chromosomes.

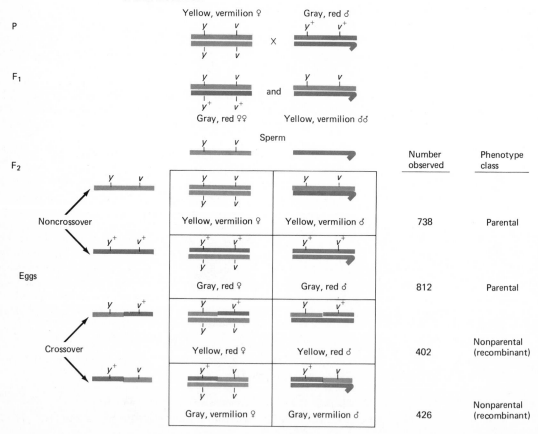

arise by fertilization of eggs carrying crossover X chromosomes. Parental phenotypic classes have noncrossover chromosomes, and in these the original parental combinations of alleles are maintained. The tendency for linked genes to be inherited together as seen in genetic analysis can be understood now on the basis of the behavior of the X chromosome during meiosis. Crossing over to produce recombinant gametes leads to the two recombinant phenotypic classes in the F_2 progeny.

4.3 Verification of Linkage

Once genes are put on a chromosome, and specifically on the X chromosome for X-linked inheritance in Drosophila, we can begin to make predictions about the behavior of these same linked genes in other crosses. If these predictions are verified in other crosses, the linkage hypothesis is strengthened.

We can predict that the reciprocal cross (gray, red ♀♀ × yellow, vermilion ♂♂) will produce parental and recombinant F_2 phenotypes in the *same* proportions as those from the cross shown in Table 4.1. Because females are XX and males are XY, however, we should find all four phenotypes only in the F_2 males in this reciprocal cross (Fig. 4.4). This is due to the fact that all the F_2 females receive one X chromosome from their F_1 fathers, and this chromosome will be y^+v^+, so that every F_2 female will be wild type in appearance. There are no such problems with F_2 males, however, since they express their hemizygous genotype according to the one maternal X chromosome which they receive through the egg.

The prediction is based on the expectation that crossing over in heterozygous F_1 females will be the same regardless of the parental source of the X chromosomes they contain. The F_1 females have the same alleles on their X chromosomes in the two reciprocal crosses, and we expect the same crossing over processes to take place in both cases.

The results shown in Fig. 4.4 illustrate one of the problems in using F_2 progeny in linkage analysis. There is no quick way to determine the chromosomal or genotypic constitutions of the F_2 females because dominant alleles lead to the same phenotype in homozygotes and heterozygotes. The same difficulties would be encountered in attempting to analyze Bateson and Punnett's F_2 progeny in sweet peas, described in Section 4.1. The single most useful method of linkage analysis in *diploid* species is the **testcross**.

In a testcross each phenotype is a unique genotype, and each phenotypic class will have a unique combination of the alleles of two linked genes in all possible pairwise arrangements. Simple inspection of testcross progenies can provide the required linkage data. The simple formula used to calculate the percentage recombination between two linked genes, and the percentage of crossover gametes represented by these recombinants is:

$$\frac{\text{number of recombinants}}{\text{total testcross progeny}} \times 100 = \% \text{ recombinants} = \% \text{ crossovers}$$

Notice here that the maximum percentage recombination which can be found for two linked genes is 50%, since the maximum proportion of re-

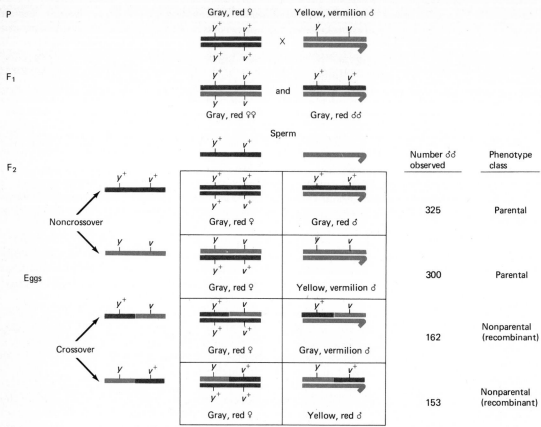

Figure 4.4 Reciprocal cross of the one shown in Fig. 4.3. In this case, only ♂♂ produce four phenotypic F₂ classes while all the F₂ ♀♀ have the wild type phenotype.

combinants would be 50% if the four phenotypic classes appeared in equal numbers. At this *upper limit* of 50% recombination, two genes on the same chromosome and two genes on different chromosomes would produce essentially the same ratio of 1:1:1:1 in the F₂, and these would be indistinguishable in dihybrid crosses (Fig. 4.5).

Figure 4.5 (Facing Page.) Origin of recombinant gametes by crossing over between linked genes. (a) Any *single* crossover event involves only two of the four chromatids of a bivalent, producing 50% parental (noncrossover) and 50% recombinant (crossover) gametes from a meiocyte. (b) The percentage of noncrossover types of gametes includes all those from meiocytes having no crossover between the specified genes, plus half the gametes from meiocytes in which there was a crossover between these genes. (c) The upper limit of recombinant gametes arising from single crossover events between two particular linked genes is 50%, since only half the gametes of each crossover meiocyte are recombinant (the remaining half contain the noncrossover chromatids of the bivalent). If the two genes were on different chromosomes there also would be 50% parental and 50% nonparental combinations (see Fig. 2.7).

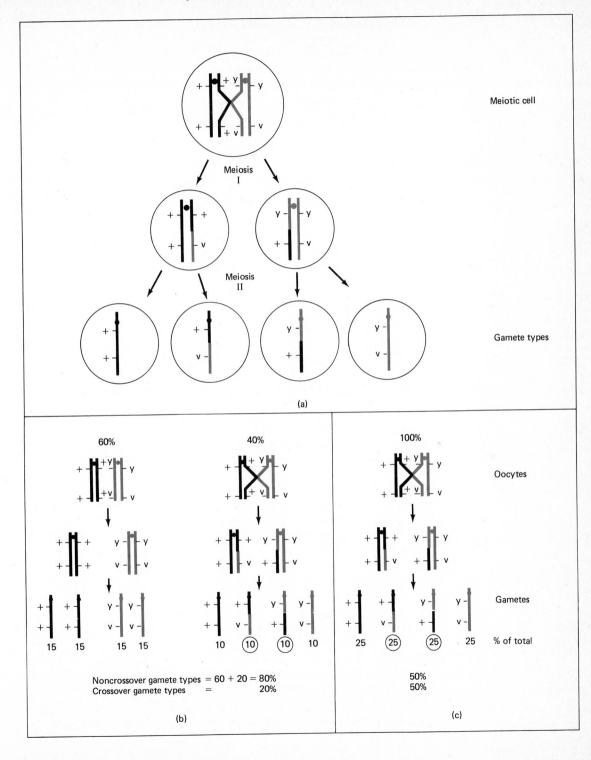

(a)

60%   40%   100%

Oocytes

15   15   15   15   10   (10)   (10)   10   25   (25)   (25)   25   Gametes

Gametes

% of total

Noncrossover gamete types = 60 + 20 = 80%
Crossover gamete types   =   20%

50%
50%

(b)   (c)

Sturtevant performed a testcross and showed that the percentage of recombinants was the same as had been found in the F_2 progeny of yellow, vermilion ♀♀ X gray, red ♂♂, which we described in Fig. 4.3. This was predicted for the special case of X-linked genes because it was known that males were hemizygous for X-linked alleles. Sturtevant's testcross data were as follows:

Parents   gray, red ♀♀ × yellow, vermilion ♂♂
F_1 gray, red ♀♀ and ♂♂
Testcross   gray, red F_1 ♀♀ × yellow, vermilion ♂ parent

Progeny class	Phenotype	No. of ♀♀	♂♂
parental	gray, red	31	23
parental	yellow, vermilion	41	21
recombinant	gray, vermilion	11	13
recombinant	yellow, red	12	8
	Totals	95	65 = 160

Percentage recombinants = $\frac{44}{160}$ = 0.28 × 100 = 28%

If we put these alleles on the X chromosome and follow their progress through the F_1 and testcross generations, we will see that the same crossovers in both this progeny and in the F_2 progeny in Fig. 4.3 lead to about the same linkage values as expressed in percentage of recombinants. The discrepancy between 28% recombination seen here and 35% recombination seen in the F_2 progeny of the other cross may be due only to the considerable differences in progeny size in the two cases. The significance of this difference can be determined using the chi-square test.

Sturtevant described another important cross involving these same two linked genes. He reasoned that if two genes are on the same chromosome, it shouldn't matter which of the two alleles of each gene is present in each chromosome to be distributed to a testcross or F_2 progeny. We would predict that the same excess of parentals and deficit of recombinants (*not* a 1:1:1:1 ratio) would be found in F_2 or testcross progeny produced by the following four combinations of parents:

1. gray, red ♀♀ × yellow, vermilion ♂♂
2. yellow, vermilion ♀♀ × gray, red males ♂♂
3. yellow, red ♀♀ × gray, vermilion ♂♂
4. gray, vermilion ♀♀ × yellow, red ♂♂

Sturtevant's data for the first two of these crosses were given in Figs. 4.3 and 4.4. Data for the fourth kind of cross, in one experiment, are given in Table 4.2. The results clearly show that the linkage pattern is expressed similarly whether the dominant alleles for both genes are in the same chromosome (called the **cis** or **coupling** arrangement, $\frac{y^+v^+}{y\ v}$), or in different ones

Table 4.2
Breeding analysis of a dihybrid cross involving two linked genes in *Drosophila melanogaster*, in repulsion

Parents	gray, vermilion ♀♀ × yellow, red ♂♂		
F₁	gray, red ♀♀ & gray, vermilion ♂♂		
F₂		♀♀	♂♂
	gray, vermilion	182	149
	gray, red	199	54
	yellow, vermilion	0	41
	yellow, red	0	119
	totals	381	363
Testcross	gray, red F₁ ♀ × yellow, vermilion ♂ (from another stock)		
	↓	♀♀	♂♂
	gray, red	50	44
	gray, vermilion	96	105
	yellow, red	68	86
	yellow, vermilion	41	47
	totals	255	282

of the pair of homologous chromosomes (called the **trans or repulsion** arrangement, $\frac{y^+\,v}{y\,v^+}$). The same kind of crossover event during meiosis must therefore characterize the exchanges between homologous chromosomes, regardless of the alleles which happen to be present on each member of the pair of chromosomes (Fig. 4.6).

From the breeding analysis described so far, we can see that the bases for recombination between linked genes seem to be:

1. chromosome behavior during crossing over in meiosis;
2. segregation of members of pairs of alleles on crossover or noncrossover chromosomes during meiosis; and
3. random combinations during fertilization between gametes carrying crossover or noncrossover chromosomes.

The method of choice in conducting linkage analysis is the testcross, since it is simple, reliable, and straightforward in comparison with F₂ progeny analysis. The number of recombinants in the total testcross progeny gives us a value which is directly related to the frequency of crossover gametes and the percentage of recombination between linked genes.

CHROMOSOME MAPPING

There was about 35 percent recombination between the body-color gene and the eye-color gene according to the preceding analysis of Drosophila. Slightly different values in different crosses usually are due to problems of sampling errors in progeny with different numbers of individuals, and to other known factors, such as lower vitality or viability of mutants when compared to wild types.

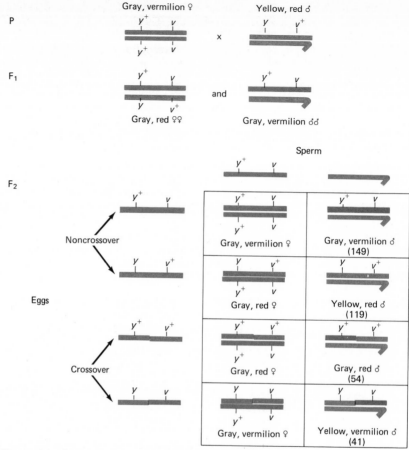

Figure 4.6 Summary of Sturtevant's study of linked genes on the X chromosome in *Drosophila melanogaster* (see Table 4.2), showing that the linkage pattern is the same for any particular linked genes whether present in the *trans*, or *repulsion*, arrangement as shown here, or in the *cis*, or *coupling*, phase of linkage shown in **Figure 4.3.**

When other pairs of genes were shown to be linked, they produced a whole range of recombination values between zero and 50%. But, significantly, any two particular genes produced the *same* values in repeated experiments in Drosophila as well as in other organisms that were studied in different laboratories. This general observation can be interpreted to mean that each gene occupies a particular location, or **locus**, on a chromosome. As Morgan first suggested, **loosely linked genes** (showing higher percentages of crossing over) and **tightly linked genes** (showing lower percentages of crossing over) may be a reflection of different distances separating two genes along the length of the chromosome. When genes are farther apart there is more chance for crossing over to occur because there is more space between the genes. If genes are situated closer together, there is less space and therefore less probability for an exchange to take place between them. These generalizations were the basis for mapping genes on a chromosome, in fixed order and at specified distances from one another on the **chromosome map.**

4.4   Mapping by Two-Factor Testcrosses

Sturtevant summarized testcross data from a number of experiments with X-linked genes in Drosophila in the form of a chromosome map. The consistency of recombination values for any two linked genes showed that the gene loci were fixed and that all the genes in the same **linkage group** occurred in a linear order along the same chromosome. Their relative distances apart, or their relative locations on the chromosome were expressed in a chromosome map based on recombination data from genetic analysis.

We still use Sturtevant's original proposal that the *percentage of recombinants arising from crossing over can be converted into a measurement of distance between two linked genes.* Specifically, *one map unit of distance equals the space between genes in which one percent recombinants arise by crossing over.* A **map unit** is a relative measurement in arbitrary units, and not an absolute or actual measurement of chromosome length in micrometers or other physical units.

Suppose we found 6% crossovers (6% recombinants) in testcross progeny produced in both the coupling and repulsion phases of linkage:

	coupling (cis)	**repulsion (trans)**
Parents	$\dfrac{A\ B}{A\ B} \times \dfrac{a\ b}{a\ b}$	$\dfrac{A\ b}{A\ b} \times \dfrac{a\ B}{a\ B}$
F_1	$\dfrac{A\ B}{a\ b}$	$\dfrac{A\ b}{a\ B}$
Testcross	$\dfrac{A\ B}{a\ b} \times \dfrac{a\ b}{a\ b}$	$\dfrac{A\ b}{a\ B} \times \dfrac{a\ b}{a\ b}$

Progeny class	Genotype	No. of individuals	Progeny class	Genotype	No. of individuals
parental	$\dfrac{A\ B}{a\ b}$	390	parental	$\dfrac{A\ b}{a\ b}$	305
parental	$\dfrac{a\ b}{a\ b}$	410	parental	$\dfrac{a\ B}{a\ b}$	295
recombinant	$\dfrac{A\ b}{a\ b}$	26	recombinant	$\dfrac{A\ B}{a\ b}$	18
recombinant	$\dfrac{a\ B}{a\ b}$	24	recombinant	$\dfrac{a\ b}{a\ b}$	22
	Total progeny	850		Total progeny	640

Percent recombinants = $\dfrac{50}{850}$ = 0.058   Percent recombinants = $\dfrac{40}{640}$ = 0.062

$0.058 \times 100 = 5.8\%$ $0.062 \times 100 = 6.2\%$

We would place these linked genes 6 map units apart on the chromosome map:

In further studies we may find that gene C is linked to A and shows 10% recombination, or crossovers. Gene C is 10 map units distant from gene A in the same linkage group, but is the order of the three genes $A\ B\ C$ or $C\ A\ B$? We know it cannot be $A\ C\ B$ since A and B are 6 units apart. We can find out which of the two possibilities is correct by determining the distance between B and C in another set of two-factor testcrosses. We can predict that the gene order is $C\ A\ B$ if there is 16% recombination between genes B and C, but that the gene order would be $A\ B\ C$ if we found 4% crossovers between B and C, as follows:

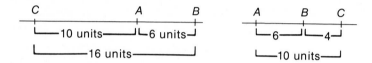

The three sets of pairwise crosses, involving $A-B$, $B-C$, and $A-C$, give consistent recombination values. This shows that genes occur in fixed positions relative to one another, that they occur in a linear order on the chromosome, and that they are found at particular distances from one another that allow predictions to be made for the numbers of recombinant progeny that will be found any time these three genes are involved in crosses with one another.

The chromosome map (or, gene map of the chromosome) has the following features:

1. It summarizes the types of progeny obtained from particular crosses. It is a summary of all the linkage data.
2. It contains two items of information: order and distance of the genes. It indicates the consistency of recombination values in crosses.
3. The gene map is a map of a linkage group, including all the genes found to be linked together on a single chromosome. A chromosome map can be derived for each linkage group of the genome in a species.
4. The same gene map will be derived no matter which alleles are carried by each parent in the crosses; the same results are obtained whether alleles are in the coupling (cis) or the repulsion (trans) phase of linkage.

5. Gene maps are reliable forecasting devices. They allow predictions about numbers and kinds of progenies in new crosses. Linkage analysis is therefore a powerful tool for describing the genome of a species.

By proceeding with pairwise combinations of linked genes, more and more genes could be added to the linear sequence, depending on the availability of mutant alleles for the wild-type alternatives. We cannot identify, much less map, a gene unless we know its inheritance pattern. To do this we must be able to identify segregation and recombination patterns involving members of pairs of alleles. Once there are a number of genes which have been shown to be linked to each other, that is, which are all in the same linkage group, the order and distances between genes are found to be *consistent* in all the combinations analyzed. This means that the genes are indeed in a linear arrangement. As Sturtevant pointed out, such an arrangement of genes made a very strong argument in favor of their location in the chromosome, which is the only known linear component in the cell that has a hereditary function.

The construction of an actual map of the chromosome can be achieved by placing the linked genes which have been analyzed into arbitrary locations, also based on the distances between them. When a gene is discovered to have linked genes only to its right and none to its left, that gene may be positioned at locus 0.0. The genes to its right are then located in accordance with the map units of distance found from linkage analysis. In Sturtevant's study of six X-linked characters in Drosophila, for example, the gene for body color was put at locus 0.0 of the X chromosome and the others were placed in relation to this gene:

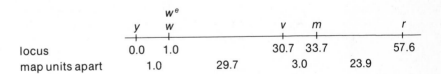

By putting the mutant allele on the map we can more easily identify the gene knowing at the same time that each of these alleles is recessive to its wild-type alternative. If a dominant mutant allele is mapped, then a capital-letter symbol is shown on the map (Fig. 4.7).

You will notice that Sturtevant's map differs somewhat in the specific locus designations from the standard map of the X chromosome in Drosophila. The standard map was constructed from numerous linkage studies, so that it is based on vast amounts of data and can therefore be more refined in its details. You will also notice that alleles w (white eye color) and w^e (eosin eye color) are positioned at the same locus. Since testcrosses involving different sex-linked genes and w or w^e consistently showed about the same percentage recombinations, there was preliminary evidence that these were two different mutant alleles of the same wild-type w^+ gene. This

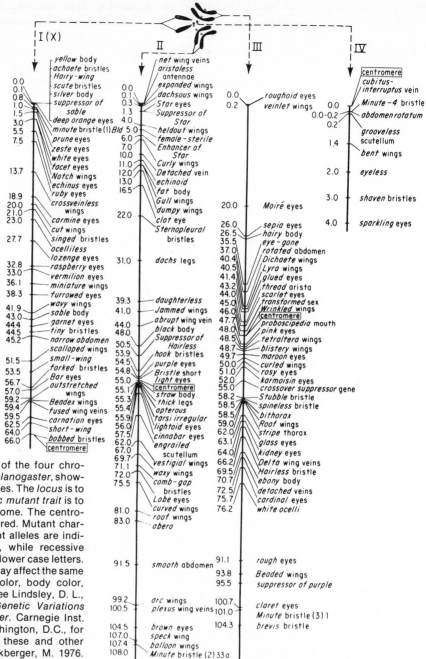

Figure 4.7 Linkage map of the four chromosomes of *Drosophila melanogaster*, showing some of the known genes. The *locus* is to the left and the *phenotypic mutant trait* is to the right of each chromosome. The centromere position is shown in red. Mutant characteristics due to dominant alleles are indicated by a capital letter, while recessive mutant traits are shown in lower case letters. Note that different genes may affect the same character, such as eye color, body color, wing shape, and others. See Lindsley, D. L., and E. H. Grell, 1968. *Genetic Variations of Drosophila melanogaster.* Carnegie Inst. Wash. Publ. No. 627, Washington, D.C., for extensive descriptions of these and other mutant traits. (From Strickberger, M. 1976. *Genetics*, 2nd ed. New York: Macmillan. Copyright © 1976 by M. Strickberger.)

tentative conclusion was verified by the more critical and reliable test for multiple alleles of the same gene versus alleles of different genes (see Fig. 2.24). Since crosses between white-eyed and eosin-eyed flies always gave mutant progeny, these alleles were interpreted to be at the same locus on the chromosome. If the situation had been mutant × mutant → some wild-type segregants, then two different genes would have been implicated in the development of the same phenotypic character (eye color, in this case), as was found for w and v.

4.5   The Double-Crossover Problem

The percentage of genetic recombinants is converted directly into percentage of crossover gametes or chromosomes, and this in turn is translated into map units of distance between two linked genes. There is a pitfall here because recombination and crossing over are not the same thing. Crossing over is a chromosomal process involving an exchange of homologous chromosome segments, while recombinations are genetically identified from genotypic constitutions in progeny. We infer that a recombination arises as the result of a crossover between two genes, but the values for genetic recombination and detectable chromosomal crossovers are not always identical and, therefore, measurement in map units is not always entirely accurate.

The main reason that we cannot always equate genetic recombinations and chromosomal crossovers is that crossing over is a random process taking place along the length of the chromosome. When there are greater distances between pairs of genes, then there are more chances for crossing over to take place, at random, between these genes. Another way of saying this is that there is a higher probability that two or more crossovers will take place between genes that are farther apart than between genes that are closer together on the chromosome.

Let us suppose that genes A and B are really 30 map units apart on a chromosome. What are the chances that one crossover will take place between them? The answer would be 30%, because 30 map units is derived from the percentage of recombinants in progenies and this is translated directly into percentage of crossover gametes. What are the chances that two crossovers will take place, at random, within this distance of 30 map units; or, what is the probability of a **double-crossover** in the region between two genes that are 30 map units apart? If the probability for one crossover is 30%, and each crossover is an independent event which takes place at random and without regard to other crossovers in the region, then the probability for two crossovers is the product of the separate probabilities. In this case, the probability for each crossover is 30% and, therefore, the probability of two crossovers between A and B is 30% × 30%, or 9% (0.3 × 0.3 = 0.09). In other words, we may expect that out of every 30 gametes per 100 produced by crossing over between A and B, 9 of these will be double-crossovers. What is the consequence of double crossovers? They yield alleles in parental combinations and therefore lead to parental, not recombinant, phenotypes. They reduce the percentage of recombinants recovered in the progeny, and therefore lead to an *underestimate* of crossing over and, in turn, to an underestimate of the map units of distance between two genes, as shown in Fig. 4.8.

Instead of 30% of the gametes from the heterozygous parent in a testcross having the *Ab* or *aB* recombinant genotype and producing *Ab/ab* or *aB/ab* recombinant testcross progeny, only 21% (30 – 9 = 21) of the gametes will lead to recombinants. The remaining 9% of these gametes will have double-crossover chromosomes and will lead to the parental types: *AB/ab* or *ab/ab*. On finding 21% recombinants in the two-factor testcross progeny, we would assume 21% of the gametes resulted from crossing over and put only 21 map units between genes *A* and *B* on the chromosome.

There is a lower probability for two crossovers to take place in the same space between two genes if the distance is smaller. If genes *C* and *D* are actually 5 map units apart, then 5% of the gametes will have crossover chromosomes. Of these, only 0.25% (0.05 × 0.05) will be double-crossovers and 4.75% will be single crossovers, on the average. The discrepancy for small distances is therefore less significant, and usually can be ignored until very fine detail and location is required for the standard map or for other purposes.

Figure 4.8 Gametic types arising from meiocytes according to crossing over in the region between two linked genes on a chromosome. Double crossovers lead to reduction in the observed frequency of recombinant gametes and, therefore, lead to underestimates of distances between linked genes.

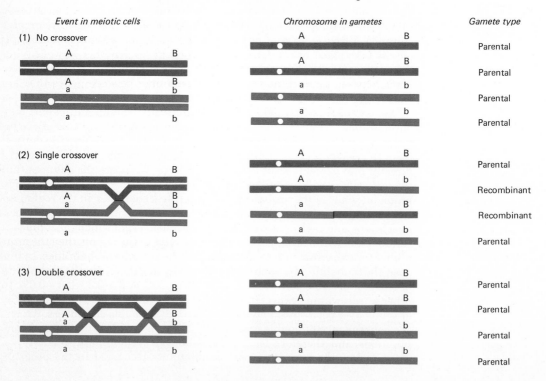

The double-crossover problem may be remedied when there is a third gene situated between *A* and *B* (Fig. 4.9). The gene in the middle serves as a "marker" for double-crossover chromosomes. If you look at the double-crossover chromosomes, you will see that the *middle pair of alleles* is reversed when compared with the parental arrangements of alleles.

The **three-point testcross** is the usual method of choice for mapping linked genes on chromosomes for a number of reasons:

1. The presence of 3 gene differences in testcross parents allows the identification of double-crossover recombinants, and makes the relationship more meaningful between percentage of recombinants and percentage of gametes resulting from crossing over, when determining map units of distance between linked genes.

2. There are eight phenotypic classes, each of which represents a unique genotype, and which is still a manageable number to analyze from reasonable numbers of progeny. Since we know that 2^n = the number of different phenotypic classes, when n = the number of pairs of heterozygous alleles, there would be 16 phenotypes for 4 pairs of alleles (2^4), 32 different phenotypes for 5 pairs of alleles (2^5), and so forth. Four- or five-factor testcrosses would require substantially larger numbers of progeny in order to recover all the phenotypic classes in the numbers needed for reliable samplings of genetic events observed from recombinations. From a practical standpoint, three-factor testcrosses are more convenient and equally as reliable as crosses involving more factors. The situation could be different, of course, for microorganisms which can be raised in huge numbers in a very brief time and in a relatively small space.

3. It is more efficient and less time-consuming to analyze three genes at one time than to analyze three genes in two-factor testcrosses. Instead of *A* × *B*, *A* × *C*, and *B* × *C* to discover the map order and distances for *A*, *B*, and *C*, we need only one three-factor testcross involving *A*, *B*, and *C* at once. This is particularly important when using organisms with a longer life cycle, or ones requiring a great deal of space and maintenance. Anything that saves time and money, and gives the same or improved results, is highly desirable.

Figure 4.9 Double crossover chromosomes can be recognized genetically if one crossover occurs to either side of the middle "marker" gene. The middle pair of alleles is reversed relative to the parental arrangement. Such double crossover types of recombinants may not be detected in two-point testcrosses.

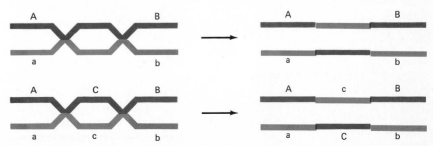

As we analyze representative three-point testcross experiments, try to keep these three features of experimental design and management in mind.

4.6   Mapping by the Three-Point Testcross Method

We can take a familiar example to begin with, and see how linkage analysis is performed when the three genes are known to be in the same linkage group. Since we want to know the relative order and distance between linked genes, we can start with X-linked genes in Drosophila, genes which are in the X chromosome. We can start with three X-linked genes already mentioned: body color (gray, y^+, versus yellow, y), eye color (red, w^+, versus white, w), and wing length (long, m^+, versus miniature, m).

If we cross $\dfrac{y\,w\,m}{y\,w\,m}$ females with $\underline{y^+w^+m^+}$ males, which we will simply abbreviate to $\underline{+\ +\ +}$ for the three wild-type alleles throughout the discussion, we obtain F_1 heterozygous $\dfrac{+\ +\ +}{y\ w\ m}$ females and $\underline{y\ w\ m}$ males. We can perform either a testcross of F_1 females to triply-recessive males from another stock, or obtain the F_2, since both crosses would be identical. In the F_2 or testcross progeny we find:

Phenotypic class	Maternal chromosome present	Number of progeny
gray, red, long	+ + +	1087
yellow, white, miniature	y w m	1042
gray, white, miniature	+ w m	17
yellow, red, long	y + +	15
gray, red, miniature	+ + m	543
yellow, white long	y w +	502
gray, white, long	+ w +	6
yellow, red, miniature	y + m	4
		3216

The first thing to find out in this progeny is the pair of parental phenotypic classes. Since these genes are linked we expect an excess of parentals, so we look for the largest two classes among the total of eight; these are + + + and $y\ w\ m$. We really know this already because we know the alleles that were present on each of the X chromosomes in the F_1 females, and the parental or noncrossover genotypes are identical with these unchanged chromosomes.

The second thing to discover is the pair of classes with the double-crossover chromosomes, since this pair will define the middle gene and give us the order of the three genes in the chromosome. The double-crossover phenotypic classes are the least numerous of all, because double-crossovers are less frequent than single crossover events. To be produced there would have been one crossover in the space between the middle gene and the gene to its right, and another crossover between the middle gene and the gene to its left. The probability of a double-crossover is the product of the separate probabilities for each single-crossover occurring, so it is less frequent than either of the single-crossover events. By comparing the parental $+ + +$ and y w m with $+ w +$ and $y + m$ in the two phenotypic classes present in the lowest numbers, we can see that w must be the middle gene and that it is flanked by y and m:

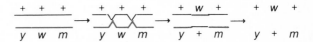

It is now a simple matter to identify each of the single-crossover pairs of classes. Crossing over between y and w would change the combination of y^+/y in a chromosome retaining the parental w m or $+ +$ alleles at these two gene loci:

$$\begin{array}{ccccccccccc}
+ & + & + & & + & + & + & & + & w & m & & + & w & m \\
\hline
y & w & m & & y & w & m & & y & + & + & & y & + & +
\end{array}$$

The single-crossover classes which remain must be those involving the space between the loci for w and m:

$$\begin{array}{ccccccccccc}
+ & + & + & & + & + & + & & + & + & m & & + & + & m \\
\hline
y & w & m & & y & w & m & & y & w & + & & y & w & +
\end{array}$$

Notice that each of the crossover events gives rise to reciprocal classes of recombinant gametes. We would expect to find approximately equal numbers of each genotype arising from two reciprocal crossover chromosomes, because approximately equal numbers of gametes will have each chromosome due to the segregation of homologous chromosomes at meiosis.

The percentages of crossovers are calculated separately for the two regions in which crossovers occurred; we usually start at the left and label region I, and call the second space region II. For more than a three-factor cross, additional regions would be identified in sequence by roman numerals. When we calculate crossovers in region I, it is necessary to *add* the total of the double-crossovers to the total of the single-crossovers for this $y-w$ region. Similarly, to obtain the total percentage of crossovers in region II we add the double-crossovers to the single-crossover events between w and m.

The reason we add double-crossovers to each of the single-crossover values is that crossing over took place in region I and in region II in the double-crossover classes. If we omit the double-crossovers, we lose one of the advantages of the three-point testcross, namely, that we can detect region I crossing over, or region II crossing over, even when a second independent crossing-over event has obscured the expected recombinations. When we total all the crossovers within a region, the percentage of crossovers (gametes or chromosomes) more accurately reflects the distance between two genes, and the translation into map units is closer to the actual distance.

For the calculations from this cross, we find:

Region	Gene loci	Proportion of crossovers	Percentage of crossovers	Distance in map units
I	$y—w$	$\dfrac{32 + 10}{3216}$	1.3	1.3
II	$w—m$	$\dfrac{1045 + 10}{3216}$	32.8	32.8
I + II	$y—m$	$\dfrac{32 + 1045 + 10 + 10}{3216}$	34.1	34.1

We can now map these three gene loci in their proper sequence and distances from each other on the X chromosome:

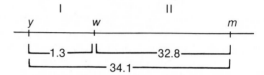

Now let us look at linkage analysis for autosomal genes in a three-point testcross. We know from previous studies in Drosophila that the genes for *gray* versus *black* body color (b^+ and b) *red* versus *purple* eye color (pr^+ and *pr*), and *long* versus *vestigial* wing length (vg^+ and *vg*) are located on autosomal chromosomes because they produce identical progenies in reciprocal crosses. X-linked genes show different reciprocal progenies. From the gene symbols you can tell that all the wild-type alleles are dominant to their mutant alternatives, as was discovered in breeding analysis. We now want to find out if these genes are in the same linkage group, each in a different chromosome, or two in one chromosome and the third in another linkage group. We cross homozygous flies from true-breeding stocks and obtain F_1 triply heterozygous for the three pairs of alleles. The F_1 ♀ heterozygotes are testcrossed to triple-recessives and the following progeny are obtained:

Phenotype	Chromosome from heterozygous parent	Number of individuals
wild type	+ + +	59
black, purple, vestigial	b pr vg	51
vestigial	+ + vg	416
black, purple	b pr +	402
purple	+ pr +	23
black, vestigial	b + vg	21
		972

The first question is: Are these genes linked? We see only six phenotypes instead of eight, with only two of the phenotypes present in very large numbers. Since these are reciprocal phenotypes (what is recessive in one is dominant in the other for each pair of alleles: + + *vg* and *b pr* +), and there is no hint of a 1:1:1:1 ratio, which means no two genes are assorting independently, we can assume that all three genes are linked. There is no evidence for independent assortment. The noncrossover or parental chromosomes are therefore $+ + vg$ and $b\ pr\ +$, since they are the most numerous classes. The missing phenotypes must be the relatively more rare double-crossovers, none of which happened to be produced, for some reason. (Perhaps a crossover in region I or in region II reduces the probability for another crossover in the other region.) In any event, we can figure out that the missing two genotypes are $+ pr\ vg$ and $b + +$, since all the other possible combinations are present.

If we assume that $+ pr\ vg$ and $b + +$ are the missing double-crossovers, we can find the middle gene by comparing these with the parental types. The transposed pair of alleles, relative to the arrangement in the noncrossover chromosomes, is $+/pr$, which is the gene in the middle $\left(\dfrac{+ + vg}{b\ pr\ +}\right.$ versus $\left.\dfrac{+ pr\ vg}{b\ +\ +}\right)$. The sequence is therefore $b\ pr\ vg$, and we can now find the single-crossovers in region I, between b and pr. We then calculate the percentage recombinants as $44/972 = 4.5\%$ and determine there are 4.5 map units in region I. The single-crossovers in region II, between pr and vg, include 110 recombinants out of a total progeny of 972, which is 11.5% crossovers, and thus there are 11.5 map units between pr and vg. The map would therefore be:

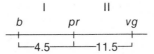

We can verify the gene order by calculating the percentage recombination between b and vg. If these are the outside members of the chromosome segment, and pr is in the middle, then the percentage of crossovers between b and vg should approximate $4.5 + 11.5$ added together. A crossover between b and vg would produce:

The recombinant phenotypic classes showing b and vg in the same chromosome are $b\ pr\ vg$ and $b + vg$; those showing b^+ and vg^+ in the same chromosome are $+ + +$ and $+ pr\ +$. When these are totaled ($51 + 21 + 59 + 23 = 154$), we can calculate $154/972 = 15.8\%$ recombinants involving b and vg. This is exactly what we would expect to find for the two genes that are farthest apart, and which are present at each end of the chromosome segment carrying these three linked genes.

We also could have taken genes in combinations of two, and determined the percentages of recombinants in each pairwise combination. By finding 4.5% for b—pr, 11.5% for pr—vg, and 15.8% for b—vg crossovers, we would have put these together on the map in the same logical order. It would be very similar to the example in Section 4.4 when we discussed mapping by two-point testcrosses for genes *A*, *B*, and *C*.

As a final example of the value of the three-point testcross, we can look at the progeny of a testcross using F_1 females heterozygous for ebony (*e*) body color, rough (*ro*) eyes, and vestigial (*vg*) wings:

e ro vg		210
+ +	+	202
e ro	+	198
+ +	*vg*	206
e +	*vg*	47
+ *ro*	+	49
e +	+	48
+ *ro vg*		50
		1010

The first thing we notice is that some linkage is involved, because we would have found a 1:1:1:1:1:1:1:1 ratio if all three genes had assorted independently. Since crossing over is infrequent, the four largest classes must be noncrossover genotypes. We can find out which two genes are linked by seeing that these are the two which do not assort in the noncrossover classes. We can check out *e* and *ro* first:

e ro	210	
+ +	202	408 *e ro*:408 + + = 1:1
e ro	198	
+ +	206	

Since there are only two classes, *e ro* and + +, these two pairs of alleles have not assorted to give a 1:1:1:1 ratio and must therefore be linked. These large classes are therefore the noncrossover, parental classes.

We can now find out whether *vg* is linked to *e* or *ro* by checking the parental classes again. If *vg* is linked to *e* (or *ro*) there will be only two parental types just as we saw before:

e vg	210
+ +	202
e +	198
+ *vg*	206

Since there is a 1:1:1:1 ratio for the two pairs of alleles, they must have assorted independently and are therefore not linked (and not to *ro* either because *ro* is linked to *e*).

We can now calculate linkage between *e* and *ro*, by looking at the smaller-sized recombinant classes:

e +	47
+ *ro*	49
e +	48
+ *ro*	50

194 recombinants/1010 total progeny = 0.192

0.192 × 100 = 19.2% recombinants = 19.2 map units

The map is:

$$\underset{19.2}{\underline{e \qquad\quad ro}} \qquad\qquad vg$$

4.7   Interference and Coincidence

The chromosome map represents a table of probabilities, which allows us to predict the percentage of gametes in which there will be a chromosome with a crossover between one gene locus and another. After all, this is a simple extension of the basis for putting two genes a certain number of map units apart on the map. It implies that crossing over is a random event, and that we may predict the probability of such a random event taking place in other meiotic cells in future crosses. We can be reasonably sure that this is the case because we find essentially similar values each time we study the same two genes. This is exactly the same as saying that we expect one coin to land heads up in approximately 50% of a large number of trials. The two situations have a definite predicted value because of the laws of **probability** governing random events happening by chance alone.

We can compare the expected and observed percentages of two crossover events occurring simultaneously, to see if the two events are independent of one another. If each crossover is a random event and does not influence the occurrence of another crossover in the same two chromatids, we should find that the **observed** frequency of double-crossovers is equal to the **expected**, or predicted, frequency. In the case of two coins, we find about 25% of the tosses consist of two heads. Since the probability of each coin alone is 50%, the product of the separate probabilites would be 25% (0.5×0.5) if each coin acted independently. Since the observed and the expected percentages, or frequencies, are the same, we can state that each toss is an independent event.

If we compare the observed frequency of double-crossovers in the first cross described in Section 4.6, with the expected frequency, we find 10/3216 = 0.31% observed. But we expected $0.013 \times 0.328 = 0.43\%$ double-crossovers in regions I and II of the $y-w-m$ segment of the X chromosome. This kind of discrepancy is found almost all of the time in different species; the observed frequency of double-crossovers is *less* than the expected value. Since the pattern is consistent, it is interpreted to mean that once crossing over has occurred, there is a lower probability of another crossover event in an adjacent region. The phenomenon is called **interference**. Two crossovers in the same region are not independent; one interferes with another's occurring. The cause of interference is unknown at present.

If we are to make more effective use of a chromosome map as a table of probabilities, we should determine the degree of interference which characterizes different chromosomes and chromosome regions. There is variation even between different parts of the same chromosome, and usually between different chromosomes. Strengths of interference are usually summarized as **coefficients of coincidence**, which are simply ratios between observed and expected frequencies of double-crossovers:

$$\frac{\text{observed frequency of double-crossovers}}{\text{expected frequency of double-crossovers}} = \text{coefficient of coincidence}$$

We can calculate the coincidence for the *y—m* region of the X chromosome map in Drosophila as 0.31/0.43 = 0.72, on the basis of the one experiment we analyzed. A more reliable value would be obtained from data collected for a number of different progenies involving the same region of the X chromosome.

Coincidence varies in inverse proportion to interference, and coincidence values generally vary from 0 to 1. When there is complete interference so that a second crossover does not occur in a region or a chromosome with one crossover present, the coincidence is 0. The coincidence value of 1 indicates a lack of interference. In studies of very closely linked genes, particularly in some microorganisms and in bacteriophages, there may be an excess of double-crossovers observed, relative to the expected frequency. In such a case, the phenomenon is called **negative interference.**

Once coefficients of coincidence have been calculated for a chromosome region, the map values are adjusted appropriately. For coincidence values which are less than 1 (some interference), the map distance is *lengthened* because the observed double crossover frequency is lower than it should be, due to interference.

4.8   Mapping by Tetrad Analysis in Haploid Microorganisms

In many of the fungi, algae, and certain other organisms, all four spore products (a tetrad) of a single meiotic cell or event may be recovered and analyzed genetically. This method is called **tetrad analysis**, and you may recall that we discussed it briefly in Chapter 2 (see Figs. 2.21 and 2.22). Whether the spores are in an *ordered* or *unordered* arrangement, and whether there are only the four immediate products of meiosis or pairs of mitotic derivatives of these four spores, we can obtain a substantial amount of information about segregation patterns and recombinations by tetrad analysis.

Since most of these organisms produce unordered tetrads, we will consider them first. Some of the same principles can also be applied to analysis of ordered tetrads, as in Neurospora and a few other fungi in the Ascomycete group. If we analyze the segregation pattern of two linked genes in a cross between haploid parents with *AB* and *ab* genotypes, we can find three kinds of *tetrad segregation patterns*. Tetrads containing *AB/AB/ab/ab* spores are called **parental ditypes** (PD) because there are only two kinds of combinations and both of these are the parental genotypes. Tetrads of the **nonparental ditype** (NPD) kind also have only two kinds of combinations, *Ab/Ab/aB/aB,* but these are recombinant and not parental genotypes. The third segregation pattern is called **tetratype** (T), and all four spores have a different genotype, *AB/Ab/aB/ab,* two of which are parental and two recombinant combinations.

Since we stated that the two genes were linked, we know that crossing over must be responsible for recombinant genotypes. Taking the simplest situation of one crossover between the two gene loci, each type of tetrad arises as follows:

1. No crossing over leads to parental chromosomes in the PD tetrad.
2. One crossover between *A* and *B* accounts for the tetratype combinations.
3. Nonparental ditypes cannot arise unless there have been two crossovers between *A* and *B*. The NPD tetrads will therefore be the rarest of the three segregation patterns for linked genes. In fact, they arise when the two exchange events involve all four chromatids of the paired homologous chromosomes (Fig. 4.10).

Since the predominant kinds of tetrads are parental PD and recombinant T, we can determine the map distance separating the two linked genes by a straightforward ratio:

$$\frac{1/2T + NPD}{total\ tetrads} = recombination\ frequency,\ \times\ 100 = map\ units$$

Figure 4.10 Mapping by tetrad analysis requires recognition of tetrad segregation patterns for two genes, producing three tetrad classes: parental ditype (PD), tetratype (T), and nonparental ditype (NPD). Each class arises as a consequence of crossover events, or lack of these, as shown.

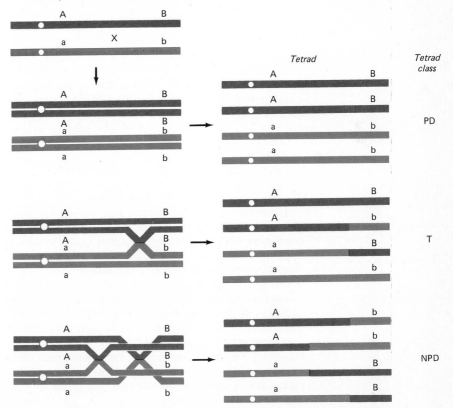

The reason we use the term 1/2T in the numerator is that only half the products of T tetrads are recombinants. All NPD products, on the other hand, are of the recombinant genotype. The numerator is therefore the number of recombinants recovered in the total progeny from unordered tetrads, and it is directly comparable to the number of recombinants obtained from randomly isolated spore progeny that have not been kept in their individual tetrad groups for analysis.

In a typical linkage analysis for the hypothetical genes a and b, we may obtain the following progeny from $a^+ b^+ \times a\, b$:

Tetrad genotypes	Tetrad type	numbers	Number of spores parental	recombinant
+ +			400	
+ +	PD	400	400	
a b			400	
a b			400	
+ +			90	
a b	T	90	90	
+ b				90
a +				90
+ b				10
+ b	NPD	10		10
a +				10
a +				10
Totals		500	1780	220

Using the ratio 1/2T + NPD/total tetrads, we find 45 + 10/500 = 11%. Genes a and b are 11 map units apart. We would have reached the same result if we had only examined isolated spores from these 500 tetrads, as follows:

$$\frac{\text{recombinants}}{\text{total spores}} = \frac{220}{2000} = 0.11, \text{ or } 11 \text{ \% recombinants} = 11 \text{ map units}$$

If genes a and b were not linked, the alleles would segregate independently and we would have found a ratio of 1:1:1:1 for the four possible genotypes, that is, 50% recombinants and 50% parental-type spores. From the standpoint of ratios of tetrad types, we would expect random segregation of chromsomes at meiosis to produce as many PD as NPD tetrads ($AB/Ab/ab/ab$ and $AB/Ab/aB/ab$), (Fig. 4.11). The proportion of T tetrads would depend on crossing over between the centromere and the gene closest to it, that is, to the distance separating the centromere and the nearest gene. Regardless of the percentage of T Tetrads produced for independently assorting genes, there would be equal proportions of PD and NPD tetrads because of random segregation of homologous chromosomes at meiosis. This means that $A + B$ and $a + b$ should arise equally as often as the segregation $A + b$ and $a + B$ in tetrads containing only two of the four possible combinations of alleles.

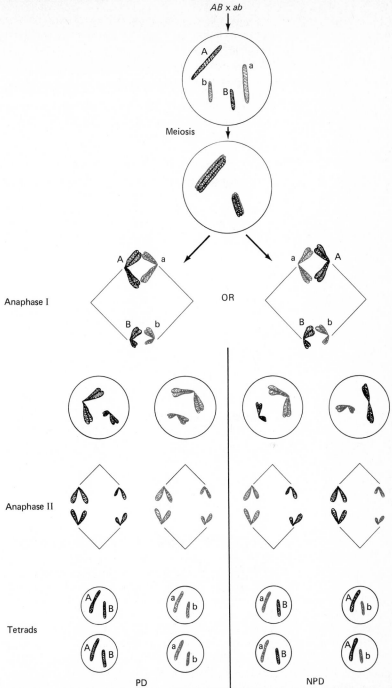

Figure 4.11   Random segregation of homologous chromosomes at meiosis produces PD and NPD tetrads with approximately equal frequency when unlinked genes are involved. Independent assortment of two genes is therefore indicated when %PD = %NPD tetrads in the progeny.

Ordered tetrads can provide more information than unordered tetrads, because each genotype can be related to the particular chromosomal events which gave rise to the chromosome present in each spore. We can relate each spore genotype to the segregation of homologous chromosomes during the first division versus separation of sister chromatids during the second division of meiosis (Fig. 4.12). So-called **first-division** and **second-division segregation** patterns can therefore provide specific information on distance between two linked genes, but they are particularly valuable in establishing the distance between a gene and the centromere of the chromosome. Since centromeres of homologous chromosomes separate at the first meiotic division, they always undergo first-division segregation. If gene *a* is located very near the centromere, then *a* will segregate from its + allele at the first division. This leads to an ordered tetrad in which *a a* + + (or + + *a a*) emerges from a heterozygous nucleus after meiosis. If there is a crossover between gene *a* and the centromere, then segregation of alleles takes place at the second meiotic division and the order of spores in the tetrad will be + *a* + *a* (or *a* + *a* +, or *a* + + *a*, or + *a a* +, depending on random orientation and sepa-

Figure 4.12 Distance between a gene and the centromere of the chromosome can be estimated from the proportions of ordered tetrads showing first-division segregation (no crossing over) versus second division segregation (crossover between gene and centromere). The closer the gene is to the centromere, the less chance of crossing over within the space and, therefore, of the production of tetrads showing the second-division segregation pattern of spore order in the ascus.

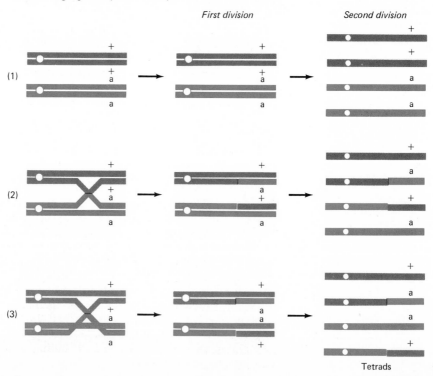

Tetrads

ration of the sister chromatids). Noncrossover tetrads have two spores with the same genotype next to two other spores with the alternative genotype. The other combinations do not have two like spores adjacent to two spores with the alternative allele. All of these combinations can be classified as crossover tetrads.

To determine the distance between the gene and the centromere, it is simply a matter of:

$$\frac{1/2 \text{ second-division tetrads}}{\text{total number of tetrads}} \times 100 = \text{percentage recombinants} = \text{map units}$$

We take only half the frequency of the second-division tetrads in the numerator because only half the spores in a tetrad have been derived from a crossover between two of the four chromatids in a meiotic bivalent. Using this method and other linkage data, the seven linkage groups of *Neurospora crassa* have been identified. Each linkage group corresponds to one of the seven chromosomes making up the genome of the species (Fig. 4.13). The correspondence in number of linkage groups determined genetically, and number of chromosomes counted by microscopy, provides one more line of cytogenetic evidence for the location of genes in chromosomes.

When considering ordered tetrad analysis in crosses involving three linked genes, there are a large number of types of tetrads which can arise as the result of crossover events during meiosis. In addition to the three kinds of tetrads which can arise as the result of double crossing over between *a* and *b* and between *b* and *c*, when two, three, or four of the chromatids of a bivalent are involved, as shown in Fig. 4.14, yet other kinds of tetrads may be produced. For example, double-crossovers involving the space between the centromere and the gene nearest to it, plus another crossover either in region I or in region II, will give a different kind of tetrad; as will single-crossover types, triple-crossover types, and so forth. There is no need for us to analyze these three-factor crosses, since there would not be any difference in the principles of linkage analysis as we have already discussed them in this chapter.

CROSSING OVER

Throughout this chapter we have freely discussed crossing over in linkage analysis, without providing evidence in support of the assumptions we have made. Crossing over is a process involving an exchange of parts of homologous chromosomes. Not only have we accepted this definition, but we have made two particular assumptions about crossing over in relation to linkage analysis: (1) that recombinations of linked genes are accomplished through the process of crossing over, and (2) that crossing over occurs after chromosomes have replicated, that is, in the "four-strand" stage when each bivalent consists of two pairs of chromatids. We should look at the evidence in support of these two assumptions, because we cannot pursue linkage analysis properly without a basic understanding of the major features of the crossing-over phenomenon.

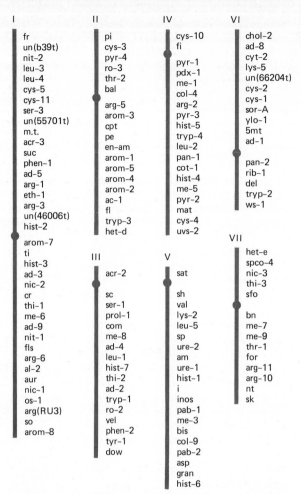

Figure 4.13 Linkage map of *Neurospora crassa* showing some of the genes known to be located on seven chromosomes of the genome. Many of the characteristics refer to biochemical activities, such as ability to synthesize amino acids and other metabolites. The centromere (solid circle) of each chromosome is shown in its most probable location. For additional information see Barratt, R. W., and A. Radford. 1970. In *Handbook of Biochemistry*, 2nd ed., H. A. Sober, ed. Cleveland, Ohio: Chemical Rubber Co.

Morgan had proposed in 1911 that new combinations of linked genes arose by exchanges between chromosomes, and that chiasmata might be the visible evidence of such exchange events. There was no experimental evidence to support this hypothesis until 1931, when two reports were published quite independently of each other. Both studies showed in the most elegant way that genetic recombinations did arise as the result of physical exchanges between homologous chromosomes in meiosis. The major difficulty in obtaining evidence for physical exchanges is that homologous chromosomes ordinarily cannot be distinguished from one another

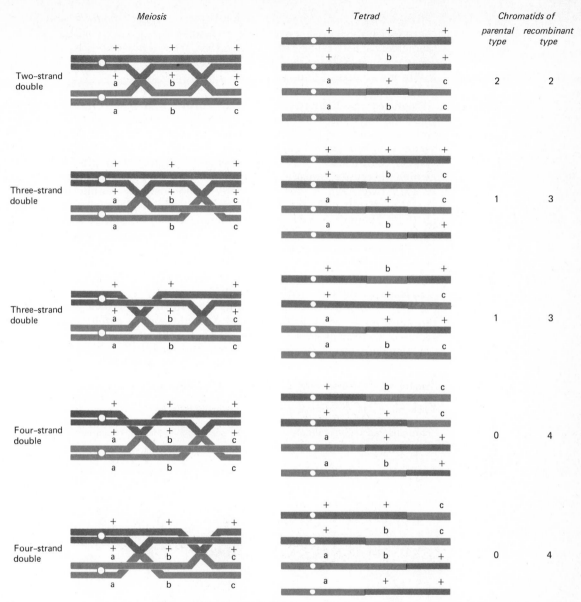

Figure 4.14 Some of the types of tetrads that may arise as the result of double crossovers involving two, three, or all four strands (chromatids) of a bivalent during meiosis.

even at the highest levels of microscopic examination. In order to establish the occurrence of exchanges, the homologous chromosomes had to be tagged or differentiated in some way so that each homologue could be identified and related to the particular alleles it carried. Curt Stern accomplished this objective using Drosophila, and Harriet Creighton and Barbara McClintock used similar logic and experimental design with corn. By coincidence, both reports appeared in 1931. We will illustrate the principles shown in one of these two equivalent analyses.

In his studies of Drosophila, Stern had come across unusual strains in which the X chromosome had undergone physical alterations and could be recognized and distinguished from the normal X. In one strain the X chromosome had a piece of chromosome number 4 attached in place of its own missing piece, and in another strain there was a portion of the Y chromosome attached to the X chromosome so that the whole structure was much longer than usual. Stern made the crosses required to obtain females in which these two unusual X chromosomes were present instead of the normal two. Each of these physically distinguishable chromosomes was made allelically different, so that Stern knew which alleles were present by both the phenotype and by seeing which X chromosomes were present (Fig. 4.15).

These special females were crossed with normal males carrying the recessive carnation (*car*) mutant allele for eye color and the recessive wild-type allele (B^+) for eye construction; the dominant mutant allele for bar eyes (*B*) leads to a reduced number of facets in the compound eye of the insect and a "bar" of color develops in part of the eye. The wild-type allele for eye color (*car⁺*) governs red eyes. The normal X from the male parent and the two altered X chromosomes from the female parent were all distinguishable cytologically by microscope observation, and genetically by the phenotypes

Figure 4.15 Diagrammatic summary of Curt Stern's 1931 cytogenetic experiments with *Drosophila melanogaster*, in which he constructed strains having physically distinguishable X chromosomes made allelically different for eye color and eye facet number. These classic studies related physical exchange between homologous chromosome segments (crossing over) as seen by microscopy, to genetic recombination as seen in progeny phenotypes.

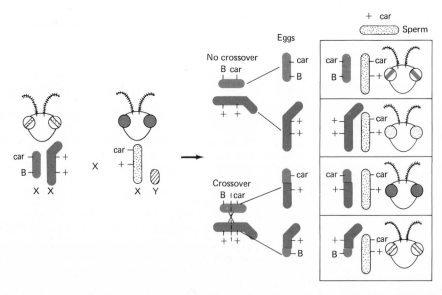

which developed from different combinations of alleles of the two marker genes.

When the progeny were examined, Stern found that noncrossover combinations of the alleles of the two genes were present (by phenotype identification) in flies with unaltered parental X chromosomes. Flies identified by phenotype as having crossover, or recombinant, combinations of alleles of the two genes *also* had a physically altered X chromosome derived from the female parent. The correlation between physically exchanged chromosomes and new combinations of alleles provided powerful evidence in support of the proposal that crossing over involved the physical exchange of homologous chromosome segments, which gave rise to new combinations of alleles of linked genes.

Evidence that crossing over took place in the four-strand stage of meiosis was obtained using Neurospora. This organism is ideally suited to such an analysis because all the products of individual meiotic cells remain associated in the order of their production during the first and second divisions of meiosis. We have already explored most of these features, so you should be able to grasp the nub of the analysis from a brief description.

Whether we look at crossing over between a gene and the centromere, or at segregation due to crossing over between two linked genes, the crucial observations will be the same (Fig. 4.16). If crossing over occurs *before* chromosome replication, a noncrossover tetrad will contain only parental (parental ditype, PD) genotypic combinations, while crossover tetrads will

Figure 4.16 Different predictions are made for the two possible alternatives shown at left. If crossing over occurs before chromosome replication, NPD tetrads may be produced. If crossing over occurs after replication, in the "four-strand" stage, T tetrads can be produced. Tetratype tetrads *cannot* be produced if crossing over between two linked genes takes place before chromosome replication. They are known to be produced and, therefore, crossing over probably occurs between two chromatids of a bivalent consisting of four chromatids, that is, after replication.

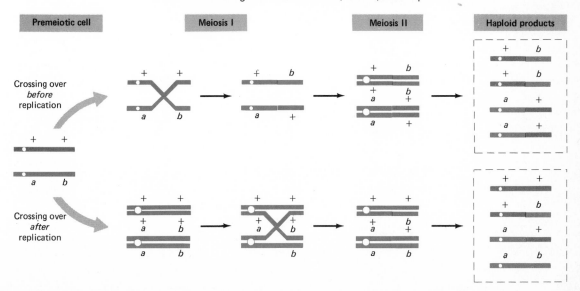

have only nonparental, recombinant genotypes (nonparental ditype, NPD). There will not be *both* parental and recombinant spores in the same tetrad (tetratype, T). If crossing over occurs in the four-strand stage, when each bivalent consists of four chromatids, then any of the three tetrad types may be produced. The relative frequencies of the three tetrad types will depend on the frequency of crossing over along the chromosomes. In further support of crossing over in the four-strand stage we have only to look back at Fig. 4.14. There is no way to get three- and four-strand double-crossovers if the bivalent has only two unreplicated strands at the time of crossing over.

Some years later we learned that DNA replicates during interphase before meiosis, and that crossing over takes place during meiotic prophase, after synapsis has occurred. The timing of replication and of crossing over are therefore clearly in the sequence of replication first and crossing over later on in the replicated pairs of homologous chromosomes (see Section 2.2).

The ordered tetrads of Neurospora were equally useful in clarifying the question of the *mechanism* of exchange between homologous chromosomes. The two major theories were: (1) **copy-choice**, and (2) **breakage and reunion** (Fig. 4.17). The copy-choice theory stated that recombinant chromatids arose *during* replication, as the newly-forming chromatids "copied" alleles partly along one chromosome and partly along the homologous chromosome of a pair. According to this theory, only two chromatids in a bivalent could ever be recombinant for two linked genes because the original two chromatids would remain intact and not undergo any genetic change during replication ("copying"). If this were true, there would be no tetrads such as the nonparental ditype kind in which all four spores contain recombinant genotypes on crossover chromosomes. Since four-strand double-crossover kinds of tetrads arise regularly, copy-choice would appear to be ruled out as a viable theory.

The mechanism of breakage and reunion is the one we accept today. It gained support from the demonstration in Neurospora that copy-choice

Figure 4.17 Diagrams showing two of the postulated mechanisms to explain crossing over, both proposed in the 1930s: (a) copy-choice, according to John Belling in 1931; and (b) breakage and reunion (at arrows) as described in 1937 by Cyril Darlington.

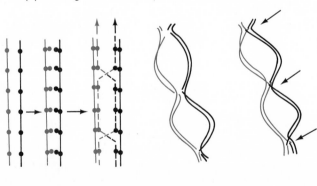

(a)   (b)

was unlikely. But tetrad analysis did not offer any direct evidence in support of breakage and reunion leading to crossover chromatids. Evidence showing that a mechanism of breakage and reunion does occur was obtained over a period of years beginning in 1961. In Chapters 7 and 10 we will discuss the precision of crossing over as it has been described from molecular studies, and see that breakage and reunion is far from being a crude chop-and-glue process, as the name might imply.

QUESTIONS AND PROBLEMS

4.1. The genes al (aristaless) and b (black body) are 48.5 units apart on chromosome 2 of *Drosophila melanogaster*. Design several crosses involving only these genes and their wild type alleles, which will demonstrate that they are physically linked.

4.2. In Drosophila, the dominant sex-linked gene for Bar eye (B) is at locus 57, and the recessive miniature wings (m) is at locus 36. The following cross is performed:

$$\frac{+\quad m}{B\quad +}\ \ ♀♀\ \ \times\ \ \overset{+\quad +}{\xrightarrow{\hspace{1.5cm}}}\ \ ♂♂$$

a. What is the expected proportion of recombinant female gametes produced by the female parents?

b. What is the expected proportion of genotypes and phenotypes in the progeny?

c. How many kinds of sperm would be produced relative to these two genes?

4.3. Explain why the genetic map of a chromosome can be greater than 50 map units long, while the maximum frequency of recombinants between two genes does not exceed 50%.

4.4. In tomatoes, round fruit shape (O) is dominant over elongate (o), and smooth fruit skin (P) is dominant over peach skin (p). Testcrosses of double recessives to F_1 individuals heterozygous for these two pairs of alleles gave the following results:

smooth, round	smooth, long	peach, round	peach, long
24	246	266	24

a. In the F_1, were the two pairs of alleles linked in the coupling or the repulsion phase?

b. What is the percentage recombination between these two genes?

4.5. In corn, a dominant gene C produces colored kernels, its recessive allele c produces colorless kernels. Another dominant gene, Sh, produces full kernels while its recessive allele (sh) produces shrunken kernels. A third dominant gene, Wx, produces normal endosperm and its recessive allele wx produces waxy starch. A testcross involving triply recessive and F_1 triply heterozygous plants produced the following progeny:

colored, shrunken, waxy	305
colorless, full, waxy	128
colorless, shrunken, waxy	18
colored, full, waxy	74
colorless, shrunken, nonwaxy	66
colored, full, nonwaxy	22
colored, shrunken, nonwaxy	112
colorless, full, nonwaxy	275
	———
	1000

Give the (a) gene sequence; (b) map distances; and (c) coefficient of coincidence.

4.6. In *Neurospora crassa* two mutant genes (*arg* and *his*) are known to interfere with the synthesis of the amino acids arginine and histidine, respectively. After a cross in which these genes were segregating, the following spore arrangements were found in the frequencies shown.

Pair 1	Pair 2	Pair 3	Pair 4	Number
arg his	*arg his*	+ +	+ +	84
+ *his*	+ *his*	*arg* +	*arg* +	80
+ +	+ +	*arg his*	*arg his*	78
arg +	*arg* +	+ *his*	+ *his*	84

How are the *arg* and *his* genes located in the chromosomes with respect to their centromeres and to each other?

4.7. A Neurospora stock which was adenine requiring (*ad*⁻) and tryptophan requiring (*tryp*⁻) was crossed to a wild type stock (++), and produced the following tetrads.

Tetrad classes	1	2	3	4	5	6	7
	ad tryp	*ad* +	*ad tryp*	*ad tryp*	*ad tryp*	*ad* +	*ad tryp*
	ad tryp	*ad* +	*ad* +	+ *tryp*	+ +	+ *tryp*	+ +
	+ +	+ *tryp*	+ *tryp*	*ad* +	*ad tryp*	*ad* +	+ *tryp*
	+ +	+ *tryp*	+ +	+ +	+ +	+ *tryp*	*ad* +
Frequency	147	21	93	6	24	3	6

a. Determine whether the two genes are linked. Explain your reasoning.

b. If they are linked, draw a linkage map including the centromere.

4.8. Vermilion eyes (*v*), lozenge shaped eyes (*lz*), and cut wings (*ct*) are recessive traits in Drosophila. A cross between females heterozygous at these three loci, and wild type males, produced the following results:

♀♀:	+ + +	1010
♂♂:	+ + +	30
	+ + *lz*	32
	+ *ct* +	441
	+ *ct lz*	1
	v + +	0
	v + *lz*	430
	v ct +	27
	v ct lz	39

    a. What is the sequence of these three linked genes in their chromosome?

    b. Calculate the map distances between the genes, and the coefficient of coincidence.

    c. In what chromosome of Drosophila are these genes carried?

4.9. Given the following two Drosophila stocks and a genetic map, predict the offspring you would obtain from 1000 progeny of a cross between triply recessive and triply heterozygous parents (assume all mutants are recessive).

$$
\begin{array}{ccc}
r & g & e \\
\mid & \mid & \mid \\
51 & 62 & 70.7
\end{array}
$$

r = rosy eyes
g = glassy eyes
e = ebony body

4.10. The cross $a\ b\ c \times +\ +\ +$ is made using an ascomycete with unordered tetrads. From analysis of 200 asci determine the linkage relationships between these three loci.

Tetrad class	1	2	3	4
	$a\ b\ c$	$a\ b\ +$	$a\ +\ c$	$a\ +\ +$
	$a\ b\ c$	$a\ b\ +$	$+\ +\ c$	$+\ +\ +$
	$+\ +\ +$	$+\ +\ c$	$a\ b\ +$	$a\ b\ c$
	$+\ +\ +$	$+\ +\ c$	$+\ b\ +$	$+\ b\ c$
Frequency	80	84	20	16

4.11. A riboflavinless strain (rib^-) of Neurospora is crossed with a tryptophanless strain ($tryp^-$), with the following results:

No. of asci	Tetrads			
258	$r\ +$	$r\ +$	$+\ t$	$+\ t$
8	$r\ +$	$+\ t$	$r\ +$	$+\ t$
124	$r\ +$	$r\ t$	$+\ +$	$+\ t$
4	$r\ +$	$+\ +$	$r\ t$	$+\ t$
2	$r\ t$	$+\ +$	$r\ +$	$+\ t$

Construct a map showing the arrangement of these two genes in relation to the centromere and to each other. Calculate the map distances.

4.12. The ABO blood groups and the nail-patella syndrome (a rare anomaly involving abnormal fingernails, toenails, and kneecaps, together with other structural abnormalities) are controlled by different genes in humans. In the pedigree shown the blood group genotypes appear below the symbols, and those individuals with the syndrome are represented by solid symbols. (Figure after Penrose, 1959)

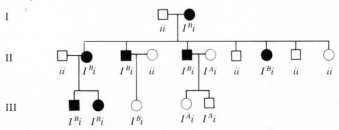

    a. Is nail-patella syndrome controlled by a dominant or recessive allele? Is the gene autosomal or sex linked?

    b. Do the above data provide any evidence for linkage between the two genes? Explain.

    c. Draw the linked genes on each of the two homologous chromosomes of both grandparents of the family (I1 and I2).

REFERENCES

Beadle, G. W., and E. L. Tatum. 1941. Genetic control of biochemical reactions in *Neurospora. Proc. Nat. Acad. Sci. U. S.* **27**:499.

Creighton, H. S., and B. McClintock. 1931. A correlation of cytological and genetical crossing-over in *Zea mays. Proc. Nat. Acad. Sci. U. S.* **17**:492.

Morgan, T. H. 1911. Random segregation versus coupling in Mendelian inheritance. *Science* **34**:384.

Srb, A. M., and N. H. Horowitz. 1944. The ornithine cycle in *Neurospora* and its genetic control. *J. Biol. Chem.* **154**:129.

Srb, A. M., R. D. Owen, and R. S. Edgar. 1965. *General Genetics*, 2nd ed. San Francisco: Freeman.

Sturtevant, A. H. 1913. The linear arrangement of six sex-linked factors in *Drosophila melanogaster. J. Exp. Zool.* **14**:43.

Extensions of Gene Transmission Analysis

In the previous chapter, we saw how linkage analysis could be used to map gene loci on eukaryotic chromosomes. The gene map summarizes the order and relative distances for known gene loci. With knowledge of chromosome behavior in meiosis and fertilization, gene transmission could be interpreted from genetic data and put into a chromosomal context. In this chapter, we will examine selected examples of situations and strategies used to map gene loci in the following systems: (1) mitotic cells in which recombinations arise by occasional occurrences of crossing over, permitting linkage analysis in parasexual cycles (nonsexual cycles which mimic sexual reproduction); (2) somatic cell genetics and family studies of human inheritance, where controlled breeding or laboratory analysis is not conducted; (3) linkage analysis in bacteria, where gene transmission between cells is effected by purified DNA, by virus vectors, and by conjugation; and (4) recombinations in phage progeny produced during the lytic cycle of infection.

In each of these situations you will find that the basic rules of linkage analysis and inheritance patterns underwrite each of the variations we discuss. Because of certain unique or different features of a life cycle and the ways by which genes are transmitted from parents to progeny, modified strategies for gene mapping have had to be devised in these systems.

The information which has come from all of these studies has reinforced the basic themes of inheritance and gene mapping. The underlying themes of genetic variation between the generations are: (1) genes are units of inheritance existing in alternative allelic forms; (2) segregation and recombination of alleles into new genotypes leads to increased genetic variety in populations of many asexual as well as sexual organisms; (3) genes are arranged in linear order, at fixed loci, on one or more chromosomes in all organisms; and (4) the genome can be mapped in virtually any organism with a sexual or parasexual cycle, because it is amenable to genetic analysis.

MITOTIC CROSSING OVER

There has been ample evidence to show that crossing over between homologous chromosomes must occur in somatic cells, which lack the capacity for meiosis. The evidence consists of observed segregation and assortment or recombination of members of pairs of alleles in heterozygous cells or tissues. We ordinarily expect lineages of somatic cells to reproduce their own genetic type exclusively, because mitosis leads to identical progeny nuclei from a parent nucleus. In most cases we see just what we expect, namely, lineages of cells with identical phenotypes. This implies that such lineages consist of cells with identical genotypes. When we find groups of cell descendants with some segregating phenotype, such as a homozygous expression in a heterozygous organism, we have preliminary evidence that alleles have segregated and then combined into new genotypes. In some of these cases, the most reasonable interpretation for the genetic alteration is that crossing over between homologous chromosomes has taken place.

5.1   Twin Spots in Drosophila

One of the first observations that could be interpreted in terms of segregation and recombination of alleles due to crossing over in somatic cells was described in 1936 by Curt Stern for *Drosophila melanogaster*. In crosses between females heterozygous for the X-linked mutant character *singed* bristles and males that expressed the X-linked mutant *yellow* body color, females in the F_1 progeny were phenotypically wild type as expected. However, in some of these F_1 flies there were small patches of cells showing the recessive mutant phenotypes of yellow or singed.

Because the yellow patches or spots and the singed spots occurred next to each other more often than they occurred singly and spaced apart on the fly's body, Stern proposed that some reciprocal event must have been responsible for the development of twin spots of mutant phenotype in an otherwise wild-type female.

The most reasonable interpretation was that crossing over had occurred between homologous chromosomes in the diploid cells, and that crossover and noncrossover sister chromatids had subsequently segregated at mitosis (Fig. 5.1). Once the daughter cells had received the crossover chromosome, they would give rise only to identical genetic copies in subsequent mitotic divisions in which no further crossing over occurred to produce variations. The cell lineage, consisting of the original modified cell and all of its mitotic descendants, would be observed as a patch or spot of phenotypically different tissue if there were enough cells to make a visible area on the fly. Cells with noncrossover chromosomes, or in which crossing over did not lead to a homozygous genotypic combination, would produce lineages of wild type color and bristle shape. The size of the spot is a reflection of the number of cells present, and would therefore indicate an earlier or a later crossover event during development. A larger spot, consisting of more cells, would imply an earlier crossover leading to more descendant cells with the crossover phenotype. A smaller spot would imply that crossing over had

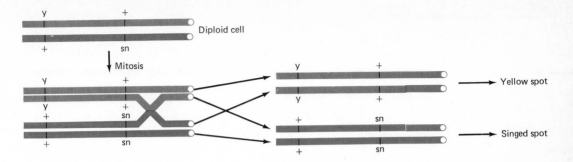

Figure 5.1 Origin of twin spots by crossing over in mitotic cells. An exchange occurred between chromatids of replicated homologous chromosomes in a diploid body (somatic) cell, and sister chromatids later will separate at anaphase (shown by direction of arrows at centromeres). Each daughter nucleus therefore will receive one chromatid of each of the homologous chromosomes, which may lead to a pair of cells that will produce twin spots from yellow and from singed cell-lineages.

occurred later during development, giving rise to fewer descendant cells in the patch.

By comparing the frequencies of twin spots, yellow spots alone, and singed spots alone, Stern was able to interpret the relative frequencies of all the possible crossover events. The higher the frequency of crossing over, the greater the distance along the chromosome in which crossovers could take place. Since twin spots mainly arise from crossing over between the singed locus and the centromere of the X chromosome, the distance should be greater in that part of the chromosome than between *y* and *sn*:

Single spots of yellow cells could arise as the result of a crossover between the *y* and *sn* loci. Single spots showing singed bristles, which were the least common of all, probably arise from a double-crossover in which there is one exchange between *y* and *sn* and a second exchange between *sn* and the centromere (Fig. 5.2). You can see from Figs. 5.1 and 5.2 that the distribution of chromosomes during mitosis may or may not lead to cells with the recombinant phenotype because of random orientation and segregation of sister chromatids during anaphase.

Mapping by mitotic or meiotic progenies has the same basis for interpretation. In each case there is a correlation between the frequency of crossover or recombinant progeny (whether cells or organisms) and distance between linked genes on a chromosome. The farther apart the genes are, the greater the probability of crossing over and the higher the frequency of recombinants produced.

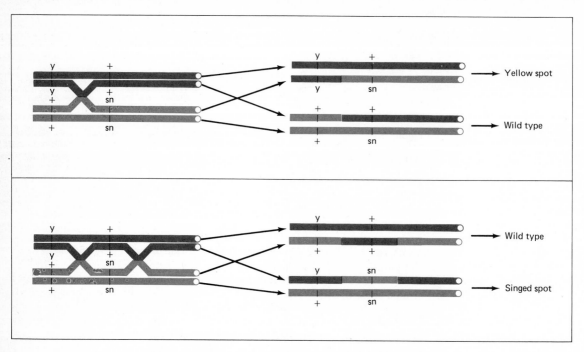

Figure 5.2 Two of the various kinds of crossover events that may occur in a mitotic cell: (a) single crossover between *y* and *sn* loci and chromatid separation as shown will lead to a single spot of yellow phenotype; and (b) double crossover as shown will lead to a single spot of singed cell-lineage in an otherwise wild type fly.

5.2 Studies with Fungi

By far the most commonly studied systems of mitotic crossing over have been among some of the filamentous fungi, particularly *Aspergillus nidulans*, an ascomycete relative of *Neurospora* and *Penicillium*. The filamentous **hyphae**, which make up the **mycelium** or body of the fungus, consist of cells with a variable number of haploid nuclei per cell. There are two particular features which provide advantages for genetic analysis of these somatic cell-systems: (1) the hyphae of different organisms can fuse together to produce **heterokaryons** (individuals or cells containing many *haploid nuclei* carrying different alleles of the set of genes), and diploid heterozygous nuclei may be formed later when pairs of genetically different haploid nuclei fuse in the heterokaryotic cells; and (2) the asexual spores which bud from the hyphae are *uninucleate*, and these spores will have a diploid nucleus if they are formed from diploid cells, or a haploid nucleus if they bud from haploid cells of the mycelium.

To illustrate how *Aspergillus* has been analyzed genetically during asexual growth and development, we have to describe the gene markers which are incorporated into the system to be studied. A haploid strain which produces white spores (*w*) instead of green (*w⁺*), and another haploid with yellow spores (*y*) instead of green (*y⁺*), are incubated together to permit heterokaryon formation by hyphal fusions. In addition to parts of the mycelium which later produce white or yellow spores, some **sectors** may produce wild-type green spores. These green spores must be diploid (*w +/+ y*) if they have one wild-type allele from each of the haploid strains, and they must have budded from a part of the mycelium in which nuclear fusions took place leading to the diploid state. The diploid nucleus can be heterozygous because there are two alleles of each gene present in the two sets of chromosomes. Interaction in the heterozygous nucleus between nonallelic genes for spore color gives rise to the wild phenotype (Fig. 5.3).

Green spores can be isolated from green sectors of the colony, and grown in pure culture for further study of the diploid mycelium which will develop. In such diploid green cultures, occasional sectors may be present which have either white or yellow spores. These uninucleate spores have either a haploid or a diploid nucleus, which can be determined by comparing the larger diameter of the diploid and smaller diameter of the haploid types using a microscope. Using the spore-color markers and spore-diameter guideline for haploids and diploids, it is possible to look for evidence of linkage among other genes included in the original heterokaryon. We will follow the transmission of six genes, all of which have their wild-type allele dominant over the mutant recessive:

haploids: *w ad⁺ pro paba⁺ y⁺ bi* and *w⁺ ad pro⁺ paba y bi⁺*

In addition to the two pairs of spore-color alleles, *w/+* and *y/+*, the other four pairs of alleles govern some metabolic requirement for growth of the fungus.

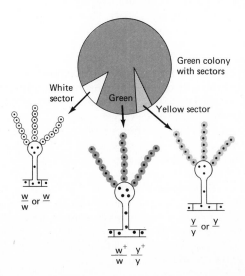

Figure 5.3 Linkage analysis by mitotic crossing over in *Aspergillus* is aided by use of selected *diploid* green colonies in which sectors appear which produce white spores or yellow spores. Such sectors indicate that changes have occurred in chromosomes of the original diploid, green, heterozygous colony, and that further studies are warranted.

If the two haploids form a heterokaryon, and we find and then isolate green diploid uninucleate spores from a colony sector, the diploid mycelium which we will analyze contains nuclei which are heterozygous for all six pairs of alleles:

$$\frac{w}{w^+} \quad \frac{ad^+}{ad} \quad \frac{pro}{pro^+} \quad \frac{paba^+}{paba} \quad \frac{y^+}{y} \quad \frac{bi}{bi^+}$$

The dominant phenotype will be expressed, since there is one wild-type allele for all six gene loci in the heterozygote.

From this green diploid mycelium we can analyze diploid (larger diameter) yellow spores which emerge in sectors within the green colonies. One usually finds that colonies which develop from such yellow spores contain recombinant phenotypes. For example, one sector type was yellow and also required "paba" for growth. Mitotic crossing over in the diploid nucleus would explain the origin of this recombinant (Fig. 5.4).

The relative frequencies of different recombinations, involving crossovers in other chromosome segments such as *paba* to *y*, or *paba* to *bi*, and so forth, can provide an estimate of distances in constructing a mitotic linkage map. As far as gene order is concerned, such mitotic maps correspond to meiotic maps, derived from conventional linkage analysis in the sexual phase of *A. nidulans*. The resulting map distances, however, may be somewhat different. Mitotic chromosome maps can be constructed and can show: (1) that these genes are indeed linked; (2) the relative order of linked genes in the chromosome; and (3) relative distances between gene loci. Mapping by somatic crossing-over data is an especially useful method of linkage analysis for organisms with no sexual cycle.

Another advantage of analysis from mitotic crossing over can be seen in the example we just discussed. By examining the recombinants we can see that five of the loci must be linked, since one crossover between a gene locus and the end of the chromosome makes every gene locus homozygous in the region in between (see Fig. 5.4). This is a more rapid method of analysis to make preliminary linkage assignments than conventional meiotic linkage studies.

Using haploid white spores isolated from white sectors of the original heterozygous green mycelium, one can show that the white spore-color locus is situated on a different chromosome from the other five genes. When a random sampling of these white haploid spores is analyzed, about half give rise to colonies with the genotype + *pro* + + *bi* and the other half to the genotype *ad* + *paba* *y* +. This shows independent assortment of *w* relative to the other five genes, and indicates that the *w* locus and the other five genes are not on the same chromosome.

The haploid spores arise by a process of random chromosome loss, called **haploidization**, from diploid nuclei of the heterozygote. Regardless of the mechanism leading to haploidization, the significant feature is the production of genotypes which are haploid for one or more chromosomes or for one or more genes in an otherwise diploid or partially diploid nucleus. The sequence of events we have been describing is called a **parasexual cycle**, so named by G. Pontecorvo about thirty years ago from his work with *Asper-*

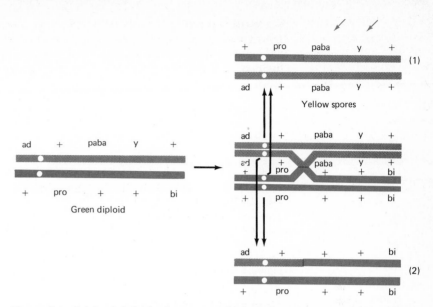

Figure 5.4 Origin of diploid yellow sector with "paba" requirement, from diploid green colony. Crossing over between chromatids of a replicated pair of homologous chromosomes, and separation of sister chromatids (centromeres) to opposite poles at anaphase, lead to a yellow, "paba" segregant (*y paba/y paba*).

gillus. The parasexual cycle involves (1) diploidization by nuclear fusions; and (2) segregation and new combinations of alleles in haploidized segregants, containing reassorted and recombined genotypes. The parasexual cycle mimics the conventional sexual cycle, since there is nuclear fusion (as in fertilization), and subsequent segregation and assortment or recombination of members of pairs of alleles (as in meiosis). The situation is very similar to analyses of haploid gamete genotypes or haploid spore genotypes in sexual cycles.

Pontecorvo pointed out the utility of a parasexual cycle in genetic analysis for various organisms. One of his predictions was especially significant, and has been realized in human genetic analysis. Pontecorvo suggested that human cells could be studied in culture, outside the body, and that linkage or independent assortment could be analyzed by taking advantage of a parasexual cycle of events. These predictions came true in the 1960s, with the beginnings of somatic cell-hybrid studies, and somatic cell genetics has since become a vital component in human chromosome mapping. We will examine such studies next.

MAPPING HUMAN GENES

Since controlled breeding analysis is out of the question for human genetic studies, two general approaches have been used to determine linkage and to map genes to particular human chromosomes. The newer method involves studies of human cells in culture, using a parasexual cycle to determine segregation and assortment or recombination of alleles. The earlier method, which has been greatly expanded through statistical and computerized data analysis, involves family studies or pedigree analysis. We gain a broader perspective and more detailed information by using both methods, since each can provide certain kinds of evidence which may be difficult to obtain using either method alone.

5.3   Mapping by Somatic Cell Hybridization

The goal of **somatic cell hybridization** is to identify and discriminate genes which are on the same chromosome and those on different chromosomes, and to assign particular loci to specific chromosomes and regions of a chromosome for the entire human haploid complement of 22 kinds of autosome and 2 kinds of sex chromosome (Fig. 5.5). The most useful information has come from cell-hybrids containing chromosomes of one mam-

Figure 5.5 Human metaphase chromosomes stained to show G-banding. Each chromosome can be uniquely identified by its G bands, once the chromosome has been identified generally according to its size and centromere location (as a member of one of the eight groups, from A-G). See Fig. 5.9 for reference.

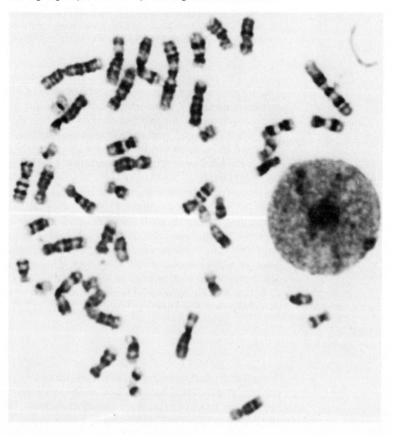

malian species, such as mouse or Chinese hamster, and chromosomes from human cells.

There are four particular reasons why rodent cells are advantageous as one parent type in hybridizations with human somatic cells:

1. Many different mutant cell-lines are readily available.
2. Rodent and human chromosomes have different sizes and shapes, and can therefore be identified easily in the hybrids.
3. Rodent chromosomes are usually retained, but the human chromosomes are lost gradually and at random from cell-hybrid nuclei by haploidization. This is especially true for human-mouse and human-hamster somatic cell hybrids.
4. Both rodent and human genes are expressed at the same time in cell-hybrids, each producing similar but detectably different proteins with the same function. If a vital enzyme is synthesized, it can be identified as rodent or human according to its molecular properties.

When different parent cells are incubated together in a culture medium, cell fusions take place only rarely. The frequency of cell fusions can be increased significantly by prior treatment using ultraviolet-inactivated *Sendai viruses*, or preferably by certain chemical agents such as *polyethylene glycol*. These treatments modify the cell surface so that cell contacts are more frequent and sufficiently intimate to permit actual fusion of cell membranes and cell contents to produce binucleate, *heterokaryon* cell-hybrids. Fusion between the two nuclei occurs shortly thereafter, yielding a **synkaryon** *heterozygote*. During subsequent mitosis, cells increase in numbers leading to formation of colonies; human chromosomes are lost at random during these divisions. Instead of finding 86 chromosomes (40 mouse + 46 human), between 41 and 55 chromosomes usually occur in a hybrid nucleus. These consist of the 40 mouse chromosomes plus 1 to 15 or more of the original human diploid complement of 46 chromosomes (Fig. 5.6).

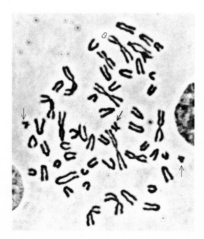

Figure 5.6 Metaphase chromosomes in mouse-human somatic cell hybrid, with only three human chromosomes remaining (at arrows). (From "Hybrid Somatic Cells" by B. Ephrussi and M. C. Weiss. Copyright © 1969 by Scientific American, Inc. All rights reserved.)

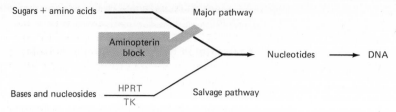

Figure 5.7 Pathways of synthesis of deoxyribonucleotides. If the major pathway is blocked by the drug **aminopterin**, nucleotides still can be made in the salvage pathway if the cells contain functional **HPRT** and **TK** enzymes.

To encourage growth of the cell-hybrids and simultaneously inhibit or retard growth of the parental cells, which would otherwise swamp the less numerous hybrids, a **selective medium** is employed. The usual selective medium contains the drug **aminopterin**, which blocks the major pathway for synthesis of DNA building blocks (Fig. 5.7). The essential purines can be made if **hypoxanthine** is provided, and pyrimidines can be made if **thymidine** is in the medium, provided the specific enzymes are available in the cell to catalyze these synthesis reactions in the so-called "salvage" pathway. The enzymes are **hypoxanthine-guanine phosphoribosyl transferase (HPRT)** and **thymidine kinase (TK)**, respectively.

Hybridizations can be accomplished by fusing mouse cells deficient in TK (phenotypically TK⁻) because they have the mutant *tk* allele, with human cells that have the mutant *hprt* allele and are therefore phenotypically HPRT⁻, or vice versa. Neither the TK⁻/HPRT⁺ parent nor the TK⁺/

Figure 5.8 Somatic cells hybrids with HPRT⁺/TK⁺ phenotype can grow and produce colonies on selective HAT medium, whereas enzyme-deficient parent cells do not grow. After nuclear fusion, the hybrid cells experience random losses of human chromosomes. The different hybrid clones (different human chromosomes lost and retained) can then be used in studies to map human chromosomes.

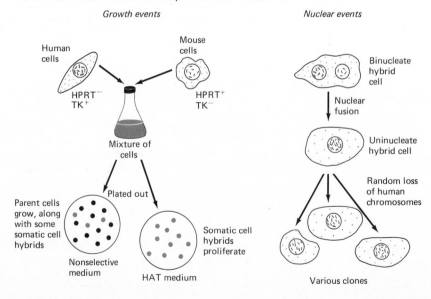

HPRT⁻ parent cells can grow in the selective medium, but any TK⁺/HPRT⁺ somatic cell-hybrids will be able to grow (Fig. 5.8). This selective medium is called the **HAT medium** because it contains Hypoxanthine, Aminopterin, and Thymidine. Hybrid colonies can be isolated from HAT medium, and then analyzed to map genes, using as many different **clones** of somatic cell-hybrids as needed.

Procedures for mapping human chromosomes involve determining whether two or more gene products and a particular chromosome are present in the same clone, and then finding which chromosome contains the genes responsible for these gene products or phenotype markers. When genes are found to be present together and the same chromosome always occurs in these cells, the genes are said to be **syntenic**, meaning that they are associated with the same chromosome. Somatic-cell geneticists use the term **synteny** to refer to genes associated in the same chromosome according to chromosome-phenotype correlations in hybridization tests. The term **linkage** is used only when recombination data have been obtained in family studies or by other gene transmission data.

The usual approach is to discover which genes are retained together and expressed in hybrid clones, and which genes are lost together. These correspondences or **concordant results** in retention and/or loss serve as the primary indicators of synteny. In the ideal situation, one would like to have 24 unique hybrid-cell clones in which a different single autosome or sex chromosome is present in each. Technical difficulties make this ideal almost impossible to attain, but as few as five properly constructed cell-hybrid clones in a **clone panel** can include 32 (2^5) unique subsets or combinations of chromosomes. These can be used to identify syntenic genes for all 24 kinds of human chromosomes (22 autosomes + X + Y). The principle can be illustrated by the more easily achieved group of three different clones, which can be selected so that there is a unique subset (2^3) for each of 8 different chromosomes in a clone panel:

Hybrid clone	Human chromosome (+ = present)							
	X	2	3	4	5	16	17	18
A	+	+	+	+	−	−	−	−
B	+	+	−	−	+	+	−	−
C	+	−	+	−	+	−	+	−

Suppose there are four different genes being monitored for synteny, and for location in a specific one or more of the eight chromosomes in these three clones. We would test each of the hybrid clones to find the pattern of retention or loss of the four enzyme activities sponsored by these genes:

Hybrid clone	Human enzyme (+ = present)			
	HPRT	GPD	PGK	TK
A	+	+	+	−
B	+	+	+	−
C	+	+	+	+

We now compare the +/– pattern for each of these enzymes, in a vertical column, with the +/– pattern for each of the eight chromosomes within clones A, B, and C in vertical columns. The vertical columns in the clone panel for the HPRT, GPD, and PGK enzymes match with the X chromosome column in the chromosome panel. The genes for the enzymes hypoxanthine-guanine phosphoribosyl transferase (*Hprt*), glucose 6-phosphate dehydrogenase (*Gpd*), and phosphoglycerate kinase (*Pgk*) are syntenic on the X chromosome. The thymidine kinase gene (*Tk*) is not syntenic with the other three genes. Comparing the clone panel for chromosomes and the clone panel for enzymes shows that the *Tk* gene is located on chromosome 17, since these two +/– patterns are concordant.

By following the abilities of hybrid cells to synthesize two or more enzymes of the human genome, synteny groups are established. If two or more enzymes or other gene products are always retained together or always lost together, they must be coded by genes which lie on the same chromosome. Once some particular gene product has been tested, we can ask about other proteins which are retained or lost together with the established protein and its gene; that is, we can look for other proteins which are concordant with a known gene product. If the chromosomal location has been assigned, other genes can be assigned to the same chromosome if tests show them to be syntenic. In the case of *Hprt* and *Gpd*, which were known to be X-linked from family studies of inheritance, somatic cell mapping provided the predicted X chromosome location for these two genes. Upon finding that *Pgk* is syntenic with *Hprt* and *Gpd*, it is immediately assigned to the X chromosome too, and this can be verified by results from a panel of known clones.

One or more genes have now been assigned to each of the 24 different human chromosomes (Fig. 5.9). Further gene assignments can be made by testing for the presence of other genes on any chromosome according to whether an unmapped enzyme or gene product marker is always inherited together with one product known to be coded by the chromosome. Cytological identification of the chromosome common to all cells with the newly-located enzyme is necessary only as a check that some structural rearrangement of the chromosome has not taken place, producing some new syntenic combination.

Gene mapping by somatic cell hybridization has progressed at an increasing rate in the past few years. Detailed mapping to locate genes in particular regions of a chromosome can be done using test systems in which one human chromosome or a piece of one chromosome is transferred selectively into a rodent cell. Studies of clones which carry a structural rearrangement, such that a part of one chromosome has been translocated to become part of a different chromosome, have provided information on *regional mapping* within a chromosome (Fig. 5.10). For example, genes for the enzymes HPRT, GPD, and PK are on the X chromosome, and a gene for the enzyme nucleoside phosphorylase (NP) was known to be present in an autosome. Using human cells from a family which had a translocated chromosome containing most of chromosome 14 and most of the long arm of the X chromosome, somatic cell hybridizations were performed with mouse cells, and clones of cell-hybrids were tested for the four enzymes. All three

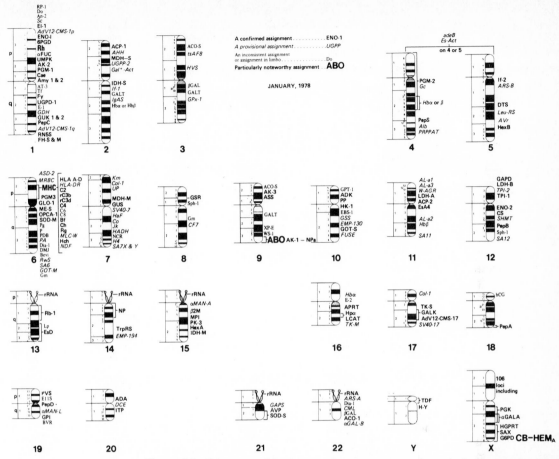

Figure 5.9 Gene map of the human chromosome complement, showing many of the important gene assignments. The gene symbols are identified in *Science* **196**;390. 1977. (From McKusick, V. A. 1978. *Amer. J. Human Genet.* **30**:105.)

X-linked markers were syntenic, showing that all three genes were present in the long arm of the X chromosome, which was represented by the X/14 translocation chromosome. In addition, the enzyme NP was concordant with the three X-linked enzymes. This showed that NP was coded by a gene on chromosome 14, which was represented in the translocated X/14 chromosome. All four genes had become syntenic as the result of the chromosome translocation.

Even more refined regional locations of particular genes can be achieved by adding viruses that are known to cause chromosome breaks leading to deletions of specific parts of specific chromosomes. By comparing concordances between enzyme markers and progressively more deleted chromosomes, the gene can be placed with greater accuracy in a part of the affected chromosome arm, as shown for the three X-linked genes in Fig. 5.11.

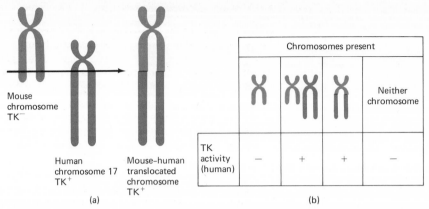

Figure 5.10   Regional mapping within a chromosome. The gene for TK must be located on the long arm of human chromosome 17, since TK enzyme activity occurs only when the cell contains that particular region of the chromosome. There is TK activity whether the whole chromosome is present or only the long arm of 17 in the mouse-human translocated chromosome.

As the repertory of techniques has increased and as these techniques have become more sophisticated, mapping in considerable detail has been made possible. These studies, together with linkage analysis by family studies, have permitted the identification of more than 100 gene loci on the X chromosome, and well over 1100 loci on the autosomes. Only a few of the 1100 loci, however, have been specifically assigned to particular autosomes.

Figure 5.11   Regional mapping within the human X chromosome. By comparing the expressed activities of the enzymes phosphoglycerate kinase (PGK), hypoxanthine-guanine phosphoribosyl transferase (HPRT), and glucose 6-phosphate dehydrogenase (GPD), with the parts of the X chromosome retained, the *Pgk*, *Hprt*, and *Gpd* loci can be assigned regionally on the chromosome. (a) These genes must be present on the long arm of the X chromosome, since all three enzymes occur in cells containing only that part of the X in an X/14 translocated chromosome. (b–e) the relative positions of the three gene loci are evident from enzyme activities correlated with amounts deleted from the long arm of the X chromosome due to breaks induced by a virus.

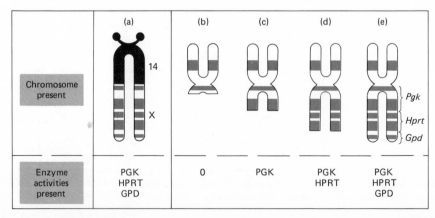

5.4   Mapping by the Family Method

The first step in gene mapping by the **family method** is to determine if the gene is on an autosome or on one of the two kinds of sex chromosomes. As we discussed in Chapter 3, there is a clear-cut difference in inheritance patterns for autosomal, X-linked, and Y-linked genes. Distances between genes can be calculated on the basis of the percentage recombinants found in one or more generations of different families.

Distances between two genes on the X chromosome can be determined more easily than distances for autosomal genes. Using the so-called **"grandfather method,"** it is possible to determine whether a mother who is doubly heterozygous for two X-linked genes has both mutant alleles in the same X chromosome (*coupling* phase of linkage) or in different X chromosomes (*repulsion* phase of linkage). If the phenotype of the maternal grandfather is known, we know his X chromosome, since males are hemizygous for X-linked genes. We can then place the pairs of alleles of both genes on the mother's two X chromosomes when we know the linkage phase; she can be genotypically *AB/ab or Ab/aB*.

Using such information from a number of families, one can look at the phenotypes of the sons of doubly heterozygous mothers and at the frequencies of noncrossover and crossover individuals. In the example shown in Fig. 5.12, about one in twenty sons of mothers doubly heterozygous for the X-linked genes for color-blindness and for GPD enzyme deficiency were found to be recombinants, according to their phenotypes. According to these family studies, the *Cb* and *Gpd* loci are about 5 units apart on the X

Figure 5.12   Determining linkage distances on the human X chromosome using the "grandfather method". Those genotypes which are recombinant can be identified and their frequency determined if it is known whether the doubly heterozygous mother of affected sons has both linked mutant alleles in *coupling* (left) or *repulsion* (right). This information can be deduced if the genotype of her father (grandfather of affected children) is known, since she obtains one X from each of her parents. Since her father's X does not undergo crossing over, it is transmitted intact to his daughters. The frequency of recombinant sons, relative to the total number of sons, provides the information for determining linkage distance between the two loci.

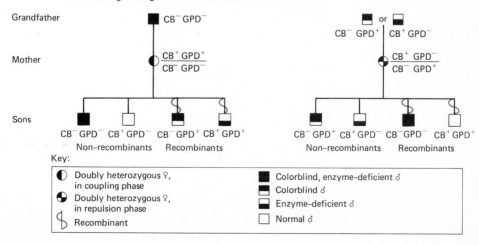

chromosome map, since 1/20 is equal to 5 percent recombination. Where such detailed information is not available, as in many cases where the phenotype of the maternal grandfather is not known, advanced statistical methods have been developed to calculate the probabilities of occurrence of particular recombinants from summed family data.

Until about 1967, the only method available for autosomal linkage analysis was the family method, also known as **pedigree analysis**. Segregations of autosomal alleles are more difficult to detect, as compared with segregations of X-linked alleles in hemizygous males. One of the more informative situations is the family in which one parent is doubly heterozygous and the other parent is doubly recessive (equivalent to a testcross situation), and the grandfather is known (Fig. 5.13). If the genes being studied have codominant alleles, or if the marker trait is governed by a dominant allele, linkage analysis becomes easier since the heterozygous phenotype can be distinguished from the homozygous phenotypes for such genes. In these cases, there is allele segregation which can be detected in *every* generation, and more information can be obtained for family studies than in cases where the altered allele is strictly recessive to normal.

Other linked autosomal genes can be placed on a particular chromosome, once the first gene locus has been determined for that chromosome. Chromosome 1 in the human complement was the first autosome to have a gene assigned. This was achieved in 1968 by Roger Donahue, who found a correspondence between a morphologically altered chromosome 1 and phenotypic expression of the Duffy blood group gene. Since the marker trait was concordant with a visibly distinct chromosome, the assignment was somewhat easier to make. Once the Duffy locus was assigned to chromosome 1, other genes found to be linked to the Duffy gene could also be assigned to chromosome 1. Because of this head start, chromosome 1 is the best mapped of all the 22 autosomes at the present time.

Gene mapping by somatic cell hybridization and by the family method are both necessary, and both methods have provided the detailed information to make the human genome the best mapped of any mammalian spe-

Figure 5.13 Determining linkage distances on autosomes using the "grandfather method". The affliction is due to a dominant allele linked to the ABO blood group gene, whose codominant I^A and I^B alleles are expressed in homozygous and heterozygous individuals. In this family, individual III-5 must be recombinant for the two genes since his father (II-1) is doubly heterozygous in the coupling phase of linkage ($D\ I^A/d\ I^B$). It happens in this family that the reciprocal recombinant type, $D\ I^B/d\ i^O$, has not been produced in generation III. Such an individual would phenotypically be afflicted and have blood type B.

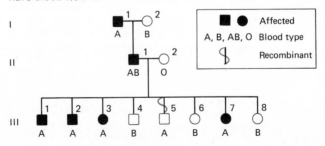

cies studied. These incredibly rapid strides have taken place over the last ten years in particular. Huge amounts of information are now stored in computer banks, from which geneticists can extract the data required to conduct the most complex kinds of linkage analysis.

5.5   Usefulness of the Map in Prenatal Diagnosis

Apart from many biologically important kinds of information we can gain from detailed maps, there is an immediate practical value in predicting risk of birth of an afflicted child in certain situations. Two examples will illustrate the principle involved.

For many inherited disorders there are no prenatal detection methods available. Suppose a mother who has had one hemophilic son wants to know the chances for having another son with this X-linked disease. The mother must be heterozygous since she has no symptoms, but one of her X chromosomes was given to her son through the egg. Knowing the pattern of inheritance for this recessive X-linked disorder, the mother can be told that there is a 50-50 chance that her next son will be hemophilic (see Fig. 3.17). If the mother's genotype is known to be doubly heterozygous for hemophilia and another X-linked trait, the "grandfather method" can provide information on whether the mutant alleles are present in the coupling or repulsion phases of linkage. Under these conditions, more reliable probabilities can be given that a male fetus will carry the hemophilia allele, or that a later son will or will not have the disease.

Suppose the woman is expecting another child and is known to be doubly heterozygous for hemophilia and for the co-dominant alleles which code for two distinct forms of the enzyme GPD, isozyme A and isozyme B (Fig. 5.14). If we know that she carries the hemophilia allele and the *Gpd-A* allele on the same chromosome, she can be told that the risk of having a hemophilic son is 95% or 5% instead of 50:50. A sample of amniotic fluid surrounding the fetus can be removed from the pregnant woman by a physician. Cells which are normally shed by the fetus into the amniotic fluid around it can be isolated and analyzed. If a Y chromosome is present, the fetus is male. A test for GPD-A and for GPD-B isozymes is then performed. If there is GPD-B present, there is a 95% chance that the fetus has received the X chromosome also carrying the normal *Hm* allele for blood clotting. Since the *Gpd* and *Hm* loci are only about 5 map units apart, the chance for a recombination by crossing over is about 5%, so there is a 5% risk that the fetus may have a recombinant X chromosome carrying the hemophilia allele and the *Gpd-B* allele.

If the male fetus has GPD-A isozyme, there is a 95% chance that this gene is on the same X chromosome as the recessive *hm* allele. Because of crossing over, there is a 5% chance that the Gpd-A allele is on a crossover chromosome and lies 5 units away from the normal *Hm* allele. With more specific risk predictions of 95% or 5% instead of 50:50, the prospective parents may have a better basis upon which to make their plans.

In a similar situation, the gene loci for *myotonic dystrophy* (a muscular disorder) and for *secretor protein* (present or absent in saliva and other body

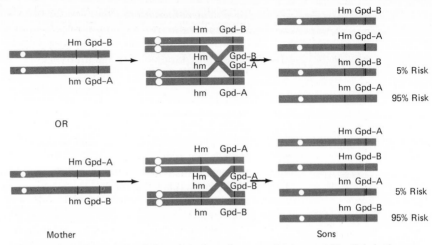

Figure 5.14 If the mother is known to carry the recessive hemophilia allele in the coupling phase with either *Gpd-A* or *Gpd-B*, according to her father's phenotype, and if we know the two loci are 5 map units apart, prediction of risk in having a hemophilc son can be given as 95% or 5% instead of 50%. Testing for the particular GPD enzyme form in fetal amniotic fluid will indicate which X chromosome the male fetus received from its mother. Once this is known, the parents can be told that the chance is 5% if the X is a crossover chromosome, or 95% if it is noncrossover. If the phase of linkage is unknown, a carrier mother and normal father can only be told there is a 50% chance that a male fetus will have the recessive hemophilia allele.

secretions) are very tightly linked on an unspecified autosome. Depending on whether the doubly heterozygous mother has the two mutant alleles of these genes in the coupling or repulsion phase of linkage, different predictions of risk can be made, after fetal cells in the amniotic fluid have been tested for secretor protein (Fig. 5.15). If the prediction of risk is about 10% or about 90%, depending on the chromosome presumed to be present according to the test of fetal cells, these are quite different odds than 50-50 for inheri-

Figure 5.15 Prediction of risk for myotonic dystrophy, an autosomal dominant muscular disorder, would be 50% in the family illustrated, if no linked gene was known. Risk can be estimated as 10% or 90% if the doubly heterozygous parent is known to carry the linked genes in coupling or repulsion, and if analysis of the amniotic fluid reveals that the fetus is (*Se/se*) or is not (*se/se*) a secretor.

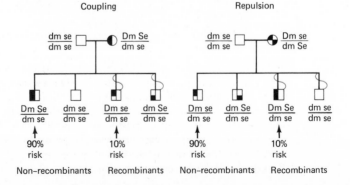

tance of the dominant autosomal disorder of myotonic dystrophy. The examples described show how important it is to construct human genetic linkage maps, and they illustrate the value of knowing linkage distances.

As more genes are mapped in particular linkage groups, and as more useful marker genes are found in various chromosomes, predictions of risk become more meaningful to the prospective parents. They can better plan the outcome of a pregnancy, and plan for their future family in situations where there is a history of some genetic disorder.

Predictions of risk based on single-gene Mendelian phenotypic ratios will continue to be needed. There are a number of inherited disorders coded by genes with no known or useful linked neighbor genes, and there are many disorders for which no tests are available for prenatal diagnosis. But where linkages have been established and map distances estimated, counseling can be more specific and more informative about a number of inherited disorders.

So far we have described parasexual cycles in eukaryotic organisms, and shown how these nonsexual systems have produced linkage and mapping data. In many of these cases, the parasexual system is a backup for the sexual cycle which is also present, or it provides a useful experimental system. In bacteria and other prokaryotic organisms there is no conventional sexual cycle; meiosis, mitosis, and fertilization are absent. In the remainder of this chapter we will examine the unique features of gene transmission in some of the bacteria and viruses. These illustrations will show that the basic principles of mapping and genome ordering are as characteristic of prokaryotes and viruses as they are of eukaryotic organisms.

GENE MAPPING IN BACTERIA

Gene transmission in bacteria involves *one-way transfer* from a **donor** to a **recipient** cell, instead of reciprocal exchanges of genes which characterize eukaryotes. There are three main avenues for gene transfer in bacteria:

1. **transformation,** in which genes enter the recipient as fragments of DNA;
2. **conjugation,** a kind of mating in which genes enter the recipient (perhaps by way of a special structure or conjugation tube called a **sex pilus**); and
3. **transduction;** in which a bacteriophage acts as the vector for getting donor bacterial genes from one bacterial cell to another.

Since a bacterial cell is invisible to the naked eye, the usual phenotypes studied are ones which involve colony growth on nutrient media. Bacterial cells can be assayed for sensitivity or resistance to drugs or virus infections; dependence or independence of amino acids, vitamins, and other supplements in the culture medium; and for differences in colony size, shape, color, and texture. These and other phenotypic characteristics make bacteria very suitable systems for genetic analysis.

Since each bacterial cell is haploid, each phenotype develops from a particular genotype. Dominance relations between alleles usually do not interfere with phenotypic expression, and each colony of haploid descendants of a single cell can be genotypically identified from its phenotype. Recombination mapping is simpler because of this feature. Also, the symbols for alleles of a gene reflect the phenotype expressed when that allele is present. For example, the gene governing cellular response to the drug streptomycin may be symbolized by the resistance allele, str^r, and the sensitivity-conferring allele, str^s. Strains which can synthesize their own amino acids, such as threonine, are threonine-independent (thr^+), while strains with the alternative allele governing dependence or requirement for threonine to be supplied in the culture medium are referred to as thr^-. Whenever we use hypothetical genes, the allele conferring nutritional independence will be shown with a + superscript, such as a^+, and the alternative allele for dependence or supplement-requirement will be a^-.

5.6   Mapping by Transformation Analysis

Evidence showing that DNA was the genetic material was first reported in 1944 by Oswald Avery, Colin MacLeod, and Maclyn McCarty of the Rockefeller Institute (now Rockefeller University) in New York. They showed that the "transforming principle" which produced genetically altered strains in their experiments was purified DNA (Fig. 5.16). Since their studies using the pneumococcus species *Diplococcus pneumoniae*, transformation has been

Figure 5.16 Diagrammatic representation of the classic 1944 experiments by O. T. Avery and coworkers, which showed that DNA was the transforming principle. This was the first significant demonstration that DNA was the genetic material. Transformation of genetically avirulent type III cells to genetically virulent type II cells was accomplished only if DNA from virulent type II cells was added to the type III culture.

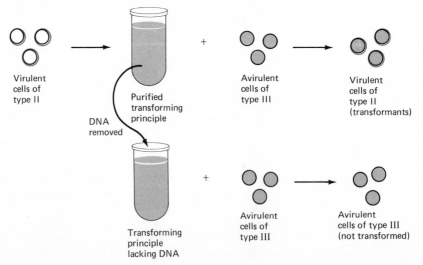

Virulent cells of type II

DNA removed

Purified transforming principle

Transforming principle lacking DNA

+

Avirulent cells of type III

+

Avirulent cells of type III

Virulent cells of type II (transformants)

Avirulent cells of type III (not transformed)

successfully accomplished in a number of other bacteria, including *Hemophilus influenzae* and *Bacillus subtilis*. The range of organisms susceptible to transformation is now increasing, and the eukaryotic yeasts have also been shown to transfer genes by transformation under strictly specified conditions. The main difficulties in demonstrating the capacity for transformation in a species are twofold: (1) strains must be in a certain state of competence to take up genes by this process: the particular conditions for the acquisition of competence and for identification of this state are uncertain or ambiguous for most organisms; and (2) certain modifications of the cell surface must be initiated if two cells are to act as a donor of DNA fragments and as recipient of these fragments of genetic material; this can only be achieved with difficulty unless prior intensive experimentation provides the detailed information needed. Since in any case gene exchange usually is accomplished by other means in most organisms, the effort to establish conditions for transformation often have not been made.

In transformation, the pieces of DNA transferred from donor to recipient must be within a particular size range. Below this size gene transfer is inefficient or unsuccessful. Above this range there is no more genetic material actually expressed in recombinants than with the optimum-sized DNA fragments. All sorts of conditions must be met, including optimum concentration of DNA extracted from donor cells as well as optimum size of these fragments. Gene transfer is accomplished in the laboratory, therefore, by providing fragments of donor-cell DNA in solution to living cells, which act as recipients of this DNA. The donor DNA must be duplex, that is, double-stranded or native DNA. Single-stranded fragments have been shown to be inefficient in subsidizing transformation.

If we perform a transformation experiment using DNA from a donor which was phenotypically (and genotypically) a^+b^+, and add this DNA extract to a population of recipient cells which are a^-b^-, there will be three new phenotype classes together with the colonies of the predominant a^-b^- recipient cells. These new classes are called **transformants**; they are descendants of recipient cells which were genetically altered or transformed, and they exhibit inherited alterations. The haploid transformant classes will be a^+b^+, a^+b^-, and a^-b^+. Each of these has had a piece of homologous DNA from the donor integrated into their own circular chromosome, as a replacement for their original segment of allelically homologous DNA. The parts of donor and recipient DNA which are not integrated or which are excised from the chromosome are usually degraded by enzymes present in the recipient cells, and exert no genetic effect.

Each event leading to the integration of a piece of DNA into an intact circle requires an *even* number of crossovers (Fig. 5.17). If there is one or some other odd number of crossovers, the circle is opened and the crossover cells are inviable. Inviable cells do not reproduce, and therefore do not develop into visible colonies to be scored among the progeny.

Knowing this, we can see that the a^+b^- and a^-b^+ classes of transformants arise through double-crossovers, one crossover in the region between a and b loci, and one between one locus and a segment on its other side away from the a—b region (Fig. 5.18). The class of a^+b^+ transformants arises as the result of two crossovers, one on either side of the a—b region, which integrates the whole donor region into the recipient chromosome.

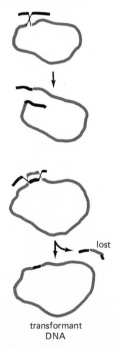

Figure 5.17 Integration of a piece of DNA (black) into an intact circle of DNA (red) requires an even number of crossovers. With an odd number of crossovers, the circle is opened. Such cells would be inviable.

lost

transformant
DNA

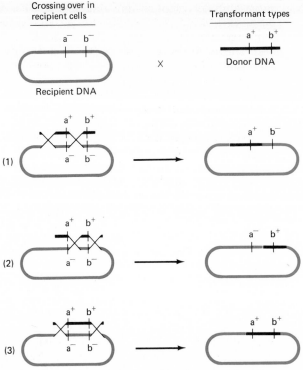

Figure 5.18 Origin of three classes of transformants by double crossovers. Only classes (1) and (2) provide data to estimate linkage distance between genes *a* and *b*.

When linkage is estimated for the *a—b* region, the only classes which are included in the calculations as recombinants are those which arose as the result of crossing over *within* the space between the *a* and *b* gene loci. Although the a^+b^+ class are transformants, there was no crossover between genes *a* and *b*. So the a^+b^+ class does not provide information about the percentage recombination between *a* and *b* and, therefore, is classified differently for mapping purposes.

In an experiment in which recipients which are a^-b^- are presented with DNA extracts from donors which are a^+b^+, the distance between gene loci *a* and *b* can be calculated from transformants, as follows:

Transformant phenotype	Number of transformants	Number of recombinants
a^+b^-	130	130
a^-b^+	70	70
a^+b^+	800	0
	1000	200

$$\frac{\text{recombinants}}{\text{total transformants}} = \frac{200}{1000} = 0.2, \text{ or 20\% recombinants, or 20 map units}$$

Notice that the two recombinant classes do not occur in equal numbers. Unlike reciprocal crossing over, leading to equal recovery of reciprocal recombinant classes in eukaryotic systems, prokaryotic recombinants are not reciprocal products. This is reflected in their different frequencies of recovery. Different double-crossover events gave rise to the two recombinant classes shown in Fig. 5.18.

Gene mapping can be accomplished by three-factor or multifactor transformations, as well as by two-gene experiments. There are few important differences between such three-factor tests and those which we descibed in eukaryotes. We will therefore only analyze one such cross, involving hypothetical $a^-b^-c^-$ recipients and DNA extracts from donors with the $a^+b^+c^+$ phenotype.

In a typical three-factor transformation experiment we might find the following kinds of transformants:

Single transformants		Double transformants		Triple transformants	
$a^+b^-c^-$	300	$a^+b^+c^-$	150	$a^+b^+c^+$	1400
$a^-b^+c^-$	60	$a^-b^+c^+$	290		
$a^-b^-c^+$	140	$a^+b^-c^+$	10		

The first order of business is to calculate the distance between two genes taken in all three possible combinations, disregarding the third gene during these calculations (Fig. 5.19). In each case, one calculates linkage as the proportion of recombinants among the total transformants for the two genes being analyzed at any one time. Since the linkage distance between genes a and c is greater than between a and b or between b and c, the gene order must be a—b—c.

The origin of each class of transformants can be traced to double-crossovers for every class except $a^+b^-c^+$, which arises through quadruple crossing over. We would predict this to be the least numerous of all the seven classes since each crossover is an independent event. This is indeed the case, as you can see from the data which have been presented. Since such a quadruple-exchange class leads to transformation of both outer genes but leaves the middle gene unchanged in relation to the recipient genotype (or changed in relation to the donor $a^+b^+c^+$), we could have identified the middle gene by finding the transposed pair of alleles and noting that such a transformant class is characterized by the lowest numbers. We might then have gone on to the a—b and b—c pairwise linkage calculations, with the knowledge of gene order already determined.

By linkage analysis in transformation and by other available methods, relatively detailed maps have been constructed. One of the best studied species, using transformation analysis, is the common soil bacterium *Bacillus subtilis*, whose linkage map is shown in Fig. 5.20.

5.7 Mapping by Conjugation Analysis in *E. coli*

You will recall that we described the first significant genetic evidence showing the existence of some kind of sexual or mating system in *E. coli* as

Recipient $a^- b^- c^-$ X $a^+ b^+ c^+$ Donor

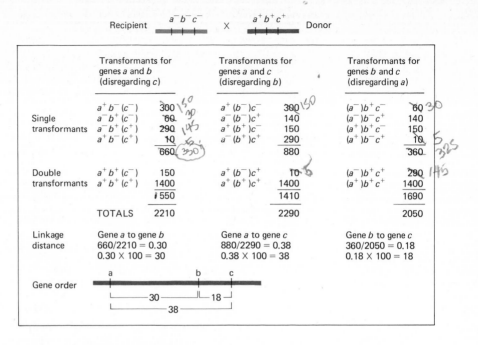

	Transformants for genes *a* and *b* (disregarding *c*)		Transformants for genes *a* and *c* (disregarding *b*)		Transformants for genes *b* and *c* (disregarding *a*)	
Single transformants	$a^+ b^- (c^-)$	300	$a^+ (b^-) c^-$	300	$(a^-) b^+ c^-$	60
	$a^- b^+ (c^-)$	60	$a^- (b^-) c^+$	140	$(a^-) b^- c^+$	140
	$a^- b^+ (c^+)$	290	$a^+ (b^+) c^-$	150	$(a^+) b^+ c^-$	150
	$a^+ b^- (c^+)$	10	$a^- (b^+) c^+$	290	$(a^+) b^- c^+$	10
		660		880		360
Double transformants	$a^+ b^+ (c^-)$	150	$a^+ (b^-) c^+$	10	$(a^-) b^+ c^+$	290
	$a^+ b^+ (c^+)$	1400	$a^+ (b^+) c^+$	1400	$(a^+) b^+ c^+$	1400
		1550		1410		1690
TOTALS		2210		2290		2050
Linkage distance	Gene *a* to gene *b* 660/2210 = 0.30 0.30 × 100 = 30		Gene *a* to gene *c* 880/2290 = 0.38 0.38 × 100 = 38		Gene *b* to gene *c* 360/2050 = 0.18 0.18 × 100 = 18	

Gene order

a   b   c

└──── 30 ────┘└─ 18 ─┘

└──────── 38 ────────┘

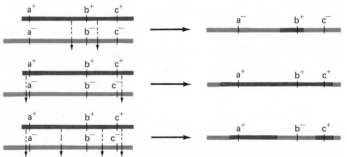

Figure 5.19 Gene mapping by three-factor transformation. From the data shown in the upper portion, crossing over events which produced transformant (recombinant) classes could be deduced, as seen in the lower part of the illustration.

reported by Lederberg and Tatum in 1946 (see Section 2.10). The two strains of triply-deficient *E. coli* (called **auxotrophs** because of their dependence on substances in the medium which they could not make in their own cells) produced wild-type **prototrophs** (no nutrient supplements needed) at a frequency of about 1 in a million cells plated out on the solid minimal nutrient medium. It appeared as though all six wild-type characteristics were expressed in these prototrophs as the result of recombination between parent auxotrophs, each carrying three wild-type and three mutant alleles ($a^+ b^+ c^+ d^- e^- f^-$ and $a^- b^- c^- d^+ e^+ f^+$ auxotrophs gave rise to $a^+ b^+ c^+ d^+ e^+ f^+$ prototrophs).

There were two other possible explanations for the origin of these proto-

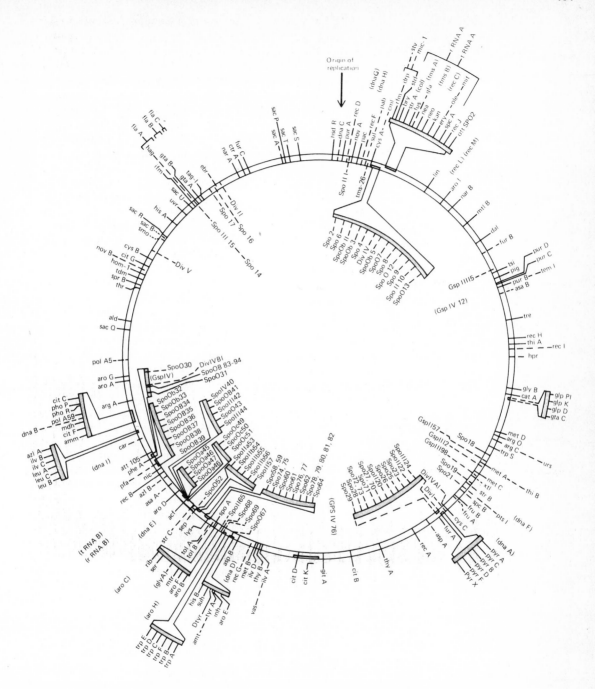

Figure 5.20 Gene map of the linkage group of the soil bacterium *Bacillus subtilis*. (From Young, F. E., and G. A. Wilson. 1974. In *Handbook of Genetics*, vol. 1, p. 69, R. C. King, ed. New York: Plenum.)

trophs, other than as recombinants produced by mating, or conjugation, between parent cells. Wild type revertants (mutants arising by reverse mutation from nutritional dependence to nutritional independence) might have arisen if three mutant alleles all mutated back to the wild type allelic forms, in the same cells; or transformation might have been responsible for the observed prototrophs. Each possibility had to be evaluated by deduction and experimental analysis.

The reverse mutations would all be independent events, which is an established feature of mutation phenomena. If the chance for any one of these genes to undergo random, spontaneous mutation were 1 in 10^5, the chances for three independent events (reverse mutations at all three gene loci happening by chance to occur simultaneously in the same cell) would be 1 in $10^5 \times 10^5 \times 10^5$, or 1 in 10^{15}. Since the prototrophs occurred with a frequency of 1 in 10^6, it would have required reverse mutation rates of 1 in 10^2 per gene ($10^2 \times 10^2 \times 10^2$) to account for the observed prototroph frequency. Such mutation rates were unknown for the genes studied. The reverse mutation hypothesis was therefore highly improbable.

Transformation was a known phenomenon in 1946, having been reported two years earlier by Avery, MacLeod, and McCarty for pneumococcus. Lederberg and Tatum ruled out the possibility of transformation by two particularly convincing kinds of experimental evidence. First, they failed to obtain prototrophs when they added DNA extracts from one strain to living cells of another strain. However, they reasoned that perhaps their unsuccessful attempts were only a reflection of improper conditions for achieving transformation. The second line of evidence was more convincing. They put each of the parent strains on a different side of a U-tube, with a filter between the two sides that had very small pores and would not permit cells to pass through (Fig. 5.21). No prototrophs were found. When the filter was removed and the cells were allowed to mingle in the common fluid medium, and after these mixed cultures were plated out and observed for colony development on minimal medium, prototrophs were observed to be present. The one condition which was shown to be essential for prototroph formation was contact between living cells. This indicated the existence of a mating system, rather than mutation or transformation events, leading to gene exchange between cells. Microscopical evidence for conjugation was obtained some years later (Fig. 5.22).

In 1953, William Hayes discovered the existence of a sex factor, or **fertility factor**, called **F**, which was present in donor cells (F^+) but absent from recipients (F^-). Transfer of genes from donor to recipient took place during conjugation, adding another system of one-way gene passage for bacteria. As it turned out, about the only genetic material passed from F^+ to F^- cells was the F factor itself. Most of the cells in a population may eventually become F^+ because the donor will retain at least one copy of F and transfer a separate copy to the F^- recipient. F^+ cells ordinarily do not engage in conjugation among themselves.

None of these events, however, led to an understanding of the genes in the bacterial chromosome itself. About 1 in every 10,000 F^+ cells will undergo a significant change, on the average, such that the F factor becomes associated with the bacterial chromosome (Fig. 5.23). In its inte-

Figure 5.21 A U-tube. Auxotrophic parents are inoculated into media on each side of the U-tube, with a glass filter between, which allows medium to pass through but not cells.

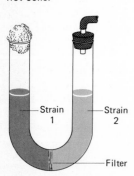

Strain 1   Strain 2

Filter

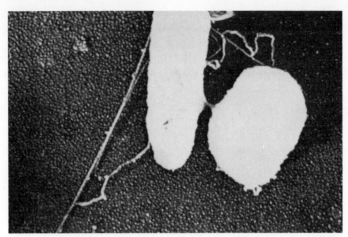

Figure 5.22 Electron micrograph of two conjugating *E. coli* cells from strains differing in cell shape. A slender bridge connects the elongated *Hfr* donor and round F^- recipient cell. (From Wollman, E. L., F. Jacob, and W. Hayes. 1957. *Cold Spring Harbor Sympos. Quant. Biol.* **21** (1956):141. Photograph by T. F. Anderson.)

grated state, the *F* factor contributes to transfer of genes on the bacterial chromosome from the donor to an F^- recipient. The *F* factor is an **episome**, which is an element of genetic material that may exist free in the cell under some conditions or be integrated into the chromosome of the cell under other conditions.

The cells with an integrated *F* factor were initially distinguished by their **high frequency of recombination** in mixed cultures of F^- and F^+ cells. These strains were called *Hfr*, and they served as the main source of materials for recombination analysis in *E. coli*. Recombinations simply were too infrequent in non-*Hfr* strains to be of maximum utility in linkage analysis.

When *F* is integrated into the bacterial chromosome, it replicates synchronously with that chromosome and is passed on from one cell generation to the next. Somehow, when conjugation is initiated between an *Hfr* and an F^- cell the *F* factor is nicked, and a part of it leads the way into the conjugation tube and into the recipient F^- cell. The significant feature is that the bacterial chromosome also moves into the F^- cell, since it is covalently linked to the leading *F* element, or some segment of this element. During the time that homologous regions of donor and recipient chromosomes are present and pair up in the recipient cell, crossing over takes place leading to recombinants for alleles of various gene loci.

The recombination data obtained from crosses between allelically different *Hfr* and F^- strains were extremely difficult to interpret in terms of a linear map of fixed gene loci in an established order. In the late 1950s, however, the difficulties began to disappear as the chromosome and gene transfer systems of different strains of *E. coli* were explored. The data which established the existence of a linear, ordered gene map for *E. coli* began with interrupted-mating experiments conducted by François Jacob and Elie Wollman in Paris.

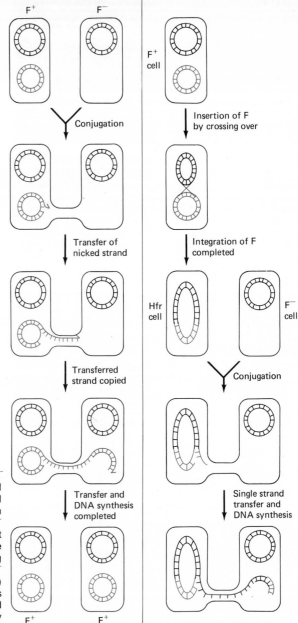

Figure 5.23 Transfer of *F* factor (red) from *F⁺* to *F⁻* recipient occurs after a conjugation bridge has joined the cells. One strand of the *F* DNA duplex is nicked, and transferred to the *F⁻* cell, where DNA replication (strand copying) occurs. When *F* has replicated, the *F⁻* cell becomes *F⁺*, and the original *F⁺* donor retains at least one copy of the episome. If *F* integrates into the bacterial chromosome, an *Hfr* cell arises. During conjugation, bacterial genes are transferred to the *F⁻* recipient with part of the integrated *F* DNA (red) leading the way. Much of the *F* DNA, however, remains at the far end of the large bacterial chromosome and does not enter the recipient because the cells usually break apart long before.

During conjugations between genetically marked *Hfr* and *F⁻* strains, Jacob and Wollman interrupted the matings by removing samples of cells at specific intervals of time and agitating them in a kitchen blender. The mating cells separated, and when they were plated out and allowed to

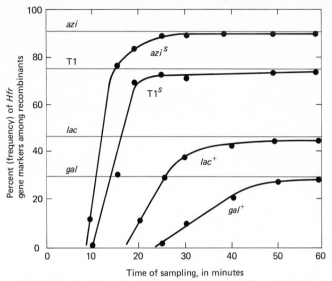

Figure 5.24 Kinetics of gene transfer from *Hfr* to *F⁻* in crosses. The frequency of *Hfr* marker genes recovered in recombinants sampled from the conjugation mixture, after blender treatment, is plotted as a function of time of sampling. (From Jacob, F., and E. L. Wollman. 1961. *Sexuality and the Genetics of Bacteria*. New York: Academic Press.)

develop overnight into colonies, recombinants were scored. The percentage of recombinants for different *Hfr* alleles were plotted as a function of time (Fig. 5.24).

There are several points to note from these summarized results:

1. Each *Hfr* allele first appears in recombinants at a different but specified time during the mating experiments. The simplest interpretation is that the *Hfr* donor chromosome moves into the recipient as a linear structure and in an orderly fashion.

2. The time interval between appearances of different *Hfr* alleles is not constant; for example, the T1ˢ marker appears one minute after the *azi*ˢ locus, whereas *lac⁺* appears at 18 minutes and *gal⁺* at 25 minutes. This can be interpreted to mean that there is a greater distance between some loci than others, if we assume that chromosome entry takes place at a relatively constant rate (present estimates are about 12 μm per minute for the 1200 to 1300 μm-long chromosome).

3. The percentage recombination for each locus reaches a plateau, or maximum value, which does not change afterward. These values were found to be the same as those obtained in non-interrupted matings. They indicate the proportion of cells which remain conjugated long enough for the marker to enter the recipient, and also confirm the time map because markers at the leading end of the chromosome are more likely to be transferred even during brief periods of conjugation. Gene loci at the far end of the chromosome, how-

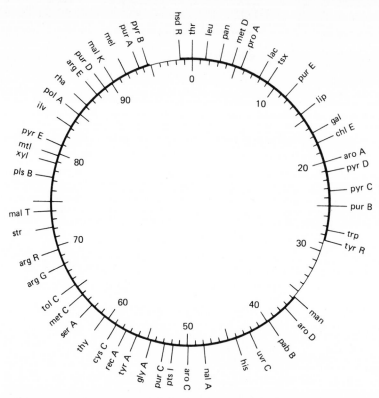

Figure 5.25 Gene map of the linkage group of *Escherichia coli* strain K-12. (a) The 100-minute map shows some of the important genes located by various means, such as interrupted matings and transduction analysis. (b) (Pages 187, 188.) Linear scale drawings represent the circular linkage map of *E. coli* K-12. Definitions of the gene symbols can be found in Bachmann,B. J., K. B. Low, and A. L. Taylor. 1976. *Bact. Rev.* **40**:116.

ever, are less likely to enter simply because conjugants rarely remain associated long enough for the whole donor chromosome to pass into the recipient.

Jacob and Wollman found that it took about 90 minutes for the entire donor complement of known genes to be transferred, in the few instances of persisting conjugation. They also found that most of the recombinants were *F⁻* (unlike *F⁺* × *F⁻*, which yields *F⁺* recombinants), but in the few instances when about 90 minutes of conjugation occurred the recombinants proved to be *Hfr*. These observations indicated that at least part of the integrated *F* factor was located at the far end of the donor chromosome during its movement into the recipient. If all or most of the chromosome were transferred, then, and only then, was the whole *F* factor transferred in its integrated state. The map based on time intervals coincided with the maps generated from more conventional recombination analysis, and it was therefore substantiated even further as a reasonable expression of the gene map for *E. coli* (Fig. 5.25). The correspondence between maps based on time and those

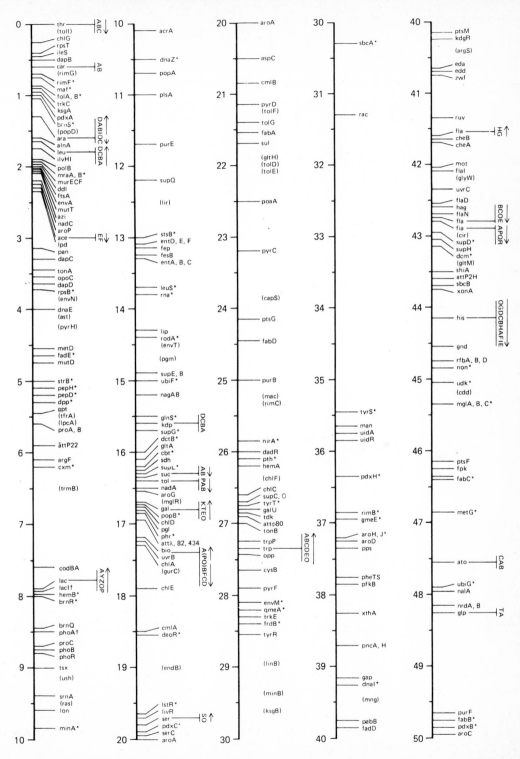

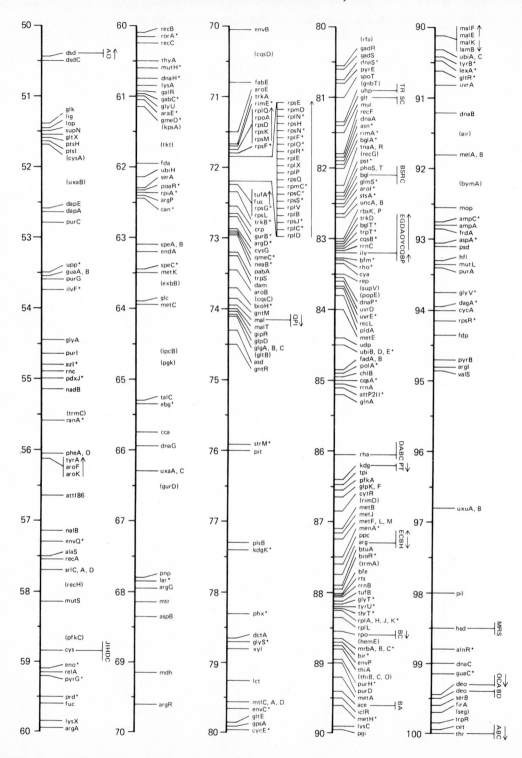

based on recombinations from linkage analysis is: one minute equals 20 map units; the most recent map has been extended from 90 minutes to 100 minutes, based on information about newly-discovered genes. In practice, general linkage relationships for *E. coli* are first established by interrupted matings. More detailed information, particularly for closely linked genes that are less than two minutes apart, is routinely obtained from transduction analysis (to be discussed shortly).

5.8 Circularity of the *E. coli* Map

Linkage relationships showed that the entire genome was organized into one linkage group in *E. coli*. We have shown a circular linkage map, but there has been no evidence presented so far to suggest the basis for this conformation. The linear entry of the *Hfr* chromosome might even suggest that the chromosome was actually a two-ended linear structure. The genetic

Figure 5.26 Gene map of *E. coli* with arcs showing the approximate chromosomal regions carried into *F⁻* recipients by various *F′* factors. The various orders of gene transfer appear to be circular permutations of one another, leading to the summarized circular linkage map shown in Fig. 5.25. (From Low, K. B. 1974. In *Handbook of Genetics*, vol. 1, p. 157, R. C. King, ed. New York: Plenum.)

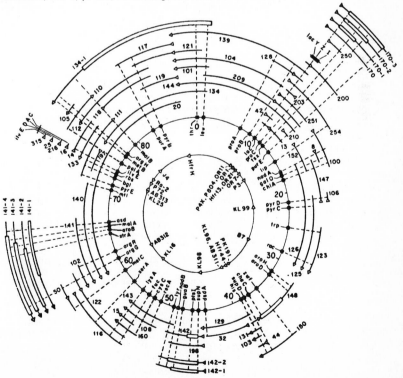

evidence for circularity of the *E. coli* gene map was obtained through studies of different *Hfr* strains. Some *Hfr* strains transferred genes in the opposite order from Jacob and Wollman's *Hfr-H* strain, while others seemed to transfer gene loci from many different starting points relative to the gene order in *Hfr-H*. From a comparison of all the data obtained using various *Hfr* strains, it appears that all the marker orders are *circular permutations* of one another (Fig. 5.26).

From what we now know, it seems that the stimulus for chromosome transfer is the integration of *F* into the bacterial chromosome. Depending on its orientation within the chromosome, *F* establishes the *polarity* of transfer and therefore may direct either end of the chromosome into the conjugation tube. From genetic analysis it was also found that *F* may integrate at many different sites along the bacterial chromosome. Since the insertion of *F* initiates the break in the circular chromosome, as well as the orientation of chromosomal entry into the recipient, all the combined data provide a consistent picture of a circular map for *E. coli* genes.

Microscopical confirmation of the circularity of the *E. coli* chromosome was obtained in 1963 by John Cairns (Fig. 5.27). We will have more to say about circularity versus linearity of bacterial and viral genomes later in this chapter and in subsequent chapters. For now, you should take note of some significant differences between bacterial and eukaryotic chromosomes (Table 5.1). We will return to these features at various times in the text, and add more items to this list. There are profound differences in organization of the prokaryotic and eukaryotic genome, even though each species we analyze possesses fixed gene loci in an ordered sequence in one or more two-dimensional structures, which are either linear or circular.

Table 5.1
Some major differences between prokaryotes and eukaryotes

Characteristic	Prokaryotes	Eukaryotes
Cell size	Mostly small (1-10 μm)	Mostly larger (10-100 μm)
Cell division	Binary fission, budding, or other means; no mitosis	Mitosis-associated furrowing, budding, and other means
Genetic system	Duplex DNA not complexed with proteins in chromosomes	Duplex DNA complexed with histones and nonhistone proteins in chromosomes
	No membrane around nucleoid	Membrane-bounded nucleus
	One linkage group per genome	Two or more linkage groups per genome
	Haploid nucleoid	Haploid, diploid, or polyploid nucleus
	Unidirectional transfer of genes, from donor to recipient; no meiosis	Equal genomic contribution to progeny from sexual parents; meiosis and gamete fusion
Internal membranes	Transient, if present	Various organelle systems and membranes
Tissue formation	Absent	Present in many groups
Reproduction	Asexual	Asexual or sexual

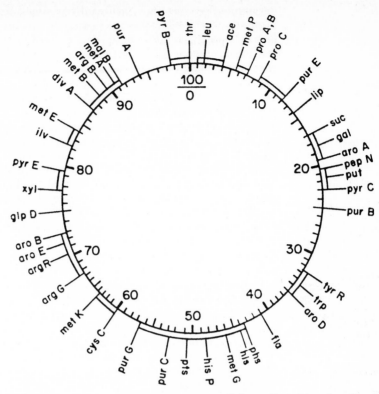

Figure 5.30 Gene map of the linkage group *Salmonella typhimurium*. (From Sanderson, K. E., and P. E. Hartman. 1978. *Microbiol. Rev.* **42**: 471.)

genes in a segment of captured bacterial DNA packaged in the virus particle. It would be very unlikely that two or three different pieces of bacterial DNA would be packaged together by chance in these rare transducing phage particles. If two gene markers are cotransduced with reasonable frequency, linkage distance can be calculated for the space between the two loci. For example, if the donor cells are a^+b^+ and the recipients are a^-b^-, any a^+b^- and a^-b^+ transductants must have arisen through recombination as the result of crossing over between the a and b loci; any a^+b^+ transductants, on the other hand, would not be recombinants because the donor segment would have been integrated when crossovers occurred to the *outside* of each marker and not in the region in between loci. This is the same situation as we described for transformation (see Fig. 5.18). To calculate distance between the a and b loci, therefore, we use the proportion of *number of recombinants/total transductants*. Once again, recombination frequencies are inversely proportional to distances between genes.

To establish gene order, one may compare two-factor transductions. For example, if a and b are cotransduced, and b and c are cotransduced, but a and c are not transduced or are rarely transduced together, the order would be a—b—c. This is nothing more than applying the same basic mapping principles we have been discussing throughout Chapters 4 and 5. Similarly, in three-factor transductions, we would expect the middle gene to be transposed in relation to the donor genotype, and to occur in the lowest frequencies among all the transductant classes. Once the middle gene has been identified and gene ordering has been determined, linkage distances can be calculated for the $a-b$ and the $b-c$ regions, in just the same way as in transformation (see Fig. 5.19). All these mapping methods are therefore extensions of the basic principles established in eukaryotic crosses.

The enormous advantage of transduction analysis is due to the relatively small size of the piece of donor genome accidentally packaged into the transducing phage. With a length of DNA that can accommodate only about 1/100 of the total bacterial genome, on the average, very closely linked loci can be identified and mapped. Such a length of donor DNA is about equal to the amount of the genome which is transferred in a little less than one minute during conjugation in *E. coli*, and may include several dozen gene loci. You can see immediately that conjugation analysis in interrupted-mating experiments only roughs in the outlines of a linkage segment, while transduction analysis fills in the details of gene order and linkage distances between individual gene loci.

It has been possible to incorporate the *E. coli* fertility factor into some strains of *S. typhimurium*, and to establish a time-of-entry map in the same way as we described for *E. coli* in interrupted mating experiments. In both species the map details are filled in by transduction analysis. Some very interesting similarities have been found in the *E. coli* and *S. typhimurium* gene maps, which reinforce previous information pointing out the close relationship between these two members of the bacterial family Enterobacteriaceae (Box 5.1).

SPECIALIZED TRANSDUCTION

In **specialized transduction**, temperate phages are again involved in the transfer of certain specific host genes. In this case, however, the particular bacterial genes transferred are those that flank the site of the integrated prophage on the bacterial chromosome. Since each specialized transducing phage in its integrated state occupies a particular place on the host chromosome, different phages will carry different but specific genes. When the integrated prophage leaves its chromosomal site, an occasional error occurs so that the piece of DNA which is packaged in the mature virus will have some bacterial genes covalently linked to some phage genes. This kind of virus is called a **specialized transducing particle** or **phage**.

In *E. coli*, for example, the integration site for prophage lambda (λ) has genes for galactose metabolism on one side and for biotin metabolism on its other side. If the excision events which lead to the separation of prophage λ are not precise, the released prophage may have host *gal* genes or host *bio* genes, leaving behind an equivalent piece of its own prophage genes (Fig. 5.31). The particles formed in this way are designated $\lambda dgal$ (*deficient for some λ genes, but carrying host *gal* genes) or $\lambda dbio$ (again: *deficient, but carrying *bio* genes). The $\phi80$ prophage of *E. coli*, on the other hand, will

Box 5.1
COMPARATIVE MAPPING

Between 22 and 45 units on the 100-unit maps of these two enteric species there is considerable similarity. Some of the loci (*pyr* C, *pur* B, *fla*, *his*) occupy identical positions on the two maps. The portion of the maps from 25.5 to 35.5 units (inside the triple lines) is inverted between the two species.

Linkage maps can be compared in order to analyze the degree of genetic homology between related species. Homology of linkage maps and of DNA nucleotide sequences can hardly be expected to arise from random, unrelated events in evolution. The greater the homology the greater the evolutionary ties between species. Maps in bacterial and viral systems have provided some of the strongest lines of evidence for genetic relationships among different organisms.

It has become possible to compare band patterns of chromosome complements of related species, and even to compare nucleotide sequences of similar genes in related species. Through all these comparative studies the case for evolutionary descent with modification has become undeniable.

Illustration from Sanderson, K. E., and P. E. Hartman. 1978. *Microbiol. Rev.* 42:471.

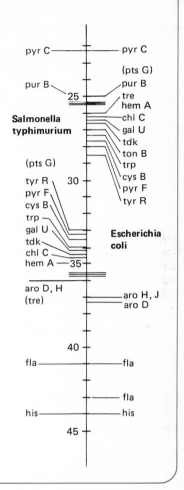

carry host tryptophan genes (φ80*dtrp*) or host suppressor genes (φ80*dsup*), depending on where the wrong crossover occurs that leads to formation of these specialized transducing particles.

All these transducing phages therefore are **episomes**, that is, pieces of DNA which may exist in the integrated prophage state or assume the free infective state in their host. The specialized transducing particles to which these phages give rise differ from generalized transducing particles in two significant features: (1) specialized transducing particles carry bacterial genes *as well as* phage genes, while generalized transducing particles carry only bacterial genes *instead of* phage genes; and (2) specialized transducing particles *add* transduced genes to the recipient bacterial genome, while gen-

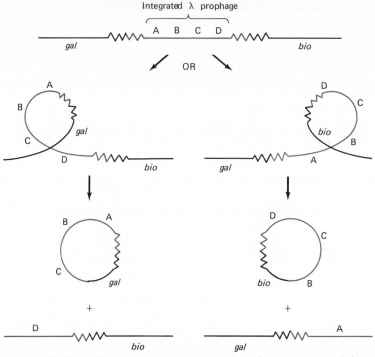

Figure 5.31 Specialized transduction. Formation of circular λ*dgal* (left) and λ*dbio* (right) DNA leads to transducing particles which carry particular bacterial genes (black) in place of some of their own DNA (red). In the case of the specialized transducing phage λ of *E. coli*, the prophage integrates between the *gal* and *bio* loci in the bacterial chromosome and, therefore, carries either *gal* or *bio* genes when inaccurate excision of the prophage takes place.

eralized transducing particles carry in genes which may *replace* those of the recipient.

Since specialized transduction leads to the creation of partial diploids in the recipients, the system can be used to:

1. Identify the dominant member of a pair of alleles; for example, gal^+ is dominant to gal^- since the merozygote phenotype is gal$^+$;

2. Provide information on complementation and functional allelism; for example, if a biotin-dependent strain is infected with λ*dbio*$^-$ specialized transducing particles, the mutant phenotype will still be expressed in the merozygote if the resident and the entering *bio*$^-$ alleles are the same; if the merozygote develops the wild-type biotin-independent phenotype, the resident and entering *bio* loci are non-allelic, each representing a different gene locus which happens to lead to the same phenotype in both cases; and

3. To identify and map closely-linked gene loci which flank the prophage attachment sites.

MAPPING BY GENETIC METHODS IN VIRUSES

Of all the organisms we have discussed so far, there was none so different in its genetic system that we could not apply essentially similar methods to gene mapping. Some of the unusual parasexual features involving gene transfer by transformation, conjugation, and transduction still lend themselves to construction of maps despite the one-way transfer of donor genes and despite the requirement for double-crossovers rather than single-crossovers to explain recombinations. We have really been dealing with variations on basic themes in mapping. In some ways, viruses present a very different system for recombination analysis, but maps can be constructed once these differences are known and taken into account.

5.11 Recombination in Viruses

The most useful phenotypes for genetic analysis of bacterial viruses are ones which can be determined easily with the naked eye. Since viruses as units can only be seen with the electron microscope, the phenotypes of choice are ones which appear as the result of virus activity in the lysis of their bacterial hosts. When bacteria are incubated on solid medium in such large numbers that they cover the entire surface as an opaque lawn of growth, we can detect lysis by the appearance of a clear or cloudy spot called a **plaque**. Each plaque is equivalent to a colony, since one original phage and all of its descendants create one plaque. *Plaque morphology* is an inherited feature of a viral strain, and can serve as a useful phenotypic character. Another useful phenotypic characteristic is *host range* of the virus. Most viruses are highly restricted in the species and cell types which they can attack, but some strains can infect a wider range of hosts and can be identified by plaque formation and certain plaque features.

Among the earliest studies of phage recombination in the late 1940s, those reported by Alfred Hershey and R. Rotman for the T2 phage of *E. coli* can provide us with important basic information. When phages are "crossed," the bacterial cultures are exposed to a *mixed infection*; that is, two or more phenotypically different phage strains are added to cells at the same time, in carefully determined concentrations to allow infection of each cell by two or more phages. The progeny phages (*phage lysate*) are recovered and added to a lawn of bacterial cells to analyze phage phenotypes according to plaque development and other characteristics.

For the two phage parents Hershey and Rotman used an r mutant which produces large, sharp-bordered plaques (r^+ phenotypes are small plaques with irregular borders), and an h mutant which can lyse *E. coli* strains B and B/2 (h^+ has a more restricted host range and only lyses strain B). The parents were therefore $r\ h^+$ and r^+h in phenotype (Fig. 5.32). From phage lysates obtained after the mixed infection with r^+h and $r\ h^+$ T2 phage strains, Hershey and Rotman found four kinds of plaques on plates containing a lawn of mixed *E. coli* strains B and B/2. The two parental types were present in greater proportion than the recombinant r^+h^+ and $r\ h$ plaques.

The results were made more significant because the **single-burst** exper-

Figure 5.32 Plaques formed by parental T2 phages rh^+ and r^+h after mixed infection on *E. coli* B + B/2 cell mixtures, and T2 recombinants r^+h^+ and *rh*.

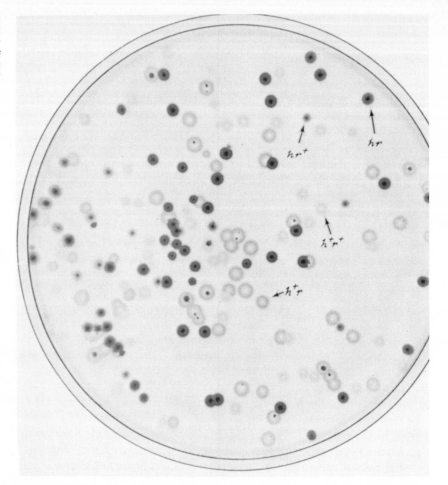

imental design had been used. In such an experiment, the bacterial culture which has been subjected to a mixed infection is later diluted into a series of tubes such that no more than one infected cell is present per tube, on the average. Hershey and Rotman found that the reciprocal classes of recombinants rarely, if ever, appeared with equal frequency from any one single burst. But approximately equal amounts of the recombinant classes could be recovered when many such single-burst progenies were examined. Recombination in T2 phage, therefore, appears to involve some non-reciprocal process, but there is an equal probability for each exchange to occur in a large sampling of phage populations. In some infected cells, both reciprocal products may not be packaged in the same burst by chance alone, even if produced.

Hershey and Rotman also showed that the same proportions of recombinant and parental types were produced in the reciprocal mixed infection, using r^+h^+ and $r\,h$ as the two parental types. Calculation of the frequency of exchange between the r and h loci was the familiar proportion of total recombinants/total plaques counted. A linear relationship was established for other gene loci, in addition to r and h, and the T2 gene map was initiated.

Further information was collected for T2 (and other T-even phages) to fill in the map, but George Streisinger and his colleagues found some peculiar results in three-factor crosses with T4. When the gene markers were relatively close together, a linear and consistent order of loci was obtained. But when widely separated markers were studied, particularly those at the "ends" of the linear map, there were inconsistencies. For example, in a cross between $a^+b^+c^+$ and $a\ b\ c$, the rare double-exchange recombinants were $a^+b\ c^+$ and $a\ b^+c$, which indicated the gene order to be $a-b-c$. Previous mapping, however, had shown that the gene order and distances were:

To resolve this apparent inconsistency, Streisinger proposed that the genetic map was circular rather than linear, and should be shown as:

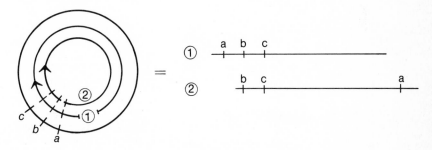

When a variety of three- and four-factor crosses were compared, every inconsistency in linkage distances could be explained by circularity of the gene map (Fig. 5.33). Several different, but related, linear maps could be generated from a single circular map. This has also been found in a number of other viruses and is not unique to T4 and other T-even phages.

5.12 Unusual Features of T2 Recombination

One of the unusual features of T2 recombination we mentioned was that single-burst experiments with T2 revealed an unequal proportion of the reciprocal recombinant classes, but equal proportions were obtained when *populations* of phage progeny were analyzed. The explanation is that during the course of a lytic cycle, DNA replications take place, since hundreds of phage may be released from one burst cell. Simultaneously, there are *repeated rounds of "mating"* between phage DNA molecules during the latent period of the lytic cycle. In addition, these pairings between replicating DNA molecules are indiscriminate. Any two molecules of any genotype may pair and undergo exchanges at any time during the infection cycle. Since initial gene exchanges may be altered during later crossover events, it is highly improbable that reciprocal recombinants would arise in equal

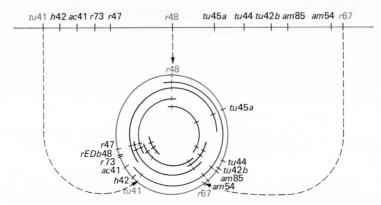

Figure 5.33 The linear sequence of genes established by recombinational analysis in phage T4 can be shown as a circular genetic map to accommodate linkage data from three- and four-factor crosses. The locations of markers used for any one cross are connected by an arc. The physical chromosome of T4 is linear, not circular, DNA. (After Streisinger, G., R. Edgar, and G. Denhardt. 1964. *Proc. Nat. Acad. Sci. U. S.* **51**:775.)

numbers from one infected cell. Since crossing over is a random event, however, a population of progenies would produce an equal number of reciprocal recombinants, on the average.

The second unusual feature we described was the circularity of the T2 gene map, when the T2 chromosome is actually a linear DNA molecule measuring about 53 μm from one free end to the other. This information was obtained by molecular studies. How does a linear genome translate into a circular gene map? The answer came from molecular studies of T2 DNA replication during the lytic cycle and from the packaged DNA in mature phage particles.

During DNA replication of T2 in an infected cell, numerous large duplex DNA molecules are produced, each of which is much longer than 53 μm. These long molecules are called **concatamers**, because they consist of repeated sequences of T2 genes arranged in tandem. For example, if there were 5 genes in the T2 genome, the concatamers could be *abcdeabcdeabcde-abcdeab*. When these molecules are cut into linear 5-gene-long pieces by enzyme action, some of the genomes would be *abcde, cdeab, bcdea, eabcd*, and so forth. Each phage will have a full complement of the 5 genes, but each of the DNA molecules of the population would begin and end at different loci. Such a collection of molecules is *circularly permuted*, and the circular linkage map arises from these circular permutations of a gene complement.

The long concatamers themselves probably arise in the vegetative pool of DNA by exchange events between homologous genes at the ends of two different molecules. Two molecules would be linked together if there were a recombination such as:

a b c d e a b
                    ⟍   a b c d e a b c d e a
                     ⟍   ⟶
         e a b c d e a

Knowing these unusual features of T2 recombination and the T2 life cycle, the recombination analyses and linkage maps are not fundamentally different from those of other organisms. The actual recombination frequencies, however, will reflect different sets of events in viruses which undergo repeated rounds of matings and others in which some DNA molecules do not undergo exchanges or in which only one or two crossovers occur during a lytic cycle. The *E. coli* phage lambda (λ), for example, is characterized by the latter pattern of little or no exchange in the pool of vegetative DNA molecules during a lytic cycle. The differences between T2 and λ in their frequencies and complexity of recombinations leads to a lack of correspondence between the units of physical distance in the two maps.

The same recombination frequencies may be found by genetic analysis of two gene loci in T2 and in λ, and the same number of map units may be shown in the two gene maps. But the actual physical distances probably are not the same because the total sets of recombination events were not the same. One should not translate map distances based on recombination frequencies into comparable physical terms when different organisms are compared.

In this chapter and in Chapter 4 we have seen that genetic analysis shows a unity of organization of genetic material. Genes are arranged at fixed places in the chromosome, which permits their relative order to be established. There may be one linkage group, as in all prokaryotes and viruses, or more than one linkage group, as we find typically in eukaryotes. Genes in the same linkage group can undergo crossing over, leading to segregation of alleles and their recombination into new genotypes. The frequency of recombinations leads to calculations of the distances separating genes in the same chromosome. Genes on different chromosomes (in different linkage groups) assort independently. Gene maps summarize all the linkage data obtained from progenies; they are generally comparable, but cannot be directly equated into identical physical units of distance. These and other mapping methods to be described in later chapters all yield the same information: genes are arranged in a linear order, at fixed locations, in the chromosome.

In the next set of chapters, we will explore the gene and the genome in greater detail. We will find that genetic and molecular analyses complement one another, and that they are both essential to a basic comprehension of the genetic system.

QUESTIONS AND PROBLEMS

5.1. Mitotic recombination analysis in Aspergillus revealed the linked order adenine (*ad-14*)—centromere. Other tests provided information for the linked order for two other loci to be biotin (*bio-1*)—proline (*pro-1*)—centromere. Mitotic recombination alone revealed no linkage between these two groups, but haploidization showed that they were all on the same chromosome since they segregated together. What is the centromere position with respect to these three genes?

5.2. From the diploid $Acr/acr^+\ w^+/w\ pro^+/pro$ in *Aspergillus nidulans*, Pontecorvo and Kafer isolated segregants resistant to high concentrations of the drug acriflavin. Of these, 62 proved to be haploids (38 $Acr\ w\ pro$ and 24 $Acr\ w\ pro^+$). A total of 726 diploids also were recovered of which 630 were $Acr/Acr\ w/w\ pro^+/pro$, and 96 were $Acr/Acr\ w^+/w\ pro^+/pro$. On the basis of these results indicate the relative order of linked genes to the centromere. Explain your reasoning.

5.3. In a diploid somatic cell of *Aspergillus nidulans* of the genetic constitution

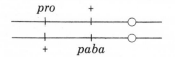

pro = proline requiring
paba = *p*-aminobenzoic acid requiring
o = centromere

a. If crossovers occur between the *pro* and *paba* loci, what genotypes could be produced in daughter cells after mitosis?
b. If there is crossing over between gene *paba* and the centromere, what daughter cells could result after mitosis?
c. If there was a two-strand double-crossover, one exchange between genes *pro* and *paba* and the other between *paba* and the centromere, what daughter cells might result after mitosis?

5.4. In *E. coli*, the following Hfr strains donate the markers shown in the order given.

Hfr strain	Marker order
1	Q R D H T
2	A X S T H
3	B N C A X
4	B Q R D H

All these Hfr strains were derived from the same F^+ strain. What was the order of these markers on the original F^+ chromosome?

5.5. You have three strains of *E. coli*, as follows:

Strain 1: $\dfrac{F'\ leu^+\ pro\text{-}1}{leu^+\ pro\text{-}1}$ (partially diploid for the two genes)

Strain 2: $F^-\ leu\ pro\text{-}2\ Z$ (lysogenic for the generalized transducing phage Z)

Strain 3: $F^-\ leu^+\ pro\text{-}1$ (an F^- derivative of strain 1, having lost F')

Strains are leucine requiring (*leu*) or not (*leu⁺*), and all require proline to grow.

a. How would you determine whether *pro-1* and *pro-2* are alleles of the same gene?
b. Suppose *pro-1* and *pro-2* are allelic, and the *leu* locus is cotransduced with the *pro* locus. Using phage Z to transduce genes from strain 3 to 2, how would you determine the genetic order of *leu*, *pro-1*, and *pro-2*?

5.6. Two independent temperature-sensitive mutations were recovered in phage T4. Both mutants formed plaques at 25° but not at 42°. If one mutant was defective in DNA replication and the other was defective in tail formation, how would you determine that these phages were mutant for different functions?

5.7. What are the characteristics that distinguish temperate and virulent phages?

5.8. Suppose that you have infected *E. coli* cells with two strains of T2 virus, one being small (s), fuzzy bordered (f), and turbid (tu), and the other being wild type for all three traits. The lysate from this infection was plated out and was classified into genotypes according to plaque morphology, as follows:

Genotype	No. of plaques
$s\ f\ tu$	6934
$+\ +\ +$	7458
$s\ f\ +$	1706
$s\ +\ tu$	324
$s\ +\ +$	1040
$+\ f\ tu$	940
$+\ f\ +$	344
$+\ +\ tu$	1930
	20,676

a. Determine the linkage distances between s and f, f and tu, and s and tu.

b. What is the linkage order for these three genes?

c. What is the coefficient of coincidence?

5.9. What genetic tests would you use to show that a bacterial chromosome is physically circular?

5.10. Discuss the contribution of viral genetic studies to the Chromosome Theory of Inheritance.

5.11. How is it possible that a physically linear chromosome produces a circular map?

5.12. The following diagram shows human-mouse hybrid clones and the human chromosomes they contain.

Human chromosomes

	X	2	11	17
Clones A	+	−	+	−
B	−	+	+	−
C	+	−	+	+

+ = present
– = absent

Four human enzymes were tested: TK (thymidine kinase), LDH (lactate dehydrogenase), PGK (phosphoglycerate kinase), and AHH (aryl hydrocarbon hydroxide). The results were as follows:

TK activity only in clone C
LDH activity in all three clones
PGK activity in clones A and C
AHH activity in clone B

What can you say about the location of the genes responsible for these human enzyme activities?

5.13. Lesch-Nyan disease is transmitted via an X-linked mutant gene. A woman gives birth to a son who is colorblind and also displays Lesch-Nyan disease. (Note: The woman's father was colorblind.)

    a. Give the possible genotypes and phenotypes of the following: (1) woman's father, (2) woman's mother, (3) woman, (4) her son.

    b. What is the probability of her having another doubly affected son?

5.14. In *E. coli* what difference in the gene transmission mechanism accounts for the following results?

$$F^+ \times F^- \longrightarrow F^+ \text{ but no chromosome transfer}$$
$$Hfr \times F^- \longrightarrow F^- \text{ but with chromosome transfer}$$

5.15. DNA was extracted from a wild type strain of *Bacillus subtilis* and was used to transform a mutant strain unable to synthesize the following amino acids: alanine (ala), proline (pro), and arginine (arg). The number of colonies produced in the different transformant classes were as follows:

4200 $ala^+pro^+arg^+$
 420   $ala^+pro^-arg^-$
1050 $ala^+pro^-arg^+$
 700   $ala^+pro^+arg^-$
 210   $ala^-pro^+arg^+$
 420   $ala^-pro^+arg^-$
 420   $ala^-pro^-arg^+$

    a. What are the linkage distances between these genes?

    b. What is the linkage order?

5.16. Five Hfr donor strains of *E. coli* (A-E) all carrying the same wild type alleles are crossed to an F^- recipient strain carrying the alternative set of alleles. Using the interrupted-mating technique, it is found that each *Hfr* strain transmits its genes in a unique sequence, as shown:

| *Hfr* strain | | | | |
A	B	C	D	E
mal^+	ade^+	pro^+	pro^+	his^+
str^s	his^+	met^+	gal^+	gal^+
ser^+	gal^+	xyl^+	his^+	pro^+
ade^+	pro^+	mal^+	ade^+	met^+
his^+	met^+	str^s	ser^+	xyl^+

Draw the genetic map of the *Hfr* strain from which these five donors were derived.

5.17. A bacterial strain-1 carrying two auxotrophic mutations, *a* and *b*, and the wild type allele for gene *c*, is infected with a generalized transducing phage. The progeny phage are used to transduce strain-2 cells which are wild type for *a* and *b* but carry an auxotrophic mutation *c*. The cells are plated on minimal media such that only those cells which are wild type for all three gene loci can survive. In a reciprocal experiment, strain-1 is transduced with phage isolated from a strain-2 infection. The following results are obtained:

strain-1 ⟶ strain-2   strain-2 ⟶ strain-1
150 wild type per   9 wild type per
10^8 cells 10^8 cells

What is the gene order for the three loci?

REFERENCES

Avery, O. T., C. M. MacLeod, and M. McCarty. 1944. Studies on the chemical nature of the substance inducing transformation of pneumococcal types. *J. Exp. Med.* **79**:137.

Brady, R. O. Aug. 1973. Hereditary fat-metabolism diseases. *Sci. Amer.* **230**:88.

Bukhari, A. I., J. A. Shapiro, and S. L. Adhya. 1977. *DNA: Insertion Elements, Plasmids and Episomes*. New York: Cold Spring Harbor Laboratory.

Caskey, C. T., and G. D. Kruh. 1979. The HPRT locus. *Cell* **16**:1.

Deisseroth, A., R. Velez, and A. W. Nienhuis. 1976. Hemoglobin synthesis in somatic cell hybrids: Independent segregation of the human alpha- and beta-globin genes. *Science* **191**:1262.

Donahue, R. P., W. B. Bias, J. H. Renwick, and V. A. McKusick. 1968. Probable assignment of the Duffy blood group locus to chromosome 1 in man. *Proc. Nat. Acad. Sci. U.S.* **61**:949.

Firshein, S. I., *et al.* 1979. Prenatal diagnosis of classical hemophilia. *New Engl. J. Med.* **300**:937.

Friedmann, T. Nov. 1971. Prenatal diagnosis of genetic disease. *Sci. Amer.* **225**:34.

Hotchkiss, R. D., and J. Marmur. 1954. Double marker transformations as evidence of linked factors in deoxyribonucleate transforming agents. *Proc. Nat. Acad. Sci. U.S.* **40**:55.

Kolodny, E. H. 1976. Lysosomal storage diseases. *New Engl. J. Med.* **294**:1217.

Macalpine, I., and R. Hunter. July 1969. Porphyria and King George III. *Sci. Amer.* **221**:38.

McKusick, V. A. 1978. Genetic nosology: Three approaches. *Amer. J. Human Genet.* **30**:105.

McKusick, V. A. Apr. 1971. The mapping of human chromosomes. *Sci. Amer.* **224**:104.

McKusick, V. A., and R. Claiborne, eds. 1973. *Medical Genetics*. New York: HP Publishing Co.

McKusick, V. A., and F. H. Ruddle. 1977. The status of the gene map of the human chromosomes. *Science* **196**:390.

Merritt, A. D., E. W. Lovrien, M. L. Rivas, and P. M. Conneally. 1973. Human amylase loci: Genetic linkage with the Duffy blood group locus and assignment to linkage group I. *Amer. J. Human Genet.* **25**:523.

Pontecorvo, G., and E. Kafer. 1958. Genetic analysis based on mitotic recombination. *Adv. Genet.* **9**:71.

Ruddle, F. H., and R. S. Kucherlapati. July 1974. Hybrid cells and human genes. *Sci. Amer.* **228**:82.

Rushton, W. A. H. Mar. 1975. Visual pigments and color blindness. *Sci. Amer.* **232**:64.

Stanbury, J. B., J. B. Wyngaarden, and D. S. Fredrickson, eds. 1978. *The Metabolic Basis of Inherited Diseases*, 4th ed. New York: McGraw-Hill.

Stern, C. 1936. Somatic crossing over and segregation in *Drosophila melanogaster*. *Genetics* **21**:625.

Streisinger, G., R. S. Edgar, and G. H. Denhardt. 1964. Chromosome structure in phage T4, I. Circularity of the linkage map. *Proc. Nat. Acad. Sci. U. S.* **51**:775.

Thomas, C. A., Jr. 1967. The rule of the ring. *J. Cell Physiol.* **70**, Suppl. 1 to No. 2, p. 13.

Wigler, M., A. Pellicer, S. Silverstein, and R. Axel. 1978. Biochemical transfer of single-copy eucaryotic genes using total cellular DNA as donor. *Cell* **14**:725.

Zinder, N. D., and J. Lederberg. 1952. Genetic exchange in *Salmonella*. *J. Bact.* **64**:679.

Gene Structure and Function

When the molecular model for DNA was presented by Watson and Crick in 1953, it had a tremendously stimulating influence on studies of the gene and its properties. The emphasis began to change from defining the gene in operational terms, such as breeding behavior, to defining these operations in molecular terms. The methods of analyzing the gene were still largely genetic, but genetic data were interpreted in terms of genes as segments of DNA.

The only way to analyze the gene in the 1950s and 1960s was by indirect methods. Since biochemical and molecular methods were available to analyze proteins, genetic and molecular studies concentrated on the protein product of the gene and then deduced the nature of the gene according to information gained from its product. The gene itself was mappable, through analysis of intragenic recombination from studies of intragenic mutations and from studies of mutant proteins. The gene was shown to be linear, with nucleotides that could be altered by mutation and by crossing-over events taking place within a single gene. These kinds of evidence also led to a changing view of the chromosome as a continuous DNA molecule, rather than a string of genes beaded together by unknown linker molecules.

The information stored in DNA sequences consists of triplets of nucleotides or codons, each specifying a particular amino acid in the polypeptide or a stop signal for genetically-coded protein synthesis. Both genetic and molecular evidence established the precise nature of the genetic code and all its 64 codons in a dazzling display of ingenious experimentation between 1961 and 1967. The coded genetic message was shown to be read in a continuous reference frame, each codon consecutively read out as an amino acid or stop signal in protein synthesis.

In the 1970s, direct sequence analysis of DNA became feasible. DNA sequencing of the gene and the genome have led to another revolutionary change in our knowledge of gene structure. These new studies are now in active progress.

GENETIC PROPERTIES OF DNA

We have known the chemical composition of DNA for over 100 years, ever since Friedrich Miescher described "nuclein" isolated from extracts of nuclei in 1871. In 1953, Watson and Crick proposed a molecular model of duplex DNA and pointed out its suitability for genetic material. The molecular model of DNA had an immediate and powerful impact on the scientific community, and it still serves as the foundation for genetic studies.

DNA meets the four main requirements for genetic material: (1) precise replication, (2) information storage, (3) information transfer, and (4) mutation. All these features had come to be generally understood through a half-century of genetic analysis. Now it became possible to analyze *how* these properties were achieved by the genes. With the new molecular perspective, new questions could be asked, new methods developed, and new insights gained into the most intimate operations of the genetic apparatus. In this chapter and in the ones to follow, we will examine these properties and operations in various organisms and see how classical studies of the gene and the genome have been put into a molecular perspective and described in molecular terms.

6.1   The DNA Duplex

As described briefly in Section 3.9, the bases in three of the four nucleotide monomers for nucleic acid polymer construction are shared by DNA and RNA: **adenine**, **guanine**, and **cytosine** (**A, G, C**). The fourth kind of base is **thymine** (**T**) in DNA, but it is **uracil** in RNA (**U**). Three major kinds of chemical bonds make DNA molecules very stable in the watery environment of the cell (Fig. 6.1):

1. **Covalent bonds** link atoms within nucleotide units, and they link nucleotides together via **3′,5′-phosphodiester bridges** extending from the 5′ carbon of one pentose sugar to the 3′ carbon of the pentose in the adjacent nucleotide. These strong bonds in the sugar—phosphate "backbone" of each strand make the polynucleotide chains relatively resistant to breakage due to the high energy requirement for such damage. Specific enzymes, called **endonucleases**, catalyze breaks in these strands at relatively specific sites in specific nucleotide groups. Such **restriction endonucleases**, or

Figure 6.1   (Facing Page.) Molecular structure of DNA. (a) Each polynucleotide chain of the duplex consists of repeating nucleotide units held together by 3′,5′-phosphodiester bridges. The antiparallel strands are hydrogen bonded between complementary base pairs. (b) The molecule is a double-stranded helix, and must be untwisted to become two single-stranded chains. (c) The constant width of 20 Å for the duplex is due to the equivalence of width of all four possible base pairs (A-T, T-A, G-C, C-G), consisting of a larger purine bonded to a smaller pyrimidine residue. (d) The individual chains of the duplex are often illustrated to emphasize the nature of the sugar-phosphate backbone to which the bases are bonded covalently.

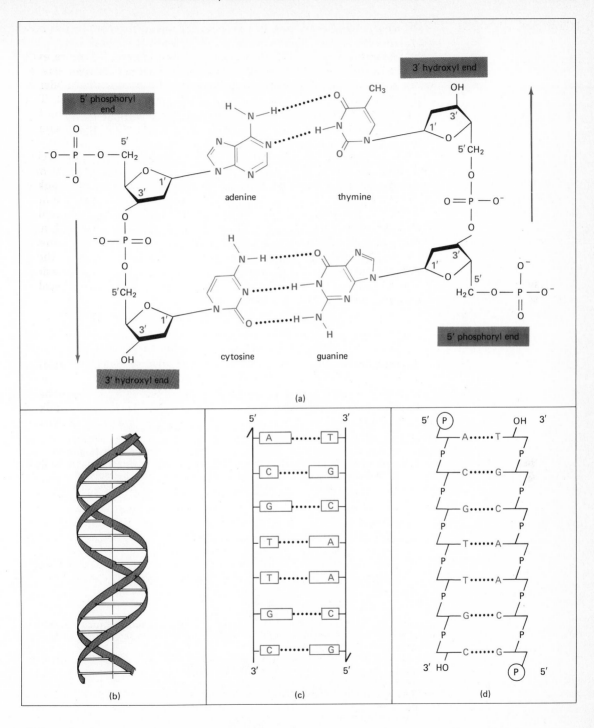

(a)

(b)

(c)

(d)

restriction enzymes, have provided a means for reproducibly cutting up a molecule into recognizable pieces. It is possible to determine the sequence of these restriction fragments and construct a map showing the whole DNA molecule, which may be tens of thousands of nucleotides long (Fig. 6.2).

2. The many weak **hydrogen bonds** within the DNA duplex are so arranged that most of them cannot break without many others breaking at the same time. This is energetically unlikely at cell temperatures, but is easily accomplished in the laboratory by heating to 100°C or less. The separation of duplex DNA into single strands by heating provides investigators with material to analyze template function, RNA copies of single DNA strands, and the unique features of each of the two complementary chains of one molecule. When native (duplex) DNA strands are separated, the molecule is **denatured.** The process of denaturation is also called **melting**, and DNA melting properties provide a useful means for identifying base composition differences between different DNAs, the presence of repeated stretches of nucleotides among unique sequences, and various molecular features of the gene and the genome (Fig. 6.3).

    Hydrogen bonding also takes place between virtually all the surface atoms in the sugar—phosphate chains and the surrounding water molecules in the cell or in solution in the test tube. These stabilizing forces help in the maintenance of molecular shape, which is essential for genetic function.

Figure 6.2 The restriction enzyme *Eco RI* is an endonuclease derived from *E. coli.* The enzyme recognizes a particular duplex nucleotide sequence and catalyzes staggered breaks in the complementary strands. Such pieces, or **restriction fragments**, can undergo recombination with each other or with any complementary sequence to become **recombinant DNA**. The restriction fragments can also be isolated and their nucleotide sequence determined, in preparation for molecular mapping of a gene or a genome. (For information on the Nobel awards in 1978 to Werner Arber, Hamilton O. Smith, and Daniel Nathans for their studies on restriction enzymes, see *Science* **202**:1069. 1978.)

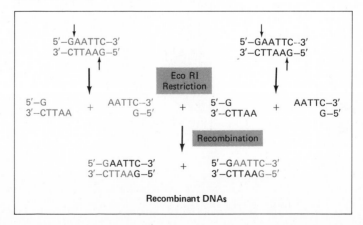

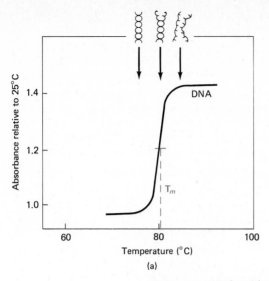
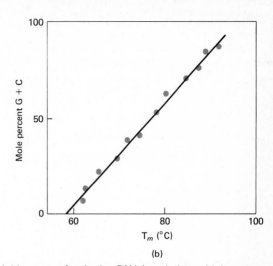

Figure 6.3 DNA melting. (a) Melting curve for duplex DNA in solution, with increase in absorbance (the hyperchromic shift) plotted as a function of temperature. The T_m of the particular DNA is the midpoint melting temperature, at which half the denaturation has occurred in the sharp transition from double- to single-strands (at top of figure). When melting is completed there is no further change in absorbance (plateau). (b) T_m is dependent on G-C content of the DNA sample, as seen by the linear relationship for various DNA sources (dots). Knowing T_m, one can deduce the G-C content of a DNA.

3. **Hydrophobic interactions** between the flat surfaces of the aromatic nitrogenous bases stacked vertically along the duplex length make an important contribution to molecular stability. These interactions lead to the exclusion of water molecules from the interior of the molecule, and from interference or competition in hydrogen bonding between complementary base pairs. Hydrophobic interactions also lend a considerable stiffness to the DNA duplex.

   The cooperative result of all these kinds of bonds and interactions is stability of molecular shape and, therefore, maintenance of molecular properties and functions under physiological conditions.

There were three important clues to DNA molecular structure, which Watson and Crick put together in 1953, along with their own information and brilliant insight. Photographs of **x-ray diffraction patterns** made by bombardments of crystalline DNA preparations, from studies by Rosalind Franklin and by Maurice Wilkins, indicated that: (1) components were spaced in highly regular fashion, as opposed to a random or haphazard order in the molecule; and (2) each molecule consisted of two helical chains held together as a duplex (Fig. 6.4). The third clue came from Erwin Chargaff's biochemical studies of DNA, which showed that there was a consistent percentage of A, T, G, and C in any particular source of DNA but that these percentages varied from one source to another. In particular, Chargaff had found that each source had equal amounts of A and T and

Figure 6.4 X-ray diffraction photograph of crystalline DNA.

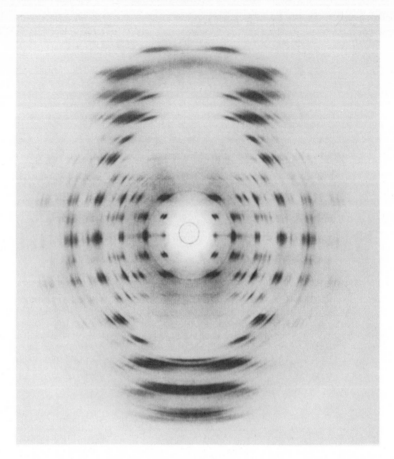

equal amounts of G and C, but different sources had varying amounts of A + T and G + C (Table 6.1). The rule therefore appeared to be that the ratio of A:T or of G:C was unity, but the ratio of AT:GC was variable. It was the brilliant conceptual achievement of Watson and Crick to build a molecular model in which all of these factors fit together logically and consistently.

By evaluating the size, shape, and theoretical bonding interactions of the four kinds of bases, Watson and Crick perceived that a double helix with a constant diameter of 2 nanometers could only be achieved if A paired with T and G paired with C across the space between the invariant sugar—phosphate chains. The ratio of 1 for A:T and for G:C was therefore due to pairing between these **complementary bases** along the length of the molecule.

6.2   DNA is the Genetic Material

The great excitement over the Watson-Crick model in 1953 was largely due to the parallels between genes and DNA, which they had pointed out clearly

Table 6.1

Molar proportions of bases (as moles of nitrogenous constituents per 100 g-atoms P) in DNAs from various sources

Source of DNA	A	T	G	C	$\frac{A+T}{G+C}$	$\frac{A+G}{T+C}$	A:T	G:C
Human liver	30.3	30.3	19.5	19.9	1.53	0.99	1.00	0.98
Human sperm	30.7	31.2	19.3	18.8	1.62	1.00	0.98	1.03
Human thymus	30.9	29.4	19.9	19.8	1.52	1.03	1.05	1.00
Bovine sperm	28.7	27.2	22.2	21.9	1.27	1.04	1.06	1.01
Rat bone marrow	28.6	28.5	21.4	21.5	1.33	1.00	1.00	1.00
Wheat germ	27.3	27.2	22.7	22.8	1.20	1.00	1.00	1.00
Yeast	31.3	32.9	18.7	17.1	1.79	1.00	0.95	1.09
Escherichia coli	26.0	23.9	24.9	25.2	1.00	1.04	1.09	0.99
Mycobacterium tuberculosis	15.1	14.6	34.9	35.4	0.42	1.00	1.03	0.98
Bacteriophage T2, T4, or T6	32.5	32.5	18.3	16.7*	1.86	1.03	1.00	1.10
Bacteriophage T3	23.7	23.5	26.2	26.6	0.89	1.00	1.01	0.98
Bacteriophage T5	30.3	30.7	19.5	19.5	1.56	1.00	0.99	1.00

*The T-even phages have hydroxymethyl cytosine in place of cytosine in their DNA.

and simply from the model. Watson and Crick particularly noted that DNA had properties which would explain four known features of genetic material: (1) stability during metabolism: (2) precise replication; (3) a variety of molecular species; and (4) capacity for mutation. They noted the following:

1. DNA does not undergo **turnover** during cell metabolism, but virtually all other molecules are made and degraded during the lifetime of a cell. DNA is stable, persisting essentially unchanged throughout the life of a cell.

2. Each one of the two complementary strands of a duplex might serve as the **template** for synthesis of an exact complementary copy of a partner strand; two identical molecules can thus arise from one parent duplex molecule (Fig. 6.5). The rule of **complementary base-pairing** underwrites the precision of DNA (and gene) replication generation after generation.

3. The variety of DNA molecules is practically unlimited, and matched this genetic requirement very well. Although base-pairing across the molecule is restricted, there is no restriction on the *linear* order of bases or base-pairs. With only 4 kinds of bases or base-pairs (AT, TA, GC, CG) in a duplex of any length, the theoretical number of different molecules is 4^n. If the average gene is 500 base-pairs from one end to the other, then 4^{500} different arrangements, or molecules, or genes, could be constructed from 500 units arranged in all permuted sequences of the 4 building blocks. DNA had more than enough variety to be the genetic material.

4. Watson and Crick indicated how mutations could arise, as the result of **base substitution** during DNA replication. An altered base

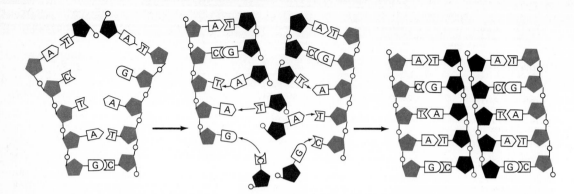

Figure 6.5 Each strand of the DNA duplex guides synthesis of a new complementary partner strand, making two molecules identical to each other and to the original parental DNA. Genetic continuity is thus ensured from generation to generation.

might be inserted in a replicating system by accident when an adenine pairs with cytosine instead of the usual thymine (Fig. 6.6). Upon separation in the next round of replication, the substituted cytosine will direct the incorporation of a guanine in its partner strand. The net result is substitution of an AT base pair by a GC pair. The alteration would be perpetuated in later generations, just as mutations are transmitted through successive generations.

Before 1953 there were two landmark experiments which specifically pointed to DNA as the genetic material: the 1944 studies of transformation in pneumococcus by Avery, MacLeod, and McCarty; and the 1952 experiments with T2 phage DNA and protein by Hershey and Chase, as described in Chapter 2. After 1953, many studies were designed to verify that DNA was indeed the genetic material and the chemical basis of heredity, by seeking parallels between genes and DNA in various genetic phenomena. Today we routinely study every genetic process with the full and basic knowledge that DNA and genes are one and the same.

GENE STRUCTURE AND FUNCTION

After the proposal for the molecular structure of DNA had been made, new kinds of questions were asked about the gene. What was its structure? Was the gene an indivisible unit, or could its molecular properties be dissected by genetic methods? Could the gene itself be mapped as chromosomes were mapped? It was generally acknowledged that proteins were products of the genes, but how did nucleotides in DNA translate into amino acids in proteins? For a period of twenty-five years after Watson and Crick proposed the molecular model of DNA, genetic research was pursued vigorously with the goals of defining gene structure in relation to mutation, recombination, and function. Genetic methods went hand in hand with molecular analysis, wherever it was possible to use or design appropriate techniques. During the

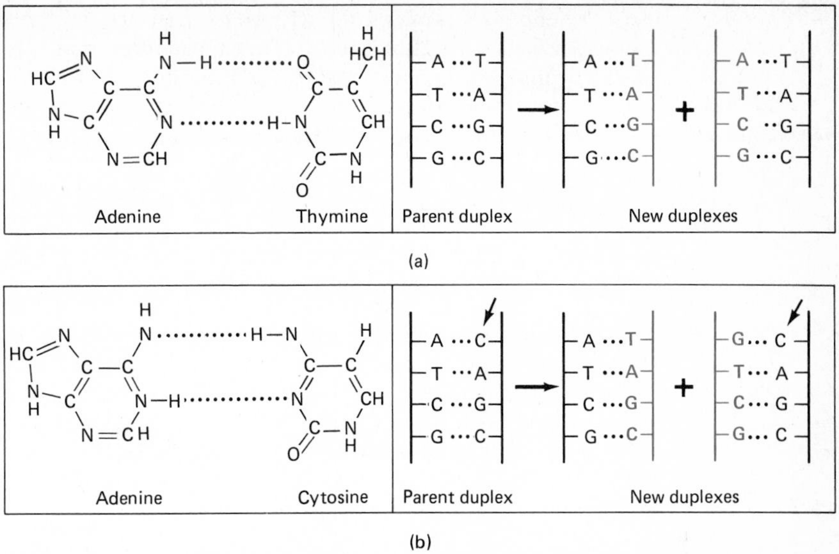

(a)

(b)

Figure 6.6 The shift of a hydrogen to another position produces a **tautomeric** form of adenine (as happens in other bases, too). In its more stable tautomeric form adenine pairs with thymine; in another tautomeric form it pairs with cytosine. Mutation by such base substitution during replication was first suggested by Watson and Crick, and verified later by experiments (see Chapter 10).

1950s and 1960s, the power of genetic analysis was elegantly demonstrated in a number of investigations, which were inspired by the molecular model of DNA and by an increasing understanding of the nature of proteins as gene products.

6.3   Fine Structure Mapping of the Gene

The detailed mapping of sites within a gene locus using genetic methods is called **fine structure mapping**. The first detailed maps of specific genes were produced by genetic analysis of the rII region in *E. coli* phage T4 by Seymour Benzer between the mid-1950s and early 1960s. Wild type T4 lyse cells in 2-3 hours and small, fuzzy-edged plaques appear about 6-10 hours after phages infect cells of strains B and K-12(λ) of *E. coli*. Mutations to the rapid lysis (r) character are recognized by lysis about 20 minutes after infection and by production of large, sharp-edged plaques. In addition, there is a change in host range, since rII mutants can infect strain B cells but not *E. coli* K-12(λ). There are several r mutants which map in different parts of the phage genome, but rII mutants were the ones studied. There are two adjacent genes in the rII region, called the A and B genes, and the rIIA and rIIB mutations were both analyzed by Benzer. Both the A and B genes affect the same phenotypic characters.

Benzer collected about 2400 different mutant strains, and he proceeded to cross different rIIA mutants two by two and to make crosses pairwise between different rIIB mutant strains. He mixedly infected *E. coli* B with an adequate number of particles from two *rIIA* or two *rIIB* mutant strains to be crossed, so that each host cell would be multiply infected by at least one phage from each parental strain. Since *r*II mutants can develop in strain B, recombinations could occur during the vegetative multiplication of the infecting viruses in repeated rounds of mating (Fig. 6.7). Progeny phages recovered from infected B cells were added to K-12 cells spread as a lawn of growth on nutrient media. Any wild-type recombinants would produce plaques, since these can infect K-12, but doubly-mutant recombinants and the mutant parental classes would not develop in this host strain of bacteria.

The assay was very sensitive, since even 1 in 10^6 wild type recombinants could be scored by this method. Because some r^+ phages also arise by reverse mutation from the mutant condition, the limit of *unambiguous* recombination which could be detected was set at a high enough level not to be confused with reverse mutations, which were more rare. A minimum frequency of 0.01% wild type recombinants could be detected. The actual

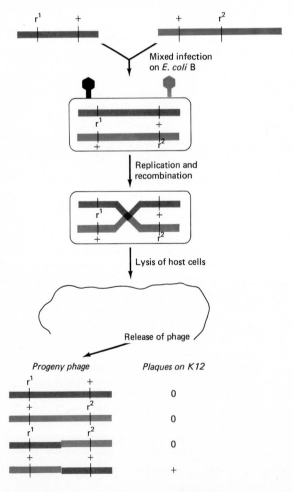

Figure 6.7 Recombination assay for phage T4 *r*II mutants in mixed infections on *E. coli* B. Wild type recombinants are the only progeny class that can infect *E. coli* K-12, as indicated by formation of plaques on this host strain.

recombination frequency observed in any cross was doubled, because the reciprocal double-mutant recombinants were not detected but were expected to be present.

The astonishing result was that recombinants arose regularly in these crosses between mutants for the *same* gene. The explanation for their appearance was that crossing over had occurred *within* the gene itself, that is, by **intragenic recombination**. Since genes were composed of linear DNA, it seemed reasonable to propose that exchanges took place between different sites in a single gene. The closer together these sites were in any cross, the lower the frequency of recombination; higher recombination frequencies characterized mutant sites that were farther apart along the length of the gene. Since crossing over is a random event, and is more likely to happen when there is a larger space between mutant sites, the gene could be mapped in exactly the same way that chromosomes were mapped . . . by recombination frequencies, equated to map units of distance. The fine structure of the *rIIA* and *rIIB* genes revealed that they were *linear assemblies of mutable sites*, which could undergo crossing over and give rise to recombinants; the gene was *not* an indivisible unit. Crossing over was *not* restricted to spaces between genes. Since the same crossover events occurred within a gene as between genes, it seemed very likely that the whole chromosome was a continuous DNA structure. A new view of the chromosome began to emerge, and new insights developed about the molecular nature of the crossing over process, as we will see later.

It was clearly impractical to proceed with the millions of pairwise crosses needed to map the 2400 mutant sites of the *r*II region. Benzer devised an original and ingenious procedure to accomplish the task in a reasonable amount of time with a reasonable amount of effort. He assembled a reference collection of **deletion mutants**. These mutants never reverted to wild type by back mutation, which had long been known to characterize deletion mutants in higher organisms. Each mutant had a piece of the *r*II region that was missing, or deleted, and these deletions were of varying lengths. The deletion regions were overlapping, so that two or more deletions in different mutants might have the same deleted segment in some part of the lesion (Fig. 6.8).

Benzer used his **overlapping deletions method** to map the *r*II region. He first established the location, length, and overlap of the deletions in the reference collection of deletion mutant strains. This was done by making crosses with a few single-site mutants which had already been mapped by recombination in the *r*II region. Once the deletion mutants had been characterized, it was possible to cross any unknown single-site mutant with known deletion mutants to locate the single-site mutation roughly at some location within the gene (Fig. 6.9). If unknown mutant *a* produced wild type recombinants with deletion mutants 1, 2, 3, and 4, but not with 5, then the single-site mutation must be located somewhere in the region deleted in strain 5. To pin down the location more closely, mutant *a* was then crossed with other reference strains which had *smaller* deletions within the same region missing in strain 5. After several crosses of unknown mutant *a* with a set of increasingly smaller overlapping-deletion mutants, it was possible to make the last cross between mutant *a* and a known, mapped, single-site

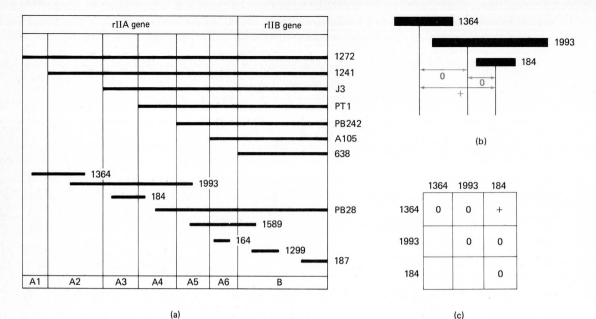

Figure 6.8 Overlapping deletion mapping in the *r*II region of phage T4. (a) The reference collection of overlapping deletion mutants defines the entire *r*II region. Each black bar indicates the extent of the deletion and its relative location in the *r*IIA and *r*IIB genes of the region. The gene lengths are subdivided into smaller segments (A1-A6 and B), and smaller ones still which are shown in Fig. 6.10. (b) Crosses between a newly isolated *r*II mutant and reference deletion mutants permit assignment of the new mutant to an approximate map location, if wild type recombinants occur. A topological map can be drawn according to these results. (c) The matrix of crosses between mutants in pairs can be drawn to show those crosses producing wild type recombinants (+) and those which do not (0), from which the order of the mutations in the topological map (shown in b) can be determined. (After Benzer, S. 1961. *Proc. Nat. Acad. Sci. U. S.* **47**:410.)

mutation in a very nearby location. Recombination frequencies between these two single-site mutants thus yielded the values to map the unknown mutant site precisely and to calculate its distance from other mutant sites in the neighborhood. In this way, 428 different sites were identified from intragenic recombination data, and the fine structure of the T4 map of the *r*II region was defined (Fig. 6.10). The linear genetic map provided very strong evidence that the gene itself was linear in construction, which coincided with the known linear construction of duplex DNA.

The *r*II region consists of two genes, yet mutations in either *r*IIA or *r*IIB produce the same rapid lysis character. Why are these considered to be separate genes, one right next to the other, and not a single gene governing a single phenotype? The basis for Benzer's interpretation of two genes in the *r*II region was the **cis-trans test** (Fig. 6.11).

When *E. coli* K-12 was infected with two *r*IIA or two *r*IIB mutant phages, no virus progeny developed. But when an *r*IIA and an *r*IIB mutant

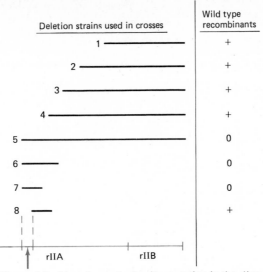

Figure 6.9 Mapping a single-site mutation in the *r*II region. The mutant is crossed with a series of known deletion mutants 1-5, from which an approximate location is determined (left end of *r*IIA, according to reference map shown at bottom of figure). Using small-deletion mutants 6-8, a more refined location can be made, according to production of wild type recombinants between the single-site and deletion mutants. The single-site mutation is then located (red arrow) on the reference map. Precise map location is later determined by crosses with other single-site mutants in this immediate part of the *r*II map.

infected strain K-12 simultaneously, virus progeny were produced even though no recombination had occurred. This showed that mutant viruses could *multiply* in K-12 because each parent phage provided one of the functions needed for development; two different functions were required for virus multiplication. The *r*IIA mutant provided a functional *B* gene product, while the *r*IIB mutant provided a functional *A* gene product. The two gene products or functions allowed growth. On the other hand, two *r*IIA mutants had a defective *A* gene function, and two *r*IIB mutants had a defective *B* gene function, and neither cross allowed mutant virus growth. The rare wild type recombinants produced in any of these three kinds of crosses were not confused with production of large numbers of mutant progeny after infection.

When each mutation is present in a different homologous chromosome, we have the **trans** arrangement. When both mutations are in the same chromosome and the wild type alternatives are in the opposite homologue, we have the **cis** arrangement. The trans arrangement is the critical one to assay, since the cis arrangement has one intact chromosome introduced by one parent, and virus multiplication can occur. The cis test serves as a formal control to see that normal experimental conditions prevail.

Benzer coined the term **cistron** (from cis-trans test) as a substitute for gene. He redefined the gene as a cistron which directed one function in

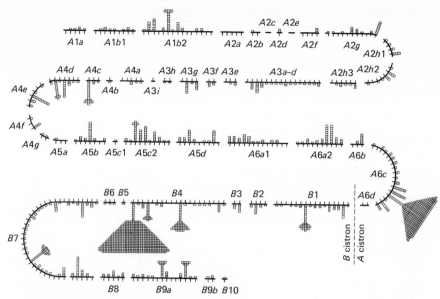

Figure 6.10 Fine structure genetic map of the *r*II region of phage T4. The region is divided into deletion segments (A1a–B10). The single-site mutants are indicated by short vertical lines; thus segment A1a contains 5 sites, A1b1 has 9 sites, etc. Each square represents one occurrence of a spontaneous mutation at the site. Sites without squares have been identified by induced mutations. Some sites are "hot spots" of spontaneous mutation, such as those in segments A6c and B4. (From Benzer, S. 1961. *Proc. Nat. Acad. Sci. U. S.* **47**:410.)

phenotypic development. Two or more cistrons might direct different but related functions in the development of a single phenotypic character, such as rapid lysis. The cis-trans test for **complementation** between mutants provides the evidence for the number of cistrons governing a single phenotypic character. Different mutations which do *not* complement each other must therefore be located in the same cistron.

Using the cis-trans test, regions previously assumed to contain a single gene were shown to consist of two or more genes or cistrons in other viruses. Similar results have been obtained for bacteria, where partial diploids can be produced through conjugation or transduction. It is fairly characteristic for clusters of related genes or cistrons to be present in viral and bacterial genomes. It is very rarely the case in eukaryotes. In fact, different genes with a known related set of functions, such as the gene for the α-globin chain and the gene for the β-globin chain of hemoglobin in human beings, are usually found in different chromosomes. These observed differences in genome organization are not fully understood, but are believed to be associated with different systems for regulation of gene expression.

The cistron concept was very important in the 1960s in many kinds of studies designed to identify genes with related functions in phenotype development. Since gene locations were not at all random, it soon became clear that the genome was a highly organized system and not just a random

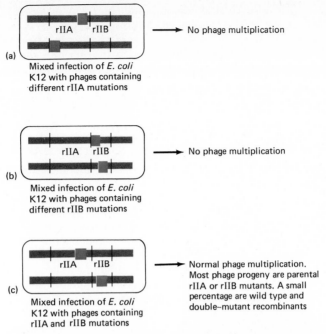

Figure 6.11 The cis-trans test for complementation distinguishes between mutants having lesions in the same or in different genes. Simultaneous infections with two mutants in (a) *rIIA*, or in (b) *rIIB* do not complement and must therefore be lesions in the same gene. Complementation as shown in (c) indicates there are two different genes in the *rII* region of phage T4, since each mutant makes up for the other's defect and together they both become capable of normal multiplication in the host.

collection of genes scattered here and there. This was especially true for viruses and bacteria. Of course, many genes which contribute to a single phenotype are not necessarily adjacent in these organisms.

With increasing information about polypeptides as products of gene expression, the term cistron has lost some of its former heuristic significance. We use the term gene once again today, but we have a better idea of its action because of the cistron concept that led to many modern insights about the gene and its product.

6.4   Colinearity of Gene and Polypeptide

Many studies, particularly in the 1960s, led to the concept that a linear sequence of nucleotides in DNA specified the linear sequence of amino acids in its protein product. The general hypothesis that one gene specified one enzyme grew out of the biochemical genetic studies of metabolic pathways in *Neurospora* by George Beadle, Edward Tatum, and others in the 1940s. Using a variety of mutants which affected metabolism, it was made clear that each step in a metabolic pathway was catalyzed by an enzyme which was under genetic control (Fig. 6.12).

Enzymes are only one of the kinds of proteins under direct genetic control. In the 1950s, Vernon Ingram had shown that the only difference between normal hemoglobin and hemoglobin from patients with sickle cell anemia was in the substitution of glutamic acid by valine at position number 6 in the chain of 146 amino acids making up the β-chain of the molecule. He had "fingerprinted" the globin molecule using **chromatography** (Fig. 6.13). By locating the one fragment of the digest which was different between the normal and mutant chains, it was possible to quickly find the molecular difference by analyzing the amino acids in the variant part of the molecule only. It was concluded that a single nucleotide change in the globin gene was responsible for the altered polypeptide.

How could the relationship between gene and protein be established? In phage T4 the fine structure of the *r*II gene had been provided, but the protein product was (and still is) unknown. In the hemoglobins the protein was well known, but the gene mutations were too few and the experimental analysis was complicated because genetic tests were not available for human beings. The required experimental evidence was provided by Charles Yanofsky and co-workers in an elegant series of genetic and molecular studies of the two adjacent genes governing synthesis of the enzyme tryptophan synthetase in *E. coli*.

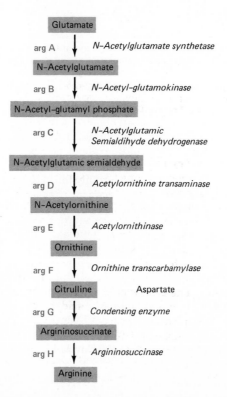

Figure 6.12 Pathway of arginine synthesis from glutamate in *E. coli*. Each step is catalyzed by a particular enzyme (right, italics), which is governed by a specific gene (left, red italics).

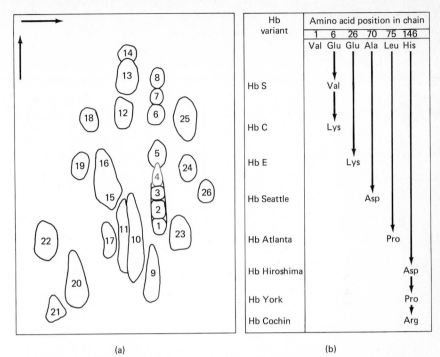

Figure 6.13 Molecular analysis of human hemoglobin variants. (a) Chromatographic separation of 26 fragments of the β chain of hemoglobin produced by tryptic digestion. Fragment no. 4 in this protein digest contains the amino-terminus of the chain, including amino acid 6. Analysis of amino acids only in the one fragment (out of 26) which chromatographs differently in a mutant compared with this fingerprint of normal Hbβ reduces the amount of work required to identify the molecular alteration. (b) Specific amino acid substitutions in human hemoglobin variants. Almost 100 of the 146 sites in the Hbβ molecule have been found to vary in one or more individuals from one or more human populations. The Hbβ gene has been mapped on chromosome 11.

The enzyme **tryptophan synthetase** catalyzes the final step in a biochemical pathway leading to the synthesis of the amino acid tryptophan (Fig. 6.14). The enzyme consists of two subunits, with two α-chains in one subunit and two β-chains in the other. Both subunits are required for enzyme function. Gene *A* of the *trp* genetic region was responsible for α-chain synthesis, while *trpB* directed β-chain synthesis. Since direct analysis of the nucleotide sequence in DNA was not possible in the 1960s, Yanofsky decided to analyze the enzyme and compare its altered amino acid composition with mutable sites in the *trpA* and *trpB* genetic fine structure maps. The goal was to determine whether gene and protein were **colinear**, that is, whether amino acid changes along the length of the protein corresponded in *location* to mutable sites within the gene.

Yanofsky isolated a large number of mutants which lacked a functional α-chain and were therefore enzymatically inactive. All of these α-chain mutants mapped at various sites in the *trpA* gene, and all were alleles according to the cis-trans complementation test. Mutants defective in the β-

Figure 6.14 Some steps in the pathway of tryptophan biosynthesis, showing the *trp* genetic region in *E. coli* (red) and the enzymes specified.

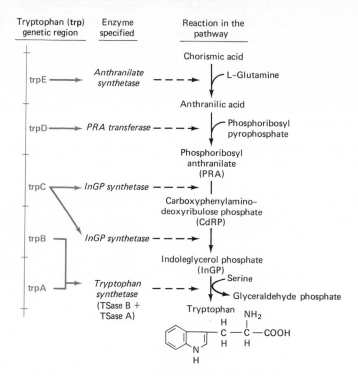

chain all mapped in the *trpB* gene and all complemented *trpA* mutants, but not one another. The inactive enzyme could be isolated from many of these mutants, and the amino acid composition could be determined for the wild type chains. Any difference between mutant and wild type protein could be analyzed by fingerprinting the protein digest, as Ingram did for hemoglobins. It was then only necessary to find the one variant peptide fragment to determine the nature and location of the amino acid alteration in the chain of 267 known units making up the α-polypeptide chain (Fig. 6.15).

From these studies it was established that there was a corresponding location of the mutant site in the gene and of the amino acid substitution in the protein. Gene and polypeptide were colinear molecules, and the gene specified the kinds of amino acids and their sequence in the polypeptide. The polypeptide, in turn, influences phenotypic expression in the organism. Mutant *trpA⁻* cells cannot make tryptophan, but wild type *trpA⁺* have this biochemical ability. The different kinds of cells will therefore have different growth properties in minimal media, since tryptophan is an essential amino acid needed to make a variety of proteins for cellular activities.

How does the gene specify the polypeptide product? The information in the gene must exist in a *coded* form based on nucleotide sequence. Somehow, this coded information stored in the gene must be made available for the synthesis of polypeptides according to the particular genetic blueprint. Deciphering the genetic code was a spectacular achievement of the 1960s.

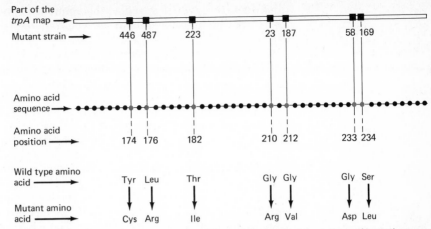

Figure 6.15 Colinearity of the gene and its protein product. Locations of mutations on the linear genetic map correspond to locations of amino acid substitutions in the linear polypeptides made by these *trpA* mutants of *E. coli*. Each square on the gene map represents a mutant site, and each red dot on the polypeptide represents the site of the substituted amino acid in that mutant. The position number of the amino acids, out of the total of 267, and the particular amino acids at these positions are shown. (After Yanofsky, C., *et al.* 1967. *Proc. Nat. Acad. Sci. U. S.* **57**:296.)

Yanofsky's studies of colinearity between gene and polypeptide also provided important information about the nature of the code, so we will discuss more of his studies shortly.

6.5 Deciphering the Genetic Code

The central problem was to identify the coding unit, or **codon**, in DNA which specified amino acids in proteins. The most obvious system of coding would be one in which groups and sequences of DNA nucleotides corresponded to groups and sequences of amino acids in a protein. The flow of information from DNA to the system for polypeptide synthesis has an intermediate stage. DNA information is first copied into RNA by synthesis of a complementary strand of RNA from the DNA template. This RNA copy of the genetic instructions is then used as the guide for polypeptide synthesis; that is, DNA ⟶ RNA ⟶ protein. It is just as relevant to study the relationship between RNA and protein as it is to study DNA and protein, since DNA and RNA are complementary to each other and the information in one molecule reflects the information in the other molecule. Since it was not possible to work directly with DNA in the 1960s, most of the information came from experiments in which artificially constructed RNA was related to amino acids incorporated into polypeptides *in vitro*, that is, in test tube systems. Once a particular set of RNA nucleotides was associated with a particular amino acid in the protein product, the DNA codon could be deduced, since it would be complementary to the observed RNA codon defined in experiments. For example, the first codon to be identified was UUU, which specified the amino acid phenylalanine (Fig. 6.16). The DNA codon for phenylalanine would therefore be the complementary triplet AAA.

In 1961, Marshall Nirenberg and Henry Matthaei showed that an artificial RNA made up only of uracil bound to the sugar-phosphate backbone of the polynucleotide chain, or **poly(U)**, could direct synthesis of a polypeptide consisting entirely of phenylalanine residues. The *in vitro* test system contained a mixture of amino acids plus all the other ingredients known to be needed for polypeptide synthesis in a test tube. Each mixture had a different single amino acid labeled with a radioactive isotope, and all the other amino acids in that mixture were unlabeled. It simply required looking for the one test tube out of the total number in which there was a *radioactively-labeled polypeptide* that had been made from poly(U) instructions. On collecting the labeled polypeptide and hydrolyzing it to its constituent amino acids, Nirenberg and Matthaei found that only phenylalanine was present in the polymer. The RNA codon for phenylalanine contained only uracil, and the complementary DNA codon contained only adenine.

The size of a codon was assumed to be **triplet**, although the poly(U) data could not be interpreted directly as showing that UUU was the codon. Since there are 20 naturally-occurring amino acids which are directly incorporated into polypeptides during their synthesis, there were assumed to be at least 3 nucleotides per codon specifying each of these 20 amino acids. Taking 4 kinds of nucleotides in all permutations of threes, 64 (4^3) unique codons can be assembled. If there were only 2 nucleotides per codon, only 16

Figure 6.16 The genetic coding dictionary, showing messenger RNA codons and the amino acids or punctuations they specify.

Second Nucleotide

	U	C	A	G	
U	UUU / UUC — Phe ; UUA / UUG — Leu	UCU / UCC / UCA / UCG — Ser	UAU / UAC — Tyr ; UAA / UAG — Stop	UGU / UGC — Cys ; UGA — Stop ; UGG — Trp	U C A G
C	CUU / CUC / CUA / CUG — Leu	CCU / CCC / CCA / CCG — Pro	CAU / CAC — His ; CAA / CAG — Gln	CGU / CGC / CGA / CGG — Arg	U C A G
A	AUU / AUC / AUA — Ile ; AUG — Met	ACU / ACC / ACA / ACG — Thr	AAU / AAC — Asn ; AAA / AAG — Lys	AGU / AGC — Ser ; AGA / AGG — Arg	U C A G
G	GUU / GUC / GUA / GUG — Val	GCU / GCC / GCA / GCG — Ala	GAU / GAC — Asp ; GAA / GAG — Glu	GGU / GGC / GGA / GGG — Gly	U C A G

First Nucleotide (left axis) — Third Nucleotide (right axis)

(a)

Abbreviation	Amino acid
Ala	Alanine
Arg	Arginine
Asn	Asparagine
Asp	Aspartic acid
Cys	Cysteine
Gln	Glutamine
Glu	Glutamic acid
Gly	Glycine
His	Histidine
Ile	Isoleucine
Leu	Leucine
Lys	Lysine
Met	Methionine
Phe	Phenylalanine
Pro	Proline
Ser	Serine
Thr	Threonine
Trp	Tryptophan
Tyr	Tyrosine
Val	Valine

(b)

(4^2) combinations arise, and only 4 (4^1) codons are possible if one base equals one codon. Neither the doublet nor the singlet codon would be adequate to specify 20 amino acids.

Between 1961 and 1964 Nirenberg, Severo Ochoa, and others reported various studies where artificially synthesized RNAs were used in *in vitro* coding tests. These synthetic RNA polymers consisted of different proportions and kinds of the four ribonucleotides (U, A, C, G). About 50 codons were identified after statistical analysis of the experimental results. The composition of codons could be determined in this way, but not the sequence within the codons. For example, poly(UG) was found to be involved in coding for leucine, valine, and cysteine, since polypeptides containing these amino acids were formed when the synthetic RNA contained twice as many Us as Gs. There was no way, however, to show that UUG coded for leucine, GUU for valine, or UGU for cysteine.

These studies were very important in leading the way to deciphering the genetic code, and they provided a clear demonstration that all or most of the 64 possible triplet codons were part of the dictionary that spelled out amino acids in proteins. They further showed that an amino acid could be specified by more than one codon, since more than 50 triplets were used to code for only 20 amino acids.

By 1964 new methods had been invented by Nirenberg, H. G. Khorana, and others, who specified the sequence of three nucleotides in most of the codons. By 1967 the last of the 64 triplet codons had been deciphered. Of this group, 61 of the codons specified amino acids and the other 3 were stop signals marking termination of a gene message. These **terminator codons** are also called punctuation codons. Just as a genetic message has a terminus, so must there be a beginning or initiation signal for the first amino acid to be positioned in polypeptide synthesis. The RNA codon AUG is the major, and in some cases the only, **initiator codon**, as well as the codon which specifies methionine.

In summary, we have found the following features for the genetic code:

1. The code is **triplet**. Each codon consists of a unique combination of three nucleotides.

2. The code has **punctuations** (start and stop) which mark the limits of each genetic instruction.

3. Most amino acids are specified by more than one codon, that is, the code is degenerate. There are codon **synonyms** for 18 of the 20 amino acids included in the code. Only methionine and tryptophan are specified by a single codon.

4. The code is **consistent**, since each one of the 61 codons is specific for only one amino acid out of the set of twenty.

5. The code is **universal**. Studies using many different kinds of organisms among viruses, bacteria, and eukaryotes have all shown that the same codons are translated into the same amino acids in every case. The same initiating and terminating codons have been demonstrated in all organisms which have been studied.

Altogether there is an overwhelming amount of evidence to support the conclusion that all organisms share a common genetic code, from viruses to human beings. It is highly unlikely that each group of organisms happened to stumble on the same genetic code by accident or coincidence. The inescapable conclusion is that life forms at every level of complexity share a common ancestry and evolutionary history, as revealed in their genetic operations. We may further deduce that the present-day code must have been established early in evolution and continued virtually unchanged for the billions of years afterward.

6.6   Genetic Evidence for the Code

Independent evidence in support of the proposed genetic code came from genetic analysis, primarily through observations on the effects of mutations on proteins of known amino acid composition. By comparing the triplet codon proposed for the correct amino acid with possible codons specifying a substituted amino acid in a mutant polypeptide, it was clear that a change in one base in the codon was adequate to account for the amino acid difference.

One of the best examples of codon—amino acid correlations *in vivo* came from Yanofsky's analysis of the known amino acid alterations in the *trpA* polypeptide and the probable codon alterations at corresponding sites in the *trpA* gene (Fig. 6.17). Some of the most detailed correlations were found in changes at amino acid number 210, where glycine occurs in the wild type polypeptide chain. While mutant A23 has arginine at this site, mutant A46 has glutamic acid. Although there are four codons specifying glycine, the one codon which could give rise to either arginine or glutamic acid through a single base substitution is the DNA codon CCT. A change in the first base produces TCT, for arginine; a change in the middle base produces CTT, for glutamic acid:

CCT (wild type) *gly*

arg (Mutant A23) T**CT**   **C**TT (Mutant A46) *glu*

If this analysis is correct, any further mutational changes in the TCT codon of mutant A23 should give rise to revertants with the original glycine at site 210, and to others with partial or full enzyme activity restored because serine (TCG or TCA), threonine (TGT), or isoleucine (TAT) were present. Using mutation-inducing agents, Yanofsky found the predicted true revertant to wild type and the other three expected types, all with the predicted amino acid at site 210. Similar results were obtained in mutation induction studies for mutant A46 (Fig. 6.18).

Although the precise codon could not always be determined, since there are codon synonyms for all the amino acids involved in this particular study, the substituted amino acid could always be accounted for by a *single*

```
                                      AGx
     xUz  CAy  GGA  UUx  GGz  AUw  UCz  GCz  CCz  GAx  CAy  GUz
    Leu —Gln —Gly —Phe —Gly— Ile  — Ser— Ala—Pro— Asp— Gln— Val
                210

     AUw  GCz  GGz  GCz  GCz  GGz  GCz  GAx  AUw  GCz  GCz  AAy
    Ile  —Ala —Gly—Ala—Ala—Gly— Ala —Asp— Ile  —Ala—Ala—Lys
          230                                                220
    AGx
    UCz  GGx  UCz  GCz  AUw  GUz  AAy  AUw  AUw  GAy  CAy  CAx
    Ser —Gly —Ser—Ala— Ile —Val—Lys— Ile — Ile —Glu—Gln —His
                                        240
```

w = U, C, or A   x = U or C   y = A or G   z = U, C, A, or G

Figure 6.17   Part of the chain of 267 amino acids in tryptophan synthetase A in *E. coli*, including amino acids 208–243. The probable codon for each amino acid is shown in red. (After Yanofsky, C., *et al.*, 1967. *Proc. Nat. Acad. Sci. U. S.* **57**:296.)

base change in one codon. It appeared that the codons derived from biochemical studies were the same ones used in the living cell.

Alan Garen and co-workers studied the alkaline phosphatase gene and protein in *E. coli* to see whether one base change in a codon was responsible for observed mutations. One particular mutant made a shorter alkaline phosphatase polypeptide since the mutant codon specified "stop" instead of the amino acid tryptophan. When this premature-termination mutant was subjected to chemicals that caused base substitutions, new mutants were obtained as well as revertants to wild type (Fig. 6.19).

Seven different amino acid substitutions were found in these induced mutants. The revertant had tryptophan restored in the proper site in the polypeptide, and the other six strains had a different amino acid present instead of the termination codon. In every case, a single base substitution in the DNA codon could explain the newly-derived mutants if the termination codon were ATC (or UAG in the complementary RNA codon).

Figure 6.18   Revertants at amino acid site 210 in the *trpA* gene of *E. coli*. (a) The amino acid and its DNA codon in wild type, its derived mutants A23 and A46, and their induced revertants are shown. (b) The corresponding RNA codons of the genetic dictionary are shown, for each strain pictured in (a).

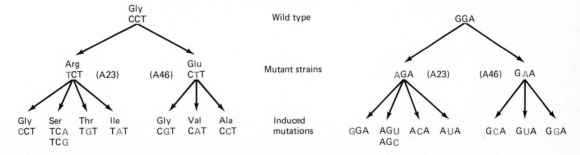

Amino acid substitutions and DNA codon changes proposed

(a)

RNA codons equivalent to altered DNA codons

(b)

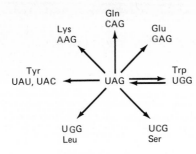

Figure 6.19 Codons arising by induced mutation at the termination codon UAG in *E. coli.* The probable single base substitution is indicated in red for each of the observed reverse mutants having an amino acid at the former termination site of the polypeptide.

These and other studies therefore showed that:

1. One base substitution in one codon was responsible for mutation, leading to a colinear modification of one amino acid site in the polypeptide.
2. Any one of the three bases could be altered by mutation, giving rise to different mutants whose altered codon caused polypeptide alterations.
3. The unit of mutation could be the minimum of one base change in one codon.

Mutants A23 and A46 provided another item of information about the gene in Yanofsky's *trpA* studies. When these two mutants were crossed, some wild type progeny were produced. These were shown to have glycine restored at site 210 in the polypeptide. How did these changes arise? The simplest explanation was that a crossover had occurred between the first and second bases of the codons (Fig. 6.20). The unit of recombination, therefore, could be the minimum distance represented by the space between two adjacent nucleotides in one codon. Benzer had also come to this conclusion in the *r*II mapping studies.

Figure 6.20 If a crossover occurs in *E. coli* between nucleotides in *trpA* DNA from mutant A23 × A46 so that a strand with the original CCT codon is produced, the amino acid glycine would be inserted in the protein at position 210 and the recombinant would show the wild type phenotype. The unit of recombination (sometimes called a *recon*) could be as small as the space between two adjacent nucleotides in a chain.

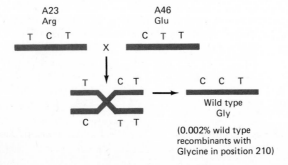

Through these kinds of genetic studies and others we have described, the concept of the gene as a linear sequence of nucleotides in DNA was strongly established. Mutations involving a single base substitution, or crossing over within a codon, could give rise to new genotypes specifying new phenotypes in the organism. Alterations in DNA or its RNA copy gave rise to amino acid changes at corresponding sites along the length of the colinear polypeptide product of the gene. The molecular concept of the gene and its product changed our views of the chromosome, the gene, and the nature of the relationship between the gene and its polypeptide product.

6.7   Readout of the Genetic Message

The genetic message is a coded sequence of DNA which specifies the amino acid sequence of a polypeptide. The message has a beginning and an end, and it is read *in sequence* from the start to the finish of the instruction, codon by codon. The instructions in DNA are copied into a complementary messenger RNA molecule, from which the codons can be translated into amino acids in the polypeptide product:

$$\text{DNA} \xrightarrow{\text{transcription}} \text{messenger RNA} \xrightarrow{\text{translation}} \text{polypeptide}$$

Genetic evidence for the sequential reading of the genetic message, that is, for the existence of a **reading frame**, was obtained by Crick and co-workers in England, using phage T4 mutants.

They exposed T4 to a chemical agent which was believed to cause mutations by its action in adding or deleting single base-pairs in the DNA sequence. The mutant strain "FCO" obtained by these treatments of wild type phage could be recognized by altered plaque morphology. The FCO mutant was then exposed to the same mutagenic agent, and wild-type revertants were sought and found. When the original wild type T4 and the revertant wild type were crossed, it was discovered that the two strains could produce recombinants with mutant plaque morphology. If these had been truly wild type revertants, there should have been only wild type progeny and no segregants. It was therefore obvious that the apparent revertant was a **pseudowild** (mimicking wild type) strain and not a true reverse mutant to the original wild type. The events were interpreted to mean that the pseudowild strain had both the original mutation and another base change at a different site in the same gene. FCO and other segregants could arise by crossing over between these two mutant sites in the gene (Fig. 6.21).

If the genetic message is read consecutively from a point of origin to the end, then we can explain the FCO mutant and its pseudowild derivative. Suppose a base had been deleted in the FCO mutant, and the reading frame shifted so the rest of the message was garbled (Fig. 6.22). If the second mutation were due to a base addition, the reading frame would be restored and a functional protein produced. There would be some remaining garble in the region between the two mutant sites in the gene, but it might not

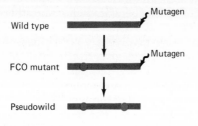

Wild type

FCO mutant

Pseudowild

Figure 6.21 When the induced FCO mutant was itself treated with a mutagen, some of its progeny appeared to be wild type phenotypically. Upon crossing these apparent wild types (pseudowilds) with true wild types, mutant recombinants may be produced as a consequence of crossing over between genetically different DNAs. Crosses between true wild types will yield only wild type progeny.

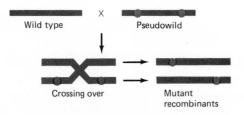

affect protein function if there were relatively few amino acids affected in this block. The **polarity** in message readout demonstrated by these and other T4 mutants was most easily interpreted to mean that there was a genetic reading frame with a particular origin from which the readout began.

George Streisinger and others provided proof that such **frameshift mutations** were responsible for mutants and pseudowild strains in the case of the lysozyme protein in T4. The complete amino acid sequence is known for this enzyme, which digests bacterial cell walls. In one pseudowild strain, the enzyme was found to have a cluster of five amino acids that differed from those in the wild type enzyme (Fig. 6.23). This was interpreted in terms of the effects of base deletion and base addition on the reading frame. As

Figure 6.22 Restoration of the genetic reading frame in a pseudowild mutant. (a) Deletion of a base in wild type DNA alters the reading frame, as shown in (b). If a base is added near the one originally deleted, the reading frame is restored, as shown in pseudowild DNA in (c). The message readout has **polarity** (readout begins at a particular origin and proceeds in a particular direction).

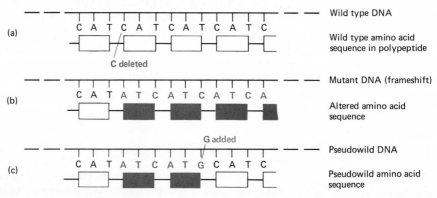

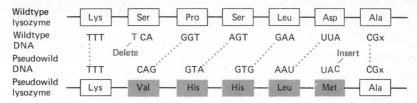

Figure 6.23 Frameshift mutations in phage T4. The difference in five amino acids (red) in the lysozyme protein of a pseudowild mutant compared with wild type is explained most easily by a compensating deletion and insertion of single bases into this part of the genetic reading frame. (After Streisinger, G. *et al*. 1967. *Cold Spring Harbor Sympos. Quant. Biol.* **31** (1966): 77.)

Crick had predicted, a small part of the pseudowild protein contained a small number of altered amino acids in a block, representing the remaining garble between the site of the original codon change and the changed codon in the pseudowild mutation event. The amino acids on both sides of the remaining garbled region were identical in wild type and in pseudowild proteins. The reading frame was altered only in between the two mutant codons in the pseudowild strain.

Direct verification of the colinear translation of codons in the gene into amino acids in a polypeptide came in 1977, using a gene which had been synthesized in the laboratory. It served as the template for making a specific polypeptide coded by this gene. Using available methods to put together specific nucleotides in a specific sequence of triplet codons, a gene was synthesized to correspond with the known sequence of amino acids in a precursor of the mammalian hormone **somatostatin** (Fig. 6.24). The precursor is biologically inactive but is processed into the 14 amino acid-long hormone, which is an inhibitor of secretion of a certain number of other hormones, including insulin. Somatostatin therefore has therapeutic value in relation to disorders such as insulin-dependent diabetes.

The synthesized gene for the hormone precursor was spliced into a segment of *E. coli* DNA and the entire complex was incorporated into *E. coli* cells by transformation. After protein synthesis had taken place, the whole protein complex was isolated and treated *in vitro* to cleave the active somatostatin molecule from the rest of the material. The hormone was then shown to have biological activity by *in vivo* tests.

There is no doubt whatsoever that DNA stores information in coded form, and that this coded information provides the blueprint for making a specific polypeptide. The polypeptide function is determined by the kinds of amino acids and their sequence in the linear molecule.

SEQUENCE ANALYSIS OF THE GENE

Most of the information accumulated about the nucleotide sequence in the gene itself was inferred from studies of natural and artificial messenger RNAs and from amino acid sequences in the polypeptide product. Very little was known directly from DNA sequencing because the available methods

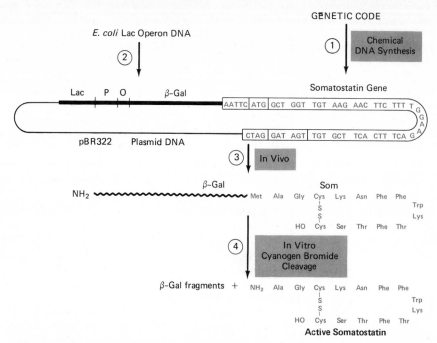

Figure 6.24 Schematic outline of the experimental plan. The somatostatin gene was synthesized in the laboratory and spliced to the *Lac* gene of *E. coli* on an episome (plasmid DNA) so transformation could be achieved. After transformation, the whole protein was cleaved *in vitro* by cyanogen bromide to yield the active mammalian hormone consisting of 14 amino acids. (From Itakura, K., *et al.* 1977. *Science* **198**:1056.)

were tedious, enormously time-consuming, and very limited. Beginning in the mid-1970s, new and unexpected kinds of information began to accumulate from studies of messenger RNAs, and these data were confirmed when new methods became available in 1977 to sequence DNA itself, rapidly and accurately (Box 6.1). Once again, our notion of the gene is undergoing a dramatic change as more sequencing data are published. We will examine some of these studies now, and continue in the following chapters.

6.8 DNA Genomes

The first hints were obtained in the mid-1970s that the sequence of nucleotides in the gene was not identical to the messenger RNA which was actually translated into a polypeptide product of the gene. When messenger RNA (mRNA) was isolated just after its transcription from the gene, the molecule was usually found to be very much longer than the mRNA isolated from systems in which polypeptides were being made. In other words, it appeared as though a larger mRNA was made first, as a complementary copy of the genetic instruction, and was later processed into a smaller molecule which then guided translation into a polypeptide. If the freshly

Box 6.1
GEL ELECTROPHORESIS

Molecules or homogenates from cells or tissues are placed in a gel made of some substance which provides a homogeneous matrix, such as starch or polyacrylamide. The gel is permeated with a buffered aqueous solution, and the biological materials move in an electrical field toward the positive or negative pole, depending on their net charge. By varying factors selectively it is possible to achieve separations differing only slightly in their electrical charge and within a useful range of molecular sizes. Afterward the gel can be stained with a dye to make the bands or spots visible, or scanned with ultraviolet light and its absorbance plotted, or placed in a solution with an appropriate substrate to assay enzyme activities of variant forms. In addition, autoradiographs can be made of polypeptides, polynucleotides, or other molecules labeled with isotopes such as ^{32}P or ^{14}C, and subjected to electrophoresis in slab gels molded paper thin, dried, and applied to film for later development showing sites of radioactivity in the sample.

(a) Tracing made of stained–gel absorbance plot, showing different size RNA molecules resolved from a mixture. Molecular size is proportional to distance the molecules have migrated in the electrical field.

(b) Autoradiograph showing ^{32}P-labeled restriction fragment of DNA sequenced by one of the current rapid sequencing methods. Slab gel electrophoresis was carried out.

(c) Separation of variant forms of an enzyme by gel electrophoresis. The spots of each sample have been made visible through reaction of the enzyme with substrate and a suitable dye marker of the reaction.

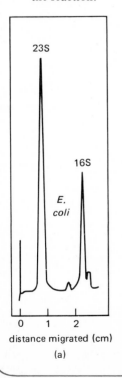

(a)

(b)

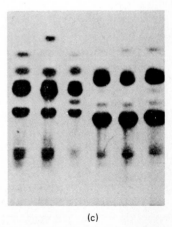

(c)

made mRNA were a longer molecule, the gene from which it was copied must also be larger than was supposed from previous analyses of polypeptide chains and from mRNA undergoing translation. *There must therefore be non-coding sequences in the gene itself.* These non-coding segments of the gene must be excised from the messenger after transcription, so that a *spliced messenger RNA* is the finished transcript molecule which acts as the colinear instruction in translation into polypeptide.

Verification of these interpretations was provided only after it became

Figure 6.25 The Maxam-Gilbert procedure for DNA sequencing. (a) A pure preparation of DNA, such as a particular restriction fragment, is labeled enzymatically with ^{32}P at the 5′ ends of both strands (black squares). The duplex strands are separated into two single-strand fractions, one of which (the "heavy" fraction) is sequenced. (b) The fraction of single strands is divided into four portions and each portion is treated specifically to give a pattern for G>A, A>G, C+T, or C, that is, to identify every G in one fraction, every A in another, every G and every C in the remaining two portions. Each treatment generates fragments (designated 1-12), and all the 5′ ends can be identified autoradiographically by ^{32}P presence (shown as black square). In G>A and A>G the break positions only are shown for each fragment remaining after treatment; for C+T and C the break positions are shown by a red mark on each fragment as it occurs before breaking.) (c) By comparison of the four autoradiographic patterns of fragments separated in gels by electrophoresis, the DNA sequence can be determined directly, as shown.

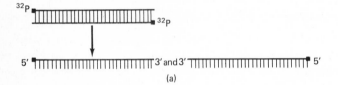

(a)

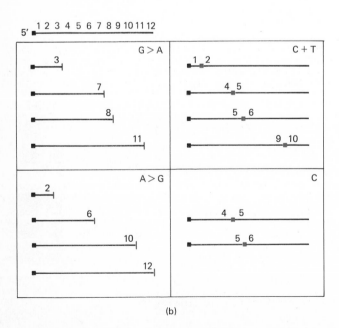

(b)

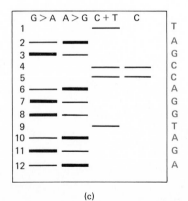

(c)

possible to sequence DNA, beginning in 1977. Using **restriction endonucleases** to chop up a DNA molecule precisely, the individual nucleotides
can be quickly determined for each fragment, in correct sequence, and all
these sequenced fragments can then be put together to find the precise
nucleotide sequence of the whole gene (Fig. 6.25). What might have taken
years to accomplish earlier could now be accomplished in days.

Studies of specific genes, such as those specifying α- and β-chains of
mammalian hemoglobin, or ovalbumin in the chicken, have shown that
there are non-coding regions interspersed among coding regions in a single
gene (Fig. 6.26). In these cases, one can sequence DNA in the gene, and RNA
codons in the newly transcribed messenger and in the final processed
messenger, and compare these with the known amino acid composition and
sequence in the polypeptide. The fact that many (all?) eukaryotic genes
have both coding and non-coding segments in their sequences of nucleotides has led to the view of **"genes-in-pieces."** The phenomenon occurs
in viruses which infect eukaryotic cells, such as simian virus 40 (SV 40), and
in various eukaryotic species, but not in prokaryotes or their viruses. The significance of this pattern of gene construction is under active investigation.

Another astonishing discovery from DNA sequencing in the last few
years was the existence of **overlapping genes**, first reported in SV40 and
in the *E. coli* phage ϕX174, after the entire genome had been sequenced (Fig.
6.27). In both of these DNA viruses there is at least one nucleotide sequence
in which a smaller gene is contained *entirely* within a larger gene. In ϕX174,
the complete gene for E protein is contained within the D gene region. In
SV40, there is an even more unusual situation involving two related
proteins, T antigen and t antigen. Both the *T* gene and the *t* gene have the
same codon origin at nucleotide 80 in the genome made up of 5,224 base
pairs (Box 6.2).

Figure 6.26 "Genes-in-pieces" is a revolutionary new concept of genetic organization
in eukaryotes and their viruses. The gene contains interspersed coding and noncoding
segments, all of which is transcribed into a precursor of messenger RNA (pre-mRNA).
The noncoding sequences of pre-mRNA are excised precisely and the remaining pieces
are spliced together precisely to yield the mature mRNA from part of which translation
into polypeptide occurs.

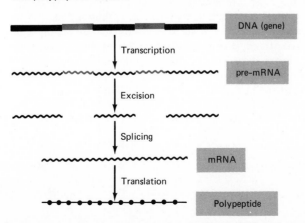

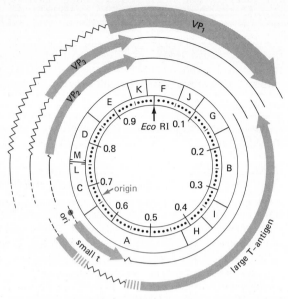

Figure 6.27 Standard physical map of simian virus 40 (SV40) showing the single break site for the restriction enzyme *Eco* RI in this duplex DNA molecule, used as a reference point for the map. The point of origin of DNA replication is indicated at position 0.663. The five virus-coded proteins are indicated relative to the parts of the map where they are coded: small t and large T-antigen overlap completely; virus proteins (VP) 1-3 also overlap completely with each other on the DNA map. The only portions of the genes translated into amino acids in these proteins are shown by thick gray arrows. The untranslated parts of the pre-mRNA are shown by thin lines and the segments excised from pre-mRNA are shown as wavy lines. The arrows point in the direction of genetic readout. (After Fiers, W., *et al.* 1978. *Nature* **273**:113.)

Box 6.2
DNA SEQUENCE INFORMATION

In most published reports of DNA sequences, the noncoding strand of DNA is the only information given. It is actually the most informative sequence possible, if a single strand is to be shown. By deducing the complementary bases one can derive the coding strand of DNA in the appropriate 3' to 5' orientation from which messenger RNA is transcribed. By simply changing all T to U in the printed noncoding DNA strand, one reads off directly the messenger RNA sequence in the correct 5' to 3' orientation. From such deduced mRNA codons, one knows the amino acids and their sequence in the polypeptide translation, from the amino-terminus to the carboxy-terminus of the chain, according to the standard coding dictionary (See Fig. 6.16).

3'	TAC	CTA	TTT	CAA	AAT	TTG	TCT	CTC	CTT	AGA	5'	Coding strand of DNA
5'	ATG	GAT	AAA	GTT	TTA	AAC	AGA	GAG	GAA	TCT	3'	Noncoding strand of DNA
5'	AUG	GAU	AAA	GUU	UUA	AAC	AGA	GAG	GAA	UCU	3'	mRNA transcript

H_2N — Met — Asp — Lys — Val — Leu — Asn — Arg — Glu — Glu — Ser • COOH   Polypeptide translation

t antigen is 174 amino acids long. Its reading frame begins at nucleotide 80 and continues until the terminator codon ATT (UAA in the RNA complementary codon) at position 602 of the genome. It seems that the 80 ⟶ 602 region contains only coded DNA, so *t* gene and *t* protein are truly colinear throughout their lengths. On the other hand, *T* gene, which also begins at nucleotide 80, is read in the same frame until about the middle of

Figure 6.28 Part of the genome of SV40, containing sequences coding for t and T antigens. (a) The *anticoding DNA strand* is shown here, proceeding from the 5′ to the 3′ end. To read off RNA codons as they would occur in the mRNA or pre-mRNA molecule it is only necessary to change T to U and retain all other bases as given. The initiator RNA codon AUG appears here as ATG (boxed) and the terminator codon UAA appears here as TAA (boxed). The same initiator codon serves for both t and T antigens, beginning at nucleotide 80. The terminator codon for t begins at nucleotide 602, and for T at nucleotide 2550. (b) The complete amino acid sequence of the 174 residues in t antigen. This can be compared with codons appearing between nucleotides 80 and 601, above in (a). (From Fiers, W., *et al.* 1978. *Nature* 273:113.)

```
CGCCTCGGCCTCTGAGCTATTCCAGAAGTAGTGAGGAGGCTTTTTTGGAGGCCTAGGCTTT
            10              20            30          40            50              60
      Hind C↓A
TGCAAAAAGCTTTGCAAAG ATG GATAAAGTTTTAAACAGAGAGGAATCTTTGCAGCTAAT
        70              80            90            100          110              120

GGACCTTCTAGGTCTTGAAAGGAGTGCCTGGGGGAATATTCCTCTGATGAGAAAGGCATA
      130              140            150          160          170              180

TTTAAAAAAATGCAAGGAGTTTCATCCTGATAAAGGAGGAGATGAAGAAAAAATGAAGAA
      190              200            210          220          230              240

AATGAATACTCTGTACAAGAAAATGGAAGATGGAGTAAAATATGCTCATCAACCTGACTT
      250              260            270          280          290              300

TGGAGGCTTCTGGGATGCAACTGAGGTATTTGCTTCTTCCTTAAATCCTGGTGTTGATGC
      310              320            330          340          350              360

AATGTACTGCAAACAATGGCCTGAGTGTGTGCAAAGAAAATGTCTGCTAACTGCATATGCTT
      370              380            390          400          410              420

GCTGTGCTTACTGAGGATGAAGCATGAAAATAGAAAATTATACAGGAAAGATCCACTTGT
      430              440            450          460          470              480

GTGGGTTGATTGCTACTGCTTCGATTGCTTTAGAATGTGGTTTGGACTTGATCTTTGTGA
      490              500            510          520          530              540

AGGAACCTTACTTCTGTGGTGTGACATAATTGGACAAACTACCTACAGAGATTTAAAGCT
      550              560            570          580          590              600

C TAA GGTAAATATAAAATTTTTAAGTGTATAATGTGTTAAACTACTGATTCTAATTGTTT
      610              620            630          640          650              660

GTGTATTTTAGATTCCAACCTATGGAACTGATGAATGGGAGCAGTGGTGGAATGCCTTTA
      670              680            690          700          710              720

ATGAAACAGGCATTGATTCACAGTCCCAAGGCTCATTTCAGGCCCCTCAGTCCTCACAGT
    2410            2420                      2440

CTGTTCATGATCATAATCAGCCATACCACATTGTAGAGGTTTTACTTGCTTTAAAAAAC
    2470            2480
                                                        Hind B↓
CTCCCACACCTCCCCCTGAACCTGAAACA TAA AATGAATGCAATTGTTGTTGTT ...3′
    2530            2540            2560            2580
```

MET-ASP-LYS-VAL-LEU-ASN-ARG-GLU-GLU-SER-LEU-GLN-LEU-MET-ASP-LEU-LEU-GLY-LEU-GLU- 20
ARG-SER-ALA-TRP-GLY-ASN-ILE-PRO-LEU-MET-ARG-LYS-ALA-TYR-LEU-LYS-LYS-CYS-LYS-GLU- 40
PHE-HIS-PRO-ASP-LYS-GLY-GLY-ASP-GLU-GLU-LYS-MET-LYS-LYS-MET-ASN-THR-LEU-TYR-LYS· 60
LYS-MET-GLU-ASP-GLY-VAL-LYS-TYR-ALA-HIS-GLN-PRO-ASP-PHE-GLY-GLY-PHE-TRP-ASP-ALA- 80
THR-GLU-VAL-PHE-ALA-SER-SER-LEU-ASN-PRO-GLY-VAL-ASP-ALA-MET-TYR-CYS-LYS-GLN-TRP-100
PRO-GLU-CYS-ALA-LYS-LYS-MET-SER-ALA-ASN-CYS-ILE-CYS-LEU-LEU-CYS-LEU-LEU-ARG-MET-120
LYS-HIS-GLU-ASN-ARG-LYS-LEU-TYR-ARG-LYS-ASP-PRO-LEU-VAL-TRP-VAL-ASP-CYS-TYR-CYS-140
PHE-ASP-CYS-PHE-ARG-MET-TRP-PHE-GLY-LEU-ASP-LEU-CYS-GLU-GLY-THR-LEU-LEU-LEU-TRP-160
CYS-ASP-ILE-ILE-GLY-GLN-THR-THR-TYR-ARG-ASP-LEU-LYS-LEU
                                                          174

the *t* region. At this point, there is a switchover (at about nucleotide 280) and the rest of the *T* gene continues in a different reading frame, until nucleotide 2550 when the ATT stop-codon appears. The end result is that both genes share an initial segment of nucleotides, but that each readout continues within a different reading frame to yield two different proteins (Fig. 6.28). The *T* gene has a non-coding segment at the switchover region. The T antigen which is made, therefore, is translated from a spliced messenger RNA, which is made after non-coding regions have been excised in the original mRNA transcript and the coding regions have been joined together in the final mRNA molecule. We will explore these phenomena in more detail in Chapter 8.

6.9   RNA Genomes

DNA is the genetic material in all eukaryotes and prokaryotes, and in many viruses. Some viruses, however, have RNA as their genetic material and no DNA is present in the infective particle. The first convincing evidence for RNA genomes was obtained by Heinz Fraenkel-Conrat and Beatrice Singer in 1957, using tobacco mosaic virus (TMV). TMV contains RNA wrapped in a protein coat, but no DNA.

Fraenkel-Conrat and Singer separated the TMV protein coat and the single strand of RNA by simple and gentle means from four strains which differed slightly in their proteins and in the nature of the lesions produced during infection of tobacco plants. They then reconstituted "hybrid" TMV using protein from one strain and RNA from another, in various combinations.

If RNA was the genetic material in TMV, the lesions of plants infected with reconstituted viruses should resemble infections produced by the RNA source and not those typical of the protein source in the "hybrid" particles (Fig. 6.29). This prediction was verified in every case. In addition, progeny viruses contained RNA like that of the parental RNA source, and their protein had an amino acid composition that also was typical of the original parental RNA strain. New viruses received their inherited characteristics, therefore, according to RNA rather than protein. RNA was the genetic material in TMV and, by extension, in other RNA viruses as well.

A number of RNA viruses have since been studied, including those which infect bacteria and various eukaryotic host species (see Table 2.3). The first RNA virus to have its genome completely sequenced was phage MS2, in 1976. The RNA phages are the smallest viruses known, containing only three genes. These code for: (1) an RNA polymerase, which is the replication enzyme; (2) a protein (A protein) needed for the RNA genome to bind to host protein-synthesizing machinery; and (3) the coat protein (CP). The three coded genetic regions are separated by non-coding sequences of ribonucleotides, and there are untranslated sequences at both ends of the genome. The *CP* gene sequence has been checked by comparison with the known amino acid sequence of the purified coat protein.

There is another class of RNA infectious agents called **viroids**. These are naked RNA molecules lacking any other associated molecules in their

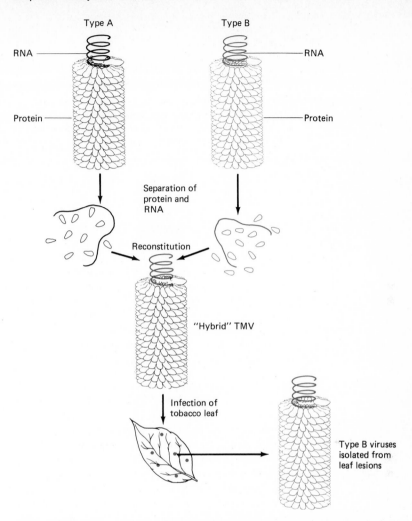

Figure 6.29 Scheme illustrating the TMV reconstitution experiments of Fraenkel-Conrat and Singer. When "hybrid" tobacco mosaic virus particles infected tobacco leaves, the lesions of infected leaves resembled those produced by Type B virus, from which the RNA had come in the reconstituted TMV particles. Afterward, type B viruses were isolated from infected leaves, showing that RNA was the genetic material in TMV. guiding RNA and protein synthesis.

construction. In 1978, Hans Gross, Heinz Sänger, and co-workers published the entire sequence of 359 ribonucleotides in the closed circular genome of potato spindle tuber viroid (PSTV). Although the primary sequence of nucleotides conforms to a closed circle, hydrogen bonding between bases leads to a unique rod-shaped secondary structure of the circular genome. **Primary structure** refers to the nucleotide sequence alone, while **secondary structure** is a three-dimensional configuration of the molecule produced by bonding between nearby units in the primary structure (Fig. 6.30).

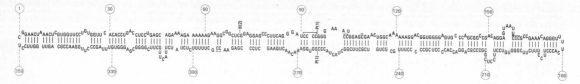

Figure 6.30 Part of the 359 ribonucleotides making up the genome of potato spindle tuber viroid (PSTV). Intramolecular hydrogen bonding, primarily between adenines and uracils and between guanines and cytosines, produces the rod-shaped secondary structure of a linear single strand of RNA. (After Gross, H. J., *et al.* 1978. Nature **273**: 203.)

The secondary structure of the viroid helps to explain many observed physical properties, particularly its high thermal stability. This appears to be due to the numerous hydrogen-bonded pairs of bases in the closed configuration. It is expected that comparisons between genomes of different viroids, and between viroids and viruses, will lead to a better understanding of their modes of infectious activity, and of the evolutionary relationship of viroids and viruses. At present, very little is known concerning the function of viroid RNA, or about the mechanism by which viroids cause diseases in plants, many of which are of great agricultural importance.

It almost seems as if we have come full circle in this chapter, from deducing gene structure and sequence according to RNA and polypeptides, to understanding the gene and genome construction without necessarily knowing anything at all about the gene products, as with PSTV and other viroids. Even if methods had been available to directly sequence DNA and RNA in the 1950s, little would have been learned from the efforts. The intervening period in the 1950s and 1960s provided the basic conceptual framework into which nucleotide sequencing studies could be placed in the 1970s. Through genetic and molecular analyses of DNA, RNA, and proteins, we have gained a firm handle on the interactions in the genetic system which lead to phenotype development. We will continue to explore the system in the chapters to follow.

QUESTIONS AND PROBLEMS

6.1. State the evidence supporting the principle that a change in phenotype is the result of a single amino acid substitution, at least in some proteins.

6.2. Three independently arising *rIIB* mutants are crossed in phage T4 and the following results are obtained:

Crosses	% Recombinants
rIIB2 × *rIIB1*	0
rIIB2 × *rIIB3*	0
rIIB1 × *rIIB3*	0.8

What is the nature of these three mutants? How are they related to each other?

6.3. Assume an average gene consisted of a linear sequence of 1000 bases and there were 2000 genes in a chromosome.

   a. How many *base-pairs* would such a chromosome contain in its duplex DNA?

   b. If 10 nucleotides measure 34 Å in length, how long would this chromosome be in centimeters (1 Å = 10^{-8} cm)?

6.4. If one DNA sample had a melting temperature (T_m) of 80°C and another sample showed a melting temperature of 88°C, what might you conclude about the base composition of the two samples?

6.5. Five deletion mutants within the *A* gene of the *rII* region of phage T4 were tested in all pairwise combinations for wild type recombinants, and gave the following results:

	1	2	3	4	5
1	0	0	0	0	0
2		0	0	0	0
3			0	+	0
4				0	+
5					0

0 = no recombination
+ = recombination

Construct a topological map for these deletions.

6.6. A number of mutations were found in the *rII* region of phage T4. From the recombination data shown in the table, determine whether each mutant is the result of a point mutational defect or a deletion. One of the four mutants has never been known to revert to wild type, while the other three have been observed to undergo reverse mutation. Draw a topological map to represent your interpretations.

	1	2	3	4
1	0	0	0	+
2		0	+	+
3			0	+
4				0

6.7. Suppose you were given two recessive mutants of *Drosophila*, claret eyes (*c*) and minute bristles (*mb*), both autosomal, both belonging to the same linkage group.

   a. What cross could you use to determine if *c* and *mb* are alleles?

   b. What F_1 phenotype would indicate allelism?

   c. Assuming allelism, what cross could you use to determine whether *c* and *mb* occupied the same or different sites within a gene locus?

   d. If the sites of *c* and *mb* were 0.1 map units apart, how many flies must you collect in progeny in order to recover 1 wild type recombinant?

6.8. An analysis of a protein shows that four mutants contain an amino acid substitution at the site normally occupied by glycine. The origin of these mutants is:

$$Gly \nearrow^{Val \rightarrow Met\text{-}1}_{\searrow Arg \rightarrow Met\text{-}2}$$

Assign the respective codons to each mutant and to the wild type strain.

6.9. A peptide was isolated containing only 4 amino acids: valine, alanine, serine, and histidine. After partial degradation, 3 kinds of dipeptides were recovered: Val-Ala, Val-His, and Ser-His. What is the amino acid sequence in the peptide?

6.10. After treatment with the mutagen nitrous acid, phage T4 produced mottled plaques (a consequence of the coexistence of two genetically different viruses in the same plaque) while ϕX174 viruses gave only non-mottled plaques on a lawn of *E. coli* cells. What do these results suggest with regard to DNA structure of the two phages?

6.11. There are tumorigenic DNA viruses known in the mouse. A scientist obtained a pure extract of virus DNA, a pure preparation of DNA extracted from mouse tumor cells, and pure DNA from normal mouse cells. When the scientist conducted molecular hybridization tests using these three sources of DNA, the viral DNA was found to hybridize with the cancer-cell DNA but not with DNA from the normal mouse cells. Explain the significance of this result from the genetical, molecular, and medical points of view.

6.12. Diagram the pattern of bands obtained in the gel for the sequence of a piece of single-stranded DNA which is 5'-G C C A T T T A A C G T-3', if the Maxam-Gilbert method is used.

6.13. The base composition and base ratios of nucleic acids from 8 different viruses are given below. For each of these viruses indicate whether the nucleic acid is DNA or RNA, and whether these molecules are single- or double-stranded. Explain in each case.

Virus	G	C	A	T	U	A+T or U / G+C	A+G / C+T or U
1	19	19	31	31			
2	19	19	31		31		
3	31	31	19	19			
4						1.00	1.26
5	25	18	25	32			
6	20	25	23		32		
7						1.26	1.00
8						1.00	1.00

REFERENCES

Benzer, S. 1961. On the topography of the genetic fine structure. *Proc. Nat. Acad. Sci. U. S.* **47**:403.

Bunn, H. F., B. G. Forget, and H. M. Ranney, (eds.). 1977. *Human Hemoglobins.* Philadelphia: Saunders.

Catterall, J. F., B. W. O'Malley, M. A. Robertson, R. Staden, Y. Tanaka, and G. G. Brownlee. 1978. Nucleotide sequence homology at the 12 intron-exon junctions in the chick ovalbumin gene. *Nature* **275**:510.

Chargaff, E. 1951. Structure and function of nucleic acids as cell constituents. *Fed. Proc.* **10**:654.

Cohen, S. N. July 1975. The manipulation of genes. *Sci. Amer.* **233**:24.

Crick, F. H. C., L. Barnett, S. Brenner, and R. J. Watts-Tobin. 1961. General nature of the genetic code for proteins. *Nature* **192**:1227.

Adams, R. L. P., R. H. Burdon, A. M. Campbell, and R. M. S. Smellie. 1976. Davidson's *The Biochemistry of the Nucleic Acids*, 8th ed. New York: Academic Press.

Fiddes, J. C. Dec. 1977. The nucleotide sequence of a viral DNA. *Sci. Amer.* **237**:54.

Fiddes, J. C., and G. N. Godson. 1978. Nucleotide sequence of the J gene and surrounding untranslated regions of phage G4 DNA: Comparison with phage ϕX174. *Cell* **15**:1045.

Fiers, W. *et al.* 1978. Complete nucleotide sequence of SV40 DNA. *Nature* **273**:113.

Fraenkel-Conrat, H. Oct. 1964. The genetic code of a virus. *Sci. Amer.* **211**:46.

Fraenkel-Conrat, H., and B. Singer. 1957. Virus reconstitution: combination of protein and nucleic acid from different strains. *Biochim. Biophys. Acta* **24**:540.

Garber, E. D., and M. S. Esposito. 1978. Defining the gene by mutation, recombination, and function. In *Cell Biology, A Comprehensive Treatise* (L. Goldstein and D. M. Prescott, eds.), Vol. 1, p. 1.

Garen, A. 1968. Sense and nonsense in the genetic code. *Science* **160**:149.

Goeddel, D. V. *et al.* 1979. Expression in *Escherichia coli* of chemically synthesized genes for human insulin. *Proc. Nat. Acad. Sci. U. S.* **76**:106.

Gross, H. J., H. Domdey, C. Lossow, P. Jank, M. Raba, and H.

Alberty. 1978. Nucleotide sequence and secondary structure of potato spindle tuber viroid. *Nature* **273**:203.

Ingram, V. I. Jan. 1958. How do genes act? *Sci. Amer.* **198**:68.

Itakura, K. *et al.* 1977. Expression in *Escherichia coli* of a chemically synthesized gene for the hormone somatostatin. *Science* **198**:1056.

Khorana, H. G. 1979. Total synthesis of a gene. *Science* **203**:614.

Little, P. F. R., R. A. Flavell, J. M. Kooter, G. Annison, and R. Williamson. 1979. Structure of the human fetal globin gene locus. *Nature* **278**:227.

Maxam, A. M., and W. Gilbert. 1977. A new method for sequencing DNA. *Proc. Nat. Acad. Sci. U. S.* **74**:560.

Meselson, M., and F. W. Stahl. 1958. The replication of DNA in *E. coli. Proc. Nat. Acad. Sci. U. S.* **44**:671.

Mirsky, A. E. June 1968. The discovery of DNA. *Sci. Amer.* **218**:78.

Nirenberg, M. W. Mar. 1963. The genetic code. II. *Sci. Amer.* **208**:80.

Nirenberg, M. W., and P. Leder. 1964. RNA code words and protein synthesis. *Science* **145**:1399.

Nirenberg, M. W., and J. H. Matthaei. 1961. The dependence of cell-free protein synthesis in *E. coli* upon naturally occurring or synthetic polyribonucleotides. *Proc. Nat. Acad. Sci.* **47**:1588.

Olby, R. 1974. *The Path to the Double Helix.* Seattle: Univ. Washington Press.

Raacke, I. D. 1971. *Molecular Biology of DNA and RNA. An Analysis of Research Papers.* St. Louis: Mosby.

Reddy, V. B. *et al.* 1978. The genome of Simian virus 40. *Science* **200**:494.

Sanger, F., *et al.* 1977. Nucleotide sequence of bacteriophage ϕX174 DNA. *Nature* **265**:687.

Sarabhai, A. S., A. O. W. Stretton, S. Brenner, and A. Bolle. 1967. Colinearity of gene with the polypeptide chain. *Nature* **201**:14.

Sasisekharan, V., N. Pattabiraman, and G. Gupta. 1978. Some implications of an alternative structure for DNA. *Proc. Nat. Acad. Sci. U. S.* **75**:4092.

Smith, M. 1979. The first complete nucleotide sequencing of an organism's DNA. *Amer. Sci.* **67**:57.

Taylor, J. H. 1965. Distribution of tritium-labeled DNA among chromosomes during meiosis. I. Spermatogenesis in the grasshopper. *J. Cell Biol.* **25**:57.

Watson, J. D., and F. H. C. Crick. 1953. A structure for deoxyribose nucleic acid. *Nature* **171**:737.

Watson, J. D., and F. H. Crick. 1953. Genetical implications of the structure of deoxyribonucleic acid. *Nature* **171**:964.

Wilkins, M. H. F., A. R. Stokes, and H. R. Wilson. 1953. Molecular structure of deoxypentose nucleic acids. *Nature* **171**:738.

Yanofsky, C. May 1967. Gene structure and protein structure. *Sci. Amer.* **216**:80.

Yanofsky, C., G. R. Drapeau, J. R. Guest, and B. C. Carlton. 1967. The complete amino acid sequence of the tryptophan synthetase A protein (α subunit) and its colinear relationship with the genetic map of the A gene. *Proc. Nat. Acad. Sci. U. S.* **57**:296.

The Molecular Nature of the Genome

The double helix model of DNA stimulated many kinds of studies of genetic phenomena from a molecular perspective. Different features of the model were immediately open to experimental tests, including the proposed mode of replication in which each parental strand of a duplex acted as a template for the synthesis of a complementary partner. This semiconservative process of DNA replication was experimentally verified in all life forms tested. A variety of enzymes cooperate to ensure the highest degree of accuracy in replicating all the genetic information needed for growth and development in every cell generation.

Recombination has been studied from a molecular viewpoint, but many aspects of the molecular mechanisms remain to be established. It has been shown that recombination arises by crossing over at the level of the DNA molecule, and that it involves many of the same enzymes which serve in replication. These enzymes catalyze DNA repair-synthesis reactions by which breakage and reunion of homologous DNAs lead to recombination. There are some differences in the details of prokaryotic, viral, and eukaryotic recombination mechanisms, since crossing over gives rise to reciprocal recombinants in eukaryotes but not in viruses or prokaryotes. Chiasma formation must be explained in any eukaryotic mechanism. Most models of recombination invoke the formation of heteroduplex DNA recombination intermediates, which arise by enzymatically catalyzed reactions and are processed into recombinant molecules.

Chromosomal DNA in the eukaryotic chromosome is organized as a single duplex molecule in association with histones and other proteins. The nucleosome is a repeating subunit of the chromatin fiber, with DNA coiled around the outside of all the nucleosomes, from one end of the chromosome to the other. Chromosomal DNA is heterogeneous in composition and in functions, and much of it apparently has no coding function.

DNA REPLICATION

Watson and Crick had suggested that each strand of duplex DNA might act as a template for making a new complementary partner strand, yielding two identical duplexes from one parental double-helix molecule. Strand separation does not require enzymatic action, and hydrogen bonds can be made and broken rather easily in the cell. Breaking of these bonds would lead to separation of the two strands, and new hydrogen bonds would act to keep the new partner strand associated with its template as replication progressed.

It all seems very simple when stated in this way. The demonstration of this mode of replication came within five years of Watson and Crick's suggestion in 1953. The rest of the story is still unfolding. An ever increasing number of genes and gene products has been found to act in DNA replication, each one required for a specific step in DNA synthesis along a template. The current view includes a complicated set of processes, all or most of which are set in motion by the requirement for high fidelity in making accurate, exact copies of all the genes in the genome, in every cell generation, in every organism throughout time.

7.1   Semiconservative Replication

The particular mode of replication suggested by Watson and Crick is called **semiconservative replication**, in which each partner strand of the duplex acts as a template directing synthesis of a new complementary strand. The new duplexes are composed of one parental and one newly synthesized strand; that is, the original duplex is partly conserved, or semi-conserved, in the new molecule. This idea was compelling, but it initially lacked experimental support. In fact, two other possible modes of replication were suggested soon afterward: conservative replication and dispersive replication. In **conservative replication**, the original duplex remains intact; that is, it is entirely conserved, and the whole duplex guides the synthesis of a completely new duplex replica of itself. In **dispersive replication**, bits and pieces of newly synthesized DNA become assembled with bits and pieces of the original duplex to reconstitute two duplexes from one original template (Fig. 7.1).

In 1958, Matthew Meselson and Franklin Stahl provided elegant and very convincing evidence in support of the semiconservative mode. Using **equilibrium density gradient centrifugation** to separate DNAs in cesium chloride (CsCl) gradients, Meselson and Stahl designed their experiments so that the possible results would match only one of the three different sets of predictions made for the three possible modes of replication.

The *E. coli* cultures had been grown in nutrient media containing the heavy isotope ^{15}N, so that both strands of all their DNA were labeled when the experiment began. These [^{15}N] cells were afterward transferred to media containing ordinary ^{14}N. After one generation during which cells and their DNA had doubled, the DNA was extracted and centrifuged to equilibrium in CsCl. Molecules with ^{15}N were heavier than [^{14}N] DNA and settled at

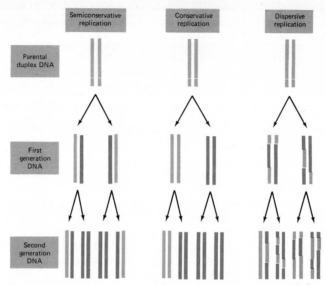

Figure 7.1   Three possible modes of duplex DNA replication. The predicted distribution of original parental strands (black) and newly synthesized strands (red) are shown for two rounds of replication.

equilibrium in a part of the gradient that corresponded to their buoyant density in CsCl (Fig. 7.2). During cell doubling only ^{14}N would be available for synthesis of new DNA (and other substances), since the bacteria had been transferred to unlabeled media at the start of the experiment. Any original DNA or parts of such DNA would retain the ^{15}N label incorporated before the experimental doubling interval.

The predictions based on the three modes of replication were that different amounts of ^{15}N and ^{14}N would be present in first-generation DNA. Because all these DNAs would have different and nonoverlapping buoyant densities in CsCl, their N contents could be determined by the positions occupied by DNAs in the gradient. If replication were semiconservative, all first-generation DNA duplexes would have one strand of original ^{15}N-containing bases while the other strand would be newly synthesized from ^{14}N-containing precursors present in the unlabeled medium. Such ^{15}N-^{14}N duplexes would be half-heavy (half as much ^{15}N as in fully labeled DNA). According to conservative replication, 50% of the molecules would be fully labeled, or heavy (^{15}N-^{15}N), representing the original conserved duplexes, and 50% would be unlabeled, or light (^{14}N-^{14}N), representing the new duplexes made in unlabeled medium. Dispersive replication was predicted to produce DNA with varying amounts of original [^{15}N] bases and newly made [^{14}N] bases, depending on how the bits and pieces of original and new DNA might assemble in a duplex.

When DNA from first generation cells was centrifuged, the contents of the centrifuge tubes were photographed with ultraviolet optics to make DNA bands visible in the photographic emulsion. The position of a DNA band in the gradient corresponded to its N content, and the results clearly showed a single band of DNA in the position expected for half-heavy duplexes (Fig. 7.3).

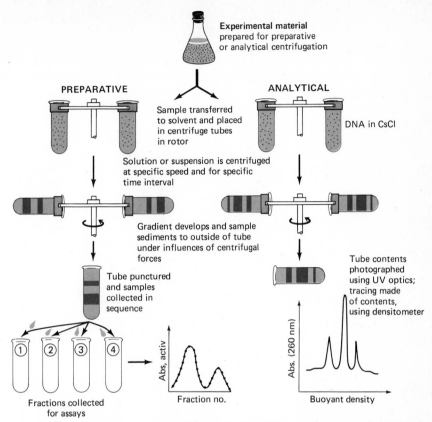

PREPARATIVE

ANALYTICAL

Experimental material
prepared for preparative
or analytical centrifugation

Sample transferred
to solvent and placed
in centrifuge tubes
in rotor

DNA in CsCl

Solution or suspension is centrifuged
at specific speed and for specific
time interval

Gradient develops and sample
sediments to outside of tube
under influences of centrifugal
forces

Tube punctured
and samples
collected in
sequence

Tube contents
photographed
using UV optics;
tracing made
of contents,
using densitometer

Abs, activ

Fraction no.

Abs. (260 nm)

Buoyant density

Fractions collected
for assays

Figure 7.2 Equilibrium density gradient centrifugation. Samples of experimental material can be sedimented in a preparative centrifuge, from which the fractions can be collected for analysis by various means. Alternatively, components centrifuged to the point of equilibrium in the density gradient in an analytical ultracentrifuge system are processed directly in the centrifuge tube or cell. DNAs in different regions of the density gradient of CsCl are visualized by photographs showing UV absorption bands, from which tracings are made using a densitometer. Each band or its trace corresponds to DNA of a particular buoyant density in CsCl, reflecting the G-C content or differences in ^{15}N incorporated into the molecules.

These results ruled out conservative replication, but did not discriminate between semiconservative and dispersive replication. By continuing the experiments for four generations of growth, or doublings, the only reasonable interpretation of all the data was that DNA replicated semiconservatively. The predictions for this replication model were fulfilled in every cell generation, and the two other possibilities were eliminated. Such instances of beautifully clear experimental design, data, and conclusions are realized all too rarely, and we appreciate them all the more when they happen.

One year before the Meselson and Stahl experiments, a report by J. H. Taylor, P. Woods, and W. Hughes showed that semiconservative replication characterized chromosomal DNA in eukaryotic cells. Cells were grown in media containing thymidine labeled with the radioactive isotope **tritium**, or ^{3}H. Since thymidine is found uniquely in DNA, original and newly made

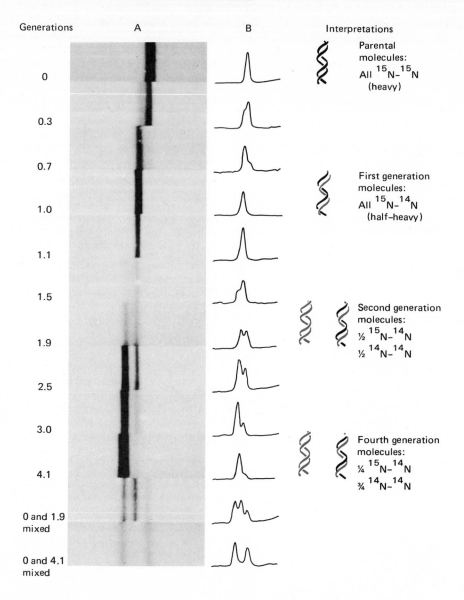

Figure 7.3 Experimental demonstration of semiconservative replication of *E. coli* DNA. (A) Ultraviolet absorption photographs from analytical centrifugation, showing distribution of DNA (bands) in samples monitored at different times in the experiments. Cells were labeled initially with ^{15}N and grown afterward in ^{14}N-containing medium for the number of generations indicated. (B) Densitometer tracings of UV absorption bands of DNA. The interpretations of the kinds of DNA and amounts of each, according to centrifugation data, fit the predictions made for semiconservative replication of DNA. (After Meselson, M., and F. W. Stahl. 1958. *Proc. Nat. Acad. Sci. U. S.* **44**:671.)

molecules could be located and identified in chromosomes of these cells by the presence or absence of radioactivity in **autoradiographs**.

Cells were first labeled with [³H] thymidine by incubation in media containing this DNA precursor. Labeled cells were then transferred to a medium containing unlabeled thymidine (with ordinary ¹H), and were allowed to undergo one cycle of doubling. The cells were removed to glass slides and coated with a photographic emulsion for subsequent autoradiography

Figure 7.4 Semiconservative replication of eukaryotic chromosomes. (a) Autoradiograph of metaphase chromosomes of the bean *Vicia faba* after one DNA replication cycle in the presence of [³H] thymidine. (b) Autoradiograph of similar root tip nucleus after one replication cycle in the presence of [³H] thymidine and a second cycle in the absence of the labeled DNA precursor. (c) Diagrammatic representation of the distribution of DNA strands and of metaphase chromosomes during two cycles of replication. ³H-labeled strands are shown in red, and red dots represent the silver grains of autoradiographs such as shown in (a) and (b). Solid and dashed black lines represent unlabeled strands. (From Taylor, J. H. 1963. *Molecular Genetics*, Part I, pp. 74–75, New York: Academic Press.)

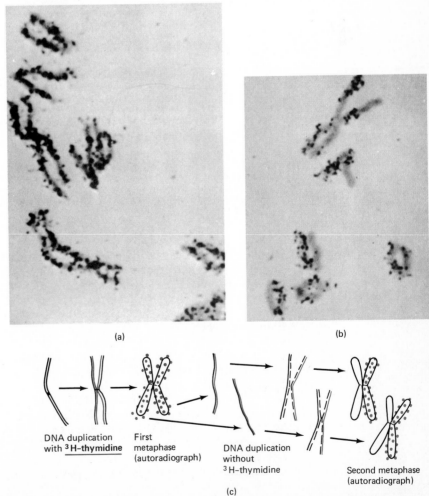

(a)   (b)

DNA duplication   First   Second metaphase
with ³H-thymidine   metaphase   DNA duplication   (autoradiograph)
                         (autoradiograph)   without
                                              ³H-thymidine

(c)

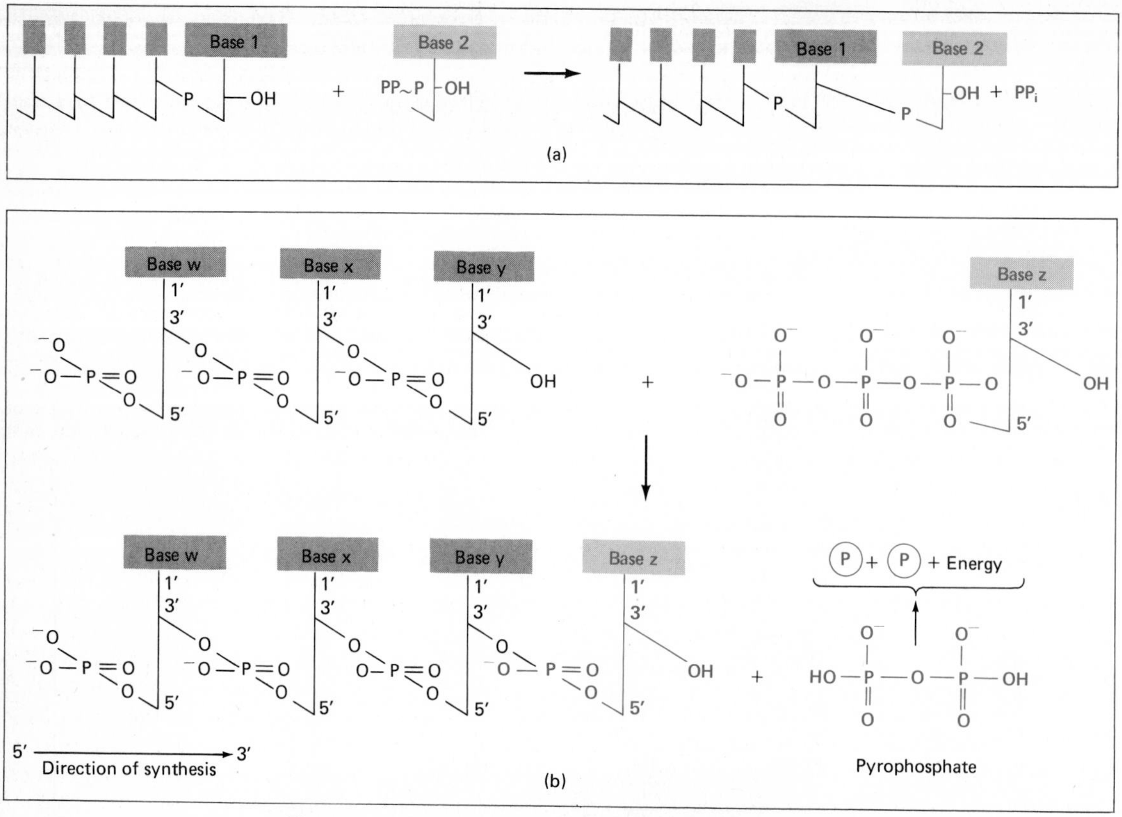

Figure 7.5 DNA synthesis. (a) New strand synthesis proceeds from 5′ to 3′, through the addition of mononucleotides derived rom triphosphate precursors. (b) Detail of a step in synthesis showing the nucleoside 5′-phosphate precursor (red) and the addition of a mononucleotide monomer. Release of pyrophosphate drives the reaction to completion.

using the light microscope. The emulsion was developed to reveal any silver grains, which indicate a radioactive decay event at that site in the cell underneath, and the chromosomes were stained to enhance contrast. Silver grains were found to be present along one chromatid of each replicated chromosome, and were absent from the sister chromatid almost entirely (Fig. 7.4). This pattern conformed to the predictions for semiconservative replication, since each chromosome was half-labeled. If replication had been conservative, 50% of the chromosomes would have been labeled along both chromatids and 50% of the chromosomes would have had no label at all. This was not found to be the case. Apparently, eukaryotic and prokaryotic DNA replicate by the same mode.

In 1958 Taylor further showed that semiconservative replication characterized DNA in meiotic cells. Within five years of the original suggestion by Watson and Crick, therefore, semiconservative DNA replication had been successfully demonstrated in bacteria and in both mitotic and meiotic cells of eukaryotes.

These and other experiments showed that progeny DNA duplexes were semiconserved, but they did not show *how* the new strands were made and incorporated into new molecules. The processes of DNA replication have been a focus of investigation for more than 25 years. Some of the highlights of these studies will be discussed in the next sections.

7.2 Synthesis of New Strands

The building blocks of DNA are deoxyribonucleoside 5'-*mono*phosphates, which become active precursors when a pyrophosphoryl group is added on to make them deoxyribonucleoside 5'-*tri*phosphates. In the triphosphate form, the units are added on to a growing chain and pyrophosphate is released in a hydrolysis reaction that drives the synthesis to completion (Fig. 7.5). The overall direction of chain growth is 5'→3', with the addition of the triphosphate at the 3'-hydroxyl end of the chain.

The two complementary strands of the DNA duplex are antiparallel, and chain growth proceeds along each template strand only in the 5'→3' direction. Both new complementary strands in a replicating duplex therefore must proceed in *opposite* directions from one another. It has been shown using labeled units that the triphosphate precursors are only added at the 3' end of a chain. The labeled units are found only at the 3' ends of the new chains, which means they were added most recently during synthesis. The replication enzyme, or **DNA polymerase**, is only capable of adding a new monomer onto the 3' free end of the growing chain, which further verifies the 5'→3' direction of chain growth in all systems which have been studied.

Since the antiparallel growing chains are growing in opposite directions, their synthesis may not be simultaneous or synchronous, that is, each chain may grow by independent steps although the same enzymes catalyze all these steps. On the other hand, the DNA strand may be synthesized in short pieces that are later assembled into lengthening stretches, until both chains of a replicating duplex are completed and two daughter replica duplexes have been made from one parental double-helix (Fig. 7.6).

This sketchy picture of DNA replication does little justice to the actual processes involved. All these replication events require specific proteins and enzymes, and all cooperate to produce an accurate pair of replicas. How is all this possible? What are these components and how is accuracy ensured?

The first of the three known DNA polymerases was **DNA polymerase I**, called the "Kornberg enzyme" after its discoverer. Although the enzyme was shown to catalyze DNA synthesis *in vitro*, its products were often branched chains, whereas linear, unbranched DNA strands are the only form made in living systems. This enzyme was therefore considered to function in some way in replication, but it was not believed to be the main replicating enzyme because of its peculiar properties in test systems. The search for other DNA polymerases was frustrated by the dominating presence and activity of DNA polymerase I, which masked other enzymes and made them difficult to isolate. The situation was improved with the discovery of polymerase-deficient or -defective mutants in *E. coli*.

In 1969 John Cairns described the *polA⁻* mutant he had discovered in *E. coli*. The mutant synthesizes DNA at normal rates even though there is barely detectable DNA polymerase I activity. Using *polA⁻* mutants, a

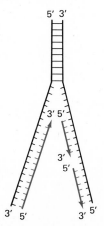

Figure 7.6 Diagram of a replicating region of duplex DNA. It is undecided whether both new strands are synthesized synchronously or not, or continuously versus discontinuously (in short pieces). We do know that two semiconserved duplexes arise from one parental duplex.

258   Chapter 7/The Molecular Nature of the Genome

search was begun for other DNA polymerases which had to be present, since replication was unimpaired in *polA⁻* strains.

Polymerase I activity is so high in wild-type cells that other polymerase activities are masked. But *polA⁻* mutants do not present this problem. They were found to have **DNA polymerase II** and, later, to also have **DNA polymerase III**. DNA polymerase II was ruled out as the main replicating enzyme when *polB⁻* mutants were isolated and shown to synthesize DNA at normal rates despite a deficiency of this enzyme. Studies of more recently isolated *polC⁻* mutants, which are deficient in DNA polymerase III, have provided some evidence for this as the main replicating enzyme in *E. coli.* But DNA polymerase I also fulfills a vital function in DNA chain growth, since mutants have never been found which totally lack this enzyme. Its function can be better understood when the nature of discontinuous chain growth is examined; it acts in reactions that lead to joining between the short pieces of DNA made by DNA polymerase III reactions. It fills in gaps.

R. Okazaki provided evidence that DNA synthesis might be discontinuous, proceeding by bursts of synthesis of small pieces of DNA, about 1000 to 2000 nucleotides long. Fragments of this size were isolated from mutants that were unable to hook these pieces together to make whole chains. When such *E. coli* mutants were presented with short pulses of labeled precursor at low temperature, almost all the label was found in small pieces of DNA. Discontinuous DNA synthesis might characterize either one or both growing strands. There is evidence showing that newly synthesized, single-stranded fragments bind to *both* parental template strands to an equal extent. Such highly specific binding between polynucleotides is possible if they are complementary to each other and join by complementary base-pairing. These replication fragments are often called **Okazaki fragments**, after their discoverer.

The short pieces are joined together in wild-type *E. coli*, which means there must be an enzyme that links Okazaki fragments to each other and to the growing chain. The enzyme **DNA ligase** fulfills this function. It

Figure 7.7 Enzymes and other protein components of DNA synthesis. Primase initiates strand synthesis, and DNA polymerase III catalyzes addition of deoxyribonucleotides to the RNA primer segment. When the RNA primer is later excised, DNA polymerase I fills in the gap, and the strand is sealed into a continuous region by DNA ligase action. Single-stranded regions at the replication fork are held taut during unwinding through bound molecules of "unwinding protein"; otherwise these regions would kink. Asynchronous, discontinuous synthesis of Okazaki fragments is depicted in this diagram.

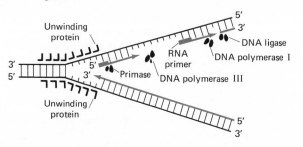

catalyzes the formation of phosphodiester links which make the chain continuous by splicing the sugar—phosphate backbone. The mutants used by Okazaki to show that synthesis was discontinuous were ligase-deficient and could not join the pieces together, so the pieces accumulated and could be isolated and analyzed.

The *initiation* of synthesis for each Okazaki fragment cannot be accomplished by DNA polymerases. This created a problem for a time, until it was discovered that chain growth was initiated or "primed" by the addition of a short stretch of RNA catalyzed by an **RNA polymerase**. Some of these RNA polymerases have been called **primases**, but there is considerable variation among these priming enzymes in different systems. Once primed, DNA polymerase III catalyzes the addition of DNA monomers to the **RNA primer**, and an Okazaki fragment is made. The same events would take place for each burst of discontinuous synthesis along both growing chains in a replicating duplex (Fig. 7.7).

Newly made DNA duplexes do not contain RNA segments, however, which means that the RNA primers must be excised from the Okazaki fragment. This leaves a gap which must be filled in with DNA monomers. DNA polymerase I appears to be the catalyst in these reactions. The polymerase has an **exonuclease** function as well as a polymerase function. It can start at a free 3' end and digest away the RNA primer in the 3'→5' direction. It can then catalyze DNA monomer additions, 5'→3', to fill in the gap. The same polymerase I is also believed to fill in gaps between Okazaki fragments and make the pieces continuous. The gap-filling activities occur throughout the period of synthesis, so chains are lengthened step by step and not all at once after the whole complementary chain has been made.

DNA polymerase I has another important function which helps to ensure accuracy of chain synthesis. It **"proofreads"** the growing chain fragments, and can excise inaccurate monomer additions, since it has the ability to work in the 3'→5' direction. If excision does occur through its exonuclease function, the DNA polymerase I can exercise its polymerase function and guide the addition of correct monomers in the 5'→3' direction, according to the base sequence in the complementary template strand.

There are many other processes and components that have been discovered, and which continue to be discovered. They are all under gene control (Fig. 7.8). The tightly wound double helix must be unwound, or destabilized, at the replicating region if all the necessary enzymes are to have access to

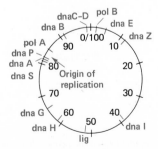

Figure 7.8 Eleven of the genes in *E. coli* that are involved in DNA replication, in mapped order.

the template strands and guide synthesis of the complementary chains. The activity of a **"gyrase"** or untwisting enzyme has been demonstrated, as well as the existence of **"unwinding proteins"** which stabilize the separated strands so they remain taut and apart from one another in the replicating region. All of these and other interacting molecules and processes contribute to the remarkably accurate synthesis of new DNA in countless cell generations in all organisms. The complexity of these processes, and the fact that there are a number of different pathways even in the same cell, all work to provide the highest possible insurance against error in replication.

All of these processes must be under very tight control in cells. We know a great deal about specific enzymes and other proteins because it was possible to isolate and identify them in test assay systems using numerous mutants in viral bacterial, and eukaryotic systems. Virtually nothing is known, however, about regulation of DNA replication. Mutants defective in regulation of replication are almost unknown, and studies of replication control have therefore lagged far behind studies of the replication processes themselves.

7.3 Direction of Replication

John Cairns provided the first experimental evidence in 1963 to show that DNA replication proceeded in a specific direction, from what is now called the **origin**, or site of initiation of replication. The particular origin has been mapped in some viruses (for example, at position 67 in the 100-unit map of SV40) and bacteria (the 82-minute site on the 100-minute *E. coli* map).

Cairns grew *E. coli* in media containing [³H]thymidine for one 30-minute generation period to label one strand of their DNA. The cells were then allowed to grow in the same labeled medium for varying lengths of time in a second 30-minute cycle before samples were removed and prepared for autoradiography. It was expected that label density would be twice as great where the molecule had undergone two rounds of replication (Fig. 7.9). In

Figure 7.9 Diagrams showing distribution of silver grains in replicating circular DNA in *E. coli*, and interpretation of such autoradiographs according to semiconservative replication. Strands A and B have replicated a second time since the experiment started, while strand C has only replicated once thus far.

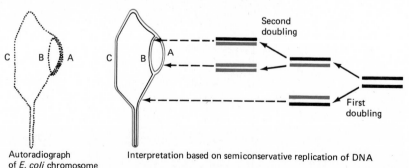

Autoradiograph
of *E. coli* chromosome

Interpretation based on semiconservative replication of DNA

other words, some parts of the molecule had both strands labeled and other parts still only had one labeled strand in their semiconservatively replicating duplex DNA. The images of these circular replicating molecules resembled the Greek letter *theta*, and for this reason they are referred to as θ-forms.

These forms were interpreted as showing that replication proceeded directionally from an origin, going around the circle until two semiconserved daughter duplexes were formed. Label densities served as markers to identify which parts of the molecule had replicated twice and which parts only once. Since two segments of the θ form were singly labeled and the third segment was doubly labeled, all three segments were measured in molecules at different stages of the second replication cycle (Fig. 7.10). In every case, two differently labeled segments were of equal length, while one of the singly-labeled segments was longer in molecules just starting the second replication and became progressively shorter as this second cycle neared its completion. These measurements served as the basis for proposing that replication proceeded directionally around the circle, beginning at some point of origin on the molecule. In most viruses, bacteria, and

Figure 7.10 Replicating DNA. (a) Electron micrograph showing a theta-form molecule; and (b) interpretation showing unreplicated part C and replicated, equal-length parts A and B of the molecule. There are two replication forks (at arrows). × 56,000. (Courtesy of D. R. Wolstenholme, from Wolstenholme, D. R., *et al.* 1974. *Cold Spring Harbor Sympos. Quant. Biol.* **38** (1973):267.)

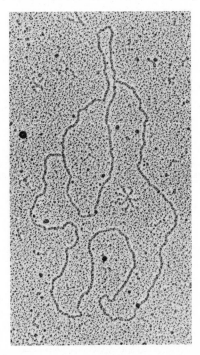

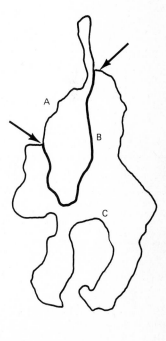

(a)   (b)

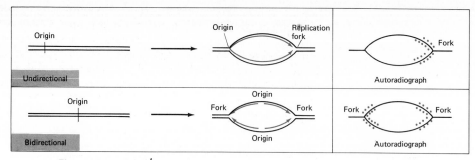

Figure 7.11   Expected labeling patterns after incorporation of [³H] thymidine for a few minutes following onset of DNA replication, reveal whether replication proceeds in one or in both directions away from the origin. Label would appear only in new DNA which had just incorporated the tritiated precursor.

eukaryotic systems which have been studied, replication proceeds in *both* directions away from the origin. There are two **replication forks** in each bidirectionally replicating "bubble" (Fig. 7.11).

There usually is one replication origin in viral and bacterial genomes, and the entire genome can be considered as a **replicon** or unit of replication. In eukaryotes, there are many replicons per genome. This has been deduced from electron micrographs showing a number of replication "bubbles" along a single chromosomal DNA segment, each "bubble" presumably having a particular origin (Fig. 7.12). From electron micro-

Figure 7.12   Electron micrograph and interpretive drawing of replicating DNA from *Drosophila melanogaster* nuclei. The portion of the molecule shown here is 119,000 base-pairs long and has 23 replication "bubbles". A kilobase (kb) is a unit of length equal to 1000 bases or base-pairs in single- and double-stranded nucleic acids, respectively. (Courtesy of H. J. Kriegstein and D. S. Hogness, from Kreigstein, H. J., and D. S. Hogness. 1974. *Proc. Nat. Acad. Sci. U. S.* **71**:135, Fig. 1.)

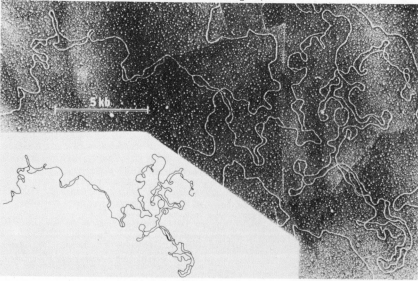

graphs and from studies of the rate of DNA synthesis, an estimated 100-200 replicons per genome may exist in a eukaryote.

Among the major accomplishments of biochemical studies of DNA replication has been the complete test tube synthesis of functional, whole DNA genomes of several viruses. Not only are these molecules complete, but they start *in vitro* at the correct origin. These completely synthesized molecules can serve as templates *in vivo* for the accurate synthesis of new generations of functional, complete DNA viral genomes.

7.4 Replication in Viruses

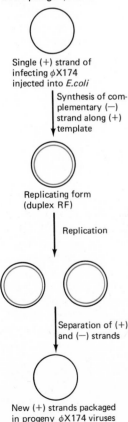

Figure 7.13 Scheme showing DNA replication of the single-stranded DNA phage φX174.

Single (+) strand of infecting φX174 injected into *E.coli*

Synthesis of complementary (−) strand along (+) template

Replicating form (duplex RF)

Replication

Separation of (+) and (−) strands

New (+) strands packaged in progeny φX174 viruses

DNA phages may have single-stranded or double-stranded DNA, and some viruses have either single-stranded or duplex RNA genomes (see Table 2.3). How do these genomes replicate? From many *in vitro* studies and from analysis of a number of mutants in either the virus or the host genetic system, it seems clear that there are a number of variations in replication. There is no single set of requirements that serves all systems. To get some sense of the diversity among these viruses, we will examine a few examples in sufficient depth to see their characteristics and their variations.

The DNA phage φX174 of *E. coli* is one of the best-studied single-stranded DNA systems. When the virus infects its host cell, the single-stranded molecule is converted to a double-stranded circular molecule called the **replicating form** (RF). The entering strand, which we will call the (+) strand, serves as a template for the synthesis of a complementary (−) strand, making the duplex RF. The RF duplex then acts as the template, in turn, to make new (+) single strands which are packaged in the virus particles later released from the cell during lysis (Fig. 7.13). In this system, therefore, complementary base-pairing serves the same function in ordering nucleotides into a precise sequence as it does in other replicating situations. The major difference is that only (+) strands are made, that is, only one strand of the duplex RF serves as a template for new chain synthesis.

There is considerable variation among viruses in the particular enzymes which function in replication. Some virus-coded enzymes are essential in one species and dispensable in another species, or an enzyme coded by a host gene may function in replicating viral DNA.

In the mammalian virus SV40, duplex DNA is always present in combination with histone proteins, and it actually resembles a miniature version of a eukaryotic chromosome. Virus replication proceeds by reactions catalyzed by host cell enzymes exclusively; the virus does not code for its own replication components. The circular viral nucleoprotein provides a model system to study eukaryotic DNA replication and chromosome organization. In double-stranded DNA phages, on the other hand, naked DNA molecules replicate semiconservatively to produce new naked duplex DNA. The *E. coli* phage λ is known to occur inside the host cell as a circle during the lytic cycle, but as a linear segment in the virus particle or when integrated into *E. coli* DNA while it is in its prophage state. Furthermore, λ DNA can be isolated in either circular or linear forms from *E. coli* cells. How can these two configurations be reconciled?

Figure 7.14 Intercon-
vertibility of linear and
circular forms of phage
λ DNA.

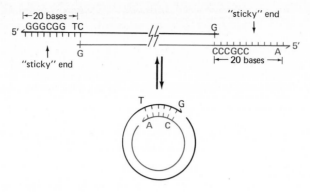

Apparently, the circular and linear forms of phage λ are interconverti-
ble. The DNA circle can be linearized, or the linear molecule can be circu-
larized (Fig. 7.14). This property of interconvertibility is made possible by
the presence of "sticky" ends of the linear form, which can undergo complementary base-pairing to constitute the circular form. The property is of
immense importance in temperate phages such as λ, since the molecule
must be able to assume either configuration in different phases of the lytic
cycle. If you will recall, recombination events which integrate or excise λ
from the *E. coli* chromosome require circular and linear forms at different
stages of the process (see Fig. 5.31). Circularity *per se* is not required for
DNA replication, however, since phages such as T2 always exist in linear
form and are never found as circles (see Section 5.12). These are only some
of the variations which have been described for viruses with duplex DNA
genomes.

RNA viruses also occur in double-stranded and single-stranded forms.
The duplex RNA viruses apparently replicate through the activities of RNA
polymerases, which are replication enzymes in such systems. The most
interesting cases, however, have been described for the single-stranded
RNA tumor viruses, such as mouse mammary tumor virus and avian (Rous)
sarcoma virus (ASV). The whole group of single-stranded RNA tumor
viruses appears to be very closely related and they have been shown to
cause tumors in many kinds of vertebrate animal species. In the case of
ASV, one of the best studied and a fairly typical virus in this group, the
infective particle penetrates into the cell cytoplasm where its RNA genome
separates from its protein coat. The single-stranded RNA genome is then
transcribed into a complementary DNA strand using the virus-specific
enzyme **reverse transcriptase**. This enzyme is an RNA-dependent DNA
polymerase, that is, it catalyzes DNA strand synthesis from an RNA
template (Fig. 7.15). The discovery of this enzyme by Howard Temin and
David Baltimore came as quite a surprise. It led to the change in the dogma

of information flow from the gene, from ⟲ DNA→RNA→protein in cells

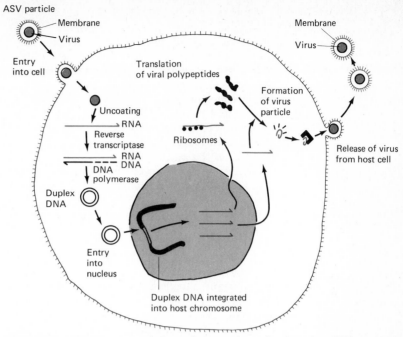

Figure 7.15 Diagram showing the major steps in replication of an RNA tumor virus, avian sarcoma virus (ASV). The enzyme **reverse transcriptase** (RNA-dependent DNA polymerase) is essential for replication in this virus.

and many viruses, to $\left(\overset{\curvearrowright}{\text{DNA}\rightleftharpoons\text{RNA}\rightarrow\text{protein}}\right.$ or $\left(\overset{\curvearrowright}{\text{RNA}\rightarrow\text{protein}}\right.$ in some viruses only.

The single-stranded DNA serves as the template for enzymatically catalyzed synthesis of a complementary DNA partner, to form a circular duplex DNA, called the **provirus**. The provirus then integrates into the host chromosome, probably by a recombination process similar to the one which integrates phage λ into the *E. coli* chromosome. After integration, the proviral DNA serves as the template for synthesis of viral RNA molecules catalyzed by the host cell's RNA polymerase II, the same enzyme responsible for messenger RNA transcription. Some of these RNA chains guide the synthesis of viral proteins much as a messenger RNA does. Eventually, several of these RNA strands combine with newly made viral proteins and new virus particles are formed, each with one RNA strand. These particles go through a series of finishing steps before they are released from the host cell surface. None of these steps in the multiplication of RNA tumor viruses interferes with normal cellular processes and functions. The host cell is not obliged to die, as happens when DNA tumor viruses multiply in host cells.

These few examples serve to show some of the variety in virus replication systems. We will explore RNA and DNA tumor viruses further in Chapter 12, when we discuss interactions between extrachromosomal genes and the host cell genome.

RECOMBINATION AT THE MOLECULAR LEVEL

In several previous chapters we discussed recombination arising by crossing over, which involves an exchange of chromosome segments. Crossing over takes place after chromosomes have replicated, and each exchange involves only two of the four chromatids in a meiotic bivalent. The two general mechanisms tested in Neurospora by tetrad analysis were copy choice, and breakage and reunion (see Fig. 4.16). The occurrence of certain kinds of tetrads was interpreted to mean that copy choice could not be the actual mechanism of crossing over, but there was neither proof nor disproof of the mechanism of breakage and reunion.

Genetic recombinants arise by crossing over in bacteria and viruses, as well as in mitotic and meiotic cells in eukaryotes. The process of crossing over must involve the DNA molecule, and presumably we can study any suitable system and derive certain generalizations that may be applied to all systems where crossing over takes place. We would expect a number of enzymes to be involved in the molecular events, since polynucleotide chains are broken and rejoined, and since these are known to be enzymatically catalyzed reactions. Crossing over phenomena also play a vital role in excision and integration of viral genomes into host chromosomes as we will see in Chapter 9. We are faced at every turn with some phenomenon involving crossing over. It is very important, therefore, to understand the molecular events behind it.

7.5   Breakage and Reunion

In 1961, Matthew Meselson and Jean Weigle provided very convincing evidence that crossing over involved breakage and subsequent reunion of DNA molecules. They used a doubly mutant strain and a wild type strain of phage λ, in which one strain had been grown in *E. coli* on media containing the heavy isotope ^{15}N and the other strain in ordinary ^{14}N. These preliminary experiments were done reciprocally so they obtained phages that were + +[^{15}N] and *c mi*[^{14}N], or + +[^{14}N] and *c mi*[^{15}N]. Crosses were made by mixedly infecting *E. coli* cells with both viruses in [^{14}N] medium. We will follow the + +[^{15}N] × *c mi*[^{14}N] cross, although similar results were obtained in the reciprocal cross. Note that each phage chromosome is genetically marked by two gene loci governing two plaque characteristics, so recombinants can be identified by their phenotypes, and each phage chromosome is distinguished physically by having ^{14}N or ^{15}N in its construction. This is a cytogenetic experiment, comparable in every way with the *Drosophila* experiment done in 1931 by Curt Stern (see Fig. 4.15). The results can be interpreted by comparing the distribution of gene markers with the distribution of isotopically distinguishable DNA molecules (chromosomes).

The experiment is designed to obtain possible results which can show that one proposed mechanism is correct and the other incorrect. The opposing mechanisms were copy choice, and breakage and reunion. Copy choice had been revived as a plausible mechanism of crossing over during the 1950s, as the result of new studies using phages and bacteria in recombination experiments. It had to be considered alongside breakage and reunion because of newer results obtained at this time.

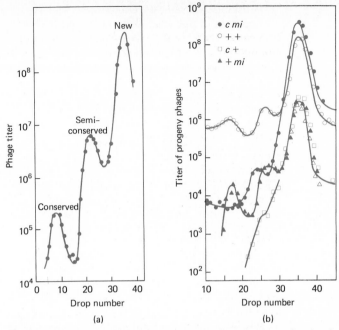

Figure 7.16 Crossing over occurs by breakage and reunion in phage λ, producing genetic recombinants. (a) Diagram showing positions in the gradient of phages containing conserved (^{15}N in both strands), semiconserved (^{15}N in one strand), and new (^{15}N in neither strand) duplex DNA depending on 0, 1, or 2 cycles of replication of heavy phage infecting light *E. coli* in light medium. (b) Note the presence of conserved and semiconserved + *mi* recombinants, in particular. These must have arisen by breakage and reunion since copy-choice would lead only to new (^{14}N only) recombinant phage progeny. (From Meselson, M., and J. J. Weigle. 1961. *Proc. Nat. Acad. Sci. U. S.* **47**:857.)

If crossing over is by copy choice, it must take place *during* DNA replication. In this case, *all* recombinants should be "light," since only ^{14}N is available for new strand synthesis during infection in the experiment. These ^{14}N viruses would be genetically recombinant as the result of the new strand switching back and forth between two parental strands as replication proceeds, but physically they would be of only one isotopic composition. If breakage and reunion is the mechanism of crossing over, at least some of the genetic recombinants would also have recombined DNA molecules, physically part ^{14}N and part ^{15}N. This would result from breakage and reunion involving parental and new strands.

Progeny phages were collected after cellular lysis, and were centrifuged in CsCl density gradients to separate phages of different densities (Fig. 7.16). Samples of these phages from different parts of the gradient were removed to determine their genotype, on the basis of plaque morphology. Meselson and Weigle found that *c* + and + *mi* genetic recombinants were also physically recombinant, according to their density positions in the CsCl gradients. They must have contained both ^{14}N and ^{15}N atoms, since completely light or completely heavy DNA-containing particles were present in less dense and more dense regions of the gradient, respectively.

Crossing over therefore took place by a mechanism involving breakage and reunion of parental and newly synthesized DNA. The molecular reactions involved in breakage and reunion could now be hypothesized, and recombination enzymes could be sought in appropriate test systems.

7.6   Recombination Mechanisms

The underlying assumption in recombination studies is that base-pairing in single-stranded regions of duplex DNA brings molecules into the intimate association which would permit exchanges to take place. Single-stranded regions would develop if one strand of a duplex were broken at a specific site, by nuclease action. If two homologous DNAs experienced breaks at nearly the same sites, both their single-stranded regions could undergo base-pairing. This would set the stage for enzymatically catalyzed reactions that would lead to rejoining of the broken molecules and to recombinant DNA. There are no known forces through which intact, homologous DNA duplexes would attract each other at specific sites. Recombination requires this kind of specific-site interaction, however, since all the genes are preserved intact within and around the recombination region. This last feature is based on many years of genetic analysis of recombinants, and on the precision which must underlie recombination within the gene as shown by Benzer, Yanofsky, and others.

There is no shortage of models for molecular recombination, but there is only a limited amount of evidence in support of any of them. However, most models share common features, and we will take a brief look at the more prominently mentioned ones.

All current models proposed to explain molecular recombination in viruses and prokaryotes state that specific **endonucleases** cut or nick one strand of a duplex. **DNA polymerase** can add nucleotides onto the free end to make a single-stranded "tail" (Fig. 7.17). If homologous DNAs are near enough for base-pairing along these "tails," a short duplex "bridge" can form connecting the two duplexes. Once this **recombination intermediate**, or **heteroduplex** (containing parts of two different DNA molecules), has formed, subsequent nicks by endonucleases would lead to a recombinant DNA duplex and fragments of the remaining strands of the parental molecules. Gaps in the nucleotide sequence of the heteroduplex would be filled in by DNA polymerase action, and the chains would be made continuous by a **DNA ligase**-catalyzed reaction. These events usually lead to *nonreciprocal* recombination; that is, if gene markers *a b* were in one parental duplex and + + in the other duplex, the single recombinant molecule would be either *a* + or + *b*. In many such recombination events, there would be an equal chance that both kinds of recombinants would arise. But the products of a single virus-infected cell, for example, might show more of one recombinant than another. You will recall that single-cell-burst virus progeny usually do not have equal numbers of both recombinant classes, but that the sum of many such populations do. Furthermore, nonreciprocal recombination is a general characteristic of bacterial systems involving transformation, transduction, or conjugation, as we discussed at length in

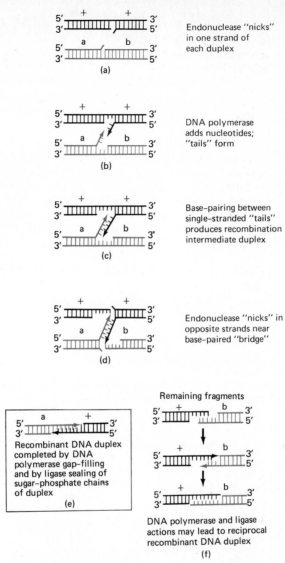

Figure 7.17 Steps involved in recombination by crossing over in prokaryotes and viruses may involve a sequence of enzymatically-catalyzed events leading from a recombination intermediate to a completed heteroduplex DNA, shown in steps (a)-(d) leading to (e). It is theoretically possible for a reciprocal recombinant duplex to be made from remaining fragments, as shown schematically in (f).

Chapter 5. This model, and others that differ in one or more particular details, apparently coincide with observations of nonreciprocal recombination in viruses and bacteria.

All the required enzymes for recombination are the same as, or are similar to, DNA replication enzymes, which are known to be present. The kind of DNA synthesis which occurs during recombination, however, involves

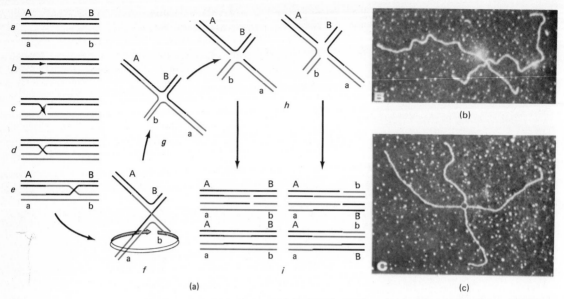

Figure 7.18 Structural intermediates of reciprocal recombination between two paired DNA duplex molecules, according to the prototype model developed by R. Holliday. (A) Genetic recombinants may arise after a series of steps shown in (a)-(f), and these would be reciprocal if the interlocked strands are first rotated by 180° before nucleases cleave the strands, as shown in (g). After nuclease-induced breaks, gap-filling by DNA polymerase I and ligase-catalyzed sealing would produce heteroduplex DNAs that were genetically recombinant (h)-(i). (B) and (C) Electron micrographs of *E. coli* plasmid DNA resembling the postulated structural recombination intermediates shown in (f) and (g), respectively. (From Potter, H., and D. Dressler. 1977. *Proc. Nat. Acad. Sci. U. S.* **74**:4168.)

reactions in only small portions of the DNA molecules. This is usually called **DNA repair synthesis**. Evidence which indicates the occurrence of DNA repair synthesis during recombination has come from the identification of enzymatic defects in recombination-deficient mutants in *E. coli* and certain phages. In *E. coli*, *recA*⁻ mutants are defective in repair of DNA which has been damaged by ultraviolet light, and they cannot undergo recombination. Mutants of the *recB*⁻, *recC*⁻, and *recB*⁻*C*⁻ genotypes also are deficient in repairing UV-induced damage to DNA, and they carry out very little recombination. The *recB* and *recC* gene products are the two subunits of a powerful endonuclease; a defect in such an enzyme could strongly influence DNA repair synthesis and recombination. Similar enzymatic defects have been found in phages, such as T4 and λ, where recombination is severely affected.

Numerous electron microscopy studies have been conducted to visualize the heteroduplex recombination intermediate (Fig. 7.18). In addition, physical evidence for heteroduplex DNA has been obtained in transformation experiments and in other studies, where isotopically-marked parental DNA molecules containing different alleles for marker genes can be monitored. Genetic recombinants have been shown to arise from physically exchanged

DNA, carrying the isotope markers of both parental DNAs as well as different alleles of the two parental duplex molecules.

These lines of evidence support the breakage and reunion mechanism, but they usually can be interpreted in various ways in relation to specific models for molecular events of recombination. No one model currently satisfies everyone, and the subject seems to get more complex as new models and new data are presented.

Recombination in eukaryotic systems involves **chromatids** rather than naked DNA molecules, and must explain the formation of **chiasmata** in meiotic bivalents, since chiasmata develop only when recombination has taken place. The problem of bringing homologous chromosomes together is not so difficult, however, because synapsis is a regular event in the early stages of meiosis. The physical basis for exact pairing, however, is still not known. The models of molecular recombination for eukaryotic systems are ones which attempt to explain recombination leading to chiasma formation. One model which has enjoyed considerable favor since it was first presented in 1964 by Robin Holliday has also had the largest amount of experimental support. Over the years, some modifications have been introduced into the Holliday model, but the basic postulates have been retained.

The **Holliday model** for molecular recombination calls for a series of enzymatically catalyzed events in which single-strand nicks by endonuclease action arise first (Fig. 7.19). Nicks are made at corresponding sites in duplex DNAs of paired nonsister chromatids, in the meiotic bivalent. The broken strands separate and then reassociate to produce a heteroduplex when ligase seals the free ends of these strands. A series of events involving digestion of DNA strand fragments, by exonuclease action, and gap-filling, by polymerase action, eventually produces two intact DNA duplex molecules which are finally made whole by DNA ligase action. The physical consequence is the development of a chiasma at the site of recombination. Two intact, *reciprocally recombinant chromatids* arise as the result of molecular events at the DNA level.

The proposed model fits all the observed recombination phenomena known for meiotic chromosomes. But whether or not the correct model is this particular mechanism, or some variation of the mechanism, or some entirely different model, has not yet been determined. The Holliday model provides a very useful working hypothesis, and it permits specific experiments to be designed which can test various features of the proposed model. Some features have been verified while others are still under investigation.

Some of the most convincing evidence showing DNA repair synthesis to be the probable basis for molecular recombination in eukaryotes has come from studies of meiosis in lily plants by Herbert Stern and Yasuo Hotta. Similar evidence has also been obtained from studies of mammalian and other animal species, and it is therefore likely to be of general significance in explaining meiotic recombination in all or most eukaryotes.

Lily flower buds undergo essentially synchronized meiosis, so that buds of a particular size are known to be in a particular stage of meiosis, and all the meiotic cells in a bud are in the same stage as well. These features permit biochemical analysis of lily meiosis, since large quantities of material in known parts of the meiotic sequence can be collected and prepared for enzymatic analysis. Stern and Hotta have shown that endonuclease, DNA

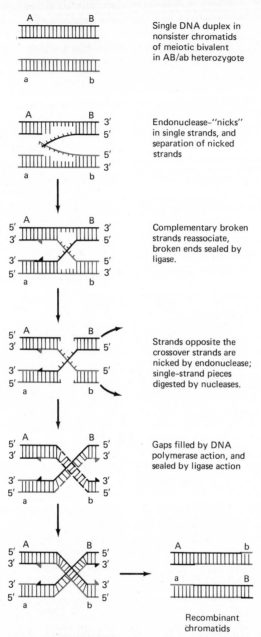

Single DNA duplex in nonsister chromatids of meiotic bivalent in AB/ab heterozygote

Endonuclease–"nicks" in single strands, and separation of nicked strands

Complementary broken strands reassociate, broken ends sealed by ligase.

Strands opposite the crossover strands are nicked by endonuclease; single-strand pieces digested by nucleases.

Gaps filled by DNA polymerase action, and sealed by ligase action

Recombinant chromatids

Figure 7.19 The Holliday model of genetic recombination applied to crossing over between nonsister chromatids in meiosis in eukaryotes. Through a series of enzymatically catalyzed steps, reciprocally recombinant chromatids would arise, and a chiasma would develop at the site of recombination. Only two of the four chromatids of a meiotic bivalent are shown here, and each chromatid has been represented as a duplex DNA molecule.

polymerase, and DNA ligase activities begin to appear in early stages of meiotic prophase I, reach a peak at pachynema (the stage when recombination probably occurs), and decline afterward. These enzymatic events coincide with the presumed timing of synapsis, crossing over, and chiasma formation in meiotic cells. Using radioactively labeled precursors, they have shown that short pieces of DNA are made in pachynema, and that some DNA digestion also occurs at this time. Because synthesis and breakdown of short pieces of DNA compensate one another, there is *no net change* in the amount of DNA present before and after pachynema. This is exactly what one expects for DNA repair synthesis . . . . a replacement of DNA and not synthesis of more DNA than was present at the beginning.

Hotta and Stern have conducted many other kinds of experiments to determine the influence of inhibition of DNA, RNA, and protein synthesis on chiasma formation, as an index to molecular recombination events. Thus far, all of their studies have strengthened the proposal that DNA repair synthesis is involved in crossing over and chiasma formation and, therefore, underlies molecular recombination events.

We now have the broad picture of molecular recombination. What is still missing are some of the specific details that contribute to this overall picture. There is every reason to expect these missing details to be discovered and the whole story of recombination to be revealed in future investigations.

7.7   Gene Conversion

The phenomenon of **gene conversion** refers to unusual patterns of allele segregation in which expected ratios of 1:1 for a pair of alleles may be distorted to give 3:1 and other ratios. The term gene conversion was coined to reflect the belief that somehow one allele was converted or transformed into its alternative allelic form. Gene conversion has been studied primarily in different species of fungi, such as yeast and Neurospora, where tetrad ratios for allele segregations can be examined directly. In Neurospora, for example, one might find 4 a^+:4 a as expected among the eight ascospores of a single ascus, or it might be 2:6 or 6:2 or 5:3 or some similar ratio distortion. Gene conversion refers to this phenomenon of aberrant ratios for a single pair of alleles of a gene segregating at meiosis.

Gene conversion reflects a recombinational event and not mutation or some other DNA modification. This is evident from crosses where outside gene markers can be followed along with incidents of gene conversion. When recombinants are examined and found to have an aberrant ratio for one pair of alleles, the alleles of genes flanking the converted region can be shown to have undergone recombination to produce 1:1 allele segregations. Because of this relationship, it is most probable that gene conversion itself arises by some recombination event which has also rearranged genes on either side. Since gene conversion is confined to heterozygotes, it hardly seems possible that mutation could be responsible for the observed modifications. Mutation would affect homozygotes and heterozygotes equally.

The favored explanation for incidents of gene conversion, which occur very frequently in yeast and some other fungi, is that there is mismatching

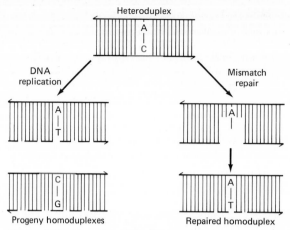

Figure 7.20   The mismatched base pair in a recombinant heteroduplex can be resolved in either of two ways: replication to produce semiconserved duplexes with matched base pairs, or mismatch repair of the heteroduplex itself. In the latter case, one strand is digested in the mismatched region, the intact strand is copied, and the repair is sealed. These two resolutions could yield aberrant tetrad ratios, if mismatch repair occurred within a sequence with a marker gene.

of nucleotide segments during DNA repair synthesis in recombination heteroduplexes; gene conversion is therefore believed to arise through what is called **mismatch repair** (Fig. 7.20). In fact, gene conversion has been proposed as one line of evidence for the occurrence of DNA repair synthesis in recombination.

Evidence showing that gene conversion rates and DNA repair are both affected in certain enzyme-deficient mutants has been provided by Holliday. He found that mutants of the smut fungus *Ustilago*, which were deficient in an endonuclease known to act on heteroduplex DNA, showed reduced rates of gene conversion and reduced efficiency of DNA repair synthesis. Similarly, other studies with yeast mutants showed that a deficiency in repair synthesis of radiation-damaged DNA was accompanied by higher frequencies of gene conversion events in the mutants. These observations are relevant to proposed mismatch repair of a heteroduplex, which can yield 2:6 or 6:2 tetrad ratios for a pair of alleles, instead of 4:4. They are also relevant to segregation and subsequent replication of mismatched heteroduplex DNA, which is believed to be responsible for observed 3:5 and 5:3 tetrad ratios for a pair of alleles (Fig. 7.21).

At the present time we have useful models which can be tested genetically and physically. Gene conversion is a very significant component of genome change by recombination in other organisms as well as in fungi. It is important to understand how these events arise, and studies with Drosophila, fungi, and other organisms have been more and more informative in recent years. The complete resolution of the molecular mechanism is theoretically accessible to experimental analysis using genetic, molecular, and physical methods.

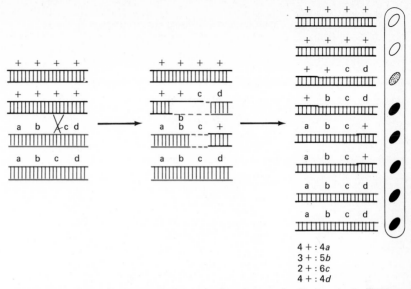

$4+:4a$
$3+:5b$
$2+:6c$
$4+:4d$

Figure 7.21   Following a crossover event, mismatch repair of heteroduplex DNA could produce 2 +:6 c, while segregation and later replication of mismatched heteroduplex DNA could be responsible for 3 +:5 b tetrad ratio. Outside markers +/a and +/d segregated 4:4, as expected. These 4:4 tetrad ratios for the outside markers emphasize the recombinational origin of **gene conversion** ratios for pairs of other alleles in the same tetrads.

CHROMOSOMAL DNA IN EUKARYOTES

Eukaryotes have their DNA distributed in separate molecules among two or more chromosomes that make up the genome, and this DNA is part of a nucleoprotein complex in each chromosome. Prokaryotes and viruses have all of the genome contained in one DNA or RNA molecule. Furthermore, there is a great deal more DNA per nucleus in the eukaryotic cell than in any bacterium or virus (Table 7.1). How is all of the DNA arranged in the eukaryotic chromosome? How is the vast amount of DNA packaged into the relatively small confines of a chromosome or a nucleus? In order to understand replication, recombination, and the operations of the genetic system in eukaryotes, it is essential to know the physical ordering of the genetic material and molecules with which genes interact in transcription into RNA, regulation of gene expression, and other phenomena.

We expect that many of the differences in chromosomal and genome organization between eukaryotic and prokaryotic organisms provide the basis for understanding the profound differences in development and differentiation of complex multicellular organisms compared with a bacterial cell or a virus particle. We also expect that similarities in metabolism and genetic operations are due to similarities in gene structure and function in all these groups.

Table 7.1
DNA content in various organisms (See also Box 7.2)

Organism	Haploid DNA content in picograms (10^{-12} g)
Viruses	
Herpes simplex	0.00011
Bacteriophage λ	0.000055
Bacteriophage T2	0.0002
Bacteria (prokaryotes)	
Escherichia coli	0.0047
Staphylococcus aureus	0.007
Salmonella typhimurium	0.013
Eukaryotes	
Yeast	0.018
Corn	7.5
Drosophila melanogaster	0.18
Rana pipiens (frog)	6.5
Mus musculus (mouse)	2.5
Human	3.2

Various sources for data, including Sober, H. A. 1970. *Handbook of Biochemistry*, 2nd ed. Chemical Rubber Co., Cleveland.

In the remainder of this chapter, we will look briefly at selected features of eukaryotic chromosome organization, as analyzed at the molecular level. This should provide the background for subsequent topics to be discussed in succeeding chapters.

7.8   One DNA Duplex per Chromosome

Interpretations of available genetic data, as well as information from replication and recombination studies, were consistent with the presence of a single duplex DNA molecule in a chromosome. Until 1973, however, there was inadequate evidence to support this working hypothesis. Two independent experimental approaches were reported in 1973, each showing that the eukaryotic chromosome contains a single duplex DNA molecule that extends from one end of the chromosome to the other.

Studies of yeast chromosomal DNA by Thomas Petes and others showed that one DNA molecule was present in each of the 17 chromosomes of a haploid nucleus. When total nuclear DNA is extracted from a known number of cells, it is a matter of simple arithmetic to figure out the amount of DNA per nucleus. There are about 10^{10} daltons of DNA per nucleus, and an average of 6×10^8 daltons of DNA per chromosome in yeast.

Petes used two independent methods to determine whether an average molecular weight of 6×10^8 daltons of DNA represented one duplex DNA molecule per chromosome:

1.   Carefully isolated yeast nuclear DNA was centrifuged in density gradients. DNA occurred in regions of the gradient which indicated that the duplex molecules had a molecular weight of about 6×10^8 daltons. This value corresponds to one DNA duplex per chromosome.

2. Nuclear DNA was examined by electron microscopy, and molecules ranging in length from 50 to 365 μm were observed. Each μm of duplex DNA has an equivalent in molecular weight of 2×10^6 daltons. Therefore, the observed molecules had a range of molecular weight between 1 and 7×10^8 daltons and averaged out close to 6×10^8 daltons in this particular genome. Once again, the evidence shows a single DNA duplex per chromosome.

In a comparable study using a totally different analytical method, Ruth Kavenoff, Lynn Klotz, and Bruno Zimm reported in 1973 that there was one DNA molecule in the chromosomes of *Drosophila* species. They used a physical method in which DNA molecular weight was determined according to the rate of recoil of a stretched molecule which is undergoing relaxation. This **viscoelastic method** provides information only for the largest molecules in the DNA solution; short or broken molecules do not register. The investigators found that the longest DNA duplex in preparations of chromosomes from *Drosophila melanogaster* had a molecular weight of about 4×10^{10} daltons. This is equivalent to a molecule which is 20,000 μm long (2 cm). Molecules of this length could be present in chromosome 2 or chromosome 3, each of which has about the same length and is much longer than the X chromosome or chromosome 4 in this species (see Fig. 4.7). It appeared that each chromosome had one DNA molecule, but another interpretation also seemed possible. Each of these chromosomes has its centromere about in the middle, so that the two arms of chromosome 2 or 3 are approximately equal in length. Was it possible that each arm had one DNA molecule that was folded in half, and that there really were two DNA molecules in each chromosome, with one chromosome-length DNA on each side of the centromere (Fig. 7.22)?

To test this possibility, Kavenoff and co-workers examined the lengths

Figure 7.22   Since there was no increase in size of DNA (red) when arm lengths were modified in inversion chromosomes compared with equal-armed wild type chromosomes of the same overall length, there must be only one DNA duplex per chromosome. The DNA molecule extends from one end of the chromosome to the other, passing through the centromere region.

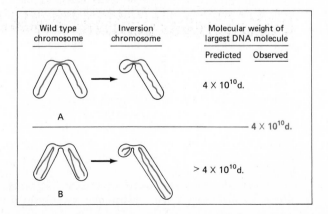

of DNA molecules from strains of *Drosophila* whose large chromosomes had been structurally rearranged. In one case the rearrangement changed the position of the centromere so that it was at one end of the chromosome, without changing the length of the whole chromosome itself. If there were only one DNA molecule in each arm, DNA should be twice as long in this particular altered chromosome, since it had one arm that was twice as long as the wild type chromosome. They found no change in DNA molecular weight between wild type chromosomes and the altered chromosome. This suggested that a single DNA molecule occurred as a continuous duplex through the centromere, from one end of a chromosome to the other. Confirming evidence for this interpretation was obtained from studies of other structurally altered chromosomes in *D. melanogaster* and in other *Drosophila* species.

The evidence from these studies in yeast and *Drosophila*, as well as other evidence reported since 1973, has amply confirmed the conclusion that each eukaryotic chromosome contains one duplex DNA molecule throughout its entire length.

7.9   Nucleosomes: Repeating Subunits of Chromosome Organization

Chromosomes are nucleoprotein structures, whose DNA molecule is bound to an assortment of proteins. The structural unit of the chromosome is called the **chromatin fiber**, which is best seen in interphase nuclei or metaphase chromosomes as greatly extended and folded threadlike structures (Fig. 7.23). This fiber folds back on itself over and over again to produce the even more condensed and compacted chromosome of a typical metaphase nucleus. Each chromatin fiber contains one DNA duplex, so each chromatin fiber is equivalent to an unreplicated chromosome, but chemically it is a nucleoprotein. How is this protein arranged in relation to DNA in the chromatin fiber? It is absolutely essential to understand this structural organization if we are to understand DNA activities in eukaryotic cells.

The current view of chromatin fiber organization began in 1974 with reports on biochemical analyses of chromatin by Roger Kornberg, and on electron microscopic analyses by A. L. and D. E. Olins. Kornberg found a repeating unit consisting of about 200 base-pairs of DNA complexed to an octamer of **histone proteins** (two each of histones H2A, H2B, H3, and H4), plus the fifth kind of histone, H1, in some undetermined association. This repeating unit of DNA plus the histone octamer was called a **nucleosome** (or nu-body). Olins and Olins produced electron micrographs showing that the chromatin fiber looked like a string of beads, each bead presumably representing a nucleosome (Fig. 7.24).

These studies created a considerable stir in the scientific community, and many laboratories became engaged in nucleosome analysis, which remains a subject of intensive study today. This breakthrough opened the way to detailed analyses of chromosome organization at the molecular level.

When isolated chromatin is partially degraded by nucleases, nucleosomes separate from the continuous chromatin fiber. Further enzymatic

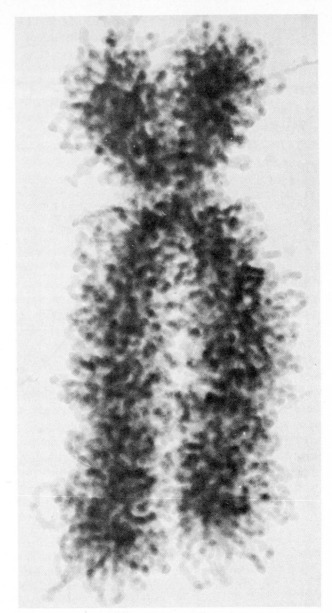

Figure 7.23 Electron micrograph of whole mount human chromosome 12, showing the extensively folded chromatin fiber making up each chromatid of the metaphase chromosome. × 27,000. Courtesy of E. J. DuPraw, from DuPraw, E. J. 1970. *DNA and Chromosomes*, Fig. 9.10, p. 144. New York: Holt, Rinehart, and Winston.)

degradation produces a nucleosome core particle of 140 base-pairs of DNA plus the histone octamer; histone H1 and 60 or more base-pairs of DNA are lost during these last stages of nuclease action. As work has progressed in

Mononucleosome   Oligonucleosome

DNA

Inner
histones

(a)

H1 class of histones
bound to spacer region

(b)

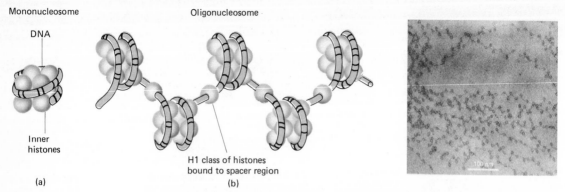

Figure 7.24   The nucleosome model of chromatin fiber organization. (a) The repeating unit of the fiber is the nucleosome, which consists of about 200 base-pairs of DNA wound around an octamer of histones (2 each of H2A, H2B, H3, and H4). (b) The nucleosomes are part of a continuous nucleoprotein (chromatin) fiber, consisting of one DNA duplex wound around histone octamers at regular intervals, and in association with histone H1 in the space of DNA between adjacent nucleosomes. When the chromatin fiber is digested by nuclease action, separate nucleosomes are recovered. The spacer DNA + histone H1 are removed by further digestion, leaving a nucleosome core particle of 140 base-pairs wrapped around the histone octamer. (c) Electron micrograph of chicken erythrocyte chromatin showing fibers artifactually stretched out during preparation, resembling a string of beads. (From Olins, D.E., and A.L. Olins. 1978. *Amer. Sci.* **66**:704.)

analyzing nucleosome composition and organization, the definitions have undergone some refinements. We now view the nucleosome as consisting only of what was formerly called the core, that is, having 140 base-pairs of DNA and an octamer consisting of two each of the four kinds of histone proteins. The 60 or more base-pairs of DNA and histone H1 are now viewed as "linking" segments between nucleosomes, and not as parts of the nucleosome itself.

The whole chromatin fiber has a *constant diameter* along its length, and is not really a string of wider beads linked by narrower nucleoprotein pieces. Pictures such as those produced in the mid-1970s are now believed to be of unraveled fibers produced by harsh treatments during preparations for electron microscopy. Duplex DNA is coiled around the outside of the nucleosomes, giving rise to a flexibly-jointed filament of repeating units. Each nucleosome around which the helical DNA is wound appears to be a roughly disk-shaped particle which is made up of two wedge-shaped, symmetrically arranged halves.

The nucleosome concept of chromatin fiber organization has several important implications. First, it provides a satisfactory model by which a rather stiff nucleoprotein fiber can be folded back on itself repeatedly to occupy a space which may be little more than one or a few micrometers of chromosome length. There is enough flexibility in such a fiber for 20,000 μm or more to fold into the tiny condensed chromosomes typical of metaphase nuclei. Second, the proposed association with histones helps to explain how DNA is protected against attack by the abundance of nucleases known to be present in nuclei of living cells. We expect that additional information on nucleosome organization will provide the needed perspective to understand how parts of the DNA molecule are accessible to enzymatically controlled transcription into RNA while other parts of the same molecule are not engaged in transcription. We will discuss this topic again in Chapter 9.

7.10   Repetitious DNAs

Eukaryotic DNA consists of two kinds of nucleotide sequences: (1) **unique-copy** sequences, present as single units represented once in a genome; and (2) **repetitious DNA** sequences, present in repeated units numbering up to millions of copies of the same nucleotide sequence in a genome. Unique-copy DNA apparently consists of all or most of the genes coding for polypeptides, representing the conventional genes analyzed by recombination and mapping methods. Repetitious DNA is highly variable, and several kinds of repeated sequences have been identified, including (1) informational DNA coding for ribosomal RNAs, transfer RNAs, and histone proteins; (2) noncoding sequences which are transcribed into RNA but which are not translated into the amino acid sequences in polypeptides; and (3) noncoding repeats which are never transcribed into RNA and which, therefore, cannot be translated into polypeptides.

When purified cellular DNA is centrifuged to equilibrium in CsCl, components with different percentages of G+C sediment to equilibrium in different parts of the gradient according to their buoyant density in CsCl (Fig. 7.25). Eukaryotic DNA invariably sediments into more than one fraction, whereas prokaryotic DNA bands as a single homogeneous population of DNA molecules. This difference reflects a fundamental distinction in the organization of eukaryotic and prokaryotic genomes, even though both are composed of DNA. In addition to a major component called **bulk nuclear DNA** in eukaryotes, a number of minor components called **satellite DNAs** can be identified after gradient sedimentation. These DNA fractions can be isolated from the gradients and purified for subsequent molecular studies.

The origin of satellite DNAs can be determined by comparisons between fractions obtained by centrifugation from whole-cell DNA and purified DNA from mitochondria, chloroplasts, and nuclei. Apart from mitochondrial and chloroplast DNAs, one or more satellite nuclear DNAs usually are separated from the bulk nuclear DNA in preparations of nuclei. The molecular characterization of nuclear DNAs was opened to detailed studies in the 1960s by Roy Britten and Eric Davidson, who developed the techniques for analysis of DNAs according to their **renaturation kinetics**, to obtain C_0t plots (Fig. 7.26).

Using these techniques, different fractions of nuclear DNA are analyzed according to the rate of **reassociation**, or **reannealing**, of melted single-strand fragments during renaturation of duplexes from these denatured pieces of DNA. DNA is denatured, or melted, to the single-strand state, and these strands are then broken down into pieces of a predetermined average size. These fragments are then allowed to pair, and the rate of duplex re-

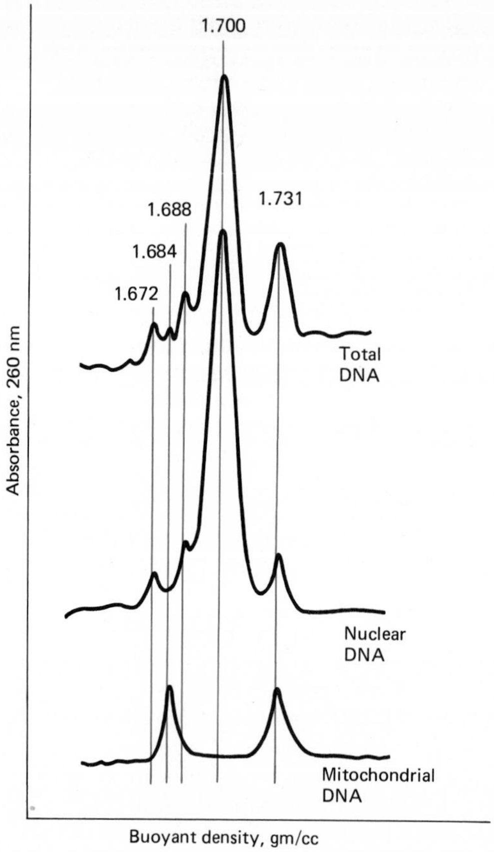

Figure 7.25 Densitometer tracings of purified DNAs from yeast, centrifuged to equilibrium in CsCl density gradients in an analytical ultracentrifuge. Buoyant density of DNA in CsCl is expressed in g/cc, and is proportional to G-C content of the DNA. Higher G-C content produces proportionately higher buoyant density values. The reference DNA bands at 1.731 g/cc, bulk nuclear DNA at 1.700 g/cc, and three satellite DNAs at 1.688, 1.684, and 1.672 g/cc. Examination of the bottom tracing reveals that the 1.684 g/cc satellite consists of mitochondrial DNA, while the other two satellites must be nuclear in origin since they appear in the middle tracing.

naturation is found to vary according to the relative degree of repetition of nucleotide sequences. Single-copy DNA is identified by its slow kinetics of renaturation; repetitive DNA renatures much more rapidly, and the more repetitious the DNA is, the faster the fragments will renature (Box 7.1).

The basis for these observed kinetic differences is interpreted as follows: if there is one copy or a few copies of a nucleotide sequence in a DNA preparation, it takes some time before partner, complementary fragments "find" each other and pair; the more copies there are of some sequence, the better the chance for complementary sequences to "find" each other and renature. The highest renaturation rates therefore define **highly-repetitive DNA**, existing in millions of copies in a genome; **middle-repetitive** or **inter-**

Box 7.1
RENATURATION KINETICS OF DUPLEX DNA

The presence of unique–copy and repetitive DNA sequences in eukaryotes stands in contrast to the virtual absence of repetitive DNA in prokaryotic and viral genomes. This difference becomes apparent from the renaturation kinetics of the different sources of DNA, that is, from the measurements of the time course of reassociation of dissociated strands of duplex DNA. The extent of reassociation is usually monitored during an experiment by passing samples of the reaction mixture over *hydroxy-apatite columns*, since only duplex DNA binds selectively to hydroxyapatite crystals under appropriate conditions. Conditions for renaturation are standardized for temperature, ionic conditions, and 300–400 nucleotides per sheared fragment of single-stranded DNA from melted duplexes; this permits comparisons among different experiments and for different DNA sources.

The rate-limiting step in the reassociation reaction is one in which collisions occur between complementary single-stranded regions such that base-pairing begins. Reassociation thus follows second-order kinetics, according to the equation $\dfrac{C}{C_0} = \dfrac{1}{1 + KC_0t}$ where C_0 is the total DNA concentration, C the concentration of DNA remaining single-stranded at time t and K the reassociation rate constant. (a) The time course of an ideal, second-order reaction to illustrate the features of the logarithmic C_0t plot, with total DNA in the initial state being single-stranded and reassociated into double strands in the final state of the reaction. The rate constant of reassociation is inversely proportional to genome size, and the C_0t is therefore proportional to genome size (See Fig. 7.26). (b) The single S-shaped (sigmoidal) curve of the second-order reaction typifies total DNA from prokaryotes, but not from eukaryotes. The C_0t plot for calf thymus (eukaryotic) DNA indicates that some sequences are reassociating faster than others. When each component is isolated from the total DNA of eukaryotic origin, each component reassociates with second-order kinetics, but with different rates of reaction. The skewed curve for calf thymus DNA indicates that the population of DNA molecules is heterogeneous with respect to its kinetics of reassociation. Very low C_0t rates characterize rapidly reassociating DNA, indicating many copies of the same sequences are present and, therefore, they can "find" correct partners relatively easily. *E. coli* DNA is typically homogeneous according to its second-order kinetics, and shows the standard prokaryotic C_0t plot. From Britten, R. J., and D. E. Kohne. 1968. *Science* **161**:529.)

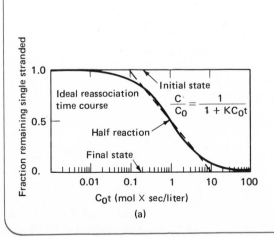

(a)

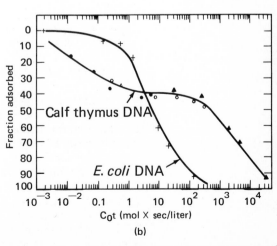

(b)

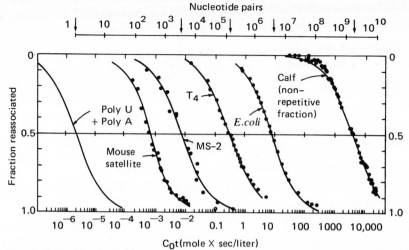

Figure 7.26   Kinetics of reassociation of dissociated fragments of duplex DNA from various sources. The genome size (in terms of nucleotide pairs) of each DNA source is indicated by arrows on the logarithmic scale at the top. Over a factor of 10^9 the genome size in nucleotide pairs is proportional to the C_0t time required for 50% reassociation (half-reaction). The shape of each curve indicates a second-order reaction and, therefore, shows that each sample was relatively homogeneous (See Box 7.1). (From Britten, R. J., and D. E. Kohne. 1968. *Science* **161**:529.)

mediate-repetitive DNA renatures more slowly, and exists in hundreds or thousands of copies per genome; while the slowest rates of renaturation define the portion of the genome consisting of unique-copy sequences.

Figure 7.27   Autoradiograph of mouse metaphase chromosomes after *in situ* hybridization with radioactively labeled RNA copied from mouse satellite DNA. Only centromeric heterochromatin is labeled (each chromosome has its centromere near one end), as seen by the distribution of dark silver grains over the lightly stained chromosomes. (Courtesy of M. L. Pardue and J. G. Gall)

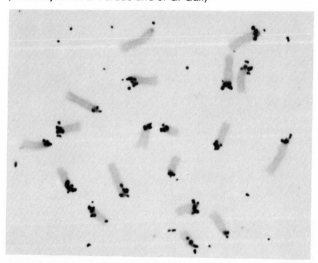

Satellite nuclear DNAs consist of highly-repetitive and intermediate-repetitive DNA, according to renaturation kinetics, while the bulk nuclear DNA consists predominantly or exclusively of unique-copy genes (Table 7.2).

How are these kinds of DNA distributed in the genome? Are there localized regions of repetitious DNA; are these sequences scattered throughout the genome; and how is unique-copy DNA arranged in relation to repetitious DNA? Some kinds of repetitious DNA have been localized specifically; for example, highly-repetitive DNA appears to be present particularly around the centromere of each chromosome. This information came from studies using the method of *in situ* **hybridization**, developed independently in 1969 by Joseph Gall and Mary Lou Pardue in the United States and by B. John in Edinburgh (Fig. 7.27). This method is an outgrowth of molecular hybridization, applied to direct observations of chromosomes on a microscope slide preparation. Radioactively labeled RNA or DNA is copied from satellite DNA strands *in vitro*, using RNA or DNA polymerase to guide the incorporation of labeled nucleotide precursors into the comple-

Table 7.2

Estimated amounts of unique-copy and repetitive DNA sequences in representative eukaryotic genomes (data from various sources)

Organism	Percent unique-copy DNA	Repetitive DNA	
		Percent	**No. of copies**
Paramecium aurelia (protozoan)	85	15	50-75
Dictyostelium discoideum (slime mold)	60	28	113
Neurospora crassa (true fungus)	80	20	60
Strongylocentrotus purpuratus (invertebrate: sea urchin)	50	27	10
		19	164
Nassaria obsoleta (invertebrate: gastropod)	38	12	20
		15	1,000
Bombyx mori (invertebrate: silkworm moth)	55	21	500
		24	50,000
Drosophila melanogaster (invertebrate: fruit fly)	78	15	35
		7	2,600
Xenopus laevis (vertebrate: amphibian; African clawed toad)	54	6	20
		31	1,600
		6	32,000
		3	high
Gallus domesticus (vertebrate: bird; chicken)	70	24	120
		3	330,000
		3	1,100,000
Bos taurus (vertebrate: mammal; cattle)	55	38	60,000
		2	1,000,000
		3	>1,000,000
Homo sapiens (vertebrate: mammal; human)	64	13	low
		12	intermediate
		10	high

mentary RNA or DNA strands. This RNA or DNA is then applied to chromosome preparations on a slide, after pretreatment to slightly denature chromosomal DNA and allow base pairing to occur. The preparation is covered by a photographic emulsion and autoradiographs are later developed to locate the silver grains, which indicate the sites where radioactive RNA or DNA has bound to complementary chromosomal DNA sequences.

Chemical analysis of highly-repetitive centromeric DNA revealed that there were between 10^5 and 10^7 repeats, in tandem, of 2-10 base-pairs in each reiterated sequence (Table 7.3). This highly-repetitive DNA is confined to regions consisting of **constitutive heterochromatin**, as determined by its properties of late replication, condensation in interphase chromosomes, and genetic stability (see Section 3.11). Furthermore, highly-repetitive DNA is not transcribed into RNA. This was shown by failure of the satellite DNA fraction to form molecular DNA-RNA hybrids with any part of whole-cell RNA. Since it does not hybridize with any cellular RNA, it must not make any RNA transcripts; otherwise some hybrid duplexes would have formed. We would not in any case expect a sequence of 2-10 nucleotides to code for polypeptide, since no more than three amino acids could be coded and this is not enough for functional polypeptide molecule construction. The function of highly-repetitive DNA is assumed to be related to chromosome structure, but there are no data to support this conjecture. In some cases, highly-repetitive DNA has been localized to noncentromeric chromatin, particularly to the Y chromosome in some species and to other parts of chromosomes with little or no known coding functions.

Middle-repetitive DNA can also be localized in the genome by *in situ* hybridization, if it forms a satellite in the gradient and can therefore be isolated and purified, or if its RNA transcripts are known. For these

Table 7.3
Characteristics of some satellite DNAs of known sequence

Organism	Base pairs per repeat	Sequence of one strand	Chromosomal location
Drosophila melanogaster	5	AGAAG	Centric heterochromatin of chromosome 2 only; arms of Y chromosome; distal end of 2L chromosome arm
	7	ATAAT ATATAAT	
	10	AATAACATAG AGAGAAGAAG	Centric heterochromatin of all chromosomes; tip of 2L chromosome arm
Drosophila virilis	7	ACAAACT ATAAACT ACAAATT	Centric heterochromatin
Cancer borealis (marine crab)	2	AT	?
Pagurus pollicaris (hermit crab)	4	ATCC	?
	3	CTG	?
Cavia poriella (guinea pig)	6	CCCTAA	Centric heterochromatin
Dipodomys ordii (kangaroo rat)	10	ACACAGCGGG	Centric heterochromatin

Source: Tartof, K. D. 1975. *Ann. Rev. Genet.* 9:355–385, Table 1.

Figure 7.28 Autoradiograph of larval polytene chromosome after *in situ* hybridization with 5S ribosomal RNA. The genes (coding DNA) for this RNA appear to be localized in region 2A at the left end of chromosome 2 in *Chironomus tentans*. (From Wieslander, L., B. Lambert, and E. Egyhazi. 1975. *Chromosoma* **51**:49.)

reasons, the best characterized DNAs of this type are sequences coding for **ribosomal RNAs, transfer RNAs,** and the genes for **histone proteins,** whose messenger RNAs can be isolated and purified from suitable cellular materials. Genes for 5S ribosomal RNA, transfer RNAs, and histone proteins may be localized in one region of one chromosome, in several different chromosomes, or even in every chromosome of the genome, according to the species studied (Fig. 7.28). Genes for the larger ribosomal RNAs, however, are always confined to the *nucleolar-organizing regions* of the chromosomes.

By chemical analysis, renaturation analysis, and nucleotide sequence measurements of the RNA transcripts or the DNA itself, middle-repetitive DNA has been found to consist of a relatively small number of repeats, numbering less than 100, or many thousands of reiterated sequences, arranged in tandem in a region of one or more chromosomes.

By molecular hybridizations and by electron microscopy of heteroduplex DNA-RNA or DNA-DNA molecules, it has also been shown that middle-repetitive DNA sequences may be separated by "spacer" segments of noncoding DNA. The organization of some repeated-DNA types will be discussed at greater length in Chapters 8 and 11. But from this preliminary survey it is apparent that eukaryotic DNA is organized into functionally distinct regions within individual chromosomes and within the genome. Each chromosome has one duplex DNA molecule, but the sequences of nucleotides are far from being arranged homogeneously in eukaryotes. There are substantial implications for gene expression and its regulation, and for development of the multicellular organism in relation to genome organization. These implications will be considered in various aspects in subsequent chapters.

7.11 How Many Genes Code for Proteins?

One of the major unanswered questions in genetics is: how many genes are there in a genome? Various attempts to answer this question have been made at various stages in our understanding of gene function. For example, when it was assumed that each gene coded for one enzyme, in the 1940s, one simply estimated the number of different enzymes in an organism and arrived at a gene number of some 3000-5000. The one-gene—one-enzyme concept was changed to one-gene—one polypeptide chain in a functional protein, in the 1960s. The estimate of gene number at that time was increased to coincide with the known fact that many proteins consist of two or more different polypeptide chains and could be coded by two or more different genes (as Yanofsky showed in *E. coli*). In the 1970s, the problem was compounded by discoveries of large amounts of noncoding DNA in the eukaryotic genome, and by the high variability in total DNA even in very closely related species (Box 7.2). We can estimate the length of an average gene, and determine total genomic DNA. But, simple arithmetic is inadequate for us to figure out how many such genes exist in the haploid genome. In order to do this we must know more about noncoding DNA and repetitious DNA that have been detected but not identified functionally.

Box 7.2

GENOME SIZE

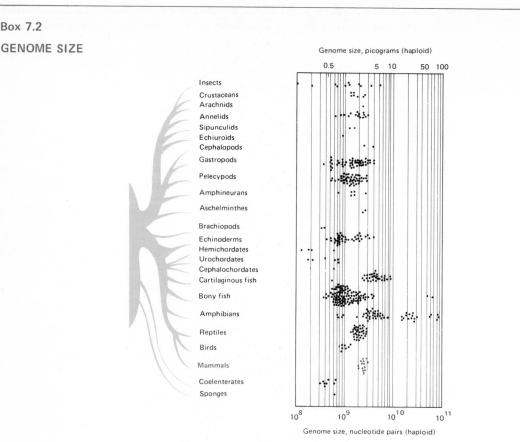

On the basis of genome size there is an enormous spread of values among animal groups, ranging from 10^8 nucleotide pairs in an insect to $8\text{-}9 \times 10^{11}$ in some amphibians. The greatest spread within a group occurs among amphibians, whereas the other groups of land vertebrates (reptiles, birds, and mammals) are far less variable. This may truly reflect group differences, or perhaps that amphibians have been studied more intensively than the other groups.

If the number of genes was reflected in genome size and in evolutionary rankings of species, we would not expect the most highly evolved animals (mammals) to have fewer genes than fish and amphibians. There is, in fact, no evident pattern showing correlations between evolutionary ranking and increase in the genome size or gene number. Some groups are quite variable and others are not, for reasons which remain uncertain. (From Britten, R. J., and E. H. Davidson. 1971. *Quart. Rev. Biol.* 46:111.)

The approximate number of genes coding for polypeptides in eukaryotes has been estimated from cytogenetic analysis, rather than from molecular studies. The experimental study which is quoted most often was reported by Burke Judd and co-workers in 1972, using specially constructed strains of

Drosophila melanogaster. They attempted to identify as many different single-gene mutations as possible within a small region of the X chromosome, and to compare the numbers of different gene mutations with the number of bands observed cytologically in larval polytene chromosomes (Fig. 7.29).

Using special strains in a series of crosses, Judd was able to isolate hundreds of different mutants for genes located in the region between the *z*este eye locus at chromosome band 3A2 and the *w*hite eye locus at band 3C2 of the X chromosome. From this collection, 121 different mutant strains were identified as having a single-gene mutation, on the basis of mutant × mutant yielding occasional wild type recombinants. Each single-gene mutant was then identified by a series of crosses as follows: (1) crosses with a set of reference deletion mutants to determine the crude location of the mutation in the *z—w* region; (2) crosses to determine the number of different

Figure 7.29 Drawing of a segment of the polytene X chromosome of *Drosophila melanogaster* showing the cytological extent of the deletions (Df) and duplications (Dp) used in determining the location of each complementation group. Each solid horizontal line shows the segment deleted or duplicated. Strain Df(1)w^{rJ1} was used in screening mutants in crosses, since the entire zeste—white region between bands 3A3 and 3C2 is missing. Strains with shorter deletions allowed rough placement of the mutation within the *z—w* region in subsequent crosses, and final location was achieved in another set of crosses. (From Judd, B. H., M. W. Shen, and T. C. Kaufman. 1972. *Genetics* **71**:139.)

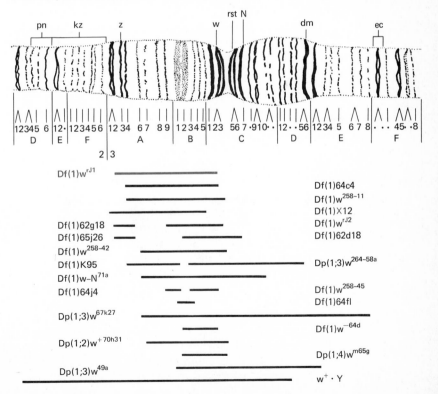

complementation groups, or gene loci, represented in the 121 different strains; and (3) finally, by pairwise crosses between different complementation group members, or single-gene mutants, to establish their order and distances apart according to recombination frequencies. These tests follow a pattern very similar to those we discussed for the *r*II region of phage T4 (see Section 6.3).

Judd found 12 complementation groups lying between the *z* and *w* loci, and 2 complementation groups just to the left of *z*. By comparing deficiencies covering known complementation groups with the cytological map, the 12 zeste-white groups of mutations were localized to a set of 11 bands in between the *z* locus at band 3A2 and the *w* locus at band 3C2 (Fig. 7.30). These results demonstrated a **correspondence between one gene and one chromosome band**. Since there are between 3000 and 5000 bands in the *D. melanogaster* haploid genome, it would appear that there are about 3000 to 5000 functional, coding genes present. These presumably represent unique-copy sequences coding for the polypeptides which govern phenotypic characteristics.

These results cannot be equated directly with the number of single-copy genes in *Drosophila* or, by extrapolation, to other eukaryotic genomes because the situation is far more complex than this study indicates. We know of single bands which seem to harbor several different genes in *Chironomus* as well as in *Drosophila* polytene chromosomes. Even more significantly, the amount of DNA per band is 7-10 times more than is needed to code for one polypeptide chain. What is the function of this excess DNA? Is it coding or noncoding? Does DNA regulate polypeptide-coding genes? These and many other questions cannot be answered at present because there are conflicting data from different experimental systems. As we will see in the chapters which follow, the complexity of genome organi-

Figure 7.30 Photograph of the part of the X chromosome in *Drosophila melanogaster* which includes the *z—w* region between bands 3A3 and 3C2. The 12 *zw* complementation groups between *z* and *w* are shown in order below, and are referred to the 11 bands (3A4, 6, 7, 8, 9; 3B1–5; 3C1) of the zeste—white region, encompassing only 0.75 map unit of distance. (From Judd, B. H., M. W. Shen, and T. C. Kaufman. 1972. *Genetics* **71**:139.)

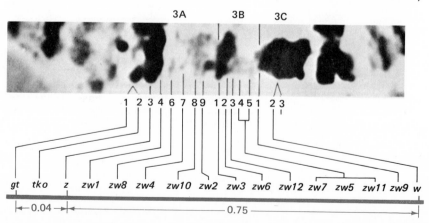

zation in eukaryotes is only just beginning to open up to experimental analysis. Far more important than knowing the number of genes in a genome is the knowledge of how coded genes function and how these functions are regulated and coordinated so that a single fertilized egg can develop over a period of many months into a complex newborn human being, and how this newborn continues to develop over many years by programs of genetic activity to become the person who is now reading this book.

QUESTIONS AND PROBLEMS

7.1. If a mixture of [^{15}N]DNA and normal [^{14}N]DNA from phage T2 is heated and then cooled slowly before density gradient centrifugation, three bands will be formed at equilibrium: two corresponding to those formed by the unheated material, and one of hybrid density. If a mixture of [^{15}N]DNA from phage T2 and unlabeled [^{14}N]DNA from phage T4 are similarly treated, only two bands are found. Explain the presence of the hybrid band in the first example and its absence in the second.

7.2. The GC content of DNA is used to characterize the molecule. Given that the A+G/T+C ratio in one strand of duplex DNA is 0.3,
   a. What is the ratio in the complementary strand?
   b. What is the ratio in the entire molecule?
   c. If the A+T/C+G ratio is 0.3, what is the ratio in the complementary strand? in the entire molecule?

7.3. A duplex DNA of the composition

C-G
A-T
G-C
T-A

produces RNA which has a base ratio of 25% A, 25% U, 25% C, and 25% G. Can you distinguish whether the RNA is formed from one or from both strands of this DNA?

7.4. The following data show the base composition of DNA and RNA of two bacteria.

Species	DNA base ratio A+T/G+C	RNA base ratio A+G/U+C
Bacillus subtilis	1.36	1.02
Escherichia coli	1.00	0.80

How can you tell whether the RNA itself is single- or double-stranded?

7.5. Messenger RNA was transcribed *in vitro* from enzymatically synthesized DNA, which was later melted to its constituent single strands.

For each strand of the DNA, the base ratio was analyzed and compared with that of mRNA. On the basis of the following ratios, which strand of the duplex DNA served as the template for mRNA synthesis?

	A	T or U	G	C
DNA-1	27.0	32.5	18.5	22.0
DNA-2	32.7	26.8	22.1	18.4
mRNA	27.0	33.0	18.0	22.0

7.6. Suppose you have a genetically determined protein in *E. coli* with a partial amino acid sequence of —Pro-Trp-Ser-Gly-Lys-Cys-His—. You recover a series of mutants that have lost the function performed by this protein, and you find the mutant proteins to include the following partial sequences:

Mutant 1   —Pro-Trp-Arg-Gly-Lys-Cys-His—
       2   —Pro—
       3   —Pro-Gly-Val-Lys-Asn-Cys-His—

a. What is the molecular basis for each of these three mutations?
b. What is the DNA sequence for the wild type protein in this particular region of the gene?

7.7. Suppose you begin with a bacterial culture whose duplex DNA has every nitrogen atom of the heavy isotope kind, or ^{15}N, instead of the usual ^{14}N. DNA replication is then allowed to occur in an environment containing only ^{14}N. Using a straight line for a heavy polynucleotide chain and a wavy line for a light chain, diagram the following:

a. The heavy parental chromosome and the products of the first replication after transfer to the ^{14}N-medium, assuming that the chromosome is a single duplex DNA molecule and that replication is semiconservative.
b. Repeat part (a) but assume that replication is conservative.
c. Suppose that the daughter chromosomes produced in the first replication in ^{14}N-medium were centrifuged in CsCl density gradient, and a single band of DNA was obtained. What would this prove?

7.8. The following sequence is found in a DNA polymer 20 bases long:
3'-C A C G T C A T T A T T C C A G C T T A-5'

a. What would be the first 10 bases of the 3' end of the complementary strand?
b. What would be the first 10 bases of the 5' end of the complementary strand?
c. Assuming the existence of complementary strands, what is the percentage composition of the polymer with respect to A-T base pairs, and G-C pairs?

7.9. A cell culture is incubated in a medium containing the thymidine analog bromodeoxyuridine (BrdU). A particular dye that binds to DNA fluoresces weakly when bound to DNA in which BrdU is substituted for thymidine in both strands of the double helix. The dye fluoresces strongly when bound to DNA that contains BrdU in only one of the strands of duplex molecules.

a. Suppose a cell containing a single chromosome went through two generations (DNA replications) in BrdU medium. Diagram the appearance of the metaphase chromosome, indicating the relative fluorescence of the two sister chromatids.

b. Diagram the metaphase chromosomes found in each daughter cell after a third generation in BrdU medium.

c. Suppose the cell had 40 chromosomes. After 4 generations in BrdU, how many brightly fluorescing *chromatids*, on the average, would be found in a given cell? (Assume a random segregation of sister chromatids during mitosis.)

REFERENCES

Alberts, B. M., and L. Frey. 1970. T4 bacteriophage gene 32: A structural protein in the replication and recombination of DNA. *Nature* **227**:1313.

Alberts, B. M., and R. Sternglanz. 1977. Recent excitement in the DNA replication problem. *Nature* **269**:655.

Britten, R. J., and D. E. Kohne. 1968. Repeated sequences in DNA. *Science* **161**:529.

Britten, R. J., and D. E. Kohne. Apr. 1970. Repeated DNA. *Sci. Amer.* **222**:24.

Cairns, J. Jan. 1966. The bacterial chromosome. *Sci. Amer.* **214**:36.

Cold Spring Harbor Symposia on Quantitative Biology
1974. *Chromosome Structure and Function.* Vol. 38.
1978. *Chromatin.* Vol. 42.
1979. *DNA: Replication and Recombination.* Vol. 43.

Davidson, E. H., G. A. Galau, R. C. Angerer, and R. J. Britten. 1975. Comparative aspects of DNA organization in metazoa. *Chromosoma* **51**:253.

Davis, B. D. 1977. The recombinant DNA scenarios: Andromeda strain, chimera, and Golem. *Amer. Sci.* **65**:547.

Dressler, D. 1970. The rolling circle for ϕX DNA replication, II. Synthesis of single-stranded circles. *Proc. Nat. Acad. Sci. U. S.* **67**:1934.

Esposito, M. S., and R. E. Esposito. 1978. Gene conversion, paramutation, and controlling elements: A treasure of exceptions. In *Cell Biology, A Comprehensive Treatise* (L. Goldstein and D. M. Prescott, eds.), Vol. 1, p. 59.

Finch, J. T., L. C. Lutter, D. Rhodes, R. S. Brown, B. Rushton, M. Levitt, and A. Klug. 1977. Structure of nucleosome core particles of chromatin. *Nature* **269**:29.

Flint, S. J. 1979. Spliced viral messenger RNA. *Amer. Sci.* **67**:300.

Friedmann, T. 1979. Rapid nucleotide sequencing of DNA. *Amer. J. Human Genet.* **31**:19.

Gall, J. G., and M. L. Pardue. 1969. Formation and detection of RNA-DNA hybrid molecules in cytological preparations. *Proc. Nat. Acad. Sci. U. S.* **63**:378.

Gilbert, W. 1978. Why genes in pieces? *Nature* **271**:501.

Gilbert, W., and D. Dressler. 1969. DNA replication: The rolling circle model. Cold Spring Harbor Sympos. Quant. Biol. **33** (1968):473.

Hall, B. D., and S. Spiegelman. 1961. Sequence complementarity of T2-DNA and T2-specific RNA. *Proc. Nat. Acad. Sci. U. S.* **47**: 137.

Hand, R. 1978. Eucaryotic DNA: Organization of the genome for replication. *Cell* **15**:317.

Jorcano, J. L., and A. Ruiz-Carrillo. 1979. H3-H4 tetramer directs DNA and core histone octamer assembly in the nucleosome core particle. *Biochemistry* **18**:768.

Judd, B. H., M. W. Shen, and T. C. Kaufman. 1972. The anatomy and function of a segment of the X chromosome of *Drosophila melanogaster. Genetics* **71**:139.

Kavenoff, R., L. Klotz, and B. Zimm. 1974. On the nature of chromosome-sized DNA molecules. *Cold Spring Harbor Sympos. Quant. Biol.* **38**(1973):1.

Kornberg, A. 1974. *DNA Synthesis.* San Francisco: Freeman.

Kornberg, A. Oct. 1968. The synthesis of DNA. *Sci. Amer.* **219**:64.

Kornberg, R. D. 1974. Chromatin structure: A repeating unit of histones and DNA. *Science* **184**:868.

Kriegstein, H. J., and D. S. Hogness. 1974. Mechanism of DNA replication in *Drosophila* chromosomes: Structure of replication forks and evidence for bidirectionality. *Proc. Nat. Acad. Sci. U. S.* **71**:135.

Laskey, R. A., B. M. Honda, A. D. Mills, and J. T. Finch. 1978. Nucleosomes are assembled by an acidic protein which binds histones and transfers them to DNA. *Nature* **275**:416.

Lauer, G. D., T. M. Roberts, and L. C. Klotz. 1977. Determination of the nuclear DNA content of *Saccharomyces cerevisiae* and implications for the organization of DNA in yeast chromosomes. *J. Mol. Biol.* **114**:507.

Meselson, M., and C. M. Radding. 1975. A general model for genetic recombination. *Proc. Nat. Acad. Sci. U.S.* **72**:358.

Meselson, M., and J. J. Weigle. 1961. Chromosome breakage accompanying genetic recombination in bacteriophage. *Proc. Nat. Acad. Sci. U. S.* **47**:857.

Müller, U., H. Zentgraf, I. Eicken, and W. Keller. 1978. Higher order structure of Simian virus 40 chromatin. *Science* **201**:406.

Olins, A. L., and D. E. Olins. 1979. Stereo electron microscopy of the 25-nm chromatin fibers in isolated nuclei. *J. Cell Biol.* **81**:260.

Olins, D. E., and A. L. Olins. 1978. Nucleosomes: The structural quantum in chromosomes. *Amer. Sci.* **66**:704.

Pardue, M. L., and J. G. Gall. 1970. Chromosomal localization of mouse satellite DNA. *Science* **168**:1356.

Polani, P. E., J. A. Crolla, M. J. Seller, and F. Moir. 1979. Meiotic crossing over exchange in the female mouse visualized by BUdR substitution. *Nature* **278**:348.

Potter, H., and D. Dressler. 1976. On the mechanism of genetic recombination: Electron microscopic observation of recombination intermediates. *Proc. Nat. Acad. Sci. U. S.* **73**:3000.

Potter, H., and D. Dressler. 1979. Biochemical assay designed to detect formation of recombination intermediates *in vitro*. *Proc. Nat. Acad. Sci. U. S.* **76**:1084.

Spiegelman, S. May 1964. Hybrid nucleic acids. *Sci. Amer.* **210**:48.

Wensink, P. C., D. J. Finnegan, J. E. Donelson, and D. S. Hogness. 1974. A system for mapping DNA sequences in the chromosomes of *Drosophila melanogaster*. *Cell* **3**:315.

Wickner, S. H. 1978. DNA replication proteins of *Escherichia coli*. *Ann. Rev. Biochem.* **47**:1163.

Winnacker, E.-L. 1978. Adenovirus DNA: Structure and function of a novel replicon. *Cell* **14**:761.

Worcel, A., S. Han, and M. L. Wong. 1978. Assembly of newly replicated chromatin. *Cell* **15**:969.

Gene Expression

The usual direction of information flow from genotype to phenotype, through processes involved in the overall phenomenon of gene expression, is shown by: $\text{DNA} \rightarrow \text{RNA} \rightarrow \text{protein}$. DNA transfers information to make new DNA in replication, DNA information is copied into RNA during transcription, and this copied information guides synthesis of coded polypeptides during translation. The coded polypeptides underwrite phenotypic development in the organism.

RNA transcripts are synthesized as larger precursor molecules, which are then processed to their final functional forms. Messenger RNA is composed of noncoding sequences at its 5′ and 3′ termini. Eukaryotic messengers are further modified at these termini and also within the coding region in between the 5′ and 3′ termini. Ribosomal and transfer RNAs are modified in different ways.

Protein synthesis takes place on polysomes, which are groups of active ribosomes bound to messenger RNA. Correct positioning of the messenger to the ribosome and to transfer RNA carriers of amino acids as well as readout of the message are based on the rule of complementary base-pairing between RNAs. The polypeptide is initiated, elongated, and terminated in steps which require processes that are coordinated and catalytically assisted by the ribosomes. Various enzymes and other proteins are identified as requirements in particular stages of the translation process. The outcome is an accurately made polypeptide, which contributes to normal phenotypic development.

Various antibiotics interfere with protein synthesis at different steps in translation. These effects are illustrated by streptomycin action.

INFORMATION FLOW FROM DNA

The genetic information encoded in DNA is expressed in three distinct steps:

1. **Replication**, in which the sequence of deoxyribonucleotides in DNA directs the synthesis of an identical replica sequence of deoxyribonucleotides;
2. **Transcription**, in which the sequence of deoxyribonucleotides in DNA directs the synthesis of a complementary sequence of ribonucleotides in RNA; and
3. **Translation**, in which the sequence of ribonucleotides in messenger RNA guides the synthesis of a corresponding sequence of amino acids in polypeptides.

Proteins, which consist of one or more polypeptide chains, contribute to cellular activities in many different ways. Proteins which function as enzyme catalysts facilitate many biochemical reactions whose products are the visible phenotypes of a cell.

In the last chapter we discussed replication. In this chapter we will look at the processes of transcription and translation, and see how genetic and molecular methods can be used to analyze these steps in **gene expression**.

8.1   An Overview of Information Flow

Using molecular analysis, we can study how information in DNA contributes to phenotypic development. The ultimate focus of all these studies is to understand how a gene in a chromosome directs the development of a phenotype such as brown eyes or blue eyes, diseases such as phenylketonuria or sickle cell anemia, and other characteristics. By biochemical studies we can often determine the chemical reactions which are involved, and we can sometimes understand how particular changes ultimately lead to an altered phenotype. We may not be able to trace all the steps in the maze of metabolism and development, but we can frequently determine the *primary* reaction that leads to the phenotype (Fig. 8.1). An altered enzyme protein results from an altered codon in the gene, so gene and protein or genotype and phenotype relations can be established by genetic analysis. But what are the intervening processes between gene and enzyme, or between the coded gene and its expression in the organism?

DNA remains fixed in its location in the cell nucleus, while protein synthesis takes place in the surrounding cytoplasm in eukaryotes. Using specific stains or autoradiography we can see that DNA is spatially separated from the sites of protein synthesis. There must therefore be an intermediary which takes DNA instructions out to these sites of protein synthesis. The logical candidate for such an intermediary or messenger is RNA, which is also a polynucleotide and can interact with DNA through complementary base-pairing. We would therefore expect to find RNA in the nucleus and in the cytoplasm, which is exactly what we do find in

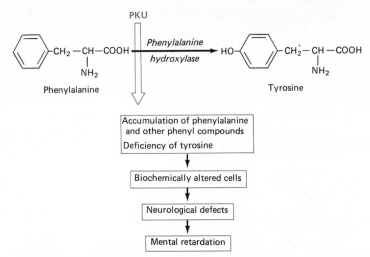

Figure 8.1 Human beings with the inherited disorder phenylketonuria (PKU) do not hydroxylate phenylalanine due to an enzyme defect. The phenotypic consequences of this primary fault in metabolism are varied, and may lead to mental retardation unless dietary correction is initiated early and maintained for about the first six years of childhood.

actively synthesizing systems. In fact, we have known for a long time that protein synthesis will not take place in the absence of RNA.

Three kinds of RNA must interact during protein synthesis: **messenger RNA (mRNA), ribosomal RNA (rRNA), and transfer RNA (tRNA).** All these RNAs are complementary copies of DNA sequences, synthesized during transcription, and they are all required for translation of genetic information into polypeptides.

Each kind of RNA has a different but related function in translation. DNA codons specifying amino acids are transcribed into mRNA complementary condons, as we implied in our earlier discussion of the genetic code. If the DNA coding sequence is ATCGGCTA, then the mRNA copy will be UAGCCGAU. Translation of the mRNA message absolutely requires the participation of ribosomes, which contain rRNA, and tRNAs, which carry amino acids to the mRNA—ribosome complexes. The system which underwrites the accuracy of interactions leading to accuracy in translation of an exact copy of the genetic instructions is complementary base-pairing (Fig. 8.2). The 5′ end of mRNA binds to the ribosome through base-pairing between parts of mRNA and rRNA. The correct amino acid is brought to the ribosome and inserted in correct sequence in the growing polypeptide through base-pairing between the mRNA codon and the **anticodon** in tRNA, to which the amino acid is attached. The recognition system therefore involves the simple molecular feature of pairing between A and T or U and between G and C.

When the allele for normal hemoglobin (*Hb A*) is transcribed into mRNA, the codon for *glutamic acid* is copied precisely into the position corresponding to amino acid 6 in the polypeptide. During translation of the

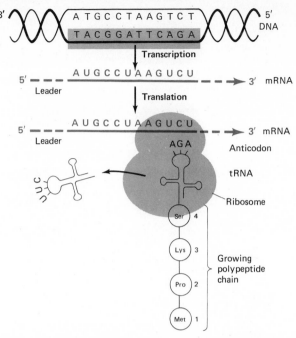

Figure 8.2 Complementary base pairing is the basic feature of the recognition system which provides for the high degree of accuracy in translation of the genetic message into polypeptide at the ribosome.

β-globin chain, glutamic acid is correctly positioned because of pairing between the mRNA codon and the anticodon of the tRNA carrying this amino acid. If mRNA is transcribed from the alternate *Hb S* allele for sickle cell β-globin, then a different codon occupies position number 6, and *valine* is installed in that site in the globin chain when a valine-carrying tRNA appears with the matching anticodon (Fig. 8.3). This seemingly simple change leads to profound alteration in protein shape, which affects the oxygen-carrying capacity of sickle-cell hemoglobin. The red blood cells carrying the altered hemoglobin are responsible in turn for circulatory problems, which are responsible for symptoms that characterize the distress of sickle cell anemia.

8.2   Transcription And Processing Of mRNA

Enzymes which catalyze transcription are **DNA-dependent RNA polymerases**, usually just called **RNA polymerases** for short. The template for synthesis is one strand of DNA, and the product of synthesis is an RNA polymer consisting of a single chain of covalently linked ribonucleotides which are complementary to template DNA. Of all the RNA polymerases, the *E. coli* enzyme has been characterized in the greatest detail, by genetic and biochemical analyses.

RNA polymerase of *E. coli* consists of six polypeptides: one each of β, β',

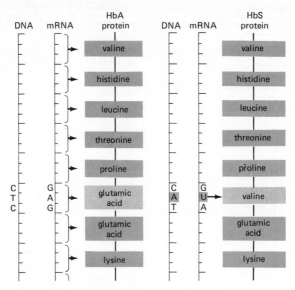

Figure 8.3 Glutamic acid is inserted at position 6 in the β chain of Hb A protein, or valine at position 6 in Hb S (sickle cell hemoglobin), according to the mRNA codon which is recognized by the transfer RNA (tRNA) anticodon which carries the amino acid to the ribosome.

ω, and σ, and two α chains. If the σ subunit is dissociated from the whole enzyme *in vitro*, transcription is initiated at random along the DNA template, instead of at its special initiation site, and both DNA strands are copied instead of the usual coding **sense strand**. When σ is added back, transcription is initiated correctly and only the sense strand of DNA is copied. These data indicate the requirement of the σ subunit for recognition of the initiation, or **promoter**, site on DNA by the RNA polymerase. The function of the β polypeptide has been interpreted from **mixed reconstitution** studies using enzyme subunits from a drug-resistant mutant and from normal *E. coli*. Transcription is not initiated in wild type *E. coli* grown with the anti-tuberculosis drug **rifampicin**; rifampicin-resistant *E. coli* mutants have been used in the reconstitution studies. The only combination of the six polypeptide subunits which produced a rifampicin-resistant RNA polymerase was one containing the β polypeptide from the mutant; it didn't matter what source had provided the other five subunits. This indicates the involvement of the β subunit in the initiation of transcription.

The gene loci for *E. coli* RNA polymerase polypeptides are not clustered in the genome. (Fig. 8.4). From the observed scatter between 66 and 89 minutes on the map, it appears that subunits may not be made coordinately and that they probably assemble into the whole functional enzyme later on in the cells. The *rpo* loci on the map (*rpo* stands for *R*NA *po*lymerase) are those for α (*rpoA*), β (*rpoB*), β' (*rpoC*), and σ (*rpoD*); the gene for ω has not yet been mapped. The *rho* locus codes for the **rho protein**, which is essential for termination of transcription of the gene sequence; its mode of action is uncertain.

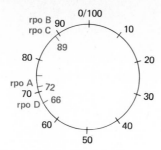

Figure 8.4 Genetic map of *E. coli* showing known genes which code for the various polypeptide components of functional RNA polymerase protein.

There are three different nuclear RNA polymerases in eukaryotes (Table 8.1). These enzymes can be distinguished by their subcellular location, sensitivity to particular antibiotic drugs, and by the functional kinds of RNA transcripts which they produce.

When separated strands of duplex DNA are allowed to interact with RNA, all or most of the RNA binds to only one of the two DNA strands. The fact that an RNA transcript will only bind to one strand indicates that this is the template strand of DNA, or the coding **sense strand**. The other DNA strand is **anti-sense** and noncoding. This information was obtained from **DNA-RNA molecular hybridization**, a method developed in the early 1960s by Sol Spiegelman and Benjamin Hall (Fig. 8.5).

The two DNA strands can be separated and identified if they contain different percentages of purines, since the heavier AG-rich strand settles in a different part of an alkaline CsCl gradient than its lighter partner which has less A and G. The isolated **heavy (H)** and **light (L)** strands can then be hybridized separately with any known kind of RNA. Their complementarity is revealed by the formation of **DNA-RNA hybrid duplexes**. Since base-pairing is highly specific, the interpretation is that the RNA was transcribed from the DNA strand with which it pairs. The anti-sense strand, therefore, is not transcribed. Molecular hybridization is a fundamental and extremely useful method in molecular genetics.

In certain viruses and in some mitochondrial and chloroplast DNAs, parts of *both* the H and L strand may code for polypeptides or for tRNAs. In other words, different genes may be transcribed from the H and the L strands. In these cases, relatively little coded information is included in the L strand, and most of the coded genome is in the H, or sense, strand. Whether the H or L strand is transcribed, *RNA polymerization proceeds in the 5' ⟶ 3' direction along the DNA template strand.* Since ribonucleotides (like deoxyribonucleotides) are added *only* at the growing 3' end, and the two chains are *antiparallel*, and since mRNA is *translated in the 5' ⟶ 3'*

Table 8.1
Characteristics of RNA polymerases from animal nuclei

Polymerase type	Nuclear location	Cellular RNAs transcribed
I	nucleolus	18S and 28S rRNAs
II	nucleoplasm	hnRNA (pre-mRNA) and mRNA
III	nucleoplasm	tRNAs, 5S rRNA

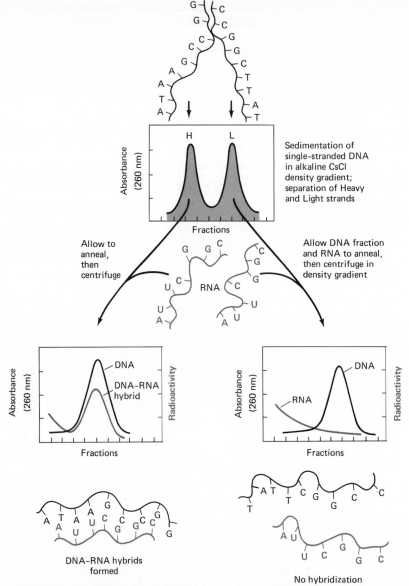

Figure 8.5 DNA-RNA molecular hybridization. Melted single strands of duplex DNA, separated by centrifugation, are mixed with radioactively labeled RNA in the annealing (association of complementary strands) phase of the procedure. The positions and amounts of DNA and of DNA-RNA molecular hybrids are revealed by absorbance at 260 nm, and distinguished by the radioactive labels carried. Curves such as these indicate whether or not hybridization has taken place.

direction, the gene sequence must start at the 3′ end of the DNA. These are important considerations when comparing DNA and mRNA sequence complementarity, and colinearity of mRNA and polypeptide.

The relationship between template DNA and its mRNA transcript is:

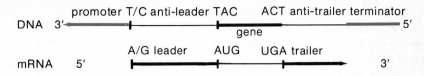

Purified-mRNA sequencing has shown that there is a non-coding **leader** consisting of a variable number of nucleotides (<20 to >600) between an invariable **5′ terminal purine** (5′-pppA or 5′-pppG) and the polypeptide initiating AUG codon. Beyond the terminator codon (UGA, UAG, or UAA), there is another non-coding segment, called the **trailer**.

While the length of the leader varies, all sequenced prokaryotic mRNAs have been shown to contain a 5′ leader segment of nucleotides which is complementary to the 3′ end of the rRNA exposed on the ribosome surface (Fig. 8.6). This suggests that part (all?) of the function of the leader sequence is to orient mRNA to the ribosome, and to promote binding between the 5′ end of mRNA and a complementary 3′ end of rRNA. These functions are important for initiation of polypeptide synthesis at the correct place on the messenger sequence bound to the ribosome.

The promoter sequences from a number of genes have been isolated, after digestion of DNA to which RNA polymerase has been bound. The parts of DNA which are protected by the bound polymerase are retained after the rest of the DNA has been digested by nuclease action. These protected DNA regions can then be sequenced. In each case, there appears to be a sequence of seven nucleotides, which represent either all or part of the promoter. In *E. coli*, as mentioned earlier, the σ subunit of RNA polymerase recognizes and binds to the DNA promoter site in initiation of transcription.

Once transcription has been initiated, mRNA synthesis proceeds at a

Figure 8.6 Homology between 5′ leader segments and initiator AUG codon locations in different genes of the *E. coli* phage φX174. The portion in mRNAs complementary to the 3′ end of 16S rRNA is shown in red letters. Such complementarity may promote binding of the 5′ end of mRNA to the exposed 3′ end of 16S rRNA of the small ribosomal subunit, just before translation begins.

φX gene	5′→3′ sequence of mRNA leader and initiator regions
A	C A A A U C U U G G A G G C U U U U U U *A U G* G U U
B	A A A G G U C U A G G A G C U A A A G A *A U G* G A A
D	C C A C U A A U A G G U A A G A A A U C *A U G* A G U
E	C U G C G U U G A G G C U U G C G U U U *A U G* G U A
F	C C C U U A C U U G A G G A U A A A U U *A U G* U C U
G	U U C U G C U U A G G A G U U U A A U C *A U G* U U U
J	C G U G C G G A A G G A G U G A U G U A *A U G* U C U
16S rRNA (3′ end only)	HO A U U C C U C C A G U A G ..... 3′ → 5′

relatively constant rate. Presumably, there is (1) a separation of DNA strands just ahead of the growing mRNA chain; (2) transcription from the DNA sense strand; (3) displacement of the mRNA; and (4) closure of the DNA duplex when transcription is completed in that segment. Transcription is terminated when the RNA polymerase reaches the DNA **terminator** sequence, beyond the anti-trailer segment of the gene. Most prokaryotic genes seem to end with a string of GC base pairs followed by a string of AT pairs. The 3′ end of sequenced prokaryotic mRNAs usually terminates with the sequence 5′-UUUUUUA-3′. It has been suggested that the difference between tightly bonded GC-stretches and more loosely bonded AT-stretches acts as a signal for dissociation of the RNA polymerase from the template DNA. There is little supporting evidence for this, however, at the present time. As we mentioned earlier, rho protein is required for mRNA termination in *E. coli*. When rho is added to an *in vitro* system, mRNA transcription is terminated much more accurately than when rho protein is absent.

8.3   Some Unusual Features of Eukaryotic mRNA

A major difference in mRNAs of eukaryotes and many of their viruses, as compared with prokaryotes and their viruses, is the occurrence of a significant amount of **post-transcriptional modification** after dissociation of RNA from the DNA sense strand. Eukaryotic messenger transcripts are modified post-transcriptionally in at least four ways:

1. by removal of up to 90 percent of the length of **pre-mRNA** to produce mRNA in the nucleus;
2. by **"capping"** of the 5′ terminus with the unusual nucleoside **7-methylguanosine** to produce 5′-m^{7}G-ppp(leader)----3′;
3. by addition of a string of adenine nucleotides, making up a **poly(A)** **"tail"** at the 3′ terminus; and
4. by **excision** of noncoding sequences, followed by **splicing** of the finished mRNA so that its sequence corresponds exactly with the amino acid sequence in the polypeptide made during translation (Fig. 8.7).

In most other respects, such as presence of noncoding leader and trailer sequences, eukaryotic and prokaryotic mRNAs are generally similar.

The differences in prokaryotic and eukaryotic messengers may be related to the timing of their translational activities and to their transport within the cell. In prokaryotes, transcription and translation are coordinated processes (Fig. 8.8). While mRNA is still being transcribed from the DNA template, the first rounds of translation begin from the 5′ end of the messenger. There is relatively little time for any extensive processing of prokaryotic mRNA before translation begins. In addition, mRNA and its DNA template are in intimate association during translation, meaning that mRNA doesn't really travel far from its site of synthesis in the bacterial nucleoid; and there is no membrane separating nucleoid from cytoplasm.

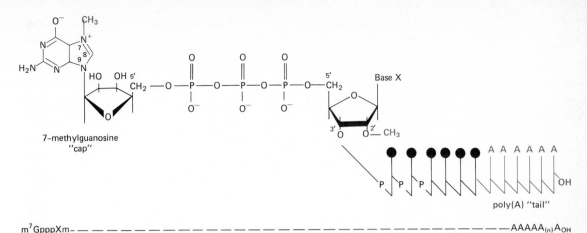

m^{7}GpppXm— —AAAAA$_{(n)}$A$_{OH}$

5'————————————————————————————————————▶3'

Figure 8.7 Post-transcriptional modification of mRNA in eukaryotes includes "capping" the 5' end with 7-methylguanosine (m^{7}G) and the addition of a polyadenylate tail (poly(A) tail) at the 3' end. These events occur in the nucleus, before mRNA exits to the cytoplasm.

In eukaryotes, mRNA is transcribed in the nucleus along chromosomal DNA, and must then be transported across the nucleus and through the nuclear membrane to enter the cytoplasm. Once in the cytoplasm, mRNA may associate with ribosomes and participate in translation. While particular aspects of mRNA processing are only speculative at present, there is

Figure 8.8 Electron micrograph of transcription-translation complexes from *E. coli*. Ribosomes bind to mRNA as the messenger "peels off" the template DNA during transcription, seen here by increasing length of the mRNA-ribosome aggregates when viewed from right to left along a gene segment. Molecules of RNA polymerase (arrows) catalyze transcription. (Courtesy of O. L. Miller, Jr., from Miller, O. L., Jr., *et al.*, 1970. *Science* **169**:392, Fig. 3.)

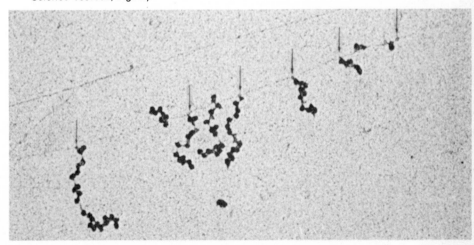

good reason to believe that large chunks of **pre-mRNA** (formerly called heterogeneous nuclear RNA or **hnRNA**) are removed in the nucleus before the remainder of the molecule enters the cytoplasm. Various studies had shown that pre-mRNA in the nucleus was 7 to 10 times larger than mRNA in the cytoplasm. In addition, the excised portions are rarely found in the cytoplasm so they must remain behind in the nucleus after processed mRNA leaves. The studies which clearly showed that hnRNA was actually pre-mRNA were done using globin genes. The large globin hnRNA was identified, and it was followed through a series of processing steps, which finally led to a globin mRNA with the size predicted according to globin mRNAs that had been isolated from reticulocytes engaged in hemoglobin synthesis. It is quite probable that pre-mRNA provides protection against nuclease degradation while the molecules are still in the nucleus, and perhaps also contributes to transport of the smaller mRNA through the nuclear membrane out into the cytoplasm. The addition of the m^{7}G cap and the poly(A) tail occur in the nucleus, along with excision and splicing to produce a continuous coded sequence between the initiator and terminator codons of the genetic message. The exact sequence of these events is currently under investigation.

The function of the m^{7}G cap is unclear, but it does prevent any nucleotides from being added at the 5′ end and it is known to be required for translation. The poly(A) tail may help bind mRNA by its 3′ end to membranes of the endoplasmic reticulum in eukaryotic cytoplasm (Fig. 8.9). This would stabilize the molecule at one end, while its 5′ end was secured through binding to ribosomes on the endoplasmic reticulum membrane. Binding of the 3′ end should also protect against its degradation by ribonucleases, which are abundant in cytoplasm. These proposals are speculative at present.

There may be relatively large stretches of noncoding sequences between coding regions of unprocessed mRNA. For example, Philip Leder found an intervening, noncoding sequence of 550 nucleotides between the codons for amino acids 104 and 105 in the β-globin gene of rabbit. This sequence must later be removed with great precision, and the coded regions must be

Figure 8.9 Scheme showing assembly of bound polysomes with mRNA (red) attached by its 3′ end to the membrane (oval shape) of a eukaryotic cell. Binding of the complex to the membrane may occur through interactions between growing polypeptide chains and the membrane in addition to, or instead of, mRNA binding as shown. (Redrawn from Lande, M. A., *et al.* 1975. *J. Cell Biol.* **65**:513.)

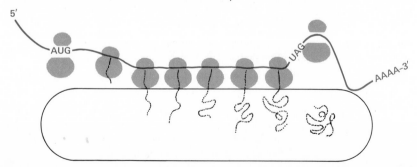

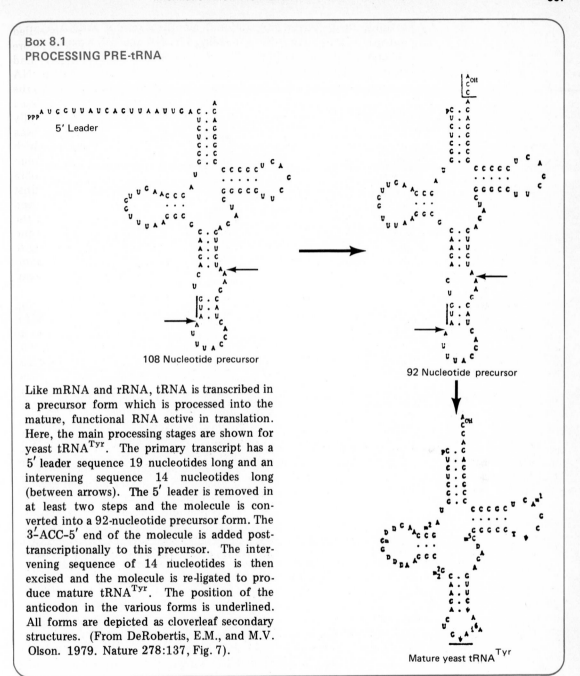

Box 8.1
PROCESSING PRE-tRNA

108 Nucleotide precursor

92 Nucleotide precursor

Mature yeast tRNA^Tyr

Like mRNA and rRNA, tRNA is transcribed in a precursor form which is processed into the mature, functional RNA active in translation. Here, the main processing stages are shown for yeast tRNA^{Tyr}. The primary transcript has a 5′ leader sequence 19 nucleotides long and an intervening sequence 14 nucleotides long (between arrows). The 5′ leader is removed in at least two steps and the molecule is converted into a 92-nucleotide precursor form. The 3′-ACC-5′ end of the molecule is added post-transcriptionally to this precursor. The intervening sequence of 14 nucleotides is then excised and the molecule is re-ligated to produce mature tRNA^{Tyr}. The position of the anticodon in the various forms is underlined. All forms are depicted as cloverleaf secondary structures. (From DeRobertis, E.M., and M.V. Olson. 1979. Nature 278:137, Fig. 7).

spliced together very precisely to yield mRNA with the codons for amino acids 104 and 105 adjacent to one another. We know little about these gene-processing events at present.

In addition to post-transcriptional modifications of mRNA, similar modifications characterize the processing of rRNA and tRNA transcripts of rRNA and tRNA genes (Box 8.1). There are important differences, however, as we will now see.

8.4   tRNA Transcription

As we mentioned in Section 7.10, there may be hundreds of copies of tRNA and rRNA genes in middle-repetitive sequences of eukaryotic DNA. There also are multiple copies of some tRNA genes in *E. coli*, and about 5-10 copies of rRNA genes according to molecular hybridization analysis (only three map sites exist). The high redundancy of eukaryotic systems far exceeds such minimal repetitiveness in bacteria.

Since tRNA interacts with mRNA through pairing between codon and anticodon triplets, we might expect 61 different tRNAs to match the 61 codons which specify amino acids. This is not the case, according to evidence showing that a single kind of tRNA may bind to several different mRNA codons *in vitro*. Furthermore, many sequenced tRNAs may have the base **inosine** in the anticodon 5′ position, instead of 5′ U, A, C, or G. Inosine is enzymatically modified from adenine by post-transcriptional deaminiation at carbon 6. There are a number of modified, minor bases in tRNAs, in addition to inosine, and all of these arise by chemical modifications in the tRNA transcripts (Fig. 8.10).

Crick developed the **wobble hypothesis** to explain the nonrandom distribution of codons specifying the same amino acid. The first two bases of the codon for an amino acid are usually the same, but the third base varies. The wobble occurs at the third base in the triplet codon, meaning that its pairing is less restricted. All pairings are not possible, however, and there is a maximum of three different base-pair combinations only when inosine occupies the wobble position in the anticodon.

The wobble hypothesis received its most substantial verification when the predicted minimum number of three tRNAs for the six serine codons (UCU, UCC, UCA, UCG, AGU, and AGC) were found. By comparing mRNA codons with their tRNA anticodons, one can calculate the *minimum* number of tRNAs for each amino acid in the code (Fig. 8.11). These features of tRNAs explain why there are fewer than 61 different tRNAs and tRNA gene types, but more than 20 different tRNA species.

8.5   rRNA Transcription

The largest RNA molecules which participate in protein synthesis are rRNAs. There may be several thousand ribonucleotides in a rRNA chain, but only 70-80 in a tRNA, and a variable number in mRNAs according to gene size and noncoding segment sizes. If we had to estimate an average-sized mRNA, it would be about 500 nucleotides if it coded for an average size polypeptide chain [150 amino acids require 450 (150 × 3) nucleotides in the coding region alone]. The usual way of describing all these molecules is according to their **sedimentation coefficient**, expressed in terms of **Svedberg units (S)**. These coefficients are calculated from analysis of

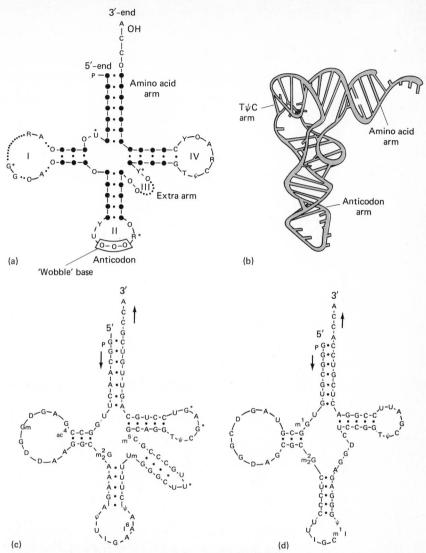

Figure 8.10 Molecular structure of transfer RNA (tRNA). (a) Generalized cloverleaf model of secondary structure of the single-stranded RNA molecule. Solid circles represent bases in the hydrogen-bonded helical regions, and open circles stand for unpaired bases. Unusual bases include ribothymidine (T), pseudouridine (ψ), and others. (b) Schematic model of tertiary structure of yeast tRNA[Phe] (From Kim, S.H., et al. 1974. *Science* **185**:435.) (c) Secondary structure of yeast tRNA[Ser] in which Inosine occupies the 5′ position in the anticodon 3′-AGI-5′. (d) Secondary structure of yeast tRNA[Ala], the first nucleic acid to be completely sequenced; by Robert Holley in 1965. The 3′-CGI-5′ anticodon should pair with mRNA codons 5′-GCA-3′, 5′-GCU-3′, and 5′-GCC-3′, according to the wobble concept.

molecule or particle sedimentation in sucrose gradient centrifugation (Fig. 8.12). Ribosomes and ribosome subunits are also discussed in terms of their **S values**. In prokaryotes there are **70S ribosomes** made up of one **50S** and

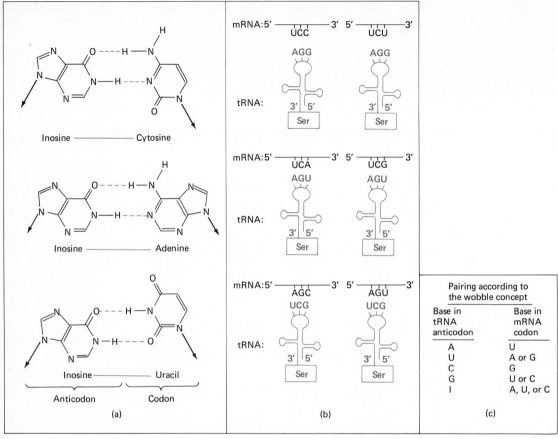

Figure 8.11 The "wobble" hypothesis. (a) Inosine pairs with C, A, or U; (b) possible pairing between the 3′ base in the anticodon and the 5′ base in the mRNA codon during translation; and (c) a minimum of three tRNAs is required to pair with six different mRNA codons for the amino acid serine. Anticodon 3′-AGU-5′ pairs with the same mRNA codons as anticodon 3′-AGI-5′, which was illustrated in Fig. 8.10c.

one **30S subunit**, while a **60S** and a **40S** subunit are associated in the **80S** eukaryotic ribosome (Table 8.2). Since shape as well as molecular weight are determining factors in sedimentations, the sum of the S values of two subunits is greater than a whole ribosome's S value. Similarly, the 23S rRNA is twice as long as the 16S rRNA, but this is not reflected in their S values.

Transcription of rRNA leads to a large precursor, or **pre-rRNA**, molecule in both prokaryotes and eukaryotes. Since there are certain differences, however, we will briefly describe each type separately. In *E. coli*, each of the rRNA genes (*rrn*) can be transcribed into a 30S pre-rRNA, although this is rarely found because the molecule is processed during transcription (Fig. 8.13). The first fragment to be cleaved is 16S rRNA, and as transcription proceeds, 23S rRNA, and finally 5S rRNA are released. It appears to be a common feature in prokaryotes, and in chloroplast and

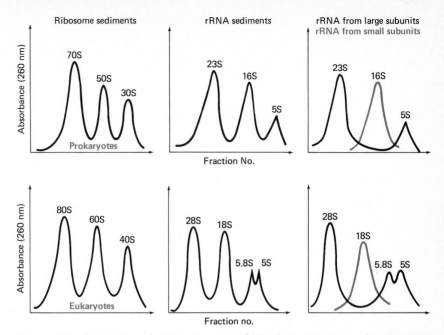

Figure 8.12 Separation of ribosomes and rRNAs from cytoplasm of prokaryotic (upper row) and eukaryotic (bottom row) cells, by centrifugation in sucrose gradients. Whole 70S or 80S ribosomes consist of two unequal size subunits (50S + 30S, or 60S + 40S) and several sizes of rRNA molecules. Purified small subunits contain one rRNA (red), and all the others are present in the larger subunit of both the 70S and 80S ribosomal types.

mitochondrial DNAs, for one or more tRNA genes to be situated in the rRNA gene region. The significance of this phenomenon is uncertain.

In eukaryotes, the size of pre-rRNA varies according to the group of species, so that insect pre-rRNA is 37S, amphibian is 40S, and mammalian pre-rRNA is 45S. In every case, however, pre-rRNA is processed into only two rRNA molecules: 18S and 25S-28S rRNAs. Pre-rRNA is transcribed from **nucleolar chromatin**, which is the portion of the chromosomal nucleolar-organizing region (**NOR**) that extends into the nucleolus proper.

Table 8.2
Some characteristics of cytoplasmic ribosomes

Source	Ribosome	Ribosomal subunits	rRNA in subunits	No. proteins in subunit
Prokaryotes	70S	30S	16S	21
		50S	23S, 5S	32-34
Eukaryotes	80S	40S	18S	~30
		60S*	25-28S, 5S, 5.8S	~50

*The large rRNA in animal 60S subunits is 28S, while the molecule is 25-26S in 60S subunits of plant, fungal, and protist ribosomes.

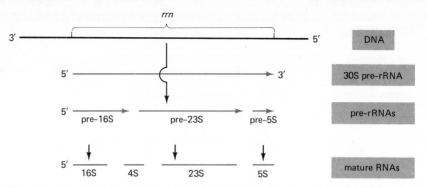

Figure 8.13 Processing of the pre-rRNA transcript of an *rrn* gene in *E. coli* results in 16S, 23S, and 5S rRNAs, along with one tRNA (4S molecule). In RNAase-deficient *E. coli* it is possible to recover 30S pre-rRNA; otherwise, the molecule is processed into smaller units *during* transcription.

Figure 8.14 Electron micrograph of actively transcribing rDNA isolated from oocyte nucleoli of the spotted newt (*Triturus viridscens*), an amphibian. Each arrow-shaped region represents one rRNA gene with rRNA transcripts "peeling off" during transcription. The longer rRNAs in a group are near the 5' end of the gene, while the shortest transcripts are still near the 3' end of the gene, where transcription begins. The rRNA genes (= rDNA) occur as tandem repeats, separated by untranscribed spacer DNA segments of uncertain function. (Courtesy of O. L. Miller, Jr., from Miller, O. L., Jr., and B. Beatty. 1969. *Science* **164**:955, Fig. 2.)

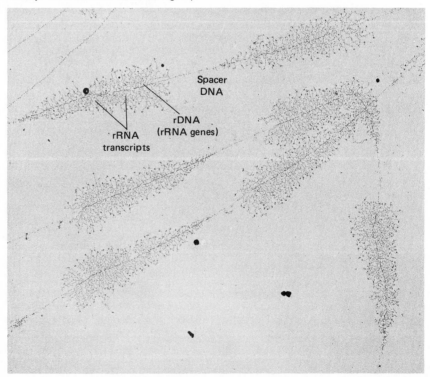

Hundreds of rRNA genes, classified as **ribosomal DNA**, or **rDNA**, are transcribed simultaneously from a continuous strand of DNA (Fig. 8.14). The molecules are processed within the nucleus, where they also may assemble with ribosomal proteins to form inactive or precursor ribosomal subunits. By processes which are not entirely understood, inactive subunits are transformed into active ribosomal subunits, probably at the nuclear envelope or in the adjacent cytoplasm.

Time studies of pre-rRNA processing showed that 18S rRNA appeared first and the remainder of the original 45S pre-rRNA was cleaved to a 32S molecule (Fig. 8.15). Sometime later, the 32S molecule was processed to the finished 28S rRNA. Genes for 5S rRNA occur elsewhere in the genome and are not necessarily near rDNA of the NOR chromosome. 5S rRNA transcription apparently is under separate control.

Localization of rDNA to the NOR of the eukaryotic chromosome was first demonstrated in 1965 by Frank Ritossa and Sol Spiegelman, using DNA-RNA molecular hybridization. There was earlier evidence from an anucleolate mutant of *Xenopus laevis* which indicated that absence of the NOR was correlated with absence of rRNA and ribosome synthesis in young embryos. Ritossa and Spiegelman therefore sought molecular evidence which might show that rRNA genes were located at the NOR.

They used four strains of *Drosophila melanogaster* which contained identical chromosomes except for having from one to four NOR per nucleus. Radioactively-labeled uridine was supplied and newly-synthesized rRNA was purified from isolated ribosomes. This labeled rRNA was then hybridized with chromosomal DNA from the same strains. The percentage of DNA-rRNA hybrids exactly paralleled the number of NOR per strain (Fig. 8.16). This showed conclusively that rDNA was located at the NOR, since

Figure 8.15 Processing of pre-rRNA and packaging of rRNAs into ribosomal subunits in eukaryotes. The 45S pre-rRNA is cleaved in at least four sites: (a) Removal of leader leaves a 41S fragment; (b) cleavage of 18S rRNA for the 40S ribosomal subunit leaves a 36S pre-rRNA fragment; (c) removal of a small region leaves a 32S fragment; and (d) processing of the 32S fragment yields 28S and 5.8S rRNAs of the larger ribosomal subunit. These latter two rRNAs are packaged together with 5S rRNA, which is coded elsewhere in the genome.

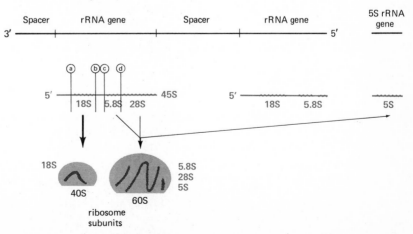

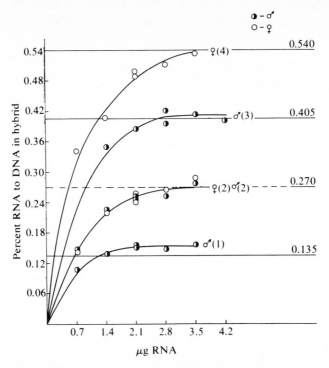

Figure 8.16 Demonstration that rDNA in *Drosophila melanogaster* is located at the nucleolar organizing region (NOR) of the chromosome. Hybridization of purified rRNA to DNA from flies carrying from 1–4 NORs per cell (2 NORs is the normal number) is shown. Horizontal lines indicate the hybridization plateau values predicted for 1, 3, or 4 NORs, on the basis of the normal plateau value of 0.270% for 2 NORs. In these saturation hybridizations, increasing amounts of RNA (μg) are added to hybridization mixtures containing a fixed amount of DNA. Once all the complementary DNA has been saturated by pairing with RNA, no additional hybrids form since no more DNA is available for hybridization regardless of the amount of RNA present. (From Ritossa, F. M., and S. Spiegelman. 1965. *Proc. Nat. Acad. Sci. U.S.* **53**:737.)

the percentage of molecular hybrids reflected the amount of rDNA present in each strain. In later studies they showed that 5S rRNA and 4S tRNA did not increase when extra NORs were present; genes for these RNAs were situated elsewhere in the genome.

8.6   Gene Amplification

Repeated replication of certain DNA sequences while others are not replicating is called **gene amplification**. The phenomenon has been best studied in amphibian oocyte development, when extra rDNA copies are replicated during meiotic diplonema. In these meiotic cells, the nucleus becomes greatly enlarged, and in the toad *Xenopus laevis* from 600-1600 free, small nucleoli appear within the periphery of the nuclear envelope. These nucleoli are made at the NOR and are released into the nucleoplasm only at this time. Each nucleolus contains DNA and ribosome precursor particles.

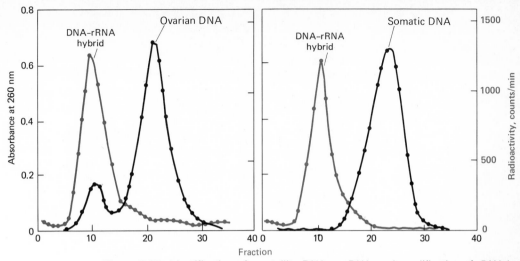

Figure 8.17 Identification of a satellite DNA as rDNA, and amplification of rDNA in oocyte nuclei. DNA-rRNA hybrids sediment in the same region of the gradient as a satellite DNA from oocytes in ovarian preparations, indicating the satellite is rDNA. Although the satellite is not evident in the absorbance curve in somatic nuclear DNA preparations, rDNA is present since molecular hybrids between rRNA and DNA from this satellite region of the DNA do form and do sediment where expected in the gradient. The increased amount of rDNA in oocytes provides evidence for gene amplification, that is, replication of certain DNA while most of the nuclear DNA does not replicate.

When DNA is extracted from the enlarged oocyte nuclei and centrifuged in CsCl, a large peak of DNA appears in the gradient in addition to bulk nuclear DNA (Fig. 8.17). This extra peak is not detectable in nuclei from ordinary somatic cells. The extra peak can be identified as rDNA because this particular DNA fraction hybridizes specifically with rRNA extracted from purified ribosomes. When DNA from somatic cell centrifugates is extracted from the same region where rDNA is expected to sediment, and this material is hybridized with rRNA, one can see that rDNA is also present in somatic cell nuclei, though in very low amounts.

In this phenomenon of gene amplification during oocyte meiosis in *Xenopus*, the original number of 900 copies of rDNA in the middle-repetitive NOR segment is increased about 600-1600 *times* this number. Gene amplification takes place in various protozoan and metazoan species, but amphibia are unusual in producing extra nucleoli to house the extra rDNA. Other species keep all the rDNA within the usual number of nucleoli typical for the species (Fig. 8.18). From the few plants that have been studied, it appears that there is no gene amplification of the thousands of copies of the rRNA genes which are normally present at the NORs of their genomes.

During an episode of gene amplification in amphibia and other species, it appears that rDNA replicates by a mechanism called the **rolling circle** (Fig. 8.19). Very large numbers of rRNA genes are produced rapidly, as multiple lengths of this DNA are synthesized and then cut out by nuclease action. Circle closure probably takes place by a crossover event in the "tail,"

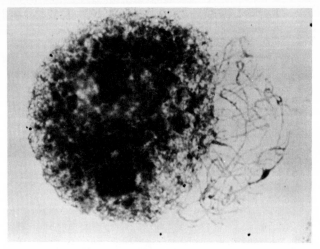

Figure 8.18 Light micrograph of an oocyte nucleus of a beetle (*Dytiscus marginalis*). A large cap of amplified rDNA is at the left, comprising about 90% of the nuclear DNA at this stage of meiotic prophase I. × 1200. (Courtesy of J. G. Gall, from Gall, J. G., and J.-D. Rochaix. 1974. *Proc. Nat. Acad. Sci. U. S.* **71**:1819, Fig. 1.)

which releases a copy of the repetitious DNA without interfering with continued replication in the rest of the rolling circle.

There are some unexplained features of gene amplification; for example, how the first rDNA circles are formed from chromosomal DNA regions where these genes are part of a continuous chromatin fiber. The obvious

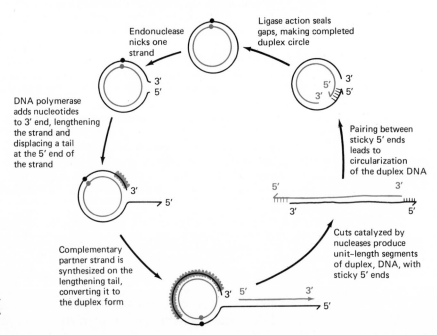

Figure 8.19 Rolling circle mechanism of rDNA replication.

Endonuclease nicks one strand

Ligase action seals gaps, making completed duplex circle

DNA polymerase adds nucleotides to 3' end, lengthening the strand and displacing a tail at the 5' end of the strand

Pairing between sticky 5' ends leads to circularization of the duplex DNA

Complementary partner strand is synthesized on the lengthening tail, converting it to the duplex form

Cuts catalyzed by nucleases produce unit-length segments of duplex, DNA, with sticky 5' ends

advantage of the rolling circle mechanism is its speed. Huge numbers of ribosomes must be made during the brief time of oocyte development. The enormous numbers of ribosomes serve during the first weeks of embryo development from the fertilized egg. By the time of gastrulation, the embryo must begin to make its own ribosomes. Before this, it depends entirely on the store of ribosomes carried over from the fertilized egg.

PROTEIN SYNTHESIS

Most proteins are coded by single-copy genes. In addition to requirements for mRNA, tRNA, and ribosomes for translation of the genetic message, a variety of enzymes and other proteins must act at specific stages during translation into polypeptides. The whole translation apparatus operates through the coordination of various components and processes, an accurate recognition system between RNAs, and special conditions to initiate, elongate, and terminate the polypeptide chain.

8.7   Amino Acids, tRNAs, and Synthetases

Before amino acids can be linked to form a polypeptide, they must be raised to a sufficiently high energy level for synthesis, and there must be a recognition mechanism to correctly insert these units in the sequence dictated by mRNA.

Energy for synthesis is provided by interaction of ATP with amino acids; this is the first step in the preparation process. The second step is accomplished when the *activated* amino acid, or **aminoacyl** residue, binds to its tRNA carrier. Both of these steps are catalyzed by the same enzyme, called an **aminoacyl-tRNA synthetase**. There is at least one synthetase for *each* of the 20 coded amino acids.

The synthetase drives the first reaction by coupling it to the hydrolysis of ATP to form adenosine monophosphate (AMP). A high-energy intermediate is formed, called an aminoacyl-adenylate, and this complex remains bound to the enzyme until the second reaction when the aminoacyl group is bonded to the terminal nucleotide of tRNA at the acceptor stem. The reactions can be summarized as:

amino acid + ATP + synthetase

$$\downarrow \qquad\qquad [8.1]$$

aminoacyl–adenylate–synthetase + pyrophosphate (PP$_i$)

followed by:

aminoacyl–adenylate–synthetase + tRNA

$$\downarrow \qquad\qquad [8.2]$$

aminoacyl–tRNA + AMP + synthetase

A particular tRNA is identified according to the amino acid it can carry; for example, tRNA^{Met} is a methionine-carrying tRNA. The particular aminoacyl-tRNA is identified by the aminoacyl group and specific tRNA; for example, met-tRNA^{Met} is the methionyl-tRNA complex which participates in adding methionine to protein.

8.8   Subunits, Monosomes, and Polysomes

Until 1962 it was generally believed that proteins were synthesized on single, free ribosomes. The true picture was discovered by Alexander Rich and co-workers, who showed that polypeptides were made at groups of ribosomes, called polyribosomes, or **polysomes**, for short. The polysome is a complex composed of a variable number of individual ribosomes, which we can refer to as **monosomes**, held together by a strand of mRNA. The length of a polysome is usually proportional to the length of the bound mRNA, or genetic message.

Their experiments involved rabbit reticulocytes which, like other mammalian red blood cell precursors, are virtual factories for hemoglobin synthesis and do little else. The advantages of this system, therefore, were suitability for bulk biochemical analysis from relatively homogeneous cell populations, and almost a single polypeptide synthesis reaction which

Figure 8.20 Sedimenting positions of a ribosomal preparation from rabbit reticulocytes to which [^{14}C] amino acids had been added for 45 seconds to determine the location of nascent polypeptides into which these amino acids were incorporated. Black circles indicate absorbance readings (optical density) at 260 nm in the 36 fractions. The bulk of the radioactivity (red) occurs in the polysome region of the gradient, where aggregates of 4, 5, and 6 ribosomes are found (170S = 5-ribosome peak aggregate). Little radioactivity is present in the monosome peak (80S). (From Warner, J. S., A. Rich, and C. E. Hall. 1962. *Science* **138**:1399.)

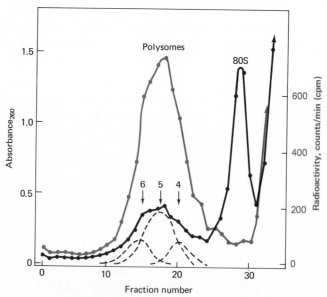

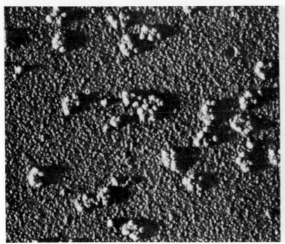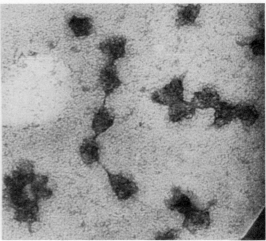

Figure 8.21 Electron micrographs of polysomes isolated from rabbit reticulocytes. (a) Clusters of 4, 5, and more ribosomes are evident in a preparation shadowed with gold. × 70,000. (b) When stained by uranyl acetate and photographed at higher magnification, a thin strand of RNA (presumably mRNA) is seen to connect ribosomes of a cluster. × 300,000. (Courtesy of A. Rich, from Slayter, H. S., *et al.* 1963. J. Mol. Biol. 7:652, Plate III.)

could be studied without screening out interference from many other polypeptides being made at the same time.

Reticulocytes were incubated in media containing radioactively-labeled amino acids, and after a suitable time the cells were broken and the cell-free lysates were separated into different fractions by centrifugation. The prediction was that growing globin chains would be found in the fractions actually engaged in their synthesis, and that they could be identified by their radioactive label (Fig. 8.20). The fraction in which most of the radioactive globin fragments were found consisted of 5-ribosome groups, not the monosome fraction.

In another experiment it was shown that the labeled polypeptides were truly in the process of synthesis and functionally associated with polysomes, rather than randomly associated or present by accident. When the drug **puromycin**, which acts as an analogue of tRNA, is added to an actively synthesizing system, chain growth is terminated *prematurely* and incomplete molecules are released from the ribosomes-mRNA complex. Such **nascent** (growing) chains would then disappear from the polysome fraction and be found in the fluid supernatant phase of the system, and be recognized by their radioactive label. In this way, it was verified that chain growth takes place at the polysomes, since only nascent polypeptides are affected by puromycin.

Supporting evidence for globin synthesis at polysomes was obtained by Rich from electron micrographs of various gradient fractions (Fig. 8.21). In the 5-ribosome fractions, groups of 5 ribosomes were seen to be held together by a thin strand. This strand was presumed to be mRNA since it was

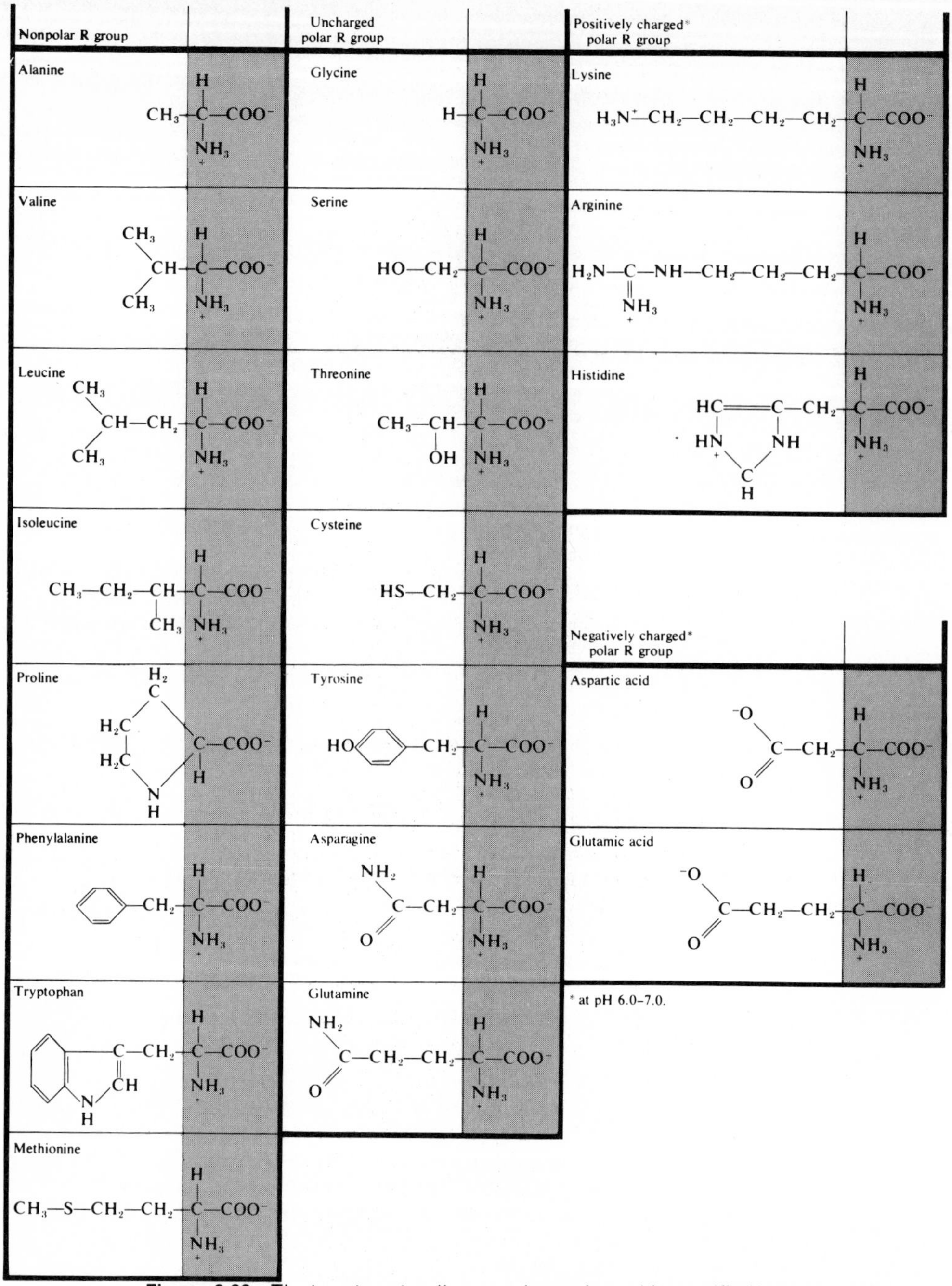

Nonpolar R group			Uncharged polar R group			Positively charged* polar R group		
Alanine			Glycine			Lysine		
Valine			Serine			Arginine		
Leucine			Threonine			Histidine		
Isoleucine			Cysteine					
Proline			Tyrosine			Negatively charged* polar R group		
						Aspartic acid		
Phenylalanine			Asparagine			Glutamic acid		
Tryptophan			Glutamine			* at pH 6.0–7.0.		
Methionine								

Figure 8.22   The twenty naturally occurring amino acids specified by the genetic code.

digested by RNase and the polysomes then dissociated into monosome units. The length of the presumed mRNA was about right for a message that should be long enough to code for 141 amino acids in α-globin or 146 amino acids in β-globin. There would be at least 146×3 nucleotides for the whole set of codons in the message, and its dimension would be about 1500 Å, since the Watson-Crick model indicated a dimension of about 10Å per 3 nucleotides in a polynucleotide chain. This is exactly what the 1500 Å-long polysome-mRNA was found to be.

8.9   Protein Structure

The twenty amino acid building blocks of proteins have a common feature in their construction, except for proline (Fig. 8.22). The first carbon, called the α **carbon**, is asymmetric since there are four different components bound to it. There are an α-**amino** (α-NH$_2$), α-**carboxyl** (α-COOH), and **H** at three sites, and the fourth site is occupied by an **R group**. Most of the chemical and conformational properties of proteins are due to R-group interactions between amino acids.

Interactions between amino acids during growth of the polypeptide chain uniformly involve **peptide bond** formation, between the α-NH$_2$ of one unit and the α-COOH of the adjacent unit, leading to the —C—N— peptide linkage (Fig. 8.23). When two or more amino acid units are thus bonded together, the product is a **peptide**. A polypeptide contains many amino acid units, with the R-groups projecting from the zigzagging "backbone" of —C—N— linkages.

The **primary structure** of a protein consists of the linear sequence of amino acids (Fig. 8.24). Three other orders of structure are also recognized:

Figure 8.23 Peptide bond formation in protein synthesis. (a) Dehydration reaction produces a dipeptide from two amino acids, and would be similar for reactions between a peptide and a free amino acid. (b) Adjacent amino acid residues are joined by peptide bonds throughout a peptide, regardless of its length. Differences are largely due to amino acid side-chains, and not to the invariant zig-zag polypeptide backbone.

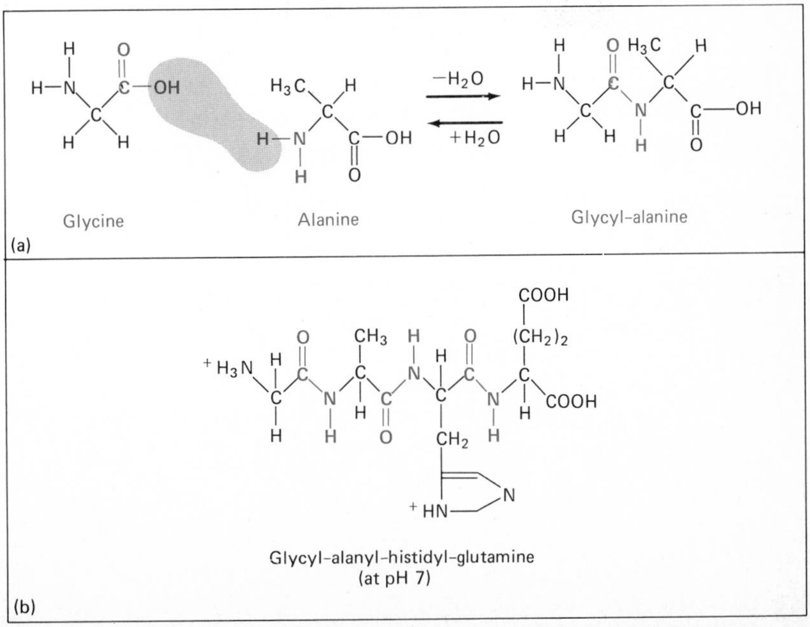

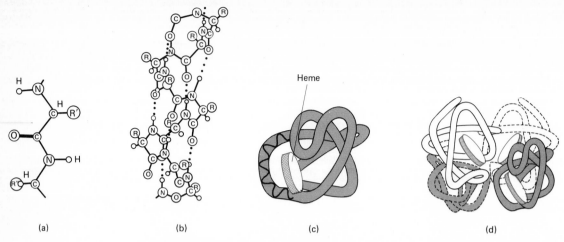

Figure 8.24 Four levels of structural organization in proteins, exemplified by hemo-globin. (a) Primary structure: the sequence of a chain of amino acids joined by peptide bonds; (b) secondary structure, and (c) tertiary structure, are both responsible for three-dimensional shape of the polypeptide; and (d) quaternary structure: the aggregation of two or more polypeptides in a single functional protein molecule. There are 4 globin chains in a hemoglobin molecule.

secondary structure, which develops from bonding between neighboring atoms; **tertiary structure**, which develops from R-group interactions at some distance from one another in the chain; and, **quaternary structure**, which develops only when two or more polypeptide chains exist as subunits in a single functional protein molecule. All these orders of structure contribute to biological activity and proper functioning of the protein, whether the protein consists of one polypeptide and has only three orders of structure or of more than one polypeptide and has four orders of structure (Box 8.2).

Mutations leading to amino acid substitutions in the primary structure may have severe effects if the substituted amino acid is important in the development of the three-dimensional shape of the protein. Otherwise, the new amino acid may have little or no effect on protein shape and, therefore, little or no demonstrable effect on protein function and phenotype development.

8.10   Polypeptide Chain Initiation

The first step in initiation of translation probably involves binding of the mRNA at its 5′ end to a homologous sequence of 16S or 18S rRNA in the small subunit of the prokaryotic or eukaryotic ribosome, respectively. The next step involves binding of the specific initiator tRNA to the AUG codon on the mRNA sequence. This initiator tRNA carries methionine (*met*) in eukaryotes and a modified methionine, called **N-formylmethionine** or **fmet** for short, in prokaryotes and in mitochondria and chloroplasts. The initiator tRNA^{Met} is different from the tRNA^{Met} which recognizes AUG

Box 8.2
CLOVERLEAF SECONDARY STRUCTURE

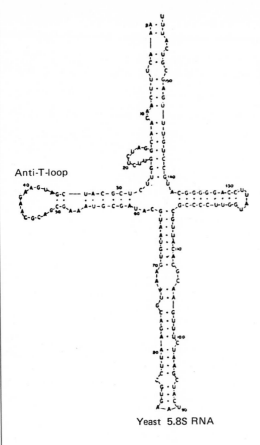

Anti-T-loop

Yeast 5.8S RNA

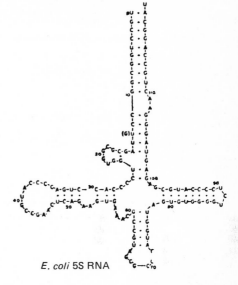

E. coli 5S RNA

It has become increasingly evident that RNA strands assume secondary and tertiary structures which we must know in order to understand molecular function in a correct perspective. The stability of eukaryotic and prokaryotic ribosomal RNAs is due in large measure to their secondary structure, now believed to be cloverleaf in conformation, like tRNAs. The shape and position of loops and arms jutting out of the backbone of a single-stranded RNA with local regions of paired bases can provide information on interactions between these RNAs and other molecules, which underwrite structure and function in the genetic system. (From Luoma, G.A., and A.G. Marshall. 1978. *J. Mol. Biol.* 125:95.)

codons at *internal* sites within the mRNA sequence. The methionine residue carried by initiator $tRNA_f^{Met}$ can be formylated by a formylase enzyme, whereas $tRNA_m^{Met}$ cannot have its methionyl formylated *in vitro* or *in vivo*. Eukaryotic initiator met-$tRNA_f^{Met}$ can be formylated *in vitro*, but there is no formylase in eukaryotic cytoplasm, so methionine is installed as the first amino acid, rather than fmet as in prokaryotes and organelles, which do have a formylase activity. The subscripts *f* and *m* indicate the initiator and non-initiator tRNAs, respectively.

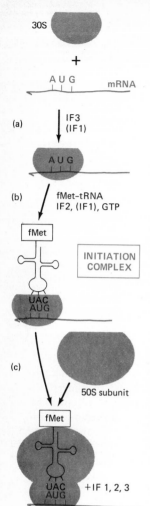

(a)

(b)

(c)

Figure 8.25 Formation of the initiation complex in protein synthesis in prokaryotes: (a) binding of mRNA to 30S ribosomal subunit in the presence of one or more initiation factors (IF); (b) binding of fmet-tRNA^{Met}, the initiating aminoacyl-tRNA, and formation of the initiation complex; (c) elongation of the polypeptide may proceed once the 50S ribosomal subunit binds to the initiation complex, and IF dissociate from the complex.

Although *met* or *fmet* is the initiating amino acid for all polypeptide chains, these may be modified or even cleaved from the polypeptide chain later on, through deformylase or aminopeptidase actions. A polypeptide, therefore, may or may not have methionine at its N-terminus. About half the polypeptides in *E. coli* have an N-terminal methionine residue.

In some cases GUG may be the initiator mRNA codon, instead of AUG, and bind met-tRNA$_f^{Met}$ or fmet-tRNA$_f^{Met}$. Internal GUG codons, however, bind only valyl-tRNA^{Val}. If fmet is the initiating amino acid, it can only form peptide bonds through its free α-carboxyl group, since its α-NH$_2$ terminus is blocked by the formyl residue (Fig. 8.25). Once the initiator tRNA has been bound to the mRNA initiating codon through base pairing between anticodon and codon, the **initiation complex** is completed. The large ribosomal subunit is not present and is not needed for chain initiation. Chain initiation can take place *in vitro* when all the components are present, even in the absence of large subunits. Among the components which are needed for formation of the initiation complex are three protein **initiation factors** (IF-1, -2, and -3), and a molecule of **GTP** which is hydrolyzed during this formation process.

Once the initiation complex is formed, the large ribosomal subunit associates with the small subunit of the complex. Chain elongation can then proceed along the mRNA which is now bound to a whole ribosome. As the ribosome moves away from the 5' end of the mRNA during polypeptide chain elongation, the mRNA can continue to participate in new initiation complex formations at its freed 5' end. The development of polysomes takes place as additional ribosomes join to a single mRNA strand, which repeatedly undergoes initiation complex formation in proportion to its length and the space taken up by bound ribosomes engaged in polypeptide synthesis.

8.11   Polypeptide Chain Elongation

Once the initiating aminoacyl-tRNA$_f^{Met}$ is in place, the next aminoacyl-tRNA can be bound to the mRNA at the **A site** of the ribosome. Since the initiator is also on the ribosome, at its **P site**, there are believed to be only these two ribosomal sites for accommodating the events of chain elongation. The initiating aminoacyl-tRNA is the only one which enters directly at the P (peptide) site of the ribosome; all others enter at the A (amino acid) site only (Fig. 8.26). It is the ribosome which *coordinates* and *catalytically assists* processes of polypeptide synthesis.

The first amino acid is joined to the amino acid of the second aminoacyl-tRNA in a peptide-linking reaction that is catalyzed by **peptidyl transferase**, an enzyme component of the ribosome. Once the **dipeptidyl** chain

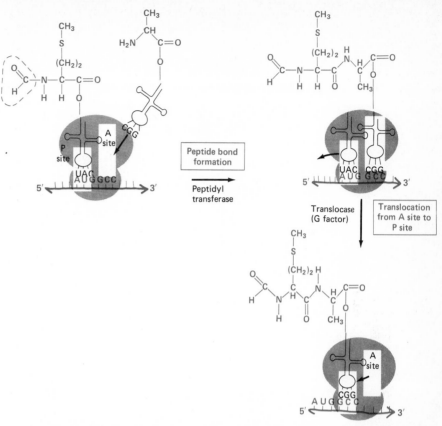

Figure 8.26 Polypeptide chain elongation at the ribosome. Incoming aminoacyl-tRNA enters at the A site; peptide bond formation takes place catalyzed by peptidyl transferase, making the peptidyl chain one unit longer. The tRNA is discharged from the P site after giving up its peptidyl chain to the incoming unit, and the new peptidyl-tRNA is translocated from the A to the P site in a reaction requiring translocase (G factor). The A site is now open for the next aminoacyl-tRNA specified by the coded sequence in mRNA. These same steps are repeated for each amino acid residue until chain termination occurs.

has been formed, the free tRNA$_f^{Met}$ is released from the P site. The entire dipeptidyl-tRNA is then translocated from the A site to the open P site, catalyzed by a **translocase** enzyme, or **G factor**, which is another component of the ribosome. The available A site can now accept the next incoming aminoacyl-tRNA, and the whole process of peptide bond formation and translocation continues repeatedly until the end of the genetic message.

During chain elongation the ribosome keeps moving from codon to codon, toward the 3′ end of mRNA. Translocation of the lengthened **peptidyl-tRNA** is an energy-requiring process, which involves GTP hydrolysis to GDP and P$_i$. If either GTP hydrolysis or translocation from the A to the P site fails to take place, further chain elongation stops, since there is no available A site for aminoacyl-tRNA entry. In addition, one or more **elongation factors (EF)** are required for polypeptide synthesis (Fig. 8.27). EF combines with GTP, and the EF—GTP complex combines with the incoming aminoacyl-tRNA. In this form of **EF—GTP—aminoacyl-tRNA**, the incoming unit is accurately brought into the A site, where it can then participate in chain growth. When complexed with EF and GTP, the incoming aminoacyl-tRNA will *only* bind to the A site of a ribosome that has its P site filled with a peptidyl-tRNA. Once bound to the ribosome, the GTP of this complex is hydrolyzed so that EF—GDP is released, and the **GTPase** component of the ribosome can bind G factor (translocase) and a free second molecule of GTP. This second GTP is hydrolyzed during translocation of the peptidyl-tRNA from the A to the P site. At the same time, GDP and G factor are released and the A site is available for the next aminoacyl-tRNA.

Figure 8.27 Summary diagram showing various components involved in lengthening the peptidyl chain by one amino acid residue during polypeptide synthesis.

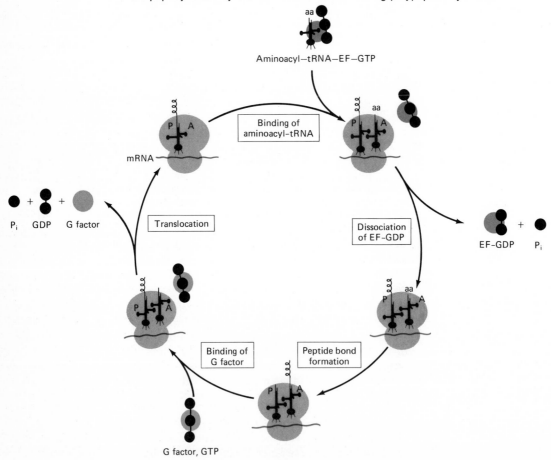

All these closely coordinated events of chain elongation provide greater insurance that few mistakes will take place. Enzymes and other proteins would be less effective or even nonfunctional if they were assembled inaccurately. Cell survival depends absolutely on the accuracy of protein synthesis, since even one incorrect amino acid can cause protein dysfunction in some cases.

8.12   Polypeptide Chain Termination

Before the finished polypeptide can be released from the ribosome, the link between the C-terminal amino acid and its tRNA must be broken. Separation is not spontaneous, nor is it efficient even when the terminator codon UAA, UAG, or UGA is exposed in the mRNA segment at the A site of the ribosome. No further amino acids can be added, however, since none of the tRNA anticodons recognize the terminator codons. There are protein **releasing factors** (**RF**) which are believed to interact at the terminator codon—A site location on the ribosome, and these RF activities apparently prevent the A site from being filled. Then a hydrolysis reaction, probably mediated by another protein, severs the link between the tRNA and the polypeptide, freeing both components from the polysome.

Upon release of the polypeptide, the two ribosome subunits *dissociate* and return to the cytoplasmic pool of subunits for further participation in protein synthesis. Whole monosomes usually are not found in an active cell, except as parts of polysome groups. In fact, if the subunits do not dissociate and the monosome persists, protein synthesis slows down and may even stop due to the deficiency of free small subunits for initiation complex formation, and of large subunits for elongation events. There is some evidence that one of the initiation factors, IF-3, aids in monosome dissociation into subunits by binding to the small subunit. At the same time, therefore, IF-3 helps to dissociate monosomes and also becomes bound to the small subunit in preparation for another round of chain initiation.

In some of the variant hemoglobins the particular modification can be traced to mutations in the normal terminator codon, leading to chains that are longer than normal. There are three particular human α-globin variants with chains longer than 141 amino acids. Hemoglobin Constant Spring (Hb CS) has 31 extra amino acids at the C-terminus, but the normal 141 amino acids are all present between the N-terminus and the extra length beginning at codon 142. Since there is a *glutamine* at position 142 in Hb CS, the most reasonable explanation is that the normal UAA or UAG terminator of α-globin mRNA has been altered to CAA or CAG, which code for glutamine. A simple base substitution, therefore, seems to have eliminated the punctuation and allowed translation of normally untranslated sequences known to exist in the trailer segment beyond the message (Fig. 8.28).

The other two α-globin variants are similar to Hb CS, except that there is a different amino acid at position 142. In Hemoglobin Icaria the first of the 31 extra amino acids is *lysine*, while it is the amino acid *serine* that is first in Hemoglobin Koya Dora. The codon change in Hb Icaria leading to lysine could have arisen by one base substitution of UAA or UAG to AAA or AAG,

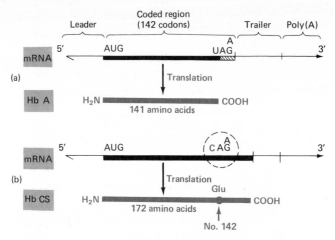

Figure 8.28 Effect of mutation in the terminator codon of the human *Hbα* gene. (a) Normal Hb α is 141 amino acids long; and (b) Hb Constant Spring (Hb CS) has 172 amino acids in its α chain, due to base substitution in the UAG terminator codon, which now codes for glutamic acid (CAG). A portion of the trailer mRNA segment is translated, adding 31 amino acids to the normal chain length.

and would therefore involve the same base as in Hb CS, an altered first base in the triplet. A single base substitution from a terminator to a serine codon in Hb Koya Dora could only involve a change in the middle base of the codon, from UAG or UGA to UCG or UCA. All other possibilities would require two substituted bases in the terminator codon. Since the one terminator codon common to all three variants was UAG, this was the most probable terminator for the α-globin message. This was verified later by direct sequence analysis of normal α-globin mRNA.

8.13   Effects of Streptomycin On Protein Synthesis

Various chemical agents, including a number of **antibiotics**, interfere with protein synthesis at one or more stages in the process (Table 8.3). These drugs are useful as therapeutic agents in health care, and as experimental probes of protein synthesis and other biological activities. We mentioned puromycin effects in Section 8.8.

In 1964 it was shown that streptomycin exerted its effect specifically on the 30S ribosome subunit in *E. coli*. In mixed reconstitution experiments using small and large subunits, in all combinations, from streptomycin sensitive (*str-s*) and resistant (*str-r*) strains, protein synthesis was monitored *in vitro* using the artificial messenger poly(U) in the presence and absence of streptomycin. When streptomycin was absent, all systems synthesized polyphenylalanine, as expected. When streptomycin was present, however, the only systems that functioned were those with a 30S small subunit derived from the *str-r* strain. The source of the 50S large subunit made no difference (Fig. 8.29).

One year later it was further shown that low concentrations of the drug caused **misreading** of codons in *str-s E. coli* strains. When poly(U) is the

Table 8.3
Characteristic action of some inhibitors of protein synthesis

Synthesis stage inhibited	Inhibitor	Mode of action of inhibitor	Effective in	
			Prokaryotes	Eukaryotes
Initiation	Aurintricarboxylic acid	Prevents association of ribosomal subunit with messenger RNA	+	+
	Streptomycin	Releases bound fMet-tRNA from initiation complex	+	−
Elongation	Streptomycin	Inhibits binding of aminoacyl-tRNA to ribosome; inhibits translocation on the ribosome	+	−
	Chloramphenicol	Stops amino acid incorporation by inhibiting peptidyl transferase	+	−
	Cycloheximide	Inhibits tRNA movement on the ribosome	−	+
	Puromycin	Acts as amino acid analog and causes premature polypeptide chain termination	+	+
Termination	Various drugs	Inhibit releasing factors; inhibit ribosome release from messenger RNA of polysome	+	+

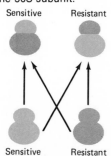

Figure 8.29 Mixed reconstitution experiments using ribosomal subunits of *str-s* and *str-r E. coli* showed that resistance or sensitivity to streptomycin depended on the source of the 30S ribosomal subunit and not on the 50S subunit.

messenger, we expect only phenylalanines to be incorporated into polypeptide, since the codon is UUU. Drug-sensitive bacteria, however, made polypeptides containing isoleucines and serines as well as phenylalanines from poly(U) messengers. Resistant strains made only polyphenylalanine. In comparisons with other studies using different artificial messengers, it was found that misreading of codons involved only the pyrimidines U and C in a codon (Fig. 8.30). For example, poly(C) promoted incorporation of the usual proline, and also serine, histidine, and threonine in sensitive strains. The U is misread as C and the C is misread as U, and occasionally either is misread as A. Misreading is not known to occur in eukaryotes, for unexplained reasons.

The lethal effect of streptomycin in sensitive strains, however, is not due primarily to misreading. This was first shown when misreading did not take place with certain artificial messengers, but protein synthesis was still inhibited. The primary effect of streptomycin is on polypeptide chain initiation.

Streptomycin causes the release of fmet-tRNA$_f^{Met}$ from the initiation complex, after the 50S ribosome subunit has joined on. Up to this point, processes take place as usual. When initiation is disturbed so that chain elongation cannot proceed to the dipeptidyl stage, the 70S ribosomes dissociate from the mRNA and accumulate as monosomes in the drugged cells. These do not dissociate into subunits, since the initiation factor IF-3 has already left the 30S subunit. As a result, there is an increase in monosomes and a decline in free subunits and polysomes, inhibiting protein synthesis.

The specific change in *str-r E. coli* was traced to one of the 21 proteins of the small ribosome subunit (proteins S1-S21), specifically to S12. Masayasu Nomura conducted mixed reconstitution experiments using

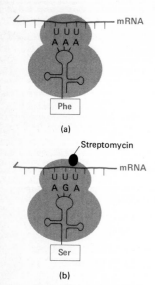

(a)

(b)

Figure 8.30 Misreading of codons in *E. coli*: (a) UUU is translated as phenylalanine under normal conditions, but (b) misreading of UUU as UCU is a frequent event in *str-s E. coli* in the presence of streptomycin. Serine instead of phenylalanine would be inserted into the polypeptide in the case illustrated.

purified rRNAs and ribosomal proteins from *str-s* and *str-r* strains. The only reconstituted small subunits that could function normally in the presence of streptomycin were ones containing protein S12 from *str-r* strains, even if all the other ribosomal proteins came from *str-s* strains (Fig. 8.31). Presumably, streptomycin binding to the small ribosomal subunit is mediated by protein S12 in sensitive strains. The mutation which confers resistance to streptomycin involves an amino acid alteration in protein S12, perhaps because of the substitution of one base in one codon.

What we have seen in this chapter fills in the molecular basis for the events which lead from the gene to the polypeptide product of gene expression. DNA is transcribed into mRNA, which directly provides a blueprint for synthesis of a polypeptide containing amino acids specified by codons, in the sequence specified by the DNA and its copied mRNA sequences. Alteration of a codon leads to a change of a single amino acid at the site in the polypeptide which corresponds to the site of codon change in the gene. Translation takes place in a reading frame (see Chapter 6), and the polypeptide product is a colinear product of the codon sequence in the final mRNA transcript. Transcription and translation processes render the genetic blueprint into the polypeptide, which influences development of the phenotype in the organism.

Figure 8.31 Summary of mixed reconstitution experiments conducted by M. Nomura, in which he showed that streptomycin-sensitive *E. coli* differed from streptomycin-resistant strains in one of the 21 proteins making up the small subunit of the ribosome.

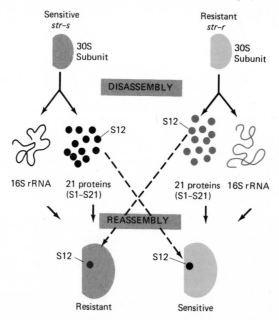

QUESTIONS AND PROBLEMS

8.1. The wobble hypothesis predicts that an A in the 3′ position of a codon can pair with either a U or an I from a tRNA anticodon. Similarly, a C in the 3′ position of a codon can pair with either a G or I from a tRNA anticodon. According to the genetic code, the codon 5′-AGA-3′ codes for the amino acid arginine and 5′-AGC-3′ codes for serine. Would you expect the serine tRNA to have the anticodon 5′-ICU-3′? Why?

8.2. When ribosomes are isolated from actively synthesizing *E. coli* cells, the polysomes are "attached" to cellular DNA. Explain the presence of the DNA in such preparations and its means of attachment to the polysomes.

8.3. Human HeLa cell chromatin can be separated into one portion with attached nucleoli and another portion without attached nucleoli. Design an experiment to test these two chromatin portions for the presence of rDNA, and describe the results you would expect.

8.4. How would you determine that the RNA detected around a puff in a polytene chromosome was directly transcribed from the puff DNA and was not simply an accumulation of RNA that had been synthesized elsewhere in the genome?

8.5. Is it possible to obtain DNA in "cloverleaf" conformation? Explain.

8.6. Suppose there was a mutation in the initiator codon of some structural gene sequence so that a single base change occurred. What would be the consequence of this alteration on translation of this gene product?

8.7. The bobbed mutant of *Drosophila melanogaster* has a low cellular concentration of ribosomes. What effect would this mutation have on the rate of development of the flies? Explain.

8.8. Using Crick's wobble hypothesis, suggest an explanation for the specificity of tRNA anticodons in distinguishing among the codons for cysteine (UGU, UGC), tryptophan (UGG), and the UGA terminator codon.

8.9. The human hemoglobin genetic variants called Constant Spring (Hb CS) and Wayne 1 (Hb W1) are known to have α chains that are lengthened at the -COOH terminus of the polypeptide, so there are more than 141 amino acids present. Hb CS amino acids are identical with normal α chains up to amino acid No. 141, but Hb W1 differs from normal Hbα beginning with amino acid No. 139. Assuming that only single nucleotide changes (substitution, deletion, or insertion) are responsible for these variant α chains, how would you explain their amino acid sequence in terms of DNA sequence?

8.10. You are given three different RNA preparations all of which have been isolated and purified from one population of eukaryotic cells. Preparation No. 1 is rRNA, No. 2 is mRNA, and No. 3 is tRNA.
   a. How would you unambiguously identify the tRNA preparation according to a function test?

   b. How would you unambiguously identify the rRNA preparation
      using autoradiography?
   c. How would you determine that preparation No. 2 was indeed
      mRNA, even though you know from the above experiments that
      it is not rRNA or tRNA?

8.11. Describe the events which lead from the primary transcript of pre-
mRNA in the nucleus to the mature mRNA which guides translation at the ribosomes in eukaryotic cells. Diagram the relevant steps
beginning with the DNA sequence of the structural gene and ending
with the mRNA ready for translation.

8.12. In an experiment designed to examine the relationship between 45S
RNA in the nucleus and 28S + 18S rRNA in cytoplasmic ribosomes,
a pulse of labeled uridine is presented at time zero to experimental
rat liver cells in culture. After 10 minutes the cells are washed and
transferred to medium containing unlabeled uridine. Samples of
cells are then removed at intervals and analyzed, with the following
results.

Portion of cell examined	Time (min)	RNA containing[³H]uridine			
		45S	32S	28S	18S
Cytoplasm	0	−	−	−	−
	10	−	−	−	−
	20	−	−	−	−
	30	−	−	−	+
	60	−	−	+	+
Nucleus	0	−	−	−	−
	10	+	−	−	−
	20	−	−	−	−
	30	−	+	−	+
	60	−	−	+	+

Which data provide evidence for the following interpretations:
   a. RNA is synthesized in the nucleus and not in the cytoplasm.
   b. 45S RNA is the precursor to 32S RNA.
   c. 32S RNA is the precursor to 28S RNA.
   d. 28S and 18S RNAs are processed from 45S RNA in the nucleus.
   e. 18S RNA is processed to mature rRNA before 28S RNA is com-
      pleted.
   f. Why is 45S RNA only labeled at 10 minutes and not afterward?

8.13. Diagram the scheme for rDNA replication by the rolling circle
mechanism.

8.14. What would be the distribution of nuclear DNA in CsCl density
gradients for cells engaged in rDNA amplification and for non-
amplifying cells? How would you identify the "satellite" DNA as
rDNA? Diagram your expected results.

REFERENCES

Bell, G. I., L. J. DeGennero, D. H. Gelfand, R. J. Bishop, P. Valenzuela, and W. J. Rutter. 1977. Ribosomal RNA genes of *Saccharomyces cerevisae*. I. Physical map of the repeating unit and location of the regions coding for 5 S, 5.8 S, 18 S, and 25 S ribosomal RNAs. *J. Biol. Chem.* **252**:8118.

Brenner, S., F. Jacob, and M. Meselson. 1961. An unstable intermediate carrying information from genes to ribosomes for protein synthesis. *Nature* **190**:576.

Brown, D. D., and I. B. Dawid. 1968. Specific gene amplification in oocytes. *Science* **160**:272.

Brown, D. D., and J. B. Gurdon. 1964. Absence of ribosomal RNA synthesis in the anucleolate mutant of *Xenopus laevis. Proc. Nat. Acad. Sci. U. S.* **51**:139.

Crick, F. H. C. 1966. Codon-anticodon pairing: The wobble hypothesis. *J. Mol. Biol.* **19**:548.

Crick, F. H. C. 1979. Split genes and RNA splicing. *Science* **204**:264.

Daneholt, B. 1975. Transcription in polytene chromosomes. *Cell* **4**:1.

Durante, M., P. G. Cionini, S. Avanzi, R. Cremonini, and F. D'Amato. 1977. Cytological localization of the genes for the four classes of ribosomal RNA (25S, 18S, 5.8S, and 5S) in polytene chromosomes of *Phaseolus coccineus. Chromosoma* **60**:269.

Federoff, N. V. 1979. On spacers. *Cell* **16**:697.

Gall, J. G. 1968. Differential synthesis of the genes for ribosomal RNA during amphibian oogenesis. *Proc. Nat. Acad. Sci. U. S.* **60**:553.

Gannon, F. *et al.* 1979. Organization and sequences at the 5' end of a cloned complete ovalbumin gene. *Nature* **278**:428.

Givens, J. F., and R. L. Phillips. 1976. The nucleolus organizer region of maize (*Zea mays* L.). *Chromosoma* **57**:103.

Gorini, L. Apr. 1966. Antibiotics and the genetic code. *Sci. Amer.* **214**:102.

Hourcade, D., D. Dressler, and J. Wolfson. 1973. The amplification of ribosomal RNA genes involves a rolling circle intermediate. *Proc. Nat. Acad. Sci. U. S.* **70**:2926.

Kinniburgh, A. J., J. E. Mertz, and J. Ross. 1978. The precursor of mouse β-globin messenger RNA contains two intervening RNA sequences. *Cell* **14**:681.

Konkel, D. A., S. M. Tilghman, and P. Leder. 1978. The sequence of the chromosomal mouse β-globin major gene: Homologies in capping, splicing, and poly(A) sites. *Cell* **15**:1125.

Kozak, M. 1977. Nucleotide sequences of 5′-terminal ribosome-protected initiation regions from two reovirus messages. *Nature* **269**:390.

Kozak, M. 1978. How do eucaryotic ribosomes select initiation regions in messenger RNA? *Cell* **15**:1109.

Lande, M. A., M. Adesnik, M. Sumida, Y. Tashiro, and D. D. Sabatini. 1975. Direct association of messenger RNA with microsomal membranes in human diploid fibroblasts. *J. Cell Biol.* **65**:513.

Lilley, D. M. J. 1978. Active chromatin structure. *Cell Biol. Internat. Repts.* **2**:1.

Lipmann, F. 1969. Polypeptide chain elongation in protein biosynthesis. *Science* **164**:1024.

Miller, D. M., P. Turner, A. W. Nienhuis, D. E. Axelrod, and T. V. Gopalakrishnan. 1978. Active conformation of the globin genes in uninduced and induced mouse erythroleukemia cells. *Cell* **14**:511.

Miller, O. L., Jr. Mar. 1973. The visualization of genes in action. *Sci. Amer.* **229**:34.

Monod, J. 1978. *Selected Papers in Molecular Biology*, (Lwoff, A., and A. Ullmann, eds.). New York: Academic Press.

Nomura, M. 1973. Assembly of bacterial ribosomes. *Science* **179**:864.

Nordstrom, J. L., D. R. Roop, M.-J. Tsai, and B. W. O'Malley, 1979. Identification of potential ovomucoid mRNA precursors in chick oviduct nuclei. *Nature* **278**:328.

Proudfoot, N. J., and G. G. Brownlee. 1976. 3′ Non-coding region sequences in eukaryotic messenger RNA. *Nature* **263**:211.

Quigley, G. J., and A. Rich. 1976. Structural domains of transfer RNA molecules. *Science* **194**:796.

Rich, A. Dec. 1963. Polyribosomes. *Sci. Amer.* **209**:44.

Rich, A., and S. H. Kim. Jan. 1978. The three-dimensional structure of transfer RNA. *Sci. Amer.* **238**:52.

Ritossa, F. M., K. C. Atwood, and S. Spiegelman. 1966. A molecular explanation of the *bobbed* mutants of *Drosophila* as partial deficiencies of ribosomal RNA. *Genetics* **54**:819.

Ritossa, F. M., and S. Spiegelman. 1965. Localization of DNA complementary to ribosomal RNA in the nucleolus organizer region of *Drosophila melanogaster*. *Proc. Nat. Acad. Sci. U. S.* **53**:737.

Safer, B., and W. F. Anderson. 1978. The molecular mechanism of hemoglobin synthesis and its regulation in the reticulocyte. *CRC Crit. Rev. Biochem.* **5**:261.

Tilghman, S. M., P. J. Curtis, D. C. Tiemeier, P. Leder, and C. Weiss-mann. 1978. The intervening sequence of a mouse β-globin gene is transcribed within the 15S β-globin mRNA precursor. *Proc. Nat. Acad. Sci. U. S.* **75**:1309.

Tsai, M.-J., S. Y. Tsai, and B. W. O-Malley. 1979. Distribution of RNA transcripts from structural and intervening sequences of the ovalbumin gene. *Science* **204**:314.

Warner, J. R., A. Rich, and C. E. Hall. 1962. Electron microscope studies of ribosomal clusters synthesizing hemoglobin. *Science* **138**:1399.

Wood, W. G., J. M. Old, A. V. S. Roberts, J. B. Clegg, D. J. Weatherall, and N. Quattrin. 1978. Human globin gene expression: Control of β, δ and $\beta\delta$ chain production. *Cell* **15**:437.

9

Regulation of Gene Expression

In the last chapter, we saw that gene expression required a flow of information from DNA-coded sequences to messenger RNA by transcription and to proteins by translation of mRNA. In this chapter, we will see some of the ways in which gene expression is regulated, leading to phenotypically different cells in genotypically identical populations. The long-range focus of these studies is to understand how the regulation of gene action produces multicellular organisms, such as human beings, whose trillions of differentiated cells have all come from one fertilized egg cell by many mitotic divisions in a lifetime. In order to approach the answers to problems of differentiation and development, however, one must use simpler and more accessible systems for genetic and molecular analysis at the start.

All cells of an organism contain a complete set of genes. The phenotypic differences which arise are due to differential gene action, that is, some genes are turned on and some genes are turned off in different cell types. The controls over gene expression are generally found to be at the level of transcription of genetic information into mRNA. In *E. coli* and other bacteria, there are negative controls in which regulatory genes determine whether or not proteins will be made by their associated structural genes in coordinated gene clusters called operons. Transcription is turned off when repressor proteins bind to DNA and is only turned on if repressors are released from DNA operator sites. Positive control is another widespread phenomenon in all organisms, involving proteins which turn on transcription after they bind to DNA or to chromatin. A knowledge of the molecular organization of the chromosome in eukaryotes is essential to an understanding of molecular interactions which regulate gene expression. These studies are only in the first stages at this time.

A new class of genetic elements has been studied by genetic and molecular methods in the past decade; these are transposable since they move onto and off the chromosome. Transposable elements influence transcription and also can lead to major restructuring of a genome.

DIFFERENTIAL GENE ACTION

The trillions of somatic cells in a human being are genetically identical mitotic descendants of the fertilized egg cell; yet there are many phenotypically different kinds of cells in the body. How can we explain the origin of phenotypically different cells from a genotypically identical cell population in multicellular and unicellular organisms? The possibilities of mutations during development, or of differential losses of genes, can be ruled out by certain kinds of experimental evidence. At the same time, the evidence supports the possibility that different genes are active in different cells, and that differential gene action is regulated by one or more control mechanisms in prokaryotes and eukaryotes. Genes are turned "on" and "off" in different cells by control switches that are part of a set of cellular regulation systems in the organism.

9.1   Cells Have A Complete Set Of Genes

There are three very general hypotheses concerning the way in which some cells may develop a different phenotype from other cells among genotypically identical members of a cell population: (1) different genes are lost or retained in different cells; (2) different mutations arise in different cells leading to different phenotypes during growth and development; and (3) different genes are active in different cells. These possibilities can be tested experimentally.

Evidence against **gene loss** has come primarily from studies of banding patterns in giant polytene chromosomes of dipteran larval tissues, and from molecular hybridizations involving DNAs from different tissues in the organism. Polytene chromosomes in dipteran larvae from *Drosophila*, *Chironomus* and others, have unique banding patterns that permit each chromosome in the genome to be identified unambiguously. From mapping studies and from comparisons between the genetic and cytological features of these insects, it appears that each chromosome band represents one gene (Fig. 9.1). On the assumption that observations of chromosome bands are equivalent to observations of the genome. Wolfgang Beermann and others examined polytene chromosomes in *Chironomus* larvae at various stages during their development toward the pupal stage. They found that chromosome bands did not change in the cells of any one organ during days of profound developmental changes, nor did chromosome bands appear any different in cells from several different kinds of larval organs that were studied. Since no chromosome bands were missing in any differentiated cells, it seemed unlikely that any large segments of genes were lost.

A more precise way of looking for loss of small segments of DNA was made possible by the introduction of molecular hybridization (see Fig. 8.5). DNAs were isolated and purified from different tissues and DNA-DNA hybrid molecules were allowed to form on filters. If one DNA source is labeled with ^{3}H and another source with ^{32}P or ^{14}C so that each source can be identified, one can seek duplex molecules which are doubly-labeled and

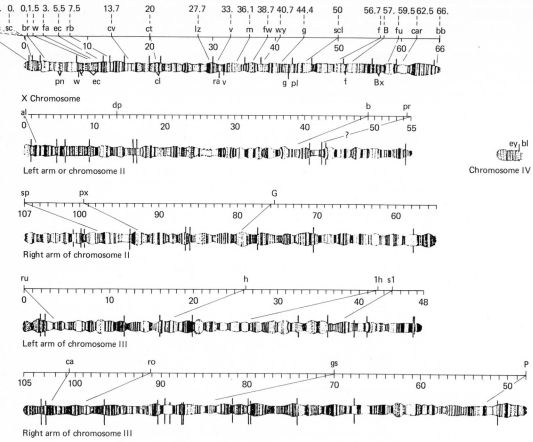

Figure 9.1 Salivary gland chromosome maps of *Drosophila melanogaster*, and locations of certain genes according to loci on the genetic map and bands on the cytological map. (From Painter, T. S. 1934. *J. Hered.* **25**:465.

therefore represent the hybrids. The extent of hybridization between DNAs from different tissues is an index to the sequences of DNA, or genes, which are present in these tissues. Such experiments have shown that essentially the same DNA sequences are present in the various tissues of the individual. Once again, it appears that gene losses do not take place.

Evidence against **mutations** leading to phenotypic differences in an initially homogeneous cell population has come primarily from experiments using plants and animals in two particular procedures. In one procedure, Frederick Steward showed that differentiated cells isolated from carrot root tissue were capable of giving rise to whole carrot plants that produce flowers at the usual time in development (Fig. 9.2). These isolated differentiated cells were therefore **totipotent**, that is, capable of producing all the kinds of differentiated cells making up the adult organism. Since this is the case, it must mean that the whole genome was retained in the differen-

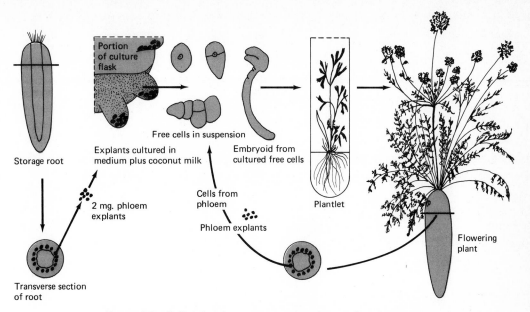

Storage root

Transverse section
of root

Portion
of culture
flask

Explants cultured in
medium plus coconut milk

2 mg. phloem
explants

Free cells in suspension

Cells from
phloem

Phloem explants

Embryoid from
cultured free cells

Plantlet

Flowering
plant

Figure 9.2 Cells taken from carrot root and grown in culture can give rise to a normal flowering carrot plant, indicating the cells are totipotent and genetically complete. (From Steward, F. C. 1964. *Science* **143**:20.)

tiated root cells and that all the genetic information was available to guide growth and development from one cell through to the adult plant. Genes had not mutated, nor were they lost; otherwise a normal carrot plant could not have developed.

In another experimental design with a similar objective to the studies with carrots, the totipotency of the nucleus in the differentiated cell was tested by **nuclear transplantation** in toads and other amphibians. Robert Briggs and Thomas King developed techniques in the 1950s for manipulating nuclei in eggs and in differentiated tissues (Fig. 9.3). They found that nuclei removed from somatic cells in the pre-blastula stage could usually support normal adult frog development, but that post-blastula nuclei could not. Their extensive studies with frogs showed that some irreversible change had occurred during development in the frog embryo, and that somatic nuclei were totipotent only up to the gastrula stage. John Gurdon, on the other hand, was later able to show that nuclei from differentiated intestinal cells in the toad *Xenopus laevis* remained totipotent long after gastrulation. The difference between the two amphibian species is not understood. In *Xenopus* there is evidence of reversible changes in the genetic material of highly differentiated cells which are put into an environment (the egg) that can support all stages of development leading to the adult toad. All the genetic information must have been retained in nonmutated form in toad somatic cells after they had differentiated. Since mutation is a permanent change in the genome, totipotency would not be possible under such a change. It must mean that mutations did not cause phenotypic changes during differentiation.

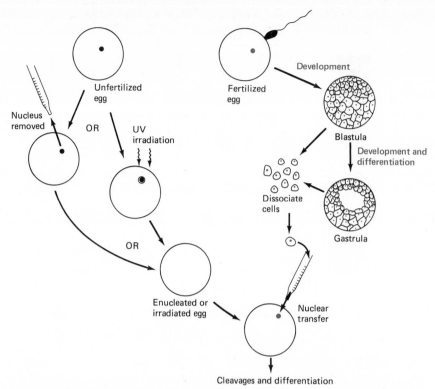

Figure 9.3 Nuclear transplantation experiments have shown that nuclei taken from differentiated cells and placed into enucleated or irradiated eggs can support normal amphibian development. Such evidence indicates that development and differentiation are not the consequences of gene losses or gene mutations in cells of the multicellular organism.

Evidence in favor of **differential gene action** has come from these studies and others. Direct observations of differential gene action have come from studies of puffing of particular bands of polytene chromosomes (see Sec. 3.12). Puffs developed and regressed at different bands, in different chromosomes, in different cells and organs of the larvae. Differential gene action was directly evident from identification of newly synthesized RNA at puffs and from its absence at unpuffed sites, and from the correlation between puffing and the appearance of a protein product of the gene known to exist at one band in *Chironomus* (see Fig. 3.30). In more recent studies of *Drosophila*, Ekkehard Bautz and co-workers have found RNA polymerase II at puffs, but not at unpuffed bands. This is the transcription enzyme for messenger RNA, and its presence signifies gene expression in progress.

DNA-RNA molecular hybridization can be used to test whether differential gene action occurs in differentiated systems. The most direct evidence has come from particular cells and tissues whose messenger RNAs have been followed during a developmental interval. For example, reticulocytes make lots of **hemoglobin** and other cells do not. Is this because globin genes are active in reticulocytes and not in most other cells? The answer is yes because globin messengers can be isolated and identified by molecular criteria, and these mRNA molecules are found in reticulocytes and not in nonblood-forming cells. Similar evidence has been obtained from other specialized cell systems, including vertebrate oviduct in which great amounts of **ovalbumin** are made. Ovalbumin mRNA is found in quantity in oviduct, but not in other cells which do not synthesize the ovalbumin egg protein. In addition to describing significant differences in globin mRNA and ovalbumin mRNA in chick oviduct and in mature hen oviduct, Pierre Chambon and co-workers have shown that substantially more RNA polymerase II is bound to ovalbumin genes in oviduct than to globin genes in the same tissues. These data indicate transcriptional differences between different genes in the same cells, that is, differential gene action during development. Different gene products arise, producing phenotypic differences in genotypically identical cells.

These studies of chromosome banding, molecular hybridizations, and nuclear totipotency, and others, point strongly to *differential gene action during development*, leading to different tissues and organs in an individual organism whose cells retain a full set of genes throughout life.

If all the genes are present but are active only at certain times in certain cells, what *regulates* their activity or inactivity? The first important evidence leading toward an answer to this fundamental question was obtained in experiments using *E. coli*. We will discuss the genetic evidence for gene regulation next.

9.2   The *lac* Operon In *E. coli*

Studies of the *lac* genetic region in *E. coli* by François Jacob and Jacques Monod in the late 1950s opened up a new view of gene functions. Using mutants they had isolated, Jacob and Monod identified three genes which governed the structure of three distinct proteins needed to metabolize lactose. The three genes were mapped in the *lac* region in the order *z—y—a*. The **structural genes** were defined as genes coding for the primary structure (amino acid sequence) of the enzyme β-**galactosidase** (*z* gene), for a membrane protein called **galactoside permease** which helped lactose molecules across the membrane and into the cell (*y* gene), and for **thiogalactoside transacetylase** whose function is still unclear (*a* gene). Mutations in any of these three genes led to amino acid changes in the protein, which altered the protein function and lactose metabolism. Biochemical and visible phenotypic changes could be analyzed.

Two other classes of mutants were isolated, whose activities determined *how much* of the three structural gene proteins were made, but which did not affect the structure of the three proteins themselves. These two classes were *regulatory* mutations, and the function of **regulatory genes** was involved with control of the activities of the structural genes *z-y-a*. The **operator** class of regulatory mutants controlled genes *z-y-a coordinately*, that is, all three proteins were influenced at the same time and in the same way by a single operator mutation. The proteins of the *z-y-a* cluster were not structurally changed, but the amounts made in response to lactose varied in mutant and wild type strains according to the allele of the operator (*o*) gene which was present. This observation suggested that the operator regulated structural gene activities but did not affect the primary structure of protein products of these activities. For example, cells with the genotype $o^+ z^+ y^+ a^+$ made galactosidase, permease, and acetylase only when lactose was present in the medium. Synthesis of these proteins was *inducible* by lactose. Cells with the **operator-constitutive** mutant allele o^c made all three proteins *constitutively* (all the time) regardless of the presence or absence of lactose, when the genotype was $o^c z^+ y^+ a^+$.

An additional feature of the o^c allele was identified in studies of partial diploids, or **merodiploids**, for the *lac* region. In strains that contained an extra copy of the *lac* region brought in by the *F′* fertility factor (see Section 5.9), the o^c allele only affected the activity of *z-y-a* genes located in the *same* chromosome (called the **cis** arrangement) and not *z-y-a* genes in the other chromosome (**trans** arrangement), as shown in Table 9.1. The o^c allele is called **cis-dominant**, since it only influences alleles in the same chromosome as itself. Operator mutations therefore define a gene cluster whose closely linked DNA sequences act as a coordinated unit of function, called an **operon**. The *o-z-y-a* operon is the set of coordinated genes within the *lac* locus on the *E. coli* map. The operator gene mapped very close to *z*.

The second class of regulatory mutants belonged to the **repressor gene** *i*. The *i* gene mapped near the *o* locus of the *lac* operon. Mutants of the repressor gene were operationally distinct from operator mutants, since they acted on the *z-y-a* cluster in the same way in *both* the cis and trans arrangements in partial diploid strains. Two kinds of *i* mutants showed this feature very clearly: i^s mutants which produced *superrepressors* that prevented induction of the *z-y-a* proteins when lactose was present, and i^-

Table 9.1
Genotypes and phenotypes of *E. coli* strains partially diploid for genes of the *lac* region and heterozygous for the cis-dominant o^c allele of the operator site. The second copy of the *lac* region is brought into the cells by *F′*, giving rise to merodiploids.

Merodiploid genotype	Phenotypes*	
	Constitutively synthesized proteins	Inducibly synthesized proteins
$\dfrac{o^+\ z^-\ y^-\ a^-}{F'\ o^c\ z^+\ y^+\ a^+}$	galactosidase permease acetylase	none
$\dfrac{o^+\ z^+\ y^+\ a^+}{F'\ o^c\ z^-\ y^-\ a^-}$	none	galactosidase permease acetylase
$\dfrac{F'\ o^+\ z^-\ y^-\ a^+}{o^c\ z^+\ y^+\ a^-}$	galactosidase permease	acetylase

*Allele o^c is cis-dominant to o^+, since o^c causes *constitutive* production only of proteins coded by structural genes on the same chromosome as itself; o^+ governs *inducible* enzyme synthesis only by structural genes on the same chromosome as itself.

Table 9.2

Genotypes and phenotypes of haploids and merodiploids for the *lac* region in *E. coli* strains. Allelic behavior can be determined from phenotypes of merodiploids carrying different *i* alleles in cis or trans arrangements with *lac* region loci.

	Phenotypes		
Genotype	Constitutively synthesized proteins	Inducibly synthesized proteins	Interpreted *i* allele behavior
Haploid			
$i^+ o^+ z^+ y^+ a^+$	none	all three	wild type
$i^s o^+ z^+ y^+ a^+$	none	none	superrepressor mutant
$i^- o^+ z^+ y^+ a^+$	all three	none	constitutive mutant
Merodiploid			
$\dfrac{i^s o^+ z^+ y^+ a^+}{i^+ o^+ z^- y^- a^-}$	none	none	i^s dominant over i^+
$\dfrac{i^s o^+ z^- y^- a^-}{i^+ o^+ z^+ y^+ a^+}$	none	none	i^s dominant over i^+
$\dfrac{i^- o^+ z^+ y^+ a^+}{i^+ o^+ z^- y^- a^-}$	none	all three	i^+ dominant over i^-
$\dfrac{i^- o^+ z^- y^- a^-}{i^+ o^+ z^+ y^+ a^+}$	none	all three	i^+ dominant over i^-

mutants which caused *constitutive* synthesis of the *z-y-a* proteins (Table 9.2).

Jacob and Monod interpreted all these and other data by brilliant reasoning, and formulated the **operon concept** of regulation of gene action. The repressor and operator genes interact in the control of structural gene activity. Since operator mutants were effective only in the cis arrangement, Jacob and Monod proposed that the operator gene controlled *coordinated transcription* of the *z-y-a* gene cluster adjacent to it in the same strand. The physical proximity required for operator influence, and its coordinated effect on all three structural genes in the same strand as itself, indicated that the operator determined whether or not all three structural genes would be transcribed simultaneously. If they were transcribed, then the three proteins would be translated from such messenger RNAs. If the operator prevented transcription of the whole cluster, none of the three proteins would be synthesized even if lactose was present because there would be no mRNAs to be translated:

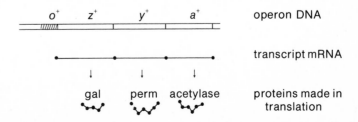

The repressor gene must act through the cytoplasm because the *i* alleles were effective in either the cis or the trans strand arrangements in merodiploids. Jacob and Monod postulated that the *i* gene specified the production of a **repressor** protein, which interacted physically with the operator gene. When the **inducer**, such as lactose, was present, the inducer combined with the repressor and altered the repressor in such a way that it could no longer interact physically with the operator site. Transcription would then take place and all three inducible enzymes would be synthesized in these

Figure 9.4   Operon concept of control over gene expression in the case of inducible enzymes of the *lac* region in *E. coli*. (a) Transcription is blocked and protein translations are not made in the absence of lactose inducer, since the *lac* repressor blocks RNA polymerase movement past the operator site. (b) In the presence of the inducer, an inactive repressor-inducer complex forms and the operator site no longer is blocked. RNA polymerase can move from its binding site at the promoter along the DNA template and catalyze transcription of the *z-y-a* genetic region. Translation occurs once mRNA is made.

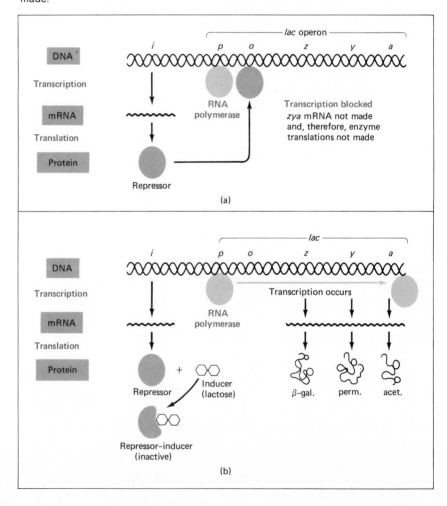

cells. When inducer was absent, repressor could physically interact with the operator and prevent transcription. When lactose was absent, therefore, the three inducible enzymes were not made because the z-y-a genes could not be transcribed when the operator was blocked by repressor (Fig. 9.4).

In the late 1960s, the postulated repressor gene product was isolated and purified by Walter Gilbert. He showed that repressor was present in i^+ but not in i^- cells, and that repressor protein binds to o^+ but not to o^c DNA. These studies, and similar studies of a phage system reported by Mark Ptashne, confirmed the model which Jacob and Monod had presented earlier.

Detection of a third kind of regulatory component of the *lac* region came from studies showing that another site, called the **promoter**, must be present to the left of the operator. Promoter mutants coordinately reduce proteins synthesized from the z-y-a cluster, but these mutants continue to respond to i gene control. In other words, the three proteins are made in reduced amounts only when lactose is present, which means that repressor control has not changed. The promoter is the specific DNA site to which **RNA polymerase** binds; this is the enzyme which catalyzes transcription into mRNA. The polymerase can move along the operon DNA if it is not blocked by a repressor bound to the operator between the *p*romoter site and the z-y-a cluster.

All the mutants of the *lac* region can be understood on the basis of this operon model of regulation of structural gene activities by regulatory genes. The direction of transcription is distally, from the promoter to the operator and on to z, y, and a, in that order. This was interpreted from genetic studies of polar mutants. A **polar mutation** reduces all wild-type activity distal to that mutation, so that a polar defect in z influences z, y, and a; a polar defect in y affects only y and a; and a polar mutation in a affects only the a gene product and not those of the z and y genes. These different polar mutations can be explained by the common feature of transcription beginning at the operator and proceeding distally through z-y-a. The result is a *single polycistronic or polygenic transcript*, with all the copied information for the three structural genes in the one mRNA molecule.

The one repressor-gene—promoter—operator complex regulates transcription of a cluster of the three genes in the *lac* operon whose proteins interact in lactose metabolism (Table 9.3). The z-y-a genes are coordinately

Table 9.3
Regulatory and structural genes of the *lac* region in *E. coli*

Component	Symbol	Function	Protein product
Structural genes	z	Codes for enzyme protein	β-galactosidase
	y	Codes for membrane protein	galactoside permease
	a	Codes for enzyme protein	thiogalactoside transacetylase
Regulatory genes			
Operator	o	Binding site for repressor	none
Promoter	p	Binding site for RNA polymerase	none
Repressor gene*	i	Codes for repressor protein	*lac* repressor

*Gene i is not part of the *lac* operon, but it has been mapped very nearby.

turned on when lactose is present, or they are coordinately turned off when lactose is absent from wild type cells. This is an example of **negative control**, since the repressor turns off the system. A similar instance of negative control characterizes the synthesis of **repressible enzymes**. Unlike inducible enzymes, repressible enzymes are made only when their substrate is depleted and *not* when this metabolite is present in excess (Fig. 9.5). In repressible enzyme systems the metabolite is called a **corepressor**, since it helps the repressor bind to the operator and prevent transcription. Sometimes inducers and corepressors are referred to generally as **effectors**, that is, metabolites which influence repressor binding in a gene regulation system.

Jacob and Monod deduced the existence of the operon and its repressor gene on the basis of genetic methods alone. Some years later, biochemical and molecular genetic studies in various laboratories verified these deductions. Later studies not only described the molecular basis for the inter-

Figure 9.5 Differential gene expression in the case of repressible enzymes coded by structural genes *A* and *B*. (a) Gene expression is turned on in the absence of the corepressor metabolite, but (b) it is turned off when repressor-corepressor bind to the operator site and block RNA polymerase movement to catalyze transcription.

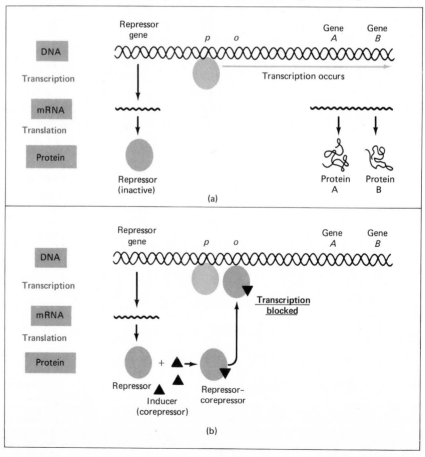

actions of genes, proteins, and metabolites of operons in different species, but have provided the exact nucleotide sequences of promoter and operator sites in some cases. These data have opened the way to a detailed analysis of the physical and chemical interactions between DNA and such proteins as repressors and polymerases.

9.3 Positive Control of Gene Action

The *lac* operon and certain other bacterial operons are also subject to **positive control** when a molecule binds to the appropriate site of the operon and turns on transcription. In fact, the positive control is required *in addition to* repressor being neutralized by interaction with an inducer in negative control, in order to achieve a maximum transcription response.

The positive control system was discovered through studies of the **glucose effect** in blocking transcription of *glucose-sensitive operons* which control the catabolism, or breakdown, of specific sugars such as lactose, galactose, arabinose, and others. When glucose is present in the medium along with one or more of the other sugars, only glucose is catabolized while the other sugars remain unutilized because their enzymes are not made in the cells. When glucose is absent or depleted, the glucose-sensitive operons become active and make breakdown enzymes, such as β-galactosidase, which will process other sugars that are present. The key metabolite which influences the glucose effect is **cyclic AMP**, which is required for transcription of all the operons which are sensitive to glucose catabolism (Fig. 9.6).

Cyclic AMP (**cAMP**) works through binding with the **catabolite activator protein** (**CAP**), which has no influence over transcription until cAMP is bound to it. When the cAMP—CAP complex binds to a specific operon site, it increases the rate of transcription of the structural genes of

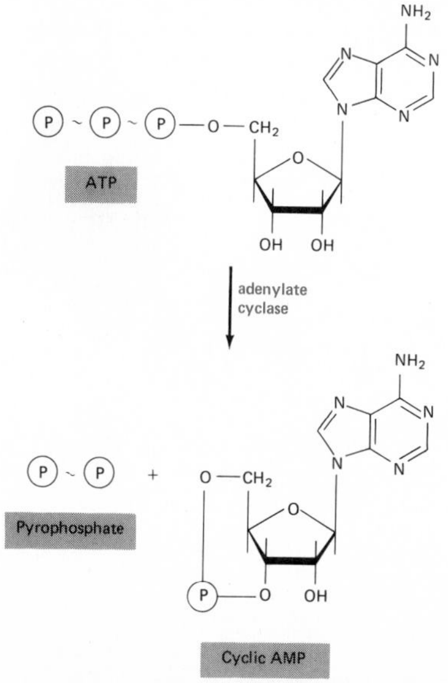

Figure 9.6 Cyclic AMP (adenosine 5′-monophosphate) is derived from ATP in a reaction catalyzed by adenylate cyclase.

that operon. Since CAP is the positive control element for all the glucose-sensitive operons, any mutations which affect its function will produce cells that simultaneously are unable to use a large number of different sugars. Such mutants include CAP-deficient strains and **adenylcyclase**-deficient strains, whose structural gene loci are known.

CAP does not act alone because adenylcyclase-deficient mutants, which do not make cAMP, make low amounts of inducible enzymes. cAMP does not act alone because CAP-deficient mutants make little inducible enzyme. Furthermore, the cAMP—CAP positive control does not act through the agency of the negative control repressor system because *i* gene mutants and *i⁺* strains of *E. coli* are stimulated to make inducible enzymes equally well if cAMP is added to these cultures. The positive and negative controls of inducible enzyme synthesis act together, but each is a separate gene regulation system for operon transcription.

The cAMP—CAP positive control is a much more efficient stimulator of operon transcription than negative control by repressor protein. In studies using isolated *lac* operon DNA it has been found that RNA polymerase binds to the *lac* promoter only infrequently, even when repressor has been removed from the adjacent operator site. Polymerase binding to the *lac* promoter is greatly enhanced when cAMP—CAP is bound to the operon. The reasons for this difference are not entirely clear yet, but may be due to more favorable steric interaction between RNA polymerase and the promoter when cAMP—CAP is also bound to the operon (Fig. 9.7). The binding site for cAMP—CAP is located proximal to the *lac* promoter, so that it not only can enhance RNA polymerase binding there, but also does not interfere with interactions between the repressor and its operator binding site distal to the promoter site.

Control over transcription of the *lac* operon, the system which has been

Figure 9.7 DNA base sequence of the regulatory region of the *lac* operon in *E. coli*. The end of the repressor gene *i* (*lac*I) and all of the promoter (*lac*P) and operator (*lac*O) are shown, along with the start of the z gene (*lac*Z). Binding sites for CAP, RNA polymerase, and the lac repressor show some overlaps. (After Dickson, R. C., J. Abelson, W. M. Barnes, and W. S. Reznikoff. 1975. *Science* **187**:27.)

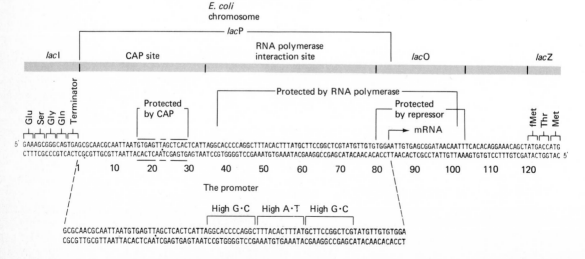

studied most intensively in bacteria, thus appears to depend on the interactions of three different proteins with particular DNA binding sites:

1. Repressors made by the *i* gene bind to the operator and turn off
   transcription. They are removed through binding with an inducer
   such as lactose, and transcription can then proceed along the structural genes *z-y-a*.

2. CAP made by the *crp* gene binds to a DNA site proximal to the promoter and turns on transcription of the *z-y-a* genes. CAP can bind
   to the operon only if it is complexed with the metabolite cAMP, after
   which transcription of the coordinated messenger RNA takes place
   along the three structural genes.

3. RNA polymerase made by the *rpo* genes binds to the promoter site
   of the operon and catalyzes transcription. It binds efficiently only
   when cAMP—CAP is bound to DNA just proximal to the promoter
   and when repressor is absent from the operator just distal to the
   promoter.

Transcriptional control is the most common system of regulation over
gene action; it determines the *amounts* of gene products made in cells whose
genes determine the *kinds* of proteins the cell can produce. There are other
gene regulation systems which also influence the amounts of gene products
a cell will contain, and thereby also control phenotypic development. Control may be exerted on the messenger RNA transcript after it has been synthesized, by **post-transcriptional controls**. Systems of **translational
control** influence the actual synthesis of the polypeptides from available
messenger RNAs. For example, the polygenic messenger of the *lac* operon
does not lead to equal amounts of the three proteins in *E. coli* cells. About
twice as much β-galactosidase is synthesized as the permease or acetylase
proteins, even though all three information sequences are carried in the
same messenger. Some post-transcriptional or translational control probably acts in this case, although the experimental evidence is somewhat
speculative. Finally, **post-translational control** also is known to influence the actual amounts of functional proteins which occur in different cells
with the same genotype. In many of these examples, the polypeptide translation must either be processed from its precursor state to some finished
functional form, or it must bind with other subunit polypeptides to make the
functional protein molecule. The amounts of functional protein available
for metabolism can therefore fluctuate in response to a variety of systems
which regulate phenotypic development through genetic processes involved in the flow of information from DNA.

Systems of nongenetic control over phenotypic development usually
affect the *activity* of proteins which are present, but do not influence the
kinds or the amounts of these proteins in the cell. Many such controls have
been described biochemically, particularly in relation to enzyme activity in
metabolic pathways. Enzyme activities may fluctuate in response to concentrations of their substrates or other metabolites, to pH variations, and to
a number of other environmental factors. The enzymes or other proteins are
already present in the cell, as a consequence of genetic processes, but their
action in metabolism is regulated afterward by nongenetic interactions.

EUKARYOTIC TRANSCRIPTIONAL CONTROL

Does the operon model help us to understand differential gene action in eukaryotes? Although the search has been extensive, there is no convincing evidence for the existence of operons in eukaryotic systems. There has been no evidence identifying regulatory genes, and the limited information from *Aspergillus* about coordinated gene transcripts in fungi is not completely convincing at present. Yet transcriptional control is a common feature of eukaryotic gene action. The mechanism(s) of this transcriptional control are unknown.

The main reason that eukaryotic gene action is so much more difficult to analyze than bacterial or viral systems is that eukaryotic DNA is part of a nucleoprotein chromatin fiber, and we are just beginning to understand how this fiber is organized. There is no suitable model for eukaryotic gene expression without the knowledge of molecular organization of the chromosome in which the DNA occurs. If we knew how chromosomes were organized and constructed, we would be able to explore how DNA in chromatin interacts with proteins and other regulatory molecules and, therefore, we would have a handle on the molecular bases for transcriptional control of gene expression.

The complexity of developmental processes poses additional problems in studying eukaryotic gene expression. In many cases there are relatively few cells of any one phenotype, and these are parts of tissues and organs made up of many cell types. A major advance toward experimental analysis of eukaryotic gene expression has been made possible, however, by new methods for the study of cells and organs cultured outside the body.

9.4 Hormone-Mediated Positive Control of Transcription

Various kinds of observations can be interpreted to show that gene expression is *turned on* at the level of transcription by some form of positive control. When active cells in culture are fused with some type of inactive cell type, the previously inactive nucleus is activated in the binucleate cell-hybrid (Fig. 9.8). For example, if human HeLa cells which are actively transcribing RNA are fused with hen erythrocyte cells that are not transcribing, the erythrocyte nucleus soon begins to enlarge and then to synthesize RNA. The highly condensed hen chromosomes become capable of nucleic acid synthesis after they expand during nuclear enlargement. This probably indicates positive control, since the hen nucleus is activated, rather than the HeLa nucleus becoming inactivated. Since the HeLa nucleus is not inhibited and the hen nucleus resumes transcriptional activity, transcription has been turned on. Negative control would turn off transcription.

These observations have been made for many kinds of cell pairs, but they do not indicate the kinds of components which directly cause specific genes to be expressed in eukaryotic organisms. The most direct information we have on this question has been obtained in studies of the influence of **steroid hormones** on transcription during development. Hormones can be purified and studied in test systems. Two particular examples will illustrate this kind of information.

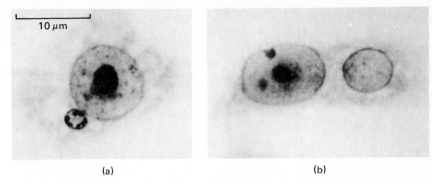

Figure 9.8 Binucleate somatic cell hybrid containing actively transcribing HeLa and hen erythrocyte nuclei. (a) The large HeLa nucleus contrasts sharply with the small, condensed hen nucleus shortly after cell fusion, but (b) the erythrocyte nucleus enlarges and becomes genetically active after an interval of coexistence in the same cytoplasm with the HeLa nucleus. (From Harris, H. 1967. *J. Cell Sci.* **2**:23.)

During larval development in Drosophila and other dipteran insects, specific chromosome bands expand by puffing and regress later on as the larva progresses toward the pupal stage of its life cycle (Fig. 9.9). The steroid hormone **ecdysone** plays a major role in turning on transcription, observed as puffing, at particular chromosome bands at certain times in development and for specific intervals of time in the developmental program. Ecdysone is a growth hormone which is made in the prothoracic gland of the early larva and then released into the bloodlike hemolymph through which the hormone circulates to all parts of the larva.

When early larvae are injected with ecdysone, existing puffs regress and new puffs appear within five minutes. Over a period of days about 125 specific chromosome bands undergo puffing, each appearing and regressing at regular intervals during development. The "early" puffs may be direct responses to the hormone, since puffing is not inhibited when protein synthesis is blocked by drugs such as **cycloheximide** (see Table 8.3). The "late" puffs do require new protein synthesis, in addition to ecdysone, since formation of these puffs can be inhibited by cycloheximide. The proteins which interact with ecdysone to turn on transcription are highly specific protein **receptors**.

Each **target cell** of hormonal induction has thousands of protein receptor molecules in the cytoplasm, as evidenced by specific interactions between the hormone and cytoplasmic proteins extracted from *noninduced* cells. After ecdysone enters the target cells, the hormone combines with specific protein receptors and the complexes thus formed move into the nucleus from the cytoplasm, and bind to chromatin. When hormone is present in these cells, the protein receptors can no longer be found in the cytoplasm, but they can be isolated from chromatin of these activated cell nuclei, in a combined form with the hormone. The protein receptors are considered to be positive control elements which turn on transcription at particular gene sites. Transcription is visible as puffing at certain sites and by RNA synthesis at puffed bands. If the drug **actinomycin** is introduced into

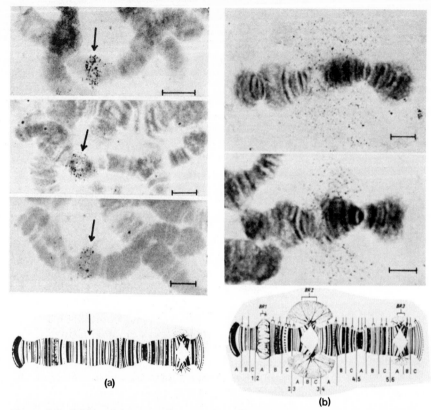

Figure 9.9 Differential gene action seen in puffing of chromosome IV of *Chironomus tentans*. (a) Rectum chromosomes hybridized *in situ* with BR 2 (Balbiani ring 2) RNA. Relatively little puffing or RNA is evident at the BR 2 locus (arrow). (b) Salivary gland chromosomes hybridized *in situ* with BR 2 RNA show a large, expanded Balbiani ring and a high count of silver grains. (From Lambert, B. 1975. *Chromosoma* **50**:193.)

activated cells, RNA synthesis is inhibited and puffs regress. Actinomycin specifically inhibits RNA polymerase activity and prevents transcription.

Drosophila larvae can be *ligatured* in such a way that part of the salivary glands are tied off from the remainder of the glands. In such ligatured larvae, the salivary gland cells which can still receive ecdysone from the neighboring prothoracic glands will undergo puffing and tissue differentiation. The salivary gland cells on the other side of the ligature constriction do not receive ecdysone. These cells show very little puffing, and the larval tissues do not continue to differentiate. The differences between the two parts of the ligatured larva, therefore, show that ecdysone is a requirement for transcription of a number of specific genes needed for a normal program of tissue development during metamorphosis.

A particular problem encountered with the dipteran larval system is that very few specific gene products have been identified for the larval genes which are active (puffed) during metamorphosis. What would be most desirable would be a cell system whose transcriptional activities could be associated with specific genes, mRNAs, and their protein products, related to the induction of gene expression by a known hormone and its protein receptors. In such a system, the actual transcripts could be isolated and identified, and their protein translations could be related to the RNA made by transcription of a particular gene. Such a system is available in the immature chick or mature hen **oviduct**, either of which can be grown in organ culture. In this system, the steroid hormone **estradiol**, an estrogen, causes changes in gene expression in the oviduct target tissues, changes which can be followed by activation of the gene for **ovalbumin** protein. The activation of this gene is analyzed through molecular studies of the ovalbumin messenger, whose entire nucleotide sequence is known (Fig. 9.10).

That the estrogenic steroid estradiol does cause changes in gene expression has been demonstrated at the level of transcription in various target tissues. Response to the hormone is blocked by drugs which inhibit RNA synthesis (actinomycin) and which inhibit translation on polysomes (puromycin and cycloheximide). RNA isolated from oviduct polysomes showed that hormone treatment results in the appearance of ovalbumin messenger RNA. The synthesis of the larger pre-mRNA has also been demonstrated, which means that the entire gene transcript is accurately made in response to estradiol and is processed to mRNA. Afterward, the finished transcript is translated on polysomes into the ovalbumin protein.

Gene activation in the chick or hen oviduct, and in other vertebrate systems of hormone-mediated positive control of transcription, requires interaction between the hormone and its specific protein receptor molecules. Transcription of DNA is turned on when the protein binds to the gene. Specific receptors are absent from cells which are not targets for the associated hormone, since they are not found in the cytoplasmic extracts of these cells. In target cells, transcription is turned on because receptors are present and can activate RNA synthesis from DNA, once the receptors have been transported to nuclear chromatin through hormonal association. Different phenotypes will then develop in the organism through differential gene expression in target and nontarget cells. The mechanism of production of specific receptors in specific cells, however, is not known.

The ovalbumin system and others of a similar nature will almost certainly be the principal models for the analysis of other questions about gene expression in chromosomes. Does the protein receptor bind to a specific site of the gene or a site somewhere near the gene which is activated? How does the protein alter inactive chromatin to the active state after it has been bound? What is the role of the histone and nonhistone proteins of the chromatin fiber in activating transcription from the DNA template? What interactions take place between chromosomal proteins and receptor proteins? These and many other questions can now be asked specifically, and they can be tested experimentally. We should have answers to many questions in a relatively brief time, now that some of the molecular features of eukaryotic gene expression are known and can be analyzed specifically.

9.5   Histone and Nonhistone Proteins In Transcription

DNA in eukaryotic nuclei is packaged together with basic **histone proteins** and acidic or neutral **nonhistone proteins** in the chromosomes. The influence of these proteins on transcription from the DNA template must be

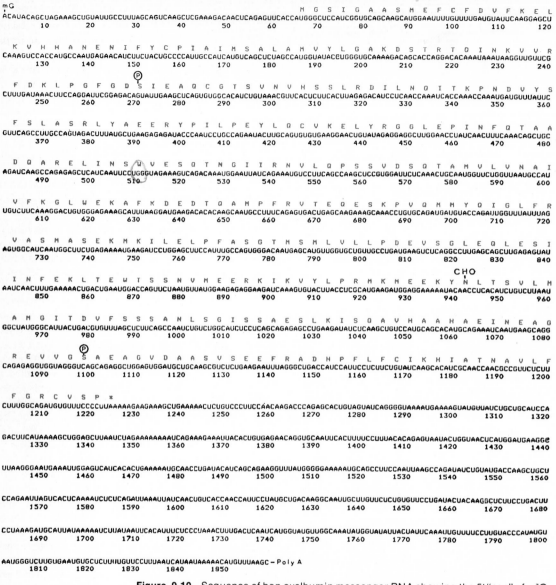

Figure 9.10 Sequence of hen ovalbumin messenger RNA showing the 5′ "cap" of m⁷G and the leader segment preceding the AUG initiator codon at nucleotide 66; the codons for the protein between nucleotides 66 and 1221, followed by the UAA terminator (*), a long trailer segment, and the poly(A) tail at the 3′ end of the molecule. There are 385 amino acid residues in the hen ovalbumin protein. (From McReynolds, L., et al. 1978. *Nature* **273**:723.)

understood if we are to understand how gene expression is regulated in the genome. These proteins may perform a regulatory function directly, by activating or repressing gene transcription, or indirectly by influencing the *conformation* of DNA so that the template may or may not be accessible to RNA polymerase for transcription.

Most of the studies so far have concentrated on discovering the molecular construction of the chromatin fiber as a first step toward understanding how the proteins are arranged in relation to each other and to the DNA duplex. Once the organization of the chromatin fiber can be described, it should be possible to see how transcribing and nontranscribing chromatin may differ, and how these differences may be related to regulation of transcription.

As we discussed in Section 7.9, the flexibly-jointed chromatin fiber is a continuous nucleoprotein strand organized as a series of repeating **nucleosome** subunits. The DNA duplex is wound around the outside of the protein core of the nucleosome, bonded to the eight histone molecules in the core. Linkers between nucleosomes consist of segments of duplex DNA and the very lysine-rich histone H1, in an association which is not yet known. The nature of the bonding and distribution of nonhistone proteins along the repeating nucleosomes and linkers is not known at present.

One way to approach the question of whether chromatin has a different conformation when it is transcribing is to isolate nucleosomes from cells which have been induced to transcribe and from cells which are noninduced and see how these systems differ. Using deoxyribonuclease digestion as a probe, it appears that DNA found in transcribing nucleosome preparations is more accessible to enzyme attack than DNA in nontranscribing preparations. This preliminary evidence leads to the suggestion that transcribing DNA is conformationally altered, and may therefore also be more accessible to RNA polymerase II for transcription of messenger RNA in the nucleus. As a further experimental approach, the structural difference between transcribing and nontranscribing chromatin can be assayed by looking for the specific genes which are induced to transcribe and seeing whether these genes are in a more accessible conformation. Such an experiment can be done using cells that can be induced to make hemoglobin, since globin genes can be identified in molecular hybridizations between DNA isolated from chromatin in the experimental cells and RNA or copied DNA (cDNA) which is complementary to these gene sequences (Fig. 9.11).

Using mouse leukemia cells in culture, James Bonner and his associates examined inducible cells and cells from a genetically noninducible strain. They found that cells which were induced to make hemoglobin contained a significant amount of hybridizable globin gene sequences, as seen by the amount of molecular hybridization with cDNA that was complementary to them. Genetically noninducible cells, however, contained very little hybridizable globin DNA in these assays. The different amounts of globin DNA available and exposed for hybridization were correlated with genes having known inducible or noninducible properties and transcriptional activity. The general conclusion from this work is that transcribing chromatin does have a conformationally different state from nontranscribing chromatin.

The roles of histones and nonhistones in regulating transcription have been studied in many systems and in many ways, but definitive evidence has been hard to get. Several groups have attempted chromatin reconstitution experiments, in which DNA, histones, and nonhistones are isolated

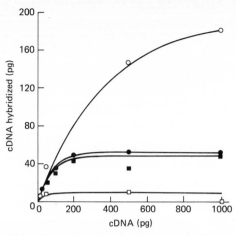

Figure 9.11　Molecular hybridization of ^{3}H-labeled globin DNA with DNAs from mouse leukemia cell cultures. Increasing amounts of the ^{3}H-labeled cDNA were hybridized to 50 μg of test DNA until saturation was approached. Hybridization of template-active whole cell DNA (●) served for comparison with results using template-active DNA from uninduced cells of an inducible strain (o), template-active DNA from genetically uninducible cells (■), and template-inactive DNA from genetically uninducible cells (□). There is barely detectable globin DNA in the uninducible strain, it being approximately the same as hybridizable globin from normal, uninduced cells. The template-inactive uninducible cellular DNA hybridizes as expected with ^{3}H-labeled globin cDNA, indicating the globin gene sequences are present but are not accessible to base-pairing in the hybridization tests. Such evidence points to conformational differences between the actively transcribing and inactive states of the same DNA sequences. (From Wallace, R. B., S. K. Dube, and J. Bonner. 1977. *Science* **198**:1166.)

from chromatin of different tissues and are then combined in all possible ways to reconstitute functioning chromatin preparations. Unfortunately, there are ambiguities in the interpretations of these experiments, and the results have been difficult to reproduce in other laboratories. At the present time, this experimental approach is not widely accepted even though it seems to be a reasonable method from a theoretical viewpoint.

A more promising approach may be one in which *specific* histone and nonhistone proteins are analyzed in systems where transcription can be turned on and off by experimentally controlled means. One such study, which is typical of others exploring the *configuration* of chromatin in transcribing and nontranscribing regions, was reported by Bautz and co-workers, as mentioned briefly above. Using *Drosophila melanogaster* larvae, puffing was induced by brief "heat shock" at 37° C. Within five minutes, existing puffs regressed and new puffs appeared. Bautz localized **RNA polymerase II** in puffs and found no detectable amounts of the enzyme in unpuffed bands. He used the **immunofluorescence method**, based on the highly specific interaction between **antigen** and **antibody** in immunity systems. Purified polymerase was injected into an animal, such as a rabbit, to elicit antibody production against the introduced foreign protein, or antigen. Antisera preparations made from the animal were tagged with a fluorescent dye by chemical means. When such tagged antibodies are presented to an unknown system, the antigen can be located by fluorescence, which develops due to the presence of bound, tagged antibody. When anti-polymerase antisera were presented to *Drosophila* chromosomes, fluorescence appeared in puffs. This showed that the polymerase molecules were located in these puffs, since no other protein would react with anti-polymerase antibodies (Fig. 9.12). Since these were new puffs, and since previous puffs had just regressed after heat shock, the polymerase molecules must have been redistributed and bound to different parts of the chromosome very rapidly, that is, transcription was turned on in new puffs and turned off in pre-treatment puffs. The same method should be useful in locating other nonhistone proteins along the chromosome and in cataloguing those which are related to the turning on and off of transcription.

Bautz also localized **histone H1** in highly condensed heterochromatin, but found no detectable amounts in euchromatin, when anti-histone H1 antibody was presented to *Drosophila* chromosomes. This confirmed many other studies which have shown by various means that histone H1 is characteristic of highly condensed, transcriptionally inactive chromatin. When the SV40 virus "minichromosome" is depleted of histone H1, the chromosome unfolds; when H1 is added back, the chromosome becomes condensed again. All these studies provide a relatively static picture of

Figure 9.12 Immunofluorescence staining pattern obtained using antiserum prepared against the ρ (rho) subunit of RNA polymerase in salivary glands of *Drosophila melanogaster*. The photographs were taken with a light microscope equipped with (a) phase contrast optics, or (b) fluorescence optics. The standard banding pattern seen in (a) provides references for fluorescent bands visible in (b). (From Silver, L. M., and S. C. R. Elgin. 1977. *Cell* **11**:971.)

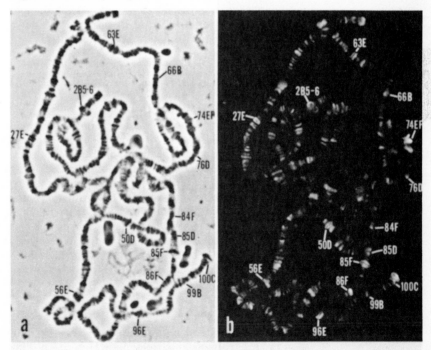

40 μm

chromosomes, and a great deal of work must still be done to find the relationships between actively transcribing chromatin and the regulatory and structural roles of histone and nonhistone proteins.

At present the opinion is that the four major kinds of histones in nucleosomes, histones H2A, H2B, H3, and H4, are primarily structural and not regulatory proteins. They are found in all nucleosomes in equal amounts, and since the whole chromatin fiber consists of repeating nucleosome subunits, there seems to be little room for variation in these four types of histone proteins. Histone H1 apparently has a structural function, since it leads to chromatin condensation, and condensation makes DNA relatively inaccessible to transcription, according to heterochromatin studies. Histones may be chemically modified, by acetylation or phosphorylation, and these modifications apparently influence DNA transcription in the associated chromatin, although the data are still rather vague.

Very little is known about the role of nonhistone proteins in transcription control. RNA polymerase II is a nonhistone protein, but it is the major transcription enzyme and hardly qualifies as a typical protein in this class of chromosomal components. Do nonhistones have a regulatory or a structural function? Do nonhistones turn on transcription, turn off transcription, or alter the conformation of chromatin in some way such that transcription is turned on or off?

These and other questions are open to experimental analysis (Box 9.1). In addition to knowing more about nonhistone and histone protein functions, we must know more about the physical biochemistry of protein-protein interactions and protein-DNA interactions. These gaps in our knowledge can only be filled in after we know the true organization of DNA and proteins in the chromatin fiber. Studies of nucleosomes represent a very promising beginning step along these lines.

TRANSPOSABLE ELEMENTS AND CONTROL OF GENE EXPRESSION

Transposable elements are unique DNA segments which can insert into several sites in a genome. There is increasing evidence showing that transposable elements play various roles in bacterial cells. They can switch transcription on and off in particular operons of the bacterial genome; they are required for chromosomal gene transfer during mating in *E. coli*; and they may be responsible for sudden and drastic rearrangements of nonhomologous gene sequences which significantly alter the bacterial phenotype. This last feature leads to particular problems in antibiotic therapy for various human diseases when pathogenic bacteria suddenly become resistant to a number of drugs simultaneously. There are also some very important evolutionary considerations involving genome restructuring, but we will delay that discussion to later chapters.

9.6   Insertion Sequences and Transposons

Simple **insertion sequences (IS)** and the more complex **transposons (Tn)** are transposable elements which can be distinguished by at least two criteria: (1) IS elements are less than 2000 base pairs (or 2 **kilobase** pairs

Box 9.1
IMMUNOGLOBULIN DIVERSITY

The ability of animals to recognize the tremendous diversity of antigenic substances depends on a vast array of antibodies, which are proteins belonging to a single group called immunoglobulins (Ig). There probably are over a million different kinds of Igs in each individual, enough to bind with any antigen and provide an immune response. How can the DNA of any genome contain enough information to encode for the millions of different Igs required for such an immune system? Many questions remain unanswered in this rapidly-advancing but complex area of study. The first clues, however, came from analysis of the chemical structure of Ig molecules, as shown in (a). Each Ig is made up of heavy (H) and light (L) polypeptide chains, and each kind of chain consists of at least two and perhaps three different regions: constant (C) and variable (V), and junction (J) in the L chain and probably in the H chain, too. These regions never interchange, so there are C_H, J_H, V_H, C_L, J_L, and V_L regions, each determined by a separate set of structural genes. In addition, there are multiple variants of each gene in each chromosome set. These Ig molecules are therefore very unusual, since *each polypeptide chain* is coded by at least three different gene sequences distributed in various parts of the genome.

The greatest variability in structure is found in the V_H and V_L regions, as one might expect from their names. By combining the multiple C, J, and V genes in various ways to make numerous H and L chains, and by combining the numerous H and L chains in various ways, it is possible to make millions of different antibodies from only a few hundred to a thousand structural genes in an organism. The high variability in the V regions is expected since this portion of the Ig includes the antigen combining site.

Joining of different C, J, and V components occurs both at the DNA level and at the RNA level, as shown schematically in (b). The Ig chain is formed from a larger number of genes than it ultimately contains, but some of the processing steps have not been demonstrated explicitly. The variability in the excision of V and J genes or transcripts accounts for the diversity in specificity of the lymphocytes in which these Igs are made. Each lymphocyte can only make one H chain and one L chain, and therefore each can make only one complete Ig out of the millions of Igs made by the animal's lymphocyte population. Differentiation in animals therefore involves sorting of structural genes specifying pieces of Ig molecules, and the establishment of millions of kinds of specified lymphocytes able to engage one antigen out of millions the animal may encounter in its lifetime. (Figures from Talmage, D.W. 1979. *Amer. Sci.* **67**:173.)

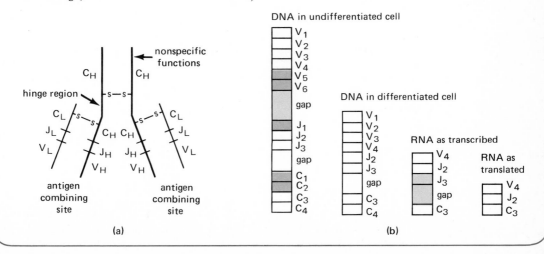

(a)   (b)

indicated as 2 **kb**) long, while Tn elements are usually much longer than 2 kb; and (2) IS elements only contain genes involved in the function of DNA insertion, while Tn elements contain genes that are unrelated to insertion, as well as insertion genes. A number of Tn elements are known to contain IS components in their construction. Both IS and Tn elements are transposable; they can move onto and off the bacterial chromosome, and they can move from place to place on chromosomes with considerable frequency. They are, therefore, called "jumping genes" by some biologists.

IS elements were discovered through studies of mutants at the *gal*actose operon in *E. coli*, and they have been studied in *lac* operon mutants as well. The mutant strains all showed a *polar* effect on structural gene transcription; all genes were turned off distal to the integration site between the *gal* operator-promoter and the three *gal* structural genes controlling three enzymes of galactose metabolism (Fig. 9.13). Strains of these polar mutants also gave rise to rare wild-type revertants (1 in 10^7 cells) and to more frequent types which had undergone some altered mutational change in *gal* and sometimes in nearby genes as well.

These genetic alterations were explained on the basis of insertion and excision of IS elements in the control region between the *gal* operator-promoter and the three structural genes of the operon. When IS inserted, it turned off transcription of all structural genes distal to its integrated site. When IS was excised precisely, the wild-type gene expression was restored to its original state. When IS was excised inaccurately, some parts of the *gal* operon were also removed, and sometimes nearby genes were deleted as well, producing altered mutant strains.

Figure 9.13 Insertion of the IS*1* element in the *gal* region of *E. coli* shuts off the *K, T,* and *E* structural genes distal to the integration site next to operator-promoter (*OP*); transcription is restored in all three genes when IS*1* leaves the site. Excisions and insertions of IS*1* may lead to deletion of the *gal* K, *gal* T, and *gal* E genes in this region, and to other effects on the genome.

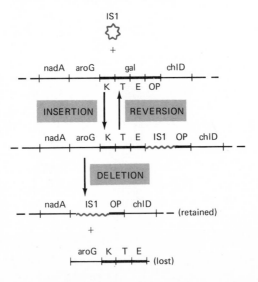

The particular element IS*1* exerted a negative control over *gal* operon transcription, turning it off by insertion and turning it on by excision from the integrated site. This kind of negative control, that is, turning off transcription when IS inserts in the genome, may occur normally in *E. coli*, since there are about eight copies of IS*1* in the normal *E. coli* genome, at various sites.

The presence of IS*1* within the *gal* operon was deduced from genetic studies, and was verified by the physical method of electron microscopy. DNA from specialized transducing phages carrying the normal *gal* operon and from specialized transducing phages carrying the *gal* polar mutant operon was extracted and purified. These DNAs were melted to single strands and then mixed to permit reannealing of duplex DNA. Reannealed duplex segments carrying one copy of normal *gal* and one copy of mutant *gal* are called **heteroduplex** molecules. Electron microscopy of heteroduplexes reveals a loop of single-stranded, unpaired DNA on the mutant DNA (Fig. 9.14). This loop consists of the IS element, for which there is no partner on the normal *gal* DNA. Similar heteroduplex mapping has revealed IS*1*

Figure 9.14 Electron micrograph of a heteroduplex molecule obtained by hybridizing a specialized transducing λ*dgal* phage with a λ*dgal* phage carrying an IS*1*-induced deletion. If IS*1* was still present after the deletion had occurred, there should be two single-stranded loops in the heteroduplex: one due to the nondeleted region which has no partner in the deleted strand, and another nearby which would be the IS*1* element still present. If the IS*1* sequence was deleted too, only one single-stranded loop would be present since neither strand would have IS*1*. This photograph shows two loops, meaning IS*1* has been retained near the deleted region, as was shown in Fig. 9.13. (From Reif, H.-J., and H. Saedler. 1977. In *DNA: Insertion Elements, Plasmids, and Episomes.* A. I. Bukhari, J. A. Shapiro, and S. L. Adhya, eds., p. 81. New York: Cold Spring Harbor Laboratory.)

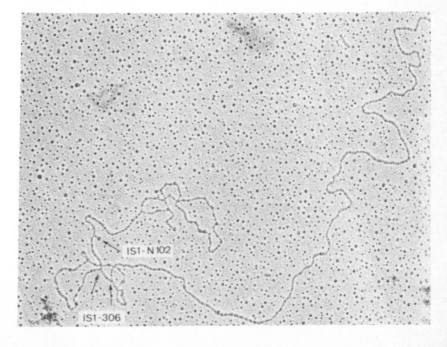

IS1-N102

IS1-306

elements in other parts of the *E. coli* chromosome. The method is used generally to analyze the extent of pairing between DNAs, deletions and insertions of DNA sequences, as well as for other purposes. The length of a deleted or inserted segment can be estimated by the length of the unpaired region of the heteroduplex molecule, since the segment can be measured directly in micrometers. The segment can then be described in terms of its molecular weight (1 μm = 2×10^6 daltons) or length in kilobases (1 μm = about 3 kb). We will refer to heteroduplex analysis on a number of occasions in this and later chapters.

IS*2* is a very interesting element, since it has the ability to implement positive control over transcription in *E. coli*. It was found that IS*2* turned on constitutive synthesis of *gal* structural genes if the element inserted in the *same* direction as operon transcription (Fig. 9.15). If IS*2* integrated in the *gal* operon in the direction *opposite* to transcription, it caused a reduction in structural gene transcription distal to the insertion site. The two orientation of IS*2* can therefore act as a simple on—off switch for transcription. Similar "flip-flop" control mechanisms have been demonstrated to regulate flagellar type in the bacterium *Salmonella* and mating type expression in the eukaryotic species *Schizosaccharomyces*, a fission yeast. **Inversions** of IS elements, from one orientation to the other and back again, may represent a fundamental mode of regulation of gene expression. IS*2* apparently may contain nucleotide sequences which act as strong promoters (start signals) and other sequences which recognize the rho protein, which terminates transcription in *E. coli* (stop signals). These sequences help to explain the different behavior of IS*2* and other IS elements, since IS*1* and IS*4* do not have promoter or rho-recognition sequences. IS*1* turns off transcription in genes distal to its integrated site whether it is in the same or the opposite direction as operon transcription.

Transposons have been described in eukaryotes as well as in prokaryotes and viruses. In fact, transposable elements were first deduced and de-

Figure 9.15 When insertion element IS*2* sits between *gal*OP and *gal*K-T-E, either of two events takes place. The *gal* enzymes remain inducible but are made in reduced amounts if IS*2* is oriented opposite the direction of *gal* transcription; but constitutive enzyme synthesis characterizes the operon when IS*2* is oriented in the same direction as operon transcription. The IS*2* orientations act like a simple on—off switch for transcription in this case.

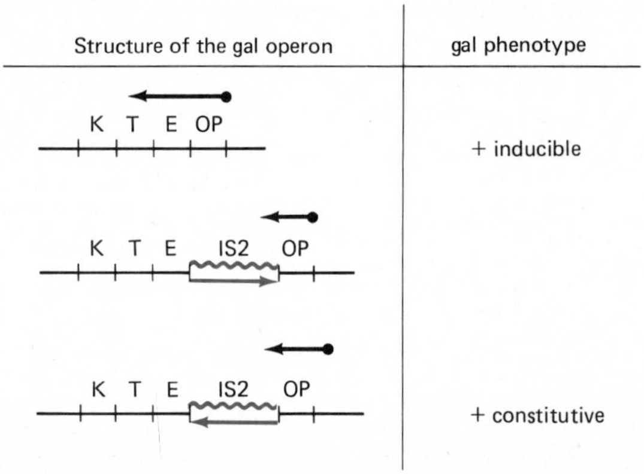

scribed from genetic studies in corn by Barbara McClintock, beginning in the late 1940s. She described sporadic occurrences of altered gene expressions as seen in variegated phenotypic patterns in kernels on the ears of corn, and brilliantly attributed these complex phenomena to the behavior of transposable elements (Fig. 9.16). A particular transposon could turn off the activity of a marker gene when the element was integrated within or near that gene. The element could subsequently be transposed to another site in the genome, which would restore the activity of the first gene, but which might influence the activity of another gene in the same cells. Transposable elements could also turn on gene action and bring the expression of nearby genes under the control of the transposon integrated in the region. The genetic analyses were relatively complicated and were not considered to be of general importance by most biologists until many similar phenomena were fully documented in bacteria and viruses in the 1970s. At this stage, molecular biologists began intensive studies of transposable elements that were not possible in complex eukaryotic systems such as corn, or Drosophila, where similar transpositions had been deduced in the 1960s.

9.7 Transposons in Plasmids

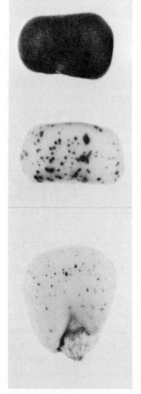

Most of the information we have on transposons has come from studies of **plasmids**, which are autonomous genetic elements that can replicate independently of the chromosome in the bacterial cells in which they occur. Certain kinds of plasmids can move onto and off the bacterial chromosome, and these plasmids are called **episomes**. Other kinds of plasmids either maintain an independent existence at all times, or they may integrate into other plasmids or into bacteriophage DNA. All plasmids are naked circular DNA duplex molecules, and there may be as many as 100 copies of the plasmid in some cells. They may consist of only a few genes or they may be many hundreds of micrometers long and contain hundreds of genes.

Plasmids are often classified according to the specialized genetic information they carry. The group known as **R plasmids** carry antibiotic resistance genes, but other kinds of plasmids may carry genes for toxin production, resistance to heavy metals, transfer ability in conjugation, and other properties (Table 9.4). Plasmids can be identified in cells by various methods, including mapping of their genes in a different linkage group from the main bacterial genes; electron microscopy showing small, circular DNAs distinct from the bacterial chromosome of much greater size; and by DNA base composition of chromosomal and nonchromosomal fractions isolated from cells and separated by centrifugation.

R plasmids can be separated into two components, each of which is capable of replicating independently of the other and of the bacterial chromosome (Fig. 9.17). The **r-determinant** is the component which retains most of the genes for antibiotic resistance, and the **RTF** (resistance transfer factor) component exclusively retains the ability to be transferred

Figure 9.16 The pattern and size of spots produced in these kernels of corn are the result of transpositions of genetic elements to various sites in the genome, at different times in development and in relation to marker genes for color.

Table 9.4
Some properties coded by naturally occurring plasmids

Property	Exemplified by*
Fertility—ability to transfer genetic material by conjugation	*F*, R1, Col1
Production of bacteriocins	CloDF13 *(Enterobacterium cloacae)* ColE1
Antibiotic production	SCP1 plasmid of *Streptomyces coelicolor*
Heavy metal resistance (Cd^{2+}, Hg^{2+})	p1258 *(S. aureus)*, R6
Ultraviolet resistance	Col1b, R46
Enterotoxin	Ent
Tumorigenicity in plants	T1-plasmid of *Agrobacterium tumefaciens*
Restriction/modification	Production of *Eco*R1 endonuclease and methylase by plasmid of RY13

*Plasmids listed are indigenous to *E. coli* unless otherwise indicated. From Cohen, S. N. 1976. *Nature* **263**:731–738, Table 1.

to other cells by conjugation. RTF components are relatively similar in R plasmids from various sources, which can be determined by heteroduplex analysis with the electron microscope. Different *r* determinants can associate with RTF units, giving rise to a great variety of R plasmids in sudden and rapid stages. The basis for association into an R plasmid is that IS elements are situated at the ends of the RTF units, and an *r* determinant can be joined on at these RTF integration sites. Excision of the *r* determinant also involves interactions with the IS elements of the RTF unit.

Different *r* determinants can be formed containing a number of antibiotic resistance genes in one or more copies, through integrations and excisions involving IS elements in the *r* determinant, and through transposons which include antibiotic resistance genes. Not only can different R plasmids arise in this way, but one or more transposons carry antibiotic resistance genes can be transferred from the plasmid or its *r* determinant to bacteriophage genomes and from these by transduction to the bacterial chromosome. In some cases plasmid transposons of the R plasmid move directly onto the bacterial chromosome in conjugating cells. The integration of transposons alters bacterial phenotypes, and excision also leads to modified gene expression, since the transposons usually are excised inaccurately and can remove bacterial genes or leave plasmid genes in the bacterial chromosome.

The discovery of R plasmids was an outcome of clinical and genetic studies in Japan due to the sudden appearance of multiply antibiotic-resistant strains of the dysentery-causing bacterium *Shigella*. Multiple resistance could be transferred from strain to strain and between different enteric bacterial species including *E. coli*, or could be lost suddenly in some strains. The enormous medical problem resulting from rapid acquisition of resistance to many different antibiotics in pathogenic bacteria is still an important worldwide issue in public health. Medical treatment of bacterial

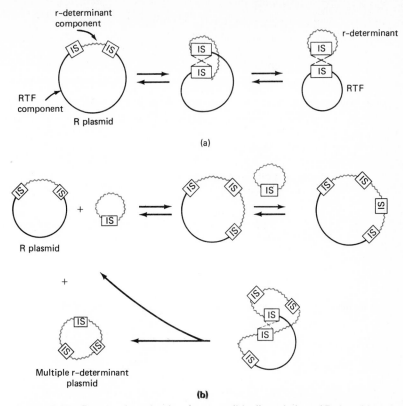

Figure 9.17 Proposed mechanism for reversible dissociation of R plasmids at the sites of IS1 insertion. (a) Independent *r* determinants and RTF units may arise, or may cointegrate to become an R plasmid. (b) Through multiple integrations, two or more transposons may be incorporated into the same R plasmid, and multiple *r* determinant plasmids may arise in this way and be transferred eventually to bacterial cells, which gain multiple antibiotic resistances in a single step. (From Ptashne, K., and S. N. Cohen. 1975. *J. Bact.* **122**:776.)

infections is seriously impeded because of the inheritance of multiple resistance and its widespread occurrence in bacteria.

Transposons can be identified by heteroduplex analysis, and their location can be determined by the site of the **stem-loop**, or "lollipop" conformation (Fig. 9.18). The presence of *inverted repeats* of IS elements flanking the transposon genes leads to these characteristic images. Specific antibiotic resistance genes have been associated with specific transposons in many R plasmids.

Through the agency of transposable elements, therefore, rapid and substantial changes may be incorporated into bacterial genomes. Control over gene expression is another significant consequence of IS and Tn integration and excision from the chromosome. In the particular case of the *E. coli* fertility factor *F*, which is an episome type of plasmid, the expression of conjugation leading to chromosomal transfer from donor to recipient cells is a function of genes in *F*. The association of *F* with the donor chromo-

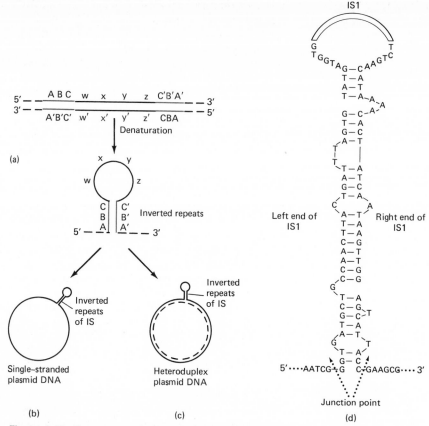

Figure 9.18 Transposons flanked by inverted repeats of IS elements provide the basis for heteroduplex analysis and mapping of these regions. (a) Transposon *W X Y Z* is flanked by inverted IS repeats, *A B C* and *C B A* in duplex DNA, which produce predicted stem-loop conformations in single strands from denatured duplexes. (b) The stem-loop would be evident in electron micrographs of single-stranded plasmid DNA, or in (c) heteroduplex DNA, where one strand loops out in the lollipop form. (d) The sequence of IS*1*, showing the inversely repeated stem of the element.

some in *Hfr* strains involves integration of the episome into the bacterial chromosome at any one of several sites. Integration of *F* to give rise to *Hfr* conjugating strains, and excision of *F* to make *F*⁺ strains from *Hfr*, both involve transposable elements which move onto and off the genome in a regular fashion (see Fig. 5.26).

9.8 Transpositions Involving Lambda and Mu Phages in *E. coli*

Both lambda and Mu are **temperate phages** of *E. coli*; they may exist integrated in the bacterial chromosome and replicate in synchrony with it, or they may initiate the lytic cycle in their lysogenic host cells when they replicate freely in the cytoplasm (see Fig. 2.26). There are many parallels between temperate phages and plasmids, since both may exist in either the integrated or nonintegrated state. Phages, however, have genes which specify unique products such as the viral coat protein; plasmids are naked DNA molecules. In addition, phages can induce cell lysis whereas plasmids are not known to have this ability, that is, plasmids do not have an infective capacity.

Since temperate phages also have properties of integration into and excision from the bacterial genome, they provide admirable model systems to study the general features of transposable elements. Phage λ integrates at a very specific site in the *E. coli* chromosome, called the λ *att*achment site, whereas Mu integrates almost anywhere in the genome in an apparently indiscriminate fashion. These two viruses therefore provide two extreme cases of transpositional specificity.

Studies of Mu have revealed the existence of **invertible DNA sequences** which are flanked by repeated IS elements (Fig. 9.19). Depending on the orientations of these IS elements, the DNA sequence found in between may be oriented so that the genes in this segment face either in one direction or in the opposite direction on the Mu duplex DNA linear molecule. When the invertible gene sequence faces in one direction the phages are viable, but when it faces in the opposite direction the phages are inviable and cannot multiply in the host cell. Mu genes are therefore turned on or off according to the orientation of the invertible segment. This is a similar situation to the ones we described earlier for IS*2* effects in the *gal* operon, and the "flip-flop" control in *Salmonella* and *Schizosaccharomyces*. The genes in the invertible Mu segment include those involved in the proteins required for the virus to adsorb to the host cell, an essential prerequisite to its penetration into the host.

Why does Mu possess a function which renders it inviable? There is no definite answer at the present time, but several possible explanations have been put forward. One explanation leads to the suggestion that inversion of the particular segment may turn off one set of adsorption proteins needed for some strains of *E. coli* and thereby allow another set of adsorption proteins to be elaborated for adsorption to a different host. In other words, the function may actually be adaptable if it serves to broaden the host range of the virus. Specific answers will be obtained once the location of control genes (operators and promoters) of these Mu structural genes has been established. Until the physical arrangements of control and structural genes for relevant operons are known, a specific explanation of the advantages of DNA inversions cannot be certain.

Mu is an unusual phage, since it essentially acts like an autonomous transposable element, integrating indiscriminately into DNA in *E. coli*, other phages, and plasmids. Studies of nucleotide sequences in the Mu

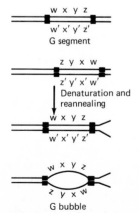

Figure 9.19 Diagram illustrating the structure of part of Mu DNA as seen in electron micrographs of denatured and reannealed duplexes. Genes *w x y z* and complementary *w′ x′ y′ z′* (hypothetical) are flanked by inverted repeat sequences (black boxes) which serve as sites of recombination for inversion. When Mu DNA mixtures reanneal after denaturation, the two orientations of the gene segment are obvious from electron micrographs showing closely paired duplexes and duplexes with the "G bubble" formation due to the heteroduplex inversion in this renatured region (the G segment).

transposable elements and of nucleotide sequences in DNAs onto which Mu can hop on and off are now in progress. With the development in 1977 of rapid sequencing methods for DNA, these studies may well have been completed by the time this book appears.

Studies of λ phage and its *att* site on the *E. coli* chromosome are considered important particularly because λ codes for its own enzyme that catalyzes its integration into the bacterial chromosome. Suitable mutant strains could provide important source material to analyze the enzymatic processes of integration, about which we know very little. For example, mutations affecting the integration enzyme cause λ to be integrated in sites other than *att*. One of the questions concerning the suitability of λ as a model system, however, is that λ forms circles before it integrates. There is no evidence thus far that IS or Tn elements form circles prior to integration into the bacterial chromosome, phage genomes, or plasmids.

Both Mu and λ alter gene expression in their host cells, and may remove host genes when they are excised from the bacterial chromosome. Both Mu and λ can pick up genes from other bacteria, other phages, or plasmids and transfer these genes to a host cell. Significant and sudden alterations in the bacterial genome as well as influences over gene expression are two important consequences of transposition phenomena. These studies have really just begun at the molecular level, and we can expect some very exciting and important concepts to emerge in the near future.

QUESTIONS AND PROBLEMS

9.1. State whether β-galactosidase synthesis is inducible or constitutive in the following haploid *E. coli* strains:
   a. $i^- \, o^c \, z^+$
   b. $i^+ \, o^+ \, z^+$
   c. $i^- \, o^+ \, z^+$
   d. $i^+ \, o^c \, z^+$

9.2. State whether β-galactosidase synthesis is inducible or constitutive in the following z^+/z^+ merodiploid strains of *E. coli*.
   a. $i^+/i^+, \, o^+/o^c$
   b. $i^+/i^+, \, o^c/o^c$
   c. $i^+/i^-, \, o^+/o^+$
   d. $i^-/i^-, \, o^+/o^+$
   e. $i^+/i^+, \, o^+/o^+$

9.3. The allele i^s codes for a super-repressor which is unable to combine with the inducer and, therefore, structural protein is not made. An allele o^0 has been found, which turns off the operon in the presence or absence of inducer. With this in mind, complete the table given below. (Use + to indicate enzyme synthesized, – to indicate enzyme not synthesized.)

Strain	Genotype	Lactose present		Lactose absent	
		β-gal.	permease	β-gal.	permease
1	$i^+ o^+ z^+ y^+$				
2	$i^s o^+ z^+ y^+$				
3	$i^- o^+ z^+ y^+$				
4	$i^+ o^0 z^+ y^+$				
5	$i^+ o^c z^+ y^+$				
6	$i^- o^0 z^+ y^+$				
7	$i^- o^c z^+ y^+$				
8	$i^s o^0 z^+ y^+$				
9	$i^s o^c z^+ y^+$				

9.4. A strain of *E. coli* exhibits constitutive synthesis of β-galactosidase. This strain remains constitutive after it is made partially diploid by the addition of an *F'* phenotype of $i^+ z^+$. Explain the basis of the genetic problem in this strain.

9.5. In *Salmonella typhimurium* three linked loci were found, given in the correct order in the table below. The mutant alleles are symbolized by *a*, *b*, and *c*, and their wild type alternatives as +. In the presence or absence of the inducer, the cells exhibit high enzyme amount or no enzyme (high and none, respectively, in the table). Which of the three mutant alleles is the structural locus, which the operator and which the regulator?

	Phenotype	
Genotype	Inducer	No inducer
a + +	high	none
+ *b* +	none	none
+ + *c*	high	high
+ + + / *a b c*	high	none
+ + *c* / *a b* +	high	high
+ *b* + / *a* + *c*	high	high
a + + / + *b c*	high	none

9.6. Tyrosine aminotransferase (TAT) activity in liver cells grown in culture increases when the cells are exposed to steroid hormones. Assume this activity is genetically regulated in a manner analogous to operon control of β-galactosidase in *E. coli*.
  a. Describe the phenotype of liver-cell mutants altered in the structural gene for TAT enzyme.
  b. Describe the phenotype of a liver-cell mutant which you could tell was altered in a regulatory gene for TAT enzyme.
  c. How could you tell whether a mutation in this system was dominant or recessive?
  d. How could you tell if two mutations affecting TAT regulation were located on the same chromosome in these cells?

9.7. In an investigation of the genetic control of enzyme synthesis, several strains of *E. coli* were constructed with different genotypes, and β-galactosidase activity was measured as a function of time. If lactose (inducer) was added at 15 minutes, there could be four possible results:

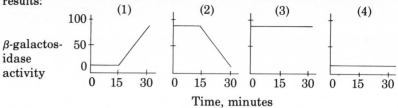

Which result would you predict for each of the following?

a. $i^+ o^+ z^-$
b. $i^- o^+ z^+$
c. $i^s o^+ z^+$
d. $i^+ o^c z^+$
e. $i^- o^+ z^+/i^+ o^+ z^+$
f. $i^+ o^+ z^+/i^+ o^c z^+$

9.8. *Chironomus tentans* is a useful insect for studies in developmental genetics because it has large polytene chromosomes which are suitable for microscopical studies.

a. When [³H]thymidine was injected into developing *Chironomus* larvae, radioactive thymidine was found to be distributed evenly all along the length of all the chromosomes in every tissue, according to autoradiography. Explain the significance of these results.

b. When [³H]uracil was injected into developing larvae it was found that only certain regions of chromosomes in only some of the tissues contained labeled uracil a short time afterward. Explain.

c. After a longer time, [³H]uracil was found in the cytoplasm of those larval cells whose chromosomes had previously been labeled in (b). Explain.

REFERENCES

Baltimore, D., and D. H. Spector. May 1975. The molecular biology of poliovirus. *Sci. Amer.* **232**:24.

Bank, A., and F. Ramirez. 1978. The molecular biology of the thalassemia syndromes. *CRC Crit. Rev. Biochem.* **5**:343.

Bertrand, K., L. Korn, F. Lee, T. Platt, C. Squires, C. Squires, and C. Yanofsky. 1975. New features of the regulation of the tryptophan operon. *Science* **189**:22.

Brown, D. D. Aug. 1973. The isolation of genes. *Sci. Amer.* **230**:20.

Bukhari, A. I., J. A. Shapiro, and S. L. Adhya. 1977. *DNA: Insertion Elements, Plasmids and Episomes.* New York: Cold Spring Harbor Laboratory.

Clowes, R. C. Apr. 1973. The molecule of infectious drug resistance. *Sci. Amer.* **229**:18.

Cohen, S. N. 1976. Transposable genetic elements and plasmid evolution. *Nature* **263**:731.

Cornelis, G., D. Ghosal, and H. Saedler. 1978. Tn951: A new transposon carrying a lactose operon. *Mol. gen. Genet.* **160**:224.

Crouse, H. V. 1968. The role of ecdysone in DNA-puff formation and DNA synthesis in the polytene chromosomes of *Sciara coprophila. Proc. Nat. Acad. Sci. U. S.* **61**:971.

de Crombrugghe, B., B. Chen, M. Gottesman, I. Pastan, H. E. Varmus, M. Emmer, and R. L. Perlman. 1971. Regulation of *lac* mRNA synthesis in a soluble cell-free system. *Nature New Biol.* **230**:37.

Dickson, R. C., J. Abelson, W. M. Barnes, and W. S. Reznikoff. 1975. Genetic regulation: The *lac* control region. *Science* **187**:27.

Farabaugh, P. J. 1978. Sequence of the *lacI* gene. *Nature* **274**:765.

Felsenfeld, G. 1978. Chromatin. *Nature* **271**:115.

Goldberger, R. F., ed. 1979. *Biological Regulation and Development.* Vol. 1: *Gene Expression.* New York: Plenum.

Guerineau, M., C. Grandchamp, and P. P. Slonimski. 1976. Circular DNA of a yeast episome with two inverted repeats: Structural analysis by a restriction enzyme and electron microscopy. *Proc. Nat. Acad. Sci. U. S.* **73**:3030.

Harris, H. 1967. The reactivation of the red cell nucleus. *J. Cell Sci.* **2**:23.

Horowitz, M., O. Laub, S. Bratosin, and Y. Aloni. 1978. Splicing of SV40 late mRNA is a post-transcriptional process. *Nature* **275**:558.

Jacob, F., and J. Monod. 1961. Genetic regulatory mechanisms in the synthesis of proteins. *J. Mol. Biol.* **3**:318.

Jamrich, M., A. L. Greenleaf, F. A. Bautz, and E. K. F. Bautz. 1978. Functional organization of polytene chromosomes. *Cold Spring Harbor Sympos. Quant. Biol.* **42**(1977):389.

Johnsrud, L. 1978. Contacts between *Escherichia coli* RNA polymerase and a *lac* operon promoter. *Proc. Nat. Acad. Sci. U. S.* **75**:5314.

Johnsrud, L. 1979. DNA sequence of the transposable element IS1. *Mol. gen. Genet.* **169**:213.

Landy, A., and W. Ross. 1977. Viral integration and excision: Structure of the lambda *att* sites. *Science* **197**:1147.

Maniatis, T., and M. Ptashne. Jan. 1976. A DNA operator-repressor system. *Sci. Amer.* **236**:64.

McClintock, B. 1965. The control of gene action in maize. *Brookhaven Sympos. Biol.* **18**:162.

McReynolds, L., B. W. O'Malley, A. D. Nisbet, J. E. Fothergill, D. Givol, S. Fields, M. Robertson, and G. G. Brownlee. 1978. Sequence of chicken ovalbumin mRNA. *Nature* **273**:723.

Miller, J. H., and W. S. Reznikoff. eds. 1978. *The operon.* New York: Cold Spring Harbor Laboratory.

Miozzari, G. F., and C. Yanofsky. 1978. The regulatory region of the *trp* operon of *Serratia marcescens. Nature* **276**:684.

Nevers, P., and H. Saedler. 1977. Transposable genetic elements as agents of gene instability and chromosomal rearrangements. *Nature* **268**:109.

Oakley, J. L., R. E. Strothkamp, A. H. Sarris, and J. E. Coleman. 1979. T7 RNA polymerase: Promoter structure and polymerase binding. *Biochemistry* **18**:528.

Pastan, I. Aug. 1972. Cyclic AMP. *Sci. Amer.* **227**:97.

Pastan, I., and R. L. Perlman. 1970. Cyclic adenosine monophosphate in bacteria. *Science* **169**:339.

Peterson, P. A. 1977. The position hypothesis for controlling elements in maize. In *DNA: Insertion Elements, Plasmids and Episomes.* A. I. Bukhari, J. A. Shapiro, and S. L. Adhya, eds. New York: Cold Spring Harbor Laboratory, p. 429.

Ptashne, K., and S. N. Cohen. 1975. Occurrence of insertion sequence (IS) regions on plasmid deoxyribonucleic acid as direct and inverted nucleotide sequence duplications. *J. Bact.* **122**:776.

Ptashne, M., and W. Gilbert. June 1970. Genetic repressors. *Sci. Amer.* **222**:36.

Reif, H.-J., and H. Saedler. 1977. Chromosomal rearrangements in the *gal* region of *E. coli* K12 after integration of IS1. In *DNA: Insertion Elements, Plasmids and Episomes.* A. I. Bukhari, J. A. Shapiro, and S. L. Adhya, eds. New York: Cold Spring Harbor Laboratory, p. 81.

Roberts, T. M., R. Kacich, and M. Ptashne. 1979. A general method for maximizing the expression of a cloned gene. *Proc. Nat. Acad. Sci. U. S.* **76**:760.

Rovera, G., J. Vartikar, G. R. Connolly, C. Margarian, and T. W. Dolby. 1978. Hemin controls the expression of the β minor globin gene in Friend erythroleukemic cells at the pretranslational level. *J. Biol. Chem.* **253**:7588.

Royal, A., *et al.* 1979. The ovalbumin gene region: common features in the organization of three genes expressed in chicken oviduct under hormonal control. *Nature* **279**:125.

Shapiro, J. A. 1979. Molecular model for the transposition and replication of bacteriophage Mu and other transposable elements. *Proc. Nat. Acad. Sci. U. S.* **76**:1933.

Silver, L. M., and S. C. R. Elgin. 1977. Distribution patterns of three subfractions of *Drosophila* nonhistone chromosomal proteins: Possible correlations with gene activity. *Cell* **11**:971.

So, M., F. Heffron, and B. J. McCarthy. 1979. the *E. coli* gene encoding heat stable toxin is a bacterial transposon flanked by inverted repeats of IS1. *Nature* **277**:453.

Stein, G. S., T. C. Spelsberg, and L. J. Kleinsmith. 1974. Nonhistone chromosomal proteins and gene regulation. *Science* **183**:817.

Tilghman, S. M., *et al.* 1978. Intervening sequence of DNA identified in the structural portion of a mouse β-globin gene. *Proc. Nat. Acad. Sci. U. S.* **75**:725.

Wallace, R. B., S. K. Dube, and J. Bonner. 1977. Localization of the *globin* gene in the template active fraction of chromatin of Friend leukemia cells. *Science* **198**:1166.

10

Mutation

Mutations are sudden, heritable changes in the genetic material. They are rare events which arise at random in any cell, but they recur and can therefore be characterized by the mutation rate from one allelic form to another. Mutations can be classified according to various criteria, such as (1) effect on the phenotype, (2) nature of the DNA molecular change, and (3) nature of the altered gene product. Mutations are usually reversible changes.

Induced mutations are identical to spontaneously occurring mutations, but they arise at a proportionally higher rate in response to physical and chemical mutagenic agents in the environment. Physical agents such as x-rays and ultraviolet (UV) light cause different kinds of damage to DNA, but the damage can be repaired by any of several known mechanisms. UV repair mechanisms have been characterized in more detail than some others. Chemical mutagens also act in various ways on DNA. Through studies of mutations induced by these kinds of environmental agents, we have been able to better understand the nature of spontaneous mutational changes. Damage induced by chemical mutagens is also subject to mutation repair in cells.

The induction of cancer by carcinogens and the induction of mutation by mutagens are closely related phenomena. Many mutagens are also carcinogenic agents. Using this relationship as a basis, preliminary screening tests for mutagenicity of physical and chemical agents can provide information on potentially carcinogenic activities. Such suspected carcinogens can then be selected for the more costly and time-consuming, but essential, tests to determine whether or not they cause tumors in live animals.

Cancer consists of a heterogeneous collection of diseases all of which are characterized by uncontrolled growth, invasiveness into other tissues, and spread to distant sites where new tumors may be initiated. All or most of these diseases apparently involve some perturbation of DNA. The exact relationships between cancer and DNA, however, are still under investigation.

THE GENERAL NATURE OF MUTATIONS

Mutations are sudden, heritable changes in the genetic material. These changes become evident when a new phenotype appears and is passed on to new generations. Inherited changes may arise as the result of alterations in single genes, which are defined as **point mutations**. In addition, there may be **chromosomal mutations** which arise by gross alterations of chromosome structure and genome restructuring. We will confine ourselves to point mutations in this chapter and discuss chromosomal mutations in Chapter 11.

Point mutations are a major source of hereditary variation in evolution, and they provide the only *new* information to subsidize species changes. They are the "raw materials" of the evolutionary pathways in past, present, and future species of organisms.

10.1   Spontaneous Mutations

Mutations can arise spontaneously in any gene at any time in any cell; this shows that mutations are *random* changes in the genes. The causes of spontaneous mutations are largely unknown, but they are generally believed to be the result of occasional mistakes in base pairing during DNA replication. The amounts of radiations or chemicals in the environment contribute to DNA damage, but have been calculated to be insufficient to account for observed mutation rates.

Mutations are *recurrent* events, a fact which permits us to determine their rates of occurrence (Table 10.1). We can see from the data that mutations are *rare* events, and that different genes and different alleles mutate at different rates. In sexual organisms, the **mutation rate** is expressed as the number of mutations per gamete per generation; in asexual organisms such as bacteria, mutation rate is expressed as the number of mutations per cell per cell-generation. The **mutation frequency**, or the number of mutations in a population, will be much higher in *E. coli* than in human beings if we count up the mutants over a period of time, such as one year. When we make comparisons on the basis of generations, regardless of their absolute duration, we can judge the general nature and properties of gene mutations in any organisms as observed in gene mutation rates.

Mutations from one allelic form to another, such as wild-type to mutant, usually yield a different mutation rate than mutations back to the original form. The rate of **forward mutation** and the rate of **reverse mutation** back to some original form can be calculated by the same methods. These data show that mutations are *reversible*, and that the rates of spontaneous forward and reverse mutation of a gene are often different. But spontaneous mutation in either direction occurs at a rate which is *characteristic* for any particular gene or allele and varies from one gene or allele to another.

Mutations are essential tools for genetic analysis, since we cannot study the gene unless we can compare allelic differences in relation to gene structure, function, and regulation. We recognize the existence of a gene through detection of its variants, from which we can then backtrack to determine the nature of the unaltered or wild-type genetic material.

Table 10.1
Mutation rates of specific genes in various organisms

Organism	Gene	Trait	Mutations per 10^6 cells or gametes
Bacteriophage T2	*h*	Host range	0.003
Escherichia coli	*str*	Streptomycin resistance	0.0004
(colon bacillus)	*lac⁻*	Lactose fermentation (to *lac⁺*)	0.2
Neurospora crassa	*ad⁻*	Adenine requirement (to *ad⁺*)	0.04
(red bread mold)	*inos⁻*	Inositol requirement (to *inos⁺*)	0.08
Zea mays (corn)	*Sh*	Shrunken seeds	1
	Y	Yellow seeds	2
	I	Color inhibitor	106
Drosophila melanogaster	*y⁺*	Body color (to *yellow*)	100
(fruit fly)	*w⁺*	Eye color (to *white*)	40
	e⁺	Body color (to *ebony*)	20
Mus musculus (mouse)	*a⁺*	Coat pattern (to *nonagouti*)	30
	c⁺	Coat color (to *albino*)	10
Homo sapiens (human)		Huntington's disease	1
		Aniridia (absence of iris)	5
		Retinoblastoma (tumor of retina)	20
		Hemophilia A	30
		Achondroplasia (dwarfness)	40–140
		Neurofibromatosis (tumor of nervous tissue)	130–250

Nonmutated genes are undetectable by genetic observations of phenotypes, but they can be identified by molecular methods.

Since mutations are random and rare but recurrent events, we can search for evidence of mutations in families, progenies, and both laboratory and natural populations. In human beings and other diploid organisms the easiest mutations to detect are dominants, because the mutant allele is

Figure 10.1 Filled symbols in this family indicate individuals with severe foot blistering, open symbols indicates people free of this affliction. The circles designate females; the squares, males; diamonds, more than one individual or unknown(s) of either or both sexes. II-5 must have inherited a mutant allele through the egg or sperm of his parents, and the allele was then transmitted to his descendants in the next generations. Autosomal dominant inheritance is apparent. (From Haldane, J. B. S., and J. Poole. 1942. *J. Hered.* **33**:17.)

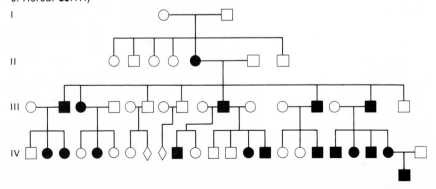

the following: C, which stands for chromosomal inverted regions on the X, that prevent crossing over and maintain this ClB chromosome intact and unchanged during the experiment; l, which stands for a lethal allele expressed only in hemizygous males or in homozygous females; and B, which stands for Bar-eye, a dominant phenotypic marker showing that the ClB chromosome is present in an individual. The second X chromosome in these ClB females is normal.

ClB females are crossed with wild type males whose individual sperm will be analyzed for occurrence of X-linked recessive mutations arising spontaneously in any of these gametes. F_1 ClB females each carry one X chromosome from one sperm contributed by their fathers. Each F_1 ClB female is mated singly in culture with a wild type F_1 male to produce an F_2 progeny. Each of these F_2 progenies then has many copies of one of the original X chromosomes to be analyzed from each of the individual sperm of the male parent in the initial crosses. By simple inspection of the culture bottle, one can see at a glance whether or not males are present. If not, the X chromosome of the original sperm cell must have carried a spontaneous lethal mutation. The frequency of F_2 progenies of this type is then used to calculate the overall mutation rate for X-linked, recessive lethal mutations. In *Drosophila*, about 2 per thousand per generation (0.2 percent, or 2×10^{-3}) is the spontaneous mutation rate for *all* X-linked recessive **lethal mutations**, derived from summed data from many experiments. Mutation rates for any one specific gene producing a lethal allele, of course, could be different.

If males are present, and if they have mutant phenotypes, then the particular phenotype which appears in a percentage of F_2 progenies among the total F_2 progenies in many experiments serves as a basis for determining the mutation rate of a particular gene which yields a morphological mutant. Summed data for all **morphological mutations** can also be used to determine the overall mutation rate for this class of gene mutations.

A third class of mutations, called **detrimental mutations**, can also be detected by the ClB method. In these cases we find present in the F_2 progenies males with the wild phenotype but in numbers significantly lower then the expected 33% of a progeny. There is no simple way to assess the kind of genetic change which has taken place, except that *on the average* there is a reduction in the life expectancy or in the relative success among these mutants in reaching the adult stage. They may be more susceptible to parasites or disease, or succumb earlier because of any one of a number of reasons. This class of mutations is of considerable importance in the evolutionary success of a species in the long run, and of immense concern in considering the damaging effects of excessive radiation or chemical agents on human populations and their descendants. Detrimental mutations are much more frequent than lethal or morphological mutations, and they contribute substantially to the **genetic load** of harmful mutant alleles carried in every diploid sexually reproducing species.

In addition to these classes of mutations, others have been identified in a variety of organisms according to the phenotypic effect they produce. There are **physiological**, or **biochemical mutations**, which alter the phenotype as the consequence of some metabolic defect, but which do not necessarily lead to a visible morphological change in the structure, color, or other outward characteristics of the individual. There is a large and diverse class of **conditional mutations** in which the alteration may or may not be expressed depending on the environment. Mutants which require some nutrient will be perfectly normal as long as the nutrient is supplied, but may grow slowly or be inviable when the nutrient is not available. Many mutants are *temperature-sensitive*, developing normally at one temperature (permissive) but abnormally or not at all at a nonpermissive temperature. Many **conditional lethal mutations** fall into this category of changes which can be detected in certain environments and not in others (Table 10.2).

Many different experimental systems have been used to detect mutations in various organisms. Drug-resistant bacterial mutants can be detected as colonies which grow in media containing a drug while the cells carrying the sensitivity allele will grow only in the absence of the chemical. Auxotrophic mutants can likewise be recognized by their growth on supplemented media and their inability to grow on minimal media. Prototrophic revertants can be detected by plating auxotrophic strains on minimal media and observing growth of wild type colonies. Many of these procedures are equally applicable to mammalian cells, fungi, and to bacteria, and they can also be used to identify mutations in viruses which lead to altered host range, plaque differences, and other phenotypic characteristics.

Because spontaneous mutations are relatively rare events, **enrichment methods** have been devised to detect and isolate mutants on a more predictable and controlled basis. For example, penicillin kills only actively growing bacterial cells. If a population of bacteria is incubated in minimal nutrient media containing this antibiotic, growing prototrophs will die. Auxotrophic mutants which may be present in small numbers in these wild type populations can be recovered because they do not grow in minimal media and are therefore not killed by the antibiotic. After washing away the penicillin, the population of surviving viable cells is transferred to media supplemented with a variety of nutrients. The auxotrophic cells that grow into colonies can be tested later for specific nutritional requirements. Similar methods can be used with fungi, such as *Neurospora*. By these and other enrichment methods, a population originally containing relatively few mutants among many nonmutants can be amplified into a population consisting largely of mutants which can be more easily detected, isolated, and characterized. Very similar procedures are widely used today to isolate mammalian mutant cells in culture, providing important materials for many kinds of experiments (Fig. 10.4).

Table 10.2
Examples of different types of mutations in human beings

Category of mutation	Mutant characteristic
Lethal	Tay-Sachs disease
Morphological	Achondroplasia (dwarfness)
Detrimental	Sickle-cell anemia
Physiological (biochemical)	Glucose 6-phosphate dehydrogenase deficiency (GPD deficiency)
Conditional	Phenylketonuria (PKU)

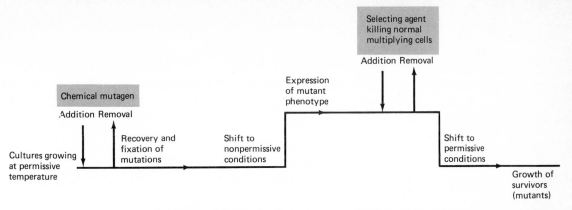

Figure 10.4 Enrichment procedure for isolation of temperature sensitive mutants in mammalian cell cultures. Mammalian cells can multiply in a temperature range between 32°C and about 40°C. It is possible to isolate temperature sensitive mutants that differ from wild type cells in that the mutants cannot grow at 38°–39°C (the nonpermissive temperature), but they can grow at 33°–34°C (permissive temperature). The desired mutants are more likely to be detected if the illustrated enrichment method is used. (From Ringertz, N. R., and R. E. Savage. 1976. *Cell Hybrids.* New York: Academic Press.)

10.3   Spontaneous Versus Directed Mutational Changes

Although most biologists believed that mutations arose spontaneously, without regard to benefit or harm in any cell anywhere at any time, some microbiologists in the 1930s and 1940s thought that bacterial mutations arose in direct response to some need in a particular environment. For example, when a population of sensitive bacteria was incubated with an antibiotic, the resulting population consisted mostly of antibiotic resistant bacteria. This appeared to be an example of the inheritance of acquired characteristics, proposed by Lamarck in 1809 and long discredited by many studies with higher organisms; but it could also be explained as selection.

In 1943, Salvador Luria and Max Delbrück designed the **fluctuation test** to settle whether bacterial mutants were *selected* over nonmutants in certain environments, or *induced* to mutate by the environmental factor. They incubated a number of separate bacterial cultures and plated these cultures onto solid nutrient media in plates containing phage T1. If preexisting mutants resistant to the phage happened to be present in these cultures, they could grow on the plates while phage-sensitive nonmutants were killed. Since such selected mutant cells could be present, by chance, in any number in the cultures, there would be a large and random fluctuation in colony numbers among the separate cultures (Fig. 10.5). If, on the other hand, cells were induced by the phage to mutate to resistance, there was an equal chance for each cell in each culture to undergo such a directed change, and approximately equal numbers of mutants should be found in each of the separate cultures. When the tests were performed, wide fluctuations in the numbers of resistant bacterial mutants were found, showing selection of preexisting, spontaneous mutations to be the correct explanation for bacteria as it was for other organisms. The fluctuation test is used as a general method to identify agents which induce mutations, in contrast with agents

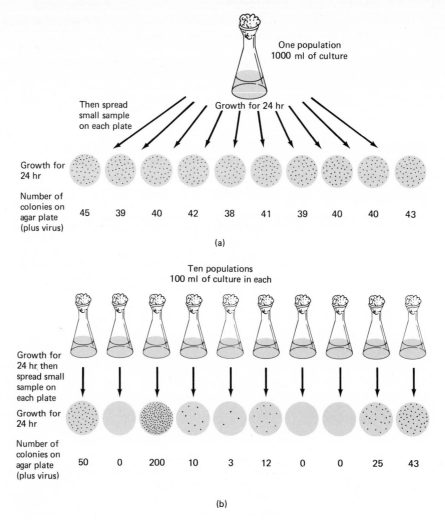

Figure 10.5 Diagrammatic representation of the experimental design for the Luria-Delbrück fluctuation test: Samples taken from a large population are compared with samples of the same total volume, but from a number of smaller populations. The test can distinguish between induction or selection of particular mutants which arise during the experimental interval.

which permit spontaneous mutants to grow in their presence and which merely mediate selective growth in the environment.

There were some difficulties at the time in accepting Luria and Delbrück's statistically-based fluctuation test as providing adequate evidence for the selection of spontaneous mutants. In addition, there was the lingering doubt that somehow the phage had induced the change since the bacteria were always incubated in the presence of the virus during the experiments. In 1952, Joshua and Esther Lederberg provided convincing evidence for the selection of spontaneous mutants which appeared in cultures that had not been exposed to the virus but which were resistant mutants nevertheless. Their method was the **replica plating test**, which has since become a standard tool in microbial genetics (Fig. 10.6).

In the experiments, large numbers of bacteria are spread on solid nutrient media so that they cover the surface as a lawn of growth. This serves as the *master plate*. Next, a velvet-covered cylinder is gently pressed to the surface of the bacterial lawn so that some cells are caught in the nap of the velvet. The velvet is then pressed onto a fresh plate such that bacterial cells are inoculated onto its surface. This second plate contains a drug or virus or some other environmental agent to which the original bacteria were sensitive, and it is a *replica* of the master plate. Only resistant cells will grow on the replica plate, and their sister cells on the original master plate can be identified according to the location of the colonies which appeared on the replica. By matching up the master and replica plates, samples of sister colonies on the master plate can be isolated and transferred to media containing the drug so that their resistance can be tested. When these cells grow in the presence of the drug or virus, to which they had not been exposed before, evidence is obtained showing that resistance arose in the absence of the specific environmental factor. Therefore, the drug or virus or other agent leads to differential survival and multiplication of mutants in a mixed population; it does not induce the mutational change.

Replica plating is a very useful and time-saving method in mutation and other microbial studies. For example, after using the penicillin enrichment procedure to isolate spontaneous mutants, as described in the preceding section, surviving cells can be grown in culture and then replica plated to many different kinds of media to determine the exact nature of the mutational change. A nutritional mutant needing some amino acid can be identified when it grows on the supplemented medium and doesn't grow on

Figure 10.6 The method of replica plating permits indirect selection of mutants which have not been in the environment containing the agent (drug, virus) to which they respond differently from wild type.

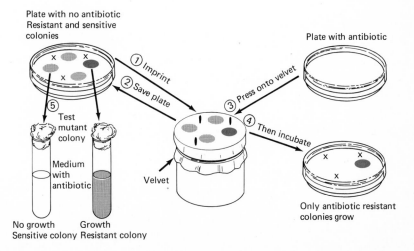

replica plates lacking amino acids. Further replica plating to media containing all amino acids but one, eventually shows the specific amino acid requirement for a specific mutant. By very simple means, it is possible to identify almost any kind of auxotrophic mutant on a routine basis by replica plating.

10.4 Mutation at the Molecular Level

Most gene mutations apparently arise as the result of mispairing or similar mistakes in DNA replication, sometimes due to the occurrence of an unstable or tautomeric form of a base and incorrect matching which follows (see Fig. 6.6). On other occasions one or another of the replication enzymes may guide the wrong base into position on the new strand and this strand will give rise in later replications to an altered set of descendant strands. In general, alterations in the base sequence of DNA lead to two types of mutations classified according to the nature of the molecular change: **base substitution** and **frameshift** classes of heritable changes.

Base substitutions may alter a codon so that it specifies a different amino acid; these are called **missense mutations**. The meaning or sense of the message has been altered, but the whole polypeptide is translated (Fig. 10.7). If, on the other hand, the substituted base changes an amino acid-specifying codon to a termination codon, this is called a **nonsense mutation**. Premature termination of polypeptide synthesis at the mutant codon results in fragments of polypeptide which do not contribute to cell functions.

Frameshifts are mutations which alter the reading frame, through addition or deletion of an existing base in the gene sequence. Since messenger RNA is read sequentially from the initiating AUG to the terminating UAG, UAA, or UGA codon in translation, the readout is garbled (see Fig. 6.23).

Mutants can be restored to the wild phenotype by **reverse mutations** or by **suppressor mutations**. True reverse mutations arise when the base alteration in a codon reverts back to the original sequence. When the codon

Figure 10.7 Human hemoglobin variants illustrating missense and nonsense mutations affecting the carboxy terminus of the β globin chain. In Hb Rainier a different amino acid is specified than in wild type, and in Hb McKees Rocks the β chain is shortened by two amino acids due to a change from a codon specifying the amino acid tyrosine to a terminator codon (UAA or UAG).

Hemoglobin Type	Residue Number				
	143	144	145	146	TERMINATOR
Normal β–chain nucleotide sequence amino acid sequence	— CAC — AAG — UAU — CAC—UAA — His — Lys — Tyr — His — COOH				
Hb Rainier (Missense)	— CAC — AAG — UGU — CAC—UAA — His — Lys — Cys — His — COOH				
Hb McKees Rocks (Nonsense)	— CAC — AAG — UAG — His — Lys—COOH				

is restored, the original amino acid is specified once again and the wild phenotype will be expressed because the wild type protein is made. The nucleotide sequence of the wild type gene and the revertant gene are identical.

Suppressor mutations are of two general classes, depending on whether the second mutation occurs in the same gene (**intragenic**) or in another gene (**intergenic**) in the mutant strain. In either case, suppression of the mutant phenotype and the appearance of the wild phenotype are the result of a second mutation. Suppressor mutants are double mutants which have a *pseudowild* phenotype, that is, the phenotype *looks like* wild type but the suppressor strain has a different nucleotide sequence from that of the wild type strain.

Intragenic suppression may arise in any one of several ways. In base substitution mutants, a nonsense mutation can be suppressed if the mutant terminator codon is altered to an amino acid-specifying codon (Fig. 10.8). The suppressor mutant has the pseudowild phenotype, but the amino acid composition of the protein product of the gene will differ by one amino acid, at the location of the nonsense codon in the nonsuppressed mutant gene. Missense mutations can also be suppressed by base substitutions in the mutant codon. In each case, a functional protein is made and a pseudowild phenotype is expressed. Frameshift mutations can be suppressed when a base is added or deleted to compensate for the first mutational deletion or addition, respectively, as described in Section 6.8. Once again, the suppressor strain makes a slightly different protein than the wild type strain, but their phenotypes may be identical or very similar. Molecular analysis of the protein or of the gene sequence can reveal the difference between the original mutant, the suppressor mutant strain, and wild type. Genetic analysis would show that segregation and recombination took place when

Figure 10.8. Intragenic suppression may arise through base substitution in a nonsense mutant, altering the terminator codon to a codeword specifying an amino acid. The suppressor mutant would then have a pseudowild phenotype.

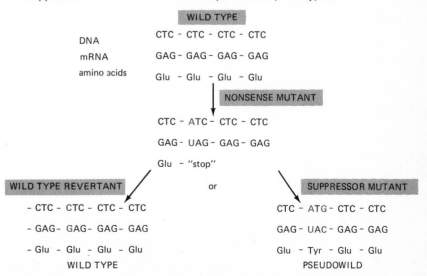

suppressors were crossed with wild types. A true revertant would not produce segregant progeny types when crossed with a wild type stock.

Intergenic suppression involves a second mutation in a different gene from the first mutation. Suppression may be *indirect* if the second mutation alters a metabolic pathway that cancels out the effect of the first mutation on a different metabolic pathway. For example, a Neurospora mutant which is sensitive to high concentrations of arginine within the cell can be suppressed indirectly by a second mutation which causes very little arginine to be synthesized in the cells. The original mutation remains unchanged, but the suppressor strain will grow well because the suppressor gene has modified the intracellular metabolism relating to arginine. Segregation of single mutant, double mutant, and wild type progeny will be found if the suppressor strain is crossed to a wild type tester strain, and if recombination takes place.

Direct intergenic suppression usually involves a second mutation which functions in the process of translation from messenger RNA. In many cases which have been analyzed, the second mutation affects a tRNA gene so that its anticodon is altered. The suppressor tRNA can then recognize a different mRNA codon. It can either insert a different amino acid from the one specified by the first mutation, or it can insert an amino acid at a mutant codon that earlier caused premature termination of protein synthesis. In other words, the direct suppressor mutation can correct a missense or a nonsense mutation through direct interaction at the site of the first mutation when translation is in progress. The altered codon caused by the first mutation remains unchanged by the mutation in the tRNA gene, but its mutational effect is corrected or suppressed by the second mutant gene product.

In suppressor mutation phenomena, therefore, the effects of the first mutation are modified by the effects of the second mutation in the same gene or in a different gene. The first mutation could have arisen by base substitution or by frameshift changes, causing missense, nonsense, or garbled messages. The second mutation directly allows a sense message to be made or it dampens the influence of a mutant message by indirect means. Suppressor mutants can be distinguished from wild type revertants by genetic analysis and by molecular analysis, as described above.

All the varieties of mutations which have been described in this section have been found in spontaneous mutants in all kinds of organisms (Table 10.3). These same kinds of mutations have been induced in experiments using particular mutagenic substances or agents. There is no essential difference between spontaneous and induced mutations either at the molecular level or at the phenotypic level of observation. Studies of the genetic material by induced mutagenesis can therefore provide detailed information about the mechanisms and consequences of spontaneous mutation, under controlled experimental conditions.

INDUCED MUTAGENESIS

In 1927 H. J. Muller reported that x-rays induced mutations in *Drosophila*, and in 1928 L. J. Stadler reported similar results using barley plants. Up to

Table 10.3
Some of the kinds of mutations recognized according to operational or molecular criteria

Kind of mutation	Observations and interpretations
Operational classes	Altered phenotype; altered inheritance pattern
point (single-site)	Change in one nucleotide
deletion	Loss of gene(s) or parts of genes
forward	Change of wild type allele to mutant alternative
reverse (back)	Change of mutant allele to wild type alternative
dominant/recessive	Mutant allele masks, or is masked by, wild type allele
sex-linked/autosomal	Location of mutated site determined by inheritance pattern
lethal	Mutant dies before age of reproduction
detrimental	Mutant has reduced average life expectancy
morphological	Visible change detected in some body feature
physiological (biochemical)	Altered metabolism; may or may not show altered morphology
conditional	Phenotypic expression varies according to environment
suppressor	Second-site alteration in presence of first-site change, leading to pseudowild phenotype and inheritance pattern
Molecular classes	Alteration in nucleotide sequence of gene(s)
base substitution	One nucleotide replaced in one codon
missense	Alteration in a codon causing altered amino acid
nonsense	Change from codon specifying an amino acid to codon specifying termination of the polypeptide
transition	Substitution of a pyrimidine by another pyrimidine, or of one purine by another purine in the codon
transversion	Substitution of a pyrimidine by a purine, or vice versa, in a codon
frameshift	One or more nucleotides added or deleted in a codon, causing altered reading frame

that time, only occasional spontaneously occurring mutants were available for genetic studies. The discovery of a useful mutagenic agent was therefore of great practical importance, but even more significantly it opened the way to studies of the molecular nature of the gene. Induced mutagenesis by chemicals was first reported in the 1940s by Charlotte Auerbach. She found that nitrogen mustard, the "poison gas" that had produced such horrible effects in World War I, induced the same kinds of mutations in *Drosophila* that had been found after radiation exposure or that had arisen spontaneously. Some progress was made in elucidating the properties of genetic material before 1953, but the proposed molecular model of DNA permitted a more systematic and primary analysis of the effects of mutagens on genes and a better understanding of the molecular nature of the gene itself.

10.5 Mutations Induced by Chemicals

There are four general groups of chemicals whose mode of action on DNA has been studied most intensively: (1) base analogues; (2) chemicals that act directly on DNA bases; (3) alkylating agents that remove purines from DNA; and (4) acridine dyes that cause deletion and addition of bases from DNA.

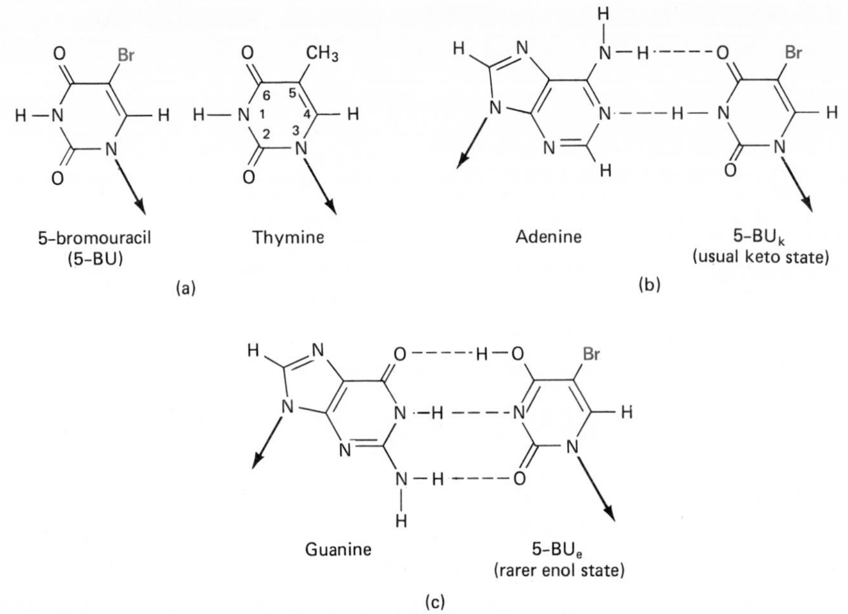

Figure 10.9 Pairing properties of the mutagenic base analogue 5-bromouracil (5-BU): (a) 5-BU closely resembles thymine, and (b) pairs with adenine as thymine does; but (c) 5-BU may pair with guanine under certain conditions, such as being in the tautomeric enol state.

Base analogues are molecules whose structure mimics the naturally occurring base so that the analogue may be incorporated instead of the usual base when DNA replicates (Fig. 10.9). Once incorporated, however, the base analogue leads to different pairings so that a base substitution may occur at the next replication of a partner strand opposite the strand with the analogue. The mutation results from a base-pair substitution at the site where the analogue originally was incorporated.

For example, 5-bromouracil (5-BU) is similar to thymine (5-methyluracil) except for a bromine atom at the place occupied by the methyl group in thymine. When 5-BU is present in the DNA strand it sometimes pairs with guanine, whereas the original thymine would have paired with adenine. The difference in pairing properties is due to the influence of the bromine atom in effecting a frequent tautomeric shift such that 5-BU may exist in an enol form leading to altered pairing properties. If we think of thymine and 5-BU as being essentially the same molecule except for the difference at carbon atom 5, we can see how a spontaneous mutation could arise when a normal thymine undergoes a tautomeric shift and a cytosine-guanine pair substitutes for the nonmutant thymine-adenine pair in DNA (Fig. 10.10).

When a purine replaces a purine or a pyrimidine replaces a pyrimidine in the mutational event, such a base-pair substitution is called a **transition**; if a purine replaces a pyrimidine, or vice versa, then a **transversion** has been responsible for the mutation:

Transitions	Transversions
AT $\longrightarrow$ GC	AT $\longrightarrow$ TA
GC $\longrightarrow$ AT	AT $\longrightarrow$ CG
TA $\longrightarrow$ CG	CG $\longrightarrow$ AT
CG $\longrightarrow$ TA	CG $\longrightarrow$ GC

In the case of 5-BU, transitions arise in either direction. When 5-BU is incorporated opposite adenine, it may lead to a transition from AT to a GC base-pair in later replications if 5-BU pairs with guanine. The analogue may cause a GC$\longrightarrow$AT transition if it is initially incorporated opposite guanine and proceeds to pair with adenine at a later replication.

Several other base analogues, such as 5-bromodeoxyuridine which mimics thymidine, or 2-aminopurine which mimics adenine, also cause mutations by transitions, which arise because of tautomeric shifts and altered pairing properties during DNA replication. All of these mutagens help us understand spontaneous mutations in normal DNA, these arising presumably through altered pairing of tautomers.

Direct acting chemicals act on the base structure of DNA rather than being incorporated into the molecule. Nitrous acid (HNO_2) is a mutagen which causes oxidative deamination of adenine, cytosine, and guanine (Fig. 10.11). When oxygen replaces the amino group at carbon atom 6, differences in hydrogen bonding properties lead to transitions in either direction. For example, cytosine pairs like thymine and causes a GC$\longrightarrow$AT transition, while adenine assumes the bonding properties of guanine and a AT$\longrightarrow$GC transition results. Since neither thymine nor uracil has an amino group in the molecule, these bases are unaffected by HNO_2.

Other chemicals which act directly on DNA bases, such as hydroxylamine or nitrosoguanidine, also cause base-pair transitions. These chemicals are potent mutagens since they are effective in very low concentrations and since they deaminate bases very efficiently. These mutagens can act on replicating or nonreplicating DNA.

Alkylating agents are very reactive compounds which can add an alkyl group (such as ethyl or methyl) at various positions on DNA bases and thereby alter base-pairing properties. These mutagens cause both transitions and transversions in either replicating or nonreplicating DNA. The nitrogen and sulfur mustards were the first chemical mutagens to be studied, and they were shown to have a delayed mutagenic effect. For example, phage mutants arose several replications after treatment with alkylating agents such as the mustards or ethyl ethanesulfonate; *Drosophila* progeny included flies with variegated or mosaic phenotypes, indicating that the mutational effect arose several generations after the sperm had

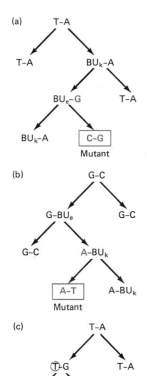

BU_k = keto form of 5–BU

BU_e = enol form of 5–BU

Ⓣ = enol–form tautomer of thymine

Figure 10.10 Origin of mutation during DNA replication. (a) 5-BU_k pairs with adenine and no change occurs in the DNA; but 5-BU_e pairs with guanine and leads to base substitution during replication. (b) A transition may arise because of 5-BU pairing in a G-C base pair, producing a A-T base pair, which is the reverse transition from the one shown in (a). (c) A base-pair substitution of the transition type may also arise if altered pairing takes place when the enol tautomer of thymine appears in the DNA sequence.

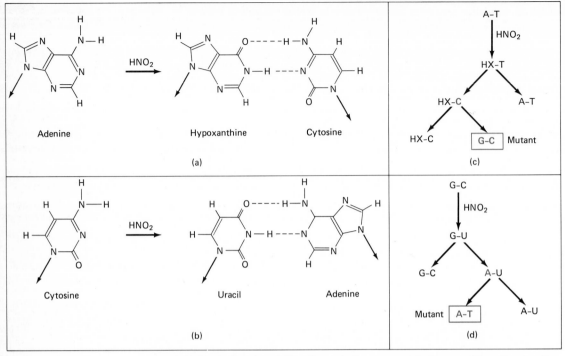

Figure 10.11 Induced mutation through the agency of nitrous acid, a direct acting chemical. Changes are instituted in a DNA sequence as the result of (a) oxidative deamination of adenine, producing hypoxanthine; this pairs with cytosine and not with thymine; and (b) oxidative deamination of cytosine, producing uracil, which pairs with adenine and not guanine. As a result of these changes in DNA structure, there is a (c) A-T to G-C transition or (d) G-C to A-T transition, respectively.

been treated and only became evident in certain mitotic cell lineages in the progeny flies.

Ethyl ethanesulfonate (EES) and ethyl methanesulfonate (EMS) are less toxic than the nitrogen and sulfur mustards, and are frequently used mutagens. Both EES and EMS act directly on guanine, adding an ethyl or methyl group at carbon 7. This weakens the linkage of guanine to deoxyribose and the guanine is lost from DNA, leaving a gap. Depending on which of the four bases fills in this gap, transitions or transversions may eventually arise (Fig. 10.12). If alkylated guanine remains in the DNA strand, it pairs like adenine and a GC to AT transition can occur. These agents therefore modify DNA even to nonreplicating molecules, but the effects appear only after subsequent DNA replications which yield altered codons.

Acridine dyes bind to DNA and they intercalate (insert themselves) between adjacent bases. They distort the DNA strand at the insertion site and either cause an extra base to be added or a base to be deleted when the DNA replicates. Acridines such as proflavine and ethidium bromide are sometimes responsible for frameshift mutations, and very often they are responsible for gross deletions or complete loss of DNA because of problems

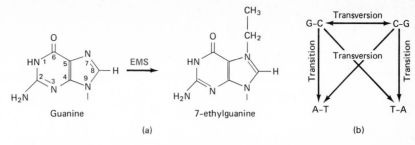

Figure 10.12 Alkylating agents lead to altered base-pairing properties. (a) EMS alters guanine at carbon 7, weakening binding to deoxyribose and leading to loss of the base from the DNA sequence. (b) When the gap left by the lost guanine is filled, transitions or transversions may arise, depending on which of the four bases replaces the guanine in the sequence.

during DNA replication when bound dye molecules interfere with new strand synthesis. Phages are very sensitive to acridines, as is mitochondrial DNA in yeast and other species. There is some doubt that acridines are mutagenic for eukaryotic nuclear genes, since the experimental evidence is either negative or ambiguous.

As we will see in Chapter 12, ethidium bromide is a powerful and very useful mutagen for mitochondrial genes in yeast. If exposure to the agent is prolonged, yeast mitochondrial DNA will be lost completely from the organelles. The mutant yeast can then be used in many kinds of genetic analysis of the mitochondrial genome. By adjusting the concentration of the mutagen and duration of exposure, deletions can be induced in mitochondrial DNA, which affect the mitochondrial phenotype.

Through chemical, physical, and genetic studies of the action by base analogues on DNA and by the several classes of mutagens which directly modify DNA, we have come to an understanding of the molecular basis for spontaneous mutations which would have been difficult or impossible to obtain from investigations of spontaneous mutants directly. Induced mutagenesis also provides the abundance of mutants which genetic analysis requires.

One of the most striking demonstrations of gene structure analysis using induced and spontaneous mutants was provided by Seymour Benzer. We discussed his analysis of the *r*IIA and *r*IIB genes in phage T4 in Section 6.3. Over two thousand independent mutations in these two adjacent genes were used in crosses to construct fine structure maps for these loci (Fig. 10.13).

These studies showed that:

1. numerous different sites of mutation occur within a gene, perhaps 1000—1500 for the *r*IIA and *r*IIB genes; some sites were "hot spots" of mutation;

2. the gene map was linear, implying that the gene has a linear construction;

3. most mutations were changes at a single site and were reversible by back mutation

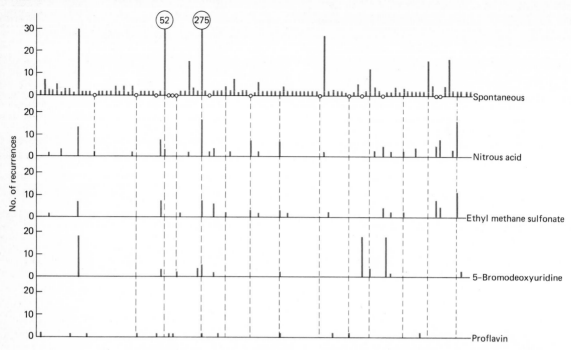

Figure 10.13 Sites of spontaneous and induced mutations in the *r*IIB gene of phage T4. Small circles on the base line in the distribution of spontaneous mutations indicate sites known only from induced mutations, primarily after treatment with the acridine dye proflavin. Sites with large numbers of recurrences ("hot spots") are evident, as well as the difference in distributions of mutations induced by different agents. (From Benzer, S. 1961. *Proc. Nat. Acad. Sci. U. S.* **47**:403.)

Mapping the genetic fine structure was a significant accomplishment twenty years ago, and provided very important insights into the nature of the gene. Similar fine structure analysis has continued to be reported, although modern experiments are more concerned with the actual sequence of nucleotides within the gene. Both approaches to gene mapping revealed the important feature that numerous mutations, and therefore numerous alleles, could arise in a single gene and produce an altered phenotype.

10.6   Radiation-Induced Mutagenesis

Radiations at wavelengths too short to be visible to us include cosmic rays, alpha and beta particles, x-rays, γ rays, and ultraviolet radiation, among others (Fig. 10.14). The most widely used **physical mutagens** are x-rays and ultraviolet (UV) light, each of which has a different mode of action on DNA. Although x-rays were the first mutagens to be identified, in the late 1920s, we know far less about their mode of action than we do about UV. The main reason for this is that UV irradiation effects can be studied more easily using biochemical methods to complement genetic analysis. In fact, we have acquired a considerable knowledge of enzymatic mechanisms of

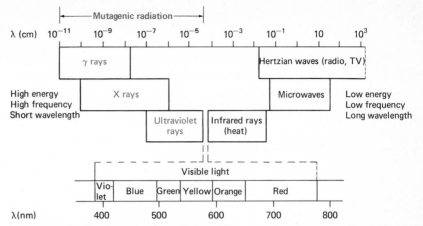

Figure 10.14 Electromagnetic radiation. The approximate ranges of radiations are plotted on a logarithmic scale of wavelength (λ) in cm, in the upper part of the diagram. The spectrum of visible light, however, is shown in nm on an arithmetic scale of wavelengths.

UV damage and its repair by an ever larger repertory of enzymes and proteins.

x-rays are *ionizing radiations,* that is, they cause an electron to be ejected from the atom, producing ionized atoms, radicals, and molecules. These ionized substances are often highly reactive in cell chemistry, and undoubtedly cause a variety of effects which lead to very complex changes in irradiated systems. x-rays generally produce gross chromosomal damage, such as breaks and rearrangements of the DNA. They also apparently cause point mutations, according to studies of inheritance patterns of x-irradiated mutants. There is some conflict in interpreting x-ray mutagenesis results, however, and there is some evidence indicating that many apparent point mutations may actually be tiny deletions of genetic material which produce similar phenotypic effects as those of base changes in DNA.

The amount of x-rays received by the organism, or *dosage,* is measured in **roentgens** (r), which are defined as the amount of radiation that yields 2.08×10^9 ion pairs per cubic centimeter of air under standard conditions of temperature and pressure. One roentgen produces two ionizations per cubic micron of tissue or water, in a biological perspective. It has been estimated that in thirty years (one human generation) we each receive a dose of about $3r$ from background radiation, and perhaps an additional $0.1r$ as the result of radioactive fallout from testing of atomic weapons in the atmosphere.

There is a directly proportional relationship between x-ray dosage and effect in inducing lethal X-linked mutations in *Drosophila* (Fig. 10.15). This same relationship is found whether the same total dosage is delivered in bursts for short periods or in small amounts over extended periods of time. We may conclude from this observation that any amount of ionizing radiation is potentially mutagenic, since a given dose will yield the same number of mutations whether it is delivered at high intensities for short times or in low intensities over months or years. The effects of ionizing radiations are

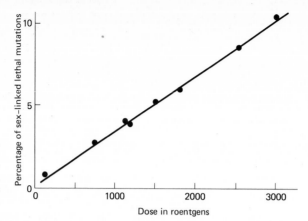

Figure 10.15 The percentage of X-linked lethal mutations induced by x-rays is directly proportional to the dosage of ionizing radiation received by the organism.

therefore *cumulative*, at least in some species. In mice, however, there seems to be less effect from chronic low-dose radiation than from a short, high-intensity exposure to the same total amount of radiation. Apparently there are repair mechanisms in mice and other mammals by which DNA can be healed if the damage inflicted at any given time has not been very extensive.

The "target theory" states that the gene is a target which is "hit" by an ionizing particle, and that one hit yields one mutation. This theory was proposed on the basis of the observed linear relationship between x-ray dosage and its induction of X-linked lethal mutations in *Drosophila*. As the dosage increases, however, a two-hit or even a multiple-hit relationship appears, since the plot yields a curve instead of a straight line. This is probably due to the fact that more than one mutation is induced but they are all recorded only as lethals. The same lethal phenotype will arise whether one or more than one mutation was induced. In the case of chromosomal damage, however, two-hit plots are usually found for radiation doses that cause breaks in chromosomes. Many of these relationships are very complicated because of a variety of events which may take place between the time of exposure to x-rays and the time the phenotypic or chromosomal effect is observed.

Ultraviolet light at the 254 nm wavelength has been used for many years as a sterilizing agent to kill bacteria. UV also induces gene mutations, primarily through photochemical changes in DNA. The wavelength which is germicidal is also the most potently mutagenic, and the two phenomena are related through the fact that DNA absorbs UV more intensively at 254-260 nm than at other wavelengths (Fig. 10.16).

The lower-energy wavelengths of the UV part of the spectrum penetrate solid materials rather poorly, unlike the higher-energy (shorter wavelengths) x-rays and other ionizing radiations which penetrate solids far more effectively. UV, therefore, is effective only for thin layers of cells or for dispersed cells.

UV induces various kinds of cellular damage, but the best known effect of UV is its induction of **pyrimidine dimer** formation in DNA, whereby pairs of adjacent pyrimidine bases in a strand become linked together by

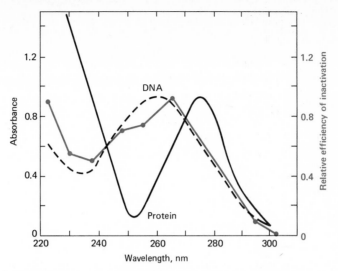

Figure 10.16 Action spectrum of UV inactivation of phage T2 (red). The action spectrum parallels the absorption spectrum for DNA very closely, but not the absorption spectrum for a typical protein. These results indicate that phage inactivation is a consequence of UV radiation damage to phage DNA.

carbon-carbon bonding (Fig. 10.17). **Thymine-thymine** dimers, abbreviated as T̂ T, are far more common than cytosine-cytosine or thymine-cytosine dimer formation. Dimerization causes a distortion or bulge in the DNA duplex in the altered region so that hydrogen bonds are broken and cross-linkages form. A large part of the killing effect of UV irradiation apparently is due to interference with DNA synthesis because of the newly formed cross links after dimerization. The mutagenic action of UV has been clarified in recent years through studies of mutation repair systems, which we will discuss next.

Figure 10.17 Pyrimidine dimer formation by UV. (a) Thymine-thymine dimer formation through carbon-carbon bonding (red lines) in DNA. (b) Dimerization causes a bulge in the altered region of the DNA duplex, where the dimer T̂T occurs.

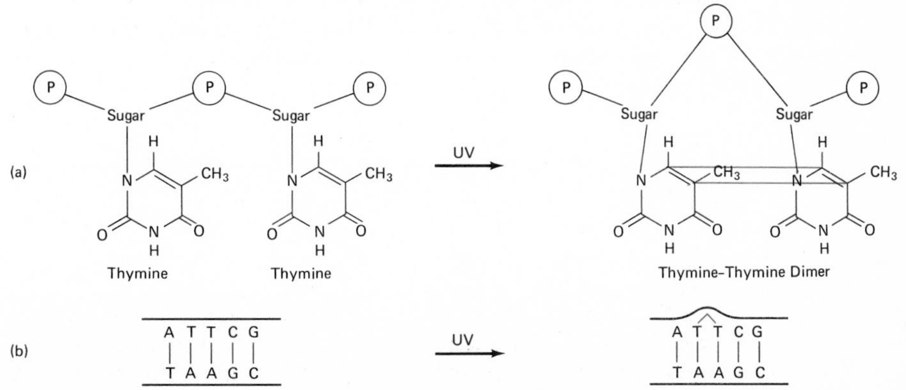

10.7   Mutation Repair

When UV-irradiated bacteria were incubated in order to locate and isolate mutants, it was found many years ago that very few mutants appeared in plates that had accidentally been left in the light when compared with the usual plates incubated in the dark. The phenomenon was called **photo-reactivation**, and it was later shown to be the result of **DNA repair** by light-dependent photoreactivating enzyme action. The most effective photoreactivation wavelengths are in the range between 310 and 400 nm. In this "light repair" process, the photoreactivating enzyme(s) splits the dimer so that single pyrimidines are restored at the altered site.

While photoreactivation is a very efficient mutation repair process, and highly accurate since there are few deaths and few mutants after UV-irradiated cells are incubated in the light, some DNA repair can also go on in the dark. The existence of "dark repair" ability was deduced from studies of *uvr* (*ultraviolet repair*) mutants in *E. coli*. These *uvr* strains give rise to many more mutations after UV irradiation than *uvr*⁺ cells which undergo the identical exposure. There are a number of different *uvr* mutants (*uvrA*, *uvrB*, and others) whose gene products are all needed for efficient and accurate **excision repair** of irradiated DNA in a number of enzymatically catalyzed steps (Fig. 10.18).

The two UV-repair systems we have mentioned so far are both enzymatically catalyzed, but by different enzymes coded by different genes. In addition, the process of dimer correction is not the same in the two pathways. In photoreactivation, the dimer itself is split so as to restore the single-base condition, and the DNA strand regains its original intact state. In excision repair, the entire dimer and some adjacent sequences are removed from the DNA strand, and the gap is accurately patched in by the action of DNA polymerase and then sealed by ligase action. The patch sequence is dictated by the complementary strand opposite the gap. Both repair processes produce undamaged DNA as an end result, and the correction processes are essentially error-free, since far fewer mutants arise in *uvr*⁺ than in *uvr*⁻ strains, and almost no mutants appear in photoreactivated cell cultures. If there were many errors in the repair pathways there would be significantly fewer surviving cells and significantly more mutants than are typically recovered in irradiation experiments.

The rare recessive hereditary disease called **xeroderma pigmentosum** (XP) is largely due to inefficient repair of UV damage, including defects in the first step in the excision repair pathway. People with this disease are characterized by a high sensitivity to sunlight, which includes the UV wavelengths, and a very high incidence of skin cancer on those body surfaces exposed to sunlight. There may be more than 100 skin cancers at one time on a single XP patient, including malignant melanomas, which are much more rare in the general population. Cultures of XP cells from different patients show a heterogeneous assortment of defects in UV-

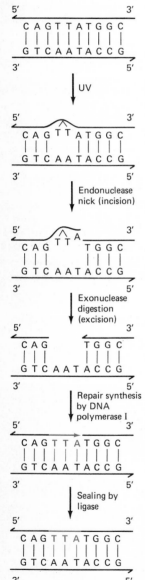

Figure 10.18 Excision repair of UV radiation damaged DNA. Dimers are excised and the accurate repair is catalyzed by DNA polymerase I using the intact strand as template. After the gap is filled, DNA ligase seals the sugar-phosphate backbone of the strand.

induced mutation repair, but some kinds of chemical agents as well as x-rays can be handled in the normal way by these mutant cells. These and similar studies are interpreted as showing that several repair pathways probably exist in mammalian systems by which damage caused by chemical and physical agents can be restored to relatively undamaged and functional DNA. Different kinds of repair deficiencies have also been found in cells cultured from patients with other recessive hereditary diseases (Table 10.4).

A third major enzymatic repair system which has been studied in *E. coli* is **postreplication repair**, whose precise pathways are not yet certain. In this system the pyrimidine dimers are retained, rather than being split or excised. An important clue to the existence of this third repair system was the discovery that *uvr* mutants kept in the dark could still carry out UV repair even when the other two systems were not functioning.

After pyrimidine dimers have formed as a primary lesion of UV irradiation in parental DNA, replication of new daughter strands leads to polynucleotide chains containing large gaps that may be 1000 nucleotides long (Fig. 10.19). These gaps in the daughter strands are found at locations that correspond to the dimers in the parental DNA strands, and they are found in approximately the same numbers. They are secondary lesions which apparently result from problems in base pairing between parental and daughter strands during replication, due to distortions caused by dimer presence in the parental strands. Postreplication repair is the process by which these "daughter strand gaps" are filled in by polymerase-directed synthesis. The filled gaps are joined to the main DNA strand segments on either side, probably by ligase action, and a continuous informational DNA is thereby produced. The pathways by which these and other events occur are still under investigation. There are, however, a number of distinct path-

Table 10.4

Some of the damaging agents or products for which genetically repair-defective cells are repair proficient or deficient

Cell type	Proficient	Deficient
Xeroderma pigmentosum	Ionizing radiation 　strand breaks 　anoxic Ethyl methanesulfonate (EMS) Proflavin + light Mitomycin C	Ultraviolet light 　dimers 　strand breaks Ionizing radiation—anoxic Chlorpromazine + light EMS HNO_2
Ataxia telangectasia	Ionizing radiation 　strand breaks 　endonuclease sites Mitomycin C Methyl methanesulfonate (MMS) Ultraviolet	Ionizing radiation 　chromosomes 　survival 　endonuclease sites Mitomycin C MMS Actinomycin D
Fanconi's anemia	MMS Ultraviolet	Mitomycin C Ultraviolet (high dose) γ-rays

Source: Setlow, R. B. 1978. *Nature* **271**:713–717. Table 1.

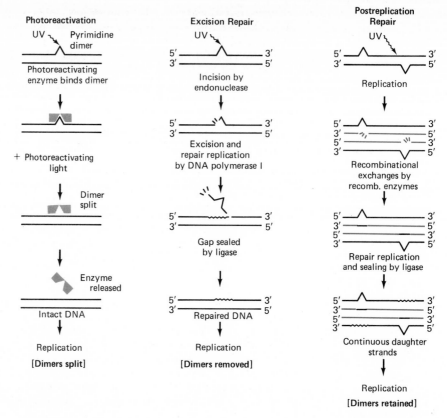

Figure 10.19 Three modes of UV repair, each leading to a different specific end result, although repair has been achieved in each case. (From Witkin, E. M. 1976. *Bact. Rev.* **40**:869.)

ways by which postreplication repair can be achieved in UV-irradiated *E. coli*. One of these requires recombination between parental and daughter strands, so that daughter strands ultimately become whole and intact while the dimer remains in a parent strand which may be left behind in the cell. Other postreplicational repair systems do not require recombinational events for the UV-induced damage to be corrected. These pathways may be either error-free or error-prone, as seen by the relative frequencies of mutants obtained after irradiation. A variety of specific repair-deficient mutants are available in *E. coli*, so that it is the best known system for the complex genetic analyses of radiation repair.

Through biochemical and genetic analysis of UV-induced mutations and mutation repair systems in viruses, bacteria, and eukaryotes, a fascinating story of biological adaptations has emerged. Cells clearly have a variety of mechanisms to clean up after damage from radiation or chemical agents. In the case of UV hazards, it is obvious that life could not exist for very long in the open air and sunlight without efficient, error-free repair systems. Since strong photoreactivating wavelengths arrive along with the dangerous UV wavelengths from the sun, photoreactivation would appear to be the first line of defense against UV-irradiation dangers. From the example of XP patients who cannot tolerate sunlight, we have a graphic demonstration of the problems that would have been encountered if there had not been evolutionary adaptations to overcome UV effects.

It is obvious that cells must be able to tolerate UV, and it makes evolutionary sense for a number of backup systems to have developed which can neutralize harmful UV effects. If one system fails, other systems can take over. These repairs must be relatively error-free, otherwise the damage caused by numerous mutations arising during repair would be equally dangerous, since most mutations are harmful to some degree. Since a variety of repair mechanisms have been found in even the simplest organisms, genetic controls over the potentially harmful effects of mutagenic agents probably evolved early in the history of life on this planet. These ancient genetic solutions were then transmitted to descendants, along with new and embellished repair systems as evolution proceeded during billions of years.

MUTAGENS AND CARCINOGENS

All of the agents which cause cancer are collectively called **carcinogens**, just as mutation-causing agents are called mutagens. In recent years there has been an increasing amount of evidence showing that some (but not all) mutagens may act as carcinogens, and that many (but not all) carcinogens are mutagenic agents. There are a number of relationships between mutagenesis and **carcinogenesis**, as phenomena, just as there are relationships between agents which act as mutagens and those which act as carcinogens. In both kinds of phenomena, a primary effect can be traced to perturbations in DNA. Once a mutation has occurred in a cell, the mutation is transmitted to descendants. Once a cell has been transformed from a normal type into a cancerous type, the transformation also is inherited in descendants of the altered cell. We are still tragically far away from understanding, much less curing or preventing, the many different diseases which all come under the single heading of cancer. There is some basic progress, however, which has come from studies of the relationships between mutagens and carcinogens, and between the phenomena of mutation induction and cancer induction.

10.8   Tests for Mutagenicity

Many carcinogens have also been shown to possess mutagenic activity, and it is of considerable medical importance to identify possible carcinogenic agents in the environment. The *in vivo* tests to demonstrate whether an agent causes cancer are expensive and time-consuming. They require large numbers of laboratory animals, animal care facilities, maintenance, personnel, and other costly items. These tests are essential, but they need not be the *first* series of tests to determine whether or not a substance is carcinogenic. The ideal situation would be to make a quick and inexpensive test showing mutagenicity, and then select such a compound for subsequent tests to determine its carcinogenicity *in vivo*. The Ames test and the Sister Chromatid Exchange (SCE) test are two such tests for mutagenicity, among others, which are widely used in preliminary screening for potentially carcinogenic compounds.

The bacterium *Salmonella typhimurium* is the test organism used in the **Ames test**, devised by Bruce Ames. The bacterial strain carries a cell wall mutation that permits most chemicals to enter the cells readily, a *uvr* mutation that abolishes most excision repair, a plasmid carrying some unknown factor that exerts mutator activity in *Salmonella* so that DNA damage is converted into mutations with high frequency, and a genetic requirement for the amino acid histidine. The *his⁻* mutation can be reverted back to *his⁺* by either base substitution or frameshift mutations. A mixture of cytoplasmic ingredients obtained as a cell-free extract from rat liver is also added to the culture dishes. The enzymes in this rat liver fraction can convert test chemicals to other products, some of which may be mutagenic even if the original substance is not. Many carcinogenic chemicals are not harmful until they have been metabolized to other products in the mammalian system, and the rat liver extract can accomplish these changes in the culture medium. The assay consists of scoring for *his⁺* revertants (or suppressor mutants which cause a pseudowild phenotype) which appear as colonies on minimal media.

The Ames test has been used for hundreds of chemicals (Table 10.5). In a

Table 10.5
Correlation between carcinogenicity in animals and mutagenicity in *Salmonella* (Ames test strains)

Category of compounds	Carcinogens detected as bacterial mutagens	Non-carcinogens not mutagenic to bacteria
Aromatic amines	23/25	10/12
Alkyl halides	17/20	1/3
Polycyclic aromatics	26/27	7/9
Esters, epoxides, carbamates	13/18	5/9
Nitro aromatics and heterocycles	28/28	1/4
Nitrosamines	20/21	2/2
Fungal toxins and antibiotics	8/9	5/5
Cigarette smoke condensate mixture	1/1	—
Azo dyes and diazo compounds	11/11	2/3
Common laboratory biochemicals	—	46/46
Miscellaneous organics	1/6	13/13
Miscellaneous heterocycles	1/4	7/7
Miscellaneous nitrogen compounds	7/9	2/4
	156/179	101/117

From McCann, J., E. Choi, E. Yamasaki, and B. N. Ames. 1975. *Proc. Nat. Acad. Sci., U. S.* **72**:5135–5139.

1975 summation of data, Ames and co-workers reported that 87% of 179 known carcinogenic chemicals in animals were also mutagenic, whereas 86% of the apparently noncarcinogenic compounds were not mutagenic (101 out of 117 tested). Because there is such a high correlation between carcinogenicity and mutagenicity, the Ames test has excellent predictive value. In other words, if a substance is found to be mutagenic there is a very good chance that it will also turn out to be a carcinogen. Once the substance is tested in animals such as mice, it can definitely be determined whether or not tumors will be produced. At that stage, the substance is a definitely identified carcinogen, and foods or cosmetics or other consumer products containing the carcinogen will be banned by the Food and Drug Administration (FDA) according to law.

Another test is chromosomal, and involves a comparison between the frequency of **sister chromatid exchange (SCE)** in control cells and in cells treated with a test substance (Fig. 10.20). The basis for chromatid exchanges remains uncertain, except that there must be breaks and rejoinings to produce the altered pattern seen in stained preparations. Many mutagens induce chromosomal breakage leading to structural rearrangements, but whether or not SCEs arise by the same processes is not known at the present time. The value of the SCE test is its speed, low cost, and high correlation between increased frequency of SCEs and known mutagenicity of some compound or radiation source.

Cultured mammalian cells are allowed to undergo two rounds of replica-

Figure 10.20 Metaphase Chinese hamster chromosomes prepared and stained to show sister chromatid exchanges (SCEs) in chromosomes whose two chromatids are differentially stained: (a) untreated control, with 12 SCEs among 20 chromosomes; and (b) chromosomes from a cell exposed to the mutagenic agent nitrogen mustard, with approximately a tenfold increase in SCEs compared with the controls. (From Perry, P., and H. J. Evans. 1975. *Nature* **258**:121, Figs. 1 and 4.)

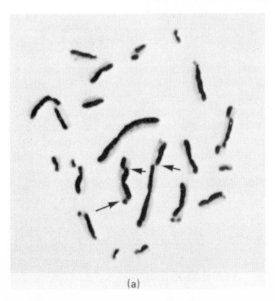

(a)

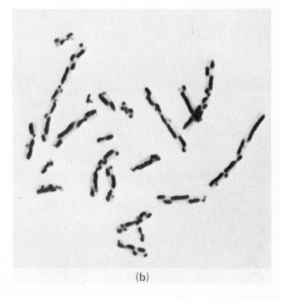

(b)

tion in the presence of 5-bromodeoxyuridine (BrdU). The test substance or treatment is provided during the second cell cycle, and cells are arrested in metaphase of the subsequent mitosis through the addition of colchicine. Colchicine disrupts spindle formation so the metaphase chromosomes are spread out through the cell in a condensed state and can be seen and photographed easily. The chromosomes are stained with ordinary Giemsa stain and examined with the light microscope. The sister chromatids of a metaphase chromosome stain differently because one chromatid has both its strands of duplex DNA loaded with BrdU, while the sister chromatid produced in the second cell cycle has only one strand of the duplex with BrdU substituted regions. The stain interacts more strongly with the doubly-brominated molecules than with the molecules having only one brominated strand, and the sister chromatids are rendered visibly distinct from each other.

Any exchange between sister chromatids will be evident by a change in staining pattern of the pair of chromatids making up a metaphase chromosome. SCEs appear in normal cells, and about 5-15 SCEs per chromosome complement has been established as the baseline frequency for untreated human lymphocytes in culture. When certain mutagenic alkylating agents, such as nitrogen mustard, are added to the lymphocyte cultures, there is a considerable increase in the number of SCEs per cell at concentrations of the test substances that produce no other visible chromosomal changes. At very high concentrations, these alkylating agents also break chromosomes. Since they seem to be effective at much lower concentrations in the SCE test, it would appear that the SCE test is a more *sensitive* assay for chromosomal breakage than tests which were used previously to detect gross structural rearrangements of whole chromosomes.

One of the difficulties with the SCE test was the uncertainty regarding the amount, if any, of genetic damage that arose in cells with high numbers of SCEs. In other words, did SCEs mean that mutations and other genetic effects had been induced, or did they simply mean that chromatid exchanges had occurred but that no genetic or inherited alteration necessarily accompanied SCE increases? In the past few years there have been stronger lines of evidence indicating that an increase in the frequency of SCEs is accompanied by an increase in genetic damage and in mutation rate. A. V. Carrano and co-workers used Chinese Hamster Ovary cells (CHO cells) that were resistant to the drug 8-azaguanine because of mutations at the X-linked locus for the enzyme hypoxanthine-guanine phosphoribosyl transferase (HPRT). Four different mutagens were applied to these cells, and each mutagen produced an increase in SCEs and in the mutation rate to drug sensitivity, in a linear relationship (Fig. 10.21). If a number of conditions can be established, including whether CHO cells can behave *in vitro* and *in vivo* in a similar manner, whether CHO results can be extrapolated to human cells, and other factors, this test system could be developed into a simple and direct quantitative assay of the mutagenicity of all sorts of agents. As with the Ames test, agents which are mutagenic can well be considered prime suspects for carcinogens. Such substances can then be tested with live animals for their ability to sponsor tumors.

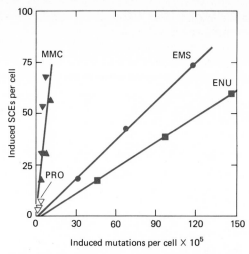

Figure 10.21   There is a linear relationship between the frequency of induced sister chromatid exchanges and the frequency of induced mutations in Chinese hamster ovary cells in culture, after exposure to four mutagens: MMC (mitomycin C, a crosslinking agent), PRO (proflavin, an intercalating agent), EMS (ethyl methanesulfonate, an alkylating agent), and ENU (*N*-ethyl-*N*-nitrosourea, an alkylating agent). (From Carrano, A. V., *et al*. 1978. *Nature* **271**:551.)

10.9   Cancer and DNA Perturbations

There is relatively little direct evidence showing that modifications in DNA can initiate **cancer**, that is, cause (1) uncontrolled growth, (2) invasion of other tissues, and (3) spread to distant sites (metastasis) where new tumors can be initiated. There is, however, a variety of indirect lines of evidence that much if not most carcinogenesis is the result of changes in DNA.

Cancer cells divide to give rise to other cancer cells like themselves. This immediately suggests that chromosomal DNA is responsible for the heritability of the cancer phenotype, or at least that gene action has been altered in the environment of the cancer cell and that as long as the altered environment is maintained the altered gene action will be maintained. That gene action rather than gene structure is altered has been demonstrated very nicely in one particular cancer by several groups working with rare teratocarinoma tumors in mice. These tumors, called embryoid bodies, arise in the gonads and contain a large variety of differentiated and undifferentiated tissues in an unorganized mass. If certain embryonal carcinoma cells are removed from the teratocarcinoma and injected into mouse blastocysts, some blastocysts proceed through normal embryo development and give rise to genetic mosaic (chimeric) mice with normal cells derived from embryonal carcinoma cells (Fig. 10.22). If the gene structure had been altered, there would be only tumor cell descendants from parental tumor cells, whereas gene action is subject to environmental influences and is reversible when the environment changes.

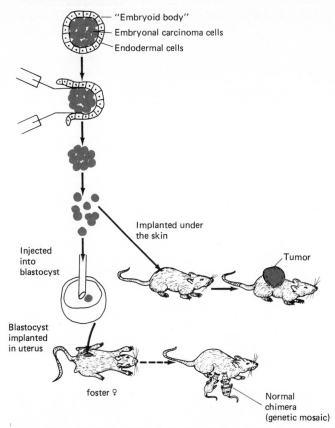

Figure 10.22 Demonstration that gene action rather than gene structure has been altered in embryoid-body tumors in mice. Embryonal carcinoma cells can be injected singly into mouse blastocyst and these can give rise to genetic mosaic, or chimeric, mice containing normal cells derived from the cancer cell. The cancerous nature of the embryonal carcinoma cell is shown in control mice which develop subcutaneous tumors from such cell implants. Reversible gene action may explain these results; the same cell type behaving differently in different environments.

As we described in the preceding section, most carcinogens have mutagenic activity. This links the induction of cancer by physical and chemical agents to alterations in DNA. The nature of the genetic changes leading to the cancerous state, however, remains unknown. It seems very unlikely that changes in a single gene could be responsible. In addition, only some exposed cells become cancerous while many others in the same population remain unaffected, or the organism succumbs if there is much cell death due to various other causes. Some carcinogens provoke changes in cell behavior only after they have been metabolized to one or more products. For example, nitrates and nitrites (food preservatives) are harmless until they are metabolically converted to powerfully mutagenic and carcinogenic nitrosoamines in the body (Fig. 10.23). Many known carcinogenic—mutagenic agents, such as x-rays, UV, nitrogen mustard, and others, cause base

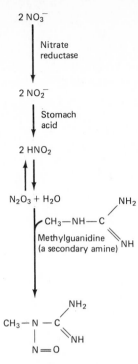

2 NO₃⁻

↓ Nitrate reductase

2 NO₂⁻

↓ Stomach acid

2 HNO₂

CH₃—NH—C⟨NH₂ / NH

Methylguanidine
(a secondary amine)

CH₃—N—C⟨NH₂ / NH
|
N=O

Nitrosoguanidine

CH₃—N—C⟨NH₂ / O
|
N
O

Methylnitrosourea

Figure 10.23 Conversion of harmless food preservatives to powerful nitrosamines, which may induce mutagenic or carcinogenic changes in the body.

substitution and frameshift mutations, chromosome breaks, and other genetic damage. But whether any of this genetic damage leads to the induction of cancer is still uncertain.

Three recessively inherited human diseases all show defects in mutation repair, although the symptoms of these diseases are very different and the repair defects also are different. In xeroderma pigmentosum (XP), ataxia telangiectasia (AT), and Fanconi's anemia (FA), different repair deficiencies have been noted (see Table 10.4). Each of these diseases, however, makes the patient cancer-prone. It would seem, therefore, that damage to DNA can be carcinogenic, and that there is a causal connection between mutagenic and carcinogenic agents.

The clinical symptoms of these disorders are characterized by extreme sensitivity of the skin to sunlight in XP patients, motor coordination and immune system problems in AT patients, and blood disorders in FA patients which lead to death as the result of hemorrhage or other blood system failure. Although approximately one in several hundred thousand births produces a child with any one of these rare diseases, there are estimated to be one in several hundred people who are heterozygous for the diseases. XP and AT heterozygotes are not cancer-prone, but there appears to be a higher risk of leukemia in FA heterozygotes than in people who are homozygous for the dominant normal allele. This inference is based on findings which show that about 5% of all people dying from acute leukemia are FA heterozygotes, which is far higher than their representation in the general population.

In addition to seeking relationships between repair deficiencies and proneness to cancer in other hereditary disorders, experiments have been done in attempts to correlate **ageing** with changes in DNA repair. The results are difficult to interpret directly, and there is a problem in making comparisons among the different experiments which have been reported. The connection remains a possible one, but there is little supporting evidence for the hypothesis. The same can be said for the hypothesis that **somatic mutations** lead to ageing, cancer induction, and other medical problems of the aged. The idea that body cells accumulate mutations over the years, or that the cellular and extracellular environments undergo such changes as to induce mutations leading to cancer and other problems in old age is unproven but recurs regularly as a hypothesis to be tested. Basic problems in designing appropriate experiments and test systems are numerous, not the least of which is our poor knowledge of the normal sequences of developmental events during a lifetime. If we do not know the normal kinds of cellular changes taking place, it is hard to detect the abnormal, much less relate some observed difference to diseases of such a varied nature as cancer.

All of these lines of study are bringing us closer to a better understanding of normal and abnormal development of cells, tissues, and organisms. It seems clear now that unrepaired damage to DNA has a high carcinogenic potential, but it seems unlikely that all cancers arise from defects in the repair of DNA. Nevertheless, we can now examine the rate and processes of DNA repair as one parameter in the steps leading to carcinogenesis. Progress may seem slow, but it is steady.

QUESTIONS AND PROBLEMS

10.1.   A mutation occurs in structural gene *Z* of the *lac* operon (*lacZ*). What would you expect if this was a nonsense mutation? a missense mutation? a frameshift mutation?

10.2.   A scientist isolates three different mutants in each of which the glycine at position 66 in the protein is replaced, by cysteine, aspartic acid, and alanine, respectively. The codons for these three amino acids include, respectively, UGU, GAU, and GCU. If each mutation only involves the change of a single base, what must the scientist deduce is the codon for glycine at position 66 in the protein?

10.3.   A laboratory group has isolated *E. coli* strains each of which is mutant for a different enzyme active in a particular metabolic pathway. When supplements of growth factors A, B, C, and D are added to the media, the bacteria respond by growth (+) or no growth (o). Using the results tabulated below, invent a pathway that could explain these data. Show the steps in the pathway at which each mutant strain is genetically blocked.

	Growth factor added			
Strain	**A**	**B**	**C**	**D**
1	o	o	+	+
2	o	o	o	+
3	+	o	+	+
4	o	+	+	+

10.4.   You wish to isolate a bacterial strain which cannot produce both leucine and tryptophan. How would you select for such double mutants?

10.5.   In the fluctuation test designed by Luria and Delbruck, bacteria were plated onto media containing the virulent phage T1 and T1-resistant bacterial mutants were sought. Had they used phage lambda, which is temperate, how would the experimental results have been different from those observed for T1?

10.6.   In corn the gene for aleurone color has a mutation rate of 11×10^{-6} while the gene for color of the corn plant has a mutation rate of 492×10^{-6}. How many plants must you use if you wish to obtain a plant with mutations at both of these gene loci?

10.7.   A normal red-eyed Drosophila male ($C^{+}l^{+}B^{+}w^{+}/Y$) is exposed to mutagen ethylmethane sulfonate (EMS), and is then mated with a red-eyed *ClB* female (*ClB* $w^{+}/C^{+}l^{+}B^{+}w^{+}$). One Bar-eyed daughter from this cross is mated to a normal male and their offspring consist of daughters that are normal, daughters with red, Bar eyes, and sons that are white-eyed.
   a.   Diagram these crosses, giving the complete genotype and phenotype of all parents and progeny.
   b.   From this pattern of inheritance, how would you describe the white-eye allele?

10.8. The wild-type coat protein of tobacco mosaic virus contains proline at position 20. Treatment with nitrous acid, which is known to deaminate cytosine to uracil, produced variants with amino acid substitution at this position in the polypeptide, according to the following scheme:

Treatment of the ultimate Phe-mutant using nitrous acid cannot induce further amino acid substitutions at this position.

a. List all possible codons for these four amino acids (using the coding dictionary in Fig. 6.16), and identify the most probable codons for these amino acids based on the assumption that each mutational change shown above was due to a single-base substitution.

b. What kinds of mutational changes were induced by nitrous acid treatment?

10.9. Pale green barley plants heterozygous for a gene determining chlorophyll production yield twice as many pale green progeny as full green progeny when self-fertilized. Explain.

10.10. A study revealed that among 735,000 children born to normal parents in a certain country, 14 of these children were brachydactylic (a dominant trait involving shortened fingers and toes). Estimate the mutation rate to brachydactyly.

10.11. As a geneticist you are asked to determine if the drinking water in your town contains industrial pollutants which are mutagenic. You decide to use *ClB Drosophila* in order to detect induced mutations.

a. Explain the genetic principles and the positive results you would expect if the water does contain significant amounts of mutagenic agents.

b. What kinds of mutations would you be able to detect using this method? Explain.

c. Describe any one kind of mutation that you could not detect in this way. Explain.

d. Suppose you were asked to use the Ames test for mutagenicity. How would you proceed, and what additional studies could you do afterward?

10.12. Compare three specific ways in which thymine dimers can be handled by cells so that UV damage can be repaired.

REFERENCES

Allen, J. W., and S. A. Latt, 1976. Analysis of sister chromatid exchange formation *in vivo* in mouse spermatogonia as a new test system for environmental mutagens. *Nature* **260**:449.

Allen, J. W., C. F. Shuler, and S. A. Latt. 1978. Bromodeoxyuridine tablet methodology for *in vivo* studies of DNA synthesis. *Somatic Cell Genet.* **4**:393.

Ames, B. N. 1979. Identifying environmental chemicals causing mutations and cancer. *Science* **204**:587.

Axelrod, D. E., R. Terry, and F. G. Kern. 1979. Cell differentiation rates of Friend murine erythroleukemia variants isolated by sib selection. *Somatic Cell Genet.* **5**:539.

Barrett, J. C., T. Tsutsui, and P. O. Ts'o. 1978. Neoplastic transformation induced by a direct perturbation of DNA. *Nature* **274**:229.

Bunn, H. F., B. G. Forget, and H. M. Ranney, eds. 1977. *Human Hemoglobins*. Philadelphia: Saunders.

Cairns, J. Nov. 1975. The cancer problem. *Sci. Amer.* **233**:64.

Cairns, J. 1975. Mutation selection and the natural history of cancer. *Nature* **255**:197.

Capecchi, M. R., S. H. Hughes, and G. M. Wahl. 1975. Yeast supersuppressors are altered tRNAs capable of translating a nonsense codon *in vitro*. *Cell* **6**:269.

Carrano, A. V., L. H. Thompson, P. A. Lindl, and J. L. Minkler. 1978. Sister chromatid exchange as an indicator of mutagenesis. *Nature* **271**:551.

Coulondre, C., and J. H. Miller. 1977. Genetic studies of the *lac* repressor. IV. Mutagenic specificity in the *lacI* gene of *Escherichia coli*. *J. Mol. Biol.* **117**:577.

Coulondre, C., J. H. Miller, P. J. Farabaugh, and W. Gilbert. 1978. Molecular basis of base substitution hotspots in *Escherichia coli*. *Nature* **274**:775.

de Serres, F. J., and M. D. Shelby. 1979. The *Salmonella* mutagenicity assay: Recommendations. *Science* **203**:563.

Devoret, R. Aug. 1979. Bacterial tests for potential carcinogens. *Sci. Amer.* **241**:40.

Evans, H. J. 1977. Some facts and fancies relating to chromosome structure in man. *Adv. Human Genet.* **8**:347.

Hanawalt, P. C., and R. H. Haynes. Feb. 1967. The repair of DNA. *Sci. Amer.* **216**:36.

Hiatt, H. H., J. D. Watson, and J. A. Winsten. 1977. *Origins of Human Cancer*. New York: Cold Spring Harbor Laboratory.

Hollaender, A., and F. J. de Serres, eds. 1978. *Chemical Mutagens*. Vol. 5: *Principles and Methods for Their Detection*. New York: Plenum.

Holliday, R., R. E. Halliwell, M. W. Evans, and V. Rowell. 1976. Genetic characterization of *rec*-1, a mutant of *Ustilago maydis* defective in repair and recombination. *Genet. Res., Cambr.* **27**:413.

Irwin, S., and J. Egozcue. 1967. Chromosomal abnormalities in leukocytes from LSD-25 users. *Science* **157**:313.

Kato, H., and H. F. Stich. 1976. Sister chromatid exchanges in ageing and repair-deficient human fibroblasts. *Nature* **260**:447.

Knudson, A. G., Jr. 1977. Genetics and etiology of human cancer. *Adv. Human Genet.* **8**:1.

Lederberg, J. and E. M. Lederberg. 1952. Replica plating and indirect selection of bacterial mutants. *J. Bact.* **63**:399.

Luria, S. E., and M. Delbrück. 1943. Mutations of bacteria from virus sensitivity to virus resistance. *Genetics* **28**:491.

Marx, J. L. 1978. DNA repair: New clues to carcinogenesis. *Science* **200**:518.

Maugh, T. H., II. 1978. Chemical carcinogens: How dangerous are low doses? *Science* **202**:37.

McElheny, V. K., and S. Abrahamson, eds. 1979. *Assessing Chemical Mutagens: The Risk to Humans.* New York: Cold Spring Harbor Laboratory.

Mintz, B., and K. Illmensee. 1975. Normal genetically mosaic mice produced from malignant teratocarcinoma cells. *Proc. Nat. Acad. Sci. U. S.* **72**:3585.

Muller, H. J. 1927. Artificial transmutation of the gene. *Science* **66**:84.

Neidle, S., *et al.* 1977. Structure of a dinucleoside phosphate-drug complex as model for nucleic acid-drug interaction. *Nature* **269**:304.

Nicolson, G. L. Mar. 1979. Cancer metastasis. *Sci. Amer.* **240**:66.

Pastan, I., and M. Willingham. 1978. Cellular transformation and the 'morphologic phenotype' of transformed cells. *Nature* **274**:645.

Perry, P., and H. J. Evans. 1975. Cytological detection of mutagen-carcinogen exposure by sister chromatid exchange. *Nature* **258**:121.

Perutz, M. F. 1976. Fundamental research in molecular biology: relevance to medicine. *Nature* **262**:449.

Ringertz, N. R., and T. Ege. 1978. Use of mutant, hybrid, and reconstructed cells in somatic cell genetics. In *Cell Biology, A Comprehensive Treatise*, Vol. 1. L. Goldstein and D. M. Prescott, eds. New York: Academic Press, p. 191.

Ringertz, N. R., and R. E. Savage. 1976. *Cell Hybrids.* New York: Academic Press.

Roberts, J. W., C. W. Roberts, and N. L. Craig. 1978. *Escherichia coli recA* gene product inactivates phage repressor. *Proc. Nat. Acad. Sci. U.S.* **75**:4714.

Scott, D., and C. Y. Lyons. 1979. Homogeneous sensitivity of human peripheral blood lymphocytes to radiation-induced chromosome damage. *Nature* **278**:756.

Setlow, R. B. 1978. Repair deficient human disorders and cancer. *Nature* **271**:713.

Stadler, L. J. 1928. Mutations in barley induced by X-rays and radium. *Science* **68**:186.

Streisinger, G., Y. Okada, J. Emrich, J. Newton, A. Tsugita, and M. Inouye. 1967. Frameshift mutations and the genetic code. *Cold Spring Harbor Symp. Quant. Biol.* **31** (1966):77.

Villani, G., S. Boiteux, and M. Radman. 1978. Mechanism of ultraviolet-induced mutagenesis: Extent and fidelity of *in vitro* DNA synthesis on irradiated templates. *Proc. Nat. Acad. Sci. U.S.* **75**:3037.

Vogel, W., and T. Bauknecht. 1976. Differential chromatid staining by *in vivo* treatment as a mutagenicity test system. *Nature* **260**:448.

Walcher, D. N., N. Kretschmer, and H. L. Barnett, eds. 1978. *Mutations: Biology and Society.* New York: Masson.

Waldren, C., C. Jones, and T. T. Puck. 1979. Measurement of mutagenesis in mammalian cells. *Proc. Nat. Acad. Sci. U.S.* **76**:1358.

Witkin, E. M. 1976. Ultraviolet mutagenesis and inducible DNA repair in *Escherichia coli. Bact. Rev.* **40**:869.

Wolff, S., and B. Rodin, 1978. Saccharin-induced sister chromatid exchanges in Chinese hamster and human cells. *Science* **200**:543.

Wolff, S., B. Rodin, and J. E. Cleaver. 1977. Sister chromatid exchanges induced by mutagenic carcinogens in normal and xeroderma pigmentosum cells. *Nature* **265**:347.

11

Cytogenetics

Cytogenetics is an area of study in which genetic and molecular features of the genes are observed in parallel with cytological features of chromosomes and chromosomal DNA using microscopy. Parallel genetic and cytological data, or cytogenetic information, provide independent lines of evidence by which some conclusion about the genetic system can be interpreted more objectively and precisely. The same principles which governed cytogenetics during its "golden era" between the 1920s and 1940s, now guide modern studies at the level of the whole chromosome as seen with light microscopy and at the DNA level as seen with the electron microscope and associated techniques. The revival of cytogenetics in the 1960s came from many new methods which permitted detailed observations to be made of chromosomes and chromosomal DNA.

Structural aberrations and numerical changes in the genome provide the major kinds of chromosomal systems by which genetic activities can be monitored and interpreted. These chromosomal changes firmly established the Chromosome Theory of Heredity, and just as firmly helped to establish that genes were sequences of nucleotides in the linear DNA double-helical molecule. Many kinds of chromosomal aberration or numerical change are considered to be important in species evolution, as well as in guiding the well-being of the individual organism. Medical cytogenetics is an increasingly important part of medical practice, and structural changes in chromosomes provide useful systems to map human genes on chromosomes.

Using a battery of sophisticated techniques to analyze the molecular features of eukaryotic genomes, information can be obtained about genes which might never be available by genetic analysis, since mutations are virtually unknown in these loci. Molecular hybridization, heteroduplex analysis by electron microscopy, and other recent methods have opened new prospects for fine structure analysis of the genome. Eukaryotic genomes have now become accessible to the same kinds of detailed dissection that previously had only been possible with bacteria and viruses.

THE CHROMOSOME COMPLEMENT

The study of eukaryotic chromosomes in the last part of the 1800s paved the way for acceptance of the Mendelian theory of inheritance in 1900, and was promptly formalized in Sutton's Chromosome Theory of Heredity. Parallels between gene behavior from genetic analysis and chromosome behavior from microscopy have been sought ever since, and **cytogenetics** is an integral component of genetics.

Chromosomes can be identified by their morphological features from metaphase preparations of somatic cells. Chromosome length, relative arm lengths as a function of centromere location, and unique features such as nucleolar organizers all contribute to specific identifications. The development of staining methods which produce unique band and interband patterns in somatic chromosomes provided the means to recognize each individual chromosome in a set regardless of their otherwise similar morphologies.

11.1   Chromosome Morphology and the Karyotype

The ordered arrangement of all the somatic chromosomes in the nucleus is called a **karyotype** (Fig. 11.1). The usual preparations of metaphase nuclei are obtained from cells in culture or from actively dividing tissues such as root tips in plants. Human karyotype studies are usually made from **lymphocytes** (a type of blood cell) or **fibroblasts** (a type of connective tissue cell) maintained or established in culture. Metaphase chromosomes are the most condensed of any division stage, and it is more likely that the chromosomes will be well spread out and easier to separate and identify than in division stages where they are longer and more tangled.

Cells in culture are stimulated to undergo mitosis in preparation for karyotyping, and colchicine is added at the proper time to arrest mitotic nuclei in the metaphase stage. Well spread metaphase chromosomes in arrested nuclei are stained, photographed, and then cut out of photographs. These are positioned according to an established convention, proceeding from the largest to the smallest chromosomes, with their centromeres aligned to emphasize differences in chromosome length and relative arm lengths of each chromosome.

Chromosomes of the human karyotype were first grouped into seven different classes, from A to G, according to chromosome length and centromere position. The three largest chromosomes, of group A, are **metacentric**, having a median centromere location and two equal-length arms (Fig. 11.2). The B and C groups of chromosomes are **submetacentric**, having one arm slightly longer than the other because of centromere location. B chromosomes are larger than C chromosomes in absolute length. Groups D and G contain the **acrocentric** chromosomes, where one arm is considerably longer than the other because the centromere is near one end of the chromosome. Group E consists of three small submetacentrics, and group F has two small metacentrics. While metacentric, submetacentric, and acrocentric types are represented in the human chromosome complement, there is no

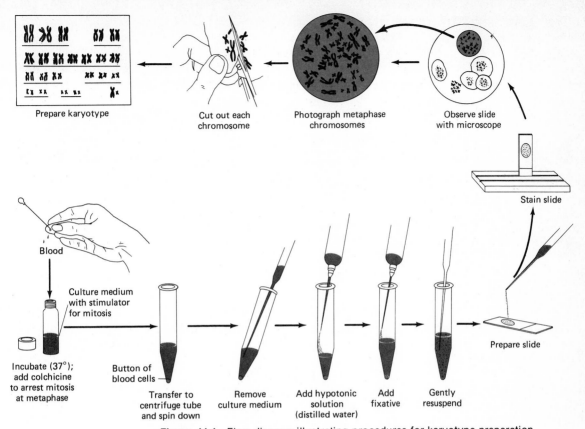

Figure 11.1 Flow diagram illustrating procedures for karyotype preparation.

telocentric type with a terminal centromere and only a single chromosome arm. This kind of chromosome is found in some species, but it is not common. The X and Y chromosomes in the human complement fall into the C and G chromosome groups, respectively, on the basis of their size and centromere location.

There are five nucleolar-organizing chromosomes in the human complement; all three D-group chromosomes and both G-group chromosomes are acrocentric and have **satellites** terminating the short arm. Satellite knobs frequently, but not always, serve as indicators of nucleolar organizing regions of chromosomes. The satellite is simply a tiny extension of the chromosome beyond the organizer region.

Karyotype analysis of human and other mammalian species was difficult to conduct before 1956. In that year, J. Tijo and A. Levan reported their new procedure to obtain human mitotic cells with well spread out metaphase chromosomes. They reported the correct number of human chromosomes in diploid nuclei to be 46, as opposed to the incorrect number of 48 which had persisted in the literature for many years. Tijo and Levan's method for preparation of somatic metaphase chromosomes is used with

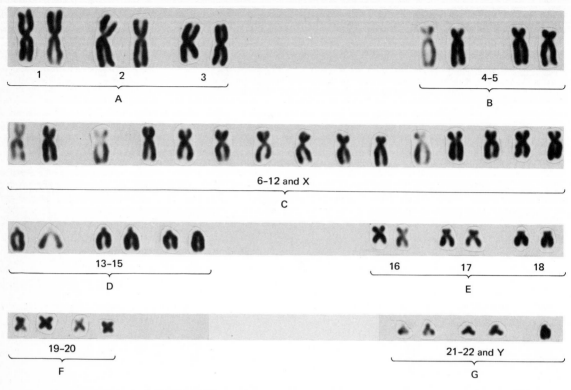

1 2 3
A

4-5
B

6-12 and X
C

13-15
D

16 17 18
E

19-20
F

21-22 and Y
G

X Chromosomes occupy the second position in the C group

Figure 11.2 Karyotype of human male. Chromosomes are arranged into 8 groups (A-G) according to size and centromere location. Group A includes large metacentrics; B, large submetacentrics; C, intermediate size submetacentrics; D, acrocentrics (and nucleolar organizing); E, smallest submetacentrics; F, smallest metacentrics; and G, smallest acrocentrics (nucleolar organizing). The X and Y chromosomes can be put into groups C and G, respectively, on the basis of morphology.

modifications today. It opened a new era of analysis of mammalian chromosomes that simply had not been possible before.

11.2 Chromosome Banding

In 1969, T. C. Hsu and others introduced new methods for staining chromosomes by which distinct patterns of stained bands and lightly stained interbands became evident (Fig. 11.3). These staining methods were enormously important, since they permitted each chromosome to be identified uniquely, even if the overall morphology was identical. Distinctions could now be made among the relatively similar C group chromosomes, for example, so that we may refer to chromosome 9 or chromosome 12 instead of merely to a C-group chromosome. It is still convenient to use the group reference in many instances, but we now more often refer to a specific chromosome by its number as set by the karyotype conventional ordering.

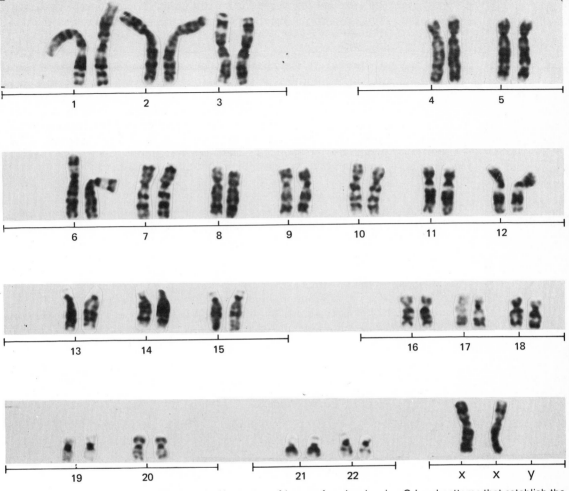

Figure 11:3 Karyotype of human female, showing G-band patterns that establish the unique identity of each chromosome in the complement.

The most useful chromosome banding method is **G-banding**. The earlier methods included some special steps in the staining procedure, but these were found to be unnecessary and no special conditions are really needed to visualize G-bands by staining with the Giemsa reagent. Giemsa staining had been used for many years to contrast nuclear material, and it was one of the first stains to delineate the bacterial nucleoid by microscopy.

Two main categories of chromosome banding patterns are recognized:

1. **G-bands** after Giemsa staining and **Q-bands**, which develop after staining with quinacrine and other fluorescent dyes, give relatively similar but not identical patterns. Fluorescent stains fade after a short time, and special microscope optics plus ultraviolet illumina-

tion are needed to see fluorescent bands. Giemsa-stained preparations are more permanent and ordinary microscope optics and illumination are used. For these reasons, G-staining is generally used routinely.

2. **C-bands** are visualized by Giemsa staining after pretreatments using HCl and NaOH to partially denature the chromosomes in a preparation. C-bands are especially evident around the centromere and in other chromosome regions which contain substantial amounts of highly-repetitive **constitutive heterochromatin** (Fig. 11.4). The Giemsa stain is not specific, but it binds to regions of DNA which have responded differently from nonbanded regions to HCl and NaOH pretreatments.

Despite many attempts to interpret banding reactions on a molecular basis, we still know relatively little about specific interactions between DNA and any staining reagents in use. Q-bands apparently result from binding between quinacrine dye and DNA regions which are rich in adenine and thymine. Since guanine and cytosine quench fluorescence, GC-rich regions of DNA generally appear as unstained interbands. Since Q-bands and G-bands are relatively similar, it would seem that a common mechanism of interaction should exist between DNA and the dye. So far, this has not been shown to be true, and G-banding mechanisms remain unclear.

Figure 11.4 Human chromosome complement showing C-bands, mainly around the centromere region of each chromosome. This pattern reflects regions containing constitutive heterochromatin, known to occur in the centromere region and various other chromosome parts in most species.

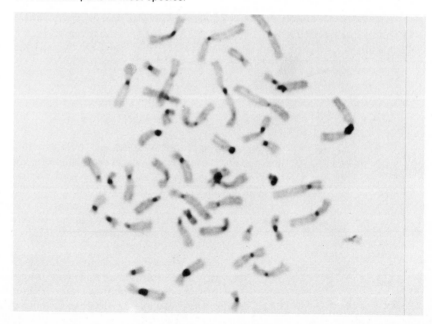

C-bands are very distinctively located, and arise as the result of binding between Giemsa stain and residual chromatin remaining after pretreatments which extract nucleoproteins. More chromatin remains in areas of constitutive heterochromatin than in other parts of the chromosomes after denaturing steps, so more material is present to bind more of the stain and yield a band that is contrasted with lightly stained or unstained regions in between. (There is little or no nucleoprotein extraction in G- or Q-banding methods.) Locations of C-bands correlate very well with localizations of constitutive heterochromatin from *in situ* hybridizations with highly repetitious DNA fractions, with autoradiography showing late replication in these same regions, and with other methods to identify constitutive heterochromatin, which is noncoding DNA in a highly condensed and compacted state (see Section 3.11).

With new methods for G-banding chromosomes, various structural and numerical aberrations of a normal complement can be identified unequivocally. These identifications have become a mainstay of human cytogenetic studies in medicine, and in map construction using somatic cell genetic methods, as we discussed in Section 5.3. The greater certainty of identifying whole chromosomes or parts of chromosomes by G-bands often allows the investigator to know exactly which chromosomes are present, and which chromosome parts have undergone structural rearrangements. Banding also provides a handle to compare karyotypes of related species and to describe differences which apparently have an evolutionary basis.

CHANGES IN GENE AND CHROMOSOME STRUCTURE

Changes in structure may involve whole chromosomes or individual genes, both of which have the same underlying basis of alterations in the linear ordering of DNA nucleotide sequences. Cytogenetic analyses of **structural aberrations** have been extended from observations at the gross level of light microscopy to the more detailed levels of DNA molecules and gene sequences. Molecular cytogenetic analyses require new tools of electron microscopy, biochemical tests, and physical methods, but they are the *same in principle* regardless of the level of observation which can be achieved.

Four general classes of structural chromosomal or genetic changes are generally recognized: (1) deficiencies or deletions, (2) duplications, (3) inversions, and (4) translocations of genetic material. Cytogenetic studies have contributed substantially to our view of the genome as a coordinated system rather than just a random collection of genes or strings of genes in chromosomes.

11.3   Deficiencies or Deletions

The loss of one or more genes or parts of genes is called a **deficiency** or a **deletion**; the terms are synonymous. Chromosomal deficiencies arise through breaks caused by one or more agents, including radiation, viruses, and chemicals. The broken region may be healed or restored with little or no subsequent effect, or all or some of the genetic material may fail to be incorporated back into the chromosome. The loss of genetic material usually has a phenotypic consequence, although its magnitude will vary according to the amount of material involved, the relative need of the material for viability and function, and the particular species involved.

When the lost piece includes the centromere of the chromosome, the **acentric** chromosome or fragment will usually not be incorporated into daughter nuclei and will eventually be degraded or eliminated from the cell. By and large, deletions are lethal when present in the homozygous state, which must mean that there is very little genetic material which does not contain some essential gene for the organism. Heterozygous deletions very often are phenotypically detectable, although it depends on the genetic lesion involved.

In human beings there are a number of disorders caused by chromosome deletions, which are detectable only in heterozygotes, since the homozygous condition is lethal. The *cri du chat* disorder is characterized by severe mental retardation and other abnormalities, as well as the peculiar mewing cry of the infant, from which the name of the disease (cat-cry) is derived. This disease is associated with a deletion of part of the short arm of chromosome 5 (Fig. 11.5). There are a few other deletion-based disorders, which generally result in mental retardation and various physical abnormalities. Apparently human beings do not readily tolerate losses of genetic material even as heterozygotes. Whether this is due to the unmasking of harmful recessive alleles on the unpaired chromosome segment whose partner has been deleted, or to genetic imbalances in the genome, or both, is uncertain.

The presence of a deficiency can be recognized cytologically in a number of ways:

1. from karyotype analysis showing the mismatched pair of chromosomes, one shorter than the other;

2. from changes or differences in banding patterns in giant polytene chromosomes of *Drosophila* and other dipteran insects when homologous chromosomes are compared in larval cells, or when banded chromosomes in a human karyotype are compared; and

3. from paired chromosomes in the pachynema stage of meiotic prophase, as one chromosome segment loops out because its partner has a deleted segment; or from similar conformations in polytene chromosomes, or in heteroduplex DNA photographed using the electron microscope (Fig. 11.6).

Figure 11.5 Group B chromosomes from a patient with *cri du chat* syndrome, showing partial deletion of the short arm of chromosome 5.

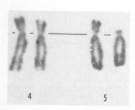

Deletion of all or part of a single gene can be detected genetically by the appearance of the recessive phenotype in a heterozygote, whose recessive allele has been unmasked when the dominant allele has been deleted entirely or in sufficient amount to be nonfunctional. This was a standard method in searching for mutant alleles in earlier years. Organisms would be irradiated to induce chromosome breaks and deletions, and recessives which were found in the irradiated wild type strains would then be exam-

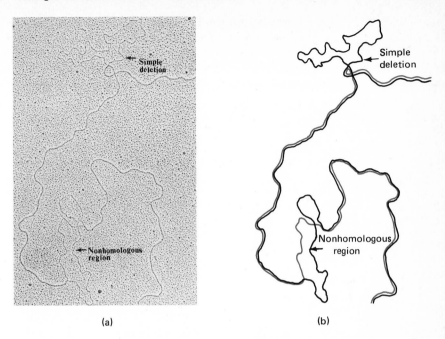

(a)   (b)

Figure 11.6 Heteroduplex DNA from annealed single strands of two phage λ strains, one of which carried a simple deletion plus a second deleted region into which a short piece of nonhomologous DNA had been incorporated instead of its own much longer sequence. (a) Electron micrograph, and (b) interpretative drawing showing that only one loop of single-stranded (unpaired) DNA occurs in the simple deletion site, but two unmatched single strands loop out in the second altered site. (Courtesy of B. Westmoreland and H. Ris, from Westmoreland, B. *et al.* 1969. *Science* **163**:1343.)

ined in detail to locate the expressed recessive allele. This was a particularly valuable approach in *Drosophila*, since the giant polytene chromosomes could be examined to find the deleted band(s) and locate the gene in that chromosome at that band (Fig. 11.7). The search was made easier because of the looped-out, unpaired segment where the deletion occurred. Through comparisons among a number of deletion mutants, many of which contained large, overlapping deletions, it was possible to fill in the details of *Drosophila* chromosome maps with more certainty. Larger deletions are more likely to occur than specific losses of one gene or one band at a time within a chromosome region. The method of **mapping by overlapping deletions**, originally developed for *Drosophila* polytene chromosomes, was extended to a standard procedure in fine structure mapping of single genes in phages and bacteria as discussed in Chapter 6. Crosses between individ-

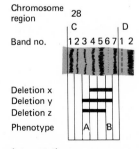

Figure 11.7 Localization of a gene to a particular band of *Drosophila melanogaster* polytene chromosome by deletion mapping. Recessive phenotype A is expressed when heterozygous with Deletion z but not with Deletion x, and recessive phenotype B is expressed when heterozygous with Deletion x but not z; both A and B recessive phenotypes are expressed when heterozygous with Deletion y. Such expression of the recessive phenotype in a deletion heterozygote is termed **pseudodominance**.

uals with different overlapping deletions produce only mutant progeny, whereas parents with different nonoverlapping deletions can complement each other's deficiencies and produce recombinants with intact genes derived partly from one and partly from the other parent.

11.4   Duplications

Duplications are repeats of chromosome segments or genes. They affect the organism in a variety of ways, ranging from negligible to considerable, and may be lethal if there is a very large amount of repeated chromosomal material. The primary evidence for duplicated genes came from polytene chromosome studies in *Drosophila*, where repeated band patterns indicated repeated genes or gene segments. These may be tandem repeats, such as ABCABC, or reverse repeats, such as ABCCBA. Although duplications have usually been found on the same chromosome and rather close together, because they are easier to spot, other repeats may be present in different chromosomes. Breakage and rejoining in the same chromosome, or insertion into another chromosome after breaking and rejoining has occurred, are often the causes for duplicated chromosome segments.

Through **unequal crossing over**, in which breakage and rejoining is not precise when nonsister chromatids exchange segments, one chromatid may acquire two copies of a gene while its nonsister has none (Fig. 11.8). A duplication and a deletion have therefore appeared by unequal crossing over. The first case of presumed unequal crossing over was analyzed in Bar-eyed *Drosophila* females in the 1930s. Both Alfred Sturtevant and Calvin Bridges, from T. H. Morgan's group at Columbia University, contributed the cytogenetic observations for females having one, two, and three copies of this X-linked dominant allele in one chromosome. The Bar-eye phenotype varies according to the number of duplicate genes in the cell and the number of copies on each chromosome. For example, when there are two gene copies on each X chromosome, there are more eye facets (68) than in females with 3 duplicates on one chromosome and a single copy on the homologous X chro-

Figure 11.8 Origin of (a) Bar and (b) ultrabar through unequal crossing over in *Drosophila*. The locus is shown as a box on the X chromosome. Recombination of the outside markers +/f and +/fu in the Bar × Bar cross giving rise to ultrabar and wild type segregants provides evidence in support of crossing over as the source of B and B^u mutations.

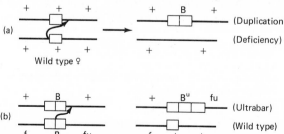

mosome (45 facets). Wild type females have almost 800 facets per eye. This is one of the examples of a **position effect**, that is, a phenomenon through which the degree of expression of a given gene or genes is modified in relation to their physical location within the genome.

Duplications of genetic material that normally occurs in one copy, such as we have been discussing, are difficult to detect cytologically or genetically in most organisms. There does exist in eukaryotes a relatively large amount of repetitious DNA, but this material is not usually the focus of duplication studies. However, we should realize that duplicates or many copies of certain genes occur normally in the nucleus. Hundreds or thousands of copies of rRNA genes, tRNA genes, and histone genes have been found in eukaryotic genomes. These repeated sequences of genetic information can be identified by methods we discussed in Chapter 7. Renaturation kinetics, molecular and *in situ* hybridizations, and other techniques identify the existence of repetitious DNA and its location in the genome.

The origin of duplications of single-copy genes or of repetitious DNA is uncertain in general. It is unlikely that all duplications have arisen by unequal crossing over, although the process certainly could have contributed to any number of duplications in the same way that Bar-eye duplications arose in *Drosophila*. Whatever the mode of origin, duplications of single-copy genes are believed to be of evolutionary significance because each copy could undergo different mutations, at random, and ultimately diverge to become quite separate genes with different gene products. The increase in gene numbers during eukaryotic evolution may be due in some measure to identical duplications diverging to become independent and different genes.

11.5   Inversions

An **inversion** is a structural change in which a segment of a chromosome is cut out and then reinserted in an orientation which is 180° different from the original sequence. If the original sequence was *abcdefgh* and breaks occurred between *b* and *c* and *f* and *g*, the inverted chromosome would have the new sequence *abfedcgh*. There is usually no loss of genetic material.

Inversions can be detected genetically by altered linkage relations between genes within the inverted segments and flanking genes on both sides of the inversion. Since recombination frequency reflects the distances between genes, any alteration in their distances will show up in altered recombination percentages and different map units of distance when compared with the standard strains.

Cytological detection of an inversion can be accomplished through examination of chromosomes in meiosis, or from comparisons between banded chromosomes in polytene nuclei or in human and other species karyotypes after staining to show bands. In meiotic cells the inversion can be seen in heterozygotes for the inverted segment, whereas karyotype analysis of somatic chromosomes can be carried out for either homozygotes or heterozygotes in comparison with standard banding patterns.

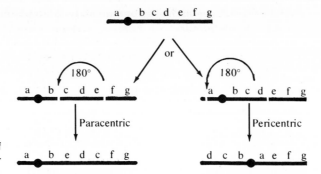

Figure 11.9 Origin of paracentric and pericentric inversions.

Inversion heterozygotes are of two general types, depending on whether the centromere is or is not included in the inverted segment. In **paracentric inversions**, the centromere occurs outside the inverted segment and is not included in the altered sequence; in **pericentric inversions**, the centromere is contained within the inverted segment (Fig. 11.9). The characteristic meiotic configuration can be seen in either paracentric or pericentric inversion heterozygotes during the pachynema stage of prophase I. During synapsis, pairing between homologous regions takes place gene for gene as usual. Since the gene order is different in the inverted and noninverted chromosomes of a pair, a characteristic *loop* develops at the inversion region (Fig. 11.10). The relative size of the loop is one indication of the extent of the inversion which is present.

Crossing over within the inverted region leads to aberrant chromatids. Depending on the site of the crossover and of other crossovers occurring within and around the inverted region, chromatids may be produced with two centromeres (dicentric) or with no centromere (acentric). Even if pachytene nuclei cannot be studied, meiotic cells in metaphase or anaphase of

Figure 11.10 Pachytene nucleus from corn (*Zea mays*) meiocyte heterozygous for an inversion in chromosome 2. (a) Inversion loop. (Courtesy of M. M. Rhoades), and (b) interpretive drawing of the inverted and noninverted chromosomes and their alignment after pairing in pachynema.

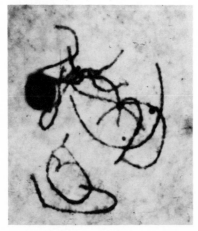

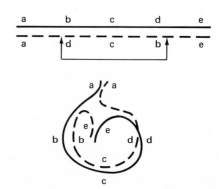

(a)   (b)

the first or the second divisions may have chromosome bridge and fragment formation which can be seen and related to crossing over events in prophase I (Fig. 11.11). Whether or not these bridge and fragment aberrations persist after metaphase I, the usual results of crossing over in inversion heterozygotes are gametes or spores which have deficiencies and duplications of chromosome segments. For this reason, inversion heterozygotes are usually partially sterile, since genetically aberrant gametes or spores often are dysfunctional.

The actual fate of acentric and dicentric chromosomes, and of cells containing these aberrations, may vary from one species to another. For example, in corn the dicentric chromosome usually breaks before metaphase I so that spores are formed with deficiencies and duplications. These give rise to inviable pollen and to partial sterility in the inversion heterozygote. In *Drosophila*, however, the aberrant chromosomes often are not included in the functional egg nucleus because of the way in which the egg and the three polar bodies form. The usual result is formation only of noncrossover egg cells (Fig. 11.12). It is this particular set of events which allows the use in genetic studies of females with heterozygous inversions, when only noncrossover gametes are required for an analysis. Crossing over does take place, but recombinant egg cells are not produced. The practical effect, therefore, is suppression of crossover eggs, and almost exclusive transmission of the noncrossover chromosome. We described such a system in the *ClB* test for mutation detection in *Drosophila* (see Section 10.2). The crossover suppressor (*C*) was an inversion which led to transmission of noncrossover *ClB* chromosomes to the progeny, since crossover chromosomes generally are not included in the *Drosophila* egg cell formed at meiosis.

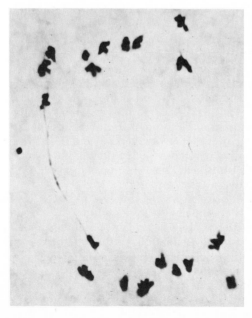

Figure 11.11 Chromosome bridge between disjoining parts of a dicentric chromosome during anaphase I of meiosis in corn. An acentric fragment lies next to the bridge. (Courtesy of M. M. Rhoades)

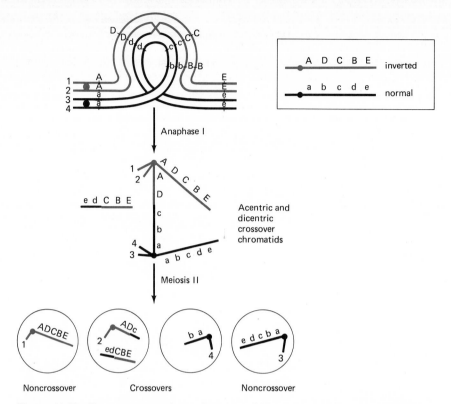

Figure 11.12 Consequences of crossing over within a paracentric inverted region in an inversion heterozygote. Gametes with crossover chromosomes have deletions or duplications, but noncrossover gametes have a complete set of the genes involved.

Karyotype analysis from banded chromosome complements in primate species has revealed the apparent existence of a number of paracentric and pericentric inversions which distinguish human chromosomes from those of the chimpanzee and other great apes, which are our closest living relatives (Fig. 11.13). The chromosomes are relatively similar except for the inversions and the chromosome number. Apparently, two of the short acrocentric chromosomes in the ape genome have fused to become the large, metacentric chromosome 2 in the human complement. Comparisons of the relative lengths of these chromosomes and of their banding pattern have led to this interpretation.

Similarities in karyotypes are matched by similarities in the protein products of a number of genes which have been analyzed. The amino acid compositions of human and ape proteins, including globins, some enzymes, and other gene products, are either identical or virtually identical. Since the protein is a reflection of nucleotide sequence in DNA, we can see that the higher primates are genetically very closely related, and the karyotype similarities provide another line of evidence in support of this conclusion. We will have more to say on this general subject in Chapter 16.

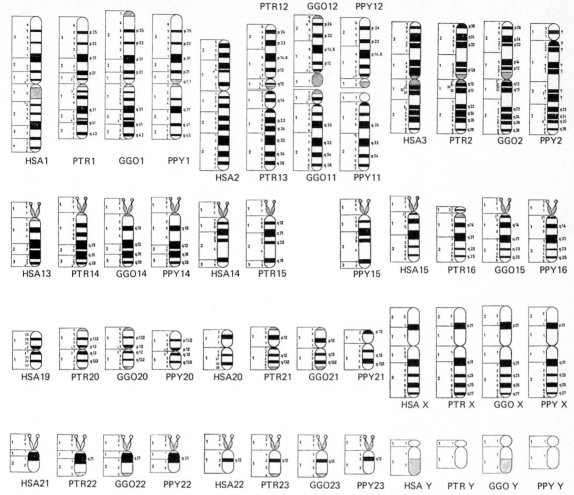

Figure 11.13 Diagrammatic representation of chromosome bands of selected chromosomes of human beings (HSA, *Homo sapiens*) and the chimpanzee (PTR, *Pan troglodytes*), gorilla (GGO, *Gorilla gorilla*), and orangutan (PPY, *Pongo pygmaeus*). The chromosomes have been arranged to show the similarities in banding pattern: solid bands are positive Q or G bands, and cross-hatched areas depict variable bands. Notice that human chromosome 2 is closely matched by two acrocentrics in all three great ape species, and that some chromosomes are astonishingly similar in all four species. (From *Paris Conference (1971), Supplement (1975); Standardization in Human Cytogenetics.* Birth Defects: Original Article Series 11, No. 9, 1975. New York: The National Foundation.)

11.6   Translocations

A **translocation** is the result of a transfer of part of one chromosome to another, nonhomologous chromosome. If the transfer involves only the attachment of part of one chromosome to an intact nonhomologue, this is called a **simple translocation**. If nonhomologous chromosomes exchange

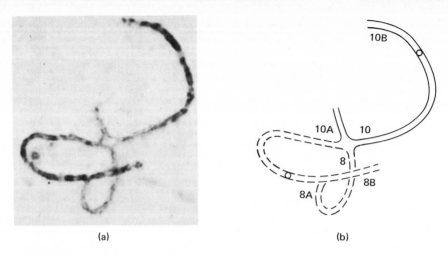

(a)   (b)

Figure 11.14 Pairing in pachytene nucleus of corn (*Zea mays*) heterozygous for a reciprocal translocation involving chromosomes 8 and 10. (a) Photograph showing two-by-two pairing within the complex of four chromosomes; and (b) interpretive drawing of the nontranslocated chromosomes 8 and 10 and the translocated 8A/10B and 8B/10A chromosomes. (Photograph courtesy of M. M. Rhoades)

Figure 11.15 Circle of fourteen chromosomes in *Oenothera*, the evening primrose. All seven pairs of chromosomes have undergone reciprocal translocations during evolution, and most wild *Oenothera* species are translocation heterozygotes.

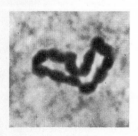

segments, this is called a **reciprocal translocation**. In either case, genes in one linkage group are transferred to another linkage group. The genetic identification of simple and reciprocal translocations involved the discovery that linked genes become independently assorting, while other independently assorting genes become linked as a direct consequence of the redistribution of chromosome segments.

Translocations require breakage and rejoining of chromosome segments, just like the other three classes of chromosome aberrations we have discussed. Like these, too, translocations can be detected cytologically in meiotic prophase (Fig. 11.14). Since synapsis is a relatively precise pairing process, homologous parts of translocated and nontranslocated chromosomes will pair in a heterozygote and produce complexes of chromosomes which can be identified easily by microscopy. Translocation configurations can be identified in pachynema as "cross-shaped" figures, and in diplonema, diakinesis, or metaphase I as groups of chromosomes in chains or rings (Fig. 11.15).

Different patterns of chromatid and gene segregation occur in translocation heterozygotes depending on the occurrence of crossing over, the location of the crossovers, and the orientation of the translocation chromosome complex on the equatorial plate at metaphase I of meiosis (Fig. 11.16). If a ring of chromosomes is twisted so that both translocated chromosomes move to one pole and both normal chromosomes go to the opposite pole (**alternate segregation**), functional gametes or spores will be produced, since each will have a full set of genes. If, however, one translocated and one normal chromosome move to the same pole at each end of the anaphase I cell (**adjacent segregation**), deficiencies and duplications will be present and the meiotic products will be nonfunctional. Adjacent segregation is

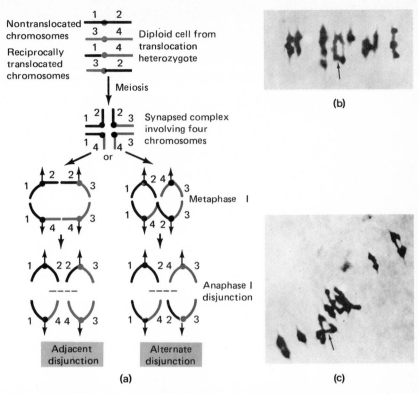

Figure 11.16 Meiosis in a translocation heterozygote. (a) Diagrammatic illustration of the consequences of the two alignments at metaphase I, producing adjacent or alternate disjunction at anaphase I. Chromosome arms are numbered, showing that deficiencies and duplications arise by adjacent but not by alternate disjunction. (b) Alignment of a ring of four chromosomes at metaphase I in corn will lead to adjacent disjunction, while (c) the "figure-8" alignment leads to alternate disjunction at anaphase I. (Photographs courtesy of M. M. Rhoades)

responsible for partial sterility in translocation heterozygotes. If the aberrant gametes or spores do participate in reproduction, they will give rise to inviable zygotes or to aberrant individuals. The reduced frequency of viable offspring in crosses involving a translocation heterozygote can be understood in relation to these processes of crossing over and chromatid segregation at meiosis. Translocation homozygotes, on the other hand, would experience no difficulties of this kind, since their chromosomes only pair two-by-two, ensuring that meiosis will be normal and give rise to functional gametes.

Translocations can be identified in human karyotypes if a simple translocation is present or if a reciprocal translocation has involved unequal lengths of chromosome segments. In either case, one or more unpaired chromosomes can be seen. About 2 or 3% of patients with Down syndrome (formerly called mongolism) have a translocated chromosome which contains parts of chromosome 21 (a G-group chromosome) and one of the three D-group chromosomes (chromosome 13, 14, or 15). Such a D/G translocated chromosome can also be found in one or more relatives of the patient, but there is no effect on the phenotype of the relative as long as there are only two copies of the genes of chromosome 21 present. Such relatives have 45 chromosomes, one of which is the D/G translocation, instead of 46 chromosomes. The second D and the second G chromosome will also be unpaired, since their homologous regions are incorporated into the larger D/G translocation chromosome. Patients with Down syndrome who have an apparently normal count of 46 chromosomes actually have three copies of chromosome 21 genes. They have a normal pair of chromosome 21, plus a third copy of these genes in their D/G translocated chromosome. The homologous D chromosome is unpaired, as is the D/G translocated chromosome (Fig. 11.17).

The vast majority of Down syndrome individuals do not have a translocated chromosome. Instead, they have a total count of 47 chromosomes, with chromosome 21 present in triplicate. These cases arise by a mistake in disjoining of homologous chromosomes during meiosis or mitosis, as we will see in a later section. Such cases do not show a familial pattern of transmission of Down syndrome. On the other hand, families with individuals having a D/G translocated chromosome do show a familial transmission pattern, since the aberrant chromosome can be transmitted through the gametes to the offspring. Years ago there was considerable confusion in interpreting familial and nonfamilial patterns of occurrence of Down syndrome. The situation became clear after human chromosome studies became possible in 1956, with the development of new methods for preparing human chromosomes for microscopic study.

All the classes of chromosomal aberrations which are due to structural changes in the genome can be identified by independent genetic and cytological criteria. The correlations between these sets of evidence strengthened the theory that genes were situated in chromosomes. These same parallels serve as well today whether studying genes at the chromosomal or the molecular level of analysis. A number of aberration types can be used directly to map genes or genetic regions to specific chromosomes and even to specific regions of a chromosome. In some species, map construction virtually depends on cytogenetic rather than purely genetic methods.

CHANGES IN CHROMOSOME NUMBER

Eukaryotic organisms have both the haploid and diploid chromosome number in nuclei of different cells in different parts of the sexual cycle. Many species have more than one or two sets of chromosomes, and the general term **euploidy** refers to the presence of any multiple of whole sets of chromosomes from the diploid number on up. Sometimes a species with more than two sets of chromosomes is a typical member of a group of related species, and sometimes only an occasional aberrant individual has extra sets of chromosomes within a population or a single species.

When there is at least one chromosome more or one less than the characteristic diploid chromosome number, it is called **aneuploidy**. In most species an aneuploid individual is different in appearance from the typical

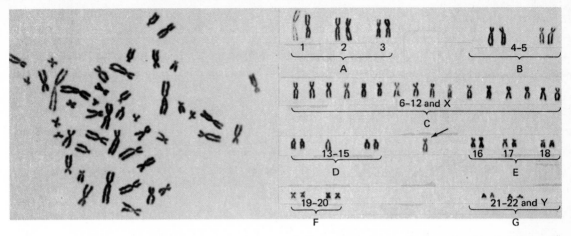

X Chromosomes occupy the second position in the C group

Figure 11.17 D/G translocation chromosome in a female patient with Down syndrome. There are three copies of chromosome 21, even though the total chromosome count is only 46. One copy of chromosome 21 genes is present in the 14/21 translocation chromosome and the other two copies exist as whole chromosomes 21. The karyotype was prepared from the metaphase spread, where only 5 chromosomes of the D group can be found in this trisomy-21 individual.

diploid individual, and aneuploids characteristically show some degree of infertility or inviability because of chromosomal imbalance.

Changes in chromosome numbers have been important in species evolution, and aberrant euploid and aneuploid types have also been important source materials for studies of genome organization and for a basic understanding of certain human disorders. We will review some of these studies in this part of the chapter.

11.7 Polyploidy

When there are more than two sets of chromosomes in a euploid individual or species, the condition is called **polyploidy** and the individual or species is a **polyploid**. The actual number of genomes which occurs is the basis for naming particular kinds of polyploids: triploids ($3n$) have three chromosome sets, tetraploids ($4n$) have four sets, hexaploids have six sets ($6n$), and so forth. About half the known species of flowering plants are polyploids, which suggests that polyploidy has been a significant factor in the evolution of higher plants. Relatively few bisexual animal species are polyploids, but a number of asexual animals and hermaphroditic species can sustain the polyploid condition.

Polyploids which have an even number of chromosomes sets (two, four, six, eight, etc.) are far more likely to be fully fertile, or at least partially fertile. The problems leading to partial sterility are usually confined to meiosis and to synapsis between homologous chromosomes in prophase I. If there are more than two homologues in the meiocyte nucleus, synapsis may involve all the homologues, although each pairing event is confined to two homologue segments in any one region (Fig. 11.18). If the synapsis events lead to associations among all the homologues, then complex meiotic chromosome configurations will be formed and abnormalities will usually arise during the meiotic divisions. A variable number of the homologous chromosomes will be distributed to the gametes, and chromosomal imbalance may cause inviability of the gametes or inviability of a zygote produced by fusions between gametes with unbalanced chromosome numbers.

Sterility is almost ensured when the polyploid has an uneven number of chromosome sets, such as in triploids or pentaploids, because segregation at meiosis will lead to variable numbers of each of the kinds of chromosomes in the gametes. Since there is some probability in tetraploids and other polyploids with an even number of genomes that an equal distribution of chromosomes may take place at meiosis to produce some gametes with the same number of copies of each chromosome, some fertility can usually be expected in these kinds of polyploids. For example, tetraploids can produce diploid gametes and these diploid gametes can fuse to restore the tetraploid adult stage. Triploids, on the other hand, may give rise to gametes with two copies of some chromosomes and one copy of others, and to a highly unbalanced chromosomal constitution in the gametes themselves. Since these gametes usually are not functional, triploids are sterile.

Polyploidy can arise because of a failure of meiosis in a diploid individual, which then produces diploid gametes. When diploid gametes unite, as in a self-fertilizing species, a tetraploid is produced. Such an individual or species is called an **autotetraploid**, since there are four copies of the same genome present. Any **autopolyploid** has multiple sets of a single genome. If, however, two different genomes come together when different species interbreed, and if such a hybrid becomes a polyploid when meiosis fails, it is called an **allopolyploid**. There are two copies of each of two different

Figure 11.18 Pairing is two-by-two among the three copies of the chromosome in this trivalent from a pachytene nucleus of castor bean, *Ricinus communis*. (Courtesy of G. Jelenkovic)

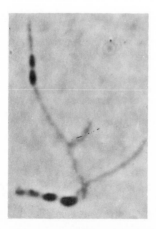
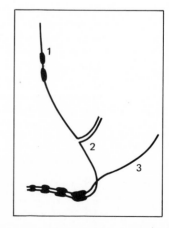

genomes in an allotetraploid, and multiple sets of two or more genomes in any allopolyploid (Fig. 11.19).

Autotetraploids generally experience problems at meiosis because of multivalent formations when more than two homologues synapse at various places along their lengths. Distorted segregations lead to inviable gametes or zygotes. Allopolyploids, on the other hand, generally are fertile because each genome has a partner genome and chromosomes generally pair in twos to produce bivalents. Little or no meiotic irregularity should result from such regular synapsis and segregation of homologues at metaphase.

There is relatively little physiological disturbance in polyploid plants because there usually are no sex chromosomes present. Most plants are hermaphroditic anyway. Even if there were some physiological difficulty, many plants can be propagated asexually, so sterile or fertile polyploids may continue to exist for many years after they have arisen. In animals, on the other hand, disturbances in the numbers of sex chromosomes and in sex chromosome—autosome balance are the usual result of breeding between polyploids or between a polyploid and a diploid. These chromosomal imbalances and the disruption of the normal sex-determining mechanisms make sexual animals very unlikely to give rise to persisting polyploids. If polyploids are produced, they usually are not perpetuated because of sexual abnormalities. These problems, of course, have little effect on asexually reproducing animals or on animals which are hermaphroditic or which have no genetic sex determination mechanism.

A number of important agricultural species are polyploid, such as wheat, cotton, tobacco, strawberries, and many of the fruit trees. In some of these species it has been possible to trace back to the probable diploid ancestors from which the polyploids arose. Wheat species are diploid, tetraploid, and

Figure 11.19 Origin of the genomes in an auto-tetraploid versus an allo-tetraploid.

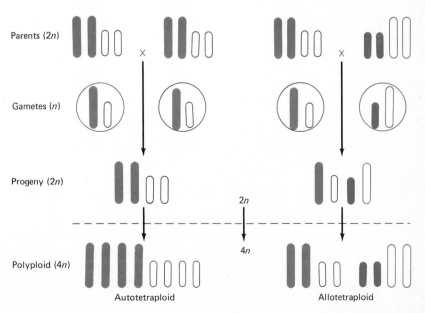

Parents (2n)

Gametes (n)

Progeny (2n)

2n

4n

Polyploid (4n)

Autotetraploid

Allotetraploid

hexaploid, but their wild ancestors in southwest Asia are diploids. Tobacco is a tetraploid species whose diploid ancestors grew in South America, and the tetraploid potato also originated from diploids in South America.

One of the great advantages of polyploidy in plants is the larger size of the plant and of its flowers, fruits, and seeds. There is better quality from the consumer standpoint and much higher yields which helps everybody from the farmer to the consumer. In the case of ornamental plants, whose desirable features usually are in foliage and flowers, polyploids are created deliberately to develop larger, more luxuriant, and more decorative plants. In many cases a sterile polyploid, such as a triploid or pentaploid, is most desirable because the flowers are larger and they last longer when there are no seeds produced in these sterile plants. A number of the prize orchids are sterile polyploids. Polyploids can be created at will by applications of colchicine, which prevents spindle formation and leads to nuclei which retain all the chromosomes within a single nuclear membrane. By adjusting the drug concentration and duration of exposure, polyploids can be made at any desired level of chromosome sets.

11.8   Aneuploidy

Aneuploids have at least one more or one less chromosome than the diploid number, but they do not have multiples of chromosome sets. If there is one extra copy of a chromosome in a diploid, the individual is a **trisomic** and the condition itself is called **trisomy** (three bodies or chromosomes of one kind); the chromosome constitution would be shown as $2n + 1$. If there are two extra copies of a particular chromosome in the diploid, it is **tetrasomic** and shown as $2n + 2$. When there is one less than a complete set of chromosomes in a diploid, it is called a **monosomic** and the condition is called **monosomy**; it is $2n - 1$. Other specific conditions of chromosome gain or loss have been found and each has been given a specific term for identification. Since trisomics and monosomics are the types encountered most often, we will discuss only these.

Aneuploids usually arise because of **nondisjunction** of homologous chromosomes at meiosis, or by nondisjunction of sister chromatids at mitosis (Fig. 11.20). The failure to disjoin or separate accurately can occur at any nuclear division, and its consequences vary according to the division in which the event occurs and the time of occurrence. Nondisjunction at meiosis gives rise to gametes with one more or one less chromosome than usual. If such gametes are viable and fuse to produce a zygote, the zygote will be trisomic or monosomic for the nondisjoined chromosome. Nondisjunction may involve any chromosomes of the complement.

We have already discussed the consequences of human aneuploidy involving the sex chromosomes (see Section 3.4). If you recall, nondisjunction can give rise to viable individuals who may be monosomic (XO, $2n - 1$), trisomic (XXX, $2n + 1$; XXY, $2n + 1$), or tetrasomic (XXXX, $2n + 2$; XXXY, $2n + 2$; XXYY, $2n + 1 + 1$), among others. Each of these conditions probably arose as the result of meiotic nondisjunction to produce a gamete containing one more or one less chromosome, or an even greater imbalance. In some

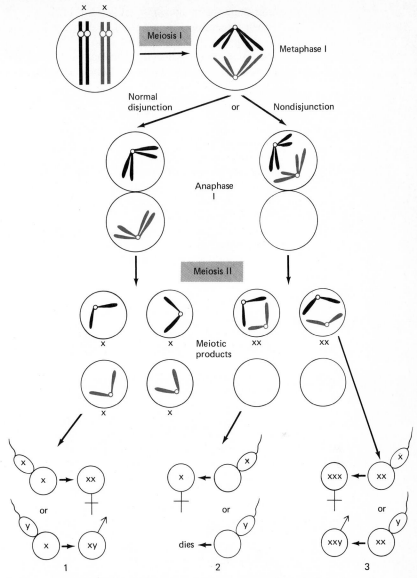

Figure 11.20 Nondisjunction at meiosis can lead to gametes with too few or too many chromosomes, and to aneuploid individuals produced by fusions involving such gametes. Nondisjunction may involve sex chromosomes as shown here, or any of the autosomes.

cases an individual may be a **sex mosaic**, having patches of tissues carrying different sex chromosome complements. These situations almost certainly are due to mitotic nondisjunction, with different cell lineages produced by chromosomally different daughter cells after the nondisjunctional event. The later the nondisjunction, the smaller the patches of aberrant tissue, since fewer divisions and fewer descendant cells would be produced late in development.

Autosomal aneuploidy in human beings has been described for several specific chromosomes, but the most common is **trisomy-21** in which chromosome 21 is present in three copies (Fig. 11.21). Such an individual has 47 chromosomes, and shows the clinical symptoms of Down syndrome. Other trisomies either are lethal early in development or in childhood. No cases of monosomy have been reported, except for monosomy of the X chromosome in Turner females, who are XO in sex chromosome constitution. Almost no species can tolerate monosomy and produce a viable individual with a missing chromosome. There is a serious genetic imbalance, and almost certainly a number of harmful recessive alleles would be expressed on the one remaining chromosome of a pair in a diploid species. An extra chromosome is better tolerated by a diploid species if it is relatively small and, presumably, carries fewer genes. But there is considerable variation from species to species.

Trisomy-21 leads to the nonfamilial pattern of Down syndrome occurrence in human beings. The risk of a woman giving birth to a child with this disorder increases with increasing age of the mother (Fig. 11.22). This pre-

Figure 11.21 Aneuploid chromosome complement of a female patient with trisomy-21, or Down syndrome. There are five G-group chromosomes instead of four, and a karyotype is not really necessary to see the chromosomal imbalance in this case of 2n + 1 aneuploidy. (Courtesy of T. R. Tegenkamp)

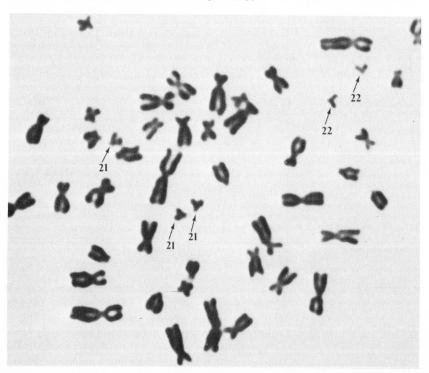

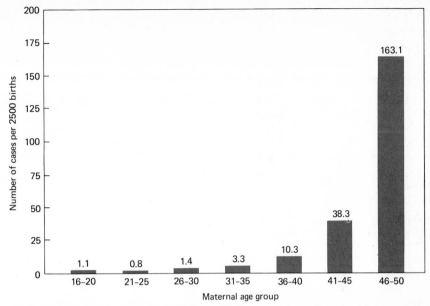

Figure 11.22   The frequency of children with Down syndrome born to older women is considerably higher than for women in the younger age groups. There is particularly high risk for women in the 46–50 age group.

sumably is due at least in part to the increasing age of the oocyte, which was produced long before the woman herself was born. As she ages, the oocytes encounter a variety of changing internal environments. These physiological factors may be responsible for higher probability of meiotic nondisjunction when the oocyte matures.

Since trisomy-21 is an autosomal disorder, it occurs equally often in both sexes. It is characterized by a number of physical abnormalities as well as mental retardation, which may be very severe in some cases. The average life expectancy has been lengthened with improved medical care, but few individuals survive into their twenties.

If an older woman wishes to know whether her pregnancy will lead to the birth of a baby with Down syndrome, she may be informed specifically after **amniocentesis** (Fig. 11.23). After a sample of amniotic fluid has been removed by the physician, the fetal cells which are shed normally into this fluid can be examined. The presence of an extra chromosome 21 in a nucleus which has 47 chromosomes is direct evidence that the child will be born with the disorder. The prospective parents may then make preparations for this birth, or elect to have the fetus aborted. The decision is theirs alone, once they have been apprised of the situation.

The incidence of aneuploidy in human births is relatively high (Table 11.1). Some aneuploidies are lethal early in life, such as trisomy for chromosomes 13 or 18. Some aneuploidies have not been observed so far, but may be found as more studies are performed. Down syndrome was the first reported autosomal aneuploidy in human beings, in 1959. One reason for this rela-

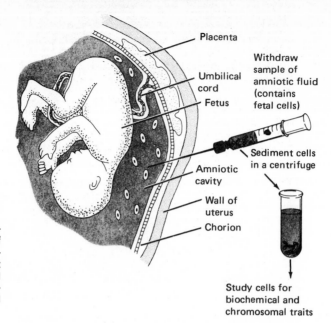

Placenta

Withdraw
sample of
amniotic fluid
(contains
fetal cells)

Umbilical
cord

Fetus

Sediment cells
in a centrifuge

Amniotic
cavity

Wall of
uterus

Chorion

Study cells for
biochemical and
chromosomal traits

Figure 11.23 Amniocentesis. A sample of amniotic fluid is withdrawn from the pregnant woman and is processed for cytological and biochemical analysis of fetal traits.

tively late information on human chromosomes and karyotypes is that suitable preparations were not achieved until Tijo and Levan's technique was applied, beginning in 1956.

11.9 Centric Fusion

Aneuploidy may also arise without gain or loss of chromatin by the process of **centric fusion**, in which two smaller chromosomes fuse to form one larger one. Usually, two smaller acrocentrics fuse to produce a large metacentric or submetacentric chromosome (Fig. 11.24).

It was originally believed that one of the two centromeres was lost during centric fusion, and that the larger derivative had only a single centromere. Electron microscopy revealed, however, that there are two centromere structures contained in the single centromere region of chromosomes known to be derived by centric fusion. This had been suspected by some investigators on the basis of their observations of various invertebrate species, since in some populations individuals had different chromosome *numbers* but they had the same number of chromosome *arms* in a genome. It has since been found that chromosomes which do undergo centric fusion, reducing the chromosome number but not the number of arms, may also dissociate into acrocentrics, increasing the chromosome number in such individuals but leaving the number of chromosome arms unchanged. There must be centromere retention to explain these reversible changes, since new centromeres cannot be created from other parts of a chromosome. Neither the mechanism for centric fusion nor the mechanism for dissociation is known.

Table 11.1

Frequency of selected aneuploidies in humans

Aneuploidy	Frequency of live-born
Sex chromosome anomalies	
Turner syndrome (45,X)	1/2500 females
Triplo-X (47,XXX)	1/1250 females
Tetra-X (48,XXXX)	very low (about 20 cases known)
Klinefelter syndrome (all types)	1/800 males
XYY male	1/900 males
Autosomal anomalies	
Trisomy 13	1/4,000-10,000
Trisomy 18	1/8,000
Trisomy 21	1/700

Source: de Grouchy, J., and C. Turleau. 1977. *Clinical Atlas of Human Chromosomes.*
New York: John Wiley & Sons.

Centric fusion has played an important role in genome evolution in many animal groups and in some of the flowering plants (Fig. 11.25). The usual trend is toward reduction in chromosome number as species groups evolve, and retention of most of the genome in structurally rearranged chromosomes of the complement. In *Drosophila*, the reduction from a haploid complement of 6 to species with only 3 chromosomes in a set has been examined in some detail from polytene chromosome band comparisons. From these detailed comparisons, it was clear that particular metacentric chromosomes had been derived from centric fusion of particular acrocentrics during evolution, since matching band patterns provided unmistakable evidence of these events.

The evolutionary significance of aneuploidy by centric fusion lies in the alterations in production of new genotype combinations and in recombination frequencies. In species with more chromosomes (linkage groups), independent assortment accounts for a high proportion of new genotype combinations in populations. If the same genes are present in fewer chromosomes, crossing over will produce recombinations for these genes. Fewer

Figure 11.24 Centric fusion may lead to one larger metacentric or submetacentric chromosome from two smaller acrocentrics. Both centromeres usually are retained in a common centromere region in the fusion chromosome product.

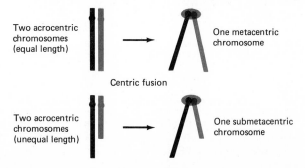

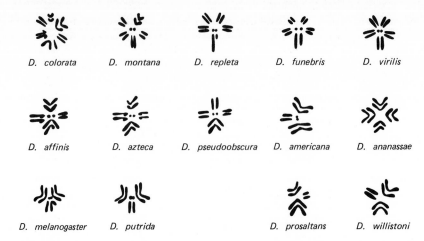

Figure 11.25 Chromosome complements of fourteen *Drosophila* species showing the aneuploid series of n = 6 to n = 3, which has arisen through centric fusions and other events in evolution of the group. The X and Y chromosomes of these male genomes are shown at the bottom of each drawing.

new genotype combinations will arise by crossing over than by independent assortment, so species with fewer chromosomes tend to be less variable than related species with the same genes in more chromosomes. Under some environmental conditions, there are advantages for low genetic variability. Centric fusions, if they occur, would be retained in such populations because of the selective advantages of the slower release of inherent genetic variability. We will discuss these phenomena in more detail in Chapter 16.

MOLECULAR CYTOGENETICS

We have described a number of molecular cytogenetic studies in earlier chapters, as well as in this chapter. The principles of cytogenetics have been extended to studies of chromosomal and genic DNA, and very detailed information has been obtained because of the high resolution achieved by new techniques. Among the most powerful of these methods is molecular hybridization and the derivative technique of *in situ* hybridization, combined with direct observations of the DNA or chromosomes by electron or light microscopy. Through these approaches it has been possible to analyze genetic material which has not undergone mutation. In these cases, conventional genetic analysis is difficult or impossible, but cytogenetic analysis can be accomplished and related back to the genome.

11.10   Organization of rRNA Repeated Genes

One of the best examples of genome analysis using molecular cytogenetic methods is provided by studies of rDNA, the part of the genome coded for rRNA. The only known mutant is the anucleolate *Xenopus* strain, which provided the basis for the discovery that the nucleolar organizing region was the site of rRNA genes, as we discussed in Section 8.5. Through molecular hybridization and *in situ* hybridization in *Xenopus* and other species, rDNA was localized in the genome and the number of repeated copies of the rRNA gene was calculated. How are the rRNA genes arranged in the repetitious DNA at the nucleolar organizing region? Are they in tandem, one next to the other? Are there regions of DNA in between rRNA gene repeats? Is the rRNA gene a continuous sequence of coded information for rRNA? These questions were answered by molecular studies, some of which will be highlighted here.

The first indication that rDNA genes were arranged in tandem but were separated by noncoding **DNA "spacers"** came from electron microscopic observations by Oscar Miller and co-workers (Fig. 11.26). Stunning photo-

Figure 11.26 Electron micrograph of active ribosomal DNA (rDNA, or rRNA genes) in the process of transcribing rRNA, which appear here as fine fibrils in each arrow-shaped grouping. The tandemly repeated rRNA genes in this newt oocyte nucleus are separated by nontranscribing spacer DNA regions. (Courtesy of O. L. Miller, Jr., from Miller, O. L., Jr., and B. Beatty. 1969. *J. Cell Physiol.* **74**, Suppl. 1:225.)

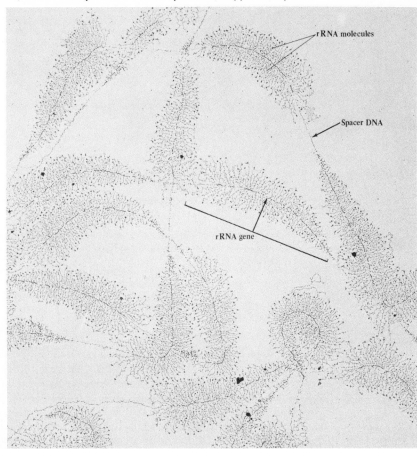

rRNA molecules

Spacer DNA

rRNA gene

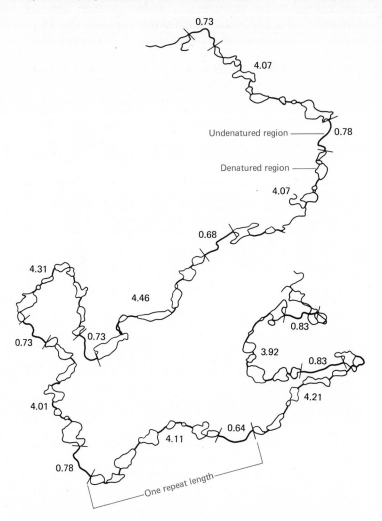

Figure 11.27 Tracing of an electron micrograph of one partly denatured segment of amplified rDNA from the toad *Xenopus mulleri*. This piece is 42 μm long and contains 8 complete repeats of the sequence coding for 40S pre-rRNA. Undenatured regions appear as solid, thicker lines, and denatured regions appear as open loops. Each repeat gene sequence contains one mainly denatured region (3.92–4.46 μm long) and one mainly undenatured region (0.64–0.83 μm long). (From Brown, D. D., P. C. Wensink, and E. Jordan. 1972. *J. Mol. Biol.* **63**:57, Plate IIb.)

graphs were obtained of isolated rDNA in the process of actively transcribing rRNA. The DNA undergoing transcription was identified by the presence of feathery collections of nascent rRNA molecules. Many transcripts were being made at the same time from each gene sequence, and the direction of transcription was evident from the relative sizes of the rRNA molecules; all the rRNA genes were transcribing in the same direction, which meant that the same template strand of the DNA duplex was being copied in each gene. The measured length of a rDNA gene corresponded to the length which was predicted from earlier studies of the length of the rRNA transcript as 40S in amphibia (45S in mammalian species).

The nontranscribing DNA in between transcribing rDNA genes in the repetitious DNA preparation was called "spacer" DNA by Miller. Its function is still a mystery, but spacer DNA is characteristic of other kinds of repetitious DNAs which have been studied. Apparently it has no coding function since it is not transcribed.

Donald Brown and others have analyzed the organization of DNA nucleotides in rDNA of *Xenopus*, using **denaturation mapping** and **heteroduplex mapping** by electron microscopy. Ross Inman had shown that virus DNA could be mapped according to controlled denaturation which distinguished A+T-rich regions from G+C-rich regions, since A+T regions were less stable and underwent strand separation much more quickly than G-C base-paired regions. You will recall that only two hydrogen bonds are involved in A-T pairs, while there are three hydrogen bonds per G-C pair, making the latter more stable to denaturing conditions. Using heat or alkali to induce denaturation in *Xenopus* rDNA, Brown and co-workers showed that a segment of repetitious rDNA contained alternating denatured and undenatured regions (Fig. 11.27). Measurements of these regions were made, and it was found that denatured regions corresponded to "spacer" DNA, while intact duplex regions corresponded to the rDNA gene segments. The gene measured about 0.8 μm and the spacer measured about 4 μm in length, which was predicted from comparisons with Miller's photographs and from other molecular studies. The spacers were therefore shown to be A+T-rich regions in between rDNA genes having much higher G+C content.

Do different species of *Xenopus* have the same nucleotide sequences in their rDNA? It was expected that the coding regions would be the same since rRNAs of different species were essentially identical or similar in base composition. When rDNAs from *Xenopus laevis* and *X. mulleri* were melted and allowed to reassociate to form heteroduplexes, the differences and similarities of these two species could be compared directly from electron micrographs of the hybrid duplex molecules (Fig. 11.28). Surprisingly, it was found that they had substantially different nucleotide sequences in spacers between repeated genes, and different nucleotide sequences in the transcribed spacer within the rDNA gene itself. Nonhomology was indicated by separated strands forming a loop or bubble, whereas homologous DNAs paired at their complementary bases and produced a thicker, duplex segment in the heteroduplex molecule.

Nucleotide sequence homologies can therefore be established by heteroduplex mapping. This method has revealed that spacer DNA between and within genes in repeated sequences usually is nonhomologous, even in very closely related species. Coding sequences, on the other hand, are very similar. In fact, repetitious DNA tends to be highly conserved in evolution. Good base-pairing can be demonstrated between sequences for repeated 5S rRNA genes and for repeated histone genes in most eukaryotic species. These genes seem to have undergone very little change over evolutionary time. Why do spacer sequences change rapidly and substantially while coding sequences for repeated genes undergo little or no change in these same

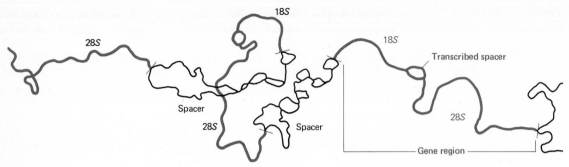

Figure 11.28 Tracing of an electron micrograph of heteroduplex DNA consisting of one strand of rDNA from *Xenopus laevis* and one from *X. mulleri*. The rRNA gene regions are shown in red and the untranscribed spacer DNA between genes is shown in black. There is very good pairing (matching of DNA sequences of the two species) in the gene region specifying the 18S and 28S rRNA sequences. There is little base pair matching in the spacers between genes, as evident from the many loops present. The rRNA sequence has been preserved in evolution of these species, but the spacer DNA has diverged almost completely *in the same time*. (From "The Isolation of Genes" by D. D. Brown. Copyright © 1973 by Scientific American, Inc. All rights reserved.)

genomes? We don't really have definitive answers to this fundamental question about changes in genome sequences, but the answers must be important since similar events have been found across a broad spectrum of eukaryotic groups (Box 11.1). The stability of these coding sequences of repeated genes is further reflected in the fact that we have no known mutations for such genes. They are extraordinarily stable parts of the genome, in both the short-term and long-term views of genetic modification of a species.

11.11   Genome Mapping Using Cloned DNA

It is possible to construct **recombinant DNA** molecules by splicing pieces of plasmid or phage DNA together with pieces of DNA from almost any species, including human genes, and introducing the spliced DNA into a suitable strain of *E. coli*. The introduced recombinant plasmid or phage DNA replicates as the cells increase in numbers, and clones of such DNA can be collected in bacterial descendants of the original cell which received the recombinant DNA molecule. Such **cloned DNA**, resident in a bacterial strain, can then be used to analyze the genes from some species which have been spliced into the plasmid or phage molecule (Fig. 11.29).

Known genes can be cloned in this way, as well as genes which have unknown function and composition and which can be analyzed using such cloned DNA populations. For example, it is possible to purify histone mRNA or hemoglobin mRNA from cells with large amounts of these identifiable molecules, and make an exact duplex DNA copy using *reverse transcriptase* to obtain the first DNA strand and *DNA polymerase* to make the second, complementary strand of the gene. Such **copied DNA (cDNA)** can

Box 11.1
R-LOOP MAPPING

Through R-loop analysis first described by Thomas, White, and Davis (1976. *Proc. Nat. Acad. Sci. U.S.* 73:2294.) it is possible to map regions of the genome and deduce sequence organization. The method includes direct visualization of RNA–DNA hybrids in the electron microscope. RNA–DNA hybrids are more stable than the corresponding DNA–DNA duplexes, so that under certain incubation conditions RNA–DNA hybrids can form at regions of partial denaturation of the DNA duplex, as shown in (a). When such incubation is performed, a single-stranded R-loop is formed in the DNA region complementary to the added RNA, having been displaced on formation of the RNA–DNA double-stranded segment just opposite the loop.

In the electron micrograph shown in (b) and the interpretive drawing shown in (c), 28S and 18S rRNA were added to duplex rDNA from *Drosophila melanogaster*. Each rRNA has hybridized to the complementary rDNA template strand, leading to looping out of displaced single stranded DNA (the anticoding strand of rDNA). These molecules can be measured precisely to show the sequence organization of 28S and 18S coding regions in rDNA, and the length and number of spacers (Sp 1, Sp 2) for which there is no mature rRNA transcript. (Photograph and drawing from Wellauer, P.K., and I.B. Dawid. 1977. *Cell* 10:193.)

R-loop mapping has proven useful in many kinds of studies involving cloned DNA and in studies of RNA processing. The R-loop pattern seen in β-globin DNA preparations to which pre-mRNA and mRNA of globin had been added clearly showed that pre-mRNA was transcribed from the entire DNA region and was later processed to a spliced mRNA complementary only to specific, identified parts of the β-globin gene sequence.

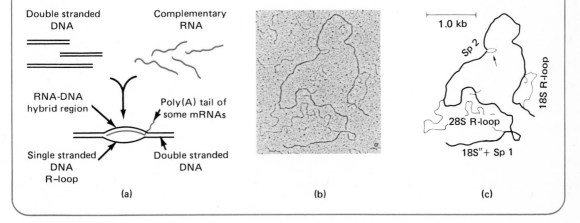

(a)   (b)   (c)

then be spliced to plasmid or phage DNA and be introduced into *E. coli* for subsequent studies. Similarly, the genome of some species can be chopped up into small fragments by a combination of restriction endonuclease treatments, and all these fragments can be spliced separately into different plasmids and be introduced into different cells to form a collection of cloned DNAs for later analysis. Cloned DNA is *amplified* DNA, since single genes or DNA segments spliced into a plasmid will be replicated in each *E. coli* cell and will be replicated countless times as this cell increases to form a popu-

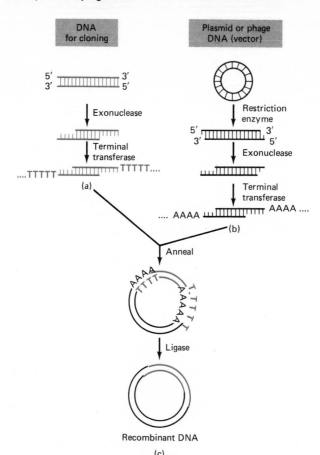

Figure 11.29   Recombinant DNA. (a) DNA fragments to be cloned are trimmed by 5'→3' exonuclease action and a poly (T) sequence is added to the single-stranded "tails" by terminal transferase action. (b) The plasmid or phage DNA used as the vector, or cloning vehicle, is cut by an appropriate restriction enzyme, nibbled by 5'→3' exonuclease, and decorated with tracts of poly (A) by terminal transferase action. (c) When these DNAs are placed together, they anneal by their poly (A) and poly (T) complementary tracts to form circular molecules, which are ligated in a final step. The recombinant plasmid or phage is then taken up by the cells in culture and such systems are analyzed according to the particular experimental design applied; for example, as was shown in Fig. 6.24.

lation of cells. Large amounts of such cloned DNA will then be available for molecular studies of one gene or of small parts of a genome.

The enormous power of this method will be illustrated by one example selected from many studies of a similar nature. This example came from experiments reported by David Hogness and co-workers in studies of *Drosophila melanogaster*. Only the broad outlines of these experiments will be described, to illustrate the principles involved and the great resolving power of the method.

The *D. melanogaster* genome was fragmented by restriction enzyme treatments, and the randomly generated segments of chromosomal DNA were spliced into a particular plasmid type to produce a collection of cloned DNAs representing the whole genome. Any of the collection could be screened to identify known or unknown gene sequences, and each clone of chromosomal *Drosophila melanogaster* (**cDm**) DNA was identified by a number. Using isolated histone mRNAs, it was found that clone cDm500 contained the histone DNA that was complementary to the histone mRNAs, according to molecular hybridizations leading to DNA-RNA hybrid duplexes. By a series of molecular tests, the histone DNA was shown to consist of about 100 repeating sequences, each measuring about 4,800 base-pairs in length, with all the repeats arranged in tandem. By *in situ* hybridization, the histone repetitious DNA was localized to region 39DE of the standard polytene chromosome map for *D. melanogaster*.

How were the five histone genes arranged in these repeated sequences? Were they all in each repeated segment or in separate segments in the 100-repeat region of the chromosome? The five different kinds of histone mRNAs were isolated and purified from *Drosophila* embryos and tissue-culture cells, and each of these mRNAs was hybridized individually to histone DNA in clone cDm500. All five mRNA types hybridized to DNA in *each* repeat unit, meaning that all five histone genes were present in each repeated segment.

How were the five histone genes arranged in a repeat unit of this DNA? The ordering of the five histone genes was determined by analyzing a portion of the nucleotide sequence in each of the five regions of homology in a repeat unit, to show the kinds of amino acids that could be produced from such a sequence of codons. Since all five histone proteins were known, the nucleotides could be matched against the amino acid sequences in these proteins to identify the five genes and their arrangement in the repeat unit (Fig. 11.30).

A further item of information was obtained by DNA-RNA molecular hybridizations of the individual RNA species to separated strands of cDm500 DNA, namely, that mRNA for histones H1, H3, and H2A was transcribed from one DNA strand, while mRNA for histones H4 and H2B was transcribed from the opposite DNA strand of the repeat unit. The

Figure 11.30 Arrangements of the five histone genes within a repeat unit in *Drosophila melanogaster* (upper) and the sea urchin *Strongylocentrotus purpuratus* (lower). In *Drosophila*, H1, H3, and H2a are transcribed from one strand and histone mRNA for H4 and H2b from the other strand of the duplex DNA. In the sea urchin, all the five genes are coded in the same DNA strand. The individual genes are separated by spacer DNA of varying lengths (thin line between block arrows). (From Lifton, R. P., M. L. Goldberg, R. W. Karp, and D. S. Hogness. 1978. *Cold Spring Harbor Sympos. Quant. Biol.* **42**(1977):1047, Fig. 1).

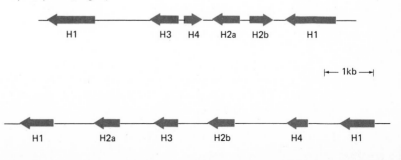

existence of coding regions on both complementary DNA strands was evident from finding two sets of hybrid duplex DNA-RNA molecules; one set of hybrid duplexes contained three homologous regions and another set of hybrid duplexes had the other two homologous regions. Independent evidence confirming this conclusion was obtained from nucleotide sequencing of portions of the DNA along each strand in the five histone gene regions of the duplex repeat unit. The DNA coding sequences were correlated with mRNA sequences of all five types, and with amino acid compositions of the five histone proteins.

In this one example, the incredibly high resolving power of molecular genetic analysis is very clear indeed. Using collections of cloned DNA, virtually any part of the genome can be analyzed, whether it includes single-copy genes or repeated gene sequences. With cloned DNA it should be possible to conduct very specific studies of genome organization, gene expression, and the regulation of gene expression in the complex eukaryotic system. Remarkable progress in molecular dissection of the genome has already been made through these methods, and we can eagerly anticipate a great deal of additional important information to be forthcoming in the next few years. Using collections or libraries of cloned DNA containing all of a eukaryotic genome, what seemed almost impossible to achieve a few years ago seems to be within our grasp today.

QUESTIONS AND PROBLEMS

11.1. When plants of the two species *Primula verticillata* and *P. floribunda* are crossed they produce hybrid offspring that are vigorous but sterile.

   a. After many vegetative propagations of the hybrid primrose, a branch with fertile seeds developed. This was the origin of *Primula kewensis*. Explain the origin of this new, fertile primrose species.

   b. If the two parent species have 18 chromosomes each in their somatic cells (that is, $2n = 18$), how many bivalents can you expect in *P. kewensis* during meiosis?

11.2. *Raphanobrassica* is a hybrid derived from a cross between radish (*Raphanus*) and cabbage (*Brassica*), but it has no economic value because the plant has the roots of a cabbage and the leaves of a radish. If the hybrid has a somatic chromosome number of 36, and its cabbage parent produces gametes with 9 chromosomes, what is the haploid chromosome number in the radish parent? Can you explain the origin of the *Raphanobrassica* hybrid?

11.3. The recessive gene bent wings (*bt*) occurs on the tiny fourth chromosome of *Drosophila melanogaster*. If a fly disomic for chromosome 4 and carrying the recessive *bt* allele on both chromosomes is crossed to a fly monosomic for this chromosome but carrying the bt^+ allele, what would be the phenotypes of the F_1 and F_2 progenies?

11.4. In tomatoes a cross is made between a normal female plant trisomic for chromosome 6 and a disomic male having compound inflorescence (s/s).

    a. Assuming the gene s is located on chromosome 6, give the kinds and ratio of phenotypes in the progeny of a trisomic F_1 female testcrossed to a disomic s/s male.

    b. What would be the result of the same cross if gene s is not located on chromosome 6?

11.5. A person with Turner syndrome was found in a family. Her brother and one uncle had glucose 6-phosphate dehydrogenase (GPD) deficiency, an X-linked condition. Which X chromosome is missing in the individual with Turner syndrome?

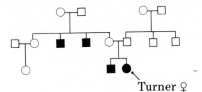

GPD deficient = shaded
GPD normal = unshaded

Turner ♀

11.6. On chromosome 2 in *Drosophila melanogaster* the normal linkage map includes purple (pr) 54.5; vestigial (vg) 67; Lobe (L) 72; arc (a) 99.2; brown (bw) 104. A cross $\dfrac{+\ \ +\ L\ +\ \ +}{pr\ vg\ +\ a\ bw}♀ \times \dfrac{pr\ vg\ +\ a\ bw}{pr\ vg\ +\ a\ bw}♂$ pro-

duced the following recombination percentages; pr-vg, 10%; vg-L, 0.2%; L-a, 1.4%; and a-bw, 5%. If the heterozygous female was an inversion heterozygote, what regions of chromosome 2 were involved in the inversion?

11.7. A corn plant homozygous for a reciprocal translocation between chromosomes 2 and 5 and for the Pr allele governing seed color was crossed with a normal pr/pr plant. The F_1 progeny were semisterile and phenotypically Pr. A testcross with the normal parent gave the following results:

              1528 semisterile Pr
               290 semisterile pr
               372 normal Pr
             1454 normal pr

How far is the Pr/pr locus from the translocation point?

11.8. Inversion heterozygosity reduces the number of recombinants recovered because there is selective elimination of products of crossing over within the inversion loop.

    a. If pairing of normal chromosomes at meiosis is represented by

diagram chromosome pairing at pachynema, without crossing over, where one chromosome has a pericentric inversion due to break points between A and B and between C and D.

    b. Diagram pairing in the inversion heterozygote in (a), with one crossover between the centromere and C.

    c. Diagram the chromosomes shown in (b) at the end of Meiosis II, and indicate which chromosomes probably would not result in viable gametes.

11.9.   Salivary chromosome preparations for *Drosophila melanogaster* are particularly useful for cytogenetic studies since these chromosomes show specific band patterns and homologous chromosomes are paired in the interphase nucleus. If bands are designated by letters on the long arm of chromosome 2, this can be represented simply in a diagram as

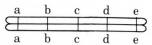

Draw a simplified diagram for paired chromosomes in which one member of the pair has

a. a large deletion

b. a large duplication

c. an inversion

d. a non-reciprocal translocation with chromosome 3

e. a reciprocal translocation with the X chromosome

11.10.   Isolation of genes *in vitro* has been achieved in various laboratories.

    a. What properties of the major ribosomal gene made it simpler to isolate?

    b. Describe the assay system which made it possible for D. D. Brown and co-workers to detect a given gene in a mixture of related DNA molecules?

    c. It is possible to introduce the gene coding for rRNA in *Xenopus* into a bacterial cell line. How can you detect the particular bacterial clones containing the *Xenopus* rRNA gene?

REFERENCES

Brown, D. D. Aug. 1973. The isolation of genes. *Sci. Amer.* **230**:20.

Bruce, E. J., and F. J. Ayala. 1978. Humans and apes are genetically very similar. *Nature* **276**:264.

Burkholder, G. D. 1975. The ultrastructure of G- and C-banded chromosomes. *Exp. Cell Res.* **90**:269.

Cohen, S. N. July 1975. The manipulation of genes. *Sci. Amer.* **233**:24.

Comings, D. E. 1978. Mechanisms of chromosome banding and implications for chromosome structure. *Ann. Rev. Genet.* **12**:25.

Crawford, R. J., P. Krieg, R. P. Harvey, D. A. Hewish, and J. R. E. Wells. 1979. Histone genes are clustered with a 15-kilobase repeat in the chicken genome. *Nature* **279**:132.

Drets, M. E., and M. W. Shaw. 1971. Specific banding patterns of human chromosomes. *Proc. Nat. Acad. Sci. U. S.* **68**:2073.

Epstein, C. J., and M. S. Golbus. 1977. Prenatal diagnosis of genetic diseases. *Amer. Sci.* **65**:703.

Evans, H. J. 1977. Some facts and fancies relating to chromosome structure in man. *Adv. Human Genet.* **8**:347.

Federoff, N. V. 1979. On spacers. *Cell* **16**:697.

Garber, E. D. 1978. Cytogenetics. In *Cell Biology, A Comprehensive Treatise*, Vol. 1 (L. Goldstein and D. M. Prescott, eds.), p. 236. New York: Academic Press.

German, J. 1970. Studying human chromosomes today. *Amer. Sci.* **58**:182.

Grobstein, C. July 1977. The recombinant-DNA debate. *Sci. Amer.* **237**:22.

Grunstein, M., and D. S. Hogness. 1975. Colony hybridization: A method for the isolation of cloned DNAs that contain a specific gene. *Proc. Nat. Acad. Sci. U. S.* **72**:3961.

Knudson, A. G., Jr., A. T. Meadows, W. W. Nichols, and R. Hill. 1976. Chromosomal deletion and retinoblastoma. *New Engl. J. Med.* **295**:1120.

Lawn, R. M., E. F. Fritsch, R. C. Parker, G. Blake, and T. Maniatis. 1978. The isolation and characterization of linked δ- and β-globin genes from a cloned library of human DNA. *Cell* **15**:1157.

Lejeune, J. R. Turpin, and M. Gauthier. 1959. Le mongolisme, premier exemple d'aberration autosomique humaine. Ann. Génét. **1**:41.

Miller, D. A. 1977. Evolution of primate chromosomes. *Science* **198**:1116.

Miller, O. L., Jr. Mar. 1973. The visualization of genes in action. *Sci. Amer.* **229**:34.

Omenn, G. S. 1978. Prenatal diagnosis of genetic disorders. *Science* **200**:952.

Orkin, S. H. 1978. The duplicated human α globin genes lie close together in cellular DNA. *Proc. Nat. Acad. Sci. U. S.* **75**:5950.

Paul, J. 1978. Gene cloning in cell biology. *Cell Biol. Internat. Repts.* **2**:311.

Phillips, R. L., and C. R. Burnham, eds. 1977. Benchmark Papers in Genetics, Vol. 6: *Cytogenetics*. Stroudsberg, Pa.: Dowden, Hutchinson, & Ross.

Rudak, E., P. A. Jacobs, and R. Yanagimachi. 1978. Direct analysis of the chromosome constitution of human spermatozoa. *Nature* **274**:911.

Schaffner, W., G. Kunz, H. Daetwyler, J. Tefford, H. O. Smith, and M. L. Birnstiel. 1978. Genes and spacers of cloned sea urchin histone DNA analyzed by sequencing. *Cell* **14**:655.

Scriver, C. R., C. Laberge, C. L. Clow, and F. C. Fraser. 1978. Genetics and medicine: An evolving relationship. *Science* **200**:946.

Shine, J., P. H. Seeburg, J. A. Martial, J. D. Baxter, and H. M. Goodman. 1977. Construction and analysis of recombinant DNA for human chorionic somatomammotropin. *Nature* **270**:494.

Swanson, C. P., T. Merz, and W. J. Young. 1967. *Cytogenetics.* Englewood Cliffs, N.J.: Prentice-Hall.

Tilghman, S. M., *et al.* 1977. Cloning specific segments of the mammalian genome: Bacteriophage λ containing mouse globin and surrounding gene sequences. *Proc. Nat. Acad. Sci. U. S.* **74**:4406.

Weatherall, D. J., and J. B. Clegg. 1979. Recent developments in the molecular genetics of human hemoglobin. *Cell* **16**:467.

Wellauer, P. K., and I. B. Dawid. 1978. Ribosomal DNA in *Drosophila melanogaster.* II. Heteroduplex mapping of cloned and uncloned rDNA. *J. Mol. Biol.* **126**:769.

Wong, V., H. K. Ma, D. Todd, M. S. Golbus, A. M. Dozy, and Y. W. Kan. 1978. Diagnosis of homozygous α-thalassemia in cultured amniotic-fluid fibroblasts. *New Engl. J. Med.* **298**:669.

Yunis, J. J., ed. 1977. *Molecular Structure of Human Chromosomes.* New York: Academic Press.

12

Extranuclear Genetics

Genes situated outside the nuclear genome may influence phenotypic expression of the cell or organism in which they occur. Extranuclear factors can be identified by unique patterns of inheritance, which differ in one or more ways from nuclear inheritance patterns. In particular, extranuclear genes often are transmitted by only one parent during sexual reproduction. Extranuclear genes segregate rapidly during mitotic divisions, whereas nuclear genes segregate during meiosis.

The principal extranuclear genes in eukaryotic cells are parts of the DNA genome in mitochondria and in chloroplasts. These organelle genomes code for rRNAs and tRNAs specific for their own translation apparatus, on which organelle-synthesized mRNA is translated into organelle-specific polypeptides. These polypeptides are parts of enzymes and membrane proteins which are essential for organelle development and for the vital processes of aerobic respiration and photosynthesis of the eukaryotic organism. While many nuclear genes control organelle traits, the organelle genes are in turn directly responsible for respiratory and photosynthetic phenotypic expressions in the whole organism and its constituent cells.

Organelle genes mutate to alternative allelic forms, and they can be mapped by genetic, molecular, and physical methods to a single linkage group which corresponds physically to a single, usually circular molecule of duplex DNA. The origin of separate organelle genomes is uncertain, but theories and speculations have been proposed.

Virus and plasmid genomes also provide extranuclear genetic information which directly influences host phenotypic expression, as well as their own inherited traits. Unlike mitochondrial or chloroplast DNAs, viral and plasmid nucleic acids may exist as free extranuclear systems in the host cell or as integrated components of the host linkage group(s).

Whether viruses and plasmids are equivalent or related systems to organelle genetic systems is unknown. They share a number of features in common, such as influence over host phenotypic expression, but they also differ in other important ways. Viruses and plasmids are dispensable, but organelle genomes are essential to host functions.

451

EXTRANUCLEAR INHERITANCE

The pattern of inheritance of extranuclear characteristics is non-Mendelian, which reflects the difference in transmission between these genes and genes on chromosomes in the nucleus of the same cells. The general criteria which describe **extranuclear inheritance**, therefore, are ones which emphasize the lack of correspondence between transmission patterns expected for genes on chromosomes and genes which are not located on chromosomes in the nucleus. The experiments are designed to *eliminate the possibility of nuclear gene inheritance*. If the nucleus can be ruled out as the location and sponsor of the inheritance pattern, the conclusion can be made that some extranuclear system is in operation and is responsible for the observed genetic phenomena.

There must, of course, be evidence showing that such extranuclear traits are indeed inherited and not simply the result of transient changes in phenotype. The principal evidence showing that such traits are inherited is that the trait persists indefinitely in populations, and is transmitted in sexual and asexual reproduction.

12.1   Extranuclear Inheritance Patterns

The nature of extranuclear inheritance can be demonstrated by the pattern of transmission from parents to progeny, and by one or more additional criteria. Although there are variations from one system to another, the basic extranuclear pattern can be demonstrated. There are various experimental tests or observations, five of which will be described briefly.

1. *Reciprocal crosses yield different progenies.* When wild type and presumptive extranuclear mutants are crossed reciprocally, each progeny may resemble only the female parent (Fig. 12.1). For example, the progeny of *poky* ♀ × wild type ♂ are *poky*, while wild type ♀ × *poky* ♂ yields wild type progeny in *Neurospora crassa*. In this example of **uniparental inheritance**, only maternal zygotes are produced. In other cases genes may be transmitted from both parents to produce biparental zygotes, or, rarely, only from the male parent to produce paternal zygotes. Whatever the nature of the progeny, reciprocal crosses give different results. By and large these differences are seen as different proportions of maternal, biparental, and paternal zygotes in different progenies, and as different overall transmission frequencies of alleles from the two parents.

    One reason for transmission mainly through the female parent is that the female gamete supplies all or most of the cytoplasm to the zygote, while the male often contributes only a nucleus. This appears to be the case in *Neurospora*, and in many plants and animals, which produce a large egg and a relatively small sperm. This is unlikely to be the explanation for other species showing uniparental inheritance, such as the isogamous alga *Chlamydomonas reinhardi* (Fig. 12.2). Mechanisms responsible for uniparental in-

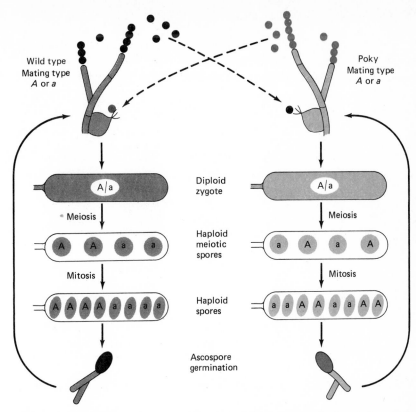

Figure 12.1   Reciprocal crosses usually yield different progenies in relation to extra-nuclear traits, but nuclear-coded traits show the expected Mendelian pattern of segre-gation in the same or in different crosses. The mating type alleles *A* and *a* segregate 4:4, but all the ascospores are either wild type or *poky*, depending on the female parent or strain of *Neurospora crassa*.

heritance, or for variable proportions of different kinds of zygotes in a single progeny, remain uncertain at the present time.

In the budding yeast *Saccharomyces cerevisiae*, extranuclear traits may be transmitted through either the *a* or *α*-mating type parent, or from both. Biparental zygotes are produced in relatively high frequencies from parents differing in alleles of structural genes. Uni-parental zygotes usually are produced in crosses between wild type, respiration-sufficient, *grande* (*rho*-plus, or ρ^+) strains and *rho*-minus (ρ^-) *petite* strains carrying deletions that are responsible for the extranuclear trait of respiration deficiency (Fig. 12.3). Some *petites* give no *petite* zygotes in crosses with *grande*; these are called **neutral petites**. Most *petites* will produce some percentage of *petite* zygotes in crosses with *grande*, and up to 99% of the progeny may be *petite* in cases involving **suppressive petite** strains. We will dis-cuss these mutants more fully later in the chapter.

The pattern of transmission through only one parent is fairly

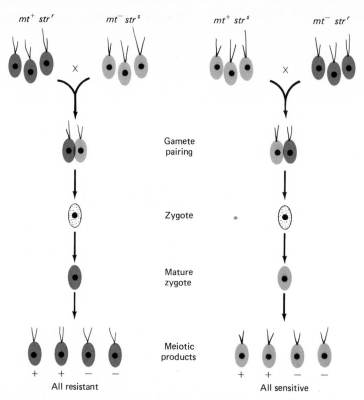

Figure 12.2 Although each parental cell seems to contribute an equal amount of nuclear and cytoplasmic materials in *Chlamydomonas* zygote formation, extranuclear traits generally show uniparental inheritance through the mating type (+) parent. Nuclear alleles, such as mt^+/mt^- segregate as expected in 2:2 tetrad ratio.

typical, but there is no consistency with regard to the particular parent which transmits; it may be always or usually through the same mating type or sex, or through either mating type or sex. Because of this variability, there is no rule of inheritance or universal prediction which will serve for all patterns of extranuclear transmission. Each case must be analyzed on its own merits.

2. *Progenies show non-Mendelian segregation ratios in a tetrad of meiotic products.* In each of the three species we have mentioned, the zygote undergoes meiosis to produce a tetrad of spores. When the four products of a single meiotic cell are examined, all four cells often have the same phenotype, that is, the phenotypic ratio of 4:0 (all like one parent) or 0:4 (all like the other parent). Pairs of alleles for nuclear gene markers, however, segregate 2:2 in these same tetrads (see Fig. 12.3). These results indicate at least two features of the system: (1) the nucleus behaves normally and meiosis is not aberrant, since known nuclear pairs of alleles segregate in the expected 2:2 ratio; and (2) extranuclear alternatives may not segregate at meiosis. We can infer from these results that extranuclear factors are not

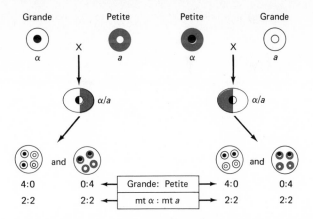

Figure 12.3 In the yeast *Saccharomyces cerevisiae*, extranuclear *petite* deletion mutants show 0:4 and 4:0 tetrad ratios in crosses with *grande* strains, while nuclear alleles segregate 2:2 in the same tetrads. Suppressive *petite* × *grande* yields varying percentages of 4:0 tetrads, whereas neutral *petite* × *grande* yields 100% 4:0 tetrads.

located on chromosomes in the nucleus; otherwise they would behave in the same way as pairs of marker alleles which are known to be on chromosomes. We cannot, however, infer where the extranuclear factors are located until there is more experimental evidence.

3. *Extranuclear factors cannot be mapped on any chromosome in the nuclear genome.* Confirming evidence can be obtained to verify that extranuclear factors are not situated in the nuclear genome, by tests showing that these factors are not linked to any known genes in any chromosome in the nucleus. Extranuclear factors assort independently of nuclear genes in every chromosome, and they therefore cannot be a part of any nuclear linkage group. Extranuclear genes will, however, show linkage to each other within one or another of the extranuclear genetic systems.

4. *Extranuclear factors are transmitted through the cytoplasm and not through the nucleus.* The **heterokaryon test** can provide evidence for a cytoplasmic rather than a nuclear location of extranuclear factors, in species which can maintain genetically different marker nuclei in a common cytoplasm. When haploid, multinucleate mycelia of *Neurospora* wild type and *poky* strains fuse together, the heterokaryon which forms will have two genetically different kinds of haploid nuclei that remain separate in the mixed cytoplasm. When spores develop asexually from different hyphae of the mycelium, a single haploid nucleus is enclosed along with some cytoplasm (Fig. 12.4). When these spores are incubated and allowed to develop, the mycelium of these asexual progeny will be either wild type or *poky*, and either kind of haploid nucleus may be present as determined by gene markers. This shows that the source of the nucleus has no influence on *poky* phenotypic development; either nucleus can be found in *poky* progeny. Since the nucleus does not

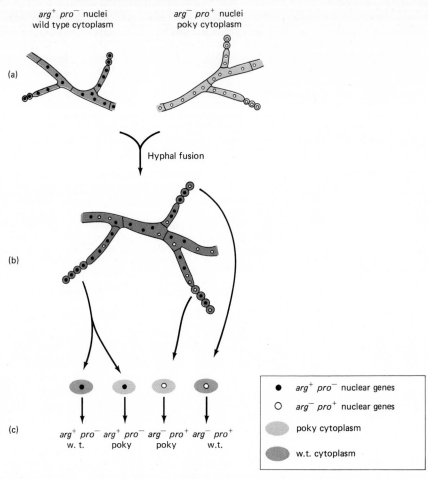

Figure 12.4 Heterokaryon test for extranuclear factor *poky*, in *Neurospora crassa*. (a) Allelically marked nuclei and cytoplasm in parent strains provide guidelines to assess genetic locations in heterokaryons. (b) Haploid nuclei carry different nuclear markers in heterokaryotic mycelium, with cytoplasm from both parental sources. (c) Germination of uninucleate, haploid spores produced by the heterokaryon reveals that the nucleus has no influence on *poky* phenotypic development, therefore, the extranuclear cytoplasm must be the source of the *poky* genetic factor.

control the *poky* phenotype, the cytoplasm remains the only other source of the inheritance factor transmitted from the heterokaryon to its asexual spore progeny.

5. Extranuclear genes in general, and organelle genes in particular, usually segregate rapidly during mitotic divisions. Such **vegetative segregation** can be seen quite clearly in variegated plants, in which green, white, and mixed cell lineages occur in variable amounts in different plants of a single progeny.

Taking these separate lines of evidence into consideration, extranuclear factors apparently are not located on chromosomes in the nucleus. They probably are situated in the cytoplasm, through which inheritance can be demonstrated. The exact cytoplasmic location can be determined by other tests, which we will discuss.

12.2   Extranuclear Genes

Are extranuclear factors equivalent to genes which are on chromosomes? If they are genes which happen to be located somewhere in the cytoplasm, we would predict that they would have genetic characteristics including (1) the capacity to mutate to alternative allelic forms; (2) different alleles of the same gene should segregate, and allelic types should breed true in the segregant populations; and (3) such genes should be physically identified with nucleotide sequences of DNA or RNA, the only known genetic molecules.

Although extranuclear mutants had been described according to inheritance and transmission patterns since 1909, there were two major problems which prevented their further analysis. First, only an occasional, single kind of extranuclear mutant had been described in various species. Second, and most importantly, only one alternative was transmitted by one of the parents to the progeny in each cross; alternatives did not segregate at meiosis. There was no way to determine if these extranuclear alternatives were unit factors or not. The situation can be compared to the problem Mendel would have faced if he had only had tall plants and short plants and the progenies were either all tall or all short in every case. The principles of genic inheritance could not have been deduced from such inheritance patterns.

Ruth Sager began the first systematic analysis of extranuclear inheritance in the early 1950s, using *Chlamydomonas reinhardi*. She discovered that streptomycin acted as a mutagen, producing extranuclear mutations which affected resistance, sensitivity, and dependence on streptomycin itself in the growth medium. Extranuclear mutations influencing cell response to other antibiotics were also isolated, as well as mutations affecting photosynthesis. Streptomycin was shown to be a mutagen in this system, by fluctuation test analysis (see Fig. 10.5).

Sager was able to conduct genetic analyses of these mutants when she found that some biparental zygotes appeared among the vast majority of uniparental zygotes, that is, some of the zygotes had received extranuclear factors through both parents. When these biparental zygotes underwent meiosis, there was no segregation of extranuclear alternatives. But segregations did take place during mitotic divisions of the haploid meiotic products. Segregant progeny types were shown to be true-breeding (Fig. 12.5). These results showed that extranuclear factors existed as pairs of allelic alternatives, which *segregated postmeiotically*, during mitotic divisions of the haploid progeny. Extranuclear factors, therefore, behaved like genes, and they could be studied by available genetic methods.

But where were these extranuclear genes located? Sager proposed that

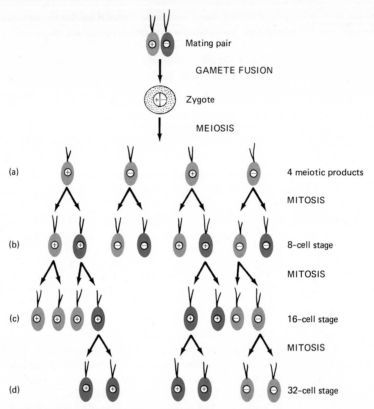

Mating pair

GAMETE FUSION

Zygote

MEIOSIS

(a) 4 meiotic products

MITOSIS

(b) 8-cell stage

MITOSIS

(c) 16-cell stage

MITOSIS

(d) 32-cell stage

Figure 12.5 Analysis of biparental zygotes in *Chlamydomonas* revealed segregation of extranuclear factors took place in postmeiotic mitotic divisions. (a) The four products of meiosis multiply asexually to produce (b) cell pairs segregating for extranuclear (gray/pink) but not for nuclear (+/−) traits. (c) Some cells continue to segregate pink and gray, while others have become homozygous and produce two gray or two pink mitotic products. (d) Segregation of extranuclear traits may be completed as early as the 32-cell stage in this species. (Only some of the 16 or 32 cells have been drawn.)

the extranuclear genes she studied were located in the chloroplast of *Chlamydomonas*, because some of the mutations affected chloroplast characteristics. The evidence in support of this inference was not particularly convincing, and it was many years later before certain of these extranuclear genes were generally acknowledged to be located in the chloroplast.

The development of extranuclear genetics was also aided substantially by studies of the *petite* extranuclear mutant in yeast, primarily by Boris Ephrussi and Piotr Slonimski in Paris. They found that the acridine dye **proflavin** acted as a specific mutgen, and up to 99% of a *grande*, respiration-sufficient strain could mutate to become *petites* (Fig. 12.6). The *petite* mutant was respiration-deficient, and it lacked some of the cytochrome enzymes required for aerobic respiration. This condition is not lethal in yeast, since the organism can gain enough energy through glycolysis to

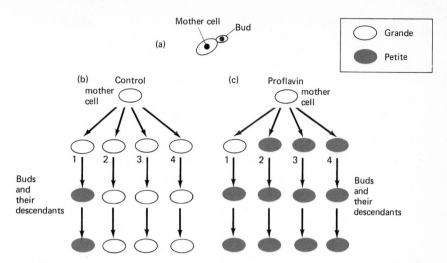

Figure 12.6 Lineage study of *grande* yeast mutation to *petite*. (a) Budding cells produce *grande* descendants, except for (b) occasional spontaneous *petite* mutants, which breed true thereafter. (c) In the presence of the acridine dye proflavin, up to 99.9% of the cells may become *petite*. The original mother cells do not mutate in the case of this particular mutagen.

sustain growth and reproduction. It grows more slowly, however, and produces small (*petite*) colonies on plates which also contain *grande* (large) wild type colonies that can metabolize sugars through aerobic respiration, a far more efficient process than glycolysis.

Petites were recognizable by colony growth, enzyme analysis, respiration tests, and by electron microscopy. Mitochondria in the mutant cells were generally abnormal in appearance, since the inner mitochondrial membrane was not organized into the typical invaginated cristae conformations (Fig. 12.7). While many differences could be recorded to identify *petites*, and their inheritance was clearly extranuclear, there were no other mutants available and genetic tests for recombination could not be conducted as they had been in *Chlamydomonas*. When it was discovered in the mid-1960s that mitochondria and chloroplasts contained DNA, Slonimski analyzed mitochondrial DNA (**mtDNA**) in *grande* and *petite* yeast. He showed that *petite* mtDNA was very different in base composition, and therefore in its sedimentation characteristic in CsCl, when compared with *grande* mtDNA (Fig. 12.8). This study in 1966 provided the first evidence which related an alteration in extranuclear DNA with mutation of a non-Mendelian inherited characteristic; the alteration in DNA paralleled the alterations in inheritance and in phenotype for *petite* mutants. This marked the beginning of studies of the physical basis for extranuclear inheritance.

12.3 Organelle DNA

The first convincing evidence for organelle DNA came from electron microscopy studies in 1963, and only one year later there already were numerous reports of the occurrence of mtDNA and chloroplast DNA (**ctDNA**) in

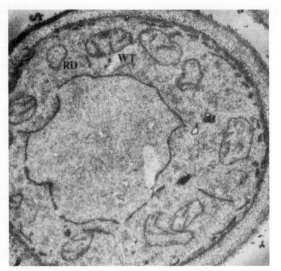
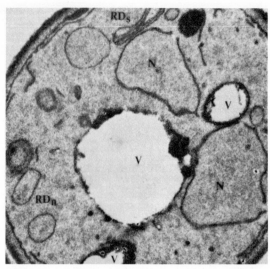

Figure 12.7 Electron micrographs of permanganate-fixed yeast cells. (a) Mitochondrial profiles in *grande* yeast show typical cristae, invaginations of the inner membrane; whereas (b) *petite* mitochondria either lack cristae or show aberrant inner membrane conformations. The nucleus (N) in b appears in two separate parts due to the plane of sectioning. Vacuoles (V) are characteristic of wild type as well as *petite* yeast cells. × 31,000. (From Federman, M., and C. J. Avers. 1967. *J. Bact.* **94**:1236.)

every species studied. At first these studies were confined to chemical and physical descriptions, which demonstrated that organelle DNA was duplex. Base composition analysis showed that A = T and G = C, as expected for base-paired duplex DNA. Physical studies confirmed the interpretation, since organelle DNA melted at higher temperatures and these single strands renatured to the duplex form when the preparation was cooled.

In 1966, individual mtDNA molecules were visualized by electron microscopy of purified DNA or of DNA released from organelles subjected to osmotic shock during preparations for microscopy (Fig. 12.9). The direct observation of organelle DNA revealed the astonishing fact that both mtDNA and ctDNA were usually circular molecules. Furthermore, every species of metazoan animal appeared to have mtDNA which measured between 4.5 and 5.9 μm in contour length (Table 12.1). Protozoan mtDNA varied from one species group to another; mtDNA in fungi was four to five times larger than the average metazoan 5 μm-long circle, and mtDNA in flowering plants measured 30 μm. Later, it was found that ctDNA molecules were about 40-45 μm in contour length in many species examined, from unicellular protists like *Euglena* on up to flowering plants.

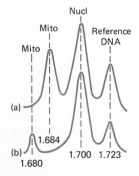

Figure 12.8 Densitometer tracings of yeast DNAs centrifuged to equilibrium in CsCl density gradients. There is a higher buoyant density (1.684) for (a) *grande* mitochondrial DNA than for (b) *petite* mtDNA, which reflects differences in base composition of the two DNAs. This difference parallels differences in the pattern of extranuclear inheritance and in phenotypic development between such strains.

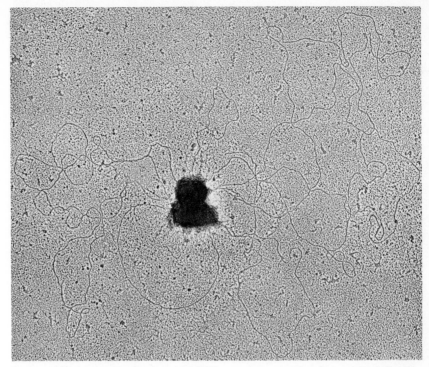

Figure 12.9 Loops of mitochondrial DNA are seen emerging from a piece of membrane from osmotically shocked yeast mitochondria photographed with the electron microscope. The contour length of mtDNA shown here is 48.5 μm. × 29,000. (From Avers, C. J., *et al.* 1968. *Proc. Nat. Acad. Sci. U. S.* **61**:90.)

Only two studies in the 1960s were reported in which mtDNA in *Neurospora* and ctDNA in *Chlamydomonas* were shown to replicate semiconservatively. Technical problems were encountered in studies of this kind using other organisms, due to large pools of DNA precursor molecules which persisted indefinitely in experimental populations. It was difficult to show that the distribution of ^{14}N and ^{15}N isotopes followed the predicted semiconservative pattern of distribution, as Meselson and Stahl had shown in *E. coli*, because ^{15}N was not used up completely when experiments began. These ^{15}N-labeled precursors continued to be available for synthesis of new strands over several generations, a condition which caused difficulties in recognizing original and newly-synthesized strands of DNA in the proportions expected (see Fig. 7.1).

Replication of mtDNA has been analyzed by electron microscopy since 1968, and mtDNA has been shown to replicate semiconservatively according to these methods. In 1968, typical *theta*-forms were found in rat liver mtDNA, similar to those described in *E. coli* by Cairns (Fig. 12.10). In 1972, however, Jerome Vinograd and co-workers reported a modified semiconservative replication pattern which is called **D-loop synthesis**. According to electron microscopy and biochemical tests, it was found that both template strands of the duplex did not replicate simultaneously; synthesis

Table 12.1
Size of circular mitochondrial DNAs in various organisms

Organism	Contour length (μm)
Animals	
Vertebrates	4.7-5.9
Invertebrates	4.5-5.9
Plants	
Flowering plants	30-34
Fungi	
True fungi	
Podospora	31
Saccharomyces	25
Neurospora	19
Aspergillus	10
Saprolegnia	14
Slime molds (*Physarum*)	19
Protists	
Protozoa	
Ciliates	14-15*
Amebae (*Acanthameba*)	13
Trypanosomes	0.2-0.8**
	6-11**
Chlamydomonas	4.6

*Molecules found in *Paramecium* and *Tetrahymena* are linear, not circular
**Minicircles and maxicircles occur together in a meshwork of DNA, which is called kinetoplast DNA (kDNA)

began along the light (L) strand and some time later the heavy (H) strand initiated synthesis of a new complementary partner (Fig. 12.11).

When replication begins along the L strand, a single-stranded displacement loop, or **D-loop**, is produced. Molecular hybridizations between iso-

Figure 12.10 Electron micrograph of replicating mtDNA from rat liver, showing a typical theta-form molecule. Arrows indicate the replication forks. Segments A and B have replicated, and segment C remains unreplicated in this 5μm-long circle. (Courtesy of D. R. Wolstenholme, from Wolstenholme, D. R., *et al.* 1974. *Cold Spring Harbor Sympos. Quant Biol.* **38**(1973):267.)

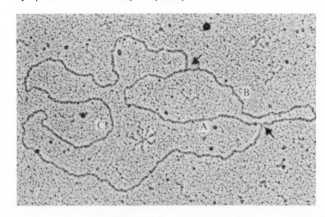

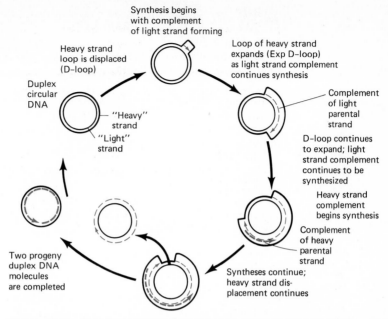

Figure 12.11   D-loop synthesis of mitochondrial DNA in diagrammatic summary. The heavy and light parental strands are shown in thick and thin black lines, respectively. The light strand complement is synthesized first (red) in the D-loop region, and the heavy strand complement (gray) is synthesized somewhat later. Each new strand is synthesized in the $5' \rightarrow 3'$ direction along the antiparallel template strands. Two identical semiconserved duplexes are produced from the parental DNA.

lated single-strand D-loops and L strand parental DNA revealed the source of these single-stranded segments. The D-loop becomes larger as replication proceeds around the circular L strand, in the 5' to 3' direction. H strand replication is initiated later, and proceeds in the 5' to 3' direction along the antiparallel strand. Ultimately, both parental strands complete their replication and two new, identical mtDNA duplexes are produced.

In addition to replication by the theta-form and D-loop processes, mtDNA and ctDNA may sometimes replicate by the rolling-circle mechanism (see Fig. 8.19). It may be that any or all of these modes of duplex DNA replication can occur in the same cells, regulated by different cellular and environmental conditions, such that *slower rates* of replication by theta-form and D-loop synthesis and *faster rates* of replication of rolling circles occur at different times in different cells. The mechanism of such regulation is not known.

ORGANELLE TRANSCRIPTION AND TRANSLATION

From genetic studies there was evidence of extranuclear genes in mitochondria and chloroplasts, and it seemed very likely that these genes were physically located in organelle DNA molecules. How were these genes expressed? Was organelle DNA transcribed and translated within the organelle itself, or was the cellular nucleocytoplasmic system required to process mtDNA and ctDNA information? It was well known that hundreds of different nuclear genes coded for various proteins and processes that were parts of mitochondrial and chloroplast phenotypes. It was not known whether organelle-coded information was also processed in eukaryotic cytoplasm.

In the 1960s and 1970s, various lines of evidence were obtained showing that mitochondria and chloroplasts were indeed **semiautonomous** components of eukaryotic cells. Not only did they contain their own DNA, which replicated and was transmitted in subsequent generations, but they also were found to transcribe coded information in these molecules, and to translate messenger RNA into organelle-specified polypeptides. Organelles are not totally autonomous or independent structures, however, since they cannot increase outside the living cell and since they depend on the nucleus for most of the genetic information specifying structure, function, and regulation of organelle components.

12.4 Protein Synthesis

In 1966, Anthony Linnane and co-workers showed that protein synthesis in the cytoplasm and in mitochondria could be selectively shut off by specific drugs. In the presence of **cycloheximide**, cytoplasmic protein synthesis is inhibited and mitochondrial activities proceed as usual; **chloramphenicol**, **erythromycin**, and certain other antibiotics inhibit mitochondrial protein synthesis and have little or no effect on cytoplasmic ribosome activities.

With these newly available methods to study organelle protein synthesis *in vivo*, it was shown that different polypeptides were made in mitochondria and chloroplasts from those made in the surrounding cytoplasm. In a typical experiment of this kind, [^{3}H]amino acids were provided during cycloheximide inhibition to label organelle-synthesized polypeptides after [^{14}C]amino acids were provided to label polypeptides made in the presence of chloramphenicol (Fig. 12.12). By selectively turning off one compartment of the cell and then the other, and distinctively labeling each set of polypeptides made in these parts of the cell, it was very clear that organelles were capable of synthesizing proteins. But were these proteins coded by the organelle genes, or were they proteins coded by nuclear genes? To answer this question it was necessary to analyze polypeptide synthesis in extranuclear mutants whose defective proteins were known. The *petite* mutant of yeast proved to be a useful system for such a specific analysis, since its cytochrome oxidase was defective when compared with the functional *grande* enzyme.

Cytochrome oxidase, the terminal enzyme of aerobic respiration, is a protein composed of seven identifiable polypeptide subunits in yeast. *Petites* can make four of these polypeptides, but not the other three. When *grande* yeast was incubated in the presence of erythromycin or chloramphenicol, the cells made only the four polypeptides known from analysis of *petites*. In the presence of cycloheximide, *grande* yeast made only the three

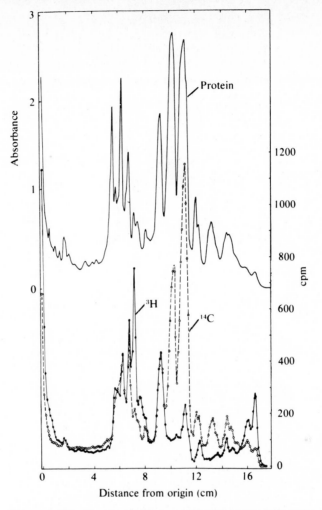

Figure 12.12 Double labeling experiment using differential inhibitors to identify location of synthesis of chloroplast membrane proteins in *Chlamydomonas reinhardi*. Absorbance of electrophoretically separated proteins from chloroplast membranes serves as the reference for the lower portion of the figure. Proteins which were made in the cytoplasm are labeled with [^{14}C]arginine, which was present during the time the cells were growing in chloramphenicol-containing medium. Proteins which were made in the chloroplast are labeled with [^{3}H]arginine, which was provided later in the experiment, when cycloheximide was the inhibiting drug for protein synthesis. Cycloheximide inhibits protein synthesis at cytoplasmic ribosomes, while chloramphenicol inhibits protein synthesis at organelle ribosomes. (From Hoober, J. K. 1970. *J. Biol. Chem.* **245**:4327, Fig. 6.)

polypeptides which *petites* were unable to synthesize (Fig. 12.13). In other words, the correspondence between drug-inhibited *grande* activities and the activities in *petite* cells showed that the three larger polypeptides of cytochrome oxidase were made in mitochondria, while the four smaller subunits

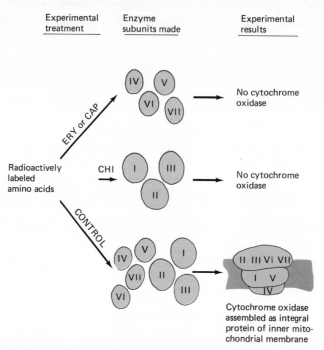

Figure 12.13 By labeling cytochrome oxidase polypeptides in wild type yeast exposed to different inhibitors of protein synthesis, it is possible to determine which polypeptides fail to be synthesized in enzyme-deficient experimental cells. In the presence of erythromycin (ERY) or chloramphenicol (CAP), mitochondrial protein synthesis is inhibited and components I-III are not made. Comparison with cycloheximide-inhibited cells (CHI) making no proteins at cytoplasmic ribosomes, and with controls that are not inhibited, reveals the different origins for the seven polypeptides of the enzyme in yeast.

were made in the cytoplasm. These seven polypeptides assemble inside the *grande* mitochondrion to form a functional respiratory enzyme which catalyzes aerobic respiration. *Petites* are unable to oxidize glucose aerobically because their mtDNA lesion involves coded information for three of the seven polypeptide subunits; they make nonfunctional enzyme proteins.

If chloroplasts and mitochondria can synthesize polypeptides from coded DNA information, there must be ribosomal machinery on which these molecules are translated. The first convincing experimental evidence showing that there were ribosomes in mitochondria and chloroplasts came in 1970. Not only were these particles isolated from organelles and purified, but their chemical, physical, and functional characteristics were described. Mitochondrial ribosomes vary in size from 55S to 80S particles, but all chloroplast ribosomes appear to be 70S (Table 12.2). These monosomes consist of two unequal-sized subunits, just like cytoplasmic ribosomes (cytoribosomes), and each subunit has one rRNA molecule. Chloroplast ribosomes apparently also have 5S rRNA, but there is no convincing evidence for the occurrence of 5S rRNA in mitochondrial ribosomes in any species which has been examined.

Table 12.2
Some characteristics of organelle ribosomes*

Organelle Organism	Ribosome monomer	Small subunit	Large subunit	rRNA from Small subunit	rRNA from Large subunit
Mitochondrion					
Animals	55-60S	30-35S	40-45S	12-13S	16-17S
Flowering plants	78S	44S	60S	—	—
Fungi	80S	40S	52S	14-17S	21-24S
Protists					
Tetrahymena	80S	55S	55S	14S + 21S**	
Euglena	71S	32S	50S	16S	23S
Chloroplast					
Various species	70S	30S	50S	16S	23S, 5S

*The reference standards are components and monomers of *E. coli* ribosomes and rat or yeast cytoplasmic ribosomes (see Table 8.2).
**There is no way to tell which rRNA comes from the two 55S ribosome subunits. It is possible that both rRNAs are present in each 55S particle, which might therefore be the actual ribosome monomer.

Ribosome function was established at first by *in vitro* tests, which showed that these particles were active in making polyphenylalanine from poly(U) messenger RNA. More stringent tests were also conducted, for example, showing that organelle ribosomes participated in making correct virus proteins when natural viral RNA was provided *in vitro* as a messenger molecule. In suitable preparations, polysomes were observed by electron microscopy (Fig. 12.14). The thin strand connecting monosomes in the polysome group was digestible with ribonuclease, and it was therefore inferred to be organelle mRNA. Direct evidence for specific RNA transcripts came from several kinds of studies, as we will see next.

12.5 Transcription in Organelles

Using molecular hybridization assays, it has been shown that mitochondria and chloroplasts transcribe their own rRNA and all or most of their unique tRNAs. Ribosomal RNA can be purified from isolated organelle ribosomes and hybridized with H and L strands of mtDNA or ctDNA. In most cases, it has been found that rRNA for both ribosome subunits is coded by the H strand of DNA, and the two coding sites are very close together. In other cases, such as yeast, 14S and 21S rRNAs are transcribed from widely separated regions of mtDNA. In chloroplasts, coding sites for rRNAs are arranged in the sequence of 16S—23S—5S (in exactly the way they occur in *E. coli*). From these molecular hybridizations, it appears that there is only one coding site for each kind of rRNA in both mtDNA and ctDNA in most species studied.

Twenty or more kinds of tRNA are transcribed from mtDNA and ctDNA. These tRNAs can be isolated from organelles and purified for molecular hybridizations and other assays. By molecular hybridizations, tRNA tran-

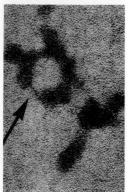

Figure 12.14 Electron micrographs of polysomes isolated from purified yeast mitochondria after preparative centrifugation in sucrose gradients. The presumptive mRNA strand is shown at the arrows. (a) × 160,000; (b) × 255,000. (From Cooper, C. S., and C. J. Avers. 1974. In *The Biogenesis of Mitochondria*, p. 289; A. M. Kroon and C. Saccone, eds. New York: Academic Press.)

scripts can be identified and located in organelle DNA (Fig. 12.15). Genes for tRNAs occur in several different regions of the mapped DNA, and usually at least one tRNA gene exists within the rRNA coded region. The significance of this consistent observation is uncertain at present.

Functional tests for organelle-coded tRNAs have also been conducted. One can bind purified organelle tRNAs to radioactively labeled amino acids for which each tRNA is specific, and look for polypeptides which are made with such labeled amino acids incorporated into the polymers. In this way, it has been shown that every tRNA made by mitochondria or chloroplasts can participate in organelle translation processes, along with organelle ribosomes and other components needed for syntheses.

Messenger RNA transcripts made in mitochondria have been identified in a few studies, in which whole-mitochondrial RNA was added to an *in vitro* system for protein snythesis. The goal was to see whether organelle-specific polypeptides would be made. If they were, it could be deduced that the organelle RNA contained messengers that were translated into organelle-coded polypeptides. In one such study using yeast, the three polypeptides known to be made from mtDNA information for cytochrome oxidase subunits was shown to be made *in vitro*. The only way these specific polypeptides could have been made was from mRNA, which must have been present in the mitochondrial RNA preparation.

Using electron microscopy and biochemical methods, transcribing mtDNA complexes from mitochondria of human cells (HeLa cell cultures) and from *Drosophila* have been isolated and studied. In both cases, the 5 μm-long circular mtDNA molecule was found to have polysome groups covering 80 to 100% of the molecule (Fig. 12.16). Each of these polysomes was inferred to represent a translation event in progress, just as these had been demonstrated in *E. coli* (see Fig. 8.8). It appears that translation begins while mRNA transcription is still under way, and transcription and translation would therefore be coordinated processes in mitochondria, as they are in bacterial cells. Whether the number of polysomes along mtDNA can be equated to the number of different structural genes coding for polypeptides, however, remains to be determined.

THE ORGANELLE GENOME

The most detailed maps have been constructed for the mitochondrial genome of yeast and the chloroplast genome of *Chlamydomonas*, using a variety of methods. Genome maps for other systems, such as human, *Drosophila, Xenopus, Paramecium*, and other mitochondrial systems, and for chloroplasts in corn, have relied more on molecular hybridizations between rRNA and tRNA with organelle DNAs, since very few extranu-

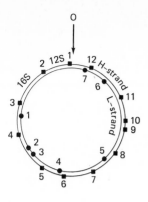

Figure 12.15 Physical and genetic maps of human HeLa cell mitochondrial DNA. The sequences for 12S and 16S rRNA are situated near each other on the heavy strand, with a tRNA gene (No. 2) between them. Genes coding for tRNAs occur on the light strand (filled circles) as well as on the heavy strand (filled squares) of the duplex DNA. The outermost circle is a physical map derived from restriction enzyme studies, and it has been aligned with the genetic map it surrounds. In the upper part of the illustration, a region of the physical map has been expanded to show the origin of replication (vertical arrow, marked 0) and of the D-loop. (From Crews, S. *et al.* 1979. *Nature* **277**:192.)

clear mutations have been identified. The large number of mutations known in yeast and *Chlamydomonas* have permitted more kinds of mapping methods to be used.

In these two model systems, genes have been shown to occur at fixed sites in a linear order on a circular map corresponding to physically circular organelle DNA molecules. Recombinations between different loci have identified different genes and different alleles for these genes in *Chlamydomonas*. Mapping by physical and molecular methods has been particularly successful only in yeast. These approaches in yeast studies have been combined with genetic analyses by deletion mapping and, to a limited extent, by recombination analysis.

12.6   Mitochondrial Mutations in Yeast

Until 1970, the *petite* mutation was the only one known in yeast. *Petites* are deletion mutants of two general types: (1) **suppressive petites**, in which varying amounts of the mitochondrial genome are missing; and (2) **neutral petites**, most of which lack mtDNA altogether (Fig. 12.17). In addition to a relatively high rate of spontaneous mutation, these *petites* can be induced by exposure to **ethidium bromide** and other acridine mutagens in 99-100%

Figure 12.16 Electron micrograph of a string of polysomes bound to mtDNA, from osmotically ruptured mitochondrion of *Drosophila melanogaster*. × 90,000. (Courtesy of C. D. Laird and W. Y. Chooi, from Chooi, W. Y., and C. D. Laird. 1976. *J. Mol. Biol.* **100**:493.)

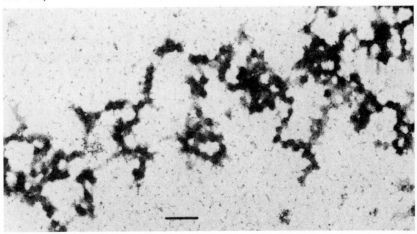

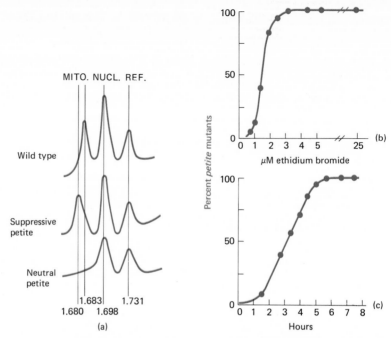

Figure 12.17   The *petite* mutation in yeast. (a) The three strains of yeast have the same nuclear DNA, according to its buoyant density in CsCl, but they differ in their mtDNA. The mtDNA base composition is altered in suppressive *petites*, and there is no mtDNA in most neutral *petite* strains. (b) Mutation induction from *grande* to *petite* by ethidium bromide is dependent on drug concentration, and 100% of the cells can become *petite*. (c) The time course of appearance of *petite* mutants exposed to ethidium bromide. In 2.5 hr (time for one cell cycle), the *petites* have increased by mutation from less than 5% to more than 90% of the population.

of treated *grande* cells. Both kinds of *petites* have the same phenotypic characteristics of slow growth, deficient aerobic respiration, and enzymatic defects. They can be distinguished by their mtDNA content and in crosses to *grande* tester strains. In *grande* × *suppressive petite*, a variable proportion of the meiotic tetrads have 4 *petite*:0 *grande* spores, as well as 0 *petite*:4 *grande* tetrad types. In *grande* × *neutral petite*, all tetrads are 4 *grande*:0 *petite*. The mechanism for variable proportions of the two kinds of tetrads in crosses involving *petites* is not known.

Little could be done until 1970, when extranuclear point mutations were found and were analyzed genetically. These point mutations could mutate back to the wild type allele, whereas *petite* deletion mutants are not revertible. Different gene loci and alleles were identified by recombination and complementation tests (Fig. 12.18). These genes were shown to be located in mtDNA by ethidium bromide mutagenesis of mutant strains, and by following the frequencies with which different mutant genes were *retained together or lost together* in *petites* induced by the mutagenic treatment. The closer together two genes were, the higher was the frequency of

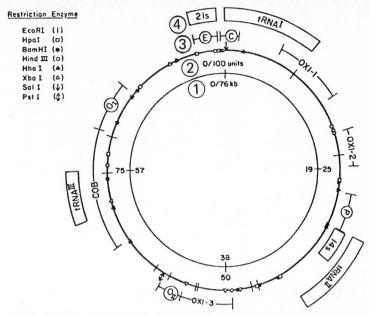

Restriction Enzyme

EcoRI	(I)
HpaI	(□)
BamHI	(●)
Hind III	(○)
Hha I	(▲)
Xba I	(△)
Sal I	(↓)
Pst I	(⌀)

Figure 12.18 Physical map of the circular genome of yeast mtDNA. Total contour length of the circle is 76 kilobases (76 kb), which is subdivided into 100 units for site references. Positions of the antibiotic-resistance loci, E, C, P, O$_{II}$, and O$_I$ (erythromycin, chloramphenicol, paromomycin, and oligomycin resistances); OXI-1, OXI-2, and OXI-3 (coding for the three cytochrome oxidase polypeptides specified by the mitochondrion); and COB (for mitochondrially-specified polypeptide of the cytochrome bc_1 complex), are shown in circle number 3. The outermost circle of designations indicates locations for the 14S and 21S rRNAs of mitochondrial ribosomes, and the three main regions in which tRNA genes are found. (From Morimoto, R., et al. 1978. *Mol. gen. Genet.* **163**:241, Fig. 15.)

their coordinated loss or retention in the induced deletion mutants. In addition, any genes that were lost when neutral *petites* were induced had to be genes physically located in mtDNA, which is known to be lost entirely in these particular *petites*. Although *petites* were of limited value before 1970, they proved to be the crucial components in later studies such as the ones just mentioned. In addition, mapping by the deletion method could be accomplished using different *petite* strains with point mutation markers incorporated into their genotype.

Yeast mtDNA is about 25 μm in contour length. Although very few intact molecules have been isolated and photographed, the size of the genome has been clearly established by restriction enzyme analysis (Fig. 12.19). According to the usual equivalents, a 25 μm-long molecule consists of 75,000 base-pairs of DNA. The entire DNA molecule derived from restriction enzyme analysis has 76,000 base-pairs of DNA, and must therefore be about 25 μm long. These restriction enzyme fragments permit one to determine the order of their occurrence in the intact molecule by comparing overlaps. These same restriction maps of the *grande* genome can then be used to determine the locations of gene loci, using *petites* with overlapping dele-

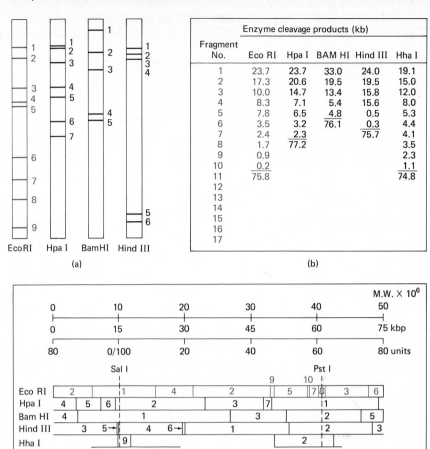

Fragment No.	Enzyme cleavage products (kb)				
	Eco RI	Hpa I	BAM HI	Hind III	Hha I
1	23.7	23.7	33.0	24.0	19.1
2	17.3	20.6	19.5	19.5	15.0
3	10.0	14.7	13.4	15.8	12.0
4	8.3	7.1	5.4	15.6	8.0
5	7.8	6.5	4.8	0.5	5.3
6	3.5	3.2	76.1	0.3	4.4
7	2.4	2.3		75.7	4.1
8	1.7	77.2			3.5
9	0.9				2.3
10	0.2				1.1
11	75.8				74.8
12					
13					
14					
15					
16					
17					

Figure 12.19 Molecular size of the yeast mitochondrial genome. (a) Cleavage pattern of yeast mtDNA by restriction endonucleases *Eco* RI, *Hpa* I, *Bam* HI, *Hind* III, and others, singly and in combination, are revealed by photographs under UV light of fragments separated by gel electrophoresis; shown here by drawings of the photographed gels. (b) Molecular size (in kb) of the products of cleavage of different restriction enzymes, corresponding to fragments on the gels in a. In each case the total genome length approximates 76 kb. (c) Linearized fragment maps obtained for different restriction enzymes have been oriented according to products of double enzyme digests. (After Morimoto, R. *et al.* 1978. *Mol. gen. Genet.* **163**:241.)

tions and with marker genes in the pieces of mtDNA which are retained in the *petite* strains.

In studies of this kind, the pieces of retained mtDNA in the deletion mutant strain of *petites* can be identified according to the restriction fragments which are generated. The genes carried in the *petites* can then be ordered on the whole 100-unit map (Fig. 12.20).

Examination of the yeast mtDNA map reveals why virtually any deletion will produce a respiration-deficient *petite*. The loci coded for polypep-

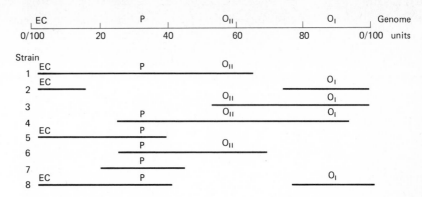

Figure 12.20 Physical mapping of yeast mitochondrial genome by molecular hybridizations using mtDNA from *petites* in which there are deletions, so that only certain combinations of antibiotic resistance markers have been retained in comparison with the *grande* genome (top). The *petite* genomes are cleaved by restriction enzymes and the fragments allowed to hybridize with *grande* restriction fragments. By comparing molecular hybrids formed, genetic markers present, and relationships of overlapping deletions, the physical map can be derived. Each *petite* strain retained only the genome segments shown, relative to the 100-unit *grande* genome.

tides of different respiratory enzymes, and loci for both rRNA genes, are widely spaced around the entire genome. The loss of almost any part of this genome will lead to some enzymatic defect or to the inability to carry out protein synthesis. The action of ethidium bromide and other acridines is through intercalation of the drug with DNA. When the drug binds to mtDNA, replication of the genome is inhibited and distorted, leading to gross alterations in the mtDNA molecule in suppressive *petites*. If the drug acts long enough in the system, treated cells or their descendants will lose all of the genome and become neutral *petites*.

All of the known loci apparently code for structural gene products. At present, virtually nothing is known about regulatory genes in the yeast mitochondrial genome.

The ctDNA molecule should code for a larger number of gene products than mtDNA, since most ctDNA is 40-45 μm in contour length, while mtDNA is only 5 μm in metazoan animals and 25 μm in yeast. Relatively few loci have been identified in ctDNA, however, and only some of these have been related directly to any feature of the chloroplast phenotype. In contrast, all of the known mitochondrial genes in yeast code for known molecular components of the mitochondrion.

Lots of the information on genes in ctDNA has come from Sager's studies of *Chlamydomonas reinhardi* using genetic analysis, and from isolated molecular analyses of some other chloroplast systems. There is some conflict between Sager and Gillham in designating the precise order of extranuclear loci in the single ctDNA linkage group of *C. reinhardi*. Sager has correlated information from different kinds of recombination mapping methods to assign the order of gene loci and their relative distances apart. When these data are compared, there is an internal consistency when various linear maps are incorporated into a single circular linkage group (Fig. 12.21). Since ctDNA is a 62 μm-long, circular molecule in *Chlamydomonas*, the genetic data indicating circularity of the linkage map are consistent with the physical conformation of ctDNA molecules.

12.7   Gene Functions in Organelles

Transcripts of genes coding for rRNAs and tRNAs remain within the organelle, where they are synthesized and where they participate in organelle protein synthesis. Most or all of the ribosomal proteins, however, are coded by nuclear genes. These organelle ribosomal proteins are translated

Figure 12.21   Maps of the chloroplast genome in *Chlamydomonas reinhardi*. (a) Physical map showing three concentric circles generated by three different restriction enzymes (*Eco* RI, *Bam* HI, and *Bgl* II). Sequences of tRNAs (4S RNAs) are shown by large letters and black arrows. The two rDNA units are indicated on the outside. Sequences coding for tRNAs and rRNAs were located by molecular hybridizations with restriction fragments. (From Malnoë, P., and J.-D. Rochaix. 1978. *Mol. gen. Genet.* **166**:269.) (b) Genetic map derived from recombination analysis and other means, showing antibiotic resistance loci and other markers. (After Singer, B., R. Sager, and Z. Ramanis. 1976. *Genetics* **83**:341.)

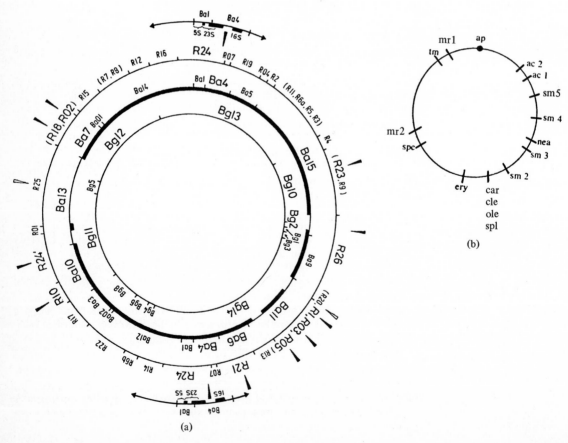

in the cytoplasm and the molecules are then transported into mitochondria or chloroplasts, where they assemble with rRNAs and emerge as functional ribosomal subunits. One or more chloroplast ribosomal proteins may be specified by ctDNA, according to the limited evidence which is available. For example, Sager showed that one of the two ribosome subunits in certain drug-resistant strains of *Chlamydomonas* was responsible for drug-resistance when mixed reconstitutions were conducted using 30S and 50S subunits from resistant and sensitive strains to make 70S monosomes (Fig. 12.22). These experiments were similar to those showing that the 30S ribosome subunit in *E. coli* was altered in streptomycin-resistant strains (see Fig. 8.29).

The polypeptides of a number of respiratory enzymes in yeast mitochondria are coded by mitochondrial genes, and these enzymes are incorporated into the structure of the mitochondrial inner membrane. In most cases, however, some of the polypeptides of the enzyme are also coded by nuclear genes. If the gene products in either cell compartment are defective, the entire enzyme has a defective or abnormal function and aerobic respiration is deficient or lacking. This may be lethal for most aerobic cells, but cells which can exist by fermentative or glycolytic carbohydrate metabolism are still able to function at a reduced level. Enzymes of electron transport and of oxidative phosphorylation are made through the cooperative actions of nuclear and extranuclear genetic systems in aerobic cells.

None of the membrane polypeptides in chloroplasts has been identified specifically, but some of these are made in the chloroplast and some are made in the cytoplasm (see Fig. 12.12). The best known protein in chloroplasts is the enzyme ribulose 1,5-diphosphate carboxylase (RuDP carboxylase), which catalyzes the first step in reduction of CO_2 to carbohydrates during the "dark reactions" of photosynthesis. The enzyme consists of a number of polypeptide chains in two subunits of the functional catalyst, and one of these subunits is coded by nuclear genes and the other by chloroplast genes in flowering plants. RuDP carboxylase is loosely associated with photosynthetic membranes within the chloroplast, but it is not a structural component of these membranes. The enzyme serves as a vital link between photosynthetic reactions, in which light energy is transformed into chemical energy, and the "dark reactions," in which this chemical energy is utilized in carbohydrate synthesis from CO_2 and H_2O.

In both mitochondria and chloroplasts, therefore, some of the polypeptides of the vital enzymes of aerobic respiration and of photosynthesis are made within the organelle. These polypeptides assemble together with others made in the cytoplasm, and the entire functional enzyme is completed in the organelle. The protein synthesizing machinery of mitochondria and chloroplasts serve as the centers for synthesis of organelle-specified polypeptides needed for the existence of the cell and the organism.

What is the advantage of having two sets of polypeptides made in different parts of the cell? One reason which has been suggested is that

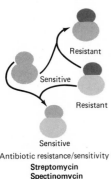

Antibiotic resistance/sensitivity to:

**Streptomycin
Spectinomycin
Neamine**

depends on the characteristics of the small subunit of the ribosome (30S)

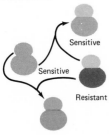

Antibiotic resistance/sensitivity to:

**Carbomycin
Cleocin**

Depends on the characteristics of the large subunit of the ribosome (50S)

Figure 12.22 Diagram summarizing results from Sager's studies, showing that one of the chloroplast ribosomal subunits is altered in extranuclear antibiotic-resistance mutants in *Chlamydomonas*. The subunit involved was identified from mixed reconstitutions.

organelle-synthesized polypeptides are highly hydrophobic in nature as a consequence of very high levels of hydrophobic amino acids used in their construction. Such molecules would move across organelle membranes with great difficulty if they were synthesized in the cytoplasm. Since they are made within the organelle, problems of their transport from the cytoplasm are avoided. Cytoplasmically-synthesized polypeptides of these organelle enzymes are far less hydrophobic, and pass across the mitochondrial or chloroplast membranes with less difficulty. This answer raises other questions, such as, why aren't all the enzyme polypeptides made within the organelle? At present we have very little information, and most of the discussions have been highly speculative.

12.8   Evolutionary Origin of Organelles

How did mitochondria and chloroplasts originate in eukaryotes such that each of these organelle types came to have some of its own DNA? Because of the unique feature of coding for some of its own RNA and polypeptides, two very general kinds of ideas have been proposed to explain the observed semiautonomous nature of the mitochondrion and the chloroplast. One proposal, which goes back to the late 1800s, is that mitochondria and chloroplasts are the modern remnants of ancient, free-living endosymbiotic organisms. The alternative proposal is that each of these organelles arose by genetic changes within the eukaryotic ancestor, leading to a differentiated subcellular structure with a piece of captured plasmid or chromosomal DNA. Each of these general theories has been stated in a number of ways, with a number of variations in the presumed details of such events during evolution.

The modern statements of the ideas about organelle origin are mostly based on comparative molecular and genetic observations. There is no experimental support, nor are there existing intermediate life forms which would show how the differences arose in the gradual stages that have been proposed.

According to the **endosymbiont theory**, stated in detail by Lynn Margulis beginning in 1967, the ancient ancestral cell was prokaryotic and anaerobic, and it had the capacity to ingest or engulf solids and other organisms. This ancestral cell engulfed a respiring bacterial cell, which established a symbiotic (mutually beneficial) relationship with its host (Fig. 12.23). The host provided needed nutrients and protection, and the endosymbiont provided the aerobic respiratory pathway by which large amounts of energy could be derived from the oxidation of organic foods. In a world undergoing an atmospheric change from anaerobic to aerobic conditions, the host benefitted considerably. Later on, other endosymbioses took place giving rise to modern flagella from a spirochetelike prokaryote, and to chloroplasts from a blue-green alga symbiont. According to this theory, the mtDNA and ctDNA we observe today are the remains of the genomes originally present in the endosymbionts, as are their protein-synthesizing ribosomal and tRNA systems.

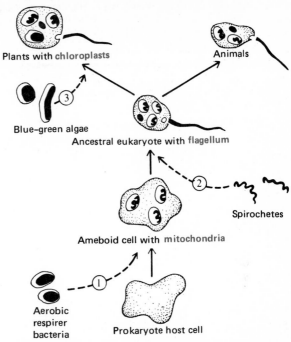

Figure 12.23 Summarized scheme of the endosymbiont theory of the origin of mitochondria, flagella, and chloroplasts in eukaryotic cells. (Adapted from Margulis, L. 1970. *Origin of Eukaryotic Cells*, p. 58. New Haven, Conn: Yale University Press. Copyright © 1970 by Yale University.)

The principal support for endosymbiosis comes from observations of similarities between prokaryotes and eukaryotic organelles. For example:

1. Genome organization is similar in bacteria and in organelles. There is a single circular duplex DNA molecule not associated with histone proteins. Eukaryotes, on the other hand, have nucleoprotein chromosomes and their genes are distributed among two or more linkage groups separated from the cytoplasm by a nuclear envelope. No membrane separates bacterial or organelle DNA from its surroundings.

2. Bacterial and organelle ribosomes respond similarly to drugs which affect the ribosomal machinery for protein synthesis, while eukaryotic cytoribosomes are inhibited by drugs which do not affect bacterial or organelle systems.

3. Specific enzymes of aerobic respiration and of photosynthesis are physically a part of the bacterial plasma membrane, and of internal membranes in the two organelle types. The eukaryotic cell has no equivalent of the enzymes for these processes other than the ones found in its organelles.

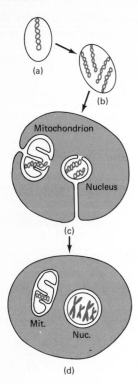

Figure 12.24 The evolutionary hypothesis for the origin of organelles postulates genome duplication and invagination of membrane to form double-membrane systems around each genome (red). (a) Prokaryotic cell; (b) duplication of prokaryotic genomes; (c) membrane invagination and formation of double membranes around genomes, all of which is destined to evolve into mitochondrion and nucleus (and chloroplast); and (d) eukaryotic cell, whose nuclear genome evolves toward greater complexity while the organellar genomes lose many duplicated genes. (After Uzzell, T., and C. Spolsky, 1974. Amer. Sci. **62**:334.

In addition to these and other specifications, endosymbiosis is a well-known phenomenon and often involves a symbiotic bacterial or blue-green algal organism within a eukaryotic host. There are no prokaryotes known, however, which act as hosts for other prokaryotic organisms in a symbiotic association. Nor are there any prokaryotes known to have the capacity of ingesting solids or other cellular organisms.

The alternatives to endosymbiosis involve evolutionary changes by which some existing parts of the cell have been altered so that they now exist as separate membranous compartments bathed in eukaryotic cytoplasm, much like other membranous compartments such as lysosomes, endoplasmic reticulum, and the nucleus itself (Fig. 12.24). Views differ about the exact nature of the prokaryotic ancestor of eukaryotes, and about the events which led to the present-day organization of eukaryotic cells. In most of the theories, however, it is proposed that some piece of the genome was separated from the bulk of the cellular DNA and became enclosed within membranes. Some of the suggested hypotheses postulate that a plasmid or plasmidlike DNA molecule carrying genes for organelle structure and function was enclosed within membranes making up the mitochondrial or chloroplast boundaries.

One of the central problems in the endosymbiosis theory is that the hundreds of genes now known to be coded in the nucleus for organelle traits must somehow have moved from the original endosymbiont genome into the host nucleus. Other difficulties with this theory have been discussed, as well as difficulties in the alternative ideas. There is no way at present of resolving these problems, and all the theories remain as possible explanations for the evolutionary origin of mitochondria and chloroplasts. In fact, it is entirely possible that mitochondria arose by one means and chloroplasts by another. The similarities between chloroplasts and blue-green algae in many details of molecular construction are striking. It is unlikely that similarities in the sequences of rRNA in chloroplast ribosomes and in blue-green algal ribosomes are the consequence of chance alone; they are more likely to indicate an ancestral relationship. Mitochondria, on the other hand, have many different features from prokaryotes and the case is less convincing for their endosymbiotic origin. Each of these theories and ideas has its enthusiastic proponents, but there is little objective evidence on which to make an unbiased choice at this time.

VIRUSES AND PLASMIDS AS EXTRANUCLEAR SYSTEMS

Genes carried by viruses and plasmids also influence host cell phenotype, and each of these can be considered as an extranuclear genetic system which interacts with the host genome in cellular growth and development. The principal difference when compared with mitochondria or chloroplasts is that the host cell can survive with or without its viruses and plasmids, whereas the organelles are vital components needed for the continued existence of the eukaryotic cell in general. Because they are dispensable we do not think of viruses or plasmids as anything other than foreign genomes in the host. Whether or not one can consider viruses of plasmids as organelles or as organelle equivalents is entirely a matter of opinion.

12.9   Infectious Inheritance

There are a number of cases in which a virus or a bacterium can be transmitted in eukaryotes through sexual reproduction, giving the impression of an extranuclear inheritance pattern in which the trait is passed from one parent to all or most of the progeny. The small bacterium called **kappa**, which occurs in certain strains of the ciliated protozoan *Paramecium aurelia*, is transmitted through the cytoplasm and not through the nuclear contribution of the parental cells (Fig. 12.25). The maintenance of kappa in these cells is dependent on the dominant nuclear allele *K*, and *kk* paramecia cannot harbor kappa even if these symbionts are introduced into *kk* cells by conjugation with *KK* or *Kk* partners which do have kappa present. Cells with kappa bacteria may be resistant to the toxin produced by these kappa elements, or they may be sensitive to the toxin and killed by it . Kappa-containing *KK* or *Kk* paramecia are "killers," and kappa therefore influences phenotypic expression in sensitive cells and in resistant cells. The presence of kappa bacteria confers immunity to the toxin in *KK* or *Kk* paramecia.

There are two examples of infectious elements transmitted by the female parent to the progeny in *Drosophila*, each demonstrating an apparently extranuclear pattern of inheritance. Flies may be phenotypically resistant to anesthesia by CO_2 and recover quickly from such exposure, or they may

Figure 12.25 Infectious inheritance in *Paramecium*. Genetic "killers" are *KK* or *Kk* and maintain kappa (red dots) in the cytoplasm. Kappa bacteria can be transmitted only through the cytoplasm, so *KK* or *Kk* paramecia remain sensitive unless they receive kappa during conjugation.

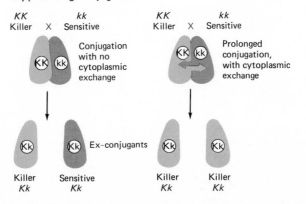

be sensitive and remain permanently paralyzed by exposure to this gas. The trait is transmitted through the female and only rarely through the male parent. Sensitive flies carry a virus called **sigma**, which alters the organism so that it becomes sensitized to CO_2; resistant organisms become sensitive to CO_2 when sigma virus is introduced during reproduction or by injection of extracts from sensitive flies. Sigma is an infectious agent which has the ability to alter the phenotype of the host organism to CO_2-sensitive, and which can be transmitted from generation to generation through the eggs of the female parent. Similarly, a trait called sex ratio (*SR*) has been traced to the effects of a symbiotic spirochete bacterium in several strains of *Drosophila*. Females harboring this spirochete produce virtually all daughters, since male embryos are killed very early in development if the spirochete is present in the cytoplasm of these cells. The *SR* trait can be introduced into normal flies through reproduction, or through injections of extracts from *SR* individuals. As with kappa, sigma virus and the *SR* spirochete can be maintained in *Drosophila* only with appropriate nuclear genes, which influence the host response to the agent in the expression of a resistant or sensitive phenotype.

Certain strains of mice are highly prone to develop mammary tumors while other strains are far less cancer-prone. The proneness to cancer appeared to be transmitted through the female parent and not through the male parent in reciprocal crosses between mice from both kinds of strains, and the pattern therefore resembled one due to extranuclear inheritance. Later, it was found that normal mice from low-cancer strains would develop mammary tumors with much higher frequency if they were *nursed* by females from high-cancer strains instead of by their own mothers. Such progeny mice would then transmit high proneness to tumor development in subsequent generations. The infectious agent, **mouse mammary tumor virus**, was eventually isolated and identified. The virus was transmitted through mother's milk, but the expression of the virus depended in part on nuclear genes in the mouse. Individuals from some mouse strains are less likely to develop these tumors even though the virus may be present.

There are a number of other RNA tumor viruses, in addition to mouse mammary tumor virus, and various DNA tumor viruses which are responsible for cancers in vertebrate animals, from fish to human beings. With all of them, the tumor virus can multiply only in certain hosts and host cell types, which are called **permissive** hosts or cells. When the same virus is introduced into a different host or cell type, called **nonpermissive**, it is unable to multiply but may **transform** the host cell into a cancerous state.

Tumor viruses induce a **lytic infection** in permissive host cells, during which virus multiplication takes place. Cell death usually follows shortly after. In cells kept in culture, usually derived from embryonic tissues, a lytic response is observed by the formation of a zone of dead cells somewhat resembling plaques produced by bacterial viruses. The **transforming response** is identified in cultured cells by the development of a disordered mass of cells which are heaped on top of one another (Fig. 12.26). In the living animal, the lytic response also leads to cell death and may cause the animal to die if there is a widespread infection. The development of tumors serves as the indicator of the transforming response in nonpermissive host animals.

Figure 12.26 Diagrammatic illustration of the growth pattern of (a) normal cells and (b) transformed cells on solid surfaces. Normal cells stop multiplying and moving when a confluent monolayer has formed, while transformed cells continue to multiply (and move) and therefore give rise to a disordered pile of cells.

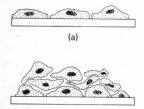

(a)

(b)

Transformed cells transmit their new phenotypes to subsequent generations indefinitely, that is, the transformed phenotype is inherited. Where
studies have been possible, it has been shown that the virus genome becomes integrated into one or more chromosomes in the transformed host cell
nucleus. As the host cell reproduces, copies of the viral genome are synthesized along with copies of the host genome, and both sets of genes are transmitted to progeny generations. In these cases, therefore, the inheritance of
the transformed phenotype can be traced to transmission of viral genes.
Only a part of the viral genome is expressed in nonpermissive cells, and this
part of the genome is coded for viral products which induce the cancerous
state in the host. Such viral genes are often called **oncogenes**, since they
are responsible for the **oncogenic** (cancer-causing) potential of the virus in
a suitable host. The integrated viruses do not multiply in nonpermissive
cells, since other genes needed for virus multiplication and infectious particle formation are turned off. In permissive host cells all the viral genes are
turned on, thus allowing multiplication to occur and a lytic response to take
place instead of transformation.

We will discuss oncogenic viruses in more detail in the next chapter.
These systems influence host development, and they also provide admirable models to investigate gene expression during eukaryotic development.

12.10   Plasmids as Extranuclear Genomes

We discussed plasmids in Section 9.7, but they should also be included here
since plasmids are prime examples of extranuclear genomes which are
transmissible from cell to cell and which influence the cellular phenotype.
While most of our information has come from plasmids in bacterial cells,
there are a few cases in which they are known to occur in eukaryotic cells.
For example, there is a 2 μm-long, circular DNA plasmid in many yeast
cells. Plasmid functions, however, are not yet known in the few eukaryotic
systems where they have been found.

The fertility factor **F** in *E. coli* confers a number of distinct phenotypic
traits on cells in which it occurs. In addition to making such cells capable of
transferring *F* plasmids themselves, integrated *F* in *Hfr* strains also causes
transfer of the host genome into conjugant partner cells. *E. coli* F^+ cells are
sensitive to infection by single-stranded RNA phages and certain single-
stranded DNA phages, but they are resistant to other phages such as T3 and
T7. These phenotypic characteristics are outcomes of phage gene action
within the host, and they are inherited when *F* is inherited by *E. coli*.

R plasmids carry antibiotic-resistance genes which confer resistance
on host cells harboring these plasmids. The plasmid genes can be incorporated into the host genome, so the resistance may remain even when the
plasmid DNA has apparently been eliminated from the host cell. This kind
of genome modification shows extranuclear inheritance when the resistance genes are in the plasmid DNA, but shows alteration to the host inheritance pattern if the genes become integrated as a part of the host
linkage group.

Bacterial cells which contain **Col plasmids** can synthesize proteins called **colicins**, which kill sensitive cells of their own species or of other species. The cells which harbor Col plasmids are immune to the effects of the toxic proteins, since they also synthesize **immunity proteins**. The Col plasmid genome contains separable regions, much like the R plasmids. The genome segment coding for colicin and immunity proteins can be separated from the transfer component. In this case, the colicin—immunity protein coding segment may be inherited along with *E. coli* genes in the single host linkage group. A pattern of extranuclear inheritance, however, would characterize *E. coli* with Col plasmids as separate genomes coexisting in the same cells with host DNA.

As with viruses, inheritance patterns of plasmid genes reflect the physical location of the extranuclear DNA. In both instances, the host phenotype is influenced by genes which are not native to the cellular linkage group but which may be integrated into this linkage group. These situations appear to be quite different from mitochondrial and chloroplast inheritance, since organelle DNA remains within the organelle and is not physically integrated into the host chromosomes. Whether the difference is only one of degree across a spectrum of variations in extranuclear inheritance, or whether these all represent different kinds of evolutionary events, is uncertain at present. The general observation which ties all these systems together is that each extranuclear genome codes for some of its own phenotypic traits and also influences phenotype expression of the cell in which it occurs. By analyzing the patterns of gene transmission, it is possible to determine whether or not these genes exist in a physically separate nucleic acid molecule or as an integrated part of the host DNA.

MATERNAL EFFECTS

The influence of maternal substances on the phenotype of the developing organism is referred to as **maternal effect**. These maternal substances, such as messenger RNAs, are made in the premeiotic oocyte under the direction of maternal genes and they therefore reflect the maternal genotype and not the zygotic genotype. When the zygote and developing organism are observed, however, it seems as though zygotic genes are responsible for the expressed phenotype. If the inheritance of such characteristics can be followed over several generations, maternal effect is usually clearly demonstrated and distinguished from true extranuclear inheritance (Fig. 12.27).

There are several classic examples of a maternal effect, which show different results in reciprocal crosses but which can be shown to be instances of *delayed Mendelian inheritance*. In the snail *Limnea peregra*, right-handed (dextral) coiling of the shell is determined by a dominant allele *D* and left-handed (sinistral) coiling by the recessive allele *d* of a single gene. The animal is hermaphroditic and is capable of self-fertilization as well as cross-fertilization. When homozygous dextral (*DD*) females are crossed with sinistral (*dd*) males, all the progeny are dextral; but in the reciprocal cross of sinistral (*dd*) females and dextral (*DD*) males, all the progeny show sinistral coiling. If *Dd* F₁ individuals in each of these reciprocal progenies

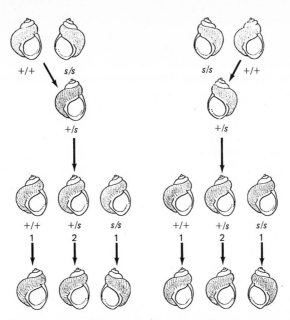

Figure 12.27 Maternal effect in the snail *Limnea peregra*. Direction of shell coiling depends on the mother's genotype rather than on the genotype of the individual itself. Dextral is dominant over sinistral coiling, but the expected F_1 and F_2 phenotypic ratios are delayed one generation, until the F_2 and F_3 generations, respectively.

undergo self-fertilization, each one produces an F_2 progeny entirely composed of dextrally-coiled snails. This seems to be non-Mendelian inheritance, but its true nature is clearly revealed when each F_2 individual undergoes self-fertilization to produce F_3 progeny. Three-fourths of the F_2 snails produce dextral progeny and one-fourth of the F_2 snails produce an F_3 generation composed entirely of sinistral types. The appearance of the same phenotypic ratio of 3 dextral:1 sinistral in reciprocal progenies points to single-gene Mendelian autosomal inheritance, but this phenotypic ratio appears in the F_3 generation instead of the F_2 generation.

The reason for the delayed expression of Mendelian phenotypic ratios is that substances produced in the egg cytoplasm by the maternal genotype govern the symmetry of the first cleavage division of the fertilized egg, or zygote. Once this division has taken place, the direction of coiling (and of the whole body) is established and lasts the lifetime of the animal. If the maternal genotype is *DD*, all zygotes will be dextral; if the maternal genotype is *dd*, all zygotes will be sinistral, regardless of the male parental genotype. Each F_1 *Dd* female in reciprocal progenies, whether dextral or sinistral in phenotype, has the dominant *D* allele. Every egg produced by these *Dd* females has the *D* gene product which directs dextral coiling in F_2 zygotes developed when these eggs are fertilized. When the F_2 snails self-fertilize, those with the *dd* genotype give rise to sinistral progeny while females with *DD* or *Dd* genotypes will produce dextral F_3 progeny. The overall result shows classical Mendelian inheritance, one generation delayed. If the pattern had been truly extranuclear, differences would have been evident in reciprocal progenies in every generation and not just in one or two generations of a lineage. In extranuclear inheritance the progeny continue to resemble only one of the two parents, and the extranuclear trait is transmitted indefinitely in subsequent generations.

The inheritance of phenotypic traits can therefore be judged by various criteria using genetic methods and molecular analyses. If the pattern of inheritance is extranuclear, the responsible extranuclear genome can be identified in many cases as belonging to organelles such as mitochondria and chloroplasts, or to viruses, or to plasmids. Investigation of some new extranuclear inherited trait in an organism is therefore guided by available methods through which the extranuclear factor can be located, and then it can be explored in greater detail in that host system.

QUESTIONS AND PROBLEMS

12.1. In certain cases it has been found that *grande* × *petite* yeast will yield normal respiration-sufficient diploids. When these diploid cells undergo meiosis and produce ascospore tetrads, each ascus is found to contain 2 *grande* and 2 *petite* spores. On the basis of these results, explain the inheritance pattern and diagram the appropriate genotypes.

12.2. *Petites* such as those described in question 12.1 are called segregational *petites*. In crosses between segregational *petites* and a neutral extranuclear *petite* strain, what percentage of the ascospores will have the *petite* phenotype after meiosis has occurred in the zygotes?

12.3. Two species of *Drosophila*, A and B, produce interesting results when crossed. If female A is crossed with male B, only female progeny occur; if female B is crossed with male A, mostly male progeny are produced and there are few or no female offspring. Suggest an explanation for these observations.

12.4. In corn there is a form of male-sterility which is inherited extranuclearly, so the *normal ♂ × male-sterile ♀* gives male-sterile offspring while the reciprocal cross gives normal offspring. Some strains of corn carry a dominant restorer gene (*Rf*), which restores pollen fertility in a male-sterile line.
   a. If pollen from a genotypically *Rf/Rf* plant is used in a cross with a male-sterile plant, what are the genotype and phenotype of the F_1?
   b. If a testcross is performed using F_1 plants described in (a) as females and pollen from a normal *rf/rf* plant, what would be the genotypes and phenotypes of these testcross progeny? What would be the nature of their cytoplasm?

12.5. Use diagrams to show how replication of mitochondrial DNA can proceed by the mechanisms of D-loop synthesis, Cairns theta-forms, and rolling circle. What electron microscopical figures would clearly permit distinction of each one of these mechanisms in populations of replicating mitochondrial DNA circular molecules?

12.6. You have isolated presumptive ribosomal particles from purified mitochondria isolated from rat liver cells.

  a. How would you demonstrate that these were ribosome monomers using a test for function?

  b. How would you demonstrate that these functional particles were composed of two subunits, both of which were needed for monosome function?

  c. What antibiotic inhibitors would you use in determining whether these ribosomes were truly mitochondrial and not merely contaminating cytoplasmic ribosomes from the same cells?

  d. List the major differences between ribosomes from mitochondria and those from the cytoplasm of animal cells.

12.7. How would you test whether rRNA in organelle ribosomes was transcribed from organelle DNA and not from nuclear DNA? How could you tell whether organelle rRNA was transcribed from one or from both strands of its template DNA?

12.8. Describe an experiment in which you could demonstrate that one subunit of a chloroplast enzyme is coded in chloroplast DNA while the other subunit of the functional enzyme is coded in nuclear DNA.

12.9. The snail *Limnea peregra* shows right-handed (dextral) or left-handed (sinistral) coiling of its shell; dextral is dominant over sinistral (*D, d* alleles). A snail produces only dextral progeny after self-fertilization. When these progeny snails undergo self-fertilization, however, they produce 25% sinistral and 75% dextral offspring. What is the genotype of the original snail?

12.10. Make a list of the major differences which distinguish extranuclear inheritance from conventional inheritance of nuclear genes in eukaryotes, using the following format:

	Inheritance	
Characteristic	Nuclear	Extranuclear
1.		

12.11. A biologist using haploid *Neurospora* notices a patch of orange mycelium on a plate containing wild type mold. The biologist constructs a heterokaryon using a non-orange, arginine-requiring haploid and the arginine-independent, orange variant, and is surprised to find some arginine-requiring, orange segregants, among several other phenotypes. Explain the probable origin of the orange phenotype.

REFERENCES

Aloni, Y., and G. Attardi. 1972. Expression of the mitochondrial genome in HeLa cells. XI. Isolation and characterization of transcription complexes of mitochondrial DNA. *J. Mol. Biol.* **70**:363.

Angerer, L., N. Davidson, W. Murphy, D. Lynch, and G. Attardi. 1976. An electron microscope study of the relative positions of 4S and ribosomal RNA genes in HeLa cell mitochondrial DNA. *Cell* **9**:81.

Birky, C. W., Jr. 1978. Transmission genetics of mitochondria and chloroplasts. *Ann. Rev. Genet.* **12**:471.

Borst, P., and L. A. Grivell. 1978. The mitochondrial genome of yeast. *Cell* **15**:705.

Borst, P., and J. H. J. Hoeijmakers. 1979. Kinetoplast DNA. *Plasmid* **2**:20.

Bos, J. L., C. Heyting, P. Borst, A. C. Arnberg, and E. F. J. Van Bruggen. 1978. An insert in the single gene for the large ribosomal RNA in yeast mitochondrial DNA. *Nature* **275**:336.

Chooi, W. Y., and C. D. Laird. 1976. DNA and polyribosome-like structures in lysates of mitochondrial of *Drosophila melanogaster. J. Mol. Biol.* **100**:493.

Datema, R., E. Agsteribbe, and A. M. Kroon. 1974. The mitochondrial ribosomes of *Neurospora crassa.* I. On the occurrence of 80S ribosomes. *Biochim. Biophys. Acta* **335**:386.

Gibbs, S. P. 1978. The chloroplasts of *Euglena* may have evolved from symbiotic green algae. *Canad. J. Bot.* **56**:2883.

Gillham, N. W. 1978. *Organelle Heredity.* New York: Raven.

Goddard, J. M., and D. R. Wolstenholme. 1978. Origin and direction of replication in mitochondrial DNA molecules from *Drosophila melanogaster. Proc. Nat. Acad. Sci. U. S.* **75**:3886.

Gray, P. W., and R. B. Hallick. 1979. Isolation of *Euglena gracilis* chloroplast 5S ribosomal RNA and mapping the 5S rRNA gene on chloroplast DNA. *Biochemistry* **18**:1820.

Hoffmann, H.-P., and C. J. Avers. 1973. Mitochondrion of yeast: Ultrastructural evidence for one giant, branched organelle per cell. *Science* **181**:749.

Horak, I., H. G. Coon, and I. B. Dawid. 1974. Interspecific recombination of mitochondrial DNA molecules in hybrid somatic cells. *Proc. Nat. Acad. Sci. U. S.* **71**:1828.

Kolodner, R., and K. K. Tewari. 1975. Chloroplast DNA from higher plants replicates by both the Cairns and the rolling circle mechanism. *Nature* **256**:708.

Ledoigt, G., B. J. Stevens, J. J. Curgy, and J. Andre. 1979. Analysis of chloroplast ribosomes by polyacrylamide gel electrophoresis and electron microscopy. *Exp. Cell Res.* **119**:221.

Linnane, A. W., and P. Nagley. 1978. Mitochondrial genetics in perspective: The derivation of a genetic and physical map of the yeast mitochondrial genome. *Plasmid* **1**:324.

Locker, J., A. Lewin, and M. Rabinowitz. 1979. The structure and organization of mitochondrial DNA from petite yeast. *Plasmid* **2**:155.

Margulis, L. Aug. 1971. Symbiosis and evolution. *Sci. Amer.* **225**:48.

Preer, L. B., and J. R. Preer, Jr. 1978. Inheritance of infectious elements. In *Cell Biology, A Comprehensive Treatise*, Vol. 1 (L. Goldstein and D. M. Prescott, eds.), p. 319. New York: Academic Press.

Robberson, D. L., H. Kasamatsu, and J. Vinograd. 1972. Replication of mitochondrial DNA. Circular replicative intermediates in mouse L cells. *Proc. Nat. Acad. Sci. U.S.* **69**:737.

Rochaix, J. D. 1978. Restriction endonuclease map of the chloroplast DNA of *Chlamydomonas reinhardii*. *J. Mol. Biol.* **126**:597.

Sager, R. 1972. *Cytoplasmic Genes and Organelles*. New York: Academic Press.

Scragg, A. H., and D. Y. Thomas. 1977. Synthesis of cytochrome *c* oxidase polypeptides in an *Escherichia coli* cell-free system directed by *Saccharomyces cerevisiae* mitochondrial DNA. *Mol. gen. Genet.* **150**:81.

Swanson, R. F., and I. B. Dawid. 1970. The mitochondrial ribosome of *Xenopus laevis*. *Proc. Nat. Acad. Sci. U. S.* **66**:117.

van Winkle-Swift, K. P. 1978. Uniparental inheritance is promoted by delayed division of the zygote in *Chlamydomonas*. *Nature* **275**:749.

van Winkle-Swift, K. P., and C. W. Birky, Jr. 1978. The non-reciprocality of organelle gene recombination in *Chlamydomonas reinhardtii* and *Saccharomyces cerevisiae*. *Mol. gen. Genet.* **166**:193.

Wesolowski, M., and H. Fukuhara. 1979. The genetic map of transfer RNA genes of yeast mitochondria: Correction and extension. *Mol. gen. Genet.* **170**:261.

Wurtz, E. A., J. E. Boynton, and N. W. Gillham. 1977. Perturbation of chloroplast DNA amounts and chloroplast gene transmission in *Chlamydomonas reinhardtii* by 5-fluorodeoxyuridine. *Proc. Nat. Acad. Sci. U.S.* **74**:4552.

Wurtz, E. A., B. B. Sears, D. K. Rabert, H. S. Shepherd, N. W. Gillham, and J. E. Boynton. 1979. A specific increase in chloroplast gene mutations following growth of *Chlamydomonas* in 5-fluorodeoxyuridine. *Mol. gen. Genet.* **170**:235.

13

Developmental Genetics

In earlier chapters we discussed a variety of evidence showing that phenotypically different cells could arise from a genotypically identical population by differential gene action. Turning genes on and off, primarily by positive and negative control over transcription, leads to differences in cellular activities, behavior, and appearance.

But is the development of organism shape and construction simply a matter of turning genes on and off? If this were the case, we would expect to find corresponding sequences of gene transcription and of phenotypic development. This is not always the case, however, since a gene may be transcribed and translated at the same time. Gene products may therefore be present at the same time even if involved in a stepwise sequence of events in a developmental pathway. Furthermore, we find that phenotypic expression may be delayed even though gene products are present in developing cells, and in some cases cells acquire and lose specificities which influence their interactions with one another as tissues and organs are put together in the embryo.

Since morphogenesis, or the development of form and function, is exceedingly complex, viruses have been used as model systems for developmental genetic study. The basic principles which were discovered in gene-controlled morphogenetic pathways in viruses have also been found to describe cellular and organismal development in eukaryotes. In these studies it is clear that morphogenesis proceeds by sequential steps which are under gene control. Interactions between molecules and between cells and molecules lead to cell-specific and stage-specific events which proceed in an orderly fashion during the time that development occurs.

In this chapter we will see how genetic methods have been applied to problems in development, and how the outlines of gene-controlled morphogenetic phenomena have been recognized and described. There is every reason to expect that these broad outlines will be filled in as new methods and new systems are exploited.

DEVELOPMENT OF BIOLOGICAL FORM

The development of functional form and structure, or **morphogenesis**, is one of the major areas of biological study. Biological structures and organisms are built up from proteins and nucleic acids specified by coded genes, and from other chemical components made in reactions which are catalyzed by genetically coded enzymes. A variety of substances obtained from the environment are also utilized in cellular metabolism and in morphogenesis.

Protein synthesis is regulated primarily at the level of transcription, leading to differential gene action. But orderly development of form and structure is not simply due to turning genes off and on in a sequence of transcriptional events which corresponds in time to the observed sequence of developmental events. In many cases, different genes involved in a developmental pathway are actively transcribing at the same time, and different proteins are being made at the same time. How do these proteins come together in particular associations and at particular times during development to make a finished structure? Important insights into this fundamental problem have emerged from studies of various model systems, such as the viruses. Through comparisons between mutants which are blocked in development at different stages, it has been possible to infer that morphogenesis proceeds in an orderly fashion as the consequence both of transcriptional events and of events which involve interactions between protein products of these transcripts.

13.1   Early Genes and Late Genes

During phage morphogenesis in infected cells, certain proteins coded by viral genes appear early in infection, while others appear later in the cycle. These "early" and "late" proteins are made from information coded in "early" and "late" genes, that is, from genes transcribed early or late in the infection cycle.

During a 25-minute infection cycle initiated by phage T4 in *E. coli* cells, the host metabolic machinery is subverted from making host molecules to making virus-specified DNA and protein molecules. Viral enzymes appear within 1 minute after infection, and viral DNA replication catalyzed by these enzymes begins within 5 minutes. About 8 minutes in the infection cycle marks the first appearance of structural head and tail proteins, and the first completed infective phage particle is made about halfway through the infection. In the remaining 12 minutes or so, about 200 phages accumulate within the cell. The phage-specified lysozyme then attacks the cell wall and free phages are liberated when the host cell bursts (see Fig. 2.25).

The sequence of events is orderly since "early" proteins consist mainly of enzymes which catalyze the synthesis of "late" proteins that are primarily the building units for phage construction. These "early" and "late" proteins are made from transcribed information coded in "early" and "late" genes, under positive transcriptional control. There is no evidence for a T4

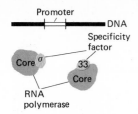

Figure 13.1 Various classes of promoters are recognized by different specificity factors (red) bound to the RNA polymerase core enzyme. For example, factor σ recognizes early promoters while factor 33 recognizes late promoters, thus leading to orderly readout of the phage T4 genome.

repressor protein and, therefore, no evidence for negative control over transcription in this phage. According to the available evidence, positive control is exerted through interactions between virus-coded protein **specificity factors** and host RNA polymerase. Different specificity factors may bind to the RNA polymerase core enzyme (made up of five polypeptide chains—see Section 8.2). Different promoters will be recognized by the different specificity factors bound to the polymerase core, resulting in a sequence of transcriptional readout of the phage genome (Fig. 13.1).

Early in infection, host-specified σ factor determines the specificity of transcription on the "e" or **early strand** of phage duplex DNA. Later in infection, σ factor dissociates from the polymerase core enzyme, after which other specificity factors bind to these cores; the activated polymerases then recognize and bind to different promoters in the phage genome. Transcription at the later stage takes place largely from the antiparallel "l" or **late strand** of phage DNA, guided by particular specificity factors bound to the RNA polymerase core. The late promoters govern genes that code for T4 structural proteins and other factors involved in phage morphogenesis (Fig. 13.2). The order of transcriptional readout is therefore specified by promoter—polymerase interactions, and this order is facilitated by the sequence of genes on the two strands of phage T4 DNA. A population of early proteins appears as transcripts of early genes are produced, and a population of late proteins appears when structural gene transcripts become available later on in infection.

In phage T7, genes are clustered according to their functions (Fig. 13.3). There are three distinct regions of the linear genome: (1) genes coded for early functions, primarily involved in the regulation of transcription; (2) genes coded for T7 DNA replication enzymes; and (3) genes coded for structural proteins involved in T7 morphogenesis. Unlike T4 in which different specificity factors associate with the host polymerase core, T7 switches from mRNA transcription of early genes to mRNA transcription of late genes through synthesis of an entirely new T7-specified RNA polymerase. Gene 1, which codes for T7 RNA polymerase, is in the early region of the map. As infection proceeds, the new polymerase continues to accumulate until it is the only transcription enzyme which acts late in infection. Products of the early genes also turn off host polymerase activity, leaving only the T7 polymerase to function, and only late promoters are recognized by the T7 enzyme. The order of transcriptional readout is governed by promoter—polymerase recognition and interaction, but in T7 there is a new enzyme in addition to the new specificity factors combined with the host polymerase.

Phage λ is more complex than the T-phages since λ is lysogenic. Not only does it have a lytic cycle characterized by early and late mRNA transcripts, but λ also can exist in the noninfectious prophage state. Phage λ must therefore be able to move on and off the bacterial chromosome, and most of its genes must be blocked while it is inserted as a prophage and while it is not producing new phage particles.

The major element which blocks transcription in the prophage state is the **λ repressor**, coded by gene C_1. Virtually no λ-specific mRNA is made when λ repressor is present, except for gene C_1 transcripts coding for the

Figure 13.2 Map of the known genes of phage T4. The numbers on the inner circle "ticks" are map distances in recombination units. The gene symbols and numbers are just outside the outer circle, and many are known to direct functions which are indicated in the rectangles by drawings of phage parts or by abbreviations (NEG, negative; DEL, delayed; ARR, arrested; HD, head; LYS, lysis; MAT, maturation; DEF, defective). The arrows within the genetic map show the direction of transcription of the known genes in that segment of the map. (From Wood, W. B. 1974. In *Handbook of Genetics*, vol. 1, p. 327; R. C. King, ed. New York: Plenum.)

repressor protein itself. λ repressor binds specifically to operators of two of the early operons in the phage genome. Since these early genes are blocked, later gene functions are not expressed because the necessary early gene

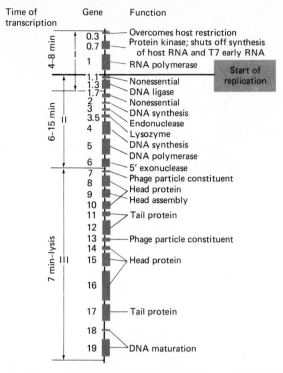

Figure 13.3 Genetic map of phage T7. The gene number is just left of each red block indicating the size of the gene, and the gene function is on the right. The roman numerals I-III mark off the early gene region, DNA replication genes, and the late genes, respectively. (After Kornberg, A., 1974. *DNA Synthesis*. San Francisco: Freeman.)

products are lacking. If the repressor is inactivated, usually under conditions which inhibit DNA synthesis (for example, exposure to UV radiation), the two early operons become accessible to the RNA polymerase and to transcription. One of these early operons contains genes largely concerned with proteins required for the recombination events which free the λ chromosome from its host chromosomal association. The other early operon contains genes needed for phage DNA replication and for other early functions. In addition to negative control over transcription via the repressor, positive control must also be exerted if all the required early operons are to be transcribed.

All the late genes code for late proteins, which are coded by about half the λ genome (Fig. 13.4). Synthesis of λ head and tail proteins is carried out by translation of a single operon, which includes about 20 functional genes coding for λ structural proteins. Transcription of this late operon is turned on by the protein product of gene Q, whose exact function is still uncertain. The product of gene Q may be a specificity factor, as we described in T4, or some other functional type of protein. The coordinated synthesis of all of the structural proteins in λ is ensured by the simple device of having all these late genes in a single operon governed by a single promoter. Once RNA

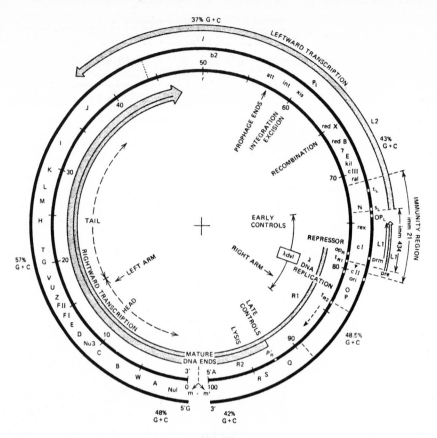

Figure 13.4 Genetic map of phage λ, showing the two complementary DNA strands (black) and the direction of transcription of regions along each strand (gray arrows). Functions of certain regions are shown within the circles. (From Szybalski, W. 1974. In *Handbook of Genetics*, vol. 1, p. 309; R. C. King, ed. New York: Plenum.)

polymerase binds to the promoter, all the gene sequences are transcribed coordinately into a polygenic mRNA. Translations which then take place lead to the variety of proteins needed to build the virus. Once DNA is packaged in the phage particle, phage lysozyme leads to dissolution of the bacterial wall and a burst of infective phage progeny particles. All these lytic cycle activities are turned off, however, as long as λ repressor is made.

In addition to early and late proteins, there are proteins which are made early and which continue to be made through all or most of a lytic cycle, as well as proteins made at different times after the early and before the late genes are turned on. These activities are facilitated in large measure by the ordering of gene sequences in the genome of phages, and by particular interactions between DNA operator and promoter sequences with repressor and enzyme proteins, respectively.

Viral morphogenesis takes place when protein products of gene action become available in the host cell. How do these proteins come together to make a specific and functional virus particle? Are proteins translated in a particular sequence guided by the transcriptional readout sequence; that is, is morphogenesis itself regulated at transcription? In order to answer this fundamental question, it was necessary to analyze a reasonably simple morphogenetic system, for which mutants with developmental blocks were available and in which the nature of these developmental blocks could be analyzed. Studies using phage T4 provided very important insights in answering this major question.

13.2 Building the T4 Virus

In relatively simple viruses and cell structures, there seems to be sufficient information in the component molecules themselves so that molecules undergo **self-assembly** into a particular biological structure. Morphogenesis in such systems needs no additional information to specify shape and size, as can be seen by *in vitro* tests. For example, when tobacco mosaic virus (TMV) particles are dissociated into their constituent RNA and protein molecules, these separate molecules will reassemble into infective viruses with the same size, shape, and properties as viruses made in the living cell. A single-stranded RNA molecule binds with thousands of molecules of the single kind of protein of the TMV coat, to produce typical TMV rods (Fig. 13.5). The shapes of the individual molecules guide the specific interactions between these molecules during morphogenesis. These molecular associations usually occur by formation of relatively weak chemical bonds, and not by covalent linkages. The inherent ability for interaction with another molecule is a property of the molecule itself in such self-assembly systems,

Figure 13.5 Reconstitution of tobacco mosaic virus (TMV) particle from dissociated coat protein molecules and single-stranded RNA. The order of assembly and the orientation of the RNA strand are shown. The final assembled particle consists of 130 turns of the helically ordered protein subunits, with 16-1/3 subunits per turn, completely enclosing the RNA strand. (After Stent, G. S., and R. Calendar. 1978. *Molecular Genetics*, 2nd ed. San Francisco: Freeman.)

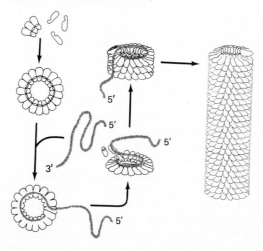

that is, the molecule has the necessary information for particular interactions.

Self-assembly of macromolecules is a fundamental mechanism involved in construction of very simple viruses like TMV, which has only five or six genes, and of cellular structures like ribosomes. Given the right collection of molecular units and the right environmental conditions, only a few kinds of structures assemble spontaneously. In most situations, structural assembly occurs only at specific times and in specific places.

When the different kinds of molecules making up T4 viruses are placed together in a test tube, virus particles do not assemble spontaneously. Phage T4 is a more complex virus, with about 50 of its approximately 100 genes coded for components involved in phage morphogenesis. It has a polyhedrally-shaped head consisting of a protein coat filled with duplex DNA; a short neck connects the head to a springlike tail consisting of a contractile sheath surrounding a central core and attached to a base plate, from which there protrude six short spikes and six long, slender tail fibers (Fig. 13.6). When T4 attaches by its spikes and tail fibers to the bacterial cell wall, the sheath contracts and drives the tubular core of the tail through the cell wall. This provides a passageway for DNA to pass from the phage head into the bacterium.

During the 1960s, Robert Edgar, William Wood, and their co-workers provided unambiguous evidence showing that T4 morphogenesis was the outcome of *interactions between gene products* and not of a sequence of transcriptional events. They isolated a large number of mutants which made altered gene products that were often nonfunctional. Phage development stopped in these mutants at the point where the altered protein was needed in phage assembly. If one were to examine all of these developmentally-blocked mutants in cells undergoing abortive infection, it would be possible to identify different genes by complementation tests and determine how many different functional genes were involved in phage development. More than 40 such mutated genes have been discovered in this way. But was there a sequence to phage assembly or did the normal parts assemble in some random fashion once the necessary normal gene products were provided by complementing mutants in a mixed infection?

Figure 13.6 Structure of T4 and the other T-even phages.

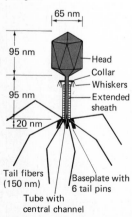

In order to determine whether there was a particular block in development at some particular time in a morphogenetic sequence, Edgar and Wood studied T4 mutants under **permissive** and **nonpermissive** conditions. When a mutant was introduced into permissive *E. coli* cells, the phage developed to the infective particle stage. In nonpermissive *E. coli* cells, development stopped at the time the altered protein was needed. The particular morphogenetic function of the genes involved in phage assembly was determined by electron microscopy of the mutant extracts taken from nonpermissive host cells, where development was blocked. For example, T4 that was mutant for gene 23 produced tails and tail fibers but no heads; so gene 23 must be involved in head assembly. Gene 34 mutants led to accumulations of heads and tails but no tail fibers in abortively infected *E. coli*; so gene 34 must be involved with tail fiber assembly. Gene 27 must control a step in tail formation, since extracts contained only heads and tail fibers, but no tails. The map shown in Fig. 13.2 reflects the morphogenetic function of various genes, which were analyzed in these **conditionally lethal**

mutants, that is, mutants whose development was blocked (lethal to the phage) in nonpermissive cells but not in permissive cells (virulent phages produced).

These and similar results indicated that a block in the formation of one of these structural components did not influence the formation of the other two structures. Heads and tails were made in tail-fiberless mutants, tails and tail fibers were made in headless mutants, and heads and tail fibers were made in tailless mutants. These results were interpreted to mean that there were three separate and distinct branches in the phage morphogenetic pathway, each branch leading to formation of a different one of the three major structures.

Did these three parts of the virus come together all at once, or was there an assembly sequence? To answer this question, extracts of different mutant lysates were collected from abortively infected cells, and the extracts were mixed together *in vitro* (Fig. 13.7). The mixtures were examined by electron microscopy to see phage morphology, and mixtures were used to infect *E. coli* in an *in vivo* assay of phage functional virulence, which would

Figure 13.7 Results of mixing extracts of T4 mutant lysates from abortively infected *E. coli* cells. (a) Different T4 mutants infect *E. coli*, and (b) lysates of the abortively infected cells are collected for (c) mixing of these lysates in various combinations. These experiments showed that there was a sequence of morphogenetic assembly in phage T4, with tails assembling onto heads and then tail fibers assembling onto the head-tail particle.

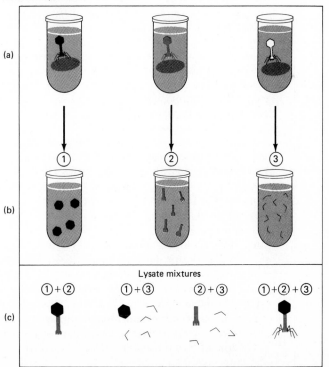

occur only if fully infective particles had assembled in the mixed extracts. From such tests it was found that heads and tails would assemble even if tail fibers were not present, but that tail fibers would only add on to head—tail combinations and not to tails alone. The virus was infective only when all three structures were combined in a phage particle, but noninfective combinations of structures could be observed with the electron microscope. The assembly of a functional virus particle apparently took place in a two-step sequence; heads and tails assembled first, and tail fibers were added in a separate step afterward.

How many steps were involved in the assembly of each of these three parts of the phage? Any head mutant produced defective heads, which would not assemble with normal tails. Any tail mutant made defective tails that would not assemble with normal heads. Any tail fiber mutant made defective fibers that would not assemble with head—tail units. In order to determine how many steps were involved in the assembly reactions, Edgar, Wood, and their associates conducted pairwise **extract complementation tests**, an *in vitro* procedure which depends on *interactions between gene products* and not on the actions of genes directly as *in vivo* complementations do.

From pairwise mixtures of extracts from lysates taken from abortively infected cells, it was found that almost all of these tests gave unambiguous positive or negative results; either there was at least a tenfold increase in infective phages or there was no detectable increase in virulent phages when compared with either extract alone. On this basis, fourteen different complementation groups were found to accommodate all of the results from the pairwise tests. Members from different groups do complement each other while members from the same group do not complement each other *in vitro* (Table 13.1). Each complementation group defined a functional component for assembly, and all fourteen of these components or reactions were needed to produce complete viruses. The extract complementations corresponded to the observed defective phenotypes of the mutants within each group; for example, all the mutants of complementation group II were defective in tail assembly and produced only completed heads and tail fibers in nonpermissive cells.

Further tests were conducted to provide more details of the assembly sequence, and from these a series of steps was derived for each of the three branches of the morphogenetic pathway leading to infective virus particles (Fig. 13.8). Some of these steps have not been worked out in as much detail as others, but the general picture is quite clear. A number of important features emerged from these studies:

1. There is a stringent sequential order to the morphogenetic process. If a step in one pathway is blocked, characteristic structural intermediates accumulate. The block cannot be bypassed. Such a block in one pathway, however, does not interfere with the morphogenetic sequence leading to the other two structures.

2. The sequence of morphogenetic events depends on interactions between gene products, and not on sequential transcription or induction of structural gene action. All of the late proteins appear in cells

Table 13.1

Complementation groups determined from results of pairwise mixing of extracts from lysates taken from abortively infected *E. coli* cells. Positive interactions between gene products, seen by tenfold increase in infective T4 phages, were interpreted to mean that the responsible genes were in the same complementation group.[1]

Extract complement-ation group	Mutant genes	Components present[2]			Inferred defect
I a	20,21,22,23,24,31	—	tail	fiber	head (formation)
I b	49,2,64,50,65,4,16,17	head	tail	fiber	head (completion)
II	53,5,6,7,8,10,25,26, 51,27,28,29	head	—	fiber	tail (baseplate)
III	48,54	head	baseplate	fiber	tail (core,sheath)
IV	13, 14 }				
V	15 }	head	tail	fiber	?
VI	18 }				
VII	9	contracted part-icle[3] (fiberless)		fiber	?
VIII	11 }	defective phage particle (fibers attached)			?
IX	12 }				
X	37, 38 }				
XI	36 }	fiberless particle	—		fiber assembly
XII	35 }				
XIII	34 }				
XIV	63	fiberless particle		fiber	fiber attachment

[1]From Wood, W. B. *et al.* 1968. Bacteriophage assembly. *Fed. Proc.* **27**(5):1160–1166.
[2]All structural components listed are unattached to each other unless otherwise indicated. Description of these as heads, tails, etc. implies only that they are identifiable in electron micrographs, not that they are complete structures.
[3]Heads with attached tails are designated particles.

at about the same time, and not in sequential order as would be expected for sequential transcription events at structural genes. This inference is supported by the observation that several extract complementation groups correspond to single gene products (see Table 13.1). These gene products interact *in vitro*, and presumably also interact *in vivo* in normal cells and in permissive cells mixedly infected with mutants from different gene complementation groups, as shown by the production of infective phages from all of these systems.

Similar interactions between gene products synthesized coordinately or independently in various phages, but appearing at about the same time during infection, probably underlie morphogenesis in all or most viruses. Similar processes very likely are responsible for orderly morphogenesis in cellular organisms, that is, development is not simply a matter of turning genes on and off through transcriptional controls. Morphogenesis also requires interactions between protein products of differential gene action, after transcripts have been translated. These interactions between gene products are also under genetic control, since mutations can block particular steps in developmental sequences.

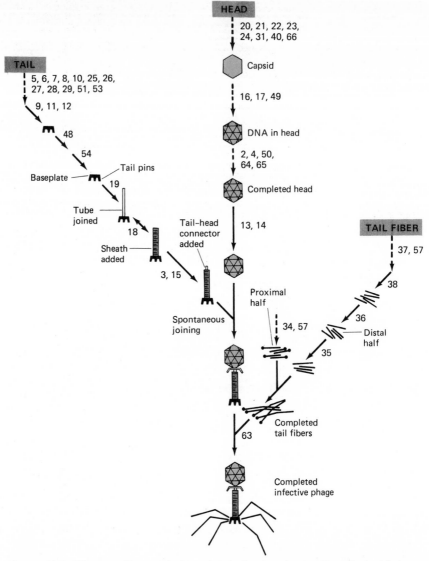

Figure 13.8 There are three main branches in the morphogenetic pathway of phage maturation, such that heads, tails, and tail fibers are formed independently and afterward combine to constitute the infective phage particle. The numbers refer to the genes whose products are involved at each morphogenetic step (see Fig. 13.2 for T4 map). (After Wood, W. B. 1973. In *Genetic Mechanisms of Development*, p. 29, F. H. Ruddle, ed. New York: Academic Press).

How can the basic principles derived from T4 studies be extended to studies of other systems? *In vitro* complementations between extracts from different mutants provide a powerful analytical tool, but these tests are clearly less sensitive than *in vivo* complementations, since only 14 complementation groups were derived from *in vitro* studies while 40 to 50 different genes were identified by *in vivo* complementations. Sorting out of the individual steps in head assembly, for example, has not yet been possible using T4.

In the next part of this chapter we will discuss genetic methods by which the timing of gene action in development has been investigated. These genetic methods have been used successfully with different systems, including eukaryotes, and they produced results which led to still deeper insights into the genetic control of morphogenetic pathways.

TIMING OF GENE ACTION IN DEVELOPMENT

As we have seen, different events occur as parts of pathways of development. Intermediates produced by gene action are processed in defined sequences, but the order of these processing events cannot be determined very easily in most species because there are too few suitable mutations available or because of technical problems in analyzing very complex systems.

There are genetic methods by which the order of events in a biological pathway can be assessed, if suitable mutants can be recognized and isolated. In one very useful experimental approach to the dissection of genetically controlled developmental sequences, advantage is taken of different responses of a mutant strain under permissive and nonpermissive conditions for development. In conditional mutants, such as those which proceed normally at one temperature but whose development is blocked at a different temperature, or whose protein products are affected differentially by inhibitors, it is possible to compare the phenotypic response in the *same cells* when they are shifted from one condition to another during development. Using temperature-sensitive mutants and other conditional mutant types it is possible to determine the developmental step which is blocked by the mutation, and to determine the time in development when this step or event takes place in normal morphogenesis.

13.3   Reciprocal Temperature Shifts in Phage P22 Studies

Phage P22 infects *Salmonella typhimurium*, and goes through a series of morphogenetic processes leading to production of numerous infective particles in the host. As we saw in phage T4, there are "early" and "late" proteins produced by action of "early" and "late" genes in the P22 genome. In 1973, Jonathan Jarvik and David Botstein described a genetic approach to analyze morphogenesis. Their method can be used to study any biological pathway in which (1) mutants can be obtained behaving normally at one temperature but abnormally at a different temperature, and (2) when different mutations can be genetically recombined.

Jarvik and Botstein collected a number of different P22 mutants which were defective in some morphogenetic feature when incubated at high or low temperatures, but which developed normally at 30°C. Temperature-sensitive (*ts*) mutants were defective at 40° but were normal at 30° or 20°, while cold-sensitive (*cs*) mutants were defective at 20° but were normal at 30° or 40° incubation temperatures. Different *ts* and *cs* mutations were recombined in mixedly infected *Salmonella*, and 30 different *ts/cs* double mutant types were collected and studied. During the experiments, each strain was shifted reciprocally from high to low and from low to high temperatures: from 20° to 30°, 20° to 40°, 40° to 30°, and 40° to 20°C. The cells infected with *ts/cs* double mutants, and with individual *ts* or *cs* mutants, were examined for phage yield at every temperature shift. Any condition or set of conditions which permitted normal morphogenesis would be evident by production of infective phage particles. Unrelieved mutational blocks would not lead to normal development or to mature infectious phage progenies.

In a double mutant whose *ts* and *cs* mutations affect events that must occur in a certain order for normal morphogenesis, there should be very different results when the shift is from the low nonpermissive temperature (20°) to the high nonpermissive temperature (40°) versus a shift from 40° to 20° (Table 13.2). For example, if the *cs* step occurs before the *ts* step in development, the shift from 20° to 40° will not result in completion of the pathway because the *ts* block will be imposed as the *cs* block is relieved at 40°. On the other hand, a shift from 40° to 20° should lead to successful completion of the pathway, since the *cs* gene product or intermediate has been made and has accumulated at 40°. When shifted to 20°, this *cs* intermediate can be processed in the next step in the pathway which is under control of the *ts* gene. The *ts* gene product can be made from the accumulated *cs* intermediate which was produced earlier in the 40° incubation interval.

Temporal order was inferred by Jarvik and Botstein for a given *ts* or *cs* action according to reciprocal temperature-shift results for 19 of the 30 *ts/cs* double mutant strains examined, *according to the execution point of the mutation*. The **execution point** (or transition point) is defined operationally as the latest time at which shift to the nonpermissive temperature will still produce a mutant phenotype. The reason for defining it as the latest time is that any thermolabile protein may be influenced either at the time it is being synthesized or at the time it is engaged in a catalytic activity. If a *ts* or *cs* enzyme activity is affected during a temperature shift, the execution point coincides with the *step* in the developmental pathway which is con-

Table 13.2
Predicted results of temperature shifts for pathways with reversible *cs* and *ts* steps[1]

Pathways[2]	Temperature shift[3]					
	20° → 20°	20° → 30°	20° → 40°	40° → 40°	40° → 30°	40° → 20°
$I_2 \xrightarrow{cs} I_2 \xrightarrow{ts} P$	−	+	−	−	+	+
$I_1 \xrightarrow{ts} I_2 \xrightarrow{cs} P$	−	+	+	−	+	−

[1]From Jarvik, J., and D. Botstein. 1973. *Proc. Nat. Acad. Sci. (U.S.)* **70**:2046–2050; Table 1.
[2]I_1 and I_2 are intermediates on a pathway with product, P.
[3]+ means that product is made after indicated shift; − means that product is not made after indicated shift.

trolled by that gene product. That particular gene product is needed for that step in the sequence to be completed. If, on the other hand, a *ts* or *cs* gene product is sensitive at the time of its synthesis, the execution point for the mutation *precedes* the step in the developmental sequence. Since it is not possible in most cases to distinguish between a temperature effect on synthesis versus activity of a thermolabile protein, gene functions were ordered according to the execution point of the mutations and not according to the time that the function intervened at a particular step in a developmental pathway. From such data, Jarvik and Botstein constructed an **order-of-function map** for phage P22 (Fig. 13.9).

Even if the nature of the gene product or of its specific function are unknown in a system, the execution point for each *ts* or *cs* mutation can be determined operationally. These data can then be used to deduce the temporal order of gene action in developmental pathways. The validity of this method was checked by Jarvik and Botstein when they showed that the order of functions derived from reciprocal temperature-shifts coincided with the temporal order of selected morphogenetic events in P22 which had been discovered using different and independent methods in other investigations. Temperature-shift studies, however, identified many more events in these morphogenetic sequences, since *ts* and *cs* mutations could be analyzed even when their gene products were unknown and could not be analyzed directly. Once there is a body of information showing temporal order of gene action, however, subsequent studies can be conducted to identify the gene product, the nature of the mutational change, and the specific function of the gene product in a morphogenetic step during development.

These studies clearly showed that specific sequences in developmental pathways contribute to phage morphogenesis, under gene control. Somewhat similar methods, based on Jarvik and Botstein experimental design, have been used successfully in studying development in other organisms, as we will now see for yeast.

13.4   Sequential Gene Action During the Yeast Cell Cycle

Unicellular, uninucleate yeast (*Saccharomyces cerevisiae*) can exist indefinitely in either the haploid or diploid state, by vegetative multiplication as bud cells arise by mitosis from mother cells. During each **cell division cycle** leading to the next generation of cells, specific steps lead to the cell-

Figure 13.9 Order-of-function map of phage P22 was constructed from temperature-shift results for *ts/cs* double mutants. Results are shown below, and the map based on these results is shown above. (From Jarvik, J., and D. Botstein. 1973. *Proc. Nat. Acad. Sci. U. S.* **70**:2046.)

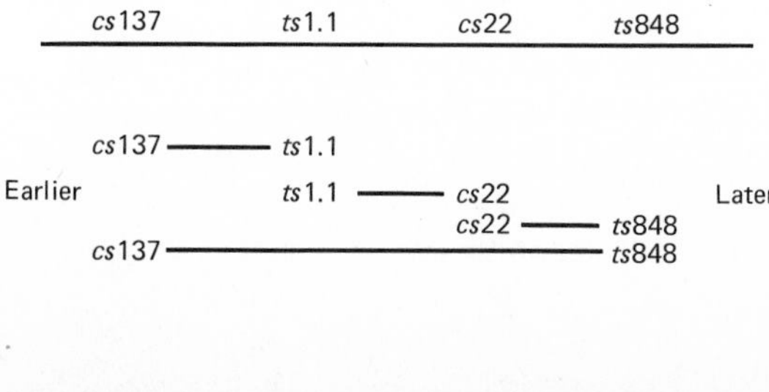

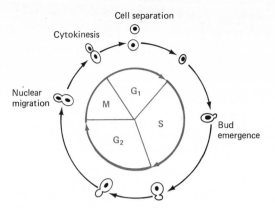

Figure 13.10 The cell cycle in yeast includes the usual four stages of G_1, S, G_2, and M. Reproductive events are shown in the outer circle, in relation to their timing in the cell cycle.

cycle-specific stages of G_1, S, G_2, and mitosis (Fig. 13.10). In addition to these specific stages, morphogenetic events are required to produce a new bud, direct nuclear migration into the bud, produce a new wall to close off the bud from the mother cell, and finally to separate the bud cell from the mother cell.

Under appropriate conditions, haploid cells of opposite mating type will fuse to produce a diploid zygote. Depending on environmental stimuli, the zygote may give rise to asexual generations of diploid cells or it may undergo meiosis (as can other diploid cells) to produce haploid ascospores (see Fig. 12.3).

One of the most significant intervals in yeast development is the G_1 phase of the cell cycle, because it is within this time period that a cell may be directed into any one of three different developmental programs. During G_1 the cell may initiate DNA synthesis and the S phase of a mitotic cycle; it may fuse with a cell of opposite mating type and produce a zygote; or it may become nondividing, or noncycling, in the quiescent state of the stationary phase of the population growth cycle. When the cell has initiated DNA synthesis, it apparently has become committed to the cell division cycle and will not undertake either of the other two developmental pathways instead. One may therefore view the initiation of DNA synthesis as an act of differentiation or determination, and the subsequent steps of the cell division cycle as elements of a developmental program. The genetic analysis of a cell division cycle should have broad implications for other eukaryotes, whether they are unicellular or multicellular, since eukaryotic growth and development generally depend in large measure on DNA synthesis in successive cell cycles.

Leland Hartwell and co-workers have identified 35 different temperature-sensitive cell-division-cycle (*cdc*) mutants in yeast. Each of these mutants could be associated with some particular interval during a cycle on the basis of the observed block in the morphological changes which take place (Fig. 13.11). For example, cells carrying the *cdc* 4 mutation stop in the G_1 phase and do not initiate DNA synthesis. In addition to tests showing that DNA synthesis does not take place, there is a morphological *landmark*: the

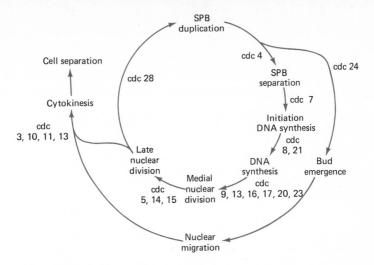

Figure 13.11 Dependent pathway of landmarks in the cell cycle of the yeast *Saccharomyces cerevisiae*, derived from phenotypes of cell-division-cycle (*cdc*) mutants. The designations for *cdc* genes are immediately preceding their diagnostic landmark. The diagram relates to mutant phenotypes as follows: Upon a shift to the restrictive temperature, mutant cells arrest synchronously at the position designated by the *cdc* number; all events flowing from this point do not occur while all other events do. (From Hartwell, L. H. 1978. *J. Cell Biol.* **77**:627.)

Figure 13.12 Determination of the execution point in temperature-sensitive mutants. First- and second-cycle arrests can be distinguished by one versus two mother-and-bud cell aggregates photographed at the time of the temperature shift and 6 hr later. (From Hartwell, L. H. 1978. *J. Cell Biol.* **77**:627.)

spindle pole body fails to separate after it has duplicated. Cells carrying the *cdc* 7 mutation also are arrested in G_1, but the morphological landmark, or terminal phenotype resulting from this mutant gene product, is a later event since spindle pole body duplication and separation both take place. The *cdc* 28 mutation precedes both of these steps, since arrested G_1 cells do not even duplicate the spindle pole body. All three *cdc* mutations block DNA synthesis, and so all three mutant types appear as unbudded cells when they are incubated at the nonpermissive temperature of 36° or 38°. When incubated at the permissive temperature of 23°, successive cell cycles proceed normally.

To determine the execution point in a temperature-sensitive mutant, cells growing at the permissive temperature are shifted to the nonpermissive temperature and photographed through an ordinary light microscope at the time of the temperature shift and about 6 hours later (Fig. 13.12). Since the size of the bud on the mother cell serves as a guide to the position of that cell in the cell division cycle, it is possible to distinguish the execution point of the mutant because cells earlier in the cycle (before the execution point) are arrested in the first cycle, while cells which were past the execution point in the first cycle would be arrested in the second cycle taking place over the 6-hour period. Since mother and bud cells remain associated during this time, first-cycle arrests and second-cycle arrests can be recognized.

The execution point defines the time at which the mutation affects a morphogenetic function. The visible effect of the mutation may occur at the time that the morphological or diagnostic landmark is completed; for example, *cdc* 8 and *cdc* 21 mutations lead to immediate cessation of DNA synthesis upon shift to the nonpermissive temperature. Both mutants have execution points near the end of the DNA synthesis phase, and both gene products probably are involved in this stage-specific event. A search for the biochemical nature of the gene products was undertaken, since it was strongly suspected to be an enzyme associated with DNA synthesis. In the case of *cdc* 21, the mutant was found to be defective in the enzyme thymidylate synthetase. Similarly, *cdc* 9 mutants were found to be defective in DNA ligase. By finding the execution point, it becomes possible to initiate more directed tests in seeking the biochemical or molecular nature of the product involved in the developmental process or event.

By cataloguing the diagnostic landmarks completed and those not completed in mutants at the restrictive temperature, the causal order or dependence of successive events can be determined. The events taking place before the mutant gene product is needed will all occur normally, while later events will not take place because of the mutational block. By determining the order of diagnostic landmark developments in different mutants, the sequence shown in Fig. 13.11 was deduced.

The dependent relationships between gene-controlled events during the cell division cycle were derived from reciprocal-shift experiments. To determine if two sequences, A and B, are *dependent* such that A cannot occur without the prior completion of B or that B cannot occur without the prior completion of A, or are *independent* so that either A or B can occur in the absence of the other, or that the two sequences are *interdependent* such that A and B must occur together, two reciprocal experiments were performed for each suitable temperature-sensitive mutant (Table 13.3). In each experiment one event was restricted and the other was permitted in the first incubation, and the conditions were then reversed in a second incubation. The order of restriction and permission in the reciprocal experiment was the opposite of the order in the first experiment. By putting these results together, the four possible models for the relationship between event A and event B could be distinguished.

These reciprocal-shift experiments were similar in concept to those used

Table 13.3
Sequencing a developmental program by reciprocal shifts to permissive and restrictive conditions*

Relationship between the two events in a pathway	Completion of developmental program	
First incubation: Second incubation:	restrict A, permit B permit A, restrict B	restrict B, permit A permit B, restrict A
Dependent A→ B→	−	+
Dependent B→ A→	+	−
Independent A→ / B→	+	+
Interdependent A, B→	−	−

*From Hereford, L. M., and L. H. Hartwell. 1974. *J. Mol. Biol.* **84**:445–461, Table 1.

by Jarvik and Botstein, but there were differences in the specific procedures used. Since there were no cold-sensitive mutations available, *cdc* mutants were exposed to some specific inhibitor to create a nonpermissive condition that could be alternated with the high temperature that was nonpermissive for these temperature-sensitive mutant strains. The results of these experiments showed that developmental events occurring during the yeast cell division cycle were temporally ordered, gene-controlled steps (Fig. 13.13). Similar studies using several different eukaryotic microorganisms have produced similar results, which amply confirm the basic principles of gene control over morphogenesis.

At present there are relatively few gene products which have been identified for these sequential morphogenetic events. As the events are defined in time and in the progress of a developmental program, biochemical and molecular methods can be used to locate, identify, and describe the products and their functions. Even when this feat is accomplished, we will not necessarily know how these pathways are regulated, and how the gene-controlled sequences of dependences are or have been established. Remarkable progress has been made, and much remains to be done.

ORDERED DEVELOPMENT OF EUKARYOTIC STRUCTURES

Eukaryotes are genetically and structurally complex systems, even in unicellular species. Genes in eukaryotes are not clustered into early and late functions; in fact, different genes on different chromosomes may code for different polypeptides which assemble into a single functional protein molecule, such as hemoglobin, whose α- and β-chains are coded by unlinked genes.

In contrast with virus development, in which all the activities in host cells produce a single kind of virus particle, and even with yeast whose cells are structurally very similar in every developmental state, many different structures and cell types develop from genetically identical cells during

Figure 13.13 Summary of dependent relationships between gene-controlled steps in yeast cell cycle, according to data from temperature-shifts. Compare with Fig. 13.11. (From Hartwell, L. H. 1978. *J. Cell Biol.* **77**:627.)

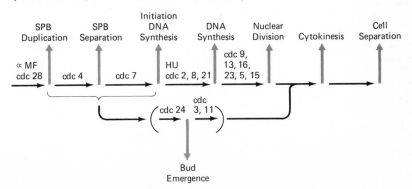

morphogenesis in multicellular eukaryotes. How do differential gene action and the enormous variety of gene products contribute to the formation and differentiation of tissues and organs and functional structures in a single organism? When do these events take place? Can a developmental pathway be established early and be delayed in expression until some later time in the life cycle? Can differentiation and development be altered or even reversed? These and other fundamental questions have been studied by genetic methods, using such experimentally suitable species as *Drosophila*, mice, and others.

13.5   Disk Determination in *Drosophila*

During development of *Drosophila* larvae, clusters of cells are set aside in groups called **imaginal disks**. These disks do not contribute at all to larval development or function. Rather they develop into external structures of the imago, or adult fly, such as head, legs, antennae, and other parts. While larval cells grow and differentiate all around them, disk cells remain in an embryonic state throughout larval development. Disk cells only begin to differentiate into adult structures during pupation, when larval tissues break down during metamorphosis into the adult individual (see Fig. 2.15). The larvae themselves can function quite well without these disks, as seen in various *Drosophila* mutants in which some or all of the imaginal disks are missing. These diskless mutants survive the larval stage, but they die in pupation, when adult structures fail to appear.

Each disk starts out as a small group of 10-50 cells, or less, and each disk is **determined** at this stage to later develop into a specific part of the adult fly (Fig. 13.14). Disk cells proliferate in the growing larvae, and several thousand cells may be present in each disk by the final stage of larval development, called the **third instar**. The individual disks can be recognized in third-instar larvae according to size, shape, and location, and each disk can be removed in whole or in part for experimental studies.

From earlier work by George Beadle and Boris Ephrussi, and from the extensive and continuing studies over many years by Ernst Hadorn, we know that imaginal disk cells are programmed for specific development long before their phenotypes are expressed in the adult. If a particular disk

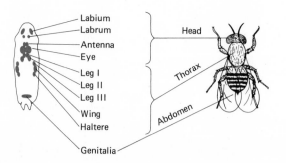

Figure 13.14 Location and identification of imaginal disks (red) in the larva of *Drosophila melanogaster*, and their structural derivatives in the adult, or imago.

is removed from a third-instar larva and transplanted into another larva, which is then allowed to develop into an adult fly, the transplanted disk will differentiate into the same structure that would otherwise have appeared had it been left in place in the original larva. If an eye disk from a larva carrying the white-eye allele is transplanted into the abdomen of a larva which is w^+, the adult will develop two red eyes in their usual location on its head, and a white eye in its abdomen. Similar transplantations using other imaginal disks lead to similar development, and the adult structure which differentiates is the same structure that would have differentiated in the original case, whether it is legs, antennae, or other external parts of the fly. When a disk is removed from a larva, other cells do not replace the lost disk cells. The donor larva, if it develops into an adult, would be missing the structure programmed by the disk taken away from it.

Through transplantation studies such as these, the different disks have been identified. Each is predetermined for a specific developmental program during metamorphosis in the pupa leading to the adult fly. The larval surroundings have no apparent influence on disk determination or on the eventual phenotype, which can be directly inferred from transplantation studies. Disks will differentiate into the determined structures regardless of where they have been inserted in the recipient larvae, and regardless of the recipient's phenotype. Disk development is *autonomous*, but development will not take place unless the proper stimulus is present or provided.

The stimulus for differentiation of the determined disks is the molting hormone **ecdysone**, which begins to be made in quantity in third-instar larvae. If isolated disks are treated with ecdysone, they will differentiate into adult structures. In addition, if determined disks are transplanted from third-instar larvae into adult flies, cell proliferation continues but the cells do not differentiate. Ecdysone is not present in adult flies. These experiments show that disk cells are determined to develop into specific gene-coded structures at a very early stage in development. Cellular differentiation will not take place in the absence of ecdysone, which is the stimulus for gene expression, or one of the important factors influencing gene expression. Differentiation proceeds normally during pupation, since ecdysone is made toward the end of larval development. There is a considerable time lag, therefore, between the time that cells are programmed to develop into certain structures and the time that development actually takes place. Development may never take place, even though the cells are already determined, if the environment is unsuitable (for example, adult instead of larval tissues).

Once determination has occurred, can disk cells retain their specific potential for differentiation indefinitely? Using **serial transplantations**, Hadorn has shown that disk cells do not de-differentiate, that is, they retain their determined state indefinitely (Fig. 13.15). By transferring part of a disk into an adult, disk cells increase in numbers and can be used over many generations as a supply of cells for transfer into larvae, where disk development can then be observed in the adult which emerges. For more than 150 such serial transfers over several years, disk cells continued to increase without differentiating in the adult hosts, but they did differentiate into the expected determined structures in the larval hosts. The determined states

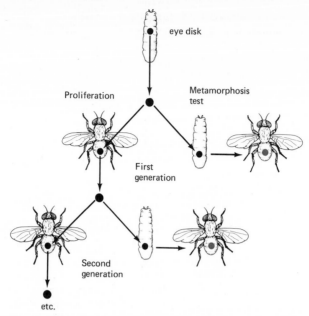

Figure 13.15 Serial transplantation procedure in *Drosophila* imaginal disk studies. Disks proliferate but do not differentiate in adult flies, but when transplanted into larvae the disk potential can be identified in the adult which emerges, in a metamorphosis test for disk specificity.

were regenerated and maintained, since disk specificities were transmitted from generation to generation. The determined state was clonally heritable.

In some of the serial transfers, Hadorn found that a disk might be altered to a different determined phenotype. For example, a leg disk might differentiate into wings in a percentage of the larval hosts. This change in determined state, or **transdetermination**, would then be regenerated and maintained in subsequent generations of serial transfer adults and larvae. The new determined state was heritable. Hadorn found that transdeterminations were not random. Certain transdeterminations were never observed to occur directly. For example, haltere disks transdetermine directly to wing, but not to genitalia or leg disks; leg disk transdetermines to wing but not to haltere (Fig. 13.16). The pathway of transdeterminations includes specific sequences, therefore, and the alterations seem to represent switches between particular determination pathways rather than a graduated range of possible alternatives.

Transdetermination is not due to mutations in somatic cells, according to the following two particular observations: (1) they arise too frequently; and (2) groups of clonally unrelated, adjacent cells may transdetermine at the same time. There is, however, a particular probability for each transdetermination event, some arising more often than others. In addition, certain transdeterminations are reversible, but the rates of change are different for the pair of changes. For example, leg disks transdetermine to wing much more often than wing disks transdetermine to leg.

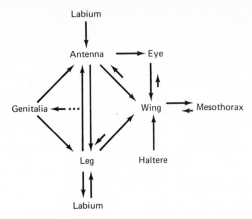

Figure 13.16 Pathways of transdeterminations in *Drosophila*. Certain disks transdetermine only into certain other potentials, resulting in apparent sequences of transdetermination rather than a range of possible alterations from one determined state to any of all others. (Based on studies by E. Hadorn.)

There is a class of inherited changes, called **homeotic mutations**, in which alterations resembling transdeterminations have been observed. In homeotic mutants, a normal structure or part of a structure develops in an abnormal location. For example, the *tetraptera* mutant has wings in place of halteres so that four-winged flies develop; in the *tumerous head* mutant, genital or leg structures develop in place of antennae; and other mutants of a similar nature have been described. The relationship between homeotic mutations and transdeterminations, however, is not known. Homeotic mutations may alter some control system, rather than causing a change in a structural protein.

When does disk determination take place in development? In experiments with embryonic systems, it was found that determinative events occurred in early blastoderms shortly after the first cleavage divisions of the fertilized egg. Blastoderms from mutant strains were cut in half at the midline, and cells from the anterior and posterior halves were put into separate suspensions. These cell suspensions were centrifuged, and clusters of sedimented cells were transplanted into wild-type adult host flies, where they multiplied. The nature of these cells was then examined by transferring some of this material into wild-type larvae to see what would develop when these larvae metamorphosed into adults. Cells that were originally taken from the anterior half of the blastoderm developed into anterior adult structures, while posterior blastoderm cells gave rise to posterior adult structures. These experiments showed that cell determination had already occurred in the blastoderm stage. Furthermore, the position of a disk and the ultimate location of the structure in the adult appear to be established at the time that blastoderm cells are determined. Form and function proceed to develop in orderly ways long before tissues and organs actually differentiate in the organism. We know there are factors present in the egg which act as stimuli for determinative events in the early cleavage divisions after fertilization, from many years of experimental embryology studies of nu-

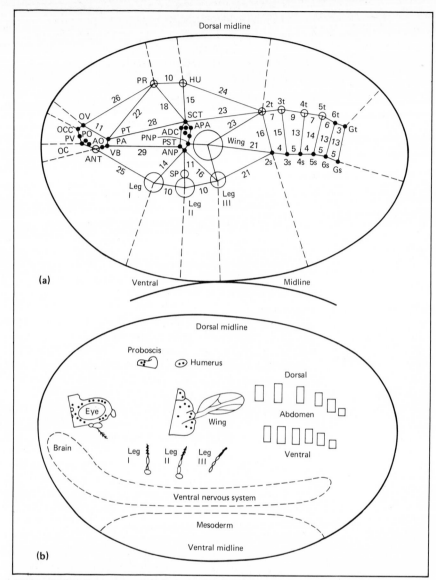

Figure 13.17 Fate map of disk precursors of *Drosophila melanogaster* blastoderm. (a) Fate map showing cells that will eventually develop into the indicated external body parts of the adult fly. The map is a projection of the right half of the blastoderm as seen from the inside of the egg. The abbreviations refer to parts shown in a pictorial sketch in (b), which is based on the fate mapping data. (From Hotta, Y., and S. Benzer, 1972. *Nature* **240**:527.)

merous species. The nature of most of these factors remains virtually unknown, however.

Through various methods it is possible to ascertain the number and position of disk precursor cells as they appear on the blastoderm surface

(Fig. 13.17). This surface is only one cell layer thick, and these cells form when nuclei produced by mitotic divisions in the fertilized egg move outward from the interior. Using a technique Alfred Sturtevant originally invented, Yoshiki Hotta, Seymour Benzer, and others have analyzed genetic and chromosomal mosaic flies and derived the relative positions and distances apart of blastoderm precursor cells which will give rise to imaginal disks and ultimately to adult structures. These "**fate maps**" of the blastoderm surface show that orderly development in *Drosophila* also depends in part on the positional information in the embryo. Imaginal disks develop in the blastoderm, and later in the larva, in places which correspond to the positions these structures will occupy in the adult fly. The developmental blueprint is therefore established quite early, long before morphogenesis takes place. At present the nature of the positional information is poorly understood. But it must ultimately be under genetic control, since homeotic mutants modify this information.

13.6   Ordered Cell-Cell Interactions in Development

In various systems, interactions between cells during development leads to ordered sequences of differentiation. In the slime mold *Dictyostelium discoideum*, John Bonner, Maurice Sussman, and others have shown that cellular differentiation and structural development are an outcome of interactions which depend on relative cell locations. Only three kinds of cells are found in this simple, haploid eukaryote: the ameboid migratory cell, the spore cell, and the stalk cell (Fig. 13.18). Large numbers of these ameboid cells generally aggregate together when their food supply of bacteria is exhausted. Depending on such environmental conditions as light and acidity, the aggregate may form a **pseudoplasmodium** which migrates or stays in place. In either case, a fruiting body eventually develops from the pseudoplasmodial aggregate. The fruiting body consists of only two kinds of cells, those making up the slender *stalk*, and the *spores* which form within a large spherical sporangium at the tip of the stalk.

Aggregation of ameboid cells appears to be initiated by the presence of **cyclic AMP**. This chemical signal occurs in a gradient of concentrations, with the highest levels of cAMP at the center of the aggregating group of cells. As cAMP diffuses outward from the center, more ameboid cells move toward this center region of higher cAMP concentration, and the pseudoplasmium enlarges. Cells adhere to one another and produce more cAMP, attracting more ameboid cells into the aggregate. Whether an ameboid cell in the group develops into a stalk cell or a spore cell apparently depends on its relative location within the aggregate. The first cells to enter give rise to the tip of the pseudoplasmodium, while those entering later give rise to the base of the system. Whether the cAMP concentration in different regions of the chemical gradient acts in some way to cause cells to differentiate, or whether it simply acts to sort out already differentiated cells is uncertain.

Whatever the basis for initial cellular differentiation may be, two kinds of cells are determined by the time the pseudoplasmodium stops migrating. Cells located at the tip move down toward the base and form the stalk cells,

Figure 13.18 Life cycle of the slime mold *Dictyostelium discoideum*, showing the three types of cells (ameboid, spore, and stalk).

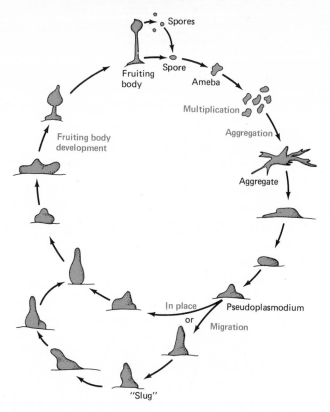

while cells located at the base move upward and develop into spore cells. These two cell types differentiate in some way according to their relative positions, rather than a specific determined state existing in each cell within the pseudoplasmodial aggregate. For example, if a pseudoplasmodium is chopped into several pieces, each cell group will produce fruiting bodies even if the original pseudoplasmodium contained cells that would have formed spores exclusively or stalk cells exclusively.

Cell differentiation in *Dictyostelium* is presumed to be under genetic control, since there are numerous mutants whose growth is affected at one particular stage and not at another. Mutations may influence growth at the ameboid stage without altering cell aggregation or cell differentiation into fruiting bodies. The rate of development may also be altered by mutations, a fact which indicates that this aspect of the life cycle is also under genetic control. The regulatory mechanisms which cause differentiation, however, are uncertain.

Present in the mouse is a large series of dominant and recessive mutant alleles at the *T*-locus region of the genome, each of which produces some observable effect on the tail in appropriate genotypic combinations (Table 13.4). All dominant mutations produce short-tailed heterozygotes (T/+) and are lethal in homozygotes (T/T). Recessive mutations have no apparent effect in +/t heterozygotes, but they interact with dominant T mutant

Table 13.4
Phenotypic effects of muta-tions at the _T_ locus in the house mouse

Genotype	Effect
_T/T_	lethal
_T/t_	tailless
+/_T_	short-tailed
_t/t_	often lethal*
_T/t_	tailless
+/_t_	normal tail
+/+	normal tail

*May be lethal, semi-lethal, or viable, depending upon the particular _t_ allele

alleles to produce a tailless phenotype in genotypically _T/t_ heterozygotes. The recessive _t_ alleles went undetected for some time, until tailless _T/t_ heterozygotes were discovered during breeding studies. When the first of the _T_-locus mutant alleles, _T_ (Brachyury), was discovered by crosses involving these short-tailed heterozygotes, the genetic basis for the phenotypic modification seemed relatively simple. As more _T_ and _t_ mutant alleles were discovered, the complexity of the _T_-locus region became evident. The precise genetic structure of the _T_-locus region remains unknown at present.

Through studies by Dorothea Bennett and others, it has been found that mutations in the _T_-locus lead to cell-specific and stage-specific alterations during embryogenesis (Fig. 13.19). The t^{12} allele acts in homozygotes at the morula stage, before blastocyst formation and implantation in the uterus. Other _T_ and _t_ mutations produce specific defects later in embryogenesis, and certain _t_ alleles may not be lethal in every homozygous individual.

According to Bennett and others, it is very likely that the spectrum of defects seen in _T_-locus mutants are due predominantly to _changes in the cell membrane_. Such alterations in the cell surface would produce alterations in cell-cell interactions and in cell-cell recognition, resulting in a variety of abnormalities during differentiation, depending on the cells affected and the time during embryogenesis at which these cells interact with one another and with other cells around them. For example, homozygotes for the t^9 allele begin differentiation of a primitive streak leading to neural development, but only a few abnormal mesoderm cells are actually formed. The embryos eventually die, presumably because of circulatory failure resulting from an inadequate mesoderm from which the circulatory system is derived. Electron microscopic observations of mesoderm cells of t^9 homozygotes show that they are abnormal in shape and do not establish _intercellular junctions_ with one another. Intercellular junctions are cell-surface differentiated regions which are required for recognition and interaction between adjacent cells. In this mutant it appears that ectoderm cells emerging from the primitive streak and destined to become mesoderm fail to

Figure 13.19 A diagrammatic representation of early development in the mouse and the defects seen in embryos homozygous for *T*-locus mutations. (From Bennett, D. 1975. *Cell* **6**:441, Fig. 1a.)

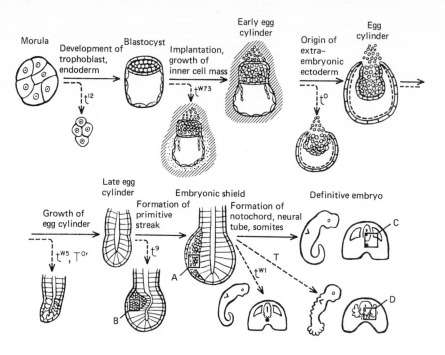

make the complete transition from one developmental state to the other.

In addition, most of the mutations in the *T*-locus region cause alterations in **serological specificities** of cell-surface components, according to cross-reactions in serological test systems. The fact that these cell-surface antigens are altered and not lost is a strong indication that *T*-locus mutant gene products are the result of codon changes in structural genes and not of deletions of genetic materials. In deletion mutants one would expect gene products to be missing rather than altered.

These studies, therefore, indicate that gene action during embryonic development causes the production of gene products which influence cell-surface characteristics. The gene products appear to be made sequentially, and they persist only for brief time periods at specific stages in development and in particular cells in the embryo. The orderly development of the embryo and the differentiation of its tissue and organ systems appears largely to be a consequence of cell-surface specificities that arise as the result of certain gene products which are incorporated into the cell membrane. The interactions between cells and cell-cell recognition depend largely on the properties of the cell membrane and the particular protein factors which appear and disappear as sequences of gene action occur during embryogenesis. While a great deal remains to be accomplished to substantiate various features of the proposed scheme, studies of the *T*-locus in the mouse have provided very strong evidence for the guiding role of gene action in ordering the complex processes of embryogenesis.

In the examples which have been discussed in this chapter, the basic theme has emerged showing that development is the outcome of gene-controlled sequential processes. Gene action is regulated primarily at transcription, but gene products are not translated in the corresponding temporal order in which development takes place. Once gene products appear, these molecules interact in temporal sequences during which the construction of the organism or its parts is determined. Gene product interactions may take place shortly after the proteins have been made in translation, as we would expect in viruses or simple cells with a short generation time and relatively limited organizational complexity. In the more complex eukaryotes, tissues, organs, and structures may be determined genetically and positionally very early in embryogenesis, but the actual morphogenetic events may take place much later in an appropriate biological or physical environment.

Gene product interactions and cell-cell interactions are cell-specific and stage-specific events, under gene control. The incredibly ordered pathways of morphogenesis can be seen in outline at the present time. We eagerly await the molecular details by which we can fill in the outline and understand how morphogenesis is regulated.

QUESTIONS AND PROBLEMS

13.1. When *E. coli* is infected by λ phage during its lytic cycle, two observations can be made: (a) the early mRNA is transcribed from the middle of the phage chromosome to the right, and (b) the later mRNA is transcribed from the middle to the left end of the λ chromosome. Suggest an explanation for this.

13.2. A geneticist has been studying four different temperature sensitive phage mutants, each of which has a defect in head protein assembly. Two of the mutants have an altered allele at locus A, one of which is heat sensitive (A^{hs}) and the other is cold sensitive (A^{cs}). There is a heat sensitive allele at locus B (B^{hs}) in a third mutant and a cold sensitive allele (C^{cs}) at locus C in the fourth mutant. A culture of *E. coli* is infected with these mutant phage strains and divided into two populations—one is grown for 15 minutes at low temperature and then for 15 minutes at high temperature, and the other population is grown for 15 minutes at high temperature and then for 15 minutes at low temperature. Then the cultures are scored for phage production (0 = none, + = phages produced). Explain the results in the following table.

	low $\longrightarrow$ high temp.	high $\longrightarrow$ low temp.
$A^{hs}\ C^{cs}$	0	0
$A^{cs}\ B^{hs}$	0	0
$C^{cs}\ B^{hs}$	+	0

13.3. A viral extract was prepared from T4 phages defective in a gene for production of either heads or tails. When complete heads were added to the extracts, infectious viruses were produced, but no viruses were produced when complete tails were added. Where is the defect in this T4 mutant assembly?

13.4. Extract complementation tests are conducted using extracts of various T4 mutants defective in one or more genes. In order to assemble a complete virus there must be present genes for normal head, tail, and tail fibers. From the following matrix, determine the nature of the defect in complementation groups B, D, E, and F. It is known that group A mutants only produce heads and complementation group C mutants only produce tails. (+ indicates phage production, 0 indicates no phages are produced)

	A	B	C	D	E	F
A	0	+	0	0	0	0
B		0	0	+	+	0
C			0	+	0	0
D				0	+	0
E					0	+
F						0

13.5. Complementation tests were performed by constructing F_1 hybrids between five strains of *Drosophila*, each of which had an abnormal wing structure. The following matrix was obtained. (+ indicates normal wing structure)

	1	2	3	4	5
1	0	0	+	+	0
2		0	+	+	0
3			0	+	+
4				0	0
5					0

Diagram the complementation map. How many different genes are defined by this set of experiments? (Assume the mutants all are recessive to wild type)

13.6. A biologist obtains evidence for a mutant gene in fruit flies, which prevents formation of sperm storage organs (spermothecae) and ovaries in females. This mutant allele, *z*, does not affect males. There is another locus at which a mutant allele, transformer (*t*), exists which is known to change XX flies into males. Flies that are XX and homozygous for *z* and *t* (*zztt*) prove to be normal males with normal sex organs. Explain these results. Which gene acts first in this developmental sequence?

13.7. George Beadle and Boris Ephrussi conducted very interesting disk transplantation experiments in the 1930s, using *Drosophila melanogaster*, marking a beginning of biochemical genetics. They transplanted eye disks reciprocally between vermilion and cinnabar larvae, and found that cinnabar disks maintained their cinnabar phenotype when developing in vermilion hosts but vermilion disks developed into wild-type eyes in cinnabar hosts. Wild-type eye color developed from wild-type disks in vermilion or cinnabar hosts, and wild-type eyes developed from vermilion or cinnabar disks in wild-type hosts. These genes act in a pathway involving synthesis of hormonelike substances needed for eye pigment production:

$$\text{tryptophan} \xrightarrow{v^+} \text{formylkynurenin} \xrightarrow{cn^+} \text{hydroxykynurenin} \longrightarrow \longrightarrow \text{pigment}$$

Use this information to explain the results observed in the eye-disc transplantation experiments described above.

13.8. Differentiated cells usually express only a few of their genes. Cite evidence showing that differentiated cells:
   a. have not lost the genes they do not express; and
   b. have not undergone different mutations in different cells leading to different phenotypes during growth and development.

13.9. A group of yeast cell cycle mutants have been grown in restrictive and permissive conditions according to the reciprocal shift method. Their ability to complete the developmental program was scored (+ and –, for completed and not completed, respectively), as follows:

cdc mutants shown as		Completion of developmental program	
A	B	1st incubation: restrict A, permit B / 2nd incubation: permit A, restrict B	restrict B, permit A / permit B, restrict A
cdc 28	*cdc* 7	–	+
cdc 28	*cdc* 4	–	+
cdc 7	*cdc* 4	+	–
cdc 2	*cdc* 24	+	+

   a. What is the developmental sequence involving *cdc* 4, 7, and 28?
   b. How are the developmental steps governed by *cdc* 2 and *cdc* 24 related to each other?

REFERENCES

Bennett, D. 1975. The T-locus of the mouse. *Cell* **6**:441.

Briggs, R., and T. J. King. 1957. Changes in the nuclei of differentiating endoderm cells as revealed by nuclear transplantation. *J. Morphol.* **100**:269.

Butler, P. J. G., and A. Klug. Nov. 1978. The assembly of a virus. *Sci. Amer.* **239**:62.

Gehring, W. J. 1969. Problems of cell determination and differentiation in *Drosophila*. In *Problems in Biology: RNA in Develop-

ment (E. W. Hanly, ed.), p. 230. Salt Lake City: Univ. Utah Press.

Gluecksohn-Waelsch, S. 1979. Genetic control of morphogenetic and biochemical differentiation: Lethal albino deletions in the mouse. *Cell* **16**:1.

Gurdon, J. B. Dec. 1968. Transplanted nuclei and cell differentiation. *Sci. Amer.* **219**:24.

Hadorn, E. Nov. 1968. Transdetermination in cells. *Sci. Amer.* **219**: 110.

Hartwell, L. H. 1978. Cell division from a genetic perspective. *J. Cell Biol.* **77**:627.

Ilmensee, K., and L. C. Stevens. Apr. 1979. Teratomas and chimeras. *Sci. Amer.* **240**:120.

Jarvik, J., and D. Botstein. 1973. A genetic method for determining the order of events in a biological pathway. *Proc. Nat. Acad. Sci. U.S.* **70**:2046.

Kauffman, S. A. 1973. Control circuits for determination and transdetermination. *Science* **181**:310.

Lewis, E. B. 1978. A gene complex controlling segmentation in *Drosophila. Nature* **276**:565.

Lindner, S., H. Brzeski, and N. R. Ringertz. 1979. Phenotypic expression in cybrids derived from teratocarcinoma cells fused with myoblast cytoplasms. *Exp. Cell Res.* **120**:1.

Markert, C. L., and R. M. Petters. 1978. Manufactured hexaparental mice show that adults are derived from three embryonic cells. *Science* **202**:56.

Meins, F., Jr., and A. N. Binns. 1979. Cell determination in plant development. *BioScience* **29**:221.

Quinn, W. G., and J. L. Gould. 1979. Nerves and genes. *Nature* **278**: 19.

Riddle, D. L., and S. Brenner. 1978. Indirect suppression in *Caenorhabditis elegans. Genetics* **89**:299.

Stamatoyannopoulos, G., and A. W. Nienhuis, eds. 1979. *Cellular and Molecular Regulation of Hemoglobin Switching.* New York: Grune & Stratton.

Stent, G. S. Sept. 1972. Cellular communication. *Sci. Amer.* **227**:42.

Susskind, M. M., and D. Botstein. 1978. Molecular genetics of bacteriophage P22. *Microbiol. Rev.* **42**:385.

Sussman, M., J. Schindler, and H. Kim. 1978. "Sluggers," a new class of morphogenetic mutants of *D. discoideum. Exp. Cell Res.* **116**:217.

Ursprung, H., and R. Nothiger, eds. 1972. *The Biology of Imaginal Disks.* New York: Springer-Verlag.

van Driel, R., and E. Couture. 1978. Assembly of the scaffolding core of bacteriophage T4 preheads. *J. Mol. Biol.* **123**:713.

Wood, W. B., and R. S. Edgar. July 1967. Building a bacterial virus. *Sci. Amer.* **217**:

Wood, W. B., R. S. Edgar, J. King, I. Lielausis, and M. Henninger. 1968. Bacteriophage assembly. *Fed. Proc.* **27**:1160.

14

Quantitative Inheritance

The principal focus of genetic analysis is on the nature and action of the individual gene. There are many inherited characters, however, which are the end result of the action of many genes on the same trait. Such multiple-gene, or polygenic, traits show a range of phenotypic variation in character expression so that it is usually impossible to separate individuals into discrete phenotypic classes. In the absence of phenotypic class ratios, different statistical and analytical methods are needed to assess quantitative inheritance.

In general, quantitative traits are highly susceptible to modification by environmental factors, which are superimposed on variability due to genetic factors. Analysis of quantitative traits must therefore distinguish between the genetic input to phenotypic expression and the influence of the environment on the trait. Various genetic approaches can be used to identify polygenic inheritance, and to assess the proportionate influences of heredity and environment on the phenotype. Quantitative traits are of immense importance in evolution and in the practical spheres of human genetics and of agriculture. It is therefore vital to understand the action of polygenic systems on measurable characters such as crop yield, behavior, mental abilities, and other traits. Since every organism displays a number of quantitative traits, these studies have great theoretical as well as practical value.

STATISTICAL ANALYSIS OF QUANTITATIVE TRAITS

Analysis of traits showing **continuous variation** across a range of values, called **quantitative traits**, requires a different set of statistical tools from those used to analyze **discontinuously varying** characters which can be sorted unambiguously into discrete, nonoverlapping phenotypic classes. The Mendelian inheritance of tall and short height is evaluated according to the ratio of tall and short individuals in progenies consisting of these two discrete phenotypic classes. In cases where there is a range of heights from taller to shorter, with no distinct separation into different phenotypic classes, there is no apparent ratio. Statistical analysis of individual measurements must be carried out in order to characterize the nature of a quantitative trait. We will examine some of the central concepts and some of the more widely-used statistics which are routinely determined in many kinds of studies.

14.1 The Mean and Variation around the Mean

The first step in analyzing quantitative data is to calculate the **arithmetic mean**, symbolized as $\bar{x}$. One simply sums up the observed values and then divides by the number of values (Table 14.1). For greater convenience of calculation, we usually group the individual values into **classes** and indicate the **frequency** of individual values in each designated class. In our example of the measured height of a sample of 100 American men, the data can be plotted in the form of a bar-graph, or **histogram**, or in the form of a **curve** constructed by connecting the plotted values (Fig. 14.1). In either representation of these data it is apparent that there is a *symmetrical distribution* of values on either side of the mean height of 69.0 inches. The familiar bell-shaped curve indicates that the spread of variation follows a normal distribution. **A normal distribution** is one in which the mean value occurs at the high point of a balanced distribution of frequencies, and these frequencies diminish regularly and symmetrically in both directions away from the mean value (Box 14.1).

The mean value is the most useful term for further statistical analysis. The *central tendency* of a sample can be described in two other ways as well: the median value and the mode. The **median** value defines the center of a set of data, such that there are as many values or numbers of measurements

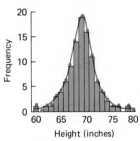

Figure 14.1 Height measurements (red dots) can be plotted in the form of a histogram or as a curve implying a continuous distribution of heights.

Table 14.1
Frequency distribution of height measurements for a sample of 100 American men

Class value, v (inches)	60	61	62	63	64	65	66	67	68	69	70	71	72	73	74	75	76	77	78
Frequency, f	1	0	1	1	3	4	6	9	14	19	16	11	6	4	2	1	1	0	1
fv	60	0	62	63	192	260	396	603	952	1311	1120	781	432	292	148	75	76	0	78

$$\text{Mean} = \frac{\Sigma fv}{N} = \frac{6905}{100} = 69.0 \text{ inches}$$

Box 14.1
THE NORMAL DISTRIBUTION

Genes with major effects tend to produce phenotypes showing discontinuous distribution. The distribution of phenotypes in the F_2 of a monohybrid cross can be plotted as tall and short, for example, or actual measurements can be made showing the influence of environmental modifications such that the phenotypic measurements cluster around some mean value for each major progeny class of tall and short. These distributions are shown in the first two plots.

If there is no dominance, the expected distribution of phenotypes in a population of individuals of different heights can be computed according to expansion of the binomial $(a + b)^n$. The third illustration shows expected distributions of phenotypic classes for F_2 ratios involving 1-4 gene loci (2-8 alleles) with additive and equal effects. The symmetrical distribution known as Pascal's triangle shows the coefficients for terms in the expanded binomials raised to different powers; for example, $(a + b)^2 = a^2 = 2ab + b^2$, and $(a + b)^6 = a^6 + 6a^5b + 15a^4b^2 + 20a^3b^3 + 15a^2b^4 + 6ab^5 + b^6$, where $a = b = 1/2$. When the relative frequencies (shown as coefficients) of these classes are plotted, the bell-shaped curve indicative of the normal frequency distribution is approached, as shown in the fourth illustration. A population with less variation (dashed line) may have the same mean as a population with greater variance (histogram plot).

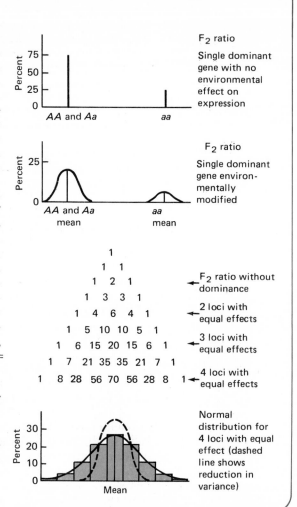

F_2 ratio

Single dominant gene with no environmental effect on expression

F_2 ratio

Single dominant gene environmentally modified

F_2 ratio without dominance

2 loci with equal effects

3 loci with equal effects

4 loci with equal effects

Normal distribution for 4 loci with equal effect (dashed line shows reduction in variance)

on one side of the mean as on the other side. In our sample of height measurements, the median value is 68.9 inches. Half the measurements were more than 68.9 inches (69.0 inches or more) and half were less than 68.9 inches. The **mode** is defined as the most frequent value in a set of data. In our sample, the mode is 69.0 inches. We can now say that the average or mean height of American men in our sample was 69.0 inches, that this was the most common measurement obtained, and that half the men were taller than the average and half the men were shorter than the average.

The mean value describes one aspect of the sample or population, but

Class value:	0	1	2	3	4	5	6	7	8	9	10	11	12
Frequency:													
Group A					3	21	52	21	3				
Group B		3	6	9	10	13	18	13	10	9	6	3	

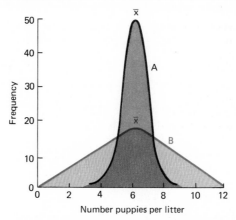

Figure 14.2 Populations having the same mean value for a quantitative feature may show very different spreads of variability around the mean. Population A is much less variable (3-9 puppies per litter) than population B (0-12 per litter), but there is the same mean value (6) in each population of 100 animals.

different *spreads of variation* may produce the same arithmetic mean (Fig. 14.2). We can provide a more complete picture of populations by measuring the **variation around the mean**. Two particular statistics can be calculated for this purpose: the statistic of **variance** (V or σ^2), which is the average squared difference from the mean, and the square root of the variance, called the **standard deviation** of the mean (σ). The formulae for these statistics and their computations for our measurements of height are shown in Table 14.2. The statistic of standard deviation has a broader use than the variance for many studies of quantitative characters. In a later part of the chapter we will see how the variance statistic is applied in genetic analysis of continuously varying traits.

With the mean and the standard deviation of the mean we have reduced the set of 100 measurements to two precise values by which the sample can be described. The average or mean height is 69.0 inches, but there is a spread of variation around this mean. In our sample, 81% of the individuals fall within the range between 3.6 inches above and 3.6 inches below the mean, 97% range between 61.8 and 76.2 inches in height, and 100% of this sample is between 58.2 and 79.8 inches tall (Fig. 14.3).

These results vary somewhat from the theoretical. In a perfect distribution we would find that one standard deviation to either side of the mean would include 68.26% of the area under the curve; two standard deviations would include 95.44% of the area; and three standard deviations would include 99.74% of the area under the curve (Fig. 14.4). These relationships

Table 14.2

Statistical analysis of height measurements in a sample of 100 American men ranging between 60 and 78 inches tall

Class	Frequency (f)	Deviation (d)	d^2	fd^2
60	1	9	81	81
61	0	8	64	0
62	1	7	49	49
63	1	6	36	36
64	3	5	25	75
65	4	4	16	64
66	6	3	9	54
67	9	2	4	36
68	14	1	1	14
69	19	0	0	0
70	16	1	1	16
71	11	2	4	44
72	6	3	9	54
73	4	4	16	64
74	2	5	25	50
75	1	6	36	36
76	1	7	49	49
77	0	8	64	0
78	1	9	81	81
	$N = 100$			$\Sigma = 1293$

$$V = \frac{\Sigma fd^2}{N - 1} = \frac{1293}{99} = 13.06$$

$$\sigma = \sqrt{\frac{\Sigma fd^2}{N - 1}} = \sqrt{13.06} = 3.6$$

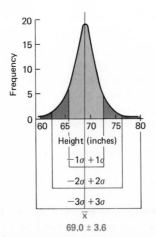

Figure 14.3 Normal distribution of measurements, showing the proportion of the distribution included between $\pm 1\sigma$, $\pm 2\sigma$, and $\pm 3\sigma$, with reference to the mean of 69.0 inches and a standard deviation of 3.6.

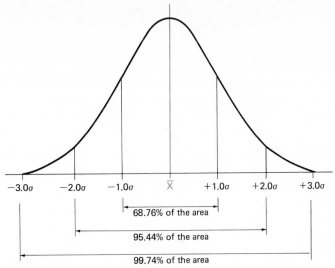

Figure 14.4 In a perfect normal distribution, regardless of the actual spread of variation around the mean, specific proportions of the area under the curve are characteristic for ±1, 2, and 3 standard deviations of the mean.

hold for any normal distribution, regardless of the actual spread of variation around the mean. A narrow spread producing a steeply-sided curve or a broader spread producing a flattened bell-shaped curve will still have one, two, or three standard deviations on either side of the mean as representing the normal distribution of the data in any particular case. Our sample of 100 men comes close to the expected distribution, although a higher percentage than the expected falls within the range of one standard deviation from the mean.

14.2   The Standard Error of the Mean

How accurately does this sample of 100 men reflect stature in the whole population? We could sample repeatedly and find the means and standard deviations for many samples or even for the entire American adult male population, but this would be tedious and unnecessary. We can take a statistical shortcut by determining the **standard error of the mean**, which can be calculated from the standard deviation of any sample, as follows:

$$\text{S.E.}_{\overline{x}} = \frac{\sigma}{\sqrt{N}}$$

where σ is the standard deviation and N is the size of the sample. In our sample of 100 individuals, where the standard deviation was 3.6, we find that the standard error of the mean value of 69.0 inches is

$$\text{S.E.}_{\overline{x}} = \frac{3.6}{\sqrt{100}} = \frac{3.6}{10} = 0.36, \text{ or } 0.4$$

We may now state that the mean height in our sample was 69.0 ± 0.4 inches.

The standard error can be considered as the standard deviation of many means. It is therefore a standard deviation of the theoretical population mean. The standard error tells us the *reliability* of the calculated mean value. There is a 68% chance that the true mean lies within one standard error of the mean, or between 68.6 and 69.4 inches. There is about a 95% chance that the true mean lies within two standard errors, or between 68.2 and 69.8 inches, and about a 99% chance that the true mean is 1.2 inches more or less than the calculated mean of 69.0 inches. You can see that we have used the standard error in much the same way that we used one, two, or three standard deviations to indicate our *confidence* in the calculated mean value. The estimates of the range within which the population mean should lie are called **confidence intervals**. We may, therefore, say that we are 95% confident or 99% confident that the true mean lies somewhere between 68.2 and 69.8 inches, or between 67.8 and 70.2 inches, respectively.

When we characterize the mean value by its standard deviation we are making a statement about the observed spread of variation around the particular mean in a particular sample. On the other hand, when we characterize the mean value in terms of its standard error, we are making a statement about the mean value in terms of an infinite population. In the usual notation, we describe the *mean plus or minus the standard error of the mean*. It is then a simple matter to add and subtract two or three standard errors from the mean value and see at a glance how the calculated mean value differs from the expected value for the entire population, at the 95% or 99% levels of confidence.

14.3   Standard Error of the Difference Between Means

The means and standard errors of two different samples or populations can also be compared to determine if the populations are the same or different. Suppose we measured stature in a population of European adult men, and found that the mean height in a sample of 100 individuals was 67.0 inches. The American and European population samples can be compared crudely by inspection of the two sets of statistics, as shown in Table 14.3. We can see at a glance that in this case the two samples do not overlap at either the 95% or the 99% confidence levels, and we would conclude that there was a *significant statistical difference between them*. In many cases, however, we might find that the values overlap. In such cases we require a more precise determination before we can say whether the difference is significant or merely due to chance.

To determine whether overlapping values are statistically significant or not, we compare the difference between the means of the two samples with

Table 14.3
Statistical information on height measurements for two different populations of adult men

Statistic	Americans	Europeans
Mean height in inches ($\bar{x}$)	69.0	67.0
Standard deviation (σ)	3.6	2.0
Standard error of the mean (S.E.$_{\bar{x}}$)	0.4	0.2
Range of variation: $\bar{x} \pm 1$ S.E.$_{\bar{x}}$	68.6–69.4	66.8–67.2
$\bar{x} \pm 2$ S.E.$_{\bar{x}}$	68.2–69.8	66.6–67.4
$\bar{x} \pm 3$ S.E.$_{\bar{x}}$	67.8–70.2	66.4–67.6

the standard error of this difference. We have already calculated means and standard errors of these means and found that the mean height in the sample of American men was 69.0 ± 0.4, while in the sample of European men it was 67.0 ± 0.2 inches. We then obtain the standard error of the difference in means (S.E.$_D$) using the equation

$$S.E._D = \sqrt{(S.E._{\bar{x}_1})^2 + (S.E._{\bar{x}_2})^2}$$

where S.E.$_{\bar{x}_1}$ is the standard error of the mean of sample 1 and S.E.$_{\bar{x}_2}$ is the standard error of the mean of sample 2.

Substituting the calculated values we determine that

$$S.E._D = \sqrt{(0.4)^2 + (0.2)^2}$$

$$= \sqrt{0.16 + 0.04}$$

$$= \sqrt{0.20}$$

$$= 0.4$$

The standard error of the difference between the two means is therefore ± 0.4. Two such standard errors would be ± 0.8, and three such standard errors would be ± 1.2. The actual difference between the means of the two samples is 2.0. When we compare these values it is obvious that the actual difference between means is much greater than even three standard errors of the difference in means (2.0 versus 1.2). We can conclude, therefore, that there is a statistically significant difference in mean height between these two samples and that they indeed represent different populations. We can be more than 99% confident that this difference in means is significant, or, we may say that there is less than a 1% probability ($P < 0.01$) that the two populations differ because of chance alone. We do not know the factors which are responsible for the observed difference, but we do know it is not simply a reflection of chance variation. We might then proceed to analyze the basis for the significant difference in mean height between the two populations. From the statistics alone we do not know whether a genetic or an environment basis underlies the difference. Other tests are required to make such assessments, as we shall see shortly.

MULTIPLE-GENE HYPOTHESIS OF QUANTITATIVE INHERITANCE

Since the pioneer studies in the early years of this century it has been presumed that most quantitative traits are the outcome of expression of three or more genes with additive effects on the phenotype. In the best-studied examples it can be shown that each allele which acts on phenotypic expression has an effect equal to that of other alleles which contribute to the trait in question. There is no dominance relationship among these active alleles. In all other respects, we assume that genes responsible for quantitative and qualitative characteristics are similar in their mode of action through enzymes, in mutability, and in susceptibility to selection. The principal distinction lies in whether they guide a trait showing continuous variation or discontinuous distribution into discrete phenotypic classes.

14.4   Inheritance of Quantitative Traits

We described briefly the classic experiments of Hermann Nilsson-Ehle on red kernel color in wheat in Section 1.8. He interpreted the results of breeding analysis as showing that three different genes contributed to phenotypic expression in an additive fashion. A very similar study was reported by Edward East and R. A. Emerson using corn.

In crosses between Tom Thumb popcorn and Black Mexican sweet corn, Emerson and East found that the F_1 progeny were intermediate between the parental types in ear length (Table 14.4). Upon interbreeding members of the F_1 generation, the F_2 progeny was obtained, and this population also produced ears that were intermediate in length between the two parental types. The spread of variability around the mean was greater in the F_2 than in the F_1 generation, however. Since both generations of plants were exposed to essentially the same environmental influences, the increase in variability in the F_2 progeny may be taken as preliminary evidence for genetic segregation and recombination (Fig. 14.5)

The multiple-gene hypothesis proposed in 1910 by East and by Nilsson-Ehle postulated that quantitative inheritance may be explained by the action and the segregation of a number of allele pairs having duplicate and cumulative effects, without complete dominance. In the example of the quantitative character of ear length in corn, as well as with many other quantitative traits, there are a number of typical observations:

1. The mean of the F_1 is approximately intermediate between the means of the two parent types.
2. The means of the F_1 and the F_2 generations are similar.

Table 14.4
Frequency distribution of ear length in corn (*Zea mays*)

	5	6	7	8	9	10	11	12	13	14	15	16	17	18	19	20	21	N	$\bar{x}$	σ	S.E.$_{\bar{x}}$
									Ear length, cm												
Parent 60 (Tom Thumb)	4	21	24	8														57	6.632	0.816	0.108
Parent 54 (Black Mexican)									3	11	12	15	26	15	10	7	2	101	16.802	1.887	0.188
F₁ (60 + 54)					1	12	12	14	17	9	4							69	12.116	1.519	0.183
F₂				1	10	19	26	47	73	68	68	39	25	15	9	1		401	12.888	2.252	0.112

Source: Emerson, R. A., and E. East, *Nebraska Research Bulletin* 2 (1913)

3. The F₂ generation is considerably more variable than the F₁, as seen by the standard deviation values and by the spread of variation in a histogram display of the measurements made for the populations.

4. There is an overlap in measurements of the extreme types in the F₂ and in the distributions of values for the two parental types.

The genetic explanation for the inheritance pattern cannot be due simply to incomplete dominance of members of a pair of alleles. If that were the case, we would expect half the population of F₂ individuals to be intermediate and one-fourth to be like one of the parental types, and the remaining one-fourth to be like the other parental type. Although we find some F₂ plants which resemble the parents, they are far fewer than the expected percentages based on the hypothesis of one pair of alleles showing incomplete dominance. The model which best fits the data is one which proposes a cumulative and equal effect of additive genes, as we can see from an

Figure 14.5 The Emerson-East experiment with popcorn × sweet corn, showing the parental and progeny frequencies of ear lengths, and the mean (red) for each population.

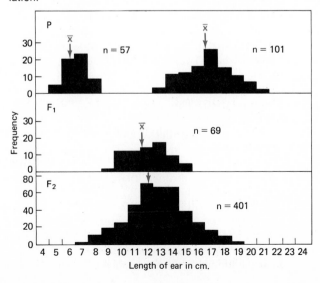

analysis of the Emerson and East experiment with corn ear length.

Each parental type was taken from true-breeding strains of corn, and we may assume that they were homozygous for the alleles in question. If we discount the effects of environment, since all the plants were grown in reasonably similar situations and conditions, we can make a number of assumptions about the genetic basis for ear length:

1. Each of the parents has the same basic genotype leading to production of ears of a minimum length, let us say 6 cm. In this regard, the two parents are identical genetically.

2. We will assume that three independent loci govern genetic differences for ear length above the minimum of 6 cm. The sweet corn parent is homozygous for alleles we will designate by capital letters, A, B, and C, and the popcorn parent is homozygous for the alternative alleles a, b, and c.

3. Each allele shown by a capital letter acts in such a way as to contribute 2 cm. of ear length in any plant in which it is present. Each allele shown by a small letter has no effect on ear length.

Under these assumptions, the sweet corn parent ($AA\ BB\ CC$) would produce ears that were 18 cm. long (6 cm. minimum plus 2 cm. for each of the six alleles involved at the three loci). The popcorn parent would produce ears that were only 6 cm. long, since all six of the alleles at the three responsible gene loci have no effect on ear length expression. The F_1 hybrid between these parental types would have the genotype $Aa\ Bb\ Cc$, and would produce ears that were 12 cm. long (6 cm. minimum plus 6 more cm. for the three alleles shown by capital letters). The F_1 would therefore be exactly intermediate between the two parental types. The F_2 progeny would show the same mean ear length as the F_1, but there would be considerably greater variability in F_2 progeny because of segregation and recombination of alleles at the three gene loci (Fig. 14.6).

The actual results of the Emerson-East experiment conform rather well with the predictions we made based on the model of three independent loci influencing ear length in an additive fashion. The actual measurements are different only because we used an increment of 2 cm. of length per active allele, instead of an increment of 1.5 cm., which would have been a closer approximation. The whole numbers were used for convenience in our discussion.

There are a number of assumptions, however, which are oversimplifications of the real situation. The influence of environment on phenotypic expression was not zero, as assumed, as we can tell from variability in all the populations obtained, including the supposedly homozygous parental types. The mean value of 12.1 cm. in the F_1 and of 12.9 cm. in the F_2 are not exactly intermediate between the 6.6 cm. and 16.8 cm. values of the two parent strains. An ear length mean value of 11.7 cm. would be more precise according to the model we have presented. This may indicate that some dominance occurs at one or more of the loci. It may indicate that each allele does not add precisely the same increment of length. Or it may indicate that

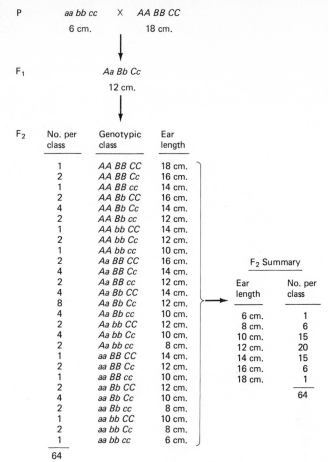

Figure 14.6 Theoretical distribution of genotypes and phenotypes in the F₂ progeny segregating for alleles at three gene loci concerned with ear length.

more than three loci are operating here. Even though the model probably is an oversimplification of the real situation, it provides us with some very useful insight into a complicated genetic situation. The model explains a great deal, but it must also be considered from the standpoint of its limitations as well as its usefulness.

14.5 Hybrid Vigor and Gene Interactions

When two different inbred lines of corn are crossed, the hybrid progeny are almost always considerably more vigorous than their parents. The phenomenon of **hybrid vigor**, or **heterosis**, is not restricted to corn. There are many examples of quantitative traits in plants and animals which show the same striking differences between parents and progeny, but far more study has been reported using corn than other species. While the F₁ hybrid progeny is much more vigorous than either parent, there is a general decline in vigor and uniformity in the F_2 and later generations. This observation should immediately suggest that genetic segregation and recombination in the F_2 and later generations takes place, and is responsible for an increasing spread of variability when compared with the F_1.

There is no consensus of opinion on the genetic explanation for hybrid vigor, and several different explanations have been proposed. According to some geneticists, heterozygosity *per se* is required for heterosis. In effect, they have proposed that the heterozygous combination of alleles at a locus is superior to any homozygous combination of alleles. The underlying implication is that the different alleles do different things, and the sum of their interaction yields some product which produces a more vigorous individual than will arise when only a single product of a single kind of allele is present. The situation is very similar to cases of intragenic complementation. A term which has been used to describe this hypothesis is **overdominance**.

Another hypothesis which is favored by many geneticists is that heterosis results from ordinary dominance and recessiveness relationships between alleles, and not from overdominance. It is explained as simply being due to dominance of alleles being favorable to vigor and recessiveness of alleles being unfavorable to vigor. Since inbreeding of normally cross-fertilizing corn will lead to homozygosity at a number of loci, there will be loci homozygous for recessive alleles and other loci which have become homozygous for dominant alleles. If the different recessive alleles are even mildly unfavorable to vigor, the inbred lines will decline in vigor during inbreeding. When two different inbred lines are crossed, however, their hybrid may have the favorable dominant alleles at *more different loci* than occurs in either parent. For example, if we consider only six different loci in a hypothetical cross, we might have the following situation:

Inbred 1   **Inbred 2**

aabbCCDDeeFF   ×   *AABBccddEEFF*

F_1 *AaBbCcDdEeFF*

In this hypothesis, heterozygosity is incidental to the expression of hybrid vigor and not a requirement. Theoretically, we should expect plants of the genotype *AABBCCDDEEFF* to be just as vigorous as those which are genotypically *AaBbCcDdEeFf*, or any other genotype in which either one or two dominant alleles are present for each gene locus concerned with vigor. It is the dominant allele which is important and not whether it occurs in homozygous or heterozygous combination.

If hybrid vigor is due to a complex of favorable dominant genes, we should be able to obtain true-breeding lines of corn that breed true for vigor. If, on the other hand, heterosis is due to allelic interactions and overdominance, then heterozygosity is a required condition and we would not expect to find stable, homozygous lines that breed true for vigor. Although it seems a simple matter of performing the appropriate crosses to test the validity of one hypothesis or the other, it is probably impossible on a practical level. The number of different genotypic classes segregating in the progeny of a cross between two individuals heterozygous at n loci is 3^n. There are 729 genotypic classes (3^6) for six heterozygous loci, and tens of thousands or even millions of genotypic classes which are possible for 10 or more heterozygous loci. The land area needed to grow an adequate progeny population could easily exceed the total land area of the Earth, and the chance of finding even one homozygous genotype is virtually zero. Attempts to isolate true-breeding lines for vigor in corn have not been successful, as we might predict, because of technical problems of progeny population size.

In addition to the practical problems in relation to population size, there are other difficulties in detecting some particular genotype among the progeny. Quantitative traits generally are influenced by environmental factors, and these would have to be sorted out from genetic variance. Furthermore, there almost certainly are linked genes involved in quantitative inheritance, and these would not sort out independently in crosses. Corn has ten linkage groups, so there is a very good chance that various loci concerned with vigor are located on the same chromosomes. Linkage would reduce the probability of recovering individuals with multiple dominants, since favorable dominants and unfavorable recessives might be inherited together more often than assorting independently during reproduction. At the present time, there is no clear evidence in favor of any proposed explanation for hybrid vigor. In fact, there may very well be some contribution by loci showing allelic interactions along with other loci which act as a complex of dominant genes, probably including a significant number of linked loci. There is no way of choosing among the several alternative and compromise explanations at present.

Although the theoretical basis for hybrid vigor remains in doubt, the practical use of heterosis is a long-standing agricultural approach. Once there are suitable inbred lines which can serve as parents for the commercial crop, the business of producing hybrid seed for the farmer can be established. In the case of corn, hybrid seed for the farmer is usually produced through double crosses between different F_1 hybrid lines (Fig. 14.7). In this procedure, F_1 hybrids are obtained from crosses between inbred lines A and B and between inbreds C and D. The F_1 AB and the F_1 CD hybrids are then interbred to yield double-cross hybrid seed which are (AB)(CD) genetically. The reason for this procedure is that inbred lines of corn are generally small plants with little vigor, and the maternal parent of the F_1 AB or F_1 CD hybrids produces small ears with a low yield of F_1 seeds. These F_1 seeds develop, of course, in the ears produced on the maternal inbred plant. If these F_1 AB and CD seeds are recovered and planted, they produce vigorous F_1 AB or CD hybrid plants. These F_1 single-cross hybrids produce large and uniform ears when pollinated by the other F_1 single-cross hybrid, used as a male parent. The double-cross hybrid seeds harvested from the single-cross F_1 maternal parent plants are then sold to the farmer. These double-cross seeds develop into vigorous, high-yielding, uniform F_1 double-cross plants.

A new batch of F_1 double-cross seeds must be purchased each year from the hybrid seed industry. If the farmer saved seeds from the F_1 double-cross plants and used these for the next year's crop, the plants which would grow from these seeds would be F_2 progeny. There would be considerable variation, rather than uniformity, in such an F_2 population, and many of the

Figure 14.7 The double cross method used to obtain (A × B) × (C × D) hybrid corn seed for planting. (After Dobzhansky)

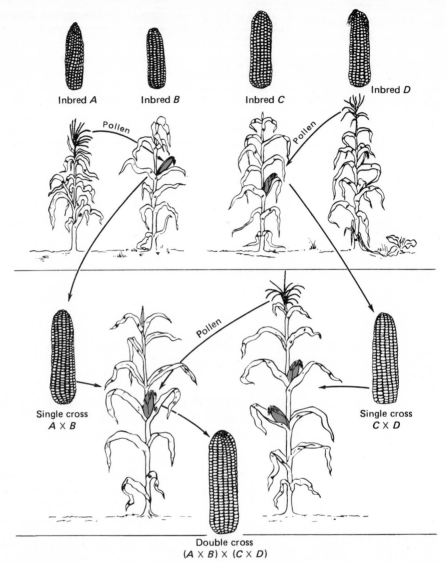

Inbred *A*   Inbred *B*   Inbred *C*   Inbred *D*

Pollen   Pollen

Single cross
A × *B*

Pollen

Single cross
C × *D*

Double cross
(*A* × *B*) × (*C* × *D*)

segregants would be less vigorous than the original F₁ double-cross plants. To profit from the advantages of hybrid vigor, the farmer must obtain a new supply of F₁ hybrid corn seeds each year.

In corn and other species showing hybrid vigor in F₁ progeny produced by inbred parent lines, many genes contribute to the expression of the quantitative trait. These polygenic systems apparently do not operate on the cumulative effects of additive genes. Instead, they appear to represent gene systems in which dominance interactions and nonallelic interactions contribute to quantitative inheritance. Vigor results from increases in quantitatively measured characteristics, such as height, yield, weight, and similar traits. The F_1 progeny greatly exceed the parental types in these measured traits, rather than being intermediate in phenotypic expression. Two short inbred corn lines, producing short ears with few seeds, can give rise to F_1 progeny of considerably greater height, producing large ears with many seeds. Whether the F_1 progeny is intermediate or considerably different from the parental types depends on the nature of gene action and interaction in phenotypic expression. Each, however, is classified as quantitative inheritance because the traits are continuously variable and not separable into discrete phenotypic classes. The genetic evidence in all cases of quantitative inheritance reveals a polygenic basis. The gradation of continuous variation from one extreme to another extreme of expression is due in all of these cases to segregation and recombination of many genes influencing the same trait.

INFLUENCES ON EXPRESSION OF QUANTITATIVE TRAITS

Populations of organisms contain a large amount of variability both in discontinuous and continuous traits. Some part of this variability is expressed as the result of environmental influences, but a large part is genetic. Quantitative traits are generally affected by both genetic and environmental factors, and it is important to determine the relative proportions of these two sets of factors in natural populations and in programs of plant and animal breeding. We will discuss some of the ways in which we can estimate the proportion of phenotypic expression which is due to the genotype and the proportion which varies according to environmental influences.

14.6   Effectiveness of Selection

Since the expression of quantitative traits varies across a range of values, we might intuitively expect that a vigorous program of selection for the most desirable type of variant could lead to an increase in the proportion of such a desirable type in later generations. This would be true, of course, only if there were at least some genetic basis for the observed variation. The effectiveness of a program of selection depends on the relative influences of genotype and environment in phenotypic expression. This fundamental principle was first demonstrated convincingly in the early years of this century by the Danish botanist, Wilhelm Johannsen.

Johannsen studied the possibilities of selecting for seed weight in experiments carried out with the Princess variety of garden bean (*Phaseolus vulgaris*). The plants are self-fertilizing, so it was only a matter of obtaining seeds and allowing these to develop into mature plants which in turn produced their own seeds. Starting with a mixture of seeds obtained from many different plants, Johannsen found that progenies derived from heavier-weight seeds produced heavier seeds than progenies obtained from lighter-weight seeds. This showed that selection had been effective.

Figure 14.8 Distribution of seed weights of 5,494 kidney beans showing a normal probability distribution, taken from records kept by Wilhelm Johannsen.

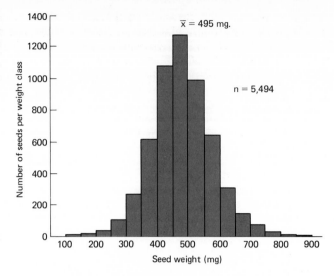

In further experiments, Johannsen selected 19 different plants and collected one seed from each. The 19 seeds grew into progeny plants which produced their own sets of seeds, all of which were kept separate from one another. Within each of the 19 lots of seeds, weights varied from one seed to another, and the total display of variation in seed weight within each lot followed an approximately normal distribution (Fig. 14.8). For a number of generations, Johannsen continued to select the heaviest and the lightest seeds from each of the 19 lines, and propagated each line every year for the duration of the experiments. He found that the average weight of seeds *within a line* was remarkably constant, year after year, regardless of whether the line was reproduced by its heaviest or by its lightest seeds. As shown in Table 14.5, in pure line number 19, the heaviest parent seeds produced a progeny with the same average seed weight as the progeny that was

Table 14.5
Seed weight in pure line No. 19 of the Princess bean over a period of six years of selection

Harvest year	Average weight of selected parent seeds, mg		Average weight of progeny seeds, mg	
	lighter seeds	heavier seeds	lighter seeds	heavier seeds
1902	300	400	360	350
1903	250	420	400	410
1904	310	430	310	330
1905	270	390	380	390
1906	300	460	380	400
1907	240	470	370	370

Source: Johannsen, W., *Elemente der Exacten Erblichkeitslehre*. Jena: Gustav Fischer, 1926.

produced by the lightest parent seeds. By the sixth generation of selection, the average weight of progeny seeds was 370 milligrams for both the heaviest and the lightest parent seeds. Clearly, selection had not been effective in this series of experiments.

We can easily understand why selection was effective in the first experiments using a mixture of seeds from different plants, and why it was not effective in the experiments using 19 separate lines. The parent seeds with which Johannsen started his second set of experiments were all homozygous, having arisen by self-fertilizations from inbred plants. Each parent seed was the basis for initiating a different **pure line**, all of which would produce genetically homozygous progeny after each round of self-fertilizations in each generation. We would not expect homozygous plants to show genetic segregation, no matter how many generations of inbreeding were studied. The variation in seed weight which was expressed among the progeny of any one pure line was due to environmental influences only. These influences have no effect on the inherited properties of the individuals, but they may cause some seeds to be heavier and others to be lighter at maturity (Fig. 14.9).

The program of selection was effective in Johannsen's first set of experiments because the population from which he obtained seeds was a mixture of pure lines, and was therefore genotypically as well as phenotypically variable. When he selected heavier and lighter seeds from the mixed population of plants, he was able to obtain plants producing heavier or lighter seeds because he had separated out different genotypes having different inherent properties relative to seed weight.

Johannsen's experiments were very important in the early years of Mendelian genetics, and contributed to our understanding of the genetic basis for evolution in a variety of ways:

1. It was possible to distinguish between heritable and nonheritable variation for quantitative traits, even where the actual genotypes were not known.

Figure 14.9 Ineffectiveness of selection in a pure line. There was no significant difference in mean weight of kidney bean seeds during six years of selection using selected smaller or selected larger seeds. Based on experiments by Wilhelm Johannsen.

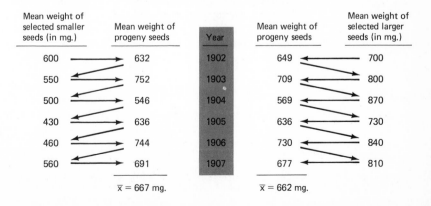

Mean weight of selected smaller seeds (in mg.)	Mean weight of progeny seeds	Year	Mean weight of progeny seeds	Mean weight of selected larger seeds (in mg.)
600	632	1902	649	700
550	752	1903	709	800
500	546	1904	569	870
430	636	1905	636	730
460	744	1906	730	840
560	691	1907	677	810

$\bar{x} = 667$ mg. $\bar{x} = 662$ mg.

2. One could predict that selection within a genetically diverse group could lead to changes in characteristics of subsequent populations. As a corollary, one could predict that selection within a homozygous population would not produce changes in subsequent populations. Selection *per se* does not create variation.

3. It was shown that inbreeding leads to genetic homozygosity, and that no amount of selection will alter the homogeneous character of the inbred population.

Johannsen's experiments and those of other investigators showed very clearly that quantitative traits were remarkably sensitive to environmental influence. These studies also showed that any meaningful program of agricultural improvement or analysis of quantitative variation in natural populations absolutely required information by which heredity and environment could be distinguished and be subjected to some sort of control.

14.7   Heritability

The value called **heritability** is used to express the degree to which the phenotypic expression of a trait is influenced by genetic factors. A heritability of 1.0 would indicate that the trait in question was produced only by the action of the genotype and was not influenced at all by environment. The ABO major blood group phenotypes are an example of traits with a heritability of 1.0. A heritability of 0 means that the phenotype is due entirely to environmental influences, such as the accidental loss of a finger or a tail. Values between 0 and 1 represent estimates of the relative contribution of heredity in the expression of a trait. A heritability of 0.65 is an estimate that 65% of the expression of the trait is due to genotype. The remainder of 35% would then be the proportionate influence estimated to be due to environmental influence on phenotypic expression. The percentage heritability, that is, *the proportion of phenotypic expression that is due to genetic factors*, varies for different traits and in different species even for the same trait. Some calculated values for particular traits of agricultural importance are given in Table 14.6.

In order to determine heritability (H), it is first necessary to determine the variance (V) of a population sample. Phenotypic variance (V_P) is considered to consist of the sum of the genotypic variance (V_G), environmental variance (V_E), and variance due to particular gene-environment interaction (V_{GE}). **Phenotypic variance** can therefore be expressed as:

$$V_P = V_G + V_E + V_{GE}$$

Genotypic variance (V_G) includes the effects of additive genes, dominant genes, and genes showing epistatic interactions. Since the major genetic component which influences genotypic variance in most cases is that due to additive genes, it is common practice to ignore dominant and epistatic gene effects in determining the value of V_G, and to use only the component of additive genetic variance (V_A) instead of V_G. In order to esti-

Table 14.6
Heritabilities for some traits of economic importance

Characteristic	Heritability
Cattle	
conception rate	0.05
milk production	0.30
slaughter weight	0.85
Corn	
ear length	0.17
yield	0.25
plant height	0.70
Poultry	
egg production	0.20
egg weight	0.60

mate this genetic input to phenotypic variance in populations which can be studied under controlled experimental conditions, one can proceed along the same lines that Johannsen did in his selection studies using beans. Individuals are selected from a given position in the normal distribution, and the mean value of these individuals is compared with the mean of the whole population from which they were taken. This difference is the **selection differential** (Fig. 14.10). The selected parents produce a progeny population, whose mean value is compared with the mean of the original parent population and of the selected parents. The difference between the means of the original parent population and of the offspring of the selected parents is called the **gain**. If there is no difference between these means (no gain), then all the variation is environmental and the heritability is 0. If the mean of the progeny population equals the mean of the selected parents, then the gain is the same as the selection differential value and heritability is 1, or 100%. Heritability can therefore be estimated from the proportion of the gain divided by the selection differential:

Heritability = Gain/Selection differential

In general, the gain represents additive genetic variance (V_A), and the selection differential represents the total phenotypic variance between parents and progeny, or V_P. A more general expression for determining heritability can therefore be shown as

$$H = \frac{V_A}{V_P}$$

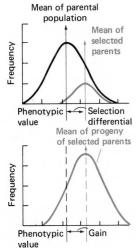

$$\text{Heritability} = \frac{\text{Gain}}{\text{Selection differential}}$$

Figure 14.10 Heritability estimate from selection studies. The proportion of change (gain) relative to the initial difference (selection differential) between means of an original population and selected parents from that population indicates the genetic contribution to the spread of phenotypic values (variability). In this example, the heritability is 1.0, indicating variability to be entirely genetic in origin. The gain represents additive genetic variance (V_A) and the selection differential represents the total phenotypic variance (V_P) between parents and progeny.

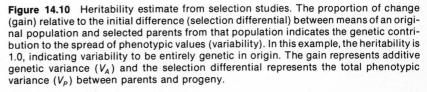

The formula states that heritability is that proportion of the total phenotypic variance which is due to the genotype, *in the population*. Heritability is a population concept, and if H is shown to be 0.5 for some trait it means that half the variation in the population is produced by genetic differences between its members. $H = 0.5$ does *not* mean that the trait is determined half by heredity and half by environment in any given individual.

In plant and animal breeding programs, heritability estimates are useful in predicting how closely the progeny will resemble the parents chosen as breeding stock. Heritability estimates are only approximations, however, since all of the contributions of the genotype are not considered in the calculations. It is the usual practice to minimize or even ignore dominant and epistatic gene effects, and the performance of genotypes in different environments (V_{GE}) is rarely determined. For these reasons, we consider heritabilities to provide only crude indications of the relative input of the genotype in phenotypic expression.

14.8   Twin Studies

Calculations of heritability for quantitative traits in human beings rely on differences between pairs of monozygotic twins and pairs of dizygotic twins. **Monozygotic twins**, or **identical twins**, arise from the division of a single fertilized egg early in development. Monozygotic twins are, therefore, genetically identical, and, of course, always of the same sex. **Dizygotic twins**, also called **fraternal twins**, develop from two different fertilized eggs that happen by chance to be ovulated at the same time. Other than being of the same age, dizygotic twins are no more genetically alike than any brothers or sisters (siblings) in the same family. Since each egg is fertilized by a different sperm, dizygotic twins may be of the same sex or of different sexes, depending on whether both fertilizations involve X-carrying sperm or both involve Y-carrying sperm, or one of each chromosomal type of sperm is involved in the dual events. The observed frequencies of 25% dizygotic twin boys, 25% twin girls and 50% twin boy and girl, show that in these cases as in others fertilizations are chance events.

Heritability estimates in twin studies are not always comparable for some particular quantitative trait. In part the difficulties are due to different ways in which heritability can be calculated, and the same statistic of heritability may mean different things in different studies. The major difficulties in interpreting heritability estimates of genetic input to phenotypic expression, however, are due to two basic assumptions: (1) that the environments of both kinds of twins are entirely equivalent; and (2) that there is no genotype-environment interaction involved. Since V_E is not accurately determined and since V_{GE} is assumed to be zero, there are substantial limitations which must be imposed on interpreting the heritability statistic as an index of genetic determination of the trait in question. Despite all these reservations, the simplest and most convenient way to summarize twin data on quantitative characters is through interpretation of heritability estimates, keeping limitations in mind.

The similarities between monozygotic twins that are due to their having a similar environment can be determined, to some extent, by comparing monozygotic twins reared apart with those reared together. Since the frequency of monozygotic twin births is only about 0.4%, and fewer than one in a thousand twins are separated early and reared apart, there are practical problems in assembling an adequate number of individuals for data analysis. In a comprehensive study reported by J. Shields in 1962, 44 pairs of separated monozygotic twins were compared for a number of quantitative characters, along with monozygotic twins raised together who served as control pairs. Comparisons with dizygotic twins were also included. The differences for height, weight, and IQ measurements between members of these three kinds of twin pairs are shown in Fig. 14.11. For the three characteristics, the similarity between monozygotic twins appeared to be only slightly decreased by their early separation, relative to the differences between dizygotic twins. This finding supports the existence of a strong genetic component in the determination of size and IQ, and similar data have been reported by others in equivalent studies. In the case of IQ, heritability values of 40-80% have been reported. Regardless of the absolute differences in this value in different studies, all the available twin data suggest that there is a fairly high heritability for IQ. Additional support for this conclusion has been obtained in more broadly-based studies in which pairs of individuals of varying genetic relationship have been compared (Box

Figure 14.11 Distribution of height, weight, and IQ differences between monozygotic twins brought up together (solid, black line) or separately (red line), and dizygotic twins (dashed line), demonstrating the relative input of genes and environment to determination of quantitative traits. (Data from Shields, J. 1962. *Monozygotic Twins Brought Up Apart and Brought Up Together.* London: Oxford University Press.)

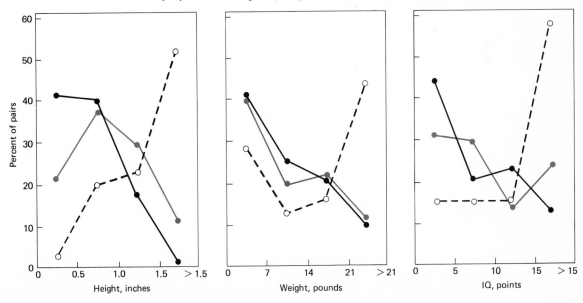

14.2). The closer the genetic relationship between members of a pair, the higher the correlation observed in their phenotypic expression of IQ scores. This kind of analysis also shows that there is a strong genetic component involved in IQ.

14.9   Heritability and IQ

In recent years there has been a flurry of controversy over the *meaning* of the difference in distribution of IQ in blacks and whites in the United States, with the mean for blacks being from 10 to 20 IQ points below the mean for whites. In one such study the mean difference in IQ was 21.1, with 95% of the blacks scoring below the white mean of 101.8 (Fig. 14.12). There was a considerable overlap in distributions, but the spread of variability was less for blacks than for whites. In this study, as in others, there are many uncontrolled variables that influence the outcome of IQ tests. Nevertheless, the differences in means are striking, and reproducible.

Since heritability estimates are rather high for IQ, attempts have been made to explain the observed differences in IQ between blacks and whites as evidence for a genetic difference in intelligence between the two races. One of the major objections to this interpretation is that heritability estimates are only valid for the particular population being studied and for the range of environmental variation to which it is subjected. Since published heritability estimates for IQ pertain to white populations, usually of the socioeconomic middle class, these data cannot be extrapolated to include a different set of populations having a different range of environmental variation socioeconomically and culturally. Proponents of the notion that blacks are genetically inferior in intelligence to whites usually minimize environmental effects on IQ performance. The majority of investigators, however, maintain that the data now available are totally inadequate to resolve this question, either as showing or not showing a genetic component underlying the mean difference in IQ between black and white Americans. In particular, we have very little information concerning the influences on

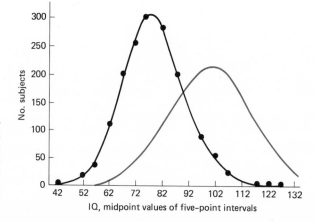

Figure 14.12 Distribution of IQ for 1800 black school children tested in the southern United States (black), compared with a "normative" sample of white Americans (red).

Box 14.2
CORRELATIONS AND RELATIONSHIPS

Genetic and nongenetic relationships studied		Genetic correlation	Range of correlations (0.00 0.10 0.20 0.30 0.40 0.50 0.60 0.70 0.80 0.90)	Studies included
Unrelated persons	Reared apart	0.00		4
	Reared together	0.00		5
Foster-parent-child		0.00		3
Parent-child		0.50		12
Siblings	Reared apart	0.50		2
	Reared together	0.50		35
Twins — Two-egg	Opposite sex	0.50		9
	Like sex	0.50		11
Twins — One-egg	Reared apart	1.00		4
	Reared together	1.00		14

Although there is considerable disagreement about the meaning of IQ, there appears to be a strong genetic component underlying whatever it is that IQ tests measure. Evidence in support of this genetic component comes from various lines of study, including studies showing that increasing genetic relationship is increasingly correlated with "intelligence" measurements between individuals. The illustration shows a summary of correlation coefficients compiled from various sources by L. Erlenmeyer-Kimling and L. F. Jarvik. Each horizontal line shows the range of correlation coefficients (dots) between individuals identified in the lefthand columns. The mean value is shown by a vertical line for each group of values. There is some environmental influence, as seen in the greater variability for one-egg twins reared apart versus those reared together, and for two-egg twins of like sex compared with all one-egg twins.

IQ of environmental variables such as educational opportunities, cultural differences, and living conditions.

In addition to these problems, we really have no firm understanding of the relationship between IQ and overall intelligence. In fact, there is no description or definition of intelligence upon which people can agree. Intelligence measurements, according to IQ, are decidedly different features from measurements of height, weight, or hip width. The individual being measured for IQ must be an active participant in the test. Performance may vary according to motivation, interaction with the person administering the test, and similar variables. Measurements of height, for example, are not subject to these influences at the time the measurement is made. Taken all together, we have found considerable variability in IQ scores within and between populations. We cannot say, however, what portion of this difference in variability is due to genetic factors and what portion of the difference is due to environmental factors. Nor can we say how IQ scores can be translated into measurements of overall human intelligence, much less into a genetic statement about mental abilities.

14.10   Concordance and Discordance

Another measure of the genetic component involved in quantitative character expression can be applied for traits that are either present or absent ("all or none") in one or both members of a twin pair. A twin pair is **concordant** with respect to a character if both twins have it or both do not. It is **discordant** for the character if one twin has it and the other does not. The **concordance frequency** is calculated as the proportion of concordant twin pairs among all twin pairs *having at least one twin with the trait*. Note that the numerator includes pairs in which both twins show the character and in which neither twin shows the character. The denominator, however, excludes those twin pairs in which neither shows the character.

$$\text{concordance frequency} = \frac{\text{both twins positive} + \text{both twins negative}}{\text{both twins positive} + \text{all discordant twins}}$$

If there is a significantly higher concordance frequency in monozygotic than in dizygotic twins, it is considered evidence for a significant genetic component in determination of some quantitatively inherited trait (Table 14.7).

Complications in genetic analysis may be introduced by single genes which show **incomplete penetrance**, that is, where only a percentage of the individuals who have the gene will express it phenotypically (Fig. 14.13). In those cases where the genetic basis for character expression is unknown or uncertain, it may be difficult to determine whether the trait is polygenic in inheritance or whether the observed variability of expression is due to one or more incompletely penetrant genes. In either situation, there will be some reduction in concordance frequency, since both members of a monozygotic twin pair may not show the same phenotype. This kind of dilemma has led to different notions about the basis for inheritance of schizophrenia, a prevalent psychotic disorder in human populations.

Figure 14.13 Demonstration of incomplete penetrance in identical twins: *left,* harelip present; *right,* harelip absent. (From Clausen, F. 1939. *Z. Abstgs. Vererb.* **76**:30.)

Table 14.7
Twin concordance for various diseases. All comparisons show a significant difference between monozygotic (MZ) twins and dizygotic (DZ) twins, except for acute infection and cancer.

Disease	MZ twins		DZ twins	
	No. pairs studied	Percent concordance	No. pairs studied	Percent concordance
Arterial hypertension	80	25.0	212	6.6
Bronchial asthma	64	47.0	192	24.0
Cancer at any site	207	15.9	212	12.9
Death from acute infection	127	7.9	454	8.8
Diabetes mellitus	76	47.0	238	9.7
Epilepsy	27	37.0	100	10.0
Mental retardation	18	67.0	49	0
Rheumatoid arthritis	47	34.0	141	7.1
Tuberculosis	135	37.2	513	15.3

Source: Harvald, B., and M. Hauge, in *Genetics and the Epidemiology of Chronic Diseases* (eds. Neel, J. V., M. W. Shaw, and W. J. Schull), U. S. Public Health Service Publication No. 1163 (1965). Washington, D. C.: U. S. Department of Health, Education, and Welfare.

The overall incidence of schizophrenia in the United States is about one percent, and of these people about a quarter of a million are in hospitals. Fully one half of all mental patients in hospitals have been diagnosed as schizophrenics, and the remaining quarter of a million patients have a variety of other mental disorders. Schizophrenia is thus a serious health problem in the United States, and in other countries as well. Diagnosis is a problem, and we are not at all certain that the disorder is precisely the same in all cases. There is also sharp disagreement as to the causes of the disorder. However, the criteria for diagnosis are reasonably definite, and schizophrenics are identified as those who show no response or an inappropriate response to other people and to their environment. There is a variable age of onset for the disorder, with a mean age of 25-30 years.

Twin data reveal a range of concordance frequencies, but it is clear that there is a significantly higher frequency for monozygotic than for dizygotic twins (Table 14.8). Those who adhere to a genetic basis for schizophrenia have interpreted the data in different ways. According to one group there may be one or two dominant genes showing incomplete penetrance, which lead to the disorder; according to another group these same data have been interpreted to mean that schizophrenia is polygenically inherited. According to the polygenic theory, there would be some point in the scale of many additive genes which would be the *threshold* beyond which the trait would be expressed. Below this threshold, the trait would not be expressed. It is also possible that phenotypic expression in appropriate genotypes is elicited by one or more environmental factors. Phenotypic variance in genotypically identical individuals, therefore, may arise from environmental variance alone.

There is another group of investigators who believe that schizophrenia is not inherited. In their view, schizophrenia results entirely from disturbances in interpersonal relations because of early social environment and

Table 14.8
Percent concordance for occurrence of schizophrenia in monozygotic (MZ) and dizygotic (DZ) twins. Data from various sources.

Year of study	Country	MZ twins		DZ twins	
		No. pairs studied	Percent concordance	No. pairs studied	Percent concordance
1928	Germany	19	58	13	0
1946	U. S. A.	174	69	296	11
1953	Great Britain	26	65	35	11
1961	Japan	55	60	11	18
1964	Norway	8	25	12	17
1965	Denmark	7	29	31	6

upbringing. This viewpoint is incorporated into yet another suggestion, which is that the disorder is caused primarily by heredity, but that social situations may trigger the appearance of schizophrenic symptoms through some undetermined developmental pathway.

We are not certain if the observed biochemical differences between excretions of schizophrenics and those of normal people are the cause of the disorder, or are an effect of the disorder on metabolism. There are no generally successful treatments of this mental disability, but recent drug therapies appear to be promising.

Overall, there is a substantial amount of evidence in support of a genetic basis for schizophrenia. At the present time, however, the precise nature of this genetic component is uncertain.

In addition to complications in analysis due to incomplete penetrance,

Figure 14.14 Pedigree of polydactyly showing variable expressivity of this dominant trait. The phenotype of individual I-1 is uncertain, but probably was polydactylous. Affected individuals are shown by black symbols, below which is shown the number of digits on each hand and on each foot (red).

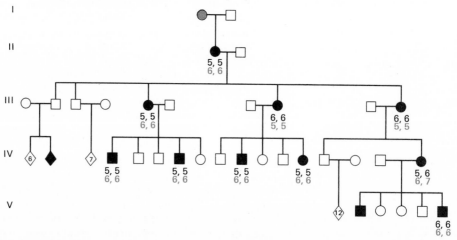

there are problems in interpreting quantitative characters because of variable expressivity of a gene, whether or not it is completely penetrant. By **variable expressivity** we mean that the same gene will produce a range of phenotypes in different individuals. In the case of **polydactyly** in humans, we know that the presence of extra digits on feet and hands is due to a single dominant gene (Fig. 14.14). The expressivity of this dominant allele varies considerably. People carrying the allele may have five digits on each hand but have six-toed feet, as do one-half of the affected people in the pedigree shown, or they may have six fingers on each hand and five toes on each foot, or different numbers of digits on both hands or on both feet or on hands and feet. If we are analyzing some measurable trait whose genetic basis is unknown, it may be difficult to determine whether the range of phenotypic expression is due to polygenic inheritance or to a gene showing variable expressivity.

Twin studies are an important part of the analysis of quantitative inheritance, but such studies *do not provide information on the nature of the inheritance pattern.* Once we know the nature of the pattern from family studies, we can calculate the portion of genetic input into phenotypic expression of quantitative traits, or the degree of penetrance or range of expressivity of single genes.

INHERITANCE OF BEHAVIOR PATTERNS

The genetic analysis of animal behavior is in many cases exceedingly complex, but we know there is a hereditary component, since many behaviors are as characteristic of a given species as its morphological and biochemical features. Each spider species spins a web of a unique pattern, by which the species can be identified as unambiguously as by its anatomical characters. Different species of honey bee display their own "language" in the dances performed by worker bees to inform other members of the hive about the location of desirable plants. There are even different "dialects" of the dance "language" among different subspecies of the honey bee *Apis mellifera.* Many species display social behaviors while other species are asocial; individuals live a solitary existence in the latter but coexist in groups in the former.

There are various genetic approaches to the study of behavior. In some cases there may be a single gene which governs a particular behavioral pattern. In other cases we can infer that a polygenic inheritance pattern is involved. We will discuss a few examples of behavioral genetic analysis.

14.11   Selection Studies of Polygenic Inheritance

Many genetically determined behavioral characteristics of insects have been studied. In Drosophila, selective breeding has produced strains which differ in courtship and mating activities, in phototaxis (tendency to move toward or away from a light), in geotaxis (tendency to fly up or down when offered a choice in a vertical apparatus), and in other quantitative traits. In one particular selection experiment reported by L. Erlenmeyer-Kimling and colleagues in 1962, a heterogeneous population was used as the original parent stock. Selection for both positive and negative geotaxis was conducted for about 65 generations (Fig. 14.15). The prolonged response to continued selection, as well as the extent of selection and the gradual nature of divergence within the strain, strongly suggested that a polygenic inheritance pattern was involved. In parallel studies, beginning with generation 25 when divergence was very wide, a series of crosses was performed using a laboratory tester stock with dominant marker genes on chromosomes 2, 3, and X. The tester stock was crossed to samples of flies from the unselected original population and from each of the selected lines. These studies showed that all three chromosomes were involved in geotactic behavior, providing additional support for the hypothesis that polygenes controlled this quantitative trait. In this case, as in many others, we have no information on the number of genes involved or on any chemical or structural differences that may exist between flies of the two selected lines.

One widely-quoted study on the inheritance of learning ability was reported in 1940 by R. C. Tryon. He conducted an extensive selection experiment for performance by rats in learning to run to the end of a maze which contained a number of choice points between blind alleys and the passageways leading to the piece of food at the finish of the run. The rats were put through 19 trials in a specialized automatic maze, and they were scored for performance according to the number of errors made (blind alleys chosen). Rats that made the smallest number of errors were selected for mating with one another, and rats that made the highest number of errors were selected

Figure 14.15 Results of selection for positive and negative geotaxis in *Drosophila*, over a period of about 65 generations. The mean score of +4.0 to −6.0 represents arbitrary units of response measurement. (From Erlenmeyer-Kimling, L., J. Hirsch, and J. M. Weiss. 1962. *Comp. Physiol. Psychol.* **55**:722.)

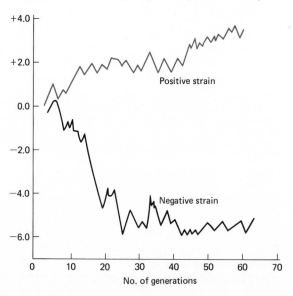

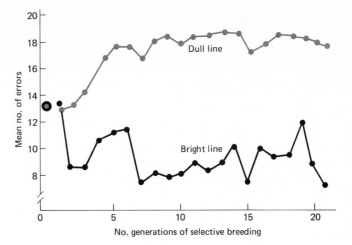

Figure 14.16 Results of selective breeding for ability of rats to run a maze, from experiments by R. C. Tryon.

and mated. This program of selection for brightness and for dullness was continued for more than 20 generations (Fig. 14.16). The results clearly showed that two different lines were established, with one being superior to the other in maze-learning ability. The gradual separation of the two selected lines indicates the operation of a polygenic inheritance system controlling this behavioral trait. Further support for this interpretation was obtained in crosses between bright rats and dull rats, since the F_1 progeny was intermediate between the two parental types in maze-learning ability. The number of genes involved, however, is unknown.

Selection studies such as these are directly comparable to studies we described earlier in the chapter, including Johannsen's classic experiment on bean seed weights. If there had been no genetic differences among individuals in the original population, selection would only have yielded progeny populations showing the same spread of variability as the parental generation. The fact that selection did yield strains showing significantly different maze-learning ability, or geotactic response, is a clear indication of the genetic variability within the original parental population. When the selected lines are interbred, further support for quantitative inheritance is obtained if the F_1 progeny is intermediate between the two parental types and shows a mean value indentical or similar to the mean of the original unselected population. Both examples we have discussed conform to these criteria.

14.12 Other Studies of Behavior Genetics

A variety of organisms have been shown to exhibit particular behaviors that are controlled by a single gene. In some of these cases it has been possible to identify the particular anatomical or biochemical difference involved in the normal and mutant individuals.

Phenylketonuric individuals may be mentally defective, unless there has been a low-phenylalanine diet instituted before the child is six years old

Table 14.9
Increase in IQ scores of phenylketonuric children after some degree of reduction in phenylalanine intake by dietary control

Age when PKU diagnosed	Initial IQ score	Change in IQ score after diet control	Present age in years
5 months	80	+ 9	2½
14 months	62	+ 5	2
22 months	98	+ 2	3
32 months	75	+ 5	5½
1 year	31	+19	3
2 years	48	+ 3	3
3 years	10	+44	4
5 years	26	+33	7

Source: Koch, R. *et al.* 1963. Clinical aspects of phenylketonuria. In *First Inter-American Conference on Congenital Defects.* Philadelphia: Lippincott, pp. 127–132.

(Table 14.9). Feeble-minded behavior in this situation may be the result of a single gene which interferes with the proper metabolism of tyrosine (see Section 1.9). Since the disorder can be suppressed by diet, which does not alter the enzyme defect in recessives, the condition probably is due to the accumulation of phenylpyruvic acid and phenylalanine and not to the presence or absence of the enzyme *phenylalanine hydroxylase* itself. The nature of the developmental pathway leading to this mental defect, however, is not known.

One of the earliest autosomal recessive traits to be analyzed in mice was the behavior called "waltzing." This single-gene defect causes the afflicted mice to run in circles for long periods of time. In addition, they display a head-shaking behavior when at rest, and they are deaf. Anatomical studies of the inner ear in "waltzer" mice have revealed abnormalities that are directly related to the unusual behavior. The semicircular canals of the inner ear are degenerated, which results in the circling and head-shaking behaviors. Deafness in these recessives is due to degeneration of the cochlea of the inner ear. While all these characters appear in the classic "waltzer"

Table 14.10
Percentage of successful single-pair matings observed for one hour in *Drosophila melanogaster* cultures

Females	Males	
	Wild	Yellow
Wild	75	47
Yellow	81	59

Source: Bastock, M. 1956. A gene mutation which changes a behavior pattern. *Evolution* **10**:421–439.

mutant, there are other mouse mutants which circle and shake their heads but are not deaf, and yet other nonallelic mutants which are deaf but do not circle or shake their heads when at rest. In each of these cases there is degeneration only of the inner ear structure controlling the respective behavior. Since a number of genetically independent factors can individually cause a similar behavioral phenotype, it seems most likely that a large number of genes control the complex processes leading to development of the inner ear.

Courtship behavior in *Drosophila melanogaster* involves a series of activities performed by the male and by the female. When the male is put with a female, he will soon approach her and tap her with his foreleg. If she stands still, the male will begin to court her in a specific sequence of the species courtship pattern. At the end of these activities, he will attempt to copulate with the female, but intromission will be accomplished only if the female allows him to mount and if she spreads her vaginal plates and permits him to penetrate.

In 1956, M. Bastock reported that *yellow* males were less successful than wild type males in mating with either wild type or yellow-bodied females (Table 14.10). Single-pair matings of wild and yellow males with wild and yellow females were observed for one-hour trials. Bastock stated that the reduced success in mating of the yellow males was not due to any change in the females' courtship behavior, but rather to slacker courtship activity on the part of the males. The explanation for the difference in mating success was that yellow males lacked sexual drive toward both kinds of females. The reasons for the altered courtship behavior remain unknown, nor is there any basis for understanding the relationship between yellow body color and altered behavior in these males. The yellow gene has a **pleiotropic** effect, that is, different phenotypic characters are altered as the result of a single gene. This, of course, is similar to other single-gene influences on behavior as discussed above.

Until we know the primary action of the gene and the developmental pathways leading to ultimate phenotypic expression, we have no way of understanding the relationship between anatomy or biochemistry and the display of a behavior pattern. At present we can say little more than that there is a genetic component involved in behavior. The fact that we can study behavior using genetic methods, however, leads us to believe that the answers to many questions should be forthcoming in the future with regard to behavior as well as other phenotypic characters.

QUESTIONS AND PROBLEMS

14.1. The following thorax length was measured in a sample of 20 *Drosophila* (in mm): 2.4, 1.9, 1.8, 1.7, 2.2, 2.1, 2.6, 2.5, 2.3, 2.9, 1.4, 1.5, 2.5, 1.8, 1.9, 1.7, 1.5, 2.7, 2.3, 1.4
Calculate the mean and standard deviation.

14.2. A sample of 2000 male college students was measured for height, with the following results.

Height (cm) midclass value	Frequency
154	4
156.5	4
159	40
161.5	96
164	150
166.5	234
169	268
171.5	314
174	280
176.5	242
178	160
181.5	114
184	52
186.5	26
189	10
191.5	4
193	2
	2000

     a. Draw a histogram of these data. Can you plot these values as a normal curve? Do these data fit a normal distribution?

     b. Calculate the mean, standard deviation, and standard error of the mean.

     c. What percentage of this sample is included within the limits of 1σ, 2σ, and 3σ?

     d. Based on the standard error, is this a representative sample of male college students?

14.3. You have two inbred lines of guinea pigs which differ in weight. You know that the difference between strains is due to three pairs of alleles, where each "plus" allele adds 40 g to the weight and each "neutral" allele adds only 20 g.

     a. If the mean weight of strain A is 120 g, and that of strain B is 240 g, what are the genotypes of these two strains?

     b. What would be the mean weight of the F_1 progeny of strain A × strain B animals?

     c. With respect to weight, what classes of progeny would occur in the F_2?

     d. How many F_2 guinea pigs must you raise to recover four individuals similar in weight to their 240 g grandparents?

14.4. Two full grown rhododendrum plants show extreme phenotypes for the quantitative character of flower size.

     a. Working in a single environmental condition (greenhouse), how could you prove whether flower size is determined by genetic or by environmental factors?

     b. If it were genetically caused, how would you determine the number of genes (pairs of alleles) that may be involved in this trait?

14.5. A cross between two inbred plants that had seeds weighing 30 and 50 g, respectively, produced an F_1 progeny with seeds that uniformly weighed 40 g. The F_2 offspring consisted of 4000 plants; 4 had seeds weighing 30 g, 4 had seeds weighing 50 g, and the remaining 3992 plants produced seeds with weights varying between these two extremes. Calculate the probable number of allele pairs involved in the determination of this trait.

14.6. In the laboratory albino rat five pairs of alleles contribute with equal and additive effect to total body weight. Two homozygous inbred strains, one with very high and the other with very low body weight, are crossed and their progeny show weights that vary between the two parental body weight extremes. Suppose that the average cost of raising a rat to maturity is $2. What will be the cost to recover in the F_2 a rat which shows the phenotype of the "high" body weight parent?

14.7. A mouse breeder notes that when pure-breeding varieties with long tail (100 mm) and short tail (50 mm) are crossed their progeny uniformly have intermediate length tails (75 mm).
   a. What is the simplest genetic explanation for this result?
   b. When F_1 mice having 75 mm-long tails are interbred, however, results such as those shown below are obtained repeatedly in the F_2 progeny.

tail length:	50	62	75	88	100 mm
no. of offspring:	5	20	30	20	5

   How must your answer in (a) be modified?
   c. What are the genotypes for each of the five tail-length phenotypes in the F_2 progeny?

14.8. In Table 14.7 showing twin concordance for various diseases, there is a significant difference between monozygotic and dizygotic twin concordances for tuberculosis infection. This indicates the influence of genetic factors in development of the disease. How can you explain this in view of the fact that tuberculosis is an infectious disease, caused by a bacterium, and is not an inherited disease?

REFERENCES

Benzer, S. Dec. 1973. Genetic dissection of behavior. *Sci. Amer.* **230**:24.

Bodmer, W. F., and L. L. Cavalli-Sforza. Oct. 1970. Intelligence and race. *Sci. Amer.* **223**:19.

Bovet, D., F. Bovet-Nitti, and A. Oliverio. 1969. Genetic aspects of learning and memory in mice. *Science* **163**:139.

Brewbaker, J. L. 1964. *Agricultural Genetics.* Englewood Cliffs, N.J.: Prentice-Hall.

Cavalli-Sforza, L. L., and W. F. Bodmer. 1971. *The Genetics of Human Populations*. San Francisco: Freeman.

Davenport, C. B. 1913. Heredity of skin color in Negro-white crosses. *Carnegie Inst. Wash. Publ. No. 554*, Washington, D. C.

East, E. M. 1916. Studies on size inheritance in Nicotiana. *Genetics* **1**:164.

Ehrman, L. 1976. *The Genetics of Behavior*. Sunderland, Mass.: Sinauer.

Feldman, M. W., and R. C. Lewontin. 1975. The heritability hang-up. *Science* **190**:1163.

Harrison, G. A., and J. J. T. Owen. 1964. Studies on the inheritance of human skin color. *Ann. Human Genet.* **28**:27.

Lerner, I. M. 1968. *Heredity, Evolution, and Society*. San Francisco: Freeman.

Srb, A. M., R. D. Owen, and R. S. Edgar. 1965. *General Genetics.* San Francisco: Freeman.

Stern, C. 1973. *Principles of Human Genetics*, 3rd ed. San Francisco: Freeman.

Thompson, J. N. 1975. Quantitative variation and gene number. Nature **258**:665.

15

Population Genetics

The application of Mendelian principles to analyze the genetic structure of natural populations comes under the general heading of population genetics. The major focus in genetic analysis at the population level is to gain perspective on those factors and forces which shape the evolutionary patterns in biological systems. Population genetics provides models and analytical tools by which the genetic composition of populations can be measured and described in quantitative terms based on mathematical analysis. Although population genetics rests on a sophisticated mathematical base, we can gain an appreciation or flavor of this approach to understanding evolutionary processes in biological systems.

By using only elementary algebra, the genetic structure or composition of a population can be described in terms of gene frequencies. By measuring gene frequencies through observations and theoretical calculations, we can estimate differences within subgroups of a species and make predictions about the evolutionary status of these populations. Once the equilibrium situations and conditions have been defined, we can evaluate those factors which sponsor nonequilibrium conditions. Since evolution involves change with time, we can distinguish between evolving and nonevolving populations through estimates of their states of equilibrium or nonequilibrium. In this way we gain deeper insight into the forces which direct biological evolution.

In this chapter we will first examine the conditions for equilibrium gene frequencies, and then we will see how specific factors influence changes in these frequencies and thereby influence evolution. In the following chapter we will pursue some of these same topics in more depth, and introduce more qualitative features of the evolutionary process.

GENE FREQUENCIES

At the beginning of this century there were various misconceptions about the relationship of Mendelian ratios found by genetic analysis and the actual proportions of different phenotypes and genotypes observed in natural populations. If brachydactyly is inherited as a dominant trait, why weren't 75% of the human population characterized by this condition and only 25% normal? If brown eyes is the dominant phenotype and blue eyes the recessive phenotype, why were some populations entirely brown-eyed and others largely blue-eyed? Should we expect populations eventually to consist of 75% dominants and 25% recessives for inherited traits under single-gene control? If that were the case, how could Mendelian genes be responsible for biological evolution when changes in inherited traits obviously occurred over long periods of time? The Mendelian 3:1 phenotypic ratio did not seem to explain events or observations in natural populations.

These perplexing problems had to be solved to see whether Mendelian inheritance could be applied to events in the natural world as well as in the laboratory, and to see if Mendelian genes were the factors responsible for biological variability during the course of evolution. The methods and concepts of population genetic analysis are concerned with measurements of gene frequencies in populations, and with interpreting the meaning of these frequencies in evolutionary terms. The core of population genetics has been developed mathematically, and models which embody population theory have been tested in experimental and natural populations.

15.1   Populations and Gene Pools

We shift our perspective from individual organisms and their individual combinations of alleles to studies of **populations**, or collections of organisms, as units, and of their combined genetic information content, or **gene pool**. Broadly defined, populations are aggregates of individuals sharing one or more features, such as living space. In genetic terms, we restrict our concept of a population to a collection of freely interbreeding individuals. In this sense we confine ourselves to groupings of members of the same species, or even to the entirety of a species, since members of different species ordinarily do not or cannot interbreed. Similarly, the sum total of genes shared by a population makes up the dynamic reservoir of information which is dealt out during reproduction to produce genotypes that lead to phenotypes, by which we can measure the population. Gametes of one generation produce zygotes of the next generation, and these zygotes develop into individuals who in turn produce new gametes and new zygotes. The gene pool is reconstituted in each generation as alleles are sorted and recombined into gametes at meiosis and into zygotes at fertilization. The population and the species persist generation after generation as long as individuals draw from and contribute to the gene pool through their reproductive activities.

Through studies of the gene pool, or of particular genes within this reservoir, we take the first steps in analyzing the evolution of the population.

Evolution involves genetic change with time, and depends on the transmission of these inherited features to successive generations. Evolution therefore depends on genetic variability, and by analyzing genetic variability within and between populations we gain leads with which to assess the occurrence and nature of biological evolution.

15.2   Equilibrium Frequencies

When we analyze a laboratory population, we study phenotypes and describe the genetic situation according to ratios or proportions of phenotypes and genotypes. If we begin with homozygous parents AA and aa, which mate and produce a uniform F_1 progeny all having the genotype Aa, and if these interbreed at random to produce F_2 progeny whose genotypic and phenotypic ratios are 0.25 AA:0.50 Aa:0.25 aa, we can deduce that the inheritance pattern is based on a pair of codominant alleles of an autosomal gene. The 1:2:1 ratio of genotypes and phenotypes is an outcome of chance combinations of gametes carrying the A or a allele, and we assume that all possible matings occur at random when we find this particular ratio. We don't always pay attention to the fact, however, that the ratio of genotypes also reflects the particular frequencies or proportions of the two alleles in the parental genotypes and in the gametes they produce (Fig. 15.1).

The frequencies of the two alleles in the gene pool are equivalent to the probabilities of gametes carrying these alleles. If the alleles are present in equal frequencies in the gene pool, then on the average half the gametes carry A and half carry a. When all possible gamete fusions take place between A and a gametes produced by both males and females, the next generation will consist of the three possible genotypes in the proportions dictated by $(0.5 + 0.5)^2$, which will be 0.25 AA:0.50 Aa:0.25 aa. Using the same binomial method, we can calculate that the F_2 gene pool with 0.5 A and 0.5 a frequencies will give rise in turn to an F_3 population in which the same three genotypes will be produced in the same ratio in which they appeared in the F_2. We can verify these calculations using the more tedious method of listing all the possible F_3 genotypes that can be produced (Table 15.1).

These calculations reveal that an equilibrium has been established after one generation of random mating among Aa individuals of the F_1 generation, that is, genotypic ratios show no further change in later generations. The frequencies of the two alleles and the three genotypes they produce will

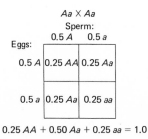

Figure 15.1 The frequency of genotypic classes of progeny is an outcome of the relative frequencies of gametes carrying alleles A and a in the cross $Aa \times Aa$.

Table 15.1

Matings and their offspring in a randomly mating F_2 population where $p(A) = q(a) = 0.5$ and the three genotypic frequencies are 0.25 AA:0.50 Aa:0.25 aa.

Type of F_2 mating	Frequency of F_2 mating	Frequency of F_3 progeny types		
		AA	Aa	aa
$AA \times AA$	$1/4 \times 1/4 = 1/16$	1/16	0	0
$AA \times Aa$	$1/4 \times 1/2 = 1/8$	1/16	1/16	0
$Aa \times AA$	$1/2 \times 1/4 = 1/8$	1/16	1/16	0
$AA \times aa$	$1/4 \times 1/4 = 1/16$	0	1/16	0
$aa \times AA$	$1/4 \times 1/4 = 1/16$	0	1/16	0
$Aa \times Aa$	$1/2 \times 1/2 = 1/4$	1/16	2/16	1/16
$Aa \times aa$	$1/2 \times 1/4 = 1/8$	0	1/16	1/16
$aa \times Aa$	$1/4 \times 1/2 = 1/8$	0	1/16	1/16
$aa \times aa$	$1/4 \times 1/4 = 1/16$	0	0	1/16
....	Totals	4/16	8/16	4/16

$$F_3 \quad p^2 \quad + 2pq \quad + q^2 \quad = 1$$
$$0.25\ AA + 0.50\ Aa + 0.25\ aa = 1$$
$$p(A) = 0.5$$
$$q(a) = 0.5 \qquad p + q = 1$$

remain unchanged through an infinite number of generations, since $(0.5 + 0.5)^2$ will continue to define the gene pool for this gene. The population will remain in equilibrium as long as the same conditions prevail: (1) large population size, minimizing sampling errors; (2) random mating; (3) equal success in survival and reproduction of all the genotypes; (4) no mutation at the gene locus; and (5) no genotypes entering or leaving the population.

Any large, randomly mating population should theoretically attain equilibrium frequencies for any pair of alleles of a gene as long as the specified conditions exist, since meiosis and fertilization events will lead to segregations and assortments for any gene in the same manner. Since this is the case, we can generalize these observations and use the principle established to characterize a population in genetic terms, according to the frequencies of alleles and genotypes produced in random matings (Fig. 15.2).

If we have only two alleles for a gene locus, their combined frequencies must add up to 100%, or 1.0. The frequency of one allele can then be p and the frequency of the other allele must be $1.0 - p$, or q for easier reference. The genotypic frequencies which arise from $(p + q)^2 = 1.0$ are the terms of the expanded binomial, or

$$p^2 + 2pq + q^2 = 1.0$$

If we analyze a population and find that $(p +q)^2 = p^2 + 2pq + q^2 = 1.0$, we can be reasonably sure that the observed genotypic frequencies provide a true indication of the frequencies of the two alleles in the gene pool of the population. This principle is the **Hardy-Weinberg law,** named for the two men

Figure 15.2 In general terms, the total frequency of genotypic classes arising from crosses in a population depends on the frequency of the alleles at that gene locus in the population.

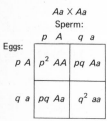

$Aa \times Aa$
Sperm:

Eggs:	$p\ A$	$q\ a$
$p\ A$	$p^2\ AA$	$pq\ Aa$
$q\ a$	$pq\ Aa$	$q^2\ aa$

$p^2\ AA + 2pq\ Aa + q^2\ aa = 1.0$

who first pointed out the generalization in independent publications in 1908. Their theoretical proposition marked the first step toward population analysis in genetic terms, or **population genetics**.

Using $(p + q)^2 = 1.0$, we can show theoretically that an equilibrium will be established after one generation of random mating between individuals which produce both kinds of gametes, in any pair of frequencies which add up to unity (Table 15.2). We can substitute any value for p and q, other than 0.5 and 0.5 as shown in Table 15.1, and we can see that an equilibrium will be established regardless of the particular allelic frequencies, as long as the specified conditions prevail in the population as listed earlier (Table 15.3).

According to this principle, we can theoretically describe the genetic structure of a population according to allelic frequencies in the gene pool and the genotypic frequencies produced in each generation. If these frequencies are in equilibrium, we can predict that the population will not change in subsequent generations. But simply finding that the three genotypes exist in the proportions which fit the Hardy-Weinberg formula is not adequate evidence that the population exists in an unchanging equilibrium. It shows that the allelic frequencies can be calculated, but the allelic frequencies themselves may change in later generations if every specified condition for an equilibrium population is not satisfied. In other words, we have a method by which we can characterize the gene pool at some moment

Table 15.2
Random matings and progeny types produced in a population where $(p + q)^2 = p^2 + 2pq + q^2 = 1$.

Type of mating	Frequency of mating	Frequencies of progeny types		
		AA	**Aa**	**aa**
$p^2\,AA \times p^2\,AA$	p^4	p^4		
$p^2\,AA \times 2pq\,Aa$	$2p^3q$	p^3q	p^3q	
$2pq\,Aa \times p^2\,AA$	$2p^3q$	p^3q	p^3q	
$p^2\,AA \times q^2\,aa$	p^2q^2		p^2q^2	
$q^2\,aa \times p^2\,AA$	p^2q^2		p^2q^2	
$2pq\,Aa \times 2pq\,Aa$	$4p^2q^2$	p^2q^2	$2p^2q^2$	p^2q^2
$2pq\,Aa \times q^2\,aa$	$2pq^3$		pq^3	pq^3
$q^2\,aa \times 2pq\,Aa$	$2pq^3$		pq^3	pq^3
$q^2\,aa \times q^2\,aa$	q^4			q^4
Totals		$p^4 + 2p^3q$ $+ p^2q^2$	$2p^3q + 4p^2q^2$ $+ 2pq^3$	$p^2q^2 + 2pq^3$ $+ q^4$

$p^4 + 2p^3q + p^2q^2$	$2p^3q + 4p^2q^2 + 2pq^3$	$p^2q^2 + 2pq^3 + q^4$
$= p^2(p^2 + 2pq + q^2)$	$= 2pq(p^2 + 2pq + q^2)$	$= q^2(p^2 + 2pq + q^2)$
$= p^2(p + q)^2$	$= 2pq(p + q)^2$	$= q^2(p + q)^2$
$= p^2 \times 1^2$ (since $p + q = 1$)	$= 2pq \times 1^2$	$= q^2 \times 1^2$
$= p^2\,AA$	$= 2pq\,Aa$	$= q^2\,aa$

$(p + q)^2 = p^2 + 2pq + q^2 = 1$ in each generation afterward
and, $p(A) + q(a) = 1$ in each generation afterward

Table 15.3
Random matings and progeny types produced in a population where
$(p_A + q_a)^2 = (0.9 + 0.1)^2 = 0.81\ AA + 0.18\ Aa + 0.01\ aa = 1.$

Type of mating	Mating frequency	Frequencies of progeny types		
		AA	Aa	aa
0.81 AA × 0.81 AA	0.6561	0.6561	0	0
0.81 AA × 0.18 Aa	0.1458	0.0729	0.0729	0
0.18 Aa × 0.81 AA	0.1458	0.0729	0.0729	0
0.81 AA × 0.01 aa	0.0081	0	0.0081	0
0.01 aa × 0.81 AA	0.0081	0	0.0081	0
0.18 Aa × 0.18 Aa	0.0324	0.0081	0.0162	0.0081
0.18 Aa × 0.01 aa	0.0018	0	0.0009	0.0009
0.01 aa × 0.18 Aa	0.0018	0	0.0009	0.0009
0.01 aa × 0.01 aa	0.0001	0	0	0.0001
		0.81	0.18	0.01

and, $p(A) = 0.9 + q(a) = 0.1 = 1$

in time, but whether this same gene pool will continue to exist in subsequent generations can only be determined by examining the population in detail. The population must be large, randomly mating, experience little or no mutation, have no selective advantage among the several genotypes, and be closed to migration of genotypes into or out of the population. Before we proceed to distinguish changing and unchanging populations, however, we should see whether the Hardy-Weinberg principle can be used to describe natural populations.

15.3   Allelic Frequencies in Natural Populations

We can first look at the distribution of the MN blood groups in human populations to see how the Hardy-Weinberg principle can be applied. The MN blood group gene exists in two codominant allelic forms, L^M and L^N, so all three genotypes can be identified unambiguously according to serological cross-reactions with anti-M and anti-N serum preparations applied to a small sample of blood. In addition to the advantage of recognizing each genotype from phenotypes of members of the population, we expect people to select mates at random with regard to their MN blood group. In fact, most people don't know their MN blood type, so matings will take place at random in relation to these alleles and genotypes. As far as we know, there is no particular selective advantage of one genotype over another in the case of this gene locus.

Since the alleles are codominant, we can calculate the frequencies of the L^M and L^N alleles directly from genotypic (phenotypic) frequencies in a sample of one or more human population groups. In a sample of 613 white Americans, there were 179 people of blood group M, 304 of blood group MN, and 130 with type N blood (Table 15.4). We can estimate the frequencies of the L^M and L^N alleles in this population sample in several ways:

1.   People of blood type M have two L^M alleles in their genotype while people with blood type MN have only one L^M allele, so the frequency of the L^M allele in this group of 613 individuals can be calculated as

$$\frac{\text{number M individuals} + 1/2 \text{ number MN individuals}}{\text{total individuals in sample}}$$

$$= \frac{179 + 1/2(304)}{613} = \frac{331}{613} = 0.54, \text{ or } 54\% \; L^M$$

and the percentage of the L^N allele = 100 − 54 = 46%. The frequency of the L^N allele, of course, can be calculated in the same way as that for L^M.

2.   The calculated percentages of the three genotypes can be used instead of the actual numbers of individuals:

percentage M + 1/2 percentage MN = percentage L^M allele
29.2% + 1/2(49.6%) = 29.2 + 24.8 = 54% L^M
100 − 54 = 46% L^N

3.   The frequency of each genotype is the product of the separate frequencies of alleles L^M and L^N, or the product of the probability that a gamete carrying one allele will fuse with a gamete carrying the same or a different allele, expressed by $(p + q)^2 = 1.0$. Since p^2 is the product of $p \times p$, we can take the square root of p^2 and derive the value for p. Similarly, $q^2 = q \times q$, so we can find q from the square root of q^2. Once we know p, or q, we simply subtract that value from 1.0 to find the value of the other allele.

$p^2 \; (L^M L^M) = 0.292$, and $\sqrt{0.292} = 0.54$; and $1.0 - 0.54 = q = 0.46$; or

$q^2 \; (L^N L^N) = 0.212$, and $\sqrt{0.212} = 0.46$

Table 15.4
Numbers and frequencies of MN blood types in a sample of a white American population.

Number in sample			Number and proportion of blood types			Allelic frequencies calculated	
			M	MN	N	$p(L^M)$	$q(L^N)$
613	Observed	No.	179	304	130	0.54	0.46
		%	29.2	49.6	21.2		
	Expected	No.	178	306	129		
		%	29	50	21		

Using $p = 0.54$ and $q = 0.46$, we can calculate the percentages of the three genotypes expected in a sample of 613 people, according to $p^2 + 2pq + q^2 = 1.0$.

$$p^2 = (0.54)^2 = 0.29; \ 613 \times 0.29 = 178 \ L^M L^M \text{ individuals}$$
$$2pq = 2(0.54 \times 0.46) = 0.50; \ 613 \times 0.5 = 306 \ L^M L^N \text{ individuals}$$
$$q^2 = (0.46)^2 = 0.21; \ 613 \times 0.21 = 129 \ L^N L^N \text{ individuals}$$

The observed and expected genotypic frequencies are essentially identical. These values are usually compared using the chi-square test, although there is no need in this case since the numbers are so similar.

From this analysis we can conclude that the frequencies of the two alleles in the gene pool of this population are 54% L^M and 46% L^N, since the observed genotypic frequencies were those expected from the Hardy-Weinberg formula. Since we are not entirely certain that every specified condition for equilibrium actually characterizes the population, we cannot be certain that these allelic frequencies are in equilibrium. We can predict, however, that the same genotypic frequencies would be found in subsequent generations sampled, if the population were in equilibrium for these allelic frequencies. If a different pair of frequencies was to be found, however, we would know that not all the conditions specified for an equilibrium population were satisfied and we could then look for those factors which influenced a change in allelic frequencies. Since changes in allelic frequencies characterize biological evolution, we would direct our analysis toward the factor or factors influencing such evolutionary change in the population. Population genetics therefore serves as a first step in the genetic characterization of a population, and leads to further studies of its evolutionary pattern.

We can also see from this analysis that a genotypic ratio of $0.25:0.50:0.25$ would arise only if the two alleles were present in equal frequency. The genotypic ratio of $0.29:0.50:0.21$ is the direct outcome of $(0.54 \ L^M + 0.46 \ L^N)^2 = 1.0$. Will these same allelic frequencies characterize any population of human beings with regard to the MN blood group gene? We can look at different groups of people to answer this question (Table 15.5).

We all know that different groups within a species, country, or region, more often tend to choose partners from within their group than from the rest of the population. The human species actually consists of many subpopulations, or **Mendelian populations**, according to data obtained

Table 15.5
Numbers and frequencies of MN blood types in samples of two human populations.

Population	Number in sample		Numbers and proportions of blood types			Allelic frequencies	
			M	MN	N	$p(L^M)$	$q(L^N)$
Aborigines (Australia)	730	No. %	22 3.0	216 29.6	492 67.4	0.178	0.822
Navaho Indians (U.S.)	361	No. %	305 84.5	52 14.4	4 1.1	0.917	0.083

Table 15.6

Observed and expected frequencies of L^M and L^N alleles and the three possible phenotypes (= genotypes) in two human populations (see also Table 15.5)

Population	Number in sample	No. phenotypes observed			Allelic frequencies		Phenotypes expected		
		M	MN	N	$p(L^M)$	$q(L^N)$	p^2(M)	$2pq$(MN)	q^2(N)
Aborigines (Australia)	730	22	216	492	0.178	0.822	23	214	493
Navaho Indians (U. S.)	361	305	52	4	0.917	0.083	304	55	2

for allelic frequencies of a gene. In fact, variations in the absolute frequencies of alleles for the same gene in different populations of a species have provided the quantitative measurements for variations within the gene pool shared by a whole species. All members of a species are *potentially* interbreeding, but truly random mating does not characterize the whole species.

The frequencies of the L^M and L^N alleles in the Navaho Indian and the Australian aborigine population samples are strikingly different from one another, and both are different from the 54% and 46% frequencies found in the white American populatioin sample. Yet, each satisfies the Hardy-Weinberg formulation. What do these differences in genotypic and allelic frequencies mean? We can find out by performing the same arithmetic for these two groups as we did for the first population, using the Hardy-Weinberg formula.

If the observed genotypic frequencies coincide with frequencies estimated by expansion of $(p + q)^2 = 1.0$, where p and q have been calculated from the observed genotypes, we will know that the calculated allelic frequencies represent the true proportions of the two alleles in the gene pools of these populations. The different proportions of the two alleles produce the different genetic compositions of the three human population groups. We expect, of course, that mating is random with respect to the alleles or genotypes of the individuals, and there is no selective advantage among the genotypes in any of these cases.

For the Aborigine population we expect to find that

$$(0.178\ L^M + 0.822\ L^N)^2 = 0.0317\ L^M L^M + 0.2926\ L^M L^N + 0.6757\ L^N L^N$$

By comparing the numbers or percentages of the three genotypes (phenotypes) in the sample of 730 individuals with the expected percentages, we find there is very close agreement between the two sets of values (Table 15.6).

The same procedure will show that the numbers expected in the Navaho population sample are in very close agreement to those actually observed, based on

$$(0.917\ L^M + 0.083\ L^N)^2 = 0.8409\ L^M L^M + 0.1522\ L^M L^N + 0.0069\ L^N L^N$$

Once again, the observed and expected numbers of genotypes can be evaluated by the chi-square test to judge the extent of numerical agreement according to the Hardy-Weinberg hypothesis. The numbers in this case are sufficiently close, however, to see that such agreement does in fact exist.

In these populations we have seen that the absolute genotypic or phenotypic ratio may vary across a rather broad range, and that each ratio is a reflection of the frequencies of the two alleles of the gene locus. These relationships can be plotted in the form of a graph, and from such a graph we can see at a glance what genotypic ratios to expect for a given pair of allelic frequencies, or what allelic frequencies we can expect to find for a particular genotypic ratio (Fig. 15.3). Indeed, if we know only one of the allelic frequencies or only one of the genotypic frequencies, we can find the other values directly from the graph, since the graph is another way of expressing the Hardy-Weinberg law of $(p + q)^2 = p^2 + 2pq + q^2 = 1.0$. The validity of these relationships has been established through studies of many gene loci in many populations for different species of sexually reproducing diploid organisms.

Upon close examination of this graph, you will see that different genotypic frequencies can arise for the same pair of allelic frequencies. We already know this from our first example of an initial parental population made up only of AA and aa individuals, which produced F_1, F_2, and F_3 generations.

	Genotypic frequencies			Allelic frequencies	
	$p^2(AA)$	$2pq(Aa)$	$q^2(aa)$	$p(A)$	$q(a)$
P	0.50	0	0.50	0.5	0.5
F_1	0	1.00	0	0.5	0.5
F_2	0.25	0.50	0.25	0.5	0.5
F_3	0.25	0.50	0.25	0.5	0.5

If observed and expected genotypic frequencies coincide, we know that these proportions can be used to describe the allelic frequencies in the gene pool. From an evolutionary viewpoint the frequencies of alleles and genotypes, however, can only be interpreted as being in equilibrium or undergoing change if we have information about more than one generation. If we can characterize the population in terms of its size, mating pattern, selective advantages of the several genotypes, mutation at the gene locus, and migration of genotypes, then we can use gene frequencies to describe the evolutionary status of the population. Since we do not expect most populations to conform to the specified equilibrium conditions, we do not expect most populations to be in a state of evolutionary equilibrium, or state of no change in allelic frequencies. We can therefore characterize populations from an evolutionary standpoint according to the nature of the gene pool in different generations, or according to the particular factors which lead to changes in the gene pool over time. Most of these studies are theoretical and are based on mathematical models which permit us to make predictions about genetic changes taking place in populations during their evolution. These points will be illustrated shortly. The main point to be

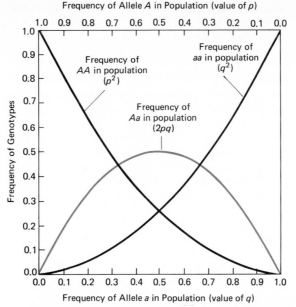

Figure 15.3 Relationships between the frequencies of alleles A and a (in values of p and q, respectively) and the frequencies of the genotypes AA, Aa, and aa as predicted by the Hardy-Weinberg formula.

made now is that we can use mathematical models to describe a particular population feature genetically, but that we must know a great deal more about the population before we can describe it in evolutionary terms or even in complete genetic terms.

Although we have looked at only one particular gene locus in one species and discussed others in general, it should be clear that we cannot determine dominance, codominance, or recessiveness of alleles from studies of their frequencies in natural populations. In the case of the MN blood group gene, we saw that very different frequencies existed for the same two alleles in different populations. It would be nonsense to conclude that the two alleles were codominant in the white American population because their frequencies were approximately equal, but that L^M was dominant among Navahos and recessive among Australian aborigines on the basis of the frequencies present. We can only discover the inheritance pattern from breeding or family studies of gene transmission and allelic behavior in phenotypic expression, not from population genetics. Population genetics is not an alternative to conventional genetic analysis of inheritance; it is, instead, an area of study in which we can *apply* known Mendelian principles to an analysis of the gene pool in natural populations. We can derive conclusions about the evolutionary situation based partly on assumptions from the mathematical model and partly from assumptions and observations using additional models in subsequent studies.

As both Hardy and Weinberg pointed out in 1908, the frequencies of dominant and recessive phenotypes depend on the frequencies of the alleles of genes in a population. We only expect 75% dominant and 25% recessive phenotypes in large, randomly mating populations where the two alleles occur with equal frequency, and one allele is dominant to the other. The population will come to equilibrium for any pair of allelic frequencies, producing a particular proportion of genotypes and phenotypes accordingly, if factors do not intervene to alter these frequencies. Equilibrium can be reached after only one generation of random mating, as long as specified factors do not change. Hardy and Weinberg therefore showed theoretically that Mendelian inheritance was as characteristic of natural populations as it was of controlled populations in the laboratory, and that the same rules could be applied in both situations. Many years later, others used the basic Hardy-Weinberg principle to extend the application of Mendelian genetics to analyze biological evolution.

15.4   Extensions of Hardy-Weinberg Analysis

We can use the Hardy-Weinberg law just as well in the case of multiple alleles at a gene locus as for two alleles, as long as all other factors remain the same. If we have three alleles at a locus, A_1, A_2, and A_3, with frequencies of p, q, and r, respectively, then $p + q + r = 1.0$. The expected frequencies of all possible genotypes can be derived by expanding the trinomial $(p + q + r)^2$, by which we predict the kinds and frequencies of genotypes that will be produced by random combinations of all kinds of gametes contributing to the next generation (Table 15.7).

The same principle of establishing equilibrium populations from initial nonequilibrium populations applies to multiple alleles as well as to a pair of alleles at a gene locus. If we find three alleles with the frequencies of $p = 0.3$, $q = 0.5$, and $r = 0.2$, an equilibrium state will be established after one generation of random mating, providing all other conditions support such an equilibrium in a large, randomly mating population.

Table 15.7
Equilibrium frequencies of genotypes produced by random matings involving three alleles of a gene, occurring in the frequencies of $(p\,A_1 + q\,A_2 + r\,A_3) = 1$.

Type of mating	Mating frequency
$p\,A_1 \times p\,A_1$	p^2
$p\,A_1 \times q\,A_2$	pq
$q\,A_2 \times p\,A_1$	pq
$p\,A_1 \times r\,A_3$	pr
$r\,A_3 \times p\,A_1$	pr
$q\,A_2 \times q\,A_2$	q^2
$q\,A_2 \times r\,A_3$	qr
$r\,A_3 \times q\,A_2$	qr
$r\,A_3 \times r\,A_3$	r^2

$$p^2 + 2pq + 2pr + q^2 + 2qr + r^2 = 1$$

Table 15.8
Phenotypes and genotypes of the ABO blood groups in human populations.

Phenotype	Genotype	Genotypic frequencies
A	$\begin{cases} I^A I^A \\ I^A i^O \end{cases}$	p^2 $2pr$
B	$\begin{cases} I^B I^B \\ I^B i^O \end{cases}$	q^2 $2qr$
AB	$I^A I^B$	$2pq$
O	$i^O i^O$	r^2

If all the genotypes are phenotypically distinguishable, the frequencies of multiple alleles can be estimated directly from the observed phenotypic (= genotypic) frequencies. The frequency of the homozygote of any one of the alleles is added to half of the proportion of each class of heterozygotes involving that allele. For three alleles of a gene, we would derive their separate frequencies by

$$p = p^2 + pq + pr \qquad q = q^2 + pq + qr \qquad r = r^2 + pr + qr$$

The major blood group ABO gene in human beings exists in a number of allelic forms, but the three major alleles are I^A and I^B, which are codominant, and i^O, which is recessive to the other two. For gene frequency analysis we can let

$$p = \text{frequency of } I^A$$
$$q = \text{frequency of } I^B$$
$$r = \text{frequency of } i^O$$
$$p + q + r = 1.0$$

Under random mating, the equilibrium frequencies of genotypes are $(p + q + r)^2 = 1.0$ (Table 15.8). We can find the value for r immediately by taking the square root of the frequency of the O blood-type group, but the values for p and q are derived less directly since homozygotes and heterozygotes are not distinguishable among people of either blood type A or B. Using the symbols, $\overline{A}$, $\overline{B}$, $\overline{AB}$, and $\overline{O}$ to denote the *frequencies* of A, B, AB, and O phenotypes, respectively,

$$\overline{A} + \overline{O} = (p^2 + 2pr) + r^2$$
$$= p^2 + 2pr + r^2$$
$$= (p + r)^2$$
$$\sqrt{\overline{A} + \overline{O}} = p + r$$

and $p + r = 1 - q$, since $p + q + r = 1.0$

therefore $1 - q = \sqrt{\overline{A} + \overline{O}}$

$$q = 1 - \sqrt{\overline{A} + \overline{O}}$$

similarly, $p = 1 - \sqrt{\overline{B} + \overline{O}}$

In a white American population sample, allelic frequencies were calculated from the proportions of the four blood types that were observed, as follows:

Individuals tested	Individuals in blood groups				Allelic frequencies		
	O	A	B	AB	$p(I^A)$	$q(I^B)$	$r(I^O)$
1849	808 (43.7%)	699 (37.8%)	259 (14.0%)	83 (4.5%)	0.24	0.10	0.66

The frequency of i^O, or r, is quickly determined by taking the square root of the O blood group class, $i^O i^O$, and $\sqrt{0.437} = 0.66$. The calculation of p, the frequency of I^A, and of q (I^B), are as follows:

$$p = 1 - \sqrt{\overline{B} + \overline{O}} \qquad q = 1 - \sqrt{\overline{A} + \overline{O}}$$
$$= 1 - \sqrt{0.14 + 0.437} \qquad = 1 - \sqrt{0.378 + 0.437}$$
$$= 0.24 \qquad = 0.10$$
$$\text{and } p + q + r = 0.24 + 0.10 + 0.66 = 1$$

These frequencies are not typical of all human populations that have been tested (Table 15.9). Once more we see the subdivision of the human species into Mendelian populations, according to the characterizations based on blood group frequencies. These also presumably represent equilibrium frequencies, since mating is random with regard to the ABO alleles and as far as we know there is little or no selective difference among the four types. Whether or not these really are populations in equilibrium with regard to these blood group alleles will require additional information on

Table 15.9
Average frequencies (%) of the ABO blood groups in various human populations.

Population	Blood groups			
	A	B	AB	O
English	42.4	8.3	1.4	47.9
French	42.3	11.8	6.1	39.8
German	42.5	14.5	6.5	36.5
Italian	33.4	17.3	3.4	45.9
Russian	34.4	24.9	8.8	31.9
American	37.8	14.0	4.5	43.7
Japanese	38.4	21.9	9.7	30.0
Chinese	30.8	27.7	7.2	34.3
Hawaiian	60.8	2.2	0.5	36.5
Aborigines (Australia)	57.4	0.0	0.0	42.6
Ute Indians (U.S.)	2.6	0.0	0.0	97.4

several generations, and on factors such as mutation, migration, and the effects of chance in modulating allelic frequencies.

If we plot these blood group frequencies geographically, we find an interesting gradient of frequencies for the I^B allele in the east-west direction across Europe and Asia (Fig. 15.4). The distribution has been correlated with historical information and with other data for human migrations, and it seems very likely that allele I^B arose in central Asia by mutation, and was spread westward during migrations and invasions by Mongols and other central Asian groups between the sixth and sixteenth centuries. American Indian populations migrated from Asia tens of thousands of years ago, but little or no I^B alleles are found in present-day Indian groups. We could interpret this to mean that the I^B mutation arose after the ancestors of American Indians had left the Asian mainland. Through these kinds of analyses, patterns of human migration and other anthropological interpretations have been made. Population genetics, therefore, provides a tool with which to analyze species history, including human history, as well as more ancient prehistorical events which occurred in species evolution.

This example also shows that mutation and migration are factors which influence changes in allelic frequencies, and that they therefore influence evolution. We will discuss this further in another part of the chapter.

Two other special cases, in addition to multiple alleles, to which we can extend the Hardy-Weinberg principle to analyze the genetic structure of populations are: (1) alleles of different gene loci, and (2) sex-linked genes.

Figure 15.4 Frequency of the I^B allele of the ABO blood group locus in populations living in Europe and parts of Africa and Asia. There is a clearcut east-west frequency gradient, which has been correlated with human migrations and invasions from Asia westward. (Adapted from Winchester, A. M. 1979. *Human Genetics*, p. 197. Columbus, Ohio: Charles E. Merrill Publishing Co.)

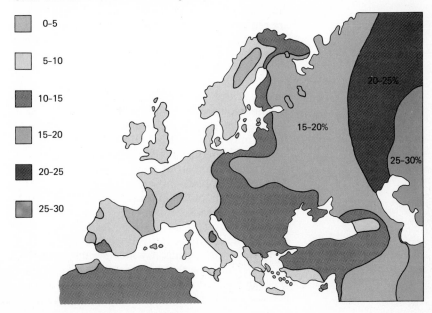

0–5	
5–10	
10–15	
15–20	
20–25	
25–30	

In effect, we can show that allelic frequencies follow the Hardy-Weinberg law in virtually any genetic situation we may wish to analyze, regardless of the number of genes we study or the particular chromosomes in which these genes may be located.

For alleles of two different genes we would simply determine the frequencies of the two pairs of alleles separately for the various genotypes and then multiply these values together to obtain the frequency of any overall genotypic class. For example, suppose alleles A and a occur in the frequencies of $p_A = 0.6$ and $q_a = 0.4$, respectively, while the frequencies for alleles B and b at another gene locus are $p_B = 0.2$ and $q_b = 0.8$, respectively. In each case, since there are only two alleles at a locus, $p + q = 1$. With the separate allelic frequencies calculated, any genotypic class frequency can be determined, as in the following three examples of the nine possible genotypes which can be produced in the population.

genotype $AABB = (p_A{}^2)(p_B{}^2) = (0.6)^2 (0.2)^2 = 0.0144 = 1.44\%$

genotype $AaBb = (2p_A q_a)(2p_B q_b) = 2(0.6 \times 0.4) \times 2(0.2 \times 0.8) = 0.1536$
$= 15.36\%$

genotype $aaBb = (q_a{}^2)(2p_B q_b) = (0.4)^2 \times 2(0.2 \times 0.8) = 0.0512 = 5.12\%$

From appropriate kinds of calculations, it has been shown that equilibrium will be reached at different speeds (numbers of generations) for loci that are linked and those that are not linked. But once in equilibrium, it is not possible to distinguish whether two pairs of alleles are linked or not. In other words, traits produced by alleles at linked loci do not show any particular association in equilibrium populations. Linkage cannot be determined directly from allelic frequencies in natural populations, any more than dominance and recessiveness. Breeding analysis and family studies are required to interpret gene transmission and allelic behavior patterns. Using these known systems, allelic frequencies can be analyzed at the population level. If we find that two known linked genes are associated more often than expected according to the equilibrium frequencies of the two pairs of alleles, we may assume that a nonequilibrium situation exists and we can search for the factor(s) responsible for the situation.

The frequencies of X-linked alleles can also be analyzed using the Hardy-Weinberg principle, with the difference that females having two X chromosomes may produce three different genotypes for one pair of alleles at a locus, while hemizygous males display only two possible genotypes. The expected proportion of genotypes in XX females is $p^2\ AA + 2pq\ Aa + q^2\ aa = 1.0$ in populations, while it is $p\ A + q\ a = 1.0$ for males in these populations. If the population under study is in equilibrium for a pair of alleles of a gene on the X chromosome, the allelic frequencies will be the same in both sexes, and $p + q = 1.0$ in both sexes (Fig. 15.5). Each sex is treated as a separate subpopulation in these calculations.

In the example shown, where $p = 0.8$ and $q = 0.2$, you can see that the frequency of males with the a genotype and, therefore, expressing the "a" trait, is considerably higher than the frequency of homozygous aa females. This accounts for the fact that many more males than females express X-linked

Sperm:

| | X-carrying | Y-carrying |
| | $p\,A$ 0.8 | $q\,a$ 0.2 |

Eggs:

$p\,A$ 0.8	$p^2\,AA$ 0.64	$pq\,Aa$ 0.16	$p\,A$ 0.8
$q\,a$ 0.2	$pq\,Aa$ 0.16	$q^2\,aa$ 0.04	$q\,a$ 0.2

Daughters   Sons

Figure 15.5 Hardy-Weinberg equilibrium frequency for two X-linked alleles, as evident from the fact that pA and qa are the same in both sexes.

Genotype frequencies
Daughters: $0.81\,AA + 0.32\,Aa + 0.04\,aa = 1.0$
Sons: $0.8\,A + 0.2\,a = 1.0$

recessive traits, such as colorblindness or hemophilia. In a population in equilibrium, the frequency of males with the a genotype should be equal to the square root of females showing the aa genotypic condition; similarly we should be able to estimate the frequency of females expected to be aa according to the squared frequency of males expressing the a genotype. If 1% of males have the recessive genotype, then we would expect $(0.01)^2 = 0.0001$, or 0.01% of females to be of the recessive phenotype. If the values for q in males and females are not equal, the population is not in equilibrium. Notice that for $q = 0.01$ in an equilibrium population, 1 in 100 males express the trait, but only 1 in 1000 females have the recessive phenotype.

In the case of X-linked alleles, as for autosomal alleles which we discussed earlier, dominance and recessiveness cannot be determined directly from allelic frequencies in natural populations. Whether a particular allele is common or rare is controlled by factors other than the dominance or recessiveness of the allele. A dominant allele will not necessarily be more common nor is it destined to become more common by virtue of its dominance; a recessive allele may be common or rare for various reasons, but not because of recessiveness itself. This was part of the message stated by Hardy and Weinberg and formulated in their simple algebraic equation.

CHANGES IN GENE FREQUENCIES

Populations whose gene frequencies do not change are nonevolving, since we define evolution as genetic change with time in biological systems. Since the Hardy-Weinberg equilibrium exists only when certain specified conditions are met, changes or modulations in one or more of these conditions will theoretically lead to changes in allelic frequencies, and to evolution of the population. The major factors or forces which influence allelic frequencies in the gene pool are:

1. **Mutation,** which is recurrent change from one allelic form to another at a gene locus;
2. **Selection,** which is responsible for differential reproduction of diverse genetic types in the population;

3. **Mating system or pattern,** which may be random or nonrandom and which therefore influences the proportions of genotypes produced in each generation;

4. **Migration** of genotypes into and out of the population, which influences the proportions of alleles contributed to the gene pool; and

5. **Random genetic drift,** which consists of fluctuations in allelic frequencies as the result of sheer chance, particularly in small populations.

We will see how each of these influences can modulate the gene pool.

15.5 Mutation

Mutations are *recurrent* heritable changes from one allelic state to another, and forward and reverse mutations usually occur at different rates. Mutation is a force affecting allelic frequencies, since mutations of allele A to allele a will slightly reduce the frequency of A and slightly increase the frequency of a in the gene pool; similarly $a \rightarrow A$ will reduce the frequency of a and increase the frequency of A. The rate of forward mutation, u, and the rate of reverse mutation, v,

$$A \xrightarrow{u} a$$
$$A \xleftarrow{v} a$$

are expressed in proportions of alleles mutating per generation. Therefore, the actual proportion of total alleles changing in one generation from A to a will be pu, and from a to A it will be qv.

The relationship between mutation rates and the frequencies of a pair of alleles in the gene pool can be illustrated as follows.

Suppose the rate of $A \rightarrow a = u = 2 \times 10^{-5}$, and
the rate of $a \rightarrow A = v = 1 \times 10^{-5}$

The increase in $A = pv$ and the decrease in $A = pu$, since the extent of the mutation effect is dependent on the frequency of A and a alleles capable of undergoing mutation. If the initial frequency of the two alleles is

$$p_0 = 0.6 \text{ and } q_0 = 0.4,$$

and the net change in the frequency of A, or Δp, is

$$\Delta p = qv - pu$$

then $\Delta p = (0.4)(1 \times 10^{-5}) - (0.6)(2 \times 10^{-5})$

$$= (4 \times 10^{-6}) - (12 \times 10^{-6})$$

$$= -8 \times 10^{-6}$$

Therefore, since the new frequency of allele A, or p_1, is the sum of the initial frequency, p_0, and the change in the frequency of A, Δp,

$$p_1 = p_0 + \Delta p$$

then $p_1 = 0.6 + (-8 \times 10^{-6})$

$$= 0.599992$$

and $q_1 = 1.0 - 0.599992$

$$= 0.400008$$

Even though the mutation rate from A to a is twice the rate of the reverse mutation, there has been a very slight effect on the gene pool in one generation, causing an increase in a of only 8 per million genes in the population.

An equilibrium point will exist when there is no further change in allelic frequencies by mutation alone, expressed as

$$\Delta p = pu - qv = 0, \text{ or } \hat{p}u = \hat{q}v$$

Solving this equation to obtain the equilibrium value of p (symbolized as $\hat{p}$),

$$\hat{p}u = \hat{q}v$$
$$\hat{p}u = (1 - \hat{p})v$$
$$\hat{p}u = v - v\hat{p}$$
$$\hat{p}(u + v) = v$$
$$\hat{p} = \frac{v}{u + v}$$

Similarly, $\qquad \hat{q} = \dfrac{u}{u + v}$

The equilibrium value, $\hat{p}$, therefore, depends only on the mutation rates and is independent of the initial value, p_0. The same equilibrium point will be reached from any initial value of p_0 and q_0, including 0 and 1.

For the example given above, the equilibrium point is

$$\hat{p} = \frac{1 \times 10^{-5}}{(2 \times 10^{-5}) + (1 \times 10^{-5})} = 0.333$$

and $\hat{q} = 1.0 - 0.333 = 0.667$

At equilibrium, therefore, there are twice as many a alleles as A in this population, but since a mutates half as often as A, the total number of mutations is the same in each direction in this particular case. The equilibrium due to opposing mutation rates is dependent on these rates, and is independent of initial gene frequencies. The change in allelic frequencies, however, is dependent both on the gene frequencies and on the mutation rates.

In general, the effect of mutation *alone* is negligible in directing changes in allelic frequencies and, therefore, on evolution. The significant feature of mutation processes is that *new genetic information* arises and increases variability in the gene pool. Mutation provides the raw material for evolution, but other factors usually provide the significant influences on the speed of evolutionary change.

15.6 Selection

The basic concept of **natural selection** proposed by Charles Darwin and Alfred Russell Wallace in 1858, and overwhelmingly documented and expounded by Darwin in 1859 in his book *On the Origin of Species*, is that of **differential reproduction** in genetically diverse populations. Any trait that has a genetic component and allows the genotypes expressing this trait to leave proportionately more progeny than other genotypes, will tend to increase in frequency in the population as the responsible genes increase in frequency. The effects of natural selection on gene frequencies can be measured, at least in the simpler genetic situations.

Suppose there are equal numbers of two homozygous types of mice, *AA* types with black fur and *aa* types with white fur, and that for every 100 black mice that survive and reproduce, only 80 white mice survive and reproduce. We may describe this situation by saying that the **fitness**, *W*, of the white mice is only 80% as much as that of the black mice. If the fitness of black mice is equal to one, the fitness of white mice is

$$W = 1 - s$$

where *s* is the **selection coefficient**. In this example

$$0.8 = 1 - s$$

$$\text{or, } s = 0.2$$

From this you can see that *s* is a measure of **selective disadvantage** of the less fit type.

If we follow this example further, but now include *Aa* heterozygotes as well as the two homozygous genotypes, and stipulate that *AA* and *Aa* genotypes are equally fit, we have a population in which the following situation exists

	Genotype		
	AA	**Aa**	**aa**
W	1.0	1.0	0.8
s	0	0	0.2

The genotypic frequencies will change after selection, since only a fraction of the *aa* genotypes contribute to the gene pool of the next generation while all the *AA* and *Aa* genotypes leave progeny (Table 15.10). The total of genotypic frequencies has changed from $p^2 + 2pq + q^2 = 1$, to become $p^2 + 2pq + q^2 - sq^2 = 1 - sq^2$. The fraction sq^2 of all the *a* gametes (alleles) is eliminated by selection against *aa* genotypes. In our example of black and white mice,

Table 15.10
Change in genotypic frequencies in one generation, where s>0 for recessive (aa) genotypes.

Genotype	Initial frequency	Fitness (W)	Contribution to the gene pool
AA	p^2	1	$1 \times p^2$
Aa	$2pq$	1	$1 \times 2pq$
aa	q^2	$1 - s$	$(1 - s)q^2 = q^2 - sq^2$
	$\overline{p^2 + 2pq + q^2}$		$\overline{p^2 + 2pq + q^2 - sq^2}$
	$= 1$		$= 1 - sq^2$

the initial frequencies, $p_0(A) = 0.6$ and $q_0(a) = 0.4$, have been changed to new frequencies in the new generation, or $p_1(A)$ and $q_1(a)$. To find these new frequencies we can calculate the change in p, or Δp

$$\Delta p = \frac{sp_0q_0^2}{1 - sq_0^2}$$

$$= \frac{(0.2)(0.6)(0.4)^2}{1 - (0.2)(0.4)^2}$$

$$= \frac{0.0192}{1 - 0.032} = \frac{0.0192}{0.968}$$

$$\Delta p = 0.02$$

and $p_1 = p_0 + \Delta p = 0.60 + 0.02$
$= 0.62$
and $q_1 = 0.38$

Therefore, the genotypic frequencies in the new generation will be derived from the new allelic frequencies, so that $(p_1 + q_1)^2 = p_1^2 + 2p_1q_1 + q_1^2 = 1.0$, or

$$(0.62 + 0.38)^2 = (0.62)^2 + 2(0.62 \times 0.38) + (0.38)^2$$

$$= 0.384 \, AA + 0.471 \, Aa + 0.144 \, aa$$

The increase in AA occurs at the expense of aa genotypes for the most part, since the genotypic frequencies were $(p_0 + q_0)^2 = 0.36 \, AA + 0.48 \, Aa + 0.16 \, aa$ in the previous generation.

The effect of selection is not necessarily very great in one generation, but the effects are cumulative. We would therefore expect a consistent decline in the frequency of allele a and a proportionate increase in A through a number of generations, if conditions do not change to alter the fitness of the three genotypes and the selective disadvantage of genotype aa.

To gain some appreciation of the speed of change in allelic frequencies under selection we can look at an extreme case in which there is a selective disadvantage of genotype aa of one, that is, $W = 0$ and $s = 1$ for the homozygous recessives, but both AA and Aa genotypes have a fitness of 1 and no selective disadvantage. Allele a, therefore, is a recessive lethal. This time we will start with a population where $p_0 = q_0 = 0.5$, and the three genotypes occur in the proportion of 0.25 AA + 0.50 Aa + 0.25 aa. The recessives make no contribution to the gene pool, since they are completely selected against and produce no gametes for the next generation, and therefore the new frequency of heterozygotes in the next generation arises only from matings between $AA \times Aa$ and $Aa \times Aa$, and the new heterozygote frequency is dependent only on $p_0^2 + 2p_0q_0$ (q_0^2 is eliminated). The new heterozygote frequency in the next generation is

$$\frac{2p_0q_0}{p^2 + 2p_0q_0}$$

or,

$$\frac{2p_0q_0}{p_0^2 + 2p_0q_0} = \frac{2q_0}{p_0 + 2q_0} = \frac{2q_0}{p_0 + q_0 + q_0} = \frac{2q_0}{1 + q_0}$$

The probability of two heterozygotes mating and producing aa offspring is one-fourth the product of the separate probabilities, or frequencies, of the heterozygote, which is

$$\frac{2q_0}{1 + q_0} \times \frac{2q_0}{1 + q_0} \times 1/4 \text{ (proportion of } aa \text{ expected)} = \frac{q_0^2}{(1 + q_0)^2}$$

This is the new frequency of aa genotypes, or q_1^2

$$q_1^2 = \frac{q_0^2}{(1 + q_0)^2}$$

so that

$$q_1 = \frac{q_0}{1 + q_0}$$

The value for q_2 in the second generation produced in this population is

$$q_2 = \frac{q_1}{1 + q_1}$$

or

$$q_2 = \frac{q_0/(1 + q_0)}{1 + [q_0/(1 + q_0)]} = \frac{q_0}{1 + q_0} \times \frac{1 + q_0}{1 + q_0 + q_0} = \frac{q_0}{1 + 2q_0}$$

and after n generations,

$$q_n = \frac{q_0}{1 + nq_0}$$

and

$$n = \frac{q_0 - q_n}{q_0 q_n}$$

Using these last two equations we can make predictions about our population as it undergoes change guided by selection against the aa

genotypes. If we start with $p_0 = q_0 = 0.5$, what will be the value of q in 10 generations?

$$q_{10} = \frac{0.5}{1 + 10(0.5)} = 0.083$$

In 10 generations of complete selection against the aa genotypes, the frequency of allele a has declined from its initial value of 0.5 to a new value of 0.083. If we use this formula to calculate events over a period of 100 generations, we learn that there is a rapid initial decrease in $q(a)$, but that this decrease occurs more and more slowly with time (Table 15.11). If we plot the changes in frequencies of all three genotypes over selected intervals for 100 generations, it becomes clear that fewer and fewer aa genotypes are exposed to selection and that most of the a alleles are protected against selection in the heterozygous genotypes, which express the dominant phenotype (Fig. 15.6).

Similarly, we can predict how many generations it will take for the initial frequency of the a allele to reach some new frequency. For example, if the initial frequency is 0.5, how many generations are required to reduce this frequency to 0.01?

$$n = \frac{0.5-0.01}{(0.5)(0.01)} = 98$$

Rounding off the number, it will take about 100 generations of complete selection against aa genotypes to reduce the frequency of a gametes from 50% of the gene pool in the initial population to 1% of the gene pool.

These calculations permit us to make some general observations concerning the role of selection in changing the frequencies of alleles in the

Table 15.11
Changes in the frequency of $q(a)$ over a period of 100 generations, when $s = 1$ for aa genotypes and $s = 0$ for AA and Aa genotypes. The population begins with $p_0 = q_0 = 0.5$, and $0.25\ AA + 0.50\ Aa + 0.25\ aa$ as genotypic frequencies.

Generation (n)	Frequency of $q^2(aa)$	Frequency of $q(a)$
0	0.25	0.50
1	0.11	0.33
2	0.06	0.25
3	0.04	0.20
4	0.03	0.17
5	0.02	0.14
10	0.007	0.08
20	0.002	0.05
50	0.0004	0.02
100	0.0001	0.01

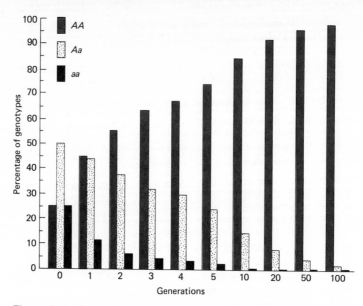

Figure 15.6 Course of complete selection against *aa* genotypes in a population which initially was composed of 0.25 *AA*, 0.50 *Aa*, and 0.25 *aa* genotypes. The decrease in frequency of allele *a* becomes slower with time, as most of the *a* alleles are protected in heterozygous genotypes and fewer *aa* genotypes are exposed to selection.

gene pool. Selection is not effective if p, q, or $s = 0$, or are very low values. Selection is most effective at intermediate values of p, q, and s. But even when s = 1, and every recessive genotype is eliminated from contributing to the gene pool, the effectiveness of selection becomes reduced over time. This is because q becomes smaller and smaller, and the lethal recessive allele is protected from selection in the heterozygotes. It should also be obvious that any program of elimination of some harmful allele from the population, as by sterilization or some other eugenic method, will be relatively ineffective if it is based only on elimination of homozygous recessives. This is especially true because most harmful alleles already exist in the population in relatively low frequencies, and most of the harmful alleles are in heterozygous members of the population.

From Table 15.12, we can also see that relatively rare recessive genotypes are present in populations along with an astonishingly high proportion of heterozygous carriers of the recessive allele. It is just because of this high proportion of heterozygous carriers that selection becomes less and less effective against a harmful allele.

Up to now we have completely ignored the effect of mutation in relation to selection against *aa* genotypes. Although selection removes *a*, mutation from *A* to *a* replaces the recessive allele in the gene pool. The opposing forces of mutation and selection should balance out at some time in the history of the population, when an equilibrium is established between the effects of the two processes. We would expect this intuitively, but we can also provide a mathematical basis for such an equilibrium.

Table 15.12
Frequencies of homozygotes and of heterozygous carriers for various recessive disorders in human populations.

Inherited disorder	Frequency of homozygotes (*aa*)	Frequency of carriers (*Aa*)	Ratio of carriers to homozygous recessives
sickle-cell anemia	1 in 400	1 in 10	40:1
cystic fibrosis	1 in 1600	1 in 20	80:1
phenylketonuria (PKU)	1 in 40,000	1 in 100	400:1
Tay-Sachs disease	1 in 100,000	1 in 160	625:1
alkaptonuria	1 in 1,000,000	1 in 500	2000:1

At equilibrium, the change in $p(A)$ can be shown as

$$\Delta p = spq^2 + vq - up = 0$$

If we ignore vq, then

$$spq^2 = up$$
$$sq^2 = u$$
$$\hat{q}^2 = \frac{u}{s} \text{ and } \hat{q} = \sqrt{\frac{u}{s}}$$

We can ignore the term vq, since the rate of mutation from a to A is usually much lower than the rate of forward mutation and vq is negligible in these cases. The balance at equilibrium depends on spq^2, the selective disadvantage of aa, and on up, the rate of mutation adding more a alleles to the gene pool. So the frequency at equilibrium of recessive genotypes, $\hat{q}^2$, is a function of u and s. Where $s = 1$, the frequency of the recessive genotypes at equilibrium will be equal only to the mutation rate of $A \longrightarrow a$, that is, $\hat{q}^2 = u/1 = u$. If the value for $s < 1$, there will be a higher frequency of aa genotypes and of the a allele in the gene pool at equilibrium. For example, if 1 per 100,000 births is of a recessive lethal genotype ($s = 1$), then

$$\hat{q}^2 = u/s = 10^{-5}/1 = 10^{-5}$$
$$\text{and } \hat{q} = \sqrt{u} = 0.003$$

But, if $s = 0.1$, then

$$\hat{q}^2 = 10^{-5}/10^{-1} = 10^{-4}$$
$$\text{and } \hat{q} = \sqrt{10^{-4}} = 10^{-2}, \text{ or } 0.01$$

By reducing the numbers of aa genotypes eliminated by selection, there has been a significant increase at equilibrium both in the frequency of aa genotypes in the population (from 10^{-5} to 10^{-4}) and in the frequency of the a allele (from 0.003 to 0.01). By increasing the frequency of aa genotypes 10-fold, there has been a 33-fold increase in the frequency of a in the gene pool. Calculations of this kind provide a basis for estimating the results of medical improvements in the treatment of hereditary disorders, and for estimating the added load of harmful alleles in the population, or the **genetic load**. Also, since the increase in the frequency of a leads to an increase in the frequency of heterozygotes, there are more carriers of the harmful allele in a population and a higher chance of heterozygotes mating and producing recessive offspring, of whom 10% die before reproduction and the remaining 90% require medical care to live and be able to reproduce.

This can be shown by calculating the frequencies of heterozygotes at equilibrium when $\hat{q} = 0.003$ versus $\hat{q} = 0.01$,

$$2pq = 2(0.997 \times 0.003) = 0.006$$
$$\text{versus } 2pq = 2(0.99 \times 0.01) = 0.02$$

and the frequencies of recessives from heterozygote × heterozygote matings is

$$(0.006 \times 0.006) \times 1/4 \text{ (proportion } aa \text{ produced)} = 0.000009$$
$$\text{versus } (0.01 \times 0.01) \times 1/4 = 0.000025$$

In other words, the chances for heterozygotes mating and producing recessive offspring has increased from 9 per million to 25 per million, in the new equilibrium population where s has been reduced from 1 to 0.1.

In these calculations it is obvious that the changes in frequency of recessive genotypes or of the recessive allele are a function of s alone, since the mutation rate, u, does not change. It should also be clear that changes in the frequencies of alleles in the gene pool are influenced predominantly by selection, rather than by mutation when p, q, or s is not zero or some negligible value (Fig. 15.7).

Figure 15.7 Individuals with the recessive genotype are eliminated more and more effectively as the intensity of selection increases. Beginning with a population which includes 1% recessives, their frequency is reduced to about 0.1% in 20 generations under a regime of complete selection, but the change is considerably less when the selection pressure is lower.

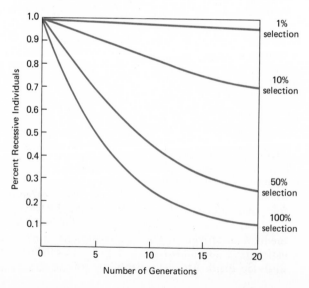

Table 15.13
Changes in genotypic frequencies in populations when there is selection against the dominant phenotypes.

Genotype	Genotypic frequency	Fitness	Contribution to the gene pool
AA	p^2	$1-s$	$p^2 - sp^2$
Aa	$2pq$	$1-s$	$2pq - 2pqs$
aa	q^2	1	q^2
Sum:	1		$1 - (sp^2 + 2pqs)$

Selection against harmful dominant alleles is obviously much quicker than it is for harmful recessive alleles, since the dominant allele is expressed in both the homozygote and the heterozygote. Complete selection against a dominant allele could theoretically be achieved in one generation, provided each allele was expressed phenotypically. All dominant alleles are not necessarily expressed in every genotype, since some genes interact in the phenomenon of **epistasis**, and others show reduced **penetrance**, by which we mean that every genotype containing the allele(s) does not produce the expected phenotype. In addition, new dominant alleles arise by recurrent mutation.

Selection against the dominant allele is shown theoretically in Table 15.13. Of the alleles which are eliminated, the proportion that are A is $sp^2 + pqs$. At equilibrium, the sum of these two terms must equal the A alleles gained by mutation, or vq. If A is rare and the frequency of a approaches 1, then $sp^2 + pqs = v$, or rearranged, the equation is $p^2 + pq = v/s$. Because q is nearly 1, p must be very small and p^2 must be negligible; therefore, we can conclude that the equilibrium state is reached when

$$pq = \frac{v}{s}$$

In the case of codominant alleles or of haploid genotypes, the force of selection acting against the genotype or the allele is shown in Table 15.14. The loss of allele a_2, qs, is balanced at equilibrium by the rate of mutation from $a_1 \longrightarrow a_2$, which is pu, the product of the frequency of allele a × mutation rate of a_1 to a_2. For a rare a_2 allele, $qs = u$, or

$$q = \frac{u}{s}$$

Table 15.14
Changes in genotypic frequencies in populations where there is selection against one codominant allele in diploids or against a haploid genotype.

Allele or genotype	Frequency	Fitness	Contribution to the gene pool
a_1	p	1	p
a_2	q	$1-s$	$q - qs$
Sum:	1		$1 - qs$

In these cases, as in the case of recessive and dominant alleles in diploids, equilibrium allelic frequencies can be reached when the forces of selection and mutation are opposable, that is, working in opposite directions. Changes in allelic frequencies, therefore, take place only in nonequilibrium situations. These are evolving populations.

15.7   Nonrandom Mating

Since one of the basic assumptions of the Hardy-Weinberg equilibrium is that of random mating, we would expect alternate mating patterns to contribute to nonequilibrium frequencies of alleles in the gene pool. In many populations there is a decided preference between partners. For example, tall people may prefer partners who are also tall, or short people may prefer one another, or tall people may choose partners shorter than themselves and vice versa. One obvious example of nonrandom mating is self-fertilization, which is a common mating pattern among plants.

In plant species which are strictly self-fertilizing, there is a very high level of homozygosity at many gene loci. We can see how this can come about by looking at an example of an initial population composed of *Aa* heterozygotes, which undergo self-fertilizations for five generations (Table 15.15). After an infinite number of generations the frequency of the heterozygotes will decrease to zero, while the frequencies of the two classes of homozygotes will be 0.5 each. The overall effect of **inbreeding**, for any number of generations, is a decrease in heterozygosity and an increase in homozygosity. Note that the allelic frequencies do not change; only the genotypic frequencies are altered directionally.

A useful measure of the degree of inbreeding in a population is provided by the **inbreeding coefficient** F, proposed by Sewall Wright. This value expresses the amount of heterozygosity that has been lost, and different

Table 15.15
Distribution of genotypes resulting from five generations of self-fertilization, beginning with one *Aa* individual.

| Generation | Genotypic frequencies | | | q | $F*$ |
	AA	*Aa*	*aa*		
0		1		1/2	0
1	1/4	1/2	1/4	1/2	1/2
2	3/8	1/4	3/8	1/2	3/4
3	7/16	1/8	7/16	1/2	7/8
4	15/32	1/16	15/32	1/2	15/16
5	31/64	1/32	31/64	1/2	31/32
n	$\dfrac{1 - (1/2)^n}{2}$	$(1/2)^n$	$\dfrac{1 - (1/2)^n}{2}$	1/2	$1 - (1/2)^n$
∞	1/2	0	1/2	1/2	1

*F is the inbreeding coefficient, representing the proportion of heterozygosity lost

Table 15.16
Genotypic frequencies in random-mating populations with different degrees of inbreeding.

Generations of inbreeding	F	Genotypic frequencies		
		AA	Aa	aa
none (Hardy-Weinberg)	0	p^2	$2pq$	q^2
one or more	$0 < 1$	$p^2 + Fpq$	$2pq - 2Fpq$	$q^2 + Fpq$
infinite number	1	$p^2 + pq$	0	$q^2 + pq$

genotypic proportions that will arise in different populations depending on the amounts of inbreeding taking place (Table 15.16). In human populations, as well as those of other species having two separate sexes, inbreeding occurs if the mating partners are related to one another, for example if they are first cousins, second cousins, and so forth. There is a loss of heterozygosity in systematic matings between relatives, but the loss is much less per generation than under self-fertilization (Fig. 15.8).

There is a general taboo in human societies against matings between close relatives. We do not know the various factors in human history which have led to this observed societal pattern, but it has been suggested that one of the reasons may have been the higher frequencies of inherited defects appearing among the children of close relatives than among the general population. In western societies, about one marriage in two hundred is between cousins; other relative pairings are found in insignificant frequencies.

We all carry a number of harmful alleles in our genotypes, our genetic load, and these alleles are usually relatively rare in populations. If two unrelated people have children, these children will have four different

Figure 15.8 Graph showing the percentage of homozygous individuals in successive generations under different degrees of inbreeding, according to closeness of relationship of the parents. (Modified from Wright, S. 1921. *Genetics* **6**:172.)

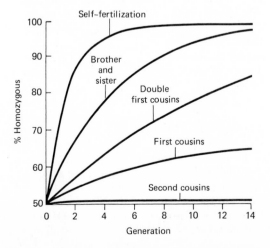

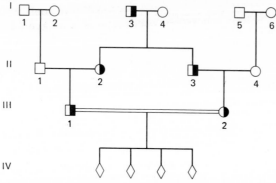

Figure 15.9 Pedigree of a family with consanguineous matings. Great-grandparent I-3 was heterozygous for a rare recessive defect, so III-1 and III-2, who are first cousins, each may have inherited the recessive allele from I-3 since he was a great-grandfather to both of them. If there is a 1/4 chance for heterozygosity at this locus for III-1 and also for III-2, then there is 1/16 (1/4 × 1/4) chance for the birth of a child with the recessive genotype in generation IV, from such first-cousin parents.

grandparents and eight different great-grandparents. If these two people are first cousins, however, their children will have only six different great-grandparents (Fig. 15.9). If one of the great-grandparents in this family happened to be heterozygous for a rare recessive defect, then both first cousins might have inherited the defective allele. The chance that each of these two people is heterozygous is 1/4 for each of them. This is due to the fact that there is a 1/2 chance that the allele was transmitted to a grandparent and, if it was, there is a 1/2 chance that the allele was transmitted in the next generation to one member of our couple. There is the same 1/4 chance that the other partner also is heterozygous, using the same line of reasoning in analyzing transmission of the allele to the second partner from the common great-grandparent. If there is a 1/4 chance that each partner is heterozygous for the harmful allele, then there is a $1/4 \times 1/4 =$ a 1/16 chance that they will produce a defective child. If these two people were not related, their chances of producing such a defective child would be $2pq \times 1/4$. Since we are discussing a rare allele, occurring perhaps with a frequency of 10^{-6}, the chances would be about 1 in 20,000,000. In fact, a good method for estimating the frequency of a rare recessive allele is to determine the incidences of cousin marriages among parents of children homozygous for the inherited disorder.

Cousin marriages, of course, are not necessarily harmful, as can be attested by numerous examples of prominent men and women whose parents were cousins. There are, however, many different, rare recessive defects in the gene pool of the human species, which are concealed for the most part in heterozygous genotypes. At the same time, desirable recessive traits are more likely to be expressed in children of related individuals. In the long run, people choose their partners for important reasons which may far outweigh the question of the likelihood of producing defective children as a hindrance to making this choice. Of course, if there is some known defective trait in the family history, cousins would have to take into consideration the greater probability of their producing a defective child than if they had selected unrelated marriage partners.

15.8   Migration and Gene Flow

Virtually every species is subdivided into a number of breeding populations, each tending to interbreed within itself more than to exchange genes with other subpopulations of the same species. If these subpopulations remain totally isolated from one another for a sufficiently long time, they may undergo enough change in their gene pools through mutation and selection so as to be no longer genetically capable of interbreeding even if the opportunity were to arise. This is the direction presumably taken toward **speciation**, that is, toward new species arising from some ancestral species population or populations. Most of the time, however, a certain amount of gene exchange, or **gene flow** between populations of a species, takes place as individuals move into or out of a population. Migration counteracts the tendency toward divergence into new species. Movements of individuals between different breeding groups also leads to changes in allelic frequencies when genotypes leave or when genotypes arrive and interbreed with resident genotypes.

If there is an influx of individuals from one population into another population, the extent of the effect of the immigrants on the gene frequencies in the recipient population is obtained from the equation for change in gene frequency:

$$p_1 = p_0(1 - m) + p_m m$$

$$\Delta p = p_1 - p_0 = p_0 (1 - m) + p_m m - p_0 = -m(p_0 - p_m)$$

where p is the frequency of the recipient or resident population, p_m is the frequency of the same allele among the migrants entering the recipient population, and m is the **migration coefficient**. The migration coefficient, or proportion of migrants, is a measure of the proportion of gametes derived from the immigrants, which is contributed to make up the next generation.

Suppose a population with allelic frequencies of $p(A) = 0.1$ and $q(a) = 0.9$ receives migrants from a different population whose allelic frequencies are $p_m(A) = 0.9$ and $q_m(a) = 0.1$; and m is 10%; the change due to migration will be

$$\Delta p = -0.1(0.1 - 0.9)$$
$$= 0.08$$
$$p_1 = p + \Delta p = 0.18$$

There is a considerable increase in the frequency of the A allele in the recipient population, from $p = 0.1$ to $p_1 = 0.18$, or almost twice the original frequency in just one generation.

When $p = p_m$, that is, when allele A (or a) occurs in equal frequency in the resident population and in the migrants, an equilibrium can be established. It is possible for very rapid changes in gene frequency to take place as the result of migration pressure, particularly when m is fairly large and p is greatly different from p_m. By migration, favorable genes or genotypes can be spread throughout the species when gene flow takes place during interbreeding between residents and migrants.

15.9   Random Genetic Drift

Although mutation, selection, and migration can be referred to as *pressures* because it is possible to predict the magnitude and direction of the changes in gene frequency which they produce, there is also a random aspect to evolution. Mutation as a process is random, of course, in the sense that any gene may mutate at any time in any cell without regard to advantage or disadvantage. Another random aspect of evolution is **genetic drift**. By genetic drift we refer to the loss of an allele or its fixation in a population by sheer chance, unrelated to selection. The most important factor involved in this phenomenon is *population size*; the smaller the population, the greater the potential for genetic drift. Since chance is the main feature underlying drift, the chance for a sampling error in constructing genotypes from the gene pool would be higher if there were fewer individuals contributing to and drawing from the gene pool.

We can illustrate this principle with an extreme example. Suppose there is a single heterozygous plant (Aa) which is self-fertilizing, and suppose it produces only one offspring which survives. The population size, N, is one and is consistent in each generation. Since three genotypes could be produced by self-fertilization of the Aa plant, there is a 50% chance that the single surviving offspring will be Aa, in which case the frequencies of alleles A and a do not change. But it is equally possible that the single offspring might be one of the homozygous genotypes, and if it is AA then the gene frequency changes to $p = 1$ and $q = 0$, while an aa survivor would produce a change to $p = 0$ and $q = 1$, each of which is different from the initial frequencies of $p = q = 0.5$.

In this way, the A allele may become fixed and the a allele lost, or the a allele may become fixed and the A allele lost from the gene pool, only because of chance and not because of the relative fitness of the genotypes. While this is an extreme example, many populations consist of relatively small numbers of breeding individuals at least during some periods in their history. It is important to note that the effective size of the population, N, is the number of breeders and not the total census of the population. N is a measure of the number of individuals actually contributing to the gene pool, from which the next generation of genotypes arises through sexual reproduction. Each diploid individual has two alleles for each autosomal gene, and in populations with equal numbers of reproductively active males and females, the rate of decrease in heterozygosity due to random genetic drift (k) has been shown to be

$$k = \frac{1}{2N}$$

In a population with 100 breeding individuals having a number of heterozygous gene loci, the expected rate of decrease in heterozygosity is 1/200.

The rate of decrease in heterozygosity should also be viewed as the rate of fixation, that is, the rate at which homozygosity is being achieved. In this population of 100 individuals, one locus in 200 would be expected to become homozygous for one allele or the other in the next generation.

As N becomes large, genetic drift becomes a very insignificant component in influencing change in the gene pool. There is no clear agreement on the limits of a "small" versus a "large" population in absolute numbers. The effective size of the breeding population is a statistical concept that allows us to estimate the amount of genetic drift.

Small, self-contained breeding units, or **isolates**, in the midst of larger populations provide the most likely situations in which genetic drift could occur. The Dunkers of eastern Pennsylvania are a very small religious sect, descended from a small group of West Germans who came to the United States in the early eighteenth century. Bentley Glass studied the community of Dunkers in Pennsylvania, a group who number about 300. The number of parents in each generation has remained relatively stable at about 90. Although the Dunkers are members of a much larger farming population in the region, they intermarry only within their own group and they are essentially genetically isolated by rigid marriage customs.

Glass compared the frequencies of certain traits among the Dunkers with those of the surrounding general population and with those of the West German population from which the Dunkers had emigrated over 200 years ago. By comparing the small isolate with its larger neighboring population and its parent population, the effectiveness of genetic drift should be evident. The relative frequencies of the ABO, Rh, and MN blood groups were determined, along with the incidences of four inherited external characteristics: left- or right-handedness, attached or free-hanging ear lobes, the presence or absence of hair on the middle segments of the fingers, and normal versus extensive flexibility of the thumb ("hitch-hiker's thumb").

These studies showed that the frequencies of some traits were strikingly different in the Dunker community when compared with the United States and West German populations. Blood group A is much more frequent, type O is somewhat rarer, and types B and AB are exceptionally infrequent in the Dunker community (Table 15.17). The I^B allele was almost lost, and most of the carriers of the I^B allele were converts who entered the isolate by marriage but were not born in the community.

Blood type M has increased and type N has decreased in frequency as compared with the other two populations. Only the Rh blood groups occur in

Table 15.17
Frequencies of ABO and MN blood group alleles in three human populations.

Population	Allelic frequencies				
	I^A	I^B	i^O	L^M	L^N
United States	0.26	0.04	0.70	0.54	0.46
West German	0.29	0.07	0.64	0.55	0.45
Dunker	0.38	0.03	0.59	0.65	0.35

Figure 15.10 Summary of events and factors which influence evolution in the direction of adaptation.

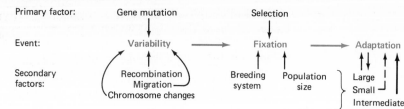

frequencies that are similar to those in the surrounding population. Similarly, in physical traits only right- and left-handedness occur in frequencies resembling those of the surrounding or parental populations. The other three external physical traits are significantly lower in the Dunker community than in the other two populations.

It would therefore seem that the particular gene frequencies, some very high, some very low, and others essentially unchanged, can best be attributed to genetic drift, that is, to chance fluctuations in gene frequencies. In these isolates, at least, drift apparently has been operative. For natural populations in general it is less certain whether random genetic drift has helped to shape the gene pool.

What we have discussed so far has shown that various factors influence gene frequencies and thereby sustain populations in nonequilibrium conditions, that is, in the state of evolutionary change. Of these factors certain ones may be particularly important in certain populations at certain times and under certain conditions, but the main force which shapes biological evolution is considered to be natural selection. Natural selection acts on genetic diversity, or variability of the gene pool, and guides the evolution of the population toward greater fitness of its genotypes, that is, in the direction of **adaptation** (Fig. 15.10). The various processes which increase genotypic diversity in populations are mutation, recombination, chromosomal changes in number and structure, and migration. Selection is usually effective, but in very small populations evolutionary changes may be either adaptive or nonadaptive, due to chance alone leading to random fixation or loss of advantageous or disadvantageous alleles when random genetic drift is in operation as an effective force. We will consider some of these concepts in more detail in the next chapter.

QUESTIONS AND PROBLEMS

(Note: Unless otherwise indicated, assume that the populations are in equilibrium.)

15.1.   Coat color in cats is governed by a pair of codominant sex-linked alleles, which give the following phenotypes:
$C^B C^B$ ♀♀ or C^B ♂♂ are black, $C^Y C^Y$ ♀♀ or C^Y ♂♂ are yellow, and $C^B C^Y$ ♀♀ are calico (mixture of yellow and black fur). A population of cats in Rome was analyzed for these alleles, with the following results:

	Black	Yellow	Calico	Total
Females	554	14	108	676
Males	622	84	0.	706

a. What are the allelic frequencies?
b. Do the genotypic frequencies for females fit the Hardy-Weinberg formula?
c. Do the genotypic frequencies for males fit the Hardy-Weinberg formula?

15.2. Vermilion eye color in *Drosophila* is due to a sex-linked recessive gene v, and wild type (red eyes) to its dominant allele v^+. A population of fruit flies reared in the laboratory was found to have 85 red-eyed males and 15 males with vermilion eye color.
a. Estimate the frequencies of the two alleles.
b. What percentage of females in this population would be expected to have vermilion eyes?

15.3. As you know, MN blood groups are determined by a pair of codominant alleles (L^M and L^N). A sample of 426 Bedouins in the Sinai peninsula was typed for MN blood group, with these results:

$$238 \text{ M}$$
$$152 \text{ MN}$$
$$36 \text{ N}$$

a. Calculate the allelic frequencies of L^M and L^N.
b. If the frequency of $L^N = 0.3$, how many individuals in a population of 1000 would be expected to belong to blood group MN?

15.4. Phenylketonuria is a metabolic disorder due to an autosomal recessive gene. If the frequency of affected individuals in the population is 1/10,000, what is the probability that two unrelated, normal parents will produce a phenylketonuric child?

15.5. In *Drosophila*, black and ebony body color phenotypes are due to recessive alleles (b and e, respectively) of gene loci on different chromosomes. A large population screened for these phenotypes gave these results:

9.69% wild type, 9.31% ebony, 41.31% black, 39.69% ebony & black

Calculate the frequencies of the ebony and black alleles of the two body color genes.

15.6. Ocular albinism is governed by a sex-linked recessive allele, and 1% of the gametes in the gene pool of a particular human population carries this allele.
a. What is the expected frequency of ocular albinism among males of this population?
b. What is the expected frequency among females of this population?

15.7. Lesch-Nyan disease is a sex-linked, recessive disorder which causes neurological damage in human beings. A survey of 500 males from a Caucasian population revealed that 20 were affected with this disorder.

    a. What is the frequency of the normal allele in this population?

    b. What percentage of the females in this population would be expected to be normal?

15.8.   In England 70% of the population are *tasters*, who can detect the bitter taste of the chemical PTC (phenylthiocarbamide), and 30% are *nontasters*. A single autosomal gene is involved, and taster is dominant over nontaster.

    a. What proportion of all marriages between tasters and nontasters have no chance (except by mutation) of producing a nontaster child?

    b. If mating is random, what is the probability of a nontaster finding a nontaster partner?

15.9.   The ABO blood group locus is on chromosome 9 in humans. In a particular population it has been found that the frequency of the i^o allele is 0.6. What would be the expected frequency of blood type 0 among individuals with trisomy-9?

15.10.   A sample of 2000 Italians was typed for ABO major blood group, with these results:

$$A = 640 \quad B = 300 \quad AB = 80 \quad O = 980$$

Calculate the frequencies of alleles I^A, I^B, and i^o

15.11.   Curly fur *versus* straight fur is governed by a single pair of autosomal alleles. A large randomly mating animal population consists of 23% with curly fur and 77% with straight fur. Which allele is dominant?

15.12.   In a sample of 2400 births at an area hospital, six babies died shortly after birth from the effects of colonic obstruction, an autosomal recessive lethal disorder.

    a. What is the frequency of the recessive *co* allele in the population?

    b. What proportion of the population is heterozygous for the *co* allele?

    c. What proportion of the population is homozygous for the normal co^+ allele?

    d. What is the rate of mutation of co^+ to *co*?

15.13.   A sheep rancher in Iceland finds that the recessive allele *y* causing yellow fat has become established in his flock of 1000 sheep, and that 1 in 25 sheep express this trait. Assume that the population is randomly mating and that all genotypes have the same reproductive fitness.

    a. How many sheep express the normal trait of white fat?

    b. How many normal sheep carry the recessive allele?

    c. Since only animals with white fat are selected for breeding,. why is it that the recessive allele has not been eliminated from the population?

    d. How long would it take to eliminate the recessive allele if selective breeding is continued, using only sheep with white fat?

REFERENCES

Cavalli-Sforza, L. L. Sept. 1974. The genetics of human populations. *Sci. Amer.* **231**:80.

Cavalli-Sforza, L. L. Aug. 1969. "Genetic drift" in an Italian population. *Sci. Amer.* **221**:30.

Cavalli-Sforza, L. L., and W. F. Bodmer. 1971. *The Genetics of Human Populations.* San Francisco: Freeman.

Dobzhansky, T. 1968. *Genetics of the Evolutionary Process.* New York: Columbia University Press.

Dobzhansky, T., F. J. Ayala, G. L. Stebbins, and J. W. Valentine. 1977. *Evolution.* San Francisco: Freeman.

Eckhardt, R. B. Jan. 1972. Population genetics and human origins. *Sci. Amer.* **226**:94.

Fisher, J. 1978. *R. A. Fisher: The Life of a Scientist.* New York: John Wiley.

Fraikor, A. L. 1977. Tay-Sachs disease: Genetic drift among the Ashkenazim Jews. *Social Biol.* **24**:117.

Hardy, G. H. 1908. Mendelian proportions in a mixed population. *Science* **28**:49.

Lerner, I. M. 1968. *Heredity, Evolution, and Society.* San Francisco: Freeman.

Lewontin, R. C., ed. 1968. *Population Biology and Evolution.* Syracuse: Syracuse University Press.

Lewontin, R. C. 1974. *The Genetic Basis of Evolutionary Change.* New York: Columbia University Press.

Mayr, E. 1970. *Populations, Species, and Evolution.* Cambridge: Harvard University Press.

Mettler, L. E., and T. G. Gregg. 1969. *Population Genetics and Evolution.* Englewood Cliffs, N.J.: Prentice-Hall.

Nei, M. 1975. *Molecular Population Genetics and Evolution.* New York: Elsevier.

Weinberg, W. 1908. Über den Nachweis der Vererbung beim Menschen. (English translation in S. H. Boyer, IV, ed. 1963. *Papers on Human Genetics*, p. 4. Englewood Cliffs, N.J.: Prentice-Hall.)

Wills, C. Mar. 1970. Genetic load. *Sci. Amer.* **222**:98.

Wright, S. 1978. *Evolution and the Genetics of Populations.* Vol. 4: Variability Within and Among Natural Populations. Chicago: University of Chicago Press.

16

Evolutionary Genetics

Natural selection acting on diversity leads to evolutionary changes in populations. The better fit individuals are those which compete successfully for the finite resources needed for life, and the better adapted genotypes become predominant through differential reproduction of fitter and less fit individuals. Selection is not simply a process for elimination of disadvantageous alleles, since advantage and disadvantage are relative and not absolute specifications. Various selection strategies modify population diversity in various ways, in relation to relative fitnesses in particular environments at particular times.

Highly adapted populations usually enjoy short-term evolutionary success, but they are less likely to succeed in meeting challenges of new or changing environments, since the price of adaptedness is lowered genetic diversity. Highly adaptable populations have more chances for long-term evolutionary success, since they preserve genetic diversity, at the cost of being less closely adapted to some particular environment at a specific moment in time. The evolutionary development of adaptedness or adaptability depends in large measure on the nature of the genetic system, especially in relation to gene recombination. The genetic system underwrites the amount of genotypic diversity which is expressed in populations, and the rate at which diversity in the gene pool is released in genotypic construction in each generation. Sexual reproduction is one mechanism for generating genotypic diversity in each generation, and the separation of the sexes into different individuals provides virtual assurance that cross-fertilization will occur and lead to genotypic diversity as long as the populations exist.

Evolutionary changes in populations ultimately lead to new species and to higher taxonomic groupings. Speciation generally is initiated in subpopulations which are spatially isolated, and which therefore proceed along divergent evolutionary pathways. If there has been adequate genetic change to prevent interbreeding between subpopulations, reproductively isolated new species may arise. Molecular analysis has provided adjunct evidence for genetic divergence in proportion to the time that taxonomic groups have evolved along their separate pathways from some common ancestor.

NATURAL SELECTION

The basic theme of biological evolution which we developed in the last chapter was that natural selection acting on genetic diversity leads to changes in gene frequencies in the gene pool. These events rest on three basic principles: (1) there must be variation to select from; (2) this variation must be heritable since there is progressive change from generation to generation; and (3) different variants leave different numbers of offspring either immediately or in later generations.

In effect we are saying that natural selection involves differential reproduction of genetically diverse types so that some types leave more offspring than others. Eventually the gene pool will be composed of a higher proportion of some types compared to some others. If we stop at this point, what have we explained? To say that inherently fitter individuals leave more offspring, and that those individuals which leave more offspring can be defined as fitter, is to state a *tautology*. We have not provided any meaningful information or explanation, and we have only defined ourselves into a circle. In order to gain insight into the biological meaning of natural selection, and to understand the nature of evolutionary changes in biological systems, we must also consider the nature of adaptation, or, the *relative fitness* of the genotype in relation to the environment. In addition, we must have a better notion about the nature and wealth of genetic diversity, since this is the raw material for evolution.

16.1   Adaptation

Darwin introduced a fourth principle underlying biological evolution, the principle of the "struggle for existence." He made it clear that the term was metaphorical in the widest sense and not simply a matter of bloody combat to the death between individuals. The fitter individuals and populations are those which compete successfully for the finite resources of life, such as space, light, food, shelter, and mates. Less fit individuals and populations are less successful in competition and they secure less of their requirements for existence and therefore decrease in frequency relative to the fitter members of the population.

The fitter individuals are better adapted to their environments, that is, they are inherently better at solving their ecological problems than are other individuals with less fit genotypes in the same environments. The concept of adaptation, that is, of the fitness of the individual or population in its environment, puts us into the real world of space and time. Once we introduce the relative fitness, or adaptedness, of the individual to its environment, we can begin to make predictions about which individuals and which populations are more likely to leave more offspring and which will leave fewer or no offspring. We can predict which individuals will be fitter according to their biological characteristics by which they solve ecological problems.

We can also see more clearly why there is a finite amount of diversity in the biological world, despite the random nature of mutation. In other words, considerable diversity arises by the random process of mutation, but only a proportion of this diversity becomes incorporated into the genetic structure of a population. That proportion of diversity which becomes incorporated is either neutral, conferring neither advantage nor disadvantage, or it is positive and enhances the fitness or adaptedness of the population in relation to environmental challenges in different places at different times in its history.

With these concepts in mind, we can expect that evolutionary changes in the gene pool will arise in different ways according to the particular nature of interactions between populations and their environments. Furthermore, environments are rarely uniform at any one time, and they also change in various ways over time. Within this space-time mosaic of the environment, we can look at ways in which adaptation is achieved. Adaptation is relative rather than absolute, so the nature of adaptations in populations will depend partly on the genetic diversity which occurs and partly on the selection strategy which acts on this diversity to modulate its quantity and quality. In some cases it is possible that diversity is maintained in the absence of selection, although this is a controversial topic.

16.2   Selection Strategies

There are a number of ways in which natural selection influences the gene pool, in addition to **normalizing natural selection** which acts to reduce or eliminate disadvantageous alleles, as we discussed in the previous chapter (Fig. 16.1). In the case of normalizing natural selection those genotypes with lowered fitness ($W < 1$) are reduced gradually, while genotypes with a fitness of 1 will increase proportionately in each generation until an equilibrium is reached. Through normalizing natural selection there is less genotypic diversity, since selection acts against one of the homozygous genotypes. For dominant, codominant, or recessive alleles which are lethal ($W = 0$, $s = 1$), the rate of elimination of the disadvantageous genotype is faster than if $s < 1$ (see Fig. 15.7). The price paid for increasing population fitness is a diminution of its gene pool diversity.

In **directional natural selection**, the population is shifted in the direction of its greatest adaptedness, or fitness, in relation to changing environmental conditions. One genotype may be favored under one set of conditions and another under a different set of conditions. In either case, there is an increase in the proportion of favored genotypes and a reduction in frequency of the less fit genotype. Since one homozygous genotype is fitter than the other, there is also a reduction in frequency of heterozygotes as one allele is reduced or eliminated and as the alternative allele may even increase to become the only variant fixed in the gene pool. The genotypic diversity is therefore reduced.

Examples of the action of directional selection are among the most spectacular because we can see evolution in action in our own lifetimes. The evolution of resistance of insect species to pesticides and of bacterial species to antibiotics in recent years have provided ample demonstrations of the ability of living species to undergo genetic changes in response to environ-

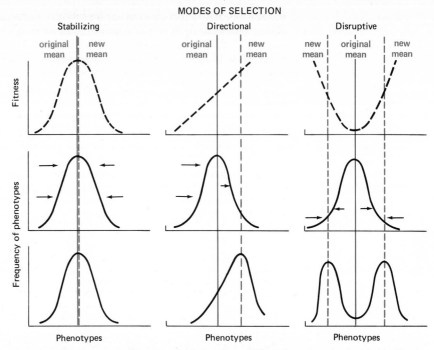

Figure 16.1 Summary diagrams depicting three different modes of natural selection in terms of influence on the gene pool. The upper set of graphs shows the distribution (dashed line) of phenotypes in relation to original and new means (red lines) under each selection regime, according to fitness of the phenotype. The influence of selection on the phenotypic frequency is indicated by arrows in the middle set of graphs, and the consequences of such selection are shown in the bottom set of graphs.

mental challenges. In each case the scenario is practically the same: when a new insecticide or a new antibiotic is introduced, a relatively satisfactory level of control can be achieved with low concentrations or infrequent treatment, but as time goes by an increasing dosage or more frequent applications are required until the results are no longer effective, economical, or safe for human beings. The problems involved in human health and survival, as well as in management of crops and domesticated animals, are of great concern and of immense practical importance to us.

Directional selection has also been observed in the spread of industrial melanism in many species of moths, and particularly detailed studies have been made of the peppered moth (*Biston betularia*) in Great Britain. Before the middle of the nineteenth century the predominant form was a "light" variant and there were rare occurrences of the "dark" or melanistic form in these populations (Fig. 16.2). The appearance and spread of the darkly pigmented form has been recorded in regions where pollution and soot have darkened the vegetation. In these industrial regions the lightly pigmented form has become greatly reduced in frequency and may even have disappeared almost entirely. In other regions where there is little or no pollution, the light form still occurs with high frequency and the dark form is rare. The main selective factor promoting directional changes in genotypic frequencies is predation of the moths by birds, according to many observations and experiments. The light varieties are protectively colored when they rest on nonpolluted vegetation; they are conspicuous on darkened vegetation, where dark varieties are protectively colored.

In genetic tests it has been shown that resistance to insecticides in insects, resistance to certain antibiotics in bacteria, and the difference between dark and light forms of many moth species are due to either a single gene with a major effect or to a set of genes with individually minor effects. In the moths, the allele producing dark color is usually dominant to the allele for light pigmentation. Also, further genetic changes have involved a system of **gene modifiers** with relatively minor phenotypic effects, but these modifiers intensify the phenotypic effect of the main gene.

Figure 16.2 Example of industrial melanism in the moth *Biston betularia*. Directional selection has modified the moth populations in industrialized regions of Great Britain toward a higher frequency of the dark phase than of the originally prevailing light phase types. Camouflage against predators is effective for the light moths in unpolluted environments (left), but not in sooty environments (right). (From studies by H. B. Kettlewell.)

In the peppered moth, directional selection has led to an increase in the dominant homozygous genotype in industrialized regions, but to relatively few homozygous dominants in nonindustrialized parts of Great Britain. In meeting these environmental challenges the diverse gene pool has been altered so that fewer heterozygotes and fewer homozygotes of one of the two types are produced in polluted and nonpolluted regions. Each population type is better adapted to its immediate environment, but the chances remain high for losing one of the two alleles since adaptation has proceeded directionally toward establishing one of the two alternative homozygotes.

In contrast with these types of selection, there are strategies by which a relatively high level of genotypic diversity is maintained despite forces acting to eliminate or reduce the frequency of a disadvantageous allele. The main types of strategy under this heading are balancing, diversifying, and frequency-dependent natural selection. While normalizing and directional selections are conservative programs in adaptation, which tend to make and keep the species relatively constant, these other types of selection act to retain diversity and therefore to maintain a higher degree of genetic flexibility in the species. In all of these kinds of selection, the relative fitness of the individual is a determining feature of genetic changes in the gene pool.

The classical example of the action of **balancing natural selection** is that of sickle-cell hemoglobin (HbS), which occurs in fairly high frequency in some parts of the world despite the low fitness of homozygous recessive individuals (Fig. 16.3). It can be shown that the *HbS* allele is maintained at a high frequency because of the selective advantage enjoyed by heterozygotes, and not because of a high rate of mutation from the *HbA* to the *HbS* allele. In parts of the world where malarial infection caused by *Plasmodium falciparum* is endemic, *HbA/HbA* homozygotes often succumb to the infection whereas *HbA/HbS* heterozygotes are not adversely affected by the pathogen. Individuals with sickle-cell anemia, *HbS/HbS* recessives, are probably resistant to malarial infection, but a very high percentage of these people die of their anemia disorder before reaching adulthood and are therefore relatively unfit. Because heterozygotes are fitter and therefore more likely to reproduce, a high frequency of recessive genotypes is maintained in these populations despite their selective disadvantage.

If we assume that the selective disadvantage of genotype *HbA/HbA* is $s_1 = 0.2$ and that of *HbS/HbS* is $s_2 = 0.9$, then the equilibrium frequency of the *HbS* allele would be $\hat{q} = s_1/(s_1 + s_2) = 0.2/(0.2 + 0.9) = 0.18$. The equilibrium frequency of the *HbA* allele would then be 0.82. In every generation, although the percentage of infants born who will develop anemia and probably die in childhood is $(0.18)^2 \times 100 = 3.24\%$, the *average fitness* of the population will be greater than that of a population consisting only of *HbA/HbA* homozygotes, since the *HbA/HbS* heterozygotes have a fitness of 1.

In nonmalarial regions, normalizing natural selection will come into operation and there will be a reduction in frequency of the *HbS* allele, since *HbA/HbS* heterozygotes enjoy no advantage over *HbA/HbA* homozygotes. In the United States sickle-cell anemia occurs mostly in the black population, with a frequency of about 0.25% (1 in 400). It has been estimated that the initial frequency of *HbA/HbS* heterozygotes among blacks brought to the United States from Africa 300 years ago was about 22%. Over approxi-

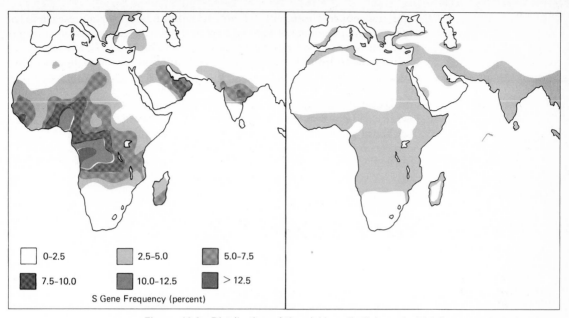

Figure 16.3 Distribution of the sickle-cell allele and of falciparum malaria in Africa and parts of Europe and Asia. (a) The sickle-cell allele is most common in central Africa, but it also occurs in considerable frequency in other areas; and (b) those areas where the falciparum malaria is prevalent coincide with the areas of occurrence of the sickle-cell allele. (From Cavalli-Sforza, L. L., and W. F. Bodmer, 1971. *The Genetics of Human Populations.* San Francisco: Freeman.)

mately 12 generations it has been calculated that the frequency of the sickle-cell allele would have declined to about 5% and that about 10% of the current black population would be heterozygotes. These are the values actually found. Since the three genotypes are found to occur in the expected Hardy-Weinberg proportions, we see that heterozygotes are no more fit than *HbA/HbA* homozygotes. We can predict a continued decline in the frequency of the *HbS* allele in subsequent generations, until the two alleles come to exist in an equilibrium proportion. The calculations are further complicated by the fact that an increasing percentage of people with sickle-cell anemia do live longer and contribute to the gene pool so that the precise equilibrium frequencies are uncertain.

Populations such as those just described for malarial regions are said to exist in a **balanced polymorphism**. In such a population several different phenotypes occur and the rarest of these phenotypes exists with a higher frequency than can be accounted for by mutation alone. Polymorphisms of various types have been described, involving morphological, physiological, biochemical, and chromosomal characteristics. We will discuss these shortly, since other issues arise in relation to polymorphisms which are not maintained by balancing natural selection.

Diversifying natural selection (also called **disruptive selection**) is a strategy which operates to diversify the gene pool so that two or more classes of genotypes have high adaptiveness in different subdivisions of a heterogeneous environment. In these situations selection operates in favor of the homozygous genotypes and against the heterozygotes, or intermediate types. Diversifying selection is believed to be a major force in the evolution of **mimicry** (also called "Batesian mimicry" in honor of the English naturalist H. W. Bates). In this type of mimicry an organism which is sought by predators comes to develop the pattern of a distasteful species and thereby gains some protection from predators that select their prey visually (Fig. 16.4). The predator learns to avoid the pattern of the distasteful species, and it will also avoid the mimic species if the two patterns are sufficiently alike. For mimicry to be successful, the distasteful

Figure 16.4 Batesian mimicry in African butterflies. Three distasteful species shown at the left are mimicked by strains of the species *Papilio dardanus* (center) and *Hypolimnas* (right). (From Wickler, W. 1968. *Mimicry in Plants and Animals.* New York: McGraw-Hill.)

species must far outnumber the edible species. Otherwise the predators will not be adequately conditioned to learn to avoid the mimics.

It has been postulated that one or a few major alleles have become predominant through diversifying selection, and that subsequent selection of modifier genes has contributed to the development of several different mimetic phenotypes in individual species. The hybrids formed experimentally between different groups are intermediate, and it is therefore believed that any hybrids in nature would be eliminated by predators. Elimination of less fit intermediates and selection of better adapted extreme phenotypes therefore produces a polymorphic situation in which different phenotypes are actively maintained by selection pressures in varied environments. The maintenance of diversity is an outcome of selection against heterozygotes, and leads to the preservation of several fitter genotypes belonging to homozygous classes.

Cases of Batesian mimicry also provide examples of the action of **frequency-dependent selection**, where a phenotype is selected against when it is more common and favored when it is rare. Selection is exerted on mimics or nonmimics depending on their relative frequencies in the population. In populations where unpalatable models are common and nonmimics are more common than mimics, the nonmimics will suffer heavier predation. However, where distasteful models are rare and mimics are more common than nonmimics, the mimics will suffer heavier predation than nonmimics.

In the above examples involving selection in natural populations, there has also been confirming evidence obtained using a variety of experimental situations, including samples captured in natural populations or samples of laboratory stocks simulating natural populations. In addition, there are numerous examples of selection practiced by plant and animal breeders which have produced improved strains of food crops, better breeds of domesticated animals, and numerous varieties of ornamental plants.

16.3   Molecular Polymorphisms

We have already discussed some polymorphisms which involve molecular differences due to the actions of different alleles of a single gene, such as those for normal and sickle-cell hemoglobins. While there are clinical symptoms by which the recessives can be recognized, homozygous HbA/HbA and heterozygous HbA/HbS individuals are generally indistinguishable phenotypically. By gel electrophoresis we can see the different patterns for the two kinds of globins, and we therefore know there is a molecular difference among all three genotypes; the situation is one involving a molecular polymorphism (Fig. 16.5). Using gel electrophoresis to obtain preliminary information on charge differences leading to differences in migration of proteins in gels, an astonishing number of allelic variants has been found for hemoglobins and for other gene products.

In the case of human hemoglobins, for example, more than 100 different allelic variants have been identified by gel electrophoresis and subsequent amino acid composition and sequence analysis of the β-globin chain alone.

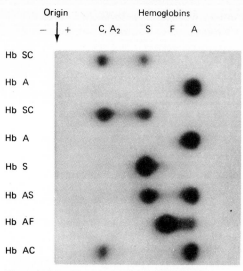

Figure 16.5 Electrophoretic mobilities of hemoglobins (from left to right) from individuals (vertical list) homozygous for Hb A, homozygous for Hb S, and heterozygous for S and C, A and S, and A and C. The sample designated Hb AF is from umbilical cord blood, showing a high percentage of fetal hemoglobin. Hb A_2 is a normal adult hemoglobin present in small amounts (about 2%) in most persons, and it is indistinguishable from Hb C under electrophoretic conditions used. All the hemoglobins consist of four globin chains in tetramer molecules: Hb A = $\alpha_2\beta_2$, Hb A_2 = $\alpha_2\delta_2$, Hb F = $\alpha_2\gamma_2$. The modification in Hb S and Hb C is at amino acid 6 in the β chains of Hb A.

In many of these cases it is clear that the allelic variation is very rare, but some variations are relatively common in particular populations. Most of these molecular variations produce no clinical symptoms at all, but some produce a mild to moderate anemia. Interestingly, the regions where some of these β-chain variants exist in high frequency are also regions where the falciparum malaria is endemic (Fig. 16.6). In addition to β-globin polymorphisms, there are polymorphisms involving the α-chain gene as well as blood group antigenic determinant genes, such as those coding for the MN, Rh, and other factors.

There are a large number of enzyme polymorphisms known for many species, including the 80 allelic variants for the human gene coding for glucose 6-phosphate dehydrogenase. In many cases there are differences in certain properties of these **isozymes**, or molecular variants of an enzyme, all variants having the same function. From such enzyme studies it has become apparent that molecular polymorphisms are common. They had gone undetected for the most part because there was little or no phenotypic difference between individuals carrying these alleles. Furthermore, since each organism carries only two alleles for a particular gene locus analysis of large samplings of populations is required in order to obtain molecular data for each series of multiple alleles. Taken altogether, molecular polymorphisms provide undeniable evidence showing that there are surpris-

Figure 16.6 Distribution of falciparum malaria and of human hemoglobin variants with modified β chains (Hb C, Hb D, Hb E, Hb S) or α chain (Hb O-Indonesia). (From Salthe, S. N. *Evolutionary Biology*. Copyright © 1972 by Holt, Rinehart, and Winston, New York.)

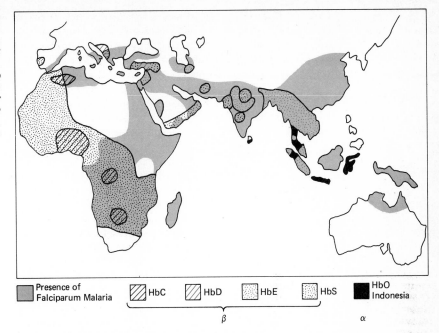

| � Presence of Falciparum Malaria | ▨ HbC | ▨ HbD | ▦ HbE | ▦ HbS | ■ HbO Indonesia |

β   α

ingly high levels of genotypic diversity in sexually reproducing species.

How is this diversity maintained in populations? By definition, the frequencies of these polymorphic genotypes are higher than can be accounted for by mutation alone. In some cases it is clear that selection operates to maintain polymorphisms, as we saw in the case of *HbA* and *HbS*. In other cases it seems unlikely that diversity is maintained by selection, and it has been suggested that some polymorphisms occur because of random genetic drift. In those cases where drift has been proposed as the mechanism, particular allelic variants are apparently **neutral mutations**, that is, mutations conferring neither advantage nor disadvantage. Mutation rate and random genetic drift, rather than selection, are most likely to influence the relative frequencies of neutral mutant alleles. Despite the abundance of experimental studies, the subject remains controversial and there is no consensus of opinion about the overall significance of random genetic drift in maintaining diversity in the gene pool. There is some question about the existence of neutral alleles, although there does seem to be evidence in support of this phenomenon. The occurrence of neutral mutations and their preservation by chance rather than by selection has been referred to as **non-Darwinian evolution**.

EVOLUTION OF GENETIC SYSTEMS

The genetic system includes all of the genetic mechanisms and controls operative in a species, such as mutation, recombination, regulation, and other components directly related to the genetic material. The genetic system itself is subject to hereditary modification, as much as the individual genes contained in the genome. We can predict that some adaptations are related directly to the genetic system itself as an outcome of mutation and selection, just as we find adaptations for the multitude of phenotypic traits in a species.

The major function of the genetic system is related to factors that provide a compromise between **fitness**, or **adaptedness** (which requires genetic constancy), and **flexibility**, or **adaptability** (which requires genetic variability). Adaptedness can be measured, as we have seen, but adaptability is difficult or even impossible to measure. Adaptedness is measured as the relative fitness of the population in relation to environment. Adaptability refers to the ability to adapt to a range of environments. Species that are highly adapted are more likely to be successful in the environment for which they are fitter at some moment in time, but we have seen that the price of adaptedness usually is a reduction in genetic diversity. With reduced diversity, and therefore higher genetic constancy, such populations may not be equally successful in meeting the challenges of new or changing environments. Adaptable species, on the other hand, are more genetically diverse. While they may not be as closely adapted to a lifestyle in the short run, they possess the genetic potential for a variety of changes in the long run and in this way they are more likely to succeed in new selection situations.

Different kinds of genetic systems manage to balance the short-term advantage of genetic constancy and the long-term advantage of genetic flexibility. We will look at some of these systems and the ways in which a balance has been achieved.

16.4   The Flow of Variability

We have seen that a considerable amount of genetic diversity can characterize the gene pool of a sexual species. We must also consider, however, how this allelic diversity is doled out when new genotypes arise in each generation. In particular, we want to know *how much* genotypic diversity is generated, and *how evenly* it is generated in successive generations; that is, we want to know how variability flows from the gene pool to actual genotypes produced in individuals making up the population. In sexual species we must therefore examine features related to meiosis, when alleles segregate into gametes, and recombination and reassortment take place.

One of the factors which influences the amount of genotypic diversity which can be generated in a species is the *number of chromosomes in the genome*. Genes which are on different chromosomes assort independently, but linked genes remain associated unless crossing over takes place between them. The higher the chromosome number, therefore, the more kinds of gametes there will be, since alleles of different unlinked genes segregate at random during meiosis. If each pair of chromosomes in the diploid nucleus contained just one pair of heterozygous alleles, then 2^n different kinds of gametes would be produced, where n is the number of different chromosomes. For 5 chromosome pairs there would be $2^5 = 32$ kinds of gametes; for 6 pairs it would be $2^6 = 64$; for 7 pairs it would be $2^7 = 128$ and so on. For each chromosome added to the genome, the number of different kinds of gametes is doubled, based on only one heterozygous locus per chromosome pair. It also follows that reduction by just one chromosome pair will reduce gamete variety by one-half. When a species with 7 chromosome pairs becomes tetraploid and then has 14 chromosome pairs, the number of kinds of gametes increases theoretically from $2^7 = 128$ to $2^{14} = 16,384$ kinds of gametes, when only one locus is heterozygous per chromosome pair. Increases in chromosome number by polyploidy are very common in the flowering plants, with about 50% of these species estimated to be polyploid today.

Reduction in chromosome number during evolution has been characteristic of a great many animal species-groups, such as *Drosophila* (see Fig. 11.25), and a substantial number of plants as well (Fig. 16.7). In these cases there has been little or no loss of genetic material, since centric fusions have been responsible for numerical reduction. Genes formerly assorting independently are segregated into different gametes only after crossing over, and fewer gametes will therefore contain recombinant genotypes in species with fewer chromosomes in the genome. With fewer new combinations of alleles in the gametes, fewer kinds of genotypes will be generated in each generation, despite the equivalence of diversity in the gene pool of a species with 3, 4, 5, or 6 linkage groups, as in *Drosophila* or *Crepis*.

In addition to genotypic diversity arising from gametes containing alleles that assort independently, the amount of crossing over between linked genes must also influence the actual diversity of genotypes which appear in successive generations. The relative amount of crossing over can be estimated by breeding analysis where marker genes are available and where breeding is possible under controlled conditions. In addition, direct cytological observations of meiotic chromosomes can provide information about crossing over frequencies. Each chiasma seen in meiotic bivalents is

Figure 16.7 Diagrams of the karyotype of 8 species of *Crepis*, a genus in the sunflower family (Compositae), showing reductions in chromosome number which have occurred during the evolution of this group. The centromere region is shown by a circle. (From Babcock, E. B. 1947. *The Genus Crepis*. Berkeley: University of California Press.)

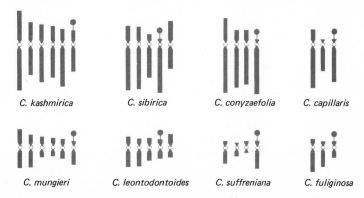

believed to represent a site of a previous crossover event. By counting the number of chiasmata per bivalent, it has been found that crossing over frequencies vary considerably among different species. Taken together with chromosome number, one can estimate the **recombination index** for a population or a species. The recombination index is derived from

$$\frac{\text{chiasma (crossover) frequency}}{\text{chromosome pairs}}$$

In a species with 5 pairs of chromosomes and an average of 10 chiasmata per meiotic nucleus, the recombination index is 2; with only 5 chiasmata for 5 pairs of chromosomes the recombination index is 1. For the same genome size, therefore, more gamete variety and more genotypic variety will be produced when there is a higher crossover frequency, or recombination index.

There are genes which are known to act to reduce crossing over in various species, and in any species we know that the occurrence of chromosome inversions can dampen recombination. Inversion heterozygotes produce fewer kinds of gametes since many of the crossover gametes are inviable (see Section 11.5). Because of their huge salivary chromosomes, *Drosophila* species are admirable systems for analysis of chromosome inversion frequencies in natural populations. Different band patterns provide unequivocal evidence for inversions, and populations may be sampled repeatedly to see if inversion chromosomes are retained intact or if they become altered by crossing over. In *D. pseudoobscura*, for example, there are four different inversion types all of which characterize chromosome 3 in the genome. In various populations there are inversion heterozygotes and inversion homozygotes present, and these same inversion chromosomes are retained year after year in the populations. The proportions of each inversion chromosome type vary from one population to another, in accordance with different adaptive values (Fig. 16.8). But for us the main point is that blocks of genes in chromosome 3 remain intact; such blocks of genes are called **supergenes**. Even though there is a high level of allelic heterozygosity for chromosome 3, genetic constancy is maintained by inversions which preserve supergenes through their effect in reducing crossover gametes. Even without banding patterns to identify inversions, it is possible to look for inversion loops in meiotic divisions (see Fig. 11.10). Following this line of analysis, we can be sure that chromosomal inversions exist in natural populations and that they influence the amount of diversity which is released in each generation. We don't know, however, how significant inversions are in general, since only a few species have been studied in relation to inversion heterozygosity. Inversions which are homozygous, of course, do not affect crossing over and recombination.

In addition to chromosome number and crossing over frequency which influence diversity at the level of meiosis, various factors act at the stage of zygote formation during fertilization. Among these are the mode of dispersal of gametes or spores, the preferences or barriers of mating between individuals, habitat differences, and other features of the lifestyle of the species. We will examine some of these features next.

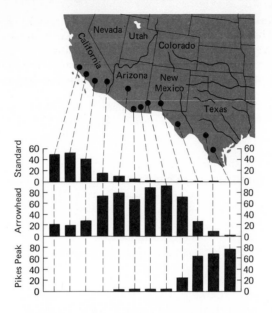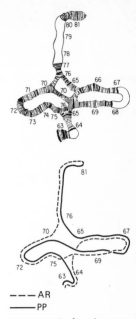

Figure 16.8 Relative frequencies of three different gene arrangements for chromosome 3 in *Drosophila pseudoobscura* in the southwestern United States. There are inverted blocks of genes in the Arrowhead (AR) and Pikes Peak (PP) chromosome types relative to each other and to the Standard pattern. The three chromosome types can be identified according to band patterns, and inversion heterozygotes in these populations can be identified by inversion loops and bands of the paired chromosomes. Pairing in a nucleus heterozygous for AR and PP types of chromosome 3 is shown at the upper right, and an interpretive drawing of the two chromosomes is just below it. The numbers refer to bands on chromosome 3. (After studies by Dobzhansky)

16.5   Variations in Reproductive Systems

Self-fertilizing species usually are highly homozygous, regardless of the degree of crossing over or of independent assortment which may take place. Inbreeding leading to homozygosity is therefore a mating system which minimizes genetic variability and enhances genetic constancy in populations. Similarly, asexual reproduction also preserves genetic constancy from generation to generation, regardless of diversity levels in the gene pool. In contrast with these extremes by which genetic constancy can be maintained, heterozygosity promoted by outbreeding serves to increase genotypic diversity in general. Heterozygosity and outbreeding or cross-fertilization would theoretically be adaptive characteristics, since diversity increases in amount and is incorporated into many new genotypes in each generation. Yet some species or groups of species have dispensed with such potential for variability and still remained successful. In most cases, however, there is some compromise between genetic constancy and genetic variability. In other words, the lifestyles of many species reveal patterns of reproduction and other features through which they attain some degree of adaptedness (constancy) and some degree of adaptability (flexibility) at the same time. Certain situations illustrate the overall consequences of compromises in genetic systems, and only a few examples will be described to emphasize the major features involved.

There are many flowering plant species which have evolved from cross-fertilizing ancestors to become self-fertilizing or even asexually reproducing by some kind of apomictic mechanism. **Apomixis** refers to an asexual substitute for sexual reproduction. One apomictic mechanism, for example, involves the production of embryos from vegetative diploid cells instead of from fusion between eggs and sperm. Apomictic plants, such as the common dandelion, produce seeds but the embryo has the same genotype as the parent plant, since the embryo develops from a maternal diploid cell. What is the advantage of asexual reproduction in a species like dandelion? If we examine this species, we find that it usually inhabits temporary spaces which undergo rapid changes, such as lawns, open fields and roadsides, or areas disturbed by human activities of other sorts. Dandelion populations fluctuate rapidly in size, and in location, as well as in time. Any dandelion seeds arriving at a suitable locale germinate quickly, produce an abundance of seeds apomictically, and can very quickly produce a large adult plant population. Genotypic constancy is highly adaptive for such a species, since one or a few suitable genotypes can multiply quickly and produce many individuals with the same suitable genotype. One or a few adapted immigrants can therefore produce a large descendant population in one or two generations in some new locality, all of which are equally well adapted to the particular environment at a particular time.

Numerous protist and invertebrate species are successful colonizers, just like the common dandelion. They produce huge numbers of progeny, often by some asexual mechanism, live for a relatively brief time, inhabit transient environments, and experience considerable fluctuations in population size at frequent intervals. In all of these cases there is a premium for adaptedness and for rapid spread of similar or identical adapted genotypes. High levels of diversity would be relatively less adaptive for such a lifestyle, since only a few genotypes out of many would usually prove to be best adapted, and any delay in establishing the population could be disastrous in the brief times available for colonizing a new, transient location.

New genotypes do arise in these species either by mutation or by an occasional episode of sexual reproduction. In the ciliated protozoan *Paramecium*, for example, reproduction usually occurs by asexual fissions. On occasion, usually when the habitat or food supply decline or become limiting, sexual reproduction is stimulated. There are many genotypes produced, and as the sexual progeny disperses there will be some genotypes that will be suitable in one location or another. The species spreads to new locations, and its spectrum of suitable locations may become expanded as genotypic diversity is produced in occasional episodes of sexual reproduction. Genetic constancy is maintained by asexual reproduction most of the time, but genetic flexibility is possible because of periodic bursts of sexual activity. These same properties also characterize many of the fungi and certain insects, which we know are capable of achieving large populations very quickly when new and suitable locations appear, and of disappearing rapidly as these habitats change suddenly.

In colonizing species there is relatively little diversity of genotypes within any one population, but there may be substantial levels of diversity among different populations. Occasional interbreeding between members of different populations would also lead to greater genotypic diversity and to overall diversity in the entire gene pool of the species.

Species with a large component of genetic flexibility and a relatively smaller component of genetic constancy would be ones with different features from the ones we have described. Adaptability in changing environments would be most likely in highly heterozygous species which release genetic diversity steadily, and at a rather slow rate. In this way there would be a continued production of new genotypes, and the chances would be rather good that some one or more of these genotypes would prove to be suitable in a new or altered environment or life situation. A higher level of adaptedness or relative fitness would not be as advantageous in a diversified environment, or in an environment with limited living space, or in one in which some particular genotype out of many would prove to be better under some specified set of conditions.

Adaptability, or genetic diversity, would be predicted to occur in species which are highly heterozygous and outbreeding, relatively long-lived, existing in relatively stable habitats, and producing a relatively large number of gametes. We would predict that such species would have a high recombination index, and probably would have higher chromosome numbers than related species which had opted for adaptedness in evolution. Such populations might produce many descendants, but only a few would survive to perpetuate the species. Good examples of such an adaptable genetic system can be found in various forest tree species, such as the oaks.

Oak populations undergo relatively little fluctuation in size, and once established the trees continue to live for a long time in the same place. Progeny as fit or fitter than the successful parents would be rare, but numerous progeny with numerous genotypes would have a higher probability of containing some one or a few acorns that would develop into seedlings that could become established in the limited amount of space available in the forest. Oak species have relatively high chromosome numbers as well as high recombination index values, and they are almost exclusively cross-fertilizing.

Annual desert-dwelling plants provide many examples of compromise between fitness and flexibility components in the genetic system. Most of these species are highly heterozygous and cross-fertilizing, qualities which underwrite the potential for genetic diversity. But these plants live in hostile terrain, and we would expect them to have some element of genetic constancy, since they must be highly adapted to their environments and since their populations fluctuate in size a great deal. In many cases it has been found that such desert species of annual plants (they live for only one year) have fewer chromosomes and lower chiasma frequencies than related species living in friendlier environments. The lower chromosome numbers of the desert annuals lead to less diversity produced by independent assortment, and the lower chiasma frequencies mean that favorable combinations of linked genes tend to be preserved as supergenes more often than not. By means of a low recombination index, therefore, such plants may maintain a highly heterozygous gene pool, but only a small portion of this diversity is actually generated in new genotypic combinations during reproduc-

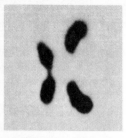

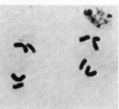

Figure 16.9 Meiosis in *Haplopappus gracilis*; *n* = 2. The two pairs of chromosomes are beginning to disjoin in very early anaphase I (above), and each of the four meiotic products (below) clearly has 2 chromosomes in its nucleus. This is the lowest known chromosome number for eukaryotic species. (From Jackson, R. C. 1959. *Amer. J. Bot.* **46**:550.)

tion. Furthermore, at times of little or no rainfall there is little or no reproduction, and genetic constancy prevails in these populations. When rain does come, there is a burst of reproductive activity and new genotypes are produced along with a high proportion of genotypes that closely resemble the parents.

In species of *Haplopappus*, a member of the sunflower family (Compositae), there may be 2, 4, or 8 pairs of chromosomes (Fig. 16.9). *Haplopappus gracilis* has only 2 pairs of chromosomes, and at least one of these has arisen by centric fusion between smaller chromosomes of an ancestral species. *Haplopappus* species with higher chromosome numbers have considerably smaller chromosomes than *H. gracilis*. Although all of these species are heterozygous and cross-fertilizing, *H. gracilis* exhibits less genotypic diversity, presumably because of its lower recombination index and related features. By reducing genetic flexibility and enhancing genetic constancy, *H. gracilis* has survived as a more highly adapted species in its desert environment. Should the environment change, this species may not be able to survive if it has evolved closer to adaptedness than to adaptability. In the short run, however, its adaptedness has been one basis for its success in the desert.

From many studies, at least for flowering plants, we can predict that there will be a relationship among the characteristics of the phenotype and the genetic system which is in operation. Specifically, we would predict that trees and other long-lived perennials would probably exist in stable habitats, be sexually reproducing and cross-fertilizing, and have higher chromosome numbers and higher crossover frequencies. These features permit maximum recombination potential and, therefore, the highest amounts of diversity and the steadiest rates of release of this diversity in each generation. Species which occupy temporary habitats and have shorter life spans would predictably have at least one of the following mechanisms by which diversity is limited in amount and in rate of flow: there would be (1) apomixis, or asexual reproduction; (2) self-fertilization; or (3) a low recombination index due to lower chromosome number and fewer chiasmata per genome at meiosis. All of these features lead to reduced amounts of diversity in the gene pool and to an erratic flow of variability into each new generation. Through any number of different compromises between fitness and flexibility, a broad range of genetic systems becomes possible, and species may evolve toward any point between the extremes of high adaptedness and high adaptability. Since adaptability involves greater genetic diversity, it is more likely to characterize populations with a higher probability for long-term evolutionary success in meeting the challenges of the ever-changing world.

16.6   Sex as an Adaptive Complex

The origins of sexual reproduction are unknown, but we believe that the earliest organisms were asexual and that sexual species first appeared a little over one billion years ago. The enormous advantages of sexual reproduction center around its property of producing new genotypes by recombination in every generation. Through sexual reproduction, high levels of genotypic diversity can be attained if genetically different parents mate and produce recombinant and parental types of progeny. The most reliable means for ensuring that parents will be genetically different is for species to produce different male and female individuals. This is the situation which characterizes all the vertebrate animals. Cross-fertilization is mandatory if the sexes are represented by different individuals.

Once separation of the sexes has been achieved during evolution, the continued production of unequivocally separate male and female individuals is secured through the development of a genetic sex determination mechanism. Determination of sex by sex chromosomes rather than by one or a few genes makes the system less prone to alterations through point mutations. And once there are sex chromosomes, there must be substantial or complete genetic differentiation between the X and Y chromosomes so that they become and remain nonhomologous. If they are nonhomologous, there will be little or no pairing between the X and Y chromosomes, and crossing over will not take place between them. The genetic constitutions of both the X and Y will remain intact and each chromosome will be transmitted as a complete X or a complete Y unit to every gamete which is produced. Blocks of sex-determining genes will be maintained as supergenes. If crossing over were possible between the X and Y chromosomes, some recombinant sex chromosome types would be produced and such X-Y recombinant chromosomes would direct development of sexual intermediates, leading to an eventual breakdown of the sex-chromosome determining mechanism.

In mammals, the Y chromosome is sex determining. There is little or no homology between the mammalian X and Y chromosomes, and no crossing over has been observed between them. In mammals, therefore, each individual with a Y chromosome is male and each individual without a Y chromosome is female. The separate sexes persist as two distinct types, and every generation is assured of being produced by parents from genetically different lineages. Heterozygosity is essentially assured, and diversity will continue to be produced and maintained in the gene pool of every vertebrate species. In this way, some degree of adaptability is guaranteed, and some degree of long-term evolutionary potential is built into the genetic system.

SPECIES FORMATION

A species is generally considered to be a group of organisms which can freely interbreed and produce healthy, fertile offspring in each generation. Members of different species cannot or do not interbreed, and gene exchange ordinarily takes place within a species but not between species. The origin and maintenance of separate species, therefore, depend on the origin and maintenance of separate gene pools. Intuitively, you would predict that speciation involved two major steps, one which prevents interbreeding between different populations of the same species so that there is no gene exchange and each gene pool diversifies independently of the others, and another step which prevents gene exchange even if populations of different species inhabit the same living space. As a further corollary, you would also expect recently diverged, closely related species to be more similar genetically and distantly related species to be more distinct genetically because of their longer times of separate evolutionary change. We will look at these situations briefly.

16.7   Isolation and Speciation

It is generally accepted that the initial event in speciation is the physical separation of subpopulations so that gene exchange cannot take place even though the potential exists. Once they are *spatially isolated*, subpopulations continue to diversify through mutation and selection, but their pathways of evolution would almost certainly not be identical. Mutations are random and we expect different mutations to arise by chance in different populations. Environments are varied, and we would expect different selection pressures to operate in different physical spaces, on different sets of mutations (Fig. 16.10).

As the separated populations become genetically differentiated during their evolution, they become *reproductively isolated*, that is, they become incapable of fruitful gene exchange. Even if the divergent populations were to come together in the future, interbreeding would be minimized and gene exchange would be abortive. The populations, now separate species, would maintain their separate gene pools and would continue to diversify into still more distantly related entities with time. In general, therefore, genetic divergence occurs in **allopatric** populations (ones separated spatially) and may continue when these populations become **sympatric** (occupying the same space), if divergence has led to some measure of reproductive isolation during the allopatric stage. Speciation continues to the stage of different and non-interbreeding populations if natural selection leads to complete reproductive isolation of the two groups.

Reproductive isolating mechanisms are often divided into two groups: **prezygotic** and **postzygotic**. Prezygotic isolating mechanisms include any ecological, physiological, or behavioral barriers that prevent or interfere with mating and gamete fusions. Mating usually does not occur at all in these cases. Postzygotic isolating mechanisms include those leading to sterility or inviability of F_1 hybrids between different groups, or to hybrid breakdown in which F_2 and backcross progeny are sterile or otherwise unfit. Once achieved, reproductive isolation is essentially irreversible and species will continue to diversify along separate evolutionary pathways. These pathways may ultimately lead to new categories of organisms, such as new genera, families, orders, and even higher taxonomic groups.

There are numerous examples of reproductive isolating mechanisms which come under the heading of prezygotic isolation. Different species of flowering plants, such as goldenrods, asters, and others, may bloom at different seasons or times during a season. Since eggs and pollen are not available at the same time for the different species, gamete fusions will not

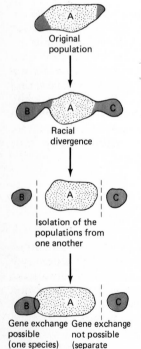

Original
population

Racial
divergence

Isolation of the
populations from
one another

Gene exchange   Gene exchange
possible   not possible
(one species)   (separate
                 species)

New species C does not
interbreed with species
A or with race B of
species A

Figure 16.10   Hypothetical population A undergoing racial divergence and speciation. If time in isolation is sufficiently long, gene exchange may no longer be possible between A and C, which implies they are separate species. When gene exchange is still possible, as between A and B, the two races constitute a single species.

take place. Similarly, animals that court and mate at different times, such as frog and toad species, would not engage in reproduction since potential partners from another species would not be sexually receptive at the same times. Species which inhabit different ecological zones in an area would be unlikely to meet and, therefore, would be unlikely to mate. Behavioral differences between species would also be very effective in keeping potential partners from different species apart, even if they were breeding at the same times in the same places.

Postzygotic isolation is not observed as often as prezygotic isolation in natural populations, but numerous examples have been documented. The classic example of a sterile F_1 hybrid is the mule, produced by mating between a horse and a jackass. Such matings are unlikely to take place in nature, but if they did there would be no further gene exchange between the two gene pools, since the F_1 hybrid is incapable of breeding either with others of its own kind or with either parent type.

In general, therefore, a variety of patterns of genetic differentiation characterize reproductive isolation. Genetic differences arise in allopatric populations and are usually maintained and strengthened even when the populations become sympatric. Some cases of sympatric speciation have been noted. One of the more obvious is the situation in which polyploids arise within a population and are unable to breed successfully with the parent types because any zygotes will have an unbalanced number of chromosomes. In tetraploid × diploid matings, the progeny will be triploid, and such individuals are sterile because of meiotic abnormalities arising from pairings and separations of three genomes during gamete formation. If the newly arisen tetraploid is self-fertilizing, seeds will be produced and the polyploids may establish their own gene pool and go on to develop into separate species isolated from the parental diploids by postzygotic isolating mechanisms. If two different diploid species produce a diploid hybrid which is sterile, and if the sterile hybrid becomes tetraploid by doubling of its chromosome number, the allotetraploid will be reproductively isolated from both diploid species because of triploid sterility, should any matings take place (see Section 11.7).

16.8   Molecular Phylogenies

Using a variety of molecular techniques, such as molecular hybridization, gel electrophoresis, amino acid sequencing, and immunological reactions, it has been possible to study phylogenetic relationships among groups of organisms belonging to different kingdoms, phyla, orders, families, and genera, as well as species. The extents of similarities and differences in nucleotide sequences and protein composition and sequences are remarkably close to the levels which are predicted on the basis of known times of evolutionary divergence and known genetic relationships among all these groups.

Using molecular hybridizations, it has been shown that DNAs isolated from representative vertebrate species show much greater similarities among animals within a particular group than among animals belonging to different taxonomic groups. DNAs from animals of the same taxonomic order or class are more similar than those of different orders or classes. In the same way, base compositions of ribosomal RNAs from organisms within a group are more similar to one another than to RNAs from different taxonomic groups. If the G + C/A + U ratios of rRNAs are plotted, it becomes even more obvious that related species are clustered together around similar ratio values and that these clusters are distinct from other groups of species belonging to different taxonomic categories. In Fig. 16.11 the six protist representatives are seen to be scattered along a gradient, indicating considerable divergence with respect to the GC/AU ratio. *Euglena* occupies the highest position among the six, and its GC/AU ratio is remarkably close to the sponge, representing the simple group of Porifera (number 7). This is in accord with the view that *Euglena* is evolutionarily close to lower multicellular animals. Looking at the central area of the GC/AU plot, divergence appears to have proceeded separately from the simpler molluscs (numbers 26 and 27) toward more highly evolved molluscs (numbers 28 to 30) on the one hand, and toward the echinoderms (numbers 31 and 32) and vertebrates (numbers 33 to 49) along another pathway. The known phylogenetic relationships among the taxonomic

Figure 16.11 Evolution of the G + C/A + U ratio of rRNA in animals and certain protists. Numbers 1–6 are the protists (*Euglena* = 6); 7–9, sponges and coelenterates; 10–12, nematodes and annelids; 13–25, arthropods; 26–30, molluscs; 31–32, echinoderms; 33–49, vertebrates (*Homo sapiens* = 49). The evolutionary pattern for rRNA base composition shown here reflects the known phylogenies of these groups. (From Lava-Sanchez, P. A., F. Amaldi, and A. La Posta. 1972. *J. Mol. Evol.* **2**:44, Fig. 2).

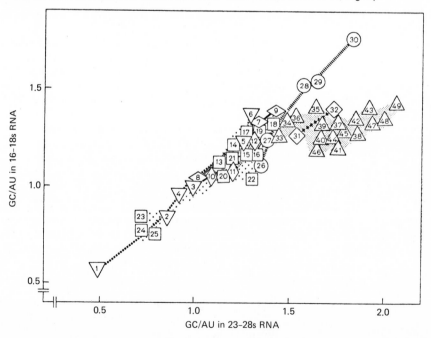

groups are reflected very well by the evolutionary pattern obtained for rRNA base composition. Similar relationships have also been found for bacterial, protist, fungal and land plant groups, in confirmation of established phylogenetic relationships.

Studies of amino acid sequences of homologous proteins from different groups of organisms have also conformed to established phylogenetic relationships previously established from comparative anatomical, physiological, and biochemical features of these groups, and from presumed times of divergence according to the fossil record. Cytochrome c is an example of a protein which has been subjected to molecular phylogenetic analysis.

Cytochrome c is a respiratory protein in aerobic prokaryotes and eukaryotes, and is presumed to have arisen about 1.2-1.4 billion years ago in some prokaryotic ancestor of eukaryotes. The protein is functionally homologous in all species tested, according to enzyme activity assays in which cytochrome c from all of these species interacts with cytochrome oxidase from any species. Since about half the amino acids of cytochrome c occupy the same positions in the molecule obtained from any of these species, the protein is presumed to be of common origin. During evolution, the remaining half of the 104 or more amino acids in the protein have undergone substitutions. These amino acid substitutions reflect changes in the gene specifying cytochrome c, changes which have arisen by mutations of the original gene during 1.2-1.4 billion years of evolution. An evolutionary tree can be constructed, based on the number of amino acid substitutions that distinguish related organisms, in accordance with branches of known phylogenetic relationships among groups of organisms (Fig. 16.12). Similar evolutionary trees have been constructed for a number of other proteins known to be homologous in origin and function in various groups of organisms.

The rate of protein change in evolution can be estimated from correlations between amino acid changes in particular proteins and the time of divergence of various organisms as seen in the fossil record. The rate of evolutionary change appears to be relatively constant for any given protein, but rates of change vary widely for different proteins (Fig. 16.13). The slowest rates of change are found in molecules that can least tolerate amino acid substitutions and still carry out vital functions. Histones bind to DNA at many sites along the protein, and modifications almost anywhere along the histone sequence would interfere with binding and therefore with DNA packaging in condensed chromosomes. Fibrinopeptides, on the other hand, are short polypeptide sequences within the fibrinogen molecule which are enzymatically excised from fibrinogen when it is converted to fibrin during blood clotting. There are far fewer functional constraints on fibrinopeptide molecules in carrying out their function, since only a small portion of the molecule is specifically required for enzymatic recognition. Amino acid substitutions in most of the fibrinopeptide molecule would have little or no effect on clotting reactions. Hemoglobin and cytochrome c show rates of change which are intermediate between fibrinopeptides and histones. These molecules have some tolerance for amino acid substitutions while retaining function, but there are portions of

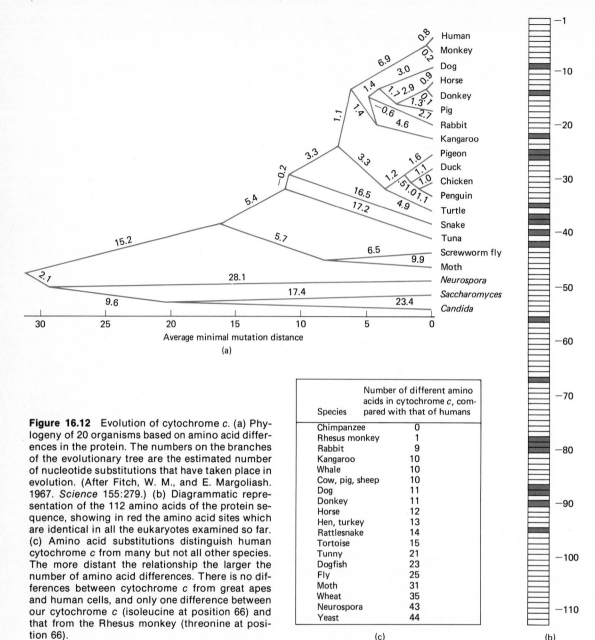

Figure 16.12 Evolution of cytochrome c. (a) Phylogeny of 20 organisms based on amino acid differences in the protein. The numbers on the branches of the evolutionary tree are the estimated number of nucleotide substitutions that have taken place in evolution. (After Fitch, W. M., and E. Margoliash. 1967. *Science* 155:279.) (b) Diagrammatic representation of the 112 amino acids of the protein sequence, showing in red the amino acid sites which are identical in all the eukaryotes examined so far. (c) Amino acid substitutions distinguish human cytochrome c from many but not all other species. The more distant the relationship the larger the number of amino acid differences. There is no differences between cytochrome c from great apes and human cells, and only one difference between our cytochrome c (isoleucine at position 66) and that from the Rhesus monkey (threonine at position 66).

Species	Number of different amino acids in cytochrome c, compared with that of humans
Chimpanzee	0
Rhesus monkey	1
Rabbit	9
Kangaroo	10
Whale	10
Cow, pig, sheep	10
Dog	11
Donkey	11
Horse	12
Hen, turkey	13
Rattlesnake	14
Tortoise	15
Tunny	21
Dogfish	23
Fly	25
Moth	31
Wheat	35
Neurospora	43
Yeast	44

(c)

each kind of molecule which cannot be modified by mutation without altering function. Substitutions in these critical regions of the protein would prove to be disadvantageous and would be selected against.

Since amino acid substitutions have taken place in parts of proteins which are not involved in active sites, or binding prosthetic groups, or

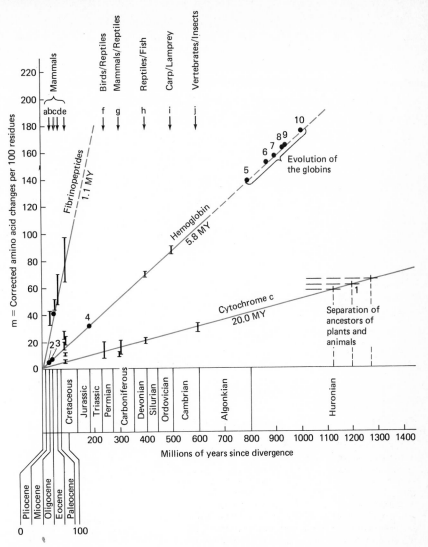

Figure 16.13 Rates of evolution in the fibrinopeptides, hemoglobins, and cytochrome c proteins. The rate of change for histones (not shown) would essentially be plotted as an almost horizontal line across the bottom of the graph. Faster rates of change characterize the molecules most able to tolerate amino acid substitutions and still maintain vital functions. Point 1 represents a date of 1200 ± 75 MY (million years) for the separation of plants and animals, based on cytochrome c data; points 2–10 refer to events in hemoglobin-gene evolution. The time in millions of years for a 1% change in amino acid sequence to show up between evolutionary lineages is shown just beneath each curve. (From Dickerson, R. E. 1971. *J. Mol. Evol.* **1**:26.)

influencing three-dimensional shape of the molecule, some would consider the observed substitutions to be the result of neutral mutations. This may explain the relatively slow but constant rate of evolutionary change which they demonstrate. It is very unlikely that these rates of change underwrite those changes in morphology, metabolism, and genetic system which have occurred during biological evolution. Structural gene mutations, such as those evident in the proteins which have been analyzed, occur too slowly to underwrite significant evolutionary pathways. Furthermore, they tend to be relatively conservative in preserving some original function. In view of such arguments, it has been proposed that mutations in regulatory genes rather than mutations in structural genes may be primarily responsible for significant changes during evolution. In contrast with this proposal is another hypothesis which has been revived recently by Stephen Gould. He has proposed that relatively few mutations of a major consequence (macromutations) have been responsible for new directions in evolution, and that the usual small-step mutations we are familiar with (micro-mutations) have enhanced and stabilized the major genetic changes sponsored by macromutations.

At this time there is insufficient evidence to judge any of the ideas which have been proposed. It does seem certain, however, that the astonishing events of biological evolution which have taken place in the past 600 million years, in contrast with the slow pace of evolution for the previous 4000 million years, cannot be explained by the oversimplified view of a few amino acid substitutions in a few proteins. Molecular phylogenies provide useful adjunct information to data obtained from the fossil record and from comparative studies of living species. By themselves, however, molecular phylogenies have provided no significant insights into understanding the observed pace of evolution nor of the biological inventions which have led to new phyla or classes or orders of organisms. These unsolved problems remain among the most exciting challenges of modern biology, and their solution may lead to new heights of intellectual and conceptual under-standing of the diversity of life, of which we form a small but significant part.

QUESTIONS AND PROBLEMS

16.1. In parts of the world where falciparum malaria is endemic there is a selective advantage of Hb^A/Hb^S over the individuals with either homozygous genotype for these hemoglobin alleles.
   a. If the selective disadvantage of genotype Hb^A/Hb^A is 0.1 and that of Hb^S/Hb^S is 0.7, what will be the equilibrium frequency of the Hb^S allele? of the Hb^A allele?
   b. What is the expected percentage of Hb^S/Hb^S infants born each year in the equilibrium population where $s_1 = 0.1$ and $s_2 = 0.7$?

16.2. Describe the changes occurring in the gene pool of a population undergoing normalizing, directional, and disruptive natural se-lection at different times in its history. What changes will occur in genotype frequencies under each of these three programs of selec-tion?

16.3. When comparing the genetic systems in *Drosophila colorata* ($n = 6$) and *D. willistoni* ($n = 3$), what might you predict to be the situation for each of the following characteristics? (Use *higher* and *lower*, comparatively)

	D. colorata	D. willistoni
Recombination index		
Frequency of inversions		
Frequency of supergenes		
Habitat stability		

Which species is probably more highly adapted (genetically constant)?

16.4. What is the evolutionary advantage of genetically differentiated X and Y sex chromosomes in species with chromosomal sex determination?

16.5. In a population of butterflies individuals with brown and yellow spots are inconspicuous in their surroundings and have a relative fitness of 1. On the other hand, insects with solid yellow wings have a relative fitness of only 0.6 since they are more likely to experience predation. The solid yellow phenotype is due to a dominant allele Y, while the spotted phenotype is due to the recessive allele y in homozygotes (yy). If the initial frequency of allele y is 0.8, what are the frequencies of alleles Y and y after one generation of selection (predation)? After ten generations?

16.6. Cross-fertilizing plants isolated from a natural population produced an average of 32 leaves per plant. By only breeding plants with high leaf numbers for fifteen generations, the mean had been raised to 58 leaves per plant. Selection was stopped for several generations and the mean leaf number was reduced to about 42, which remained the mean for the next sixteen generations during which time selection still was not practiced.

a. Suggest an explanation for these observations.

b. Why didn't the mean number drop to the original value of 32?

16.7. In comparing cytochrome c from various species, it is possible to calculate a minimum number of single nucleotide pair changes necessary to get from one cytochrome c molecule to another by mutations. The number of nucleotide changes for a group of organisms might be as follows:

	Species A	B	C	D	E
Species A	0	20	20	20	20
B		0	10	10	10
C			0	8	8
D				0	2
E					0

a. Draw an "evolutionary tree" for these species, so that each line represents mutational distance.

b. Which species is probably most ancient in this group? Why?

16.8. During the 1930s an English scientist released a large number of *Drosophila* heterozygous for the recessive allele for ebony body color (+/e) near a locality normally without these flies. After 8 generations the frequency of allele e was only 0.11. How would you explain this change from 0.5 to 0.11?

16.9. Upon landing on an island which had not been explored previously you find three populations of frogs which can be distinguished by spotting pattern.
   a. How would you determine whether they are members of 1, 2, or 3 species?
   b. Suppose you discover that all these populations represent a single species of frog. How would you explain the absence of any frog hybrids on the island?

16.10. The number of amino acid differences between the four kinds of human globins are as follows:

	α	β	δ	γ
*(141) α	0	84	85	89
(146) β		0	10	39
(146) δ			0	41
(146) γ				0

*Total amino acids in the chain shown in parentheses

   a. Construct an "evolutionary tree" for these globins.
   b. The gene for α-globin is located on chromosome 16 while the loci for β- and δ-globins are situated on chromosome 11 in the human genome. How would you explain this in view of the postulated origin of all these globins?

REFERENCES

Allison, A. C. Aug. 1956. Sickle cells and evolution. *Sci. Amer.* **195**: 87.

Ayala, F. J., ed. 1976. *Molecular Evolution*. Sunderland, Mass.: Sinauer.

Ayala, F. J. Sept. 1978. The mechanism of evolution. *Sci. Amer.* **239**: 56.

Bishop, J. A., and L. M. Cook. Jan. 1975. Moths, melanism, and clean air. *Sci. Amer.* **232**:90.

Bonen, L., and W. F. Doolittle. 1976. Partial sequences of 16S rRNA and the phylogeny of blue-green algae and chloroplasts. *Nature* **261**:669.

Brown, W. M., M. George, Jr., and A. C. Wilson. 1979. Rapid evolution of animal mitochondrial DNA. *Proc. Nat. Acad. Sci. U.S.* **76**:1967.

Bush, G. L., S. M. Case, A. C. Wilson, and J. L. Patton. 1977. Rapid speciation and chromosomal evolution in mammals. *Proc. Nat. Acad. Sci. U.S.* **74**:3942.

Clarke, B. Aug. 1975. The causes of biological diversity. *Sci. Amer.* **233**:50.

Crow, J. F. Feb. 1979. Genes that violate Mendel's rules. *Sci. Amer.* **240**:134.

Davidson, E. H., G. A. Galau, R. C. Angerer, and R. J. Britten. 1975. Comparative aspects of DNA organization in metazoa. *Chromosoma* **51**:253.

Dayhoff, M. O. July 1969. Computer analysis of protein evolution. *Sci. Amer.* **221**:86.

de Grouchy, J., C. Turleau, and C. Finaz. 1978. Chromosomal phylogeny of the Primates. *Ann. Rev. Genet.* **12**:289.

Dickerson, R. E. Apr. 1972. The structure and history of an ancient protein. *Sci. Amer.* **226**:58.

Faye, G., F. Sor, A. Glatigny, F. Lederer, and E. Lesquoy. 1979. Comparison of amino acid compositions of mitochondrial and cytoplasmic ribosomal proteins of *Saccharomyces cerevisae*. *Mol. gen. Genet.* **171**:335.

Graham, J. B., and C. A. Istock. 1979. Gene exchange and natural selection cause *Bacillus subtilis* to evolve in soil culture. *Science* **204**:637.

Kimura, M., and T. Ohta. 1971. On the rate of molecular evolution. *J. Mol. Evol.* **1**:1.

Lava-Sanchez, P. A., F. Amaldi, and A. La Posta. 1972. Base composition of ribosomal RNA and evolution. *J. Mol. Evol.* **2**:44.

Levin, D. A. 1979. The nature of plant species. *Science* **204**:381.

Lewontin, R. C. Sept. 1978. Adaptation. *Sci. Amer.* **239**:212.

Lucchesi, J. C. 1978. Gene dosage compensation and the evolution of sex chromosomes. *Science* **202**:711.

Maynard Smith, J. 1977. Why the genome does not congeal. *Nature* **268**:693.

Maynard Smith, J. 1978. *Evolution of Sex*. Cambridge: Cambridge University Press.

Mayr, E. Sept. 1978. Evolution. *Sci. Amer.* **239**:46.

Miller, D. A. 1977. Evolution of primate chromosomes. *Science* **198**:1116.

Miozzari, G. F., and C. Yanofsky. 1979. Gene fusion during the evolution of the tryptophan operon in Enterobacteriaceae. *Nature* **277**:486.

Monroy, A., and F. Rosati. 1979. The evolution of the cell-cell recognition system. *Nature* **278**:165.

Riley, M., and A. Anilionis. 1978. Evolution of the bacterial genome. *Ann. Rev. Microbiol.* **32**:519.

Roth, E. F., M. Friedman, Y. Ueda, I. Tellez, W. Trager, and R. L. Nagel. 1978. Sickling rates of human AS red cells infected *in vitro* with *Plasmodium falciparum* malaria. *Science.* **202**:650.

Schwartz, R. M., and M. O. Dayhoff. 1978. Origins of prokaryotes, eukaryotes, mitochondria, and chloroplasts. *Science* **199**:395.

Thompson, J. N., Jr., and R. C. Woodruff. 1978. Mutator genes—pacemakers of evolution. *Nature* **274**:317.

White, M. J. D. 1978. *Modes of Speciation.* San Francisco: Freeman.

Zuckerhandl, E. May 1965. The evolution of hemoglobin. *Sci. Amer.* **212**:110.

ANSWERS TO QUESTIONS AND PROBLEMS

Chapter 1

1.1. a. red

      b. $RR \times RR$ or $RR \times Rr$, $Rr \times Rr$, $RR \times rr$, $rr \times rr$, $Rr \times rr$

          ↓   ↓   ↓   ↓   ↓

          all RR or   1 RR: all Rr all rr 1 Rr:1 rr

          1 RR:1 *Rr*   2 *Rr*:

                            1 *rr*

1.2. a. red

      b. 3 red:1 scarlet

      c. 1 red:1 scarlet

1.3. a. black, dominant; white, recessive

      b. $BB \times bb$

      c. *Bb*

      d. *Bb*

      e. 1 black:1 white

1.4. Cross to recessive (white): if it is heterozygous the progeny will segregate 1:1, and if it is homozygous the progeny will all be black.

1.5. a. 9 green, starchy:3 green, waxy:3 yellow, starchy:1 yellow, waxy

      b. 1 green, starchy (*GG Wxwx* and *Gg Wxwx*); 1 green, waxy (*GG wxwx* and *Gg wxwx*); 1:1:1:1 genotype ratio

      c. *GG Wxwx*; *GG Wx Wx*; *Gg Wxwx*; *Gg Wx Wx*

1.6. a. both pink, both *Rr*

      b. (1) 2 pink:1 red:1 white, (2) all red, (3) all pink, (4) 1 pink:1 white. Incompletely dominant pair of alleles.

1.7. a. *RRpp* and *Rrpp*

      b. *RrPp* × *Rrpp*, since the 3:3:1:1 ratio of phenotypes indicates 1 pair of alleles segregates 3:1 and the other pair 1:1.

1.8. a. $\chi_1^2 = 20.54$; $\chi_2^2 = 7.8$; $\chi_3^2 = 2.52$; $\chi_4^2 = 3.59$; $\chi_5^2 = 18.8$; nos. 2, 3, and 4 fit the 9:3:3:1 ratio

      b. nos. 1 and 5

1.9. a. all *Tt*, short tail

      b. 12

1.10. a. 2/3, since he may be *EE* or *Ee*

       b. 1/4, since the mating is *Ee* × *Ee*

1.11.

Parents		Babies	
Phenotypes	**Genotypes**	**Phenotypes**	**Genotypes**
B × O	$I^B I^B \times i^O i^O$, or $I^B i^O \times i^O i^O$	B, O	$I^B i^O$, $i^O i^O$
A × B	$I^A I^A$ or $i^A i^O \times$ $I^B I^B$ or $I^B i^O$	A, B, AB, or O	$I^A i^O$, $I^B i^O$, $I^A I^B$, $i^O i^O$
AB × O	$I^A I^B \times i^O i^O$	A, B	$I^A i^O$, $I^B i^O$

Impossible to tell which parents produced the twins. But if parents of the twins are known, the other two babies can be assigned unambiguously.

1.12. a. Two pairs of alleles, A_1/a_1 and A_2/a_2, with the dominants having equal (5 cm) and additive effects on the phenotypes

b. Cross $A_1a_1A_2a_2 \times A_1a_1A_2a_2$ produced 1:4:6:4:1 phenotypic ratio in progeny:

Tail length class		No. dominant alleles	Genotypes present
1/16	2.5 cm	0	$a_1a_1a_2a_2$
4/16	7.5 cm	1	$A_1a_1a_2a_2$, $a_1a_1A_2a_2$
6/16	12.5 cm	2	$A_1A_1a_2a_2$, $A_1a_1A_2a_2$,
			$a_1a_1A_2A_2$
4/16	17.5 cm	3	$A_1A_1A_2a_2$, $A_1a_1A_2A_2$
1/16	22.5 cm	4	$A_1A_1A_2A_2$

c. $a_1a_1a_2a_2 \times A_1A_1A_2a_2$ or $A_1A_1A_2a_2$ would produce 50% 7.5 cm and 50% 12.5 cm offspring types.

1.13. The white-kernel strains were $AAbb$ and $aaBB$, producing $AaBb$ F_1 progeny. The 9:7 phenotypic F_2 ratio indicates this epistatic inheritance pattern depends on two genes. Dominants of both genes must be present for the red phenotype. χ^2 confirms the hypothesis.

1.14. One pair of alleles, since the ratio is 1 small:2 intermediate:1 large in the F_2. Each A allele adds an increment of size, so AA = large and Aa = intermediate. This can also be interpreted as incomplete dominance, since only one gene is involved.

Chapter 2

2.1. There would be membranous organelles in the cytoplasm, such as mitochondria, chloroplasts, endoplasmic reticulum, etc.

2.2. G_1, S, and G_2; macromolecular syntheses and intermediary metabolism.

2.3. Chromatids are parts of one chromosome, while chromosomes are independent structures; S phase, when DNA replicates; Prophase.

2.4. Identical nuclei arise by mitosis, genetically different nuclei may arise by meiosis (if genotype is heterozygous).

2.5. a. $(1/2)^{23}$
b. $1-2(1/2)^{23}$

2.6. a. 23
b. 46
c. 46
d. 23

2.7. a. 5 pg
b. 2.5 pg
c. 10 pg
d. 5 pg
e. 2.5 pg
f. 10 pg

2.8. Because the SC begins to form during zygonema and is completed when this stage ends. SC formation and synapsis are parallel events, not sequential.

2.9. Parallel behavior of pairs of alleles and homologous pairs of chromosomes.

2.10. The two mutants must have formed a heterokaryon, whose haploid nuclei from both strains were able to complement each other's deficiencies and produce wild type mycelium. Genetic tests would include isolating individual, haploid, uninucleate spores and seeing whether they produce the two parental kinds of phenotypes. Each strain had the wild type alleles missing in the other.

2.11.
a. *FFf*
b. *Ff*
c. *f*
d. *F*
e. *Fff*

2.12.
a. Types 1 & 2 are first-division segregations, types 3-6 are second-division segregations
b. See Figs. 2.21 and 2.22.

2.13. $(1 \times 10^{-7})^3 = 1 \times 10^{-21}$, since each mutation at each of the 3 loci is an independent event.

2.14. Haploid organisms have only one allele of each gene per nucleus, so dominance or recessiveness is irrelevant since the one allele is expressed in each case.

2.15. Labeled DNA was found inside the host cells while labeled protein was not. Genetic material must enter the host, otherwise it cannot direct synthesis of new viruses like the infecting particles. The basis of genetic material resides in its direction of continuity; like produces like.

Chapter 3

3.1.
a. $v/v\ c^+/c$
b. $v^+/\ c/c$
c. ♀♀ are $v^+/v\ c^+/c$ and $v^+/v\ c/c$, ♂♂ are $v/\ c^+/c$ and $v/\ c/c$. Gene v is X-linked, gene c is autosomal.

3.2. Parents are Cc ♀ × c ♂.
a. 1/2
b. 1/2
c. 1/2 × 1/2 = 1/4

3.3.
a. male
b. 24
c. XX ♀, XO ♂

3.4.
a. Ll ♀♀ × l ♂♂ → 1/3 Ll ♀♀ (dark green):1/3 L ♂♂ (dark green): 1/3 l ♂♂ (yellow-green). The ll ♀♀ are lethals and are not produced
b. Ll ♀♀ × L ♂♂ → 1/2 LL ♀♀ and Ll ♀♀ (dark green):1/4 L ♂♂ (dark green):1/4 l ♂♂ (yellow-green).

3.5.
a. 1 ♂:2 ♀
b. 1/3 $X^B X^b$ ♂♂:1/3 $X^B Y$ ♀♀:1/3 $X^b Y$ ♀♀ [males all are barred, 1/2

the females are barred and one-half are nonbarred; cross was X^bY "male" with X^BY female].

3.6. a. A different eye color gene is mutant in each strain, since the progeny are wild type ($a^+a^+bb \times aab^+b^+ \to a^+ab^+b$ progeny).

b. The mutant gene is X-linked in strain A and autosomal in strain B, and the scarlet allele is recessive to its wild type alternative at each locus.

c. F_1 a^+/a b^+/b ♀♀ × F_1 $a^+/$ b^+/b ♂♂ produce 3 wild type:1 scarlet F_2 ♀♀ and 3 wild type:5 scarlet ♂♂.

3.7. a. Each trait is X-linked; colorblind is fully recessive to normal, enzyme levels are determined by incompletely dominant alleles, and blood group XG presence is dominant over its absence.

b. I1 = c Gpd xg; I2 = C/C Gpd/gpd xg/xg; II1 = C Gpd Xg; II2 = C/c Gpd/gpd xg/xg; III1 = C gpd xg; III5 = C/C Gpd/Gpd Xg/xg or C/c Gpd/Gpd Xg/xg

3.8. a. The trait is an X-linked recessive, transmitted from carrier mother to about half her sons.

b.
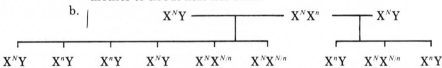

(The daughters could have received either X^N or X^n from their mother, but must have received X^N from their father, in either marriage.)

3.9. a. Autosomal dominant

b. X-linked recessive trait

c. none, none

d. I1 is D/d b/b, I2 is $D/$ B/b (He is free of the dental disease, and some of his children are not short-fingered, indicating he is heterozygous for this gene.)

3.10. a. 3/4

b. $(3/4 \times 1/2) + (1/4 \times 1/2) = 1/2$

3.11. a. Hm/hm ♀ and $Hm/$ ♂ (Every daughter receives his X chromosome carrying a normal, dominant allele.)

b. $1/2 \times 1/2 = 1/4$

c. $1/4 \times 1/4 = 1/16$

3.12. a. $a^5 = (1/2)^5 = 1/32$

b. $a^5 + b^5 = 1/32 + 1/32 = 1/16$

c. $5a^4b$ or $5ab^4$

d. $1/5$ of $5a^4b$ (since there are 5 sequences which will result in 1 boy and 4 girls) = 1/32

3.13. a. C^BC^O (calico) ♀ × $C^O/$ (orange) ♂

b. Calico or orange, if it received one of its X chromosomes from each parent, calico if it received both X chromosomes from its mother and only the Y from its father. It couldn't be black, since one of the two Xs must carry the C^O allele.

3.14. a. Egg must have been XX, carrying recessive alleles on each chromosome, and sperm carried a Y chromosome.

    b. his mother, having one Barr body in the nucleus

    c. 100%, since he must get his X from his mother and she is color-blind

Chapter 4

4.1. There is no crossing over in male *Drosophila*. One takes advantage of this unusual situation in determining linkage versus independent assortment of genes on different chromosomes. In the cross *al b/al b* ♀♀ × *al +/+ b* ♂♂, the progeny will consist of aristaless and black individuals if the genes are linked but there will be all four phenotypic classes (aristaless; black; wild type; aristaless, black) if the genes are on different chromosomes and, therefore, assort independently to produce four kinds of sperm (*al +, + b, + +,* and *al b*).

4.2. a. The two genes are 21 map units apart, so 21% of the eggs will be recombinant + + and *B m* (10.5% each)

    b. The ♀ progeny will be 50% Bar and 50% wild type, and ♂ progeny will consist of 39.5% miniature (+ *m*), 39.5% Bar (*B +*), 10.5% wild type (+ +), and 10.5% Bar, miniature (*B m*)

    c. two (X-carrying + +, and Y-carrying)

4.3. The genetic map is constructed from many experiments involving two-, three-, and four-factor crosses, among others, so that additivity can be estimated. Even if 100% of the meiocytes experienced a cross-over between two particular linked genes the maximum recombination would be 50% of the gametes, since only two chromatids of each bivalent engage in a crossing over event.

4.4. a. repulsion

    b. 8.6%

4.5. a. *wx—c—sh*

    b. *wx—c*, 28 m. u., *c—sh*, 18 m. u.

    c. 0.8

4.6. The genes assort independently and must therefore be on different chromosomes, and since there are no second-division segregations each gene must be very close to the centromere on its respective chromosome. (This information leads to the conclusion of the genes being in different linkage groups, since they could not be 50 or more map units apart on the same chromosome and at the same time each be near the single centromere.)

4.7. a. The two genes are linked since PD tetrads (147 + 24) far outnumber NPD tetrads (21 + 3); independently assorting genes would be found in crosses producing equal proportions of PD and NPD tetrads

    b. The order of the linkage map is *ad*—centromere—*tryp*, since only 39 tetrads (6 + 24 + 3 + 6) show second-division segregations for *ad/+* while 126 tetrads (93 + 24 + 3 + 6) show second-division segregations for *tryp/+*. The distance between *ad* and the centromere is 1/2 second-division tetrads/total tetrads × 100 = 6.5 map units, between centromere and *tryp* = 21 map units, and between *ad* and *tryp* the distance is $1/2$ T + NPD/total tetrads × 100 = 25.5 map units.

4.8.   a.   sequence is $v—lz—ct$

        b.   distance between v and lz is 6 map units, and between lz and ct, 7 map units; coefficient of coincidence is 0.25

        c.   the genes are in the X chromosome

4.9.   Progeny expected from $\dfrac{r\ g\ e}{+\ +\ +}\ ♀♀ \times \dfrac{r\ g\ e}{r\ g\ e}\ ♂♂$

Phenotypic classes	No. offspring
r g e	406.5
+ + +	406.5
r + +	50
+ g e	50
r g +	38.5
+ + e	38.5
r + e	5
+ g +	5
	1000

4.10.   Class 1 is PD for all genes taken two by two ($a\ b, a\ c, b\ c$); class 2 is PD for $a\ b$, but NPD for $b\ c$ and $a\ c$; class 3 is T for $a\ b$ and $a\ c$, and NPD for $b\ c$; class 4 is T for $a\ b$ and $a\ c$, and PD for $b\ c$. Using these observations, we can arrange the data as follows:

	Tetrad types		
Gene pair	**PD**	**NPD**	**T**
$a\ b$	164/200 = 0.82	0	36/200 = 0.18
$b\ c$	96/200 = 0.48	104/200 = 0.52	0
$a\ c$	80/200 = 0.40	84/200 = 0.42	36/200 = 0.18

For the $a\ b$ pair, PD and NPD are not equal and therefore genes a and b are linked. Gene c assorts independently of a and of b (PD = NPD) so it is on a different chromosome from the other two genes. The distance between genes a and b is

$1/2$ T + NPD/Total tetrads = $1/2(36)/200$ × 100 = 9 map units

4.11.

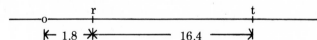

4.12.   a.   autosomal dominant

        b.   The trait seems to be linked to the ABO gene since the I^B characteristic appears together with it in all afflicted members of the three generations shown.

        c.   I1 (grandfather) is: $\dfrac{i\ n}{i\ n}$, and grandmother is: $\dfrac{I^B\ N}{i\ n}$

(Note: the recessive allele of the ABO gene is symbolized i or i^O.)

Chapter 5

5.1. *ad-14*—centromere—*pro-1*—*bio-1*

5.2. During haploidization, *pro$^+$/pro* segregates from *Acr* while *w* does not, and, therefore, *pro* is on a different chromosome. *Acr* and *w* must be linked in coupling, since the alleles segregate together more often than not in diploids, and are found together in haploid segregants. The most likely order is: centromere—*w*—*Acr*, since the majority class is recombinant for *w* (*w/w*) due to crossing over between centromere and *w* locus, while the minority class (96 *Acr/Acr* *w$^+$/w*) must arise from exchanges between these two gene loci.

5.3. a. *pro* +/*pro paba* and + +/+ *paba*, or *pro* +/+ *paba* and + +/*pro paba*, depending on sister chromatid orientations toward the poles at mitosis

  b. *pro* +/*pro* + and + *paba*/+ *paba*, or *pro* +/+ *paba* and *pro* +/+ *paba*, depending on orientation of sister chromatids

  c. *pro* +/+ *paba* and *pro paba*/+ +, or, *pro* +/+ + and *pro paba*/+ *paba*

5.4.

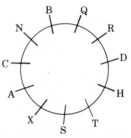

5.5. a. Perform a complementation test. Allow strains 1 and 2 to conjugate and plate on minimal medium to observe colonies. Strain 1 is proline-requiring and will die. Strain 2 is leucine-requiring and will die. Strain 2 cells that have received F^I from strain 1 during conjugation will be merodiploid (F^I *leu$^+$ pro-1/leu$^-$ pro-2*), and will live to produce colonies if *pro-1* and *pro-2* are not alleles. If *pro-1* and *pro-2* are allelic, the merodiploids will not be viable and colonies will not be produced.

  b. Infect strain 3 with phage Z and use the progeny phage to infect strain 2 (which is immune). Plate these cells on two different growth media: minimal and minimal + leucine. The relative frequency of prototrophs on minimal media and of leucine-requiring recombinants on minimal + leucine media will indicate whether the order is *leu—pro-1—pro-2* or *leu—pro-2—pro-1*, according to:

Minimal medium   **Minimal + leucine medium**

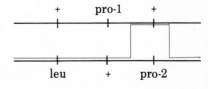

vs.

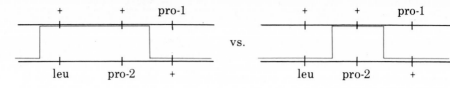

Minimal medium   **Minimal + leucine medium**

vs.

5.6. Grow each mutant at 25° during the early stage of the cycle and switch to 42° at the later stage. Only the mutant defective in DNA replication (an early function) will form plaques. In the reciprocal experiment (harvest phage growing at 42° in early stage and switch to 25° for later stage), only mutants defective in tail formation (a late function) will form plaques.

5.7. Temperate phages can enter into a lysogenic relationship with the host cells, while virulent phages have very brief latent period and always proceed through the lytic cycle.

5.8. a. *s—f*, 12.8 map units, *f—tu*, 20.8 map units, *s-tu*, 33.7 map units
b. the gene order is *s—f—tu*
c. coefficient of coincidence = observed double crossovers/expected doubles = 668/550 = 1.2

5.9. Conjugation experiments using *Hfr* and *F⁻* strains.

5.10. Among other things, viral genetics showed that DNA was the genetic material, that genetic and physical mapping could be correlated, that various means could be used to produce comparable or almost identical genetic maps, and that various mechanisms exist as substitutes for sexual reproduction in the generation of genetic diversity among bacteria and viruses.

5.11. Physically linear chromosomes produce circular genetic maps if the chromosomes are terminally redundant and circularly permuted molecules.

5.12. *Tk* on chromosome 17, *Ldh* on 11, *Ahh* on 2, and *Pgk* on the X chromosome.

5.13. a. The woman's father is colorblind (*cb +*/Y); the woman's mother is normal (*+ +/+ ln*); the woman is normal (*cb +/+ ln*); her son has inherited a crossover X chromosome from his mother, and he is (*cb ln*/Y)
b. probability would be equal to the percentage of crossing over between the two X-linked loci.

5.14. *F⁺* donors have *F* factors in the free, episomal state while *Hfr* strains have *F* integrated into the bacterial chromosome. In *F⁺* × *F⁻*, the episome is transferred and the recipient becomes *F⁺*. In *Hfr* × *F⁻*, the bacterial chromosome leads the way and *F* is the last component to enter the recipient. Most of the time conjugation terminates before *F* enters, and the recipient is *F⁻*

5.15. a. *pro—ala*, 30 units; *ala-arg*, 25 units; *pro—arg*, 37 units
b. the linkage order is *pro—ala—arg*

5.16.

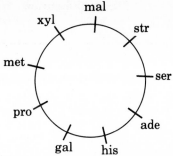

5.17. The gene order is $a—c—b$. Strain-1 transduction of strain-2 ($a^-b^-c^+$ into $a^+b^+c^-$) produces prototrophs when only c^+ is transferred; in the reciprocal, prototrophs arise if transfer a^+ and b^+ and not c^- of strain-2 into strain-1. If c is the middle gene, one predicts more wild type recombinants ($a^+b^+c^+$) from strain-1 → strain-2, than from strain-2 → strain-1 transduction. It takes only a double crossover to get $a^+b^+c^+$ in the first, but quadruple crossover for wild type recombinants in the second case. Double crossovers occur with higher frequency than quadruple crossovers.

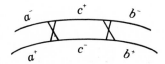

→ $a^+c^+b^+$ vs.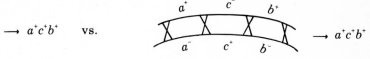

strain-1 → strain-2   strain-2 → strain-1

Chapter 6

6.1. Evidence from various α- and β-chain variants of hemoglobin in humans and in other animals; mutants for tryptophan synthetase in *E. coli*; many others.

6.2. rIIB1 and rIIB3 are point mutations 0.8 units apart; rIIB2 appears to be a deletion mutant since it produces no recombinants with the other strains.

6.3. a. 2×10^6
b. 0.068 cm

6.4. There was a higher percentage G + C in the second sample than the first.

6.5.

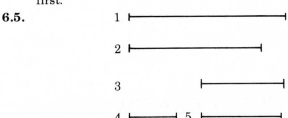

6.6. Strain 1 is a deletion mutant and strains 2, 3, and 4 have point mutations. The topological map would be:

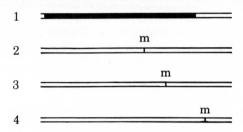

6.7. a. *c/c* × *mb/mb*
      b. mutant eyes or mutant bristles
      c. *c/mb* × *c/c*, or *c/mb* × *mb/mb*, to see if there are recombinants (different sites in the locus) or not (same locus site)
      d. 2000

6.8.

$$GGG \nearrow \begin{array}{l} GUG \rightarrow AUG \\ AGG \rightarrow AUG \end{array}$$

6.9. Ala—Val—His—Ser

6.10. T4 is a duplex-DNA phage, and nitrous acid induces mutations in one of the strands which, upon replicating, segregates one normal and one mutant daughter duplex after semiconservative replication. Phage ϕX174 is a single-stranded DNA virus and mutations in its single strand yield only mutant phage progeny.

6.11. The viral DNA has probably integrated within the mouse DNA, and exists there in provirus form. This may be responsible for altered cellular metabolism in the mouse host, and perhaps even contribute to cancer induction.

6.12.

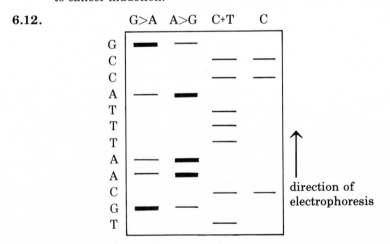

6.13. (1) d.s. DNA, (2) d.s. RNA, (3) d.s. DNA, (4) s.s. DNA if T present or RNA if U present; (5) s.s. DNA; (6) s.s. RNA; (7) d.s.; (8) s.s. or d.s.

Chapter 7

7.1. Duplex DNA melts to single strands on being heated, and double-stranded molecules will form if complementary single strands are cooled. Phage T4 mixtures produce heavy, light, and hybrid duplex DNA molecules, since the strands are able to undergo complementary base-pairing regardless of the N isotope present. DNA from phage T2 and phage T4 are not sufficiently complementary to form hybrid duplex molecules.

7.2. a. The frequency of purines (A + G) in one strand must equal the frequency of pyrimidines (T + C) in the complementary strand, so the ratio for the complementary strand in this example is $1/0.3 = 3.3$

    b. A = T and G = C in duplex DNAs, so A + G/T + C = 1 in the entire molecule

    c. The sum of A + T in one strand must equal the sum in the complementary strand, and the same is true for G + C in the two strands; therefore, A + T/G + C ratio is 0.3 for each strand, and for the entire molecule.

7.3. No; one or both strands of this DNA would transcribe the same RNA base ratio.

7.4. If double-stranded, RNA base ratio (A+G/U+C) would be 1.00. *E. coli* RNA is therefore single-stranded, but *B. subtilis* RNA might be double-stranded unless there are equal numbers of purines and pyrimidines in the template DNA strand from which a single stranded RNA is transcribed.

7.5. DNA-2, since it is complementary to the mRNA.

7.6. a. Mutant 1 has a missense mutation: Ser (AGU) → Arg (AGA or AGG); Mutant 2 has a nonsense mutation: Trp (UGG) → UGA or UAG (stop codons); Mutant 3 has two frameshift mutations (the fourth base is deleted, and U or C is inserted making Asn codon:

5'-CCx UGG AGU GAA AAA UG$_\text{C}^\text{U}$ CA$_\text{C}^\text{U}$-3' (wild type mRNA)

5'-CCx GGA GUG AAA AA$_\text{C}^\text{U}$ UG$_\text{C}^\text{U}$ CA$_\text{C}^\text{U}$-3' (mutant-3 mRNA)

    b. Wild type DNA in this region is:

3'-GGx ACC TCA CTT TTT AC$_\text{G}^\text{A}$ GT$_\text{G}^\text{A}$-5'.

7.7.

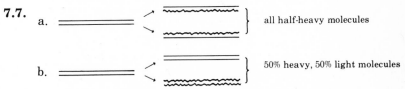

a. all half-heavy molecules

b. 50% heavy, 50% light molecules

    c. This would show that DNA replicated semiconservatively, as shown in part a, since the single band signifies isotopically identical molecules and this could only mean that all the DNA duplexes were half-heavy.

7.8. a. 3′-T A A G C T G G A A—5′
 b. 5′-G T G C A G T A A T—3′
 c. 60% A-T and 40% G-C base pairs

7.9. a.

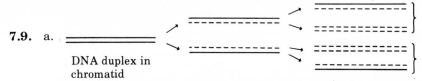

DNA duplex in
chromatid

 b. One daughter nucleus would have 1 bright and 1 dull chromatid
 in its chromosome, and both chromatids would be dull in the
 other daughter nucleus after 3 replications in BrdU medium.
 c. 10 chromatids, since there are 80 chromatids (40 replicated chromosomes) and 1/8 of these would be brightly fluorescent after 4
 generations in BrdU.

Chapter 8

8.1. No. According to the wobble hypothesis, ICU anticodons recognize
 either AGA or AGC codons. Therefore, if ICU was the anticodon of
 tRNA^{Ser}, both AGA and AGC codons would code for serine. AGC is a
 serine codon, but AGA codes for arginine.

8.2. Polysomes consist of mRNA and ribosomes, and polysomal mRNA
 is held to its template DNA through attachment to RNA polymerase
 molecules bound to the DNA.

8.3. Obtain single-stranded DNA by denaturing each chromatin fraction, and then hybridize with rRNA. The fraction producing DNA-
 rRNA molecular hybrids is the rDNA-containing chromatin. It
 should be the fraction with attached nucleoli.

8.4. Conduct *in situ* hybridization, using labeled RNA isolated from
 chromosome puffs identical to the ones under study. Silver grains
 will appear over the puffed chromosome regions if the template
 DNA is located there and has hybridized with the added RNA.

8.5. If single-stranded DNA is synthesized from tRNA or other cloverleaf RNAs, in reactions catalyzed by reverse transcriptase, then the
 single-stranded DNA should assume the same secondary and
 tertiary structure as its tRNA model.

8.6. If translation occurred at all and an amino acid other than methionine or fMet initiated the polypeptide chain, the N-terminus would
 not be blocked and chain elongation might take place in either
 direction.

8.7. The ratio of ribosomes to mRNA will decrease. This decrease will
 lower the efficiency of translation of mRNA and as a direct result
 there will be a lowered rate of protein synthesis (translation) and of
 larval development.

8.8. The cysteine codons UGU and UGC will pair with ACG (wobbly),
 and UGU will pair with anticodon ACA, as well. The tryptophan
 codon UGG pairs only with tRNA anticodon ACC, since 5′-C does

not wobble. There is no tRNA for the UGA terminator codon, so this codon is distinct from the codons for cysteine and tryptophan, which interact specifically with different tRNA anticodons.

8.9. Both mutant hemoglobins have arisen because of changes in the terminator codon following the codon for amino acid 141, leading to a lengthened α chain. The Hb CS terminator codon itself appears to have been modified by a nucleotide substitution, creating an amino acid-specifying codon instead. The Hb W1 alteration is probably due to a frameshift mutation resulting from addition or deletion of a nucleotide and thereby causing an altered reading frame.

8.10. a. tRNA will accept aminoacyl group addition in reactions catalyzed by aminoacyl-tRNA synthetase *in vitro* or *in vivo*, whereas other RNAs will not.

b. *in situ* hybridization should be carried out to see if the presumptive labeled rRNA binds to the NORs of the chromosomes, where rDNA is localized.

c. mRNA should bind to small subunits of ribosomes, and the mRNA—subunit aggregate should bind initiator aminoacyl-tRNA in turn. Polypeptide chain elongation should proceed in a preparation containing this RNA and other components of protein synthesis.

8.11. See Section 8.2 and 8.3. Pre-mRNA is trimmed and spliced, capped with m^7G, and has a tail of poly(A) added on, all before leaving the nucleus.

8.12. a. RNA appears first in the nucleus and afterward in the cytoplasm

b. 45S RNA is labeled first and this label later appears in 32S RNA; this is the expected precursor-product relationship

c. Labeled 32S RNA appears first, and it disappears as labeled 28S appears (precursor-product)

d. 45S RNA is found only in the nucleus, not in the cytoplasm, and the labeling sequence shows precursor-product relationships

e. 18S rRNA appears in the cytoplasm at 30 minutes, whereas 28S rRNA takes 60 minutes

f. 45S RNA loses its label after 10 minutes because the early labeled 45S RNA is processed to other RNAs (which appear labeled afterward), and newly made 45S RNA is synthesized from unlabeled precursors during the remainder of the experiment.

8.13. See Fig. 8.19.

8.14. There would be a large satellite rDNA peak in amplifying nuclear DNA, and not in non-amplifying material. If molecular hybrids form with rRNA, then the "satellite" DNA must be complementary and must therefore be rDNA template.

Chapter 9

9.1. a. constitutive

b. inducible

c. constitutive
d. constitutive

9.2. a. constitutive
b. constitutive
c. inducible
d. constitutive
e. inducible

9.3.

Strain	Lactose present		Lactose absent	
	β-gal	permease	β-gal	permease
1	+	+	0	0
2	0	0	0	0
3	+	+	+	+
4	0	0	0	0
5	+	+	+	+
6	0	0	0	0
7	+	+	+	+
8	0	0	0	0
9	+	+	+	+

9.4. It has an o^c mutation.

9.5. regulator (repressor) = a, structural = b, and operator = c

9.6. a. altered protein synthesized, perhaps nonfunctional TAT
b. the mutant would make TAT constitutively, in presence and absence of steroid hormones
c. If both homozygotes and heterozygotes for the mutant allele produce the same phenotype, the mutant allele is dominant over its wild-type alternative. If only homozygous mutant genotypes produce the mutant phenotype, the mutant allele is recessive to the wild-type allele
d. perform synteny tests using somatic cell hybrids (mouse-human)

9.7. a. 4
b. 3
c. 4
d. 3
e. 1
f. 3

9.8. a. DNA replication occurred, without subsequent separation by mitosis
b. transcription occurred only at certain gene loci and not at others
c. RNA transcribed in the nucleus (mRNA, rRNA, tRNA) enters the cytoplasm and functions there. Product RNA obtains label later, when pre-RNA is processed into product.

Chapter 10

10.1. A nonsense mutation would cause a shortened protein, and could lead to nonfunctional enzyme; missense mutations cause nonfunctional or weakly effective enzymes if the amino acid substitution occurs in critical regions of the protein, but many substitutions have little detectable effect on protein function. Frameshift mutations alter the reading frame and usually cause enzyme to be defective since many different amino acids occur in frameshift polypeptides.

10.2. The codon for glycine is GGU. In Gly → Cys, a transversion occurred (GGU → UGU); in Gly → Asp, a transition occurred (GGU → GAU); in Gly → Ala, a transversion occurred (GGU → GCU).

10.3.

precursor $\xrightarrow{③}$ A
precursor $\xrightarrow{④}$ B
A, B $\xrightarrow{①}$ C $\xrightarrow{②}$ D

10.4. Isolation of the double mutant *leu⁻ trp⁻* can be performed using a two-step penicillin selection method:

(1) Inoculate bacteria into complete media lacking tryptophan and containing penicillin. Only the *trp⁻* mutants survive, since they cannot divide and are therefore not killed by the drug. Plate these mutants on tryptophan-supplemented media lacking penicillin, in order to obtain stock culture.

(2) Plate the above *trp⁻* strain in media with penicillin but lacking tryptophan and leucine. The double mutants will be the only survivors, and these *leu⁻ trp⁻* mutants will grow on media only if supplemented with both amino acids they cannot produce.

10.5. Phage λ is temperate, not virulent. Once phage λ exists in its host in prophage form, further infection by other λ phages is inhibited. Resistance to temperate phages arises after the bacteria have established contact with these viruses, so the results would have shown environmental induction of mutations instead of selection of pre-existing, randomly arising mutations.

10.6. $(11 \times 10^{-6})(492 \times 10^{-6}) = 5412 \times 10^{-12}$, since each mutation is an independent event and for both to occur together, by chance, one multiplies the separate probabilities (mutation rates).

10.7. a. See Fig. 10.3, adding w^+ alleles to the genotypes shown there

b. The white-eye allele is an X-linked mutant gene, producing a morphological effect. It arose in the original male parent who was mutagenized by EMS.

10.8. a. Pro: CCU, CCC, CCA, CCG; Ser: UCU, UCC, UCA, UCG, AGU, AGC; Leu: UUA, UUG, CUU, CUC, CUA, CUG; Phe: UUU, UUC. The probable sequence of mutational changes is:

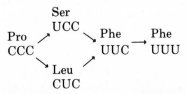

b. Nitrous acid caused transitional changes in TMV (replacement of one pyrimidine by another pyrimidine).

10.9. The recessive genotype must be lethal, so $Gg \times Gg$ produces only GG and Gg offspring in the usual proportion of $1/3:2/3$ for monohybrid inheritance of one pair of alleles showing dominance and recessiveness.

10.10. 14 children/1,470,000 gametes = about 1×10^{-5} mutation rate.

10.11. a. There will be an increase in percentage mutants over control crosses in which a source of pure water was used to make the fly food in which *Drosophila* lives and multiplies

b. Mutations affecting phenotypic appearance, phenotypic ratios, lethals, etc.

c. Molecular mutations which produce no visible effect on the organism or on progeny ratios in breeding analysis would be undetectable

d. Search for his^+ revertants and where there is a significant increase over controls, initiate carcinogenicity studies using mice or other suitable animals to search for tumor induction.

10.12. See Fig. 10.19 for schemes showing photoreactivation, excision repair, and postreplication repair processes for UV radiation damage via thymine dimers.

Chapter 11

11.1. a. Allopolyploidy: a sterile diploid species-hybrid became tetraploid and could undergo normal meiosis to produce viable gametes

b. 18

11.2. a. $n = 9$

b. *Raphanus* ($n = 9$) × *Brassica* ($n = 9$) produce hybrid *Raphanobrassica* ($2n = 18$), which is sterile. Spontaneous doubling of the chromosome number gave rise to $2n = 36$ and to the fertile allotetraploid hybrid.

11.3. F_1: 1 wild type ($+/bt$):1 bent ($bt/-$)

F_2: 1 wild type ($+/bt$ and $+/-$):1 bent (bt/bt and $bt/-$)

11.4. a. If the wild-type allele S is dominant over s in any dosage, the expected results are 5 wild type:1 compound inflorescence

b. standard testcross ratio of 1 wild type:1 compound inflorescence.

11.5. The Turner female is hemizygous (XO) and GPD deficient, so she must have the X chromosome carrying the mutant *gpd* allele. She and her brother are identical in X chromosome constitution. She is lacking her father's X chromosome, since only her mother carries the GPD deficiency allele on one X chromosome.

11.6. The intervals showing lowered recombination frequencies are $vg—L$ and $L—a$, so the inversion probably includes these two segments of the chromosome. Pairing at pachynema in the inversion heterozygote would lead to an inversion loop at the segment carrying gene *L*. Since *pr—vg* and *a—bw* show expected recombination frequencies, their distances are unchanged and, therefore, the inversion cannot include the two genes flanking *L*.

11.7.

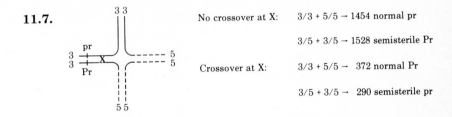

No crossover at X: $3/3 + 5/5 \rightarrow$ 1454 normal pr

$3/5 + 3/5 \rightarrow$ 1528 semisterile Pr

Crossover at X: $3/3 + 5/5 \rightarrow$ 372 normal Pr

$3/5 + 3/5 \rightarrow$ 290 semisterile pr

The locus is $662/3644 \times 100 = 18.2$ map units from the translocation point

11.8.   a.

11.9.

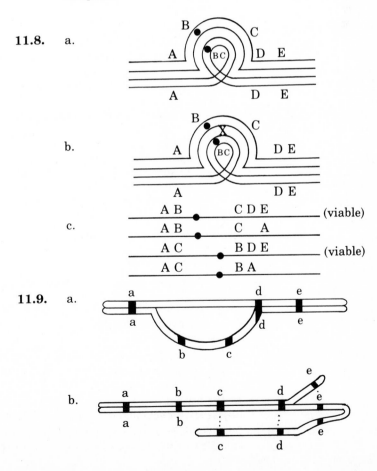

c.

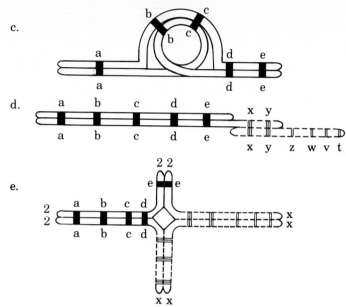

d.
a   b   c   d   e   x y
a   b   c   d   e   x y z w v t

e.

11.10. a. The major rRNA gene was simpler to isolate because its high G-C content causes rDNA to sediment in a different part of the CsCl gradient from bulk nuclear DNA; it is present in repeated copies and can be detected because of amplification of these repeated genes, or as repetitious DNA; purified rRNA was available for DNA-RNA molecular and *in situ* hybridizations, as well as heteroduplex mapping by R loops

b. specificity of DNA-RNA molecular hybridization between genes and gene products

c. various methods can be used, for example, heteroduplex analysis showing the *Xenopus* DNA region present; gel electrophoresis revealing the rDNA within the bacterial DNA material; and other methods, including observation of rDNA gene-product (*Xenopus* rRNA) in the clones carrying toad genes.

Chapter 12

12.1. Mendelian inheritance for one pair of alleles, with *grande* dominant over *petite* (F_1 diploid has *grande* phenotype and $+/p$ genotype), yielding 2:2 tetrad ratio.

12.2. Half will be *grande* and half will be *petite*, due to segregation of nuclear alleles, since *grande × neutral petite* produces *grande* only, in 4:0 tetrad ratio.

12.3. In the hybrid A ♀ × B ♂, an X chromosome from the B parent is necessary for survival of a hybrid with cytoplasm from parent A. Since male offspring do not receive their X chromosome from the B (♂) parent, they do not survive and all offspring are females. In the

reciprocal cross, there is a generally lethal effect of an X chromosome from species A in hybrids with cytoplasm from species B.

12.4.   a. *Rf/rf* individuals are normal
      b. progeny would segregate 1 normal:1 male-sterile, according to
         Rf/rf and *rf/rf* genotypes in male-sterile cytoplasm.

12.5.   See appropriate figures for diagrams. Electron micrographs for
each replication mechanism would show:

Cairns theta-forms: All segments double-stranded, and
                                            A = B in length.

D-loop synthesis: Most of molecule double-stranded,
                                            but a single-stranded region occurs
                                            opposite the D loop.

Rolling circle:

                                            All parts double-stranded, "tail"
                                            usually long and circle usually the
                                            size of one genome in contour
                                            length.

12.6.   a. Add poly(U) or other appropriate messenger in a protein-
         synthesizing system and observe for polypeptide chain syn-
         thesis
      b. Using poly(U) *in vitro*, see that either subunit fraction alone
         cannot sponsor polypeptide chain synthesis, but that mono-
         somes made of unequal-sized subunits can sponsor such syn-
         thesis
      c. chloramphenicol or erythromycin will inhibit mitochondrial
         ribosome functions, but not cytoplasmic ribosome activity
      d. mitochondrial ribosomes are small in size (55S-60S), sensitive
         to chloramphenicol but not to cycloheximide, have no 5S or
         5.8S rRNA molecules present; have 12-13S and 16-17S small
         and large subunit rRNAs, respectively; compared with cyto-
         plasmic 80S ribosomes that are sensitive to cycloheximide,
         contain 28S, 5.8S, and 5S rRNAs in the 60S subunit and 18S
         rRNA in the small subunit.

12.7.   Conduct molecular hybridizations using organelle rRNA with
organelle DNA (forms hybrids) and nuclear DNA (no hybrids);
and do a control using cytoplasmic rRNA with nuclear DNA
(hybrids) and organelle DNA (no hybrids). When organelle rRNA
is hybridized with each DNA single-stranded fraction, hybrids
forming in only one fraction indicate the template DNA strand,
or hybrids with both DNA single-stranded fractions indicate two
template strands in duplex DNA.

12.8.   Grow cells in media supplemented with chloramphenicol, cycloheximide, neither drug, and both drugs. Upon electrophoresis, one

should see the chloroplast-coded unit present in cycloheximide-media and the nuclear-coded enzyme subunit in chloramphenicol-supplemented media. Neither subunit forms in media with both drugs, and the whole enzyme is synthesized in drug-free media; the last two systems serve as experimental controls.

12.9. The original Parent was heterozygous (D/d).

12.10. See Section 12.1.

12.11. The orange phenotype is the result of an extranuclear mutation.

Chapter 13

13.1. In virus chromosomes it is commonly observed that genes active in the same part of the life cycle often are clustered together, and often are transcribed together. The genome is ordered sequentially and so is transcription.

13.2. Gene *A* products are needed at all times during phage maturation, or the involvement of gene *A* in head protein assembly is independent of genes *B* and *C*. Genes *B* and *C* act sequentially (dependently) in head assembly, as follows:

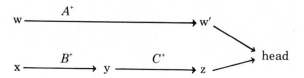

13.3. The heads must be defective in this T4 mutant, while it makes normal tails.

13.4. Group B makes tails and tail fibers;
Group D makes heads and tail fibers,
Group E makes heads and tails, and
Group F makes tail fibers.

13.5. Complementation map is:

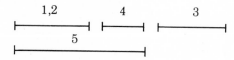

Three unique gene loci are defined: locus 1-2, 4, and 3.

13.6. The transformer (*t*) gene probably acts first, since normal male sex organs are produced in XX, homozygous males. If the *z* gene acted first, there would be defective female structures produced and the *t* gene would then direct formation of defective male structures from these defective female structures.

13.7.   *Vermilion* eye disks cannot synthesize formylkynurenin, but they do develop pigment when supplied with this substance in the body of a *cinnabar* host (is v^+). *Cinnabar* flies require hydroxykynurenin in order to make pigment, but *cinnabar* eye discs do not receive this substance in *vermilion* hosts, since *vermilion* flies themselves are blocked in its production (at an earlier developmental stage). These results define the sequence.

13.8.   See Section 9.1, where evidence is described and discussed.

13.9.   a.   *cdc* 28 → *cdc* 4 → *cdc* 7
           b.   they are independent of each other

Chapter 14

14.1.   Mean = 2.06 mm; standard deviation = 0.46

14.2.   a.   A normal curve can be plotted, and the data do fit a normal distribution
           b.   mean = 171.94 cm, standard deviation = 6.29 cm, and standard error = 0.14
           c. 1σ range = 165.65-178.23, and includes 68% of the students; 2σ ranges from 159.36-184.52 cm, and includes 95.4% of the students; and 3σ ranges from 153.07-190.81 and includes 99.7% of the sample
           d.   yes

14.3.   a.   Strain A is *aabbcc*, and strain B is *AABBCC*
           b.   180 g
           c.   7 classes: 120 g, 140 g, 160 g, 180 g, 200 g, 220 g, and 240 g weights
           d.   256 (only 1 in 64, on average, is *AABBCC)*

14.4.   a.   If flower size is determined by environmental factors then large × small will give rise to progeny resembling the parents; on the other hand, if the offspring are somehow different from their parents it means genetic factors influence flower size
           b.   Obtain F_2 offspring and determine the ratio of progeny classes; for example, 3:1 or 1:2:1 indicates 1 pair of alleles of a gene, 1:4:6:4:1 indicates 2 pairs of alleles with additive effects, etc.

14.5.   The proportion of individuals in any homozygous genotypic class in F_2 populations is $(1/4)^n$, where n is the number of genes (allele pairs) involved. If 4/4000 had seeds weighing 30 g (one of the homozygous classes), there must be 5 genes (allele pairs) involved since 1/1000 is approximately $(1/4)^5$.

14.6. $2 \times (1/4)^5 = 2 \times 1024 = \$2048$

14.7.   a.   simple monohybrid inheritance with incomplete dominance
           b.   there would only be three phenotypic classes for one pair of alleles, so these data must indicate two pairs of alleles producing $(1/4)^2 = 1/16$ in a homozygous class (5/80)
           c.   *aabb* (50 mm); *Aabb* and *aaBb* (62 mm); *AAbb, AaBb, aaBB* (75 mm); *AABb, AaBB* (88 mm); and *AABB* (100 mm). Each *A* or *B* allele adds an increment of 12-13 mm to tail length.

14.8.   Probably signifies genetic factors contributing to susceptibility to tuberculosis infection, in an environment conducive to disease induction and development. There is known to be genetic influence in immunity against many kinds of diseases, infectious and otherwise caused.

Chapter 15

15.1.   a. Total C^B alleles is 1838 [622 + 2(554) + 108], and total alleles at this X-linked locus in the sample is 1958. Frequency of C^B is 1838/2058 = 0.893, and frequency of C^Y is 1-0.893 = 0.107

        b. expected ♀♀ = $(0.893)^2$ + 2(0.893 × 0.107) + $(0.107)^2$; observed ♀♀ = 0.82 + 0.16 + 0.02 [fits Hardy-Weinberg predictions]

        c. expected ♂♂ = 0.893 + 0.107, observed ♂♂ = 0.88 + 0.12 [fits Hardy-Weinberg predictions]

15.2. $p(v^+)$ = 85/100 = 0.85, and $q(v)$ = 1-0.85 = 0.15

        b. q^2 = $(0.15)^2$ = 0.0225, 0.0225 × 100 = 2.25%

15.3.   a. L^M = 0.737, L^N = 0.263

        b. $2pq$ = 2(0.7 × 0.3) = 420

15.4. q^2 = 1/10,000, q = 1/100, p = 1-0.01 = 0.99; heterozygote frequency is $2pq$ = 2(0.99 + 0.01) = 0.0198, probability of heterozygote × heterozygote mating is $(0.0198)^2$ = 0.0004, and probability of recessive child is 1/4 (0.0004), or 0.0001 = 0.01% (1 in 10,000).

15.5. q^2(black, bb) = 0.4131 + 0.3969 = 0.81, and $q(b)$ = 0.9; q^2(ebony, ee) = 0.0931 + 0.3969 = 0.49, and $q(e)$ = 0.7.

15.6.   a. 1/100

        b. 1/100 × 1/100 = 1/10,000

15.7.   a. 480/500 = 0.96

        b. all but $(0.04)^2$ females would be homozygous and heterozygous normal, that is, 99.84% would be normal phenotypically

15.8.   a. Only TT × tt marriages between tasters and nontasters can produce taster children exclusively (all Tt). Since q^2 = 0.3, $q(t)$ = 0.55 and $p(T)$ = 0.45; $p^2(TT)$ = 0.20, $2pq$ = 2(0.45 × 0.55) = 0.495. Marriages between tasters and nontasters include TT × tt (0.20 × 0.30 = 0.06) and Tt × tt (0.495 × 0.30 = 0.148); and 0.06/0.06 + 0.148 = 0.39, or 39% of all marriages between tasters and nontasters have no chance of producing a nontaster child.

        b. $(0.3)^2$ = 0.09 = 9%

15.9. $(0.6)^3$ = 0.216, or 21.6%

15.10. $p(I^A)$ = 0.2, $q(I^B)$ = 0.1, $r(i^O)$ = 0.7

15.11.   It is not possible to determine dominance and recessiveness from genotypic frequencies in populations, as Hardy and Weinberg discussed. Breeding tests must be conducted.

15.12.   a. q^2 = 6/2400 = 1/400 = 0.0025; q = $\sqrt{0.0025}$ = 0.05

        b. $2pq$ = 2(1-0.05)(0.05) = 0.095

    c. $p^2 = (0.95)^2 = 0.9025$

    d. 12/4800 gametes carried the *co* mutant allele, so the mutation rate of co^+ to *co* is 0.0025. In fact, the mutation rate equals the birth rate for recessive lethals, since $\hat{q}^2 = u/s$ and for lethals, $s = 1$ and $\hat{q}^2 = u/1$.

15.13. a. $q^2 = 1/25 = 4\%$ are y/y, so 96% have white fat

      b. $2pq = 2(0.8)(0.2) = 0.32$

      c. recessives continue to be produced in heterozygote × heterozygote matings, and the recessive allele is protected against selection in the heterozygote

      d. cannot be eliminated, since $\hat{q}^2 = u/s$; recessive alleles would be maintained in the gene pool by recurrent mutation

Chapter 16

16.1. a. $\hat{q} = s_1/(s_1 + s_2) = 0.1/(0.1 + 0.7) = 0.12$; $\hat{p}(Hb^A) = 1.00 - 0.12 = 0.88$

      b. $(0.12)^2 \times 100 = 1.44\%$

16.2. See Fig. 16.1 and Section 16.2

16.3.

Characteristic	*D. colorata*	*D. willistoni**
Recombination index	higher	lower
Frequency of inversions	lower	higher
Frequency of supergenes	lower	higher
Habitat stability	higher	lower

*most highly adapted of the two species

16.4. Crossing over will not take place between genetically differentiated X and Y sex chromosomes, and their separate supergene systems are maintained generation after generation.

16.5

Relative fitness	Genotype			
	YY	Yy	yy	
W	0.6	0.6	1.0	$p(Y) = 0.2$
s	0.4	0.4	0	$q(y) = 0.8$

For dominant alleles with $s > 0$, the proportion of the dominant allele lost in each generation from the population is $sp^2 + pqs$ (see Table 15.13). In this case, $p_0(Y) = 0.2$, and $p_1(Y) = p - (sp^2 + pqs) = 0.2 - [(0.4)(0.2)^2 + (0.2)(0.8)(0.4)] = 0.2 - 0.08 = 0.12$. In 10 generations of predation, the frequency of Y would be $p_{10}(Y) = p_0/1 + 10(p_0) = 0.2/1 + 10(0.2) = 0.067$, as discussed in Section 15.6, and the frequency of Y after n generations would be $p_n = p_0/1 + n(p_0)$.

16.6. a. The effect is achieved through directional selection of polygenes affecting leaf number

      b. The original mean is not attained because some alleles governing "low leaf number" have been eliminated from the population during the 15 years of selection leading from 32 to 58 leaves per plant.

16.7.   a.

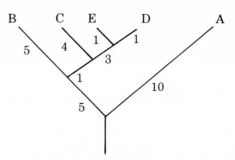

b.   Species A is probably most ancient, since it differs from every other species by the highest number of nucleotides.

16.8.   Genotype e/e was completely lethal, and allele e was reduced in frequency by selection against e/e according to the formula:

$$p_n = \frac{p_0}{1 + np_0} = \frac{0.5}{1 + 8(0.5)} = \frac{0.5}{5.0} = 0.1$$

16.9.   a.   Interbreed members of the three populations and determine whether they produce hybrids (same species) or do not produce hybrids (different species)

b.   If there are no hybrids produced by the three populations of the single species, there must be one or more isolating mechanisms preventing interbreeding. They may reproduce at different seasons, show different sexual behaviors, occupy different habitats on the island, and so forth, thereby producing no hybrids even though they are genetically close according to experimental breeding tests.

16.10. a.

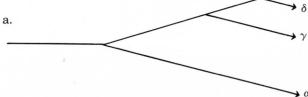

b.   The loci occupy different chromosomal sites presumably because of translocations during genome evolution.

Author Index

Numbers in italic are article references.

Adelberg, E. 192
Ames, B. N. *400, 408*
Attardi, G. *486*
Auerbach, C. 387
Avery, O. T. 176, *207*

Baltimore, D. 264
Bastock, M. 552
Bateson, W. 118-119
Bautz, E. 340, *371*
Beerman, W. 105-109, *115*, 337
Bennett, D. 515, *519*
Benzer, S. 217-223, *247*, *392*, 513, *555*
Bonner, J. 355, *373*
Botstein, D. 502, *520*
Briggs, R. 339
Britten, R. 281, *293*
Brown, D. D. 441, *449*

Cairns, J. 190, 257, 260, *293*
Carrano, A. V. 403
Cavalli-Sforza, L. L. *555, 556, 593*
Chambon, P. 341
Chargaff, E. 213, *247*
Chase, M. 67-70, *73*
Crick, F. H. C. 210, 233, *247, 248, 249*, 308, *333*

Davenport, C. B. 20-21
Davidson, E. H. 281, *293*
Dawid, I. B. *443*
Delbrück, M. 381, *409*
Donahue, R. 172, *207*

East, E. M. 530, *556*
Edgar, R. 496, *521*
Emerson, R. A. 530
Ephrussi, B. 458

Fraenkel-Conrat, H. 242-243, *247*

Gall, J. G. 285, *294*
Garen, A. 231, *247*

Gilbert, W. *238, 248*
Gillham, N. W. 473, *486, 488*
Glass, B. 589
Gross, H. 243, *244, 247*
Gurdon, J. 339

Hadorn, E. 508, *520*
Hartwell, L. H. 504, *520*
Hayes, W. 182
Hershey, A. 67-70, *73*, 199
Hogness, D. S. *445*
Holliday, R. 271
Hotta, Y. 513
Hsu, T. C. 414

Ingram, V. 224, *248*

Jacob, F. 183-193, 341-347, *371*
Janssens, F. 121
Jarvik, J. 502, *520*
Johannsen, W. 537-540
Judd, B. H. 289-290, *294*

Kavenoff, R. 277, *294*
Kettlewell, H. B. 599
Khorana, H. G. 229, *248*
King, T. 339
Kornberg, A. 257, *294*
Kornberg, R. 278, *294*

Leder, P. 306, *335*
Lederberg, J. 64-65, 193, *208*, 382, *409*
Linnane, A. W. *487*
Luria, S. E. 381, *409*
Lyon, M. 102

Margulis, L. 476
Matthaei, H. 228, *248*
Maxam, A. M. *238, 248*
McClintock, B. 363, *372*
Mendel, G. 2, 11, *35*
Meselson, M. 251, 266, *295*
Miller, O. L., Jr. 305, 312, 439, 450
Monod, J. 341-347, *371*

Morgan, T. H. 77-80, 119-122
Muller, H. J. 378, 386, *409*

Nilsson-Ehle, H. 17, *35*, 530
Nirenberg, M. W. 228, 229, *248*

Ochoa, S. 229
Okazaki, R. 258
Olins, A. L. and D. E. 278, *280, 295*

Pardue, M. L. 285, *294*
Petes, T. D. 276
Punnett, R. C. 118-119

Rich, A. 318, *334, 335*
Ringertz, N. R. *409*
Ritossa, F. M. 313, *334*

Sager, R. 457, 473, 475, *487*
Slonimski, P. P. 458, 459
Spiegelman, S. 301, 313, *334*
Stahl, F. W. 251
Stern, C. 150, 158, *208*
Stern, H. 271
Steward, F. C. *339*
Streisinger, G. 202, *208*, 234, 235
Sturtevant, A. 119, 126-128, *156*
Sutton, W. 77

Tatum, E. 64-65
Taylor, J. H. 255, 256
Temin, H. 264
Tryon, R. C. 551

Watson, J. D. 210, *248, 249*
Weigle, J. J. 266
Wilkins, M. H. F. 213, *249*
Wood, W. 496, 499, 500, *521*
Wright, S. *594*

Yanofsky, C. 224-227, 230-231, *249*

Zinder, N. 193, *208*

Subject Index

Pictorial information indicated by italics.

650